<u>Funky French</u>

Rosalyn Secor, PhD

First Edition Design Publishing

Funky French
Copyright © Rosalyn Secor

ISBN 9781506900360

LCCN 2015948329

October 2016

Published and Distributed by
First Edition Design Publishing, Inc.
P.O. Box 20217, Sarasota, FL 34276-3217
www.firsteditiondesignpublishing.com

ACKNOWLEDGMENTS

To all students- I am delighted to offer a unique approach for learning French. I hope that you find it both enlightening and entertaining.

To the late Richard Weiner, a cherished friend and prolific author. His expertise in leading me through the formatting and publishing labyrinths was invaluable.

To Farzin and Faraz Yashar, my 'on call' father-son team, who so capably provided computer assistance. This book would not have become a reality without them.

To Shana Bruno who wove her computer magic to revive a defunct computer and to teach me how to use its replacement. Her many "eleventh hour house calls" will forever be appreciated.

To Melanie Vazquez, my personal support system, whose endless patience and objective advice were truly appreciated.

To Margo Egol and Rita Striar, my lifelong best friends. Their understanding of what this project has involved is immeasurable.

To Charles Martel, my beloved father, who labeled me early on as "a mechanic of words" and nourished my love of learning.

And most of all, to my wonderful children David, Douglas, Naomi and Jeffrey. I love you more than words in any language can say.

Unique Features of Funky French

As the title indicates, <u>Funky French</u> is not a typical, comprehensive foreign language textbook. The positive educational value of the humorous approach is "a given." Its surefire mnemonics, engaging exercises and entertaining stories serve a dual purpose; the learning process is more enjoyable while the subject matter is reinforced. Even the headings of structure explanations, the titles of practice assignments and the names of many characters, which are most effective when pronounced aloud, are clever. We tend to remember what makes us smile.

The chapter sequencing is another novel aspect of <u>Funky French.</u> Organized to reflect how a student actually learns to speak, read and write a language, this textbook is arranged neither by unrelated terms and usages nor by grammatical clusters. Instead, the material is presented by interlocking concepts.

Additionally, because repetition is imperative for language acquisition, vocabulary (first shown in bold type) and structures are not given just one shot, cameo appearances. After their introduction, these terms and grammar points stay 'on stage' throughout the book. Review sections precede the more advanced corresponding chapters. Following every twenty-five or so pages, students can check their progress by doing mastery exercises. The Answer Key found at <u>www. funkyfrenchbook.com</u> has the final say.

<u>Funky French</u> is a multipurpose, invaluable resource for school, business and travel. Students who want to learn the basics, supplement classroom instruction or converse on a rudimentary level will find this textbook to be a colorful cornucopia of information. Others may view it as a self-study guide and a means to 'dust off and polish up' skills learned in high school or college. Students taking AP and IB courses will notice that all major concepts are covered in detail to insure excellent results. Moreover, readers engaged in careers involving the use of French will be far better equipped to speak the language. Lastly, anyone planning a trip or a stay abroad should not leave home without <u>Funky French</u>.

LA TABLE DES MATIÈRES - THE TABLE OF CONTENTS

the Eiffel Tower

FUNKY FRENCH

LA PRONONCIATION FRANÇAISE - French Pronunciation

Do you find it ironic that this language textbook, unique in its methodical and entertaining approach, begins with what many consider to be a difficult concept, namely French pronunciation? (Perhaps, it just sounds that way.)

Because we need to be on bilingual speaking terms for the journey ahead, please keep the following in mind:

a. You do not have to be born with Gallic vocal chords to have a good French accent.

b. It makes sense to be familiar with French pronunciation before being introduced to structures and conversation. By taking that route, students don't have to figure out how to say each word as they go along or mispronounce words and have to backtrack to review their correct sounds.

THIRTEEN TIPS OF THE TONGUE

1. The three options for dividing French words into syllables are between two vowels, between two consonants and between a vowel and a consonant. Separating the syllables between consonants and vowels is a *non-non*.

Notice how that three-choice rule applies to the following words, and say them aloud!

fran-çais, l'A-mé-rique, l'im-per-mé-a-ble (the raincoat), la ma-de-moi-selle (Don't make her 'mad' by dividing the word between the consonant and the vowel!)

You should be able to separate the following words into syllables in 'a split second':

Paris, le café, le restaurant, le théâtre, la liberté, Pompidou, économique, l'indépendance, la révolution, l'administration

2. The French oi is pronounced like the English wa.

'Oi' not say these French words *à haute voix*- aloud?

Exs. trois- three, moi- me, l'oie- the goose, le roi- the king, la soie- the silk

Oi appears to be crying out in these sentences:

Ex. Moi, je crois que je vois trois rois. > Me, I believe that I see three kings.

Ex. La mademoiselle en soie boit beaucoup ce soir. > The mademoiselle in silk is drinking a lot this evening.

An exception: *L'oignon- the onion does not start with wa. Rather, it has its 'own' sound.**

3. A single s between two vowels is pronounced like an English z, even if one word ends with an s and the next one starts with a vowel. Linking two words is termed a *liaison*. (Incidentally, the s in *liaison* has a z sound.)

Try pronouncing these 'ea-z-y' French nouns!

la chaise- the chair, **choisir**- to choose, **la maison**- the house, **les arbres**- the trees, **les enfants**- the children, **les usines**- the factories, **les États-Unis**- the United States

Say the following two phrases *à haute voix*, and underline the seven z sounds!

Ex. Françoise adore des maisons roses. > Françoise adores pink houses.

Ex. Lise choisit des éclairs et des fraises. > Lise chooses some éclairs and some strawberries.

4. An h is not pronounced in French. (Think of the consonant as standing for hush!) If there is a very brief pause between the first word and the next one that starts with an h, that consonant

is referred to as <u>aspirant</u>. **The article in front of that <u>h</u> does not have an apostrophe.**
Exs. **le haricot**- the bean, **le hibou**- the owl, **le huitième étage**- the eighth floor
4a. With no hesitation indicated between the two words, the <u>h</u> is considered mute.
Exs. **l'herbe**- the herb, the grass, **l'histoire**- the history, the story, **l'homme**- the man
5. The following letter combinations sound like a long <u>a</u> sound said quickly: ai, ais, ait, aient, é, ée, eil, er, es, est, et, ez
Say these French words aloud!
vrai- true, **mais**- but, **le lait**- the milk, **le café**- the coffee, **le soleil**- the sun, **parler**- to speak, **et**- and, **chez**- at the home of (You probably never had all A's with such little effort.)
In the next two examples, underline six, long <u>a</u> sounds said briefly in each!
Ex. Vous parlez français et anglais chez Émilie. > You speak French and English at Emiy's.
Ex. Le monstre est laid. Il a un nez cassé et une oreille. > The monster is ugly. He has a broken nose and one ear.
6. The following letter combinations resemble a long <u>o</u> pronounced quickly in English: au, aux, eau, eaux, ôt. Some French words containing this sound are beau- handsome, **chaud**- warm, hot, **l'agneau**- the lamb, **les rideaux**- curtains, **bientôt**- soon
Show what you know by underlining the four long <u>o</u> sounds said briefly in each phrase!
Ex. Les beaux bateaux de M. Rimbaud sont au quai. > Mr. Rimbaud's beautiful boats are at the pier. (They are OK *au quai.*)
Ex. À bientôt et au revoir, Claude Goudreaux. > See you soon and goodbye, Claude Goudreaux.
<u>An important note</u>: **The <u>x</u> on -aux elides to the next word as a <u>z</u> if it precedes a vowel or a mute <u>h</u>. The phrase forms a liaison just as an <u>s</u> becomes a <u>z</u> in the same cases.**
Exs. **aux aéroports**- to, at the airports, **aux écoles**- to, at the schools **aux églises**- to, at the churches, **aux universités**- to, at the universities, **aux hôpitaux**- to, at the hospitals,
7. If a French word ends with any of the consonants in the word <u>careful</u>, that letter is generally pronounced. (The helpful hint includes 'a silent warning' for consonants other than c, r, f and l.)
Repeat these French words 'carefully'!
sec- dry, **noir**- black, **le mur**- the wall, **vif**- lively, **neuf**- nine, new, **l'œuf**- the egg, **l'arc-en-ciel**- the rainbow, **le fusil**- the gun, **le sel**- the salt
Underline and say "the special consonant words" in the examples below!
Ex. Il y a un flic au fusil près du Pont-Neuf. > There is a cop with a gun near le Pont-Neuf.
Ex. La femme chic et le bel homme sont chez Dior pour choisir des bijoux. > The stylish woman and the handsome man are at Dior to choose some jewels.
<u>Careful Exceptions</u>
a. <u>C</u> is not pronounced, even though it is the last letter in these words: blanc- white, **le banc**- the bench, **le franc**- the French franc (former currency), **le tabac**- the tobacco
b. <u>R</u> following an <u>e</u> with no accent mark calls for a long <u>a</u> sound said quickly. This combination is found in infinitives of -<u>er</u> verbs.
8. When the last letter of a word is an unaccented <u>e</u>, the consonant in front of it is pronounced. Unless the speaker enunciates very clearly, the vowel is not heard. However, it is *une lettre très importante*. One use of the enabling <u>e</u> is to signal feminine agreement.
Saying this set of adjectives aloud will reveal the feminine touch.
petit (masc.) > petite (fem.)- little, small
grand (masc.) > grande (fem.)- big, great

haut (masc.) > haute (fem.)- high

mauvais (masc.) > mauvaise (fem.)- bad (The s between the two vowels produces a z sound.)

9. An œ combination is typical in written French. The joined letters are pronounced much like the ur in purse.

Nasal Sounds

10. And now for what makes the French sound so French! Though there are four sets of nasal sounds, they share one formula: a vowel + m or n + a consonant other than m or n or no letter at all. The m or n can be the last letter of the word.

10a. The four combinations am, an, em and en have the same pronunciation. (If said together, they sound similar to a foghorn.) *L'enfant*- **the child contains two nasal pairs.** (The kids' combos include 'a two-for-one deal.')

Think how an English person would pronounce <u>can't</u> or <u>France</u>! Then say these words aloud: le champagne- the champagne, chanter- to sing, **danser-** to dance, **la tante-** the aunt, **le croissant, employer-** to employ, to use, **seulement-** only, **mentir-** to lie, **l'encre-** the ink

10b. With your top and bottom lips in a straight position, voicing the <u>im/in</u> variation produces a smile. *Le pain,* **the bread, a 'staple' word of reference, can be shared with la faim-** the hunger, **simple-** simple, **le timbre-** the stamp, **grimper-** to climb, **la fin-** the end, **le lapin-** the rabbit, **mince-** thin, **le prince-** the prince

10c. The nasal combination <u>om/on</u> is not difficult to pronounce since your mouth forms an <u>o</u> in the process. While it is open, you might pop in *des bonbons-* **some candy, and say these French words aloud: le nombre-** the number, **tomber-** to fall, **le pompier-** the fireman, **mignon-** cute, nice **le mouton-** the sheep, **le pont-** the bridge, **l'oncle-** the uncle

10d. Looking in a mirror, you will notice your bottom lip making a U-turn for the <u>um/un</u> duo. Because *un* **means <u>one</u> and is also the masculine form for <u>a</u> and <u>an</u>, French speakers get plenty of mileage from this nasal sound. Start out by saying these French words aloud: emprunter-** to borrow, **le rhum-** the rum, **brun-** brown, **lundi-** Monday

<u>An interesting note</u>: If you pronounce the nasal sounds in order (10a. thru 10d.), you form the sequence emitted from the UFO in the movie *Encounters of the Third Kind.* (That might explain why nasal combinations sound alien.)

<u>A reminder</u>: A consonant other than m or n or nothing at all must follow one of those letters to produce a nasal sound. *Pommes* **in** *les pommes frites-* **the French fries are not in a nasal combo. <u>Underline the seventeen nasal sounds in the following sentences</u>!**

Le printemps et l'automne sont deux saisons. > Spring and fall (autumn) are two seasons.

La mince femme blonde a trente et un ans. > The thin blond woman is thirty-one years old.

Nous n'en avons que cinq. > We have only five of them.

Mme Lebrun prend du vin blanc et du champagne. > Mrs. Lebrun takes some white wine and some champagne.

---

11. When an <u>i</u> is not included in a nasal combination, its pronunciation is close to a long <u>e</u> said quickly. You'll get *l'idée* **as you hear yourself say le midi-** noon, **le minuit-** midnight, **joli-** pretty, **bâtir-** to build, **venir-** to come, **vite-** quickly

3

12. A <u>y</u>, like the non-nasal <u>i</u>, has a quick long <u>e</u> sound. 'Y' not listen for it in **typique**- typical, **le cygne**- the swan, **le gymnase**- the gymnasium and **le mystère**- the mystery?

Accent Marks

13a. The hook under a <u>c</u> in front of an <u>a</u>, <u>o</u> or <u>u</u> is a cedilla (*une cédille*). Its presence makes the consonant retain its soft pronunciation. (The harsh sound of 'a sea' appeals neither to gulls nor to Gauls.) Familiar words 'hooked on' the <u>c</u> are *François, le garçon*- the boy, *la salade niçoise* and *(le) français*.

<u>**Accent marks frequently top off French Es.**</u>
13b. The accent *aigu* (é) slants from right to left and signals a clipped long <u>a</u> sound. This slash, meaning <u>sharp</u>, ominously leaves marks over two <u>es</u> in *l'épée*- the sword.
<u>A very helpful hint</u>: To find the English translations of many French words beginning with an <u>é</u>, switch that first letter to an <u>s</u>.
Some examples are **l'épice**- the spice, **l'éponge**- the sponge, **l'école**- the school, **l'étudiant**- the student, **étudier**- to study.
13c. The accent *grave* (è) slants from left to right and gives the <u>e</u> a short vowel sound. You may find it ghoulish that the accent *grave* rests in *le cimetière*- the cemetery.
Repeat these French words with accents pointing left and right until you get them straight:
désolé- sorry, **l'élève**- the pupil, **Genève**- Geneva, **l'été**- summer, **l'infirmière**- the female nurse, **le médecin**- the doctor, **la mère**- the mother, **le musée**- the museum, **le père**- the father, **le thé**- the tea, **marié**- married, **tiède**- lukewarm
13d. A word with *un accent circonflexe* (^) over a vowel typically has an English cognate with <u>s</u> as the next letter. See what happens to *la forêt, l'interêt, l'hôpital* and *les vêtements*- the clothing when the roof (^) is lifted off, and the consonant is let in! (The circumflex is *l'hôte*- the host.)
Instead of an imaginary <u>s</u> after a vowel with a circumflex, the French usually offer '<u>t</u>.' (It is not just a British custom.)
Without the translations given, try to decipher the meanings of the following words!
le plâtre, la fête, la bête, l'île, le maître, coûter
13e. *Un tréma,* ë, the pair of dots above the second of two consecutive vowels, indicates that the word is split into syllables between them. This accent mark distinguishes two terms that would otherwise look and sound identical. *Mais*- but becomes *le maïs*- the corn. (It has been 'popped'.)
In addition, Noel, a first name, converts into *le Noël* for Christmas. (Were you previously *naïve* about this?)

<u>**What's in a Name?**</u>- Using the above explanations, write the numbers and numbers with letters (2-13e.) included in the pronunciation of these French names. The key sounds are underlined. The numbers in parentheses indicate how many rules apply.
Exs. Gu<u>y</u> de M<u>au</u>pass<u>an</u>t (3) 11, 7, 10a   Th<u>é</u>oph<u>i</u>le G<u>au</u>t<u>ie</u>r (6) 4, 5, 11, 6, 11, 5

1. Marc<u>el</u> Marc<u>eau</u> (2) _____   9. S<u>i</u>mon<u>e</u> de B<u>eau</u>v<u>oi</u>r (5) _____
2. G<u>é</u>rar<u>d</u> Depard<u>ie</u>u (3) _____   10. P<u>ie</u>rre <u>Au</u>gust<u>e</u> Ren<u>oir</u> (5) _____
3. Le Corbu<u>sier</u> (3) _____   11. <u>É</u>d<u>ith</u> P<u>ia</u>f (5) _____

4

4. Cla<u>ude</u> Mon<u>et</u> (3) _____
5. <u>Y</u>ves M<u>ont</u>a<u>nd</u> (3) _____
6. Bl<u>aise</u> Pasca<u>l</u> (3) _____
7. Napol<u>éon</u> Bonapart<u>e</u> (3) _____
8. <u>H</u>onor<u>é</u> de Balza<u>c</u> (4) _____

12. Fra<u>n</u>ço<u>is</u> M<u>i</u>tterr<u>and</u> (5) _____
13. C<u>é</u>lin<u>e</u> D<u>ion</u> (5) _____
14. <u>H</u>enri de Toulou<u>se</u> L<u>au</u>tre<u>c</u> (6) _____
15. <u>A</u>nto<u>ine</u> de Sa<u>int</u>-<u>E</u>xup<u>é</u>r<u>y</u> (6) _____

'From the Sound of It'- Label the statements *vrai* or *faux*.

_____ 1. French words can be divided into syllables between consonants and vowels.
_____ 2. The French sound <u>oi</u> is similar to <u>wa</u> in English.
_____ 3. A double <u>s</u> between two vowels in French is pronounced like a <u>z</u> in English.
_____ 4. There are two liaisons in *Les États-Unis*.
_____ 5. The article preceding an aspirant <u>h</u> does not have an apostrophe.
_____ 6. A long <u>a</u> sound is heard only in French letter combinations starting with an <u>a</u>.
_____ 7. The French <u>au</u> makes a clipped English <u>o</u> sound.
_____ 8. A French word ending in an <u>x</u> cannot form a liaison to the next one.
_____ 9. The consonants in <u>careful</u> are silent when they are the last letters of French words.
_____ 10. A final <u>e</u> without an accent mark serves no purpose.
_____ 11. The pronunciation of French adjectives often varies according to the gender.
_____ 12. <u>M</u> or <u>n</u> is always present in a nasal combination.
_____ 13. The shape of one's mouth does not change to produce different nasal sounds.
_____ 14. A vowel plus a double <u>m</u> or double <u>n</u> constitutes a nasal combo.
_____ 15. If <u>i</u> is not in a nasal set, it sounds like a long English <u>e</u> said quickly.
_____ 16. <u>Y</u>s and <u>i</u>s, not in nasal combinations, have different French pronunciations.
_____ 17. A cedilla goes under a <u>c</u> when that consonant is followed by an <u>a</u>, an <u>o</u> or a <u>u</u>.
_____ 18. An accent *aigu* and an accent *grave* both produce a clipped English <u>e</u> sound.
_____ 19. The English meaning of a French word is often found by changing the first <u>é</u> to an <u>s</u>.
_____ 20. An <u>s</u> usually follows a vowel topped with a circumflex.

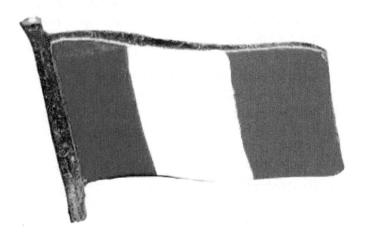

the French Flag

LES SALUTATIONS - The Greetings

Though a good French accent is *très important*, if the correct sounds are not applied in conversation, the speaker is limited to impressing French animals. Knowing how to address people is your chance to get in the first and last words.

Calling the Meeting to Order

1. When approaching or being approached by a French-speaking person whom you know well, expect to kiss or to be kissed on both cheeks. (Either party may start the exchange. There isn't any 'pecking order.')

2. One not familiar with an individual proceeds directly to *bonjour*. "Hello" is its most common translation, but it actually means <u>good day</u>. *Bon après-midi-* good afternoon can only be used at a specific time of day, whereas *bonjour* serves from sunrise until sunset. *Bonsoir-* good evening starts or ends a conversation. *Bonne nuit-* good night is the final greeting of the day. (However, the conversation is still very 'light.')

<u>Important notes:</u> You will not make *un faux pas-* a mistake if you add a title of address such as *Monsieur-* Mr., *Madame-* Mrs., and *Mademoiselle-* Miss/Ms to all greetings. An example of the correct format is *"Bonjour, Mademoiselle LaFrance."* An older woman should be addressed as *Madame.* (Referring to her as *mademoiselle* infers that she 'missed the boat.')

By not adhering to *la politesse française-* French politeness, a speaker might encounter another kind of 'cross culture.'

3. Abbreviations are perfectly acceptable in written French. You will not be considered 'short' with people for writing *M.* for *Monsieur, MM.* for *Messieurs, Mme* for *Madame, Mmes* for *Mesdames, Mlle* for *Mademoiselle* and *Mlles* for *Mesdemoiselles.*

4. When meeting somebody the first time, an obvious question is, What is your name? The two translations are *Quel est votre nom?* > What is your name?, and *Comment vous appelez-vous?*, which literally means "How do you call yourself?"

The answer for the first form starts, *Mon nom est _____.* > My name is _____. The response for the second begins, *Je m'appelle _____.* > My name is/I call myself _____.

4a. The above individual should be addressed in the formal *vous* form at the first meeting.

4b. However, when you are being introduced to someone your age or younger, it is appropriate to use the informal *tu* form.

The questions in 4. become *Quel est ton nom?*, and *Comment t'appelles-tu?*

5. Hi! is expressed by *Salut!* (That's a short salutation.)

6. One frequently hears *Ça va?* exchanged among friends and family. That is an informal way of saying "How are you?" Its literal translation is "It's going?"

<u>Typical responses to *Ça va?* are:</u>

Ça va (bien.) > I am doing (well.)/It is going (well.) The intonation in the speaker's voice distinguishes the question from the answer.

Ça va comme ci comme ça. > It's going so-so./I'm doing just OK.

Ça va mal. > It's not going well./I'm not doing well.

7. There are two very popular ways to express "How are you?" in French.

7a. When speaking to a stranger or to more than one person, regardless of how well you know him/her/them, the appropriate question is *Comment allez-vous?* Its exact meaning is "How are you going?" *Vous* is a formal form and the only plural pronoun for <u>you</u>.

7b. To ask somebody with whom you are familiar how he or she is, the most typical question is *Comment vas-tu? Tu* **is the informal subject pronoun in "How are you going?"** *Comment* **means** <u>how</u>. When answering, the person(s) will <u>comment</u> on how he/she/they is/are.

8. The most common responses to the questions in 7a. and 7b. are:

Je vais (très) bien, merci. **> I am (very) well, thank you.**

Je vais comme ci comme ça. **> I am doing so-so.** *Je ne vais pas mal.* **> I am not doing badly.**

Je ne vais pas (très) bien. **> I am not (very) well.**

Je vais mal. **> I am doing poorly.** (The prefix *mal* has nothing good to say in either language.)

<u>A very important note</u>: *Ne* before a verb and *pas* after it make a sentence negative.

9. Dialogues are often peppered with the following phrases:

9a. *S'il te plaît* **and** *s'il vous plaît!* **> Please! The word-for-word translation for both terms said before or after a request is "If it pleases you."** (Pronounced correctly, *s'il vous plaît* won't sound like an outdated wedding gift.)

Ex. S'il te plaît, apporte-moi du vin rouge! > Please bring me some red wine!

Ex. Parlez lentement, s'il vous plaît! > Speak slowly, please!

9b. *Merci* **and** *Merci beaucoup.* **> Thank you and Thank you very much. Choose either** *de rien* **or** *pas de quoi* **to say, "You are welcome." The former means** <u>of/from nothing</u>; **the latter translates as** <u>not of what</u>. **"Think nothing of it" draws from both French responses.**

Ex. La boîte de chocolats est pour moi? Merci beaucoup. > The box of chocolates is for me? Thank you very much.

De rien or *pas de quoi* would be a tasteful way to acknowledge gratitude for the sweet gesture.

10. Even a brief *rendez-vous* **precedes a choice of closing remarks. Of course, the most popular goodbye is** *au revoir*. **Because its exact translation is "to see again," it implies that there will be another meeting.** *Adieu,* **(Go) with God, is more formal and more final.**

You can also leave 'a lasting impression' with *à bientôt!* **or** *tout à l'heure!*- **See you soon! Those anticipating meeting again soon might say** *à demain*- **until tomorrow or** *à* + **the scheduled time. The international** *ciao* **can replace all of the previous possibilities.**

<u>PS</u>: **Before leaving relatives and friends, it is appropriate to plant one more** *bisou*- **kiss on each other's cheeks.**

<u>Let's Talk!</u>- **Circle the letters of the correct answers to complete the sentences below.**

1. *Bonjour* is an appropriate greeting for _____.
a. the morning only   b. the afternoon only   c. anytime of the day   d. the evening

2. Good night is translated by _____.
a. bonne soir   b. bonne nuit   c. bon après-midi   d. bonbons

3. The written abbreviation for *madame* is _____.
a. M.   b. MM.   c. Mlle   d. Mme

4. One who asks the question *Comment vous-appelez-vous?* _____.
a. wants to know a young person's name   b. has already asked *Quel est votre nom?*
c. is using informal pronouns   d. wants to know the name of someone older

5. When greeting friends, children or young adults, one often says _____!
a. Salut   b. Ciao   c. Ça ne va pas bien   d. Adieu

6. *Comment allez-vous?* is the formal form of _____?

a. Allez-vous mal?   b. Ça ne va pas bien.   c. Comment vas-tu?

d. Allez-vous comme ci comme ça?

7. *Je vais mal* is similar in meaning to _____.

a. Vous allez mal   b. Ça va comme ci comme ça   c. Ça va   d. Ça ne va pas bien.

8. To request a favor from more than one family member, one should add, _____.

a. s'il te plaît!   b. s'il vous plaît!   c. Comment ça va?   d. Vous allez bien

9. You are welcome is expressed in French by *de rien* or _____.

a. pas de quoi   b. la politesse   c. un bisou   d. merci beaucoup

10. *À bientôt* and *tout à l'heure* are synonyms which translate as _____!

a. Please go   b. See you soon   c. See you tomorrow   d. With God

---

La France

LES NOMBRES 1-30

So many conversations include numbers that they are a mainstay for all languages. While the whimsical hints in this section are memory aids, some of the pronunciation associations might be considered 'Frenglish!'

1. *Un* is the only number with a feminine form. In addition to meaning one, *un* and *une* translate as <u>a</u> and <u>an</u>.

2. *Deux* sounds like a simpleton's response to a question above his level.

3. *Trois* includes the <u>wa</u> sound and contains the beginning of trio, triplet and trilogy.

4. *Quatre* is the only one of the first ten French numbers consisting of two syllables. It shares its stem with quadruple, quadruplet and so forth.

5. *Cinq* is pronounced like the outcome of The Titanic.

6. *Six* sounds like <u>cease</u>, but it does not stop at that. It rhymes with *dix* (10).

7. *Sept* has a silent <u>p</u> and a very slightly pronounced <u>t</u>. September was the seventh month of the Julian calendar.

8. *Huit* with its silent <u>h</u> and very soft <u>t</u> is a homonym for *oui*- yes.

9. *Neuf*, which also means <u>new</u>, ends with an <u>f</u>. Handle the pronunciation carefully!

10. *Dix* is the origin of Dixie. *Les dix* referred to the $10 banknotes formerly used in that region of the US. The number is attributed to December, the tenth month of the Roman calendar.

11. *Onze* is the first in a series of numbers ending with -<u>ze</u>. Anyone who possesses eleven things *onze* them.

12. *Douze*, a cognate of <u>dozen</u>, is pronounced like the fee paid by members of a club.

13. *Treize*, which begins like *trois*, rhymes with *seize*- 16.

14. *Quatorze*, with the first four letters of *quatre*, sounds like a less expensive option offered by a travel company. (Those who do not pay full price get 'cut tours.')

15. *Quinze* has a pronunciation similar to the food containers stored in a pantry.

16. *Seize*, the last of the -<u>ze</u> sequence, sounds just like the second word of the exercise game led by Simon.

17., 18., 19. *Dix-sept, dix-huit* and *dix-neuf* add single numbers preceded by hyphens to *dix*. It is not unlike the teen concept in English. (They are known to hang out in groups.)

20. *Vingt* is identical in pronunciation to *le vin*- the fruit of the vine. The last two letters of the number are silent. *Vingt bouteilles de vin* > twenty bottles of wine. (Although all of *le vin* is there for drinking, the <u>g</u> and <u>t</u> are there only for your viewing enjoyment.)

21. *Vingt et un*, a popular casino card game in France (Black Jack in the United States), is the only number in the twenties holding *et* instead of a hyphen.

22-29. *Vingt-deux* through *vingt-neuf* include a hyphen and a single-digit number added to the *vingt* base. So, twenty-five is *vingt-cinq*. (It sounds like an SUV that went under water.)

30. *Trente* begins like its counterparts *trois* and *treize*.

<u>Important notes</u>

a. Zéro is 0. It makes its presence known with an é.

b. The <u>t</u> on *sept, huit* and *vingt* elide to the next word when it begins with a vowel or a mute <u>h</u>. If you appear to be smiling after saying one of those numbers, your mouth is in the correct position to add a word. (*Vingt étudiants*- twenty students consider it amusing.)

c. To differentiate it from #1, the European #7 has a horizontal line through its stem.
d. *Un chiffre* is a figure/a numerical symbol.

A Number of Possibilities- Write the French words for *les chiffres* below.
a. 2 _____   b. 4 _____   c. 5 _____   d. 7 _____
e. 8 _____   f. 10 _____   g. 11 _____   h. 13 _____
i. 16 _____   j. 18 _____   k. 20 _____   l. 23 _____
m. 25 _____   n. 26 _____   o. 29 _____

Fill in the blanks with French names of the numbers from 1 to 30 not written above!
_____, _____, _____, _____, _____,
_____, _____, _____, _____,
_____, _____, _____,
_____, _____, _____

le Chambord (the Loire Valley)

LES JOURS DE LA SEMAINE - The Days of the Week

Les sept jours de la semaine were named for gods, goddesses and planets. <u>Di</u> is the abbreviated form of the Latin word for day.

lundi- Monday: Because the base of its name is lunar, this is 'moon day.'
mardi- Tuesday: We can thank Mars for this day and the French for *Mardi Gras* which means <u>Fat Tuesday</u>.
mercredi- Wednesday: Mercury gets 'credi-t' for the name of this day.
jeudi- Thursday: My guess is that this word comes from Jupiter, but I could be 'far off.'
vendredi- Friday: This most welcomed day of the week was a gift from Venus.
samedi- Saturday: The origin of its name is Saturn. (Snow White pinned her hopes on this day in the song "*Samedi* My Prince Will Come.")
dimanche- Sunday: If taken apart, it says "day sleeve." (For the other six days, one has 'the right to bare arms.')

Daily Reminders
1. The French week starts with *lundi*, leaving no question about a two day weekend.
2. French days of the week begin with lowercase letters.
3. The days are masculine in gender, but there is usually no need to put a definite article before them. However, when they are used in a general sense, *le* precedes the named day. The corresponding concept is expressed by <u>on and/or s</u> in English.
Ex. M. Bruyant va aux boums le samedi soir. > M. Bruyant goes to parties (on) Saturday evenings. (Loud ones, from the sound of it.)
4. Although the other six days end with -<u>di</u>, that is how *dimanche* begins.

Strong Support for the Week
1. le jour- the day: Seen previously in *bonjour*, it can now be read in *le journal*- the newspaper.
2. la semaine- the week: Other than noting that *semaine* is a seven letter word, you are on your own for the week.
3. aujourd'hui- today: *Jour* and the uncommon French apostrophe are inside the adverb.
4. combien de- how much/how many: <u>Combine</u> numbers or things to get the total amount.
5. il y a- there is/ there are: When a question starts with *combien de*, the answer usually begins with *il y a*. Its word-for-word translation is "it has there."
Ex. Combien de jours de la semaine? Il y en a sept. > How many days of the week? There are seven of them. ('Twos-day' is counted only once.)
6. la fin de la semaine- the weekend: That's the finishing touch to the work week.
7a. *Quel jour est-ce aujourd'hui?* > What day is it today?
    C'est aujourd'hui _____. > It is today (Today is) _____.
The inverted verb phrase *est-ce?* > is it? loses an <u>e</u> in the response which is *c'est* > it is.
7b. *Quel jour sommes-nous aujourd'hui?* > What day is it today? Its word-for-word translation is "What day are we today?" The answer is *Nous sommes aujourd'hui* _____.

<u>**Making the Most of Free-Time**</u>- **Replace the blanks with correct answers.**
1. Lundi, _____, mercredi, _____, vendredi, _____, dimanche
2. _____ jours de la semaine?
3. Il y a _____ jours de _____.
4. Samedi et dimanche sont les deux jours du _____.
5. Quel jour _____ / _____ aujourd'hui?
6. C'est aujourd'hui _____.
7. _____ est le premier jour de la semaine française.
8. M. Bruyant va aux boums _____.

<u>LES MOIS DE L'ANNÉE - The Months of the Year</u>

It is not necessary to learn *les mois de l'année* from scratch. Since the French spelling for many of them is so close to their English cognates, students can take several months off.

<u>**Les Douze Mois de l'Année**</u>
1. **janvier- January: The words begin the same in both languages, but then they split up.**
2. **février- February: This is Cupid's 'fev-rite' month.**
3. **mars- March: The <u>s</u> at the end of *mars* is pronounced.** (The French word reveals its origin.)
4. **avril- April: Only the second letter and the weather vary.**
5. **mai- May: The French and English spellings 'correspond' to each other. They have already exchanged one letter.**
6. **juin- June: This month starts with the first two letters of its English translation, but it ends with a nasal sound.**
7. **juillet- July: The French celebrate Independence Day on the fourteenth- *La Fête Nationale*. (Bastille Day).**
8. **août- August: Picturing a phantom <u>s</u> after the <u>u</u> makes the month look more like the English version. As the <u>a</u> is optionally silent and the <u>t</u> is pronounced only if linked to a word beginning with a vowel or a mute <u>h</u>, *août* sounds like a brief cry of pain. (Or the forementioned phantom.)**
9. **septembre- September: The cognates are so close in spelling that you only need to swap the last two letters and a beach bag for a book bag.**
10. **octobre- October: By reversing the endings and the clocks, you assure an accurate reading for this month.**
11. **novembre- November: This is the third consecutive month with an English/French last two letter switch. (That is something to be thankful for.)**
12. **décembre- December: After adding an accent *aigu* to the first <u>e</u>, just exchange the last two letters and some holiday gifts.**

<u>**'An Annual Checkup'**</u>
1. **French months begin with lowercase letters.**
2. **The first two months, *janvier* and *février*, end the same way.** (Often very cold)
3. ***Juin* and *juillet* begin the same way.** (Usually very hot)
4. **The two months starting with <u>m</u>, *mars* and *mai*, each have one syllable.**

5. The names of five French months consist of a clipped long <u>a</u> sound produced from the letters or letter combinations <u>ai</u>, <u>é</u>, <u>er</u> and <u>et</u>.

Those months are _____, _____, _____,

_____, _____.

6. The names of five French months have nasal combinations; the sounds formed with a vowel + <u>m</u> or <u>n</u> + any consonant other than <u>m</u> or <u>n</u> or no additional letter.

The months are _____, _____, _____,

_____, _____.

7. *Le is* placed before the date of the month. So, one whose birthday is (on) the twenty-eighth of December celebrates it *le 28 décembre.* (With no on, no of and a reduced number of gifts.)

8. The first day of a month is *le premier. La première* **applies to the initial showing of a movie.**
Ex. Les vedettes célèbrent la première le premier avril. > The stars celebrate the première April 1.

9. *En* expresses <u>in</u> before a month.
Ex. Il y a trois lettres en mai. > There are three letters in May. (But February is the shortest month.)

Timely Terms

1. *Le mois* and the month share their first two letters. *L'année* is related to <u>annual</u>.

2. To ask what month it is you can say, *Quel mois est-ce?* **The answer is "***C'est* _____."
A second option is *Quel mois sommes-nous?* > What month is it/are we? The response is "*Nous sommes* _____." (Some things do not change with time.)

3. Although *l'anniversaire* **is actually** <u>the anniversary</u>, **many use the same noun to refer to** <u>the birthday</u>. *L'anniversaire de naissance* > the anniversary of birth is the 'dressed up' term.

4. *La date* refers neither to a small fruit nor to what one does socially; rather, it is found on *le calendrier*- the calendar.

Nice Dates for You- Explain in French what you think of them!

1. Saturday, January 1 _____
2. Tuesday, February 14 _____
3. Wednesday, March 17 _____
4. Friday, April 20 _____
5. Sunday, May 12 _____
6. Thursday, July 4 _____
7. Monday, September 6 _____
8. Wednesday, October 31 _____
9. Thursday, November 23 _____
10. Saturday, December 25 _____

Choosing Your Own Dates- Fill in the blanks with correct responses.

1. Il y a douze _____ de _____.
2. C'est aujourd'hui _____, _____.
3. Nous sommes aujourd'hui _____, _____.
4. Mon anniversaire de naissance est _____.
5. La date de la Fête de l'Indépendance en France est _____.
6. Le jour **après (after)** le trente et un janvier est _____.

7. La Fête des **Mères (Mothers)** est ____ mai.
8. Il y a trente jours ____ avril, juin, septembre et novembre.
9. Le Noël est _____.
10. Les mois des vacances pour les étudiants sont _____ et _____.

_____

Metro Entrance at Porte Dauphine (Paris)

LES ARTICLES DÉFINIS - LE, LA, L', LES: The Definite Article - THE

As in English, French nouns are singular or plural. However, when speaking of people, places, things and ideas in French, one must be specific. Our 'one-size-fits-all the' is tailored four ways to accommodate genders, vowels, silent <u>h</u>'s and plurality.

<u>Singular</u>
le (masculine) - precedes a consonant
la (feminine) - precedes a consonant
l' (masc. and fem.) - precedes a vowel or a mute <u>h</u>

<u>Plural</u>
les (masculine and feminine) - precedes consonants, vowels and mute <u>h</u>s

<u>Sorting out THE Articles</u>
1. *Le* precedes masculine singular nouns. It was 'the featured article' in *le banc, le boulevard, le café, le croissant, le lait* and *le soleil*.
2. *La* goes in front of feminine singular nouns and provides a built in mnemonic as it showcases the first two letters of <u>la</u>dy. She has left articles during *la semaine* in *la maison*, with *la tante*, on *la chaise* and inside *la boîte*.
3. *L'* goes in front of masculine and feminine singular nouns that begin with a vowel or a mute <u>h</u>. Consecutive vowel sounds are not heard in *l'école, l'église, l'opéra* or *l'hôpital*. (The public is also encouraged to be quiet in those locations.)
<u>An important note:</u> Most singular French nouns beginning with a <u>y</u> are preceded by *le*.
4. *Les* is the plural of *le, la* and *l'*. Because *les* has only one form, gender is never an issue. Furthermore, although there are several exceptions, the majority of singular French nouns can be made plural by adding an <u>s</u>.
Exs. le livre- the book > les livres- the books, la porte- the door > les portes- the doors, l'université- the university, l'hôtel- the hotel > les hôtels- the hotels
<u>A reminder:</u> The <u>s</u> in *les* has a <u>z</u> sound when the next word begins with a vowel or a mute <u>h</u>.
Listen to the liaisons in these French words: les arbres- the trees, les heures- the hours, les hommes- the men, les idées- the ideas. Correctly pronounced, the last French noun sounds like a long stretch of idle time. (lazy day).

<u>Little 'Noun' Facts</u>
1. *États* spelled backwards is state.
2. *Les vacances*- the vacation(s) has no singular form. (Perhaps because so many are needed.)
3. The spelling of masculine singular nouns and adjectives ending with -<u>s</u>, -<u>x</u> and -<u>z</u> remain as is in the plural. It's "the sxz (sexy) rule." (Why bother to change anything?)
Exs. le mois > les mois, **le prix- the price, the prize > les prix- the prices, the prizes**, le nez- the nose > les nez- the noses, mauvais- bad, joyeux- joyous, heureux- happy

----

<u>And THE Answer Is</u> ... Using *le, la* or *l'*, write the words in their singular forms.
1. les rois _____
2. les bouteilles _____
3. les oies _____
4. les murs _____
9. les mères _____
10. les œufs _____
11. les timbres _____
12. les usines _____

5. les ponts _____   13. les mesdames _____
6. les bêtes _____   14. les messieurs _____
7. les fusils _____   15. les prix _____
8. les pains _____

GENDER EXPLANATIONS

Since the only choices for labeling the gender of a noun are masculine or feminine, you have a 50 percent chance of getting it correct without any guidelines. But by following the tips below, you significantly increase the odds in your favor.

The Birds and the Bees of the French Language
The gender of a noun can often be determined by its ending.

Typical masculine endings
1. -eau: It is seen everywhere including in *le bureau-* **the desk/the office,** *le bateau-* **the boat and** *le château.* **A common exception is** *l'eau-* **water.** (Don't let that feminine word 'trickle' you!)
2. -o: *Le lavabo-* **the sink and** *le stylo-* **the pen are two nouns that fill the description. Exceptions are usually abbreviated forms of feminine words such as** *la disco-* **the discotheque and** *la moto-* **the motorcycle. However,** *le métro-* **the subway stays on 'the masculine track.'**
3. -acle: *L'article, le miracle* **and** *le spectacle* **are examples.** *Le spectacle* **might refer to anything as mundane as a movie.**
4. -age: *Le mirage, le village, le garage* **and** *l'âge* **are four such words, but** *le fromage-* **the cheese offers the tastiest sample.** *La page* **and** *la plage-* **the beach are exceptions.**
5. -al: *Le bal-* **the formal dance,** *le cheval-* **the horse and** *le journal* **have a masc. 'termin-al.'**
6. -ier: *L'acier-* **the steel,** *le papier-* **the paper and** *le cahier-* **the notebook have the ending in, on and with them.**
7. -ment: *L'établissement-* **the establishment,** *le gouvernement-* **the government and** *le bâtiment-* **the building are 'supported by' this final syllable.**
8. -oir: *Le boudoir-* **the formal bedroom,** *le miroir-* **the mirror,** *le tiroir-* **the drawer and** *le soir-* **the evening have a masculine ending.**

Typical feminine endings
1. -ade: *L'orangeade,* **available during** *la parade* **near** *la façade,* **is offered with these letters.**
2. -ance: *La connaissance-* **the acquaintance,** *la circonstance-* **the circumstance and** *la chance-* **the luck are also found in** *La France.*
3. -ence: *La diligence, l'intelligence* **and** *la résidence* **are shown with this ending. The spelling of the French nouns is identical to their English cognates, while the adjectives derived from them end with -ent in both languages.**
4. -ette: *L'assiette-* **the plate,** *la fourchette-* **the fork and** *la serviette-* **the napkin/the small towel have the same 'pattern on the border.'**
5. -ie: *La joie-* **the joy,** *la pâtisserie-* **the pastry/the pastry shop and** *la plaisanterie-* **the joke can provide a smile with their last two letters.**

6. -ique: *La boutique, la clinique*- the private hospital and *la musique* share one final sound but in different settings. An exception to 'the feminine mystique' is *le pique-nique*- the picnic.

7. -oire: *La gloire*- the glory of *la victoire*- the victory lived on in *la memoire*- the memory of the knight who battled near *La Loire. Le pourboire*- the gratuity is not added to the -<u>oire</u> list.

8. -sion: *La confusion, la discussion* and *la tension* are household words on *occasion*. (Although the scenes play out differently, -<u>sion</u> is always the finale.)

9. -tion: *L'éducation, la pronunciation* and *la traduction*- the translation frequently results in *les variations*, but the -<u>tion</u> has a permanent *fonction*.

10. -ure: *La coiffure*- the hairstyle, *la manucure* and *la pédicure* show good grooming as long as the -<u>ure</u> ending is not 'clipped.'

<u>Vive la Différence</u>!- Put *le, la* or *l'* in front of the words below. If the answer is *l'*, write masc. or fem. after the noun. New vocabulary words are in bold print.
Ex. <u>le</u> manteau (the coat)

1. _____ mariage
2. _____ **histoire** _____ (the history, the story)
3. _____ **chameau (the camel)**
4. _____ république
5. _____ monument
6. _____ animal _____
7. _____ **sucette (the lollipop)**
8. _____ **couloir (the corridor)**
9. _____ marmalade
10. _____ **inondation** _____ (the flood)

11. _____ Congo
12. _____ **cadeau (the gift)**
13. _____ **argenterie** _____ (the silverware)
14. _____ **espoir** _____ (the hope)
15. _____ télévision
16. _____ Afrique _____
17. _____ distance
18. _____ **grenier (the attic)**
19. _____ biologie
20. - _____ **peignoir (the bathrobe)**

'<u>Members Only</u>'- Circle the letter of the word that does not in the group. Do not eliminate the nouns based on their genders!

1. a. le restaurant   b. le pourboire   c. le bistro   d. le café
2. a. la maison   b. le bâtiment   c. la connaissance   d. le château
3. a. la semaine   b. le mois   c. le prix   d. l'année
4. a. le journal   b. le cahier   c. le papier   d. la plage
5. a. la plaisanterie   b. le jour   c. le soir   d. la nuit
6. a. le vin   b. l'orangeade   c. le cheval   d. l'eau
7. a. la gloire   b. le boudoir   c. l'espoir   d. la joie
8. a. le mur   b. la façade   c. la porte   d. le bateau
9. a. le boum   b. la fête   c. le pont   d. le bal
10. a. le livre   b. le lait   c. l'œuf   d. le fromage
11. a. le lapin   b. l'oie   c. le mouton   d. le timbre
12. a. l'herbe   b. la serviette   c. le soleil   d. l'arc-en-ciel

LES ARTICLES INDÉFINIS - UN, UNE, DES
The Indefinite Articles - A, An, Some

When someone wants to talk about people, places, things or ideas in general terms, indefinite articles definitely do the job. Nouns typically 'have words with them.' Yet, they always end up agreeing with indefinite articles.

The Specifics Re: Nonspecific Articles

1. *Un,* **translated as <u>a</u> and <u>an</u>, precedes masculine singular nouns. In addition, count on** *un* **to be <u>number one</u>.**
Exs. **un crayon- a pencil**, un stylo- a pen, un élève- a young student, un médecin- a doctor
2. *Une,* **meaning <u>a</u> and <u>an</u>, is used before feminine singular nouns. Since the article ends with an <u>e</u>, there is no nasal sound; the <u>n</u> is pronounced.**
Exs. une femme- a lady/woman/wife, **une rue- a street**, **une ville- a city**, une fête- a party/festival
(One can live with, on, in or for them 'indefinitely.')
3. *Un* **precedes masculine singular nouns beginning with a vowel or a mute <u>h</u>.** *Une* **goes before feminine singular nouns in the same instances. With the definite article** *l,'* **it is not necessary to know the gender.** (However, *un* and *une* provide an opportunity to become better acquainted with the noun.)
Exs. une année- a year, un anniversaire de naissance- a birthday, un insecte- an insect, un hasard- a chance, une idée- an idea. (There are indefinite numbers of each.)
4. The plural of *un* **and** *une* **is** *des.* **To remember that it means <u>some</u>, say aloud, "some day!"**
Exs. des étudiants- some older students, **des jardiniers- some gardeners,** des pompiers- some fire-men, des infirmières- some nurses (They are all seen carrying plural articles.)

What Small Change Adds Up To- Put indefinite articles before the nouns, and translate them.
Ex. la cuisine > une cuisine- a kitchen

1. la maison _____
2. le bâtiment _____
3. la rue _____
4. les stylos _____
5. la porte _____
6. les assiettes _____
7. le tiroir _____
8. l'impression _____
9. les greniers _____
10. le mouton _____
11. l'église _____
12. le miroir _____
13. le village _____
14. les fromages _____
15. l'histoire _____
16. la fourchette _____
17. les villes _____
18. le téléphone _____
19. la plage _____
20. les oignons _____
21. le pourboire _____
22. l'espoir _____
23. les usines _____
24. la pâtisserie _____

LA FAMILLE - The Family (Part 1)

May I present the Stick family? They are branches of a larger family tree whom you will meet later. The parents are Carver and Peggy. Their 'whittle' children are Woody and Twiggy.

The French Connection- Generic Labels for Family Members
1. l'homme- the man: The h is silent, but the association with *Homo sapiens* speaks for itself.
2. la femme- the woman/the wife: Notice the resemblance to feminine. *La femme* and *l'homme* end with -mme, the abbreviation for *madame*.
3. le garçon- the boy: The term also applies to a waiter, but referring to him as *le serveur* might prompt better service.
4. la jeune fille- the girl: The literal translation is "the young daughter." It proves that French daughters of all ages are really little girls at heart.
5. le père- the father: The same word applies to the priest in a Catholic Church.
a. le Papa- Dad or Daddy.
6. la mère- the mother: While *la mère* and *le père* rhyme, *la mère* and *la mer*- the sea share the same pronunciation.
a. la Maman- Mom or Mommy.
7. le frère- the brother: This family member is sleeping in *Frère Jacques*- "Brother James." He pledges his allegiance to a fraternity.
8. la sœur- the sister: This noun is also the nun who belongs to a special type of sorority.
9. le mari and l'époux- the husband: The first term appears at the beginning of *le mariage*. The last four letters of the second, *les poux*, mean lice. (So, if a woman refers to her husband or her ex as a louse …)
10. la femme- the wife, the woman: She also goes by *l'épouse*. (The relationship to *l'époux* should not be 'scratched.')
A helpful reminder: To find its translation, picture the é at the beginning of a word as an s.
Ex. *l'époux/l'épouse* > spouse
11. le fils- the son: The s in *fils* is pronounced and differentiates this male family member from *le fil*- the thread. (Otherwise, he might 'make something out of it.')
12. la fille- the daughter: Recently seen in *la jeune fille*, she has now lost her youth. However, a daughter retains her status at any age.
13. l'enfant- the child: Very similar to infant, the French word applies to a child of any age and either gender. *Le bébé*- the boy or girl baby does not need to be 'changed' either.
14. les grands-parents- the grandparents: They include *le grand-père* and *la grand-mère*. (With their prestigious place in the family, they merit 'a dash' of something extra.)
15. le parent/la parente- the parent, the relative (The second meaning may not be 'a-parent.')
16. la famille- the family and relatives in general

'Calling Them Names'- Identify the members of the Stick family in generic terms.
A note: One of the vocabulary words listed on the preceding page will be used twice.

<u>Carver</u>	<u>Peggy</u>	<u>Woody</u>	<u>Twiggy</u>
_____	_____	_____	_____
_____	_____	_____	_____
_____, _____	_____, _____	_____	_____
_____	_____	_____	_____

-- --

Match 'Sticks'- Write the answers to the following questions.

1. Which five family names rhyme? _____

_____

2. Which four family names start with <u>f</u>? _____

3. Which three family names start with <u>e</u> or <u>é</u>? _____

4. Which three names begin with <u>m</u>? _____

5. In which two names is there a double <u>m</u>? _____

6. In which five words is the last letter pronounced? _____

_____

7. Which seven family terms have nasal sounds? _____

_____

8. Which three terms apply to masculine and/or feminine family members? _____

_____

_____

Family Reunion by Frédéric Bazille (le Musée d'Orsay, Paris)

UNE REVUE - A Review

La Prononciation Française, Les Salutations, Les Nombres, Les Jours de la Semaine, Les Mois de l'Année, Les Articles Définis et Indéfinis, Les Membres de la Famille

'Taking Sides'- Match the letters to the numbers of their antonyms.

_____ 1. oui
_____ 2. la jeune fille
_____ 3. blanc
_____ 4. s'il vous plaît
_____ 5. et
_____ 6. la sœur
_____ 7. le soleil
_____ 8. aujourd'hui
_____ 9. beau
_____ 10. salut
_____ 11. bon
_____ 12. la mère
_____ 13. petit
_____ 14. bien
_____ 15. vrai

A. mais
B. laid
C. le père
D. la lune
E. faux
F. le garçon
G. mauvais
H. grand
I. merci beaucoup
J. le frère
K. non
L. mal
M. ciao
N. noir
O. demain

'Next Please!'- Circle the letters of the words or phrases that follow those listed on the left.

1. Salut!   a. Ça va comme ci comme ça   b. Ça va?   c. À demain!
                                                                          d. très bien

2. Bonjour   a. Je vais mal.   b. bonne nuit   c. ciao   d. madame/monsieur/
                                                                           mademoiselle

3. mercredi   a. lundi   b. mardi   c. jeudi   d. samedi

4. janvier   a. février   b. décembre   c. mars   d. mai

5. juillet   a. juin   b. août   c. janvier   d. avril

6. quatorze   a. trois   b. treize   c. quinze   d. seize

7. vingt   a. onze   b. dix-neuf   c. trente   d. vingt et un

8. le bébé   a. le parent/la parente   b. l'enfant   c. le grand-père/la grand-mère
                                                                      d. la famille

9. la jeune fille   a. la sœur   b. la femme   c. la mère   d. l'épouse

10. le garçon   a. le frère   b. le fils   c. l'homme   d. le mari/l'époux

'Beginner's Luck'- Label the statements *vrai* or *faux*.

_____ 1. An s̲ between two vowels makes a z̲ sound, even if the consonant is between two words.

_____ 2. *Un circonflexe* and *un tréma* serve the same purpose for French pronunciation.

_____ 3. *De rien* and *pas de quoi* are antonyms.

_____ 4. *Comment vous appelez-vous?* and *Quel est votre nom?* are synonyms.

_____ 5. All teen numbers begin with *dix* in French.

_____ 6. The French numbers for twenty and thirty both have nasal sounds.

_____ 7. French names of day and months begin with lowercase letters.

_____ 8. The French words for the day, the week, the month and the year are feminine.

_____ 9. The French days of the week all end with -d̲i̲.

_____ 10. French nouns ending with -e̲a̲u̲ and -i̲e̲r̲ are typically masculine.

_____ 11. French nouns ending with -s̲i̲o̲n̲ and -t̲i̲o̲n̲ are typically feminine.

_____ 12. French nouns ending with -e̲r̲i̲e̲ and -e̲t̲t̲e̲ are usually masculine.

_____ 13. There are four ways to express t̲h̲e̲ in French.

_____ 14. There are separate masculine and feminine plural definite articles.

_____ 15. *Une* is not used before a feminine singular noun beginning with a vowel or a mute h̲.

_____ 16. The indefinite article *des* means s̲o̲m̲e̲.

_____ 17. Both the husband and the wife have two French translations.

_____ 18. No French names of family members contain hyphens.

_____ 19. *Le père* and *la sœur* have religious as well as familial meanings.

_____ 20. *La femme* has two translations.

le Mont Saint-Michel (on the Brittany-Normandy Border)

FRENCH SUBJECT PRONOUNS

Subjects and verbs are "the meat and potatoes" of every language. When served together, they express what is cooking in the sentence.
These pronouns are offered as a first course.

Singular	Plural
je- I	nous- we (masculine and feminine)
tu- you (informal)	vous- you (singular and plural formal and informal)
il- he, it	ils- they (masculine for persons or things)
elle- she, it	elles- they (feminine for persons or things)
on- one, you, we, they, people, somebody, anybody, etc.	

For Starters

1. The *j* in *je*- I is capitalized (upper case) only if it is the first word of a sentence.
Ex. Je vais comme ci comme ça. > I am feeling so-so. (I must be 'on the mend.')

2. The *tu* form is used when addressing a family member of any age, a person of the speaker's age or younger or an animal. It is frequently referred to as "the informal you." Because *tu* is a singular pronoun, it applies when speaking to one individual or one animal at a time. (There is no two with *tu*.)
Ex. Tu vas bien, Maman? Oui, tu vas bien. > Are you well, Mom? Yes, you are well. (The child did not want to take "no" for an answer.)

3a. Il, the third person singular masculine pronoun, is pronounced like eel. Its meaning 'slips' from he to it as it can replace a living or a nonliving noun.
Ex. M. Alter est français. > Il est français. (Mr. Alter is French. > He is French.)
Ex. Le parfum est français. > Il est français. (The perfume is French. > It is French.)

3b. Elle, the third person singular feminine pronoun, is pronounced like the letter L. Since *elle* replaces a previously named person or thing, its meanings are she and it.
Ex. Madame Cadeau est ici. > Elle est **ici**. (Mrs. Cadeau is here; She is **here**.)
Ex. La surprise de Madame Cadeau est ici. > Elle est ici. (Mrs. Cadeau's surprise is here; It is here.) (She made her presence known, and she is known for her presents.)
An interesting note: *Elle* is the name of a popular French magazine.

3c. *On*, with multiple translations including one, you, we, they, people, somebody and anybody, is appropriately labeled an indefinite pronoun. Whether it refers to one or to more individuals, the verb following *on* is always in the third person singular form.
Ex. On a faim? > Is one, anybody, anyone etc. hungry? (*On* has several mouths to feed.)

4. *Nous*, we, the first plural subject pronoun, is the product of you and I. (For those who never thought of it that way before, it's a *nous* concept.) *Nous* refers to more than one male, more than one female or a combination of both genders.

5. *Vous*, which rhymes with *nous*, is both a singular and a plural pronoun. "The formal you" is busy catering to:
a. a person older than the speaker or anyone whom the speaker does not know well.
b. more than one person or animal, regardless of how well the speaker knows them.

Ex. Comment allez-vous, M. Tuned? > How are you, Mr. Tuned?

Ex. Comment allez-vous M. et Mme Tuned? > How are you Mr. and Mrs. Tuned? (Chances are that they are 'fine.')

Ex. Comment allez-vous **mes amis**? > How are you **my friends**?

6a. *Ils,* **which means** <u>they</u>, **is the third person plural masculine subject pronoun. Since it refers to people and to objects,** *ils* **may replace masculine or a combination of masculine and feminine subjects.** *Il* **and** *ils* **share one pronunciation unless the latter elides with a vowel or a mute** <u>h</u>**.**

Ex. Yves et cinq amies sont au cinéma. > Yves and five female friends are at the movies.

Ils sont au cinéma. > They are at the movies.

6b. *Elles,* **which means** <u>they</u>, **is the third person plural feminine subject pronoun. It applies exclusively when speaking of people or things feminine in gender.** *Elle* **and** *elles* **have an identical pronunciation unless the latter elides with a vowel or a mute** <u>h</u>**.**

Ex. Les cinq amies sont au cinéma. > The five female friends are at the movies.

Elles sont au cinéma. > They are at the movies. (When they were asked what happened to Yves, the friends said that they wanted 'to change the subject.')

<u>**A very important note**</u>: **If neither gender is specified,** <u>they</u> **should be translated as** *ils***.**

le Jeu de Quilles, Revermont (the Jura Region)

PRESENT TENSE CONJUGATION - REGULAR -ER VERBS

A conjugation consists of matched subject pronouns and verb forms. In order for this union to take place, the verb is taken out of its infinitive form. (Saying "I to love you," even Cupid would have trouble 'getting his point across.') **The subject determines the ending of the verb. Consider the two parts of speech as mates who cannot change partners!**
-ER verbs, so named because of their infinitive endings, are also called <u>first conjugation verbs</u>. Have fun with this one!

Jouer - To Play

<u>Singular</u>	<u>Plural</u>
je jou<u>e</u>- I play, do play, am playing	nous jou<u>ons</u>- we play, do play, are playing
tu jou<u>es</u>- you play, do play, are playing	vous jou<u>ez</u>- you play, do play, are playing
il jou<u>e</u>- he/it plays, does play, is playing	ils jou<u>ent</u>- they play, do play, are playing
elle jou<u>e</u>-she/it plays, does play, is playing	elles jou<u>ent</u>- they play, do play, are playing

----

<u>A Beginner's Guide to Endings</u>
1. While there are three ways to form the present tense in English, there is only one in French. It might take some practice neither to translate am, is, are, do and does nor to wonder what to do with -ing. (Not to worry! Everyone can get used to doing nothing.)
2. The remaining letters minus the infinitive ending are <u>the stem</u> or <u>the root</u> of the verb. That is the base to which -<u>e</u>, -<u>es</u>, -<u>e</u>, -<u>ons</u>, -<u>ez</u> and -<u>ent</u> are attached.
3. The entire singular and the third person plural -<u>er</u> verb forms share one pronunciation. The -<u>ons</u> ending is a nasal combination; the -<u>ez</u> ending has a clipped long <u>a</u> sound.
4. It is a coincidence that -<u>ons</u> contains several letters of its matching subject pronoun _nous_.
5. The verb form is unchanged when a subject pronoun replaces a noun.
Ex. Homer joue au baseball. > Homer plays/does play/is playing baseball.
    Il joue au baseball. > He plays/does play/is playing baseball. (_Il_ 'went to bat for' Homer.)

COMMON REGULAR -ER VERBS

<u>Basic Training</u>
1. aimer- to like, to love: Followed by _bien_, the phrase is "to like well." When _aimer_ is <u>to love</u>, no adverb is necessary. ("All you need is love.")
2. apporter- to bring: <u>Portable</u> and even <u>a porter</u> are on hand to help with this verb.
3. chanter- to sing: <u>Chant</u> is seen and heard in this one.
4. chercher- to look for: Don't look for the translation of <u>for</u>! The preposition is included in the French verb which contains some of the letters in <u>search</u>.
5. coûter- to cost: The circumflex serves as a reminder to picture the next letter as an <u>s</u>.
6. danser- to dance: Only one 'step' differs between _danser_ and its English cognate.
7. donner- to give: The stem of the verb is similar to <u>donate</u>. (The ending is 'dropped off.')
8. dépenser- to spend: What one buys depends on how much one has to spend.
9. écouter- to listen to: If good acoustics are available, listen to this 'sound advice': Don't try to translate <u>to</u>! It is included in the verb.

10. entrer (dans)- to enter (into): Forms of this verb are followed by *dans*. (The preposition is a French entrance fee.)

11. étudier- to study: Substitute an <u>s</u> for the <u>é</u>, and this verb will not require further study.

12. fermer- to close, to shut: Almost everyone is familiar with the French command, "Fermez la bouche!" > "Close/Shut your mouth!"

13. gagner- to earn, to gain, to win (Two gs and three stacked translations make for no losers.)

14. habiter- to live, to reside: <u>Habitat</u> and <u>inhabit</u> are two of its cognates. Meanwhile, each conjugated form contains 'a beet' to fortify you.

15. laver- to wash: The derivative, <u>lavatory</u>, will 'sink' this one into your memory.

16. monter- to go up, to get on (to mount), to ride: <u>Mountain</u>, <u>mound</u> and <u>mount</u> will help you come up with the meaning of this verb!

17. montrer- to show: So as not to confuse *monter* with *montrer*, note the second <u>r</u> for <u>reveal</u> in the latter. Besides, there is a correlation between *montrer* and <u>demonstrate</u>.

18. parler- to speak, to talk: *Parlez-vous français?* is a most popular French question.

19. passer- to spend time, to take an exam: *On passe un examen* but may nevertheless fail it.

20a. penser à- to think about: Rodin's famous sculpture, *Le Penseur*- <u>The Thinker,</u> is in a pensive mood. Associate the accompanying preposition *à* with <u>about</u>!

20b. penser de- to think of, to have an opinion of: What do you think of *(penser de)* that?

21. porter- to carry, to wear: Do not confuse this verb with *apporter*- <u>to bring</u>! The often heard phrase, *prêt-à-porter* > ready-to-wear, is a 'suitable' mnemonic.

22. regarder- to look at, to watch: With dual interpretations, this verb is highly regarded. Look carefully! <u>At</u> is hiding inside one translation.

23. rester- to remain, to stay: Connect the meaning to the sound of the last four letters of *rester* rather than with the entire infinitive! (You have the key. Enjoy your '-ster!')

24. travailler- to work: The verb obviously has nothing to do with travel. (I don't have a trick 'to make it work.')

25. trouver- to find: Everyone would like to find a treasure trove. (Isn't that 'trou'?)

Several French verbs closely resemble their English cognates. Examples are *arriver, composer, continuer à, désirer, informer, inviter, préparer, téléphoner à* and *visiter*.

<u>A very important note</u>: The <u>e</u> in *je* is changed to an apostrophe before verbs that begin with a vowel or a mute <u>h</u>.

Exs. j'apporte- I bring, I do bring, I am bringing
      j'habite- I live, I do live, I am living

<u>'More Than Words Can Say'</u>- Using the information above, answer the following questions.

1. How many translations are there for each conjugated verb form? _____

2. What is the difference in pronunciation among the first, second, third person singular and third person plural forms of -<u>er</u> verbs? _____.

3. The verb form that contains a nasal sound is _____.

4. Which five verbs begin with vowels? _____

_____

5. Which infinitive starts with a mute <u>h</u>? _____

6. Three French verbs with English prepositions included in their translations are _____

_____ .

7. Which verb changes its meaning according to the preposition that follows it? _____

8. Which two infinitives have a difference of only one letter in their stems? _____

_____ .

9. Two verbs that contain others inside them with different meanings are _____ and

_____ .

10. Which two verbs are *de faux amis* > **false friends** whose French spellings betray their English
translations? _____

Filling Out the Forms- Put the correct verb forms beside the subject pronouns. Then, write the
three translations for each answer.

	1.	2.	3.
1. (désirer) je _____	1. _____	2. _____	3. _____
2. (donner) vous _____	1. _____	2. _____	3. _____
3. (étudier) tu _____	1. _____	2. _____	3. _____
4. (laver) nous _____	1. _____	2. _____	3. _____
5. (montrer) ils _____	1. _____	2. _____	3. _____
6. (penser) elle _____	1. _____	2. _____	3. _____
7. (préparer) tu _____	1. _____	2. _____	3. _____
8. (trouver) on _____	1. _____	2. _____	3. _____
9. (entrer) vous _____	1. _____	2. _____	3. _____
10. (visiter) elle _____	1. _____	2. _____	3. _____
11. (aimer) j'_____	1. _____	2. _____	3. _____
12 (habiter) nous _____	1. _____	2. _____	3. _____
13. (écouter) ils _____	1. _____	2. _____	3. _____
14. (rester) elle _____	1. _____	2. _____	3. _____
15. (coûter) il _____	1. _____	2. _____	3. _____

'In Other Words'- **Translate these sentences.**

1. She loves the child. _____ .
2. They speak French. _____ .
3. You (*tu*) are working. _____ .
4. I am living in Paris. _____ .
5. He carries some books. _____ .
6. You (*vous*) enter the house. _____ .
7. The family watches (the) television. _____ .
8. The grandparents stay in (à) Lyon. _____ .
9. The daughter listens to the mother. _____ .
10. A boy is looking for three girls. _____ .
11. The husband and the wife sing badly. _____

_____ .

12. A brother and a sister visit two cities. _____

_____ .

_____

NE PAS = NOT

The negative is positively simple. When *ne* is put in front of a verb and *pas* is placed after it, an affirmative sentence becomes negative. An about-face is caused by just a couple of words.

A Few Not Notes
1. If the first letter of a verb is a vowel or a mute <u>h</u>, the <u>e</u> is deleted from *ne* and replaced by an apostrophe. (It seems that the French do a lot of '<u>es</u> dropping.')
Ex. M. Sax n'écoute pas la musique classique. > Mr. Sax does not listen to classical music. (Nobody sees him in music stores with 'a Chopin Liszt.')
2. The indefinite articles *un, une* and *des* often change to *de* or *d'* after verbs in negative sentences. It is the equivalent of switching a, one and some to <u>any</u>.
Ex. Des jeunes hommes ne portent pas **de cravates.** > Some young men do not wear **(any) ties.** (One 'k-not' is enough for them.)
3. A positive response to a negative statement or question starts with *si* rather than *oui*.
Ex. Frankenstein n'est pas laid. > Frankenstein is not ugly.
    Si, il est laid. > Yes, he is ugly.

<u>NOT Allowed Here</u> - Put the following sentences into the negative form.
Ex. Maga Zin et moi passons des heures dans les boutiques. > Maga Zin et moi ne passons pas d'heures dans les boutiques. (Maga Zin and I do not spend hours in the shops.)

1. Le roi danse au bal. _____.

2. Les étudiants étudient beaucoup. _____.

3. M. Neuf-Heures travaille dans un bureau. _____
_____.

4. Nous téléphonons à Pierre aujourd'hui. _____
_____.

5. Mlle de Versailles monte à bicyclette. _____
_____.

6. Tu trouves des stylos dans le tiroir. _____
_____.

7. J'aime bien des bonbons. _____.

8. Vous restez ici le samedi. _____
_____.

QUELLE HEURE EST-IL? - What Time Is It?

Even those who never committed a crime will now 'do time.' (However, 'the sentences' will not be very long.)

Timely Tidbits

1. l'heure- the hour (o'clock): The h is not pronounced in either language.

1a. *Une* precedes *heure* because that noun is feminine singular.

Ex. Il est une heure. > It is one o'clock.

1b. An s is added to *heure* **to signify plural hours.**

Ex. Il est six heure<u>s</u>. > It is six o'clock.

2. le midi- (the) noon: It refers to <u>the middle</u> of the day.

3. le minuit- (the) midnight: The term actually means "half night."

3a. *Midi* and *minuit* are not followed by *heure*. (It is 'two-timing' to say noon o'clock or midnight o'clock.)

3b. *Douze heures* is used less frequently to specify twelve o'clock.

4. Minutes go directly after the hour. Neither <u>past</u> nor <u>after</u> is translated. A few exceptions are listed in #5 and #6 below.

Ex. La femme **éclopée** ferme la boutique à cinq heures vingt. > The **lame** woman closes the shop at 5:20. (It takes her a few minutes 'to straighten up.')

5. et quart- and a quarter: This term equals <u>quarter past</u> and <u>quarter after</u>.

5a. *Quinze* can replace *et quart*.

Ex. **Les joueurs** du football gagnent **le match** à sept heures quinze. > The football **players** win **the game** at 7:15. (It was the last quarter that mattered.)

6. et demi(e)- and a half: This term turns to <u>half-past</u> or <u>thirty</u> in English.

6a. *Trente* can replace *et demi(e)*.

6b. An e is added to *demi* **when** *heure(s)* **is used.** (So much for having nothing to do after hours!)

Ex. Ashton Kutcher arrive à six heures et demi<u>e</u>/à six heures trente du soir. > Ashton Kutcher arrives at half past six/6:30 in the evening. (On that occasion, *'Demie'* was also there.)

7. moins- minus/less: The word means <u>to</u> or <u>of</u> when it applies to time.

7a. To tell time past the half-hour mark, identify the upcoming hour, insert *moins* **and subtract the minutes. The exceptions are listed in #7b. below.**

Ex. Le grand-père écoute la radio à dix heures moins dix. > The grandfather listens to the radio at ten minutes of/to ten. (That's his chance 'to turn back time.')

7b. Just as some people say "quarter of" and others use "quarter to," French offers a choice of *moins le quart, moins un quart* **or** *moins quinze***.**

Ex. **Une bande** entre dans **la salle de classe** à midi moins le/un quart/moins quinze. > **A gang** enters (into) **the classroom** at quarter of/quarter to noon. (Nobody dares 'to come after it.')

8. Adding the number of minutes after a half hour is an option, but it's not as common as using *moins, moins le quart* **or** *moins un quart***.** (However, all choices have the same 'show of hands.')

Ex. **L'autobus** de Mme Waite arrive à trois heures quarante-cinq aujourd'hui et pas à trois heures et demie. > Mrs. Waite's **bus** arrives at 3:45 today and not at 3:30. (It does 'get to her.')

Numbers 31-60
1. For 31, 41 and 51, *et un* **is added to** *trente, quarante* **and** *cinquante* **respectively.**
Exs. trente et un- 31, cinquante et un- 51
2. For 32-39, 42-49, and 52-59, a hyphen and a digit are attached to the base number.
Exs. trente-huit- 38, cinquante-quatre- 54

Time for Additional Vocabulary
1. de bonne heure- early: The phrase literally says "of good hour." Tôt **means early in the day.**
2. à l'heure- on time: As expected, it translates as "on the hour."
3. en retard- late: *Tard,* **appropriately found at the end of the word, is almost 'tard-y.'**
Ex. **Les factures** arrivent **toujours** à l'heure, mais les chèques arrivent en retard. > **The bills always arrive on time, but the checks arrive late.**
4. Because clocks show the same time twice in a twenty-four hour period, French differentiates am. from pm. by adding *du matin-* **in the morning,** *de l'après-midi-* **in the afternoon,** *du soir-* **in the evening and** *de la nuit-* **in the night (at night).**
Ex. Sol téléphone à Dawn à six heures du matin. > Sol phones Dawn at six o'clock in the morning. (They must have some plans 'on the horizon.')
4a. When specific times are not mentioned, in the morning, in the afternoon, in the evening and at night are preceded by definite articles.
Ex. La nuit, des enfants parlent à l'homme dans la lune. > At night, some children talk to the man in the moon. (They must be 'going through a phase.')
5. The time is usually expressed based on a twenty-four hour clock for departures, arrivals and events. If a play is scheduled to start at 19 heures 30, expect the curtain to go up at 7:30 pm.

If the Time Is Right- Label the statements *vrai* or *faux.*
_____ 1. *Heure* is used after *midi* and *minuit.*
_____ 2. The only time *heure* does not end with s is *une heure.*
_____ 3. There is no e on *demi* after *midi* and *minuit.*
_____ 4. *Quinze* cannot replace *et quart* to express quarter after/quarter past.
_____ 5. *Et demi(e)* is the only way to express half past the hour.
_____ 6. *Moins* is typically used to express of or to the hour.
_____ 7. *Moins le quart* and *moins un quart* are used interchangeably.
_____ 8. *Quarante-cinq* cannot be added to an hour to express quarter of/to.
_____ 9. The translation for *à l'heure* is "at one o'clock."
_____ 10. All French numbers from thirty-one thru fifty-nine contain *et.*
_____ 11. The French words for thirty, forty and fifty end with -nte.
_____ 12. There is no way to differentiate am. from pm. in French.

Clock Work- Write the listed times in French.
Ex. 4:50 Il est cinq heures moins dix. Il est quatre heures cinquante.

1. 12:00 _____ . _____ . _____ .
2. 3:00 _____ .
3. 5:10 _____ .

4. 7:05 _____.
5. 9:25 _____.
6. 1:15 _____. _____.
7. 6:15 _____. _____.
8. 12:15 _____. _____. _____.
         _____. _____. _____.
9. 2:30 _____. _____.
10. 4:30 _____. _____.
11. 8:30 _____. _____.
12. 11:55 _____. _____.
         _____.
13. 2:40 _____. _____.
14. 5:35 _____. _____.
15. 10:50 _____. _____.
16. 1:45 _____. _____.
         _____. _____.
17. 7:45 _____. _____.
         _____. _____.
18. 9:45 _____. _____.
         _____. _____.

'Time Will Tell'- Translate the sentences below.

1. Mom, what time is it? _____?
2. Some students enter the classroom at eight o'clock in the morning. _____
_____.
3. I watch (the) television at nine-thirty in the evening. _____
_____.
4. The friends do not study at noon. _____.
5. A boat arrives here at ten forty-five at night. _____
_____.
6. Today is Friday. It is five o'clock. We are thinking about Saturday and Sunday. _____
_____.
7. The president is speaking at twenty o'clock. _____.
8. It is seven twenty in the evening, and Dad is working in the office. _____
_____.
9. The sister always washes the baby in the morning. _____
_____.
10. The grandmother does not stay in the house in the afternoon. _____
_____.
_____.

ÊTRE - TO BE

Although *être* is an irregular verb, meaning that its conjugation is unique, its forms are used so frequently that you will master them quickly. I AM sure of it.
Here WE ARE!

Singular	**Plural**
je suis- I am	nous sommes- we are
tu es- you are	vous êtes- you are
il est- he is, it is	ils sont- they are
elle est- she is, it is	elles sont- they are

'To Be Announced'

1. The conjugation of <u>to be</u> is almost as irregular as *être*.
2. There is only one meaning for each form of *être*. (Helping verbs try to be independent.)
3. To pronounce *suis* correctly, you could pretend to beckon a pig.
4. The second and third person singular, *es* and *est*, are pronounced the same. *Il est* is familiar from telling time in French. "*Elle est*" is the largest city in California.
5. Three forms begin with an <u>e</u>, and three start with an <u>s</u> while four mean <u>are</u>.
6. Each plural form of *être* deserves special mention.
6a. *Sommes* has the distinction of being the only French verb that does not end with -<u>ons</u> in the *nous* form. (Well, aren't <u>we</u> special?)
6b. Being between two vowels, the <u>s</u> in *vous êtes* is pronounced like a <u>z</u>.
6c. *Ils/elles sont* contain nasal sounds.

'To Be Continued'- Fill in the blanks with the correct forms of *être*.

1. Sophie et Sylvie _____ des sœurs.
2. Paul habite à Paris, mais il ne (n') _____ pas français.
3. Nous travaillons dix heures par jour, et nous _____ fatigués.
4. L'examen de français _____ à deux heures de l'après-midi.
5. Je passe des jours à la plage. Je _____ en vacances.
6. Tu gagnes beaucoup d'**argent m. (money)**, mais tu ne (n') _____ pas riche.
7. Bonnie et Ben _____ les enfants de M. et Mme Lemieux.
8. Il _____ midi et demi. Vous ne (n') _____ pas en retard.
9. LA _____ une grande ville en Californie.
10. Nous _____ ici de New York.
11. Quel jour _____-ce aujourd'hui?
12. Quel mois _____-nous?
13. M. Pourboire travaille dans un restaurant. Il _____ serveur.
14. Les cravates ne (n') _____ pas dans le tiroir.
15. Je _____ un étudiant de français.

'To Be Sure'- Translate the following sentences.

1. Today is Tuesday, October 16. _____.

2. Jean and Jeanne are not the parents. _____.

3. Some mirrors are in the bedrooms. _____
_____.

4. The king is in the castle. _____.

5. Three eggs are in the omelet. _____.

6. The festival is in the street. _____.

7. The factory is not in a village. _____.

8. We are not French. _____.

9. Some doctors and (some) nurses are in the clinic. _____
_____.

10. You (*tu*) are in the class in the afternoon. _____
_____
_____.

le Palais de Chaillot- le Trocadéro (Paris)

LES COULEURS - Colors
Basic French Adjective Formation

The names of colors are adjectives. French colors are placed after the nouns they modify. After the president of France visits Washington, D.C., he might say that he was a guest at *La Maison Blanche*- The White House. *Les adjecrtifs français* are diplomatic about agreeing in gender and in number with the nouns they describe.

'Brushing Up'
1. French adjectives have four (occasionally five) forms: masculine singular, feminine singular, masculine plural and feminine plural. (The colors always stay inside those lines.)
2. Adjectives that end with an e have the same masculine singular and feminine singular forms.
Ex. rouge- masc. sing., rouge- fem. sing.
Moreover, their singular and plural forms are pronounced the same. (It can be 'red' either way.)
Other adjectives in this category include *jaune*- yellow, *pourpre*- purple and *rose*- pink. French/ English *beige* and *turquoise* also belong in this group.
3. Adjectives ending with consonants in the masc. sing. typically add an e to become fem. sing..
Exs. un béret vert- a green béret, une feuille vert*e*- a green leaf
Additional examples are *brun*- dark brown and *noir*- black. They become *brune* and *noire* after **'a touch-up' is applied.**
4. The majority of adjectives are made plural by attaching an s to both singular gender forms.
Ex. bleu- masc. sing. > bleu*s*- masc. plural; bleue- fem. sing. > bleue*s*- fem. plural (Those are a few of Blue's Clues.)
An important reminder: Nouns and adjectives that end with -s, -x or -z in the masculine singular keep the same spelling in the masculine plural. Their risqué label is "the sxz rule."
Ex. gris (gray)- masc. sing., gris- masc. plural; grise- fem. sing., grises- fem. plural
For this adjective, you need only be concerned with feminine a-'gris'-ment.
5. When two or more nouns of different genders are used together, the accompanying adjective is masculine.
Ex. La porte et le toit sont brun*s*. > The door and the roof are brown.

A Colorful Exercise for 'Hue'- Write the colors listed in the feminine singular, the masculine plural and the feminine plural forms.

masculine singular	feminine singular	masculine plural	feminine plural
1. beige			
2. bleu			
3. brun			
4. gris			
5. jaune			
6. noir			
7. pourpre			
8. rose			
9. rouge			

10. turquoise _____

11. vert _____

'Red Alerts'

1. Unique colors were purposefully omitted from the previous section. The feminine singular of *blanc-* **white is** *blanche*; **the feminine singular of violet is** *violette*. **Both 'tone down' their plurals by adding an s to the masculine and feminine singular forms.**

(Exs. **les nuages** blancs > the white clouds, **les fleurs** violettes > the violet flowers.)

2. *Marron-* **(chestnut) brown and** *orange* **have invariable forms because they are also the names of edible nouns.**

Ex. Les oranges sont orange, et les marrons sont marron.

3. *De quelle couleur est* _____ *? and De quelles couleurs sont* _____ *? = (Of) What color is/are* _____ **?**

Ex. De quelle couleur est l'océan? > What color is the ocean? (The answer is actually "clear.")

4. It is quite common in English and in French for family names to be colors. Additionally, it is not unusual in either language for females to have 'colorful' first names such as Blanche, Rose and Violette.

Ex. Mme Leblanc- Mrs. White, M. Lebrun- Mr. Brown

<u>An interesting aside:</u> **Snow White is a reversed name in English. (She must have 'drifted.') But, with the French flip, she 'comes clean' as** *Blanche Neige*.

'What Do You Make of This?'- Write the masculine singular forms of the colors created when combining the listed pairs.

1. rouge + blanc = _____

2. noir + blanc = _____

3. bleu + jaune = _____

4. pourpre + blanc = _____

5. brun + blanc = _____

6. bleu + vert = _____

7. noir + orange = _____

8. bleu + noir = _____

A Splattering of Words

1. le chocolat- the chocolate

2. ou- or

3. la tomate- the tomato

4. la souris- the mouse

5. les signaux lumineux- the traffic lights

6. la rose- the rose

7. le ciel- the sky

8. l'encre (m.)- the ink

9. le drapeau- the flag

10. souvent- often

11. l'arc-en-ciel (m.)- the rainbow

12. l'automne (m.)- the autumn/the fall

'Dashes of Color'- Fill in the blanks with the appropriate colors in their correct forms.

1. La banane est un fruit _____.

2. **Le chocolat** est _____ **ou** _____.

3. **Les tomates** sont _____.

4. L'éléphant et **la souris** sont _____.

5. Le zèbre est _____ et _____.

6. **Les signaux lumineux** sont _____, _____ et _____.

7. **Les roses** sont _____, _____, _____ ou _____.

8. Le soleil _____ est dans **le ciel** _____.
9. **L'encre** dans un stylo est **souvent** _____ ou _____.
10. **Les drapeaux** américains et français sont _____, _____ et _____.
11. **Un arc-en-ciel** est _____, _____, _____, _____, _____, _____ et _____.
12. **En automne** les feuilles sur les arbres sont _____, _____, _____, _____ et _____.

_____

la Cathédrale de Notre Dame (Paris)

INTERROGATIVE TERMS

Handy Interrogative Words

1. Comment?- How?- This adverb introduces questions such as *Comment vas-tu?* and *Comment allez-vous?*, prompting one to <u>comment</u> on how he/she/they is/are.

1a. Comment?- Used by itself, *Comment?* is the equivalent of <u>What?/Say that again!</u>

2. Combien (de)?- How much/How many? By <u>combin</u>ing things, one gets a total amount.

Ex. Combien de **personnes** travaillent ici? > How many **people** work here? (At times, not everyone.)

3. Où?- Where? This little word is pronounced like 'the discreet sound' that people make when stubbing their toes. Without an accent mark, *ou* means <u>or</u>.

Ex. Où est le métro ou l'autobus? > Where is the subway or the bus?

4. Pourquoi?- Why? This term combines *pour*- for and *quoi*- what. *Pourquoi pas?* > Why not?

5. Quand?- When? The sound of this word minus the <u>d</u> is rather similar to a native Londoner's pronunciation of <u>can</u>.

6. Que?/Qu'est-ce que?- What? The basic translation will suffice for now. (You will soon learn to decipher what's what.)

7. Qui?- Who?/Whom? In French, one does not need to decide <u>who</u> or <u>to whom</u> it may concern as one *qui* opens both cases.

le Musée des Automates (Dole)

WHAT MORE COULD HE ASK?

Choose among *À quelle heure, Combien (de), Comment, Où, Pourquoi, Quand, Qui* **and** *Qu'est-ce que* **to complete the dialogue between Payne, an overly inquisitive moviegoer, and Madame Guichet, a cashier who loses patience with him.**

Du Vocabulaire du Conte (Some Vocabulary from the Story)

1. **le guichet**- the ticket booth/window
2. **finit-il?**- does it end/finish?
3. **la vedette**- the movie star
4. **le billet**- the ticket
5. **la monnaie**- the change, the coin

6. **la carte de crédit**- the credit card
7. **Ça ne fait rien.**- It does not matter.
8. **comme**- as, like, for
9. **l'entrée**- the entrance
10. **à droite**- on the right ('rite' is inside)

Madame Guichet: Bonsoir, monsieur.

Payne: Bonsoir, Madame. _____ allez-vous?

Madame Guichet: Pas mal merci et toi?

Payne: Bien merci. _____ le film commence-t-il?

Madame Guichet: à 14 heures 30.

Payne: _____ **finit**-il?

Madame Guichet: à 17 heures.

Payne: _____ spectacles y a-t-il aujourd'hui?

Madame Guichet: Quatre monsieur.

Payne: _____ sont **les vedettes**?

Madame Guichet: Gérard Depardieu joue un rôle important.

Payne: _____ coûte **un billet**?

Madame Guichet: Huit euros.

Payne: Préférez-vous de **la monnaie** ou **une carte de crédit**?

Madame Guichet: Cela ne fait rien.

Payne: _____ vous aimez **comme** les films?

Madame Guichet: Je regarde la télévision.

Payne: _____ est **l'entrée**?

Madame Guichet: À la gauche.

Payne: Et _____ sont les toilettes?

Madame Guichet: À la droite.

Payne: _____ vous appelez-vous?

Madame Guichet: (speaking to herself) _____ est-ce que je travaille ici?

FORMER LES QUESTIONS FRANÇAISES - Forming French Questions

There are four ways to pose a question in French. The formats offered below are 'yours for the asking.' When a speaker's voice goes up at the end of a sentence, he/she wants to know "what's going down."

Room for Interrogation
1. <u>Intonation</u>- A lilt in one's voice at the end of a statement makes it into a question.
Ex. Ton anniversaire de naissance est aujourd'hui? > Your birthday is today?
2. <u>Est-ce que/qu'</u>- This phrase, placed at the beginning of a question, means <u>Is it that</u>? Intonation is in effect at the end of the phrase. *Est-ce-que/qu'* is the inverted form of *C'est*- It is.
<u>A helpful hint</u>: To remember that *est-ce que/qu'* is an interrogative option, keep this in mind: If a man wants to go out with a woman, he must first *est-ce que.* (Ask her)
Ex. Est-ce que la Bête aime les femmes **sans attraits**? > Does the Beast love **unattractive** women? (He must know that "Beauty is not just skin deep.")
2a. When the subject begins with a vowel or a mute <u>h</u>, the <u>e</u> is deleted from *que.*
Ex. Est-ce qu'on reste dans **la chambre d'amis**? > Is anyone staying in **the spare bedroom**? (Your 'guest' is as good as mine.)
3. <u>N'est-ce pas?</u>- Spoken at the end of a sentence, it includes the subject in its translation.
(Exs. aren't you?, isn't she?, aren't they?)
Intonation is heard at the end of the question.
3a. *N'est-ce pas* is the negative-interrogative form of *est-ce?*- is it?
Ex. M. Fric dépense beaucoup d'argent, n'est-ce pas? > Mr. Fric spends a lot of money, doesn't he? (He apparently doesn't 'keep it to himself.')
3b. The previously listed interrogative words are not included in sentences with *n'est-ce pas?*
(Why would you want to do that, wouldn't you? sounds strange, *n'est-ce pas?*)
4. <u>Inversion</u> involves placing the verb before the subject. (It's similar to the mathematical process of the same name in which $^5/_8$ becomes $^8/_5$.)
Tu visites encore le Louvre changes to *Visites-tu encore le Louvre?* > Are you visiting the Louvre again? (He or she will notice that things have been 'switched around.')
4a. <u>Inversion with a "t"</u>- When the third person singular of the verb ends with a vowel, a <u>t</u> preceded and followed by a hyphen is inserted in front of *il, elle* or *on.* (The <u>t</u> is for third.)
Ex. Joue-t-il au golf? > Is he playing/Does he play golf? (Speaking of adding 'a tee!')
4b. <u>Inversion with a noun subject</u>- If a noun is the subject of the question, it goes in front of the inversion. The pronoun following the verb matches the subject in number and in gender.
Ex. M. Vert joue-t-il au golf? > Is Mr. Vert playing golf?/Does Mr. Vert play golf? (Mr. Vert and *il* use 'the same club.')

'Asking Around'- Using the models as a reference, change the statements into questions.
Ex. Gustave habite sur la rive gauche. > Gustave lives on the Left Bank.
a. Gustave habite sur la rive gauche?
b. Est-ce que Gustave habite sur la rive gauche?
c. Gustave habite sur la rive gauche, n'est-ce pas? (A briefer translation is "Gustave lives on the Left Bank, right?")
d. Gustave habite-t-il sur la rive gauche?

1. Ils parlent **espagnol (Spanish)**.

_____?
_____?
_____?
_____?

2. Vous passez les week-ends à Versailles.

_____?
_____?
_____?
_____?

3. Tu portes toujours les couleurs **claires (bright)**, Claire.

_____?
_____?
_____?
_____?

4. M. Chalet est toujours aux Alpes.

_____?
_____?
_____?
_____?

5. **Un passager (a passenger)** monte dans l'autobus.

_____?
_____?
_____?
_____?

6. Rose aime bien les fleurs jaunes.

_____?
_____?
_____?
_____?

7. M. Hasard et Mme Chance trouvent de l'argent dans la forêt.

_____?
_____?
_____?
_____?

LES NÉGATIFS-INTERROGATIFS FRANÇAIS - French Negative-Interrogatives

Wouldn't you like to know what the title means? In negative-interrogative sentences, the verbs are often surrounded by *ne(n') pas*. Three interrogative formats apply. (Different ones might be chosen for each job.)
The responses can begin with *si* or *non*.

<u>**With intonation**</u>
Ex. Vous n'êtes pas français? > You are not French? (Si, je suis français.)
<u>**With est-ce que (qu')**</u>
Ex. Est-ce que vous n'êtes pas français? > Aren't you French? (Si, je suis français.)
<u>**With inversion**</u>
Ex. N'êtes-vous pas français? > Aren't you French? (Non, je ne suis pas français.)
<u>**An important note:**</u> **Because *n'est-ce pas* is worded as a negative-interrogative, it is not used to form another one.**

<u>**Won't You Do This Exercise?**</u>- Use *est-ce que* and inversion to change the following sentences into negative-interrogative forms.

1. Tu arrives de bonne heure. _____ ?
_____ ?

2. On porte un imperméable. _____ ?
_____ ?

3. L'entrée est à droite. _____ ?
_____ ?

4. Les billets sont au guichet. _____ ?
_____ ?

5. Mme Fric donne la monnaie pour un pourboire. _____ ?
_____ ?

6. Claude et François passent un examen d'**anglais (English)** le matin. _____
_____ ?

7. La famille Langues parle français, anglais et espagnol. _____
_____ ?
_____

AVOIR - TO HAVE

Avoir is a very important irregular verb. It permeates the French language and makes its way into several tenses. Imagine an **h** in front of the infinitive to help remember its meaning!

Singular	Plural
j'ai- I have, do have, am having	nous avons- we have, do have, are having
tu as- you have, do have, are having	vous avez- you have, do have, are having
il a- he/it has, does have, is having	ils ont- they have, do have, are having
elle a- she/it has, does have, is having	elles ont- they have, do have, are having

----

Important Facts to Have
1. The **e** is dropped from *je*. (**J** and a clipped long **a** sound are all I have.)
2. The *tu* and *il/elle* forms, *as* and *a*, are pronounced the same.
An amusing aside: *Tu n'as pas* sounds like the Dad of a common fish.
3. The written *nous* form, *avons*, resembles the name of a cosmetic company. Its -**ons** ending is a nasal combination.
4. The *vous* form, *avez*, starts with a short **a**, but its -**ez** ending is a quick long **a**. (Ave Maria, the well known hymn, echoes these sounds.)
5. The stems of *avons* and *avez* resemble the infinitive.
6. The third person plural is the only form that does not begin with an **a**. *Ont* features a second exception; even though the **s** in *ils ont* and *elles ont* is not between two vowels, it has a **z** sound. Here's the 'reazon': If that were not the case, *ils/elles sont* and *ils/elles ont* would have identical pronunciations. (There you are, and there you have it.)

'To Have on Display'- Fill in the blanks with the correct forms of *avoir*.
1. Les pâtisseries _____ des éclairs et des gâteaux.
2. Quel mois _____ vingt-huit jours? **Tous. (All of them.)**
3. Je n' _____ pas de montre. Quelle heure est-il?
4. "Sir Prize, qu' _____ vous à la main?"
5. Est-ce que les étudiants _____ des questions?
6. Kent Wright n' _____ pas de stylo.
7. "Combien de frères _____-tu Jacques?"
8. Nous _____ une fête nationale le quatorze juillet.

LA VIE DE LA FAMILLE BANALE - The Banale Family's Life

Du Vocabulaire du Conte

1. la vie- the life
2. banal(e)- commonplace
3. l'appartement (m.)- the apartment
4. la pièce- the room (in general)
5. la chambre à coucher- the bedroom (less formal than *le boudoir*)
6. aussi- also
7. le chat- the cat (The <u>h</u> is its chair.)
8. le chien- the dog
9. le boulot- the job
   le travail- the work (comes from *travailler*- to work)
10. le passe-temps- the pass-time, the hobby
11. l'ordinateur- the computer
12. sur- on
13. avec- with
14. le copain- the buddy, the pal
15. le voisin- the male neighbor
    la voisine- the female neighbor
16. prochain(e)- next
17. la voiture- the car
18. l'auto (f.)- the automobile
19. cher- expensive

Monsieur et Madame Banale et deux enfants habitent à Paris dans un appartement de cinq **pièces.** Il y a trois **chambres à coucher.** Les parents ont un boudoir. Louis, le fils de treize ans, a une chambre à coucher bleue et Louise, la fille de dix ans, a une chambre à coucher rose.

La famille a **aussi un** petit **chien** noir, Aboyer, et **un chat** blanc, Griffer.

Le père travaille dans un bureau cinq jours par semaine. La mère cherche **un boulot.**

Les enfants étudient le soir. Ils n'ont pas beaucoup de **passe-temps.** Louis a **un ordinateur.** Il aime bien "surfer" **sur** le net. Louise adore écouter la musique.

Les parents passent le samedi **avec** les amis quand les enfants sont avec **les copains.**

Le dimanche matin on trouve la famille dans l'église. L'après-midi les Banale sont avec les voisins, M. et Mme Porte-**Prochaine.** Ils ont **une voiture.** C'est un Citroën jaune.

M. et Mme Banale n'ont pas **d'auto.** La vie dans une grande ville est **chère.**

Your Side of the Story- Using *La Vie de la Famille Banale* as a reference, answer the following questions in complete French sentences.

1. Où la famille Banale habite-t-elle? _____.

2. Qui sont Louis et Louise? _____.

3. Comment sont les chambres à coucher de Louis et Louise? _____
_____.

4. Où le père travaille-t-il? _____.

5. Qu'est-ce que Mme Banale cherche? _____.

6. Comment la famille passe-t-elle le samedi? _____
_____.

7. Où est la famille le dimanche matin? _____
_____.

8. Qui sont M. et Mme Porte-Prochaine? _____.

9. De quelle couleur est **leur (their)** voiture? _____.

10. Comment est la vie dans une grande ville? _____.

EXPRESSIONS WITH *AVOIR*

Temporary personal conditions are expressed in French with a form of *avoir*. (To have is not to be. There is no question.)

Avoir **Idioms No Longer Meant 'To Be'**
1. avoir faim- to be hungry: <u>Famine</u> is a clue for this nasal sounding word.
2. avoir soif- to be thirsty: The <u>f</u> is not swallowed.
3. avoir chaud- to be hot: A hot tip is needed here.
4. avoir froid- to be cold: <u>Frigid</u> and <u>frozen</u> are good memory joggers.
5. avoir raison- to be right: Good reasoning can help one make the right choices.
6. avoir tort- to be wrong: Tort Law refers to little wrongs. (Just ask 'Miss Demeanors'!)
7. avoir honte- to be ashamed: *Ils ont honte.* > They are ashamed. The French equivalent 'rubs it in' with consecutive sounds.
8. avoir peur- to be afraid, to be scared: Turning petrify into 'peur-trify' might be helpful.
9. avoir sommeil- to be sleepy, to be tired: A <u>somnambulist</u> with <u>insomnia</u> is an eye-opener.
10. avoir de la chance- to be lucky: Its actual translation is "to have some luck." (The Sum Luck Chinese restaurant offers realistic fortune cookies.)
11. avoir _____ ans- to be _____ years old (Those lines always reveal one's age.)
Quel âge as-tu?/Quel âge avez-vous? > How old are you? Anyone familiar with the person need not ask his/her age. One who does not know him/her well probably should not ask.
<u>A note</u>: Though *l'an* and *l'année* both mean <u>the year</u>, *an* and *ans* are frequently preceded by a number. <u>Annual</u> and <u>anniversary</u> are yearly reminders.

<u>What Do We Have Here?</u>- Complete the sentences using the forms of *avoir* and its expressions.
1. C'est le mois de juillet en Floride. Nous _____ .
2. Je donne des céréales aux bébés quand ils _____ .
3. M. Bravo trouve 1,000 euros à la rue. Il _____ .
4. Je n'_____ pas _____ de souris.
5. Il est minuit. M. et Mme Fatigués sont dans le boudoir. Ils _____ .
6. Tu passes un examen. **La note (the grade)** est 0. Tu _____ .
7. Des cocas, de l'eau minérale et de l'Orangina sont sur la table. On _____ .
8. C'est le mois de janvier au Canada. Qui n'_____ pas _____ ?
9. Quarante et vingt **font (make)** cinquante? Non, vous _____ .
10. C'est aujourd'hui le premier anniversaire de naissance de Guillaume. Il _____ .
11. Le serveur apporte une omelette au fromage, deux croissants et des fruits à Mlle Prendtout. Elle _____ .
12. Le soir du 31 octobre des enfants _____ .
13. M. et Mme Roulette gagnent beaucoup au casino. Ils _____ .
14. Je travaille de neuf heures du matin **jusqu'à (until)** cinq heures de l'après-midi. À dix heures du soir j' _____ .

Positive vs. Negative Sentences - A Review

Un, une and *des* become *de* or *d'* in negative sentences to express <u>a</u>, <u>an</u> or <u>any</u>.

+ Ex. Superman porte **un manteau** quand il a froid. > Superman wears **a coat** when he is cold.

- Ex. Superman ne porte pas de manteau quand il a froid. > Superman does not wear a coat when he is cold. (It would slow him down unless it had a 'zip-out' lining.)

+ Ex. Il y des ordinateurs **bon marché** dans **le magasin**. > There are some **inexpensive** computers in **the store**. (And they are under warranty 'to boot.')

- Ex. Il n'y a pas d'ordinateurs bon marché dans le magasin. > There are not any inexpensive computers in the store.

'Say It Isn't So!'- Change the following affirmative sentences into negative form.

1. J'ai des amis en France. _____.

2. Nous avons un appartement à Marseille. _____
_____.

3. Madame Fortune a toujours de la chance. _____
_____.

4. Vous avez un passe-temps? _____?

5. M. Sansargent cherche un boulot. _____
_____.

6. Est-ce que tu visites des musées le dimanche? _____
_____?

7. Les enfants montrent des notes aux parents. _____
_____.

8. Les voisins ont des filles qui travaillent en ville. _____
_____.

9. Tu as peur des chats noirs. _____.

10. M. et Mme Banale ont une maison. _____
_____.
_____

A French Clown

UNE REVUE - A Review

Subject Pronouns and Regular -ER Verbs, Telling Time, Être, Les Couleurs, Question Formation, Ne .... Pas, Avoir, Expressions with Avoir

Three Against One- Circle the letters of the responses that do not belong in the groups.

1. a. tu	b. il	c. elle	d. nous
2. a. l'œuf	b. l'oignon	c. l'encre	d. l'haricot
3. a. le boulot	b. l'ami	c. le voisin	d. le copain
4. a. anglais	b. espagnol	c. français	d. prochain
5. a. vert	b. joli	c. gris	d. jaune
6. a. la feuille	b. le jardinier	c. l'arbre	d. l'herbe
7. a. haut	b. froid	c. tiède	d. chaud
8. a. le manteau	b. l'imperméable	c. l'agneau	d. la cravate
9. a. le pourboire	b. la monnaie	c. l'argent	d. le magasin
10. a. la cuisine	b. le sommeil	c. le grenier	d. la chambre à coucher
11. a. ai	b. avons	c. ont	d. sont
12. a. suis	b. as	c. sommes	d. êtes
13. a. moins	b. quand	c. pourquoi	d. qui
14. a. intonation	b. n'est-ce pas?	c. qu'est-ce que?	d. inversion

----

Sentences Made to Order- Unscramble the phrases to form sentences.
Ex. quelle heure/ -t-il/ l'autobus/ À / arrive? > À quelle heure l'autobus arrive-t-il?

1. couleur/ une souris/ est/ De quelle

_____?

2. les portes/ Un étudiant/ de la salle de classe/ ferme

_____.

3. beau/ n'est-ce pas/ L'arc-en-ciel/ est

_____?

4. et le petit garçon/ honte/ ont/ de mauvaises notes/ La jeune fille

_____.

5. les chambres/ Pourquoi/ chères/ dans l'hôtel Ritz/ sont-elles

_____?

6. penses/ les enfants/ Qu'est-ce que/ avec/ tu/ des vacances

_____?

7. mais/ au café / n'ont pas/ Les copains/ ils / soif/ sont

_____.

8. de billets/ le film/ y a pas/ au guichet/ pour/ Il n'

_____.

'Ready for Picking'- **Circle the letters of the correct responses for the sentences below.**

1. Il y a des drapeaux français sur les boulevards de Paris.
a. C'est aujourd'hui le Noël.　　　　　　　b. C'est aujourd'hui le 14 juillet.
c. Nous sommes aujourd'hui la Fête des Mères.　　d. On ne danse pas dans les rues.

2. Le lait et la neige sont _____.
a. blanc　　　　b. blanches　　　　c. blancs　　　　d. blanches

3. Normalement, les bébés portent des couleurs comme _____.
a. noir et pourpre　　b. rouge et vert　　c. orange et marron　　d. bleu et rose

4. La famille n'est pas à table quand elle _____.
a. n'a pas peur　　b. n'a pas honte　　c. n'a pas faim　　d. n'a pas tort

5. M. Banale ne travaille pas dans le bureau, et les enfants ne sont pas en classe.
a. C'est aujourd'hui samedi ou dimanche　　b. On cherche le chat et le chien.
c. Louis surfe sur le net.　　　　　　　　d. Louise a un passe-temps.

6. Il est deux heures et demie de l'après-midi est aussi _____
a. Il est deux heures trente du matin.　　b. Il est quatorze heures et demie.
c. Nous sommes toujours en retard.　　　d. Il est trois heures moins un quart.

7. Combien coûte un billet pour l'opéra?
a. Cela ne fait rien.　　b. Tenor a de la monnaie.　　c. On chante bien ici.　　d. Le prix est cher.

8. Pourquoi Corinne et Karine n'étudient-elles pas?
a. Elles jouent avec des amis.　　　b. Les jeunes filles ont onze ans.
c. Elles n'ont pas raison.　　　　　d. Elles ont du papier et des crayons

9. Où sont les entrées au cinéma?
a. Elles sont bon marché.　　　　　b. Elles sont à droite et à gauche du guichet.
c. On ferme le musée le lundi.　　　d. La famille est sur le deuxième étage.

10. C'est bien! Les vedettes sont au spectacle à Cannes.
a. Ont-elles de bonnes notes?　　　b. Pourquoi sont-elles dans les chambres à coucher?
c. Qu'est-ce que les femmes portent?　　d. Combien d'argent dépensent-elles?

_____

LA FAMILLE - The Family (Part 2)

The Stick family is having a family reunion and would like you to meet their relatives. (Did you expect the Stick Family 'to thin out'?)

The Extended Family Tree
1. l'oncle- the uncle
2. la tante- the aunt
3. le neveu- the nephew
4. la nièce- the niece
5. le cousin- the male cousin
6. la cousine- the female cousin
7. le beau-père- the father-in-law
8. la belle-mère- the mother-in-law
9. le beau-frère- the brother-in-law
10. la belle-sœur- the sister-in-law
11. le gendre- the son-in-law
12. la belle-fille- the daughter-in-law
13. le beau-père- the stepfather
14. la belle-mère- the stepmother
15. le demi-frère- the stepbrother
16. la demi-sœur- the stepsister
17. le beau-fils- the stepson
18. la belle-fille- the stepdaughter
19. le petit-fils- the grandson
20. la petite-fille- the granddaughter

A Family Resemblance
1. French relatives numbers #1 through #4 and #6 on the above list have 'shaved off' letters or added curls to distinguish themselves from English family members. #5 keeps the same look.
2. All the in-laws except *le gendre* are diplomatically labeled *beau* or *belle*- handsome or beautiful. (*Le gendre* is "on the outs" with the others.) **Only two of the step relatives, *le demi-frère* and *la demi-sœur*, are not described as attractive.** (The ugly stepsister has 'made a name for herself.')
3. French in-laws and stepparents share one translation. (Jeff Foxworthy could have 'a field day' with that fact.) **However, it is clear from the context of the conversation to whom the speaker is referring.** (That is an advantage because mothers-in-law and stepmothers could be spoken of in the same tone of voice.)
4. Although the grandchildren are preceded by *petit* and *petite*, they get a lot of attention.
5. Hyphens separate the compound names of family members. (That enables them 'to keep their distance.')

No Identity Crisis- Label the statements *vrai* or *faux*.
_____ 1. La mère d'une tante est une grand-mère.
_____ 2. Les enfants d'un oncle ne sont pas les neveux et les nièces.
_____ 3. La belle-sœur est l'épouse du frère.
_____ 4. La belle-mère est la sœur du beau-père.
_____ 5. L'oncle est le frère du père.
_____ 6. Le beau-fils est le frère de la belle-fille.
_____ 7. Le cousin est un fils d'un grand-père.
_____ 8. Le mari de la fille est un gendre.
_____ 9. La demi-sœur est la fille de la belle-mère.
_____ 10. Le demi-frère et la demi-sœur ne sont pas les beaux-enfants.

'Putting in a Few Good Words'

1. garder- to keep: Though obviously related to <u>guard</u>, the French *garde* keeps <u>u</u> out.
2. *manger- to eat: This activity is managed without any reminder.
3. marcher- to function, to walk, to work: Whatever is not running in English is not walking in French. (Actually, it is not going anywhere in either case.)
<u>An interesting note</u>: *Ça marche? and Ça va?* are synonyms.
4. *nager- to swim: The verb begins like <u>nautical</u> before it 'goes off the deep end.'
5. payer- to pay/to pay for: The preposition may come with the translation at no extra charge.
6. rencontrer- to meet: An encounter is going on inside without <u>u</u> in the middle.
7. rentrer- to reenter, to return: September entails *la rentrée*- the going back in France.
8. *voyager- to travel: The English cognate takes you where you need to go. *Bon voyage!*
9. chez- at the home of: With a clipped long <u>a</u>, *chez* sounds like the name of a former New York City baseball stadium. This preposition is followed by nouns and pronouns.
Exs. Chez Marie- at Marie's home/place, chez moi- at my house
10. maintenant- now: Taken apart, this adverb means "hand holding," but it can be thought of as *maintenant* for now.
11. souvent- often: This adverb is seen and heard *assez souvent*- often enough to be listed without another clue.
<u>An important note</u>: *Manger, *nager* and *voyager* are preceded by asterisks because they have irregular *nous* forms. (You were warned about swimming right after eating, but until now, *voyager* let you 'get away with it.')

le Palais Omnisports de Bercy- A Sports Arena (Paris)

LES ADJECTIFS POSSESSIFS - Possessive Adjectives

Possessive adjectives identify whom or what belongs to whom. Just like definite and indefinite articles, *les adjectifs possessifs* precede nouns and agree with them in gender and in number. (Being possessive, they form attachments.)

Possessive Adjectives

Singular	Plural
mon, ma, mes- my	notre, notre, nos- our
ton, ta, tes- your	votre, votre, vos- your
son, sa, ses- his, her, its	leur, leur, leurs- their

Possessive Facts to Keep

1. The first syllables of *monsieur*, *madame* and *Mesdemoiselles* are possessive adjectives. Those nouns actually mean "my sir, my dame/lady, and my damsels." (Sometimes it is permissible 'to pick people apart.')

2. The first letters of the *mon-ton-son* trio form the abbreviation mts. Meanwhile, 'on another level,' *ton, notre, votre* and their accompanying adjectives correspond to the subject pronouns *tu, nous* and *vous*.

3. *Son, sa* and *ses* share three translations- his, her and its. *Son père* expresses both <u>his and her father</u>, and *sa mère* means both <u>his and her mother</u>. That is why a French person who does not speak English fluently might inadvertently say, "François is not feeling well. He is spending the evening in her bedroom."

4. Here is your once in a French time opportunity! To avoid two consecutive vowel sounds, the masculine singular adjectives *mon, ton* and *son* precede feminine singular nouns starting with a vowel or a mute <u>h</u>. A few examples are *mon amie, ton église* and *son opinion*.

5. One also clarifies ownership by using *de* + a noun or a pronoun. Many French grammarians would give "their salary of a month" not to hear consecutive nouns. With no 's in French, our son's apartment is shown as *l'appartement de notre fils*. This word order switch is 'parroted' in the movie title, *Pirates of the Caribbean*. Other examples are *la leçon de ballet*- the ballet lesson, *la raquette de tennis*- the tennis racket and *la chanson d'amour*- the love song.

6. Possessive adjectives must be repeated before each noun that they modify.
Ex. mon petit frère et ma petite sœur > my little brother and (my) little sister (Neither one can stand on his/her own.)

<u>An important reminder</u>: When *tu* is the subject, *ton, ta* and *tes* are the coordinating possessive adjectives. With *vous* as the subject, *votre* or *vos* must be used. (Those are 'no crossing' zones.)

Treasured Possessions- Circle the best choices to complete the sentences.

1. (ma, ta, sa) J'adore **la langue (the language)** française. C'est _____ langue préférée.

2. (sa, ses, leur) Bill et Hillary sont les parents de Chelsea. Elle est _____ fille.

3. (mon, son, notre) Giselle et _____ mari sont en vacances en **Belgique (Belgium)**.

4. (nos, ses, leurs) Le chien et le chat de Buddy sont _____ **animaux de compagnie (pets)**.

5. (ton, son sa) Une fête pour Chantal? Oui, c'est _____ anniversaire de naissance.

6. (ses, nos, vos) Martin arrive toujours en retard à _____ classes.

7. (notre, votre, leur) Nous montrons des attractions de _____ ville aux touristes.
8. (mon, ma, ton) Qui est _____ actrice préférée?
9. (mes, tes, ses) Quand Allée voyage, elle téléphone à _____ parents le soir.
10. (tes, vos, leur) Est-ce que vous cherchez _____ livres?

'Showing Your Stuff'- Translate the following phrases.

1. my grades _____
2. her flowers _____
3. his/her child _____
4. our week _____
5. their university _____
6. my exam _____
7. its home _____
8. their kitchen _____
9. his/her family _____
10. his wife _____

11. your (plural) professors _____
12. your (sing.) anniversary _____
13. his/her computer _____
14. our bedrooms _____
15. your friend (f. sing.) _____
16. my father's office _____
17. his/her sister's job _____
18. their parent's attic _____
19. our dog's color _____
20. your neighbor's car _____

'Staying in Touch with the Family'- Translate the following sentences.

1. Her mother-in-law pays for their vacations. _____
_____.

2. My stepson does not eat at my house. _____
_____.

3. Your (formal form) nieces swim often, don't they? _____
_____?

4. Venus de Milo is meeting her son-in-law in the museum. _____
_____.

5. Dad, where do you keep your change? _____
_____?

6. When are our cousins arriving? _____?
7. His stepdaughter's car is not running well. _____
_____.

8. Their grandson is ten months old, and he walks now. _____
_____.

9. At what time does her uncle return? _____
_____?

10. Why do your (informal form) stepfather and your stepmother travel a lot? _____
_____?
_____

LES ADJECTIFS DÉMONSTRATIFS - Demonstrative Adjectives

Demonstrative adjectives might have been introduced into both languages to keep people from pointing fingers. However, since the French are known for *leur politesse,* credit for this concept should be given to them. (Not that I'm pointing fingers!)

Demonstrative Adjectives
ce (masculine singular)- this, that
cet (masculine singular)- this, that
cette (feminine singular)- this, that
ces (masculine and feminine plural)- these, those

Showing off the Demonstrative Adjectives
1. *Ce* precedes any masculine singular noun beginning with a consonant to express <u>this</u> or <u>that</u>. Without additional clarification, the demonstrative adjectives can go in either direction.
Ex. ce grand magasin- this/that department store (It's 'open' to both.)
2. *Cet* is used before any masculine singular noun starting with a vowel or a mute <u>h</u> and means <u>this</u> or <u>that</u>. This form has the '*cet*' function of blocking two consecutive vowel sounds.
Ex. cet avis- this/that opinion (It could be construed either way)
3. *Cette*, meaning <u>this</u> or <u>that</u>, goes in front of any feminine singular noun.
Ex. cette traduction- this/that translation (The exact interpretation is not clear.)
3a. *Cet* and *cette* share the same pronunciation.
Exs. Cet hôtel- this/that hotel, cette auberge- this/that inn
4. *Ces* goes before all masculine and feminine plural nouns and means <u>these</u> and <u>those</u>. With its clipped long <u>a</u> sound, *ces* is pronounced like *ses*. (There are no delays with the <u>a</u> when you say *ses* and *ces!*)
Ex. ces avions- these/those airplanes: The <u>s</u> between the vowels calls for a liaison between the two words. (*Ces avions* are meant to collide.)
5. Two adverbs attached to nouns differentiate this from that and these from those. *Ci*-here is added to indicate <u>this</u> or <u>these</u>; *là*-there is added to specify <u>that</u> or <u>those</u>. (The cure for ambiguity 'comes to an end.')
5a. *-Ci* and *-là* can be linked to different nouns in the same sentence. These adverbs can also be used in reverse order.
Ex. Est-ce que leur maîtresse **gronde** ces garçons-là ou ces jeunes filles-ci? > Is their school teacher **scolding** those boys or these girls? (They have more than *-ci* and *-là* coming after them.)
<u>An interesting note</u>: The well known exclamations *Voici!*- Here it is! and *Voilà!*- There it is! are contractions of See here! and See there!

'Here's a Switch!'- Exchange the nouns and attached adverbs for those in parentheses. Then, translate the finished products.

Ex. cet oiseau-ci (l'arbre) > cet arbre-là- that tree

1. ces minutes-ci (les heures) _____
2. cet hôpital-ci (la clinique) _____
3. ces océans-là (les plages) _____
4. ce professeur-là (l'étudiant) _____
5. ce beau-père-ci (le beau-fils) _____
6. ces mois-là (les années) _____
7. cette péninsule-ci (l'île) _____
8. ces nations-là (les langues) _____
9. ce neveu-ci (le gendre) _____
10. ce train-là (l'avion) _____
11. cette copine-ci (l'amie) _____
12. ces idées-ci (les avis) _____

Demonstrate What You Know about Demonstratives!- Translate the sentences below.

1. That passenger is very handsome. _____.
2. Her father loves this boat. _____.
3. These doctors do not work in that hospital. _____
_____.
4. Eight films are playing in that movie theater. _____
_____.
5. Where are those tourists traveling? _____
_____?
6. Is Mlle Degas in this ballet class? _____
_____?
7. Those teachers are talking with my parents now. _____
_____.
8. Why does she keep these papers in her kitchen? _____
_____?
9. Aren't you (*tu*) eating that French cheese? _____
_____?
10. I spend the weekends in this city often. _____
_____.
11. Is Mme Byer in this department store or in that boutique? _____
_____?
12. Raye Fléchir is thinking about these questions. _____
_____.
_____

ALLER - TO GO

Aller is the third irregular, high priority verb. Because it is needed in conversation from "the get go," several of its forms were introduced in French greetings. This multipurpose verb enables us to travel everywhere including into the near future.

<u>Singular</u>	<u>Plural</u>
je vais- I go, do go, am going	nous allons- we go, do go, are going
tu vas- you go, do go, are going	vous allez- you go, do go, are going
il va- he/it goes, does go, is going	ils vont- they go, do go, are going
elle va- she/it goes, does go, is going	elles vont- they go, do go, are going

---

What Makes *Aller* Go?

1. The entire singular and the third person plural form the outline of an elongated boot. Verbs fitting this shape start with the same letter(s) and are termed "boot verbs." Moreover, the *nous* and *vous* forms resemble the infinitive. (How's that for fancy footwork?)

2. Several forms of *avoir* including *ai, as, a* and *ont* are inside *aller*.

3. The boot gets narrower with each singular form. The <u>i</u> in the first person singular is missing from the second person singular, while the <u>s</u> ending on that verb is deleted in the third person singular. (If we lost an <u>i</u> and an <u>s</u>, we would be rushed to an emergency room.)

'Having a GO at It'- Fill in the blanks with the correct forms of *aller*.

1. Je _____ bien merci et vous?

2. Comment _____ ta famille?

3. _____-vous à Paris samedi? Non, nous restons chez nous.

4. Nous ne (n') _____ pas **parce que (because)** notre train ne marche pas.

5. Mon mari _____ comme ci comme ça, mais nos enfants _____ bien.

6. À quelle heure _____-tu chez Fifi?

7. Qui _____ à Nice avec votre nièce?

8. Les Foyer ne (n') _____ pas souvent en ville.

9. Où M. Lune _____-t-il le matin?

10. Pourquoi ne (n') _____-vous pas ce soir?

LOCATIONS, LOCATIONS, LOCATIONS!

In addition to *le bar, le club, le gymnase* and *le spa*, many French places have English cognates. Check into the destinations listed below!

Masculine Nouns
1. l'aéroport- the airport
2. l'arrondissement- the division of a city
3. le bistro- the café/restaurant
4. les bois- the woods
5. le bureau de poste- the post office*
6. le centre commercial- the shopping center
7. le champ- the field
8. le cinéma- the movie theater*
9. le collège- the high school (usually)
10. le dortoir- the dormitory
11. l'édifice- the building*
12. l'endroit- the place*
13. l'étang- the pond
14. le fleuve- the river*
15. le gratte-ciel- the skyscraper
16. l'immeuble d'habitation- the apt. building
17. le lac- the lake
18. le lieu- the place*
19. le lycée- the high school*
20. le marché- the market, le supermarché- the supermarket
21. le parc- the park
22. le quartier- the area of a city*
23. le théâtre- the theater

Feminine Nouns
1. la banlieue- the suburbs
2. la banque- the bank
3. la bibliothèque- the library
4. la boîte de nuit- the nightclub
5. la campagne- the countryside
6. la ferme- the farm
7. la gare- the train station
8. la librairie- the bookstore
9. l'île- the island
10. la mer- the sea
11. la montagne- the mountain
12. la piscine- the swimming pool
13. la place- the square, the seat
14. la poste- the post office*
15. la rivière- the river/stream

A Few Words about a Few Words- Clarifying the Words with Asterisks
1. *Le bâtiment* and *l'édifice* are synonyms for <u>the building</u>. (Several edifices together could be referred to as an 'edifice complex.')
2. Both *le bureau de poste* and *la poste* mean <u>the post office</u>. (The second one has a longer line.)
3. *Le cinéma* refers to <u>the movie theater</u> and not to the movies which are *les films*.
4. Young children are educated in *l'école primaire*. *L'école secondaire* and *le lycée* both refer to <u>the high school</u>. Although *le collège* is also attended by high school-age students, the term may apply to an elementary school or a college. Older teens and adults take classes *à l'université* or *à l'institut*. (Knowing all those terms is an education in itself.)
5. An area of a French city is *un quartier*. The <u>quarter</u> is similar to our <u>district</u>. *Un arrondissement*, identified by a number with an elevated <u>e</u>, designates a postal zone. *Un quartier* is inside *un arrondissement*. Paris's twenty *arrondissements* form an uneven circle <u>around</u> that city.
6. *Le fleuve* and *la rivière* both mean <u>the river</u>, but the former flows into a sea.
7. *L'endroit* and *le lieu* are synonyms for <u>a place or a general location</u>. (One can be said in lieu of

the other.) *L'endroit* and *le lieu* cannot be replaced with *la place*- a city square or a seat.

'What's the Good Word?'- Circle the letters of the correct responses.
1. Il y a des boutiques et des grands magasins dans _____.

a. un champ   b. un centre commercial   c. un étang   d. une pièce

2. On regarde les rives de la Seine d' _____.

a. un miroir   b. une montagne   c. une fontaine   d. un pont

3. On trouve souvent des livres intéressants _____.

a. sur un étage   b. dans une librairie   c. chez nos voisins   d. dans une rivière

4. Je rencontre mon ami à _____. Il voyage par le train.

a. l'endroit   b. la boîte de nuit   c. la gare   d. la place

5. Les campeurs mangent leur dîner dans _____.

a. les bois   b. le guichet   c. le grenier   d. le supermarché

6. Des étudiants de l'université restent dans _____.

a. une campagne   b. une auberge   c. un lac   d. un dortoir

7. _____ sont les très hauts édifices dans une grande ville.

a. Les bâtiments   b. Les gratte-ciel   c. Les fleuves   d. Les mers

8. Marie regarde son agneau, des moutons et des oies. Elle est _____.

a. à une ferme   b. à un lac   c. dans un cinéma   d. dans une forêt

9. Anne Eau nage, mais elle n'est pas à la plage. Où est-elle?

a. dans un aéroport   b. dans une piscine   c. dans un arrondissement   d. dans une poste

10. Rémy et René passent des examens cet après-midi. Ils étudient maintenant _____.

a. dans un bistro   b. dans une banque   c. dans une bibliothèque   d. sur une île

11. Je rentre chez moi par métro. J'habite une heure de Paris _____.

a. en banlieue   b. dans un château   c. dans un quartier cher   d. au parc

12. Jean et Jeanne ont seize ans. Il va à un collège, et elle va à _____.

a. un marché   b. un immeuble d'habitation   c. une école primaire   d. un lycée

LES CONTRACTIONS FRANÇAISES - French Contractions

Contractions provide links to nouns. Being word combinations themselves, contractions make the perfect blend.

<u>Contractions</u>
au (masculine singular) - to the, in the, at the
à la (feminine singular) - to the, in the, at the
à l' (masc. and fem. singular) - to the, in the, at the
aux (masc. and fem. plural) - to the, in the, at the

<u>Squeezing in a Few Words</u>
1. The single letter preposition *à* means <u>to</u>, <u>in</u> and <u>at</u>. Consequently, it would not be unusual to hear a nonfluent speaker of English say, "I want to come at your house." Before leaving for the closest home repair store, understand that the speaker chose "at" because it resembles *à*.
2. Contractions are formed with *à* + a definite article. All four mean <u>to the</u>, <u>in the</u> and <u>at the</u>.
2a. *Au* is a combination of *à* + *le*. It goes in front of all masculine singular nouns beginning with a consonant. (Ironically, *au* is the sound heard from a woman having a contraction.)
Exs. au jardin, au lac, au marché
2b. *À la* is considered a contraction even though no letters are deleted. It precedes all feminine singular nouns starting with a consonant.
Exs. à la banque, à la gare, à la poste
2c. *À l'* is a contracted contraction. This form is used before all masculine or feminne singular nouns beginning with a vowel or a mute <u>h</u>.
Exs. à l'endroit, à l'île, à l'hôpital
2d. *Aux* is derived from *à* + *les*. This plural contraction goes in front of all masculine and feminine nouns regardless of their first letters.
Exs. aux États-Unis, aux montagnes, aux supermarchés
<u>Important notes:</u> The <u>x</u> in *aux* forms a liaison to the following vowel or mute <u>h</u> and produces a <u>z</u> sound. (Ex. aux étangs) Otherwise, *au* and *aux* are pronounced identically.
Ex. au quai, aux quais (It's nice that everyone agrees.)
3. Interpretations sometimes lend themselves to *dans le/la/l'/les* rather than *au, à la, à l'* or *aux*. (By their very nature, contractions have to give up something.)
4. The accent *grave* on *à la* and *à l'* distinguishes them from the third person singular of *avoir-il/elle/on a.*

<u>'Writing a Couple of Letters'</u>- Put the correct contractions in front of the nouns.

1. _____ métro
2. _____ opéra
3. _____ toilettes
4. _____ cinéma
5. _____ poste
6. _____ spa
7. _____ agence

11. _____ clubs
12. _____ dortoirs
13. _____ mer
14. _____ Louvre
15. _____ auberge
16. _____ gymnase
17. _____ universités

8. _____ immeubles d'habitation
9. _____ quartier
10. _____ Arc de Triomphe

18. _____ usine
19. _____ place
20. _____ attraction

la Fontaine Saint-Michel (Paris)

ALLER et LE FUTUR PROCHE - To Go and The Near Future

Le futur proche consists of any present tense form of *aller* followed by an infinitive. It tells what one **is going to do**. An identical construction, the near future, is used in English.

Preparing for *Le Futur Proche*

1. *Le futur proche* is not an actual tense in either language. Although it does not offer a definite time frame, its expiration date is within the foreseeable future. Any action occurring after that is expressed by *le temps futur* and translated by **will**. (That tense will be discussed in the future.)

2a. *Le futur proche* consists of two consecutive verbs. The first is a conjugated form of *aller*; the second is an infinitive.

Ex. Nous allons manger du dessert. > We are going to eat some dessert.

2b. In negative, interrogative and negative-interrogative sentences, *ne/(n')* and *pas* surround a conjugated form of *aller* which is followed by an infinitive.

Ex. Nous n'allons pas manger de dessert. > We are not going to eat any dessert. (Regardless of what they claim, *du dessert* was 'picked at.')

3. A conjugated form of *aller* can be followed by the infinitive *aller* to express **going to go**.

Ex. Alain et Suzette vont aller à une boîte de nuit samedi soir. > Alain and Suzette are going to go to a nightclub Saturday evening. (It might be 'packed.')

'How's It Going?'- Use the correct forms of *aller*, and choose among *avoir, aller, dépenser, garder, laver, manger, montrer, nager, passer, porter, rester* and *travailler* to fill in the blanks.

1. _____-tu _____ dans un hôtel à Lyon?
2. Mme Fauchée _____ _____ son argent dans le centre commercial aujourd'hui.
3. Où _____-vous _____ le cadeau de votre mère?
4. Sponge Bob est fatigué. Il ne _____ pas _____ sa voiture maintenant.
5. _____-tu _____ ce manteau rouge à l'église?
6. Ils ont honte. Ils ne _____ pas _____ les notes à leurs parents.
7. Notre belle-sœur _____ _____ un bébé demain.
8. On a faim? On _____ _____ à un bistro avec moi?
9. Je ne _____ pas _____ au boum. Je _____ _____ tard.
10. Mme Repose et ses enfants _____ _____ des heures à la piscine, mais ses petits ne _____ pas _____ là.

CONJUGATED VERBS + INFINITIVES

The concept of a conjugated verb + an infinitive is not restricted to *le futur proche*. Most conjugated French verbs can be followed by infinitives.

Ex. Mon grand-père n'aime pas écouter la musique forte. > My grandfather does not like to listen to loud music. (He prefers his own version of 'Rock.')

Verbs with Backup Support- Translate the following sentences.

1. We are going to meet our pals at the café. _____

_____.

2. Whom are you (*tu*) going to scold? _____?

3. Smokey likes to spend his vacations in the woods. _____

_____.

4. Mr. and Mrs. Vendeur are preparing to go to the market. _____

_____.

5. I do not always prefer to study in a library. _____

_____.

6. Is Penny going to pay for the tickets now? _____

_____?

7. My mother is going to be fifty years old Saturday. _____

_____.

8. Who does not like to travel **to (en)** Europe? _____

_____?

9. When you (*tu*) do not feel well, you do not like to go to clubs. _____

_____.

10. It is one o'clock. I am going to be sleepy in my morning class. _____

_____

_____.

the Port of Honfleur

LES PARTITIFS FRANÇAIS - French Partitives

These little multiform, multimeaning terms burrow into even the most basic French sentences. Take <u>some</u> time to get "a heads up" <u>of the</u> concept <u>from the</u> list below!

Partitives
du (masculine singular)- from the, of the, some
de la (feminine singular)- from the, of the, some
de l' (masculine and feminine singular)- from the, of the, some
des (masculine and feminine plural)- from the, of the, some

<u>Pulling Partitives Apart</u>
1. The translations for *du, de la, de l', de, d'* and *des* are <u>from (the)</u>, <u>of (the)</u>, <u>some</u> and <u>any</u>.
Each has its own function. ('Part-itives' cannot be explained as a whole.)
2a. *Du* precedes all masculine singular nouns beginning with a consonant and is the product of *de + le*.
Exs. du pain- some bread, du jardin- from/of the garden, la spécialité du jour- the day's specialty/the specialty of the day
2b. *De la* is used before all feminine singular nouns starting with a consonant.
Exs. de la viande- some **meat**, de la pluie- from the/some **rain**
2c. *De l'* goes in front of all masculine and feminine singular nouns beginning with a vowel or a mute <u>h</u>.
Exs. de l'inondation- from/of the flood, de l'histoire- from/of the story/history
2d. *Des* is formed from *de + les* and goes before all masculine and feminine plural nouns.
Exs. des **prêtres**- from/of the **priests**, some priests, des **répondeurs**- from the **answering machines**, some answering machines
3. One very common use of partitives is uniquely French. Nouns that are not preceded by other modifiers require <u>some</u>. Dinner might consist of *du bifteck et des frites*- (some) steak and (some) fries topped off by *du gâteau et de la glace*- (some) cake and (some) ice cream.
<u>Important reminders</u>
a. As the plural of *un* and *une, des* means <u>some</u>.
Ex. Elle a des idées **étranges**. > She has some **strange** ideas. (There too, one word says it all.)
b. When partitives express <u>from the</u>, they are the flip side of contractions meaning <u>to the</u>.
c. *De/d'* by itself or followed by an adjective is <u>of</u>. It substitutes for '<u>s</u> and separates two nouns.
Ex. La plume de ma tante est sur le bureau de mon oncle. > My aunt's pen is on my uncle's desk.
(Part of a popular French verse for over one hundred years, that pen has signed everything but 'off.')
d. *De/d'* expresses <u>any</u> in negative sentences.
Exs. Il y a de la glace sur la table. > There is some ice cream on the table.
     Il n'y a pas de glace sur la table. > There isn't any ice cream on the table.
Notice that <u>some</u> was 'wiped up' in the second example!
<u>A helpful hint:</u> Thinking of <u>part</u> in <u>partitives</u> as <u>some</u> is a good clue for one of the translations.

Partitives- Part 1- Fill in the blanks below with *du, de la, de l'* or *des*.

1. _____ lits
2. _____ institut
3. _____ banque
4. _____ fautes
5. _____ chance
6. _____ langues
7. _____ argent
8. _____ feu
9. _____ enfants

10. _____ océan
11. _____ toit
12. _____ champs
13. _____ lessive
14. _____ aéroport
15. _____ gâteau
16. _____ hôtel
17. _____ neige
18. _____ ans

Partitives- Part 2- Translate the following sentences.

1. Hy Kalory loves to eat hamburgers and fries. _____

_____.

2. Some computers do not cost a lot. _____

_____.

3. Our parents' friends are having a party. _____

_____.

4. My sister-in-law does not like any cats. _____

_____.

5. The waiter brings (some) bread and (some) water to our table. _____

_____.

6. There is rain on my neighbor's newspaper. _____

_____.

7. You (*tu*) do not have any messages on your answering machine. _____

_____.

8. We are not sleepy. We are watching movies on television. _____

_____.

9. Mr. Banks is not afraid of a flood. He lives on a boat on this river. ____

_____.

10. Anthony (Antoine) and Cleopatra's (Cléopâtre) love story is in that book. _____

_____

_____.

FAIRE - TO MAKE, TO DO

Faire is the last in the set of most prominent French verbs. With dual translations, it enables us to make/to do a myriad of things. By the end of this chapter, students will be able to discuss the weather, talk about sports, take a trip and even go shopping. *Faire* is the most frequently used verb in the French language.

To fare much better with *faire,* keep in mind that each form has six translations!

<table>
<tr><td colspan="2" align="center">**Singular**</td><td colspan="2" align="center">**Plural**</td></tr>
</table>

Singular
je fais- I make, do make, am making
    I do, do do, am doing
tu fais- you make, do make, are making
    you do, do do, are doing
il fait- he/it makes, does make, is making
    he/it does, does do, is doing
elle fait- she/it makes, does make, is making
    she/it does, does do, is doing

Plural
nous faisons- we make, do make, are making
    we do, do do, are doing
vous faites- you make, do make, are making
    you do, do do, are doing
ils font- they make, do make, are making
    they do, do do, are doing
elles font- they make, do make, are making
    they do, do do, are doing

'A *Faire* Analysis'

1. *Fais, fait* and *faisons* 'make do' with a clipped long <u>a</u> sound.
2. *Faites* does not have a typical -<u>ez</u> ending. If its uncommon -<u>es</u> reminds you of another irregular verb, *vous <u>êtes</u> correct.*
3. Admittedly, the 'do do' translation does sound strange, but in a sentence such as *Faites-vous la cuisine?* > Do you do the cooking?, it serves its purpose.
4. A review: The third person plural of *être* is *sont.* The third person plural of *avoir* is *ont.* The third person plural of *aller* is *vont,* and the third person plural of *faire* is *font.* (Say those forms aloud to create a novel Chinese dish!)

'Easy Does It'

The following phrases can be translated word for word from English:
1. faire une faute (une erreur)- to make a mistake: One who does not want to be blamed could say, "It's not my *faute."*
2. faire une faveur- to do a favor: *Faveur* looks like <u>favor</u> with a little added flavor.
3. faire un feu- to make/to build a fire: *Un feu* starts like a fire but 'dies out' quickly.
4. faire un gâteau- to make a cake: Forms of *faire* can be put into any food that one prepares.
5. faire une lessive- to do a wash: This chore requires <u>less</u> time than *laver* by hand.
6. faire un lit- to make a bed: Learn the meaning of *un lit,* and it will be 'covered'!
7. faire la vaisselle- to wash the dishes: The singular French noun refers to the set.

'What Do You Make of This?'- Fill in the blanks with the correct forms of *faire* + expressions.

1. Les scouts ont froid le soir. Ils _____.
2. M. Dosnu n'a pas de chemise à porter. Il va _____.
3. Quand tu **aides (help)** un ami, tu _____.
4. Il n'y a pas de plats à table parce que nous _____.

5. Le professeur donne l'examen de Christophe à Cristelle. Il _____.
6. Pour **fêter (celebrate)** l'anniversaire de vos parents, vous _____.
7. Est-ce que tu _____ le matin?

IDIOMATIC EXPRESSIONS WITH *FAIRE*

'More Than *Faire*'
1. faire attention (à)- to pay attention (to) (It costs nothing, but it's worth a lot.)
2. faire de son mieux- to do one's best: Any possessive adjective can substitute for *son*.
3. faire des achats, faire des courses, faire des emplettes, faire des magasins- to do/go shopping (That's quite a shopping list!)
4. faire des progrès- to make progress, to improve (With *des* included, the French infer that there is still a ways to go.)
5. faire la connaissance de- to make the acquaintance of, to become acquainted with someone: The most typical thing to say when you meet someone for the first time is, "Je suis enchanté(e) de faire votre connaissance." > I am delighted to make your acquaintance.
6. faire un tour/faire une promenade- to take a walk
7. faire des exercices- to do exercises: As in English, this phrase applies to physical and mental activities. (Taken to the extreme, one could pull a muscle or an all-nighter.) **Notice that the French noun has two çs!**
8. faire une valise- to pack a suitcase (And 'make-do' with what is in it.)
9. faire un voyage- to take a trip (The French translation makes more sense as the trip is not going with the traveler.)
10. faire la cuisine- to cook, to do the cooking: Un cuisinier/une cuisinière fait la cuisine dans la cuisine. > A male/a female cooks/does the cooking in the kitchen. (The French prefer one 'cuisin' recipe because they know that 'too many cooks ...')
11. faire des devoirs- to do homework (With *des*, one gets off by doing only some.)

Making/Doing One's Own Thing- Use the correct idiomatic expressions from the preceding list to write conclusions for the scenarios below.
Ex. Nous étudions quatre heures avant l'examen de français. > We study/do study/are studying four hours before the French exam.
   Nous faisons de notre mieux. > We do/are doing/do do our best.

1. Mme Tendue est au gymnase ce matin. Elle _____.
2. Stu Dieux est très diligent. Il rentre du lycée, et il _____.
3. Nous sommes à l'aéroport pour aller en Afrique. Nous _____.
4. Tu n'as pas une mauvaise note en espagnol. Je pense que tu _____.
5. Vous allez du Louvre aux Tuileries. Vous _____ ou vous

_____.
6. J'écoute bien quand le professeur parle à la classe. Je _____.
7. Les copines vont manger, mais elles ne vont pas à un restaurant. Elles _____ dans leur appartement.

8. Nous n'apportons pas de bagages pour les voyages d'affaires. Nous _____
_____.

9. Mlle Veuttout va des magasins aux boutiques. Elle _____, ou elle
_____, ou elle _____.

10. Vous rencontrez la femme de votre médecin dans son bureau. Votre salutation est " _____
_____."
_____

le Jeu de Pelote (the Basque Region)

QUEL TEMPS FAIT- IL? - How Is the Weather?, What Is the Weather?

The first title literally says, "What weather is it making?" If that phrase sounds strange to you, imagine a French person trying to decipher the meaning of "It is raining cats and dogs." <u>Prediction</u>: You will use the following weather expressions very frequently.

1. **Il fait beau. > It is nice weather. The first four letters of <u>beau</u>tiful provide a convenient way to remember the phrase.**
2. **Il fait mauvais. > It is bad weather.** (There is no good mnemonic for *mauvais*.)
3. **Il fait chaud. > It is warm or It is hot.** (The exact translation is 'tempered' by degrees.)
4. **Il fait froid. > It is cold. <u>Fro</u>st is forming at the beginning of the French word.**
5. **Il fait frais. > It is cool.** *Frais* also means <u>fresh</u>. (Pick it for a memory tip!)
6. **Il neige. > It snows/does snow/is snowing. This idiom was forecasted in** *la neige*- the snow.
7. **Il pleut. > It rains/does rain/is raining. Imagine that the sound of** *pleut* **is similar to that of a raindrop, or think of** *la pluie*- the rain! *Le parapluie* is the umbrella.
8. **Il fait (du) soleil./Il y a du soleil. > It is sunny. With** *il fait*, **the idiom can be used without** *du* **for a solar panel.**
9. **Il fait du vent./Il y a du vent. > It is windy. Remembering** *vent* **is 'a breeze' if it is associated with <u>vent</u>ilator.**
10. **Il y a des nuages. > It is cloudy. Yet, the meaning is seen through** *les nuages.*

<u>Inside Information Re: The Outside</u>
1. **To make weather expressions starting with** *Il fait* **vs.** *Il y a* **less foggy:**
1a. *Beau, mauvais, chaud, froid* **and** *frais* **are adjectives which take** *fait.*
1b. *Neige* **in** *Il neige* **and** *pleut* **in** *Il pleut* **are verbs. The two expressions can endure the weather without** *fait.*
1c. **It is sunny, and It is windy provide a choice of** *Il fait* **or** *Il y a. Les nuages* **have many forms, but** *Il y a des nuages* **has only one.**
2. **The expressions** *avoir* + *chaud* **or** *froid* **describe conditions adjustable by a thermostat. With** *il fait chaud* **and** *il fait froid*, **one just has 'to weather it.'**
3. **By inserting** *très*- **very or** *un peu*- **a little in front of the adjective, the speaker can control the climate.**
Exs. Il fait un peu chaud. > It is warm.
   Il fait très chaud. > It is very hot.
4. *Le temps* **also means <u>time</u> in a nonspecific sense.** (That will be discussed *en temps opportun*- in due time.)
5. **Europeans use the Celsius scale to record temperatures.** (They might interpret 'Fahrenheit' to mean someone neither short nor tall.)

LES SAISONS DE L'ANNÉE - The Seasons of the Year

Les quatre saisons, the four seasons, are linked together but are not related to the hotel chain.

1. **le printemps**- the spring (le 21 mars au 20 juin): Picture an <u>s</u> in front of the first syllable to recall the meaning of the noun.
2. **l'été (m.)**- the summer (le 21 juin au 20 septembre): This is a short word for a season full of long days.
3. **l'automne (m.)**- the autumn/the fall (le 21 septembre au 20 décembre): As the leaves change colors, the cognates reverse the pronounced consonants. (<u>M</u> is not pronounced in *l'automne*; <u>n</u> is silent in autumn.)
4. **l'hiver (m.)**- the winter (le 21 décembre au 20 mars): Imagine an <u>s</u> in front of *hiver* to form <u>shiver</u> and 'know this season cold.'

Added 'Season-ing'
1. Like the days of the week and the months of the year, the names of the French seasons begin with lowercase letters.
2. The seasons are masculine nouns.
3. *Quelle saison est-ce?/Quelle saison sommes-nous?* both mean <u>What season is it?</u> The answers start with *C'est* or *Nous sommes*.
4. The nouns are prefaced without definite articles when they're <u>in season</u>; *au printemps*- in the spring, *en été*- in the summer, *en automne*- in the fall, *en hiver*- in the winter
It seems that *au printemps* is the only one 'out of season.' Ironically, the other three are exceptions. Because they begin with a vowel or a mute <u>h</u>, they are not preceded by *au*.

'A Weather Watch'- Label the statements *vrai* or *faux*.
_____ 1. Il fait froid en été aux États-Unis.
_____ 2. Quand il pleut, il y a des nuages.
_____ 3. Il neige à Paris en hiver.
_____ 4. Il fait mauvais quand il y a du soleil/il fait (du) soleil.
_____ 5. Avril et mai sont en automne.
_____ 6. Il fait beau quand il fait un peu chaud.
_____ 7. Il ne fait pas froid quand il neige.
_____ 8. Il fait (Il y a) du vent quand il fait frais.
_____ 9. Il fait mauvais quand il pleut.
_____ 10. Il fait chaud en Floride au printemps.
_____ 11. Le Noël n'est pas en hiver.
_____ 12. **Chaque (each)** saison a trois mois.

'A Change in the Atmosphere' - Circle the letters of the words or phrases that do not belong.
1. a. l'été   b. le temps   c. l'automne   d. l'hiver
2. a. l'imperméable b. les bottes   c. le parapluie   d. le ciel
3. a. la saison   b. les nuages   c. la pluie   d. la neige
4. a. Il fait du vent. b. Il pleut   c. Il a froid.   d. Il fait beau.

5. a. Il fait très froid.   b. Il fait un peu chaud.   c. Il neige.   d. Il fait mauvais.
6. a. Il fait du soleil.   b. Il fait chaud.   c. Il fait beau.   d. Il pleut.
7. a. Il fait très beau.   b. Il y a beaucoup de vent.   c. Il fait très frais. d. Il y a beaucoup de nuages.

le printemps

l'été

l'automne

l'hiver

LES SPORTS ET LES RÉCRÉATIONS (Avec Faire)

There is no bidding farewell to *faire* without mentioning the outdoor activities that it offers.
These expressions provide 'a warm up' before a toning exercise.

1. **faire de l'alpinisme**- to mountain climb: The prefix -**alp** is the 'top' way to recall this.
2. **faire du camping**- to go camping (The equipment is reusable.)
3. **faire du ski/skier**- to ski (Said aloud, the idiom resembles a Russian last name.)
3a. **faire du ski nautique**- to water ski: *Nautique* and *nautical* are cognates.
4. **faire un tour à bicyclette**- to bike ride. *Faire du cyclisme* and *faire du vélo* are 'spin offs.' The competitors in *Le Tour de France font du cyclisme.*
5. **faire une promenade en bateau**- to go for a boat ride: It literally says "to take a stroll on the boat." Excursions are not canceled even though there is *de l'eau dans le bateau.*
5a. **faire une promenade en bateau à voile**- to go sailing: It is possible to 'navigate around' the long phrase with *faire la voile.* Currently, the related sport, *faire de la planche à voile*, to wind-surf, 'goes over big' across 'the big pond.'
6. **faire un pique-nique**- to go on a picnic: As long as you are not *piqué*- stung, this is fun to do.
7. **faire du jogging**- to jog
8. **faire de la chasse**- to go hunting (A sport for those who prefer a 'wild' outdoor activity.)
9. **faire la lutte/lutter**- to wrestle (Clues for this one are 'on hold.')
10. **faire la natation**- to go swimming: It's within an arm's reach of *nager*- to swim. *Les nageurs* can 'give a little wave' to *les surfeurs.*
11. **faire une randonnée**- to go hiking (Advocates of this exercise choose a 'randon' location to get away from it all.)

'Activities for the Open Spaces'- Complete the sentences by using the correct forms of idioms with *faire*.

1. Des touristes _____ sur le Lac Genève.
2. Bambi est dans la forêt. Elle a peur des hommes qui _____.
3. Les Parka vont aux montagnes en hiver où ils _____.
4. Tu es à la mer, et il y a du vent. Tu _____.
5. Ces deux hommes-là au gymnase _____.
6. Herbert et **sa petite amie (his girlfriend)** sont dans la campagne. Ils apportent des sandwichs, des fruits, et de l'eau minérale. Ils vont _____.
7. _____-vous _____ dans l'océan ou dans une piscine?
8. Nous portons les sweats au parc. Nous _____.
9. Les scouts _____ dans les bois les soirs. Les jours ils aiment bien _____.
10. Est-ce que tu _____ quand tu restes dans un chalet en **Suisse (Switzerland)** en été?
11. Lance Armstrong _____ dans le Tour de France.
12. Je tombe toujours en eau quand je _____.

_____

LES SPORTS ET LES RÉCRÉATIONS (Avec Jouer)

For sports and other recreational activities that are not expressed with *faire* idioms, the French might 'toss around' a form of *jouer* plus a contraction.

Prominent Team Members
1. jouer au base-ball- to play baseball (Except for *au* and the hyphen, the score is tied.)
2. jouer au basket- to play basketball (Notice how well the French 'guard the ball'!)
3. jouer aux billes- to play marbles (When children lose them, it is not very serious.)
4. jouer aux boules- to bowl (The French spelling has a couple of letters 'to spare.')
4a. le jeu de quilles- Very similar to bowling, this sport is played outdoors. (A field is the typical location, but 'an alley' is possible.)
5. jouer aux cartes- to play cards (People see familiar faces even while playing solitaire.)
6. jouer aux dames- to play checkers (Despite its French name, this game is enjoyed by both sexes of all ages.)
7. jouer aux échecs- to play chess (Strategy must be used not to confuse it with checkers.)
8. jouer au football américain- to play American football (The French sport is 'padded' to differentiate it from #9.) **Rugby (union), a style of football, also scores well in France.**
9. jouer au football, jouer au foot, jouer au soccer- to play soccer (Do the French 'get a kick out of' the multiple names?)
10. jouer au golf- to play golf (Although it is played in France, its popularity is not 'on a par with' the sport in the United States.)
11. jouer au hockey- to play hockey: There is a slight pause between the last two words. So, *au* (not *à l'*) is in front of the aspirant h. ('A time out' is needed.)
12. jouer au tennis- to play tennis. (Except for *au*, the two terms make 'a perfect match.')
13. jouer au tennis de table, jouer au ping-pong- to play table tennis, to play ping pong (Choose the idiom that 'serves' you better.)

How to determine whether idioms are on the *faire* or the *jouer* team:
1. With the exception of *faire de la lutte/lutter*, *faire* activities are not performed inside. However, one can *jouer* under a roof or under the sky.
2. No ball is used *quand on fait une sport ou une récréation*, but a player always has something in his hands *quand il joue*.

Organizing Activities- Put the phrases in the correct order to make sentences.

Du Vocabulaire de l'Exercice
1. la basketteurs- the basketball players
2. les culottes (f.)- the shorts
3. l'équipe (f.)- the team

4. le jeu- the game
5. lancer- to throw
6. le stade- the stadium

1. dans le champ/ au soccer/ **L'équipe**/ en automne/ joue _____

_____.

2. **les culottes/ Les basketteurs**/ vertes/ portent/ de notre lycée _____

3. en hiver/ populaire/ est/ au Canada/ Le hockey _____ .

4. beaucoup/ on/ aux échecs/ On/ quand/ joue/ on/ pense _____ .

5. **un jeu**/ Des américains/ de base-ball/ vont / regarder/ **au stade** _____ .

6. Les parents/ quand/ leurs enfants/ il neige/ avec/ aux dames/ jouent _____ .

7. ne fait pas/ au tennis/ Aimes-tu/ très chaud/ quand/ jouer/ il _____ ?

8. il/ les petites balles/ mon grand-père/ **lancer**/ aux boules/ préfère/ Quand/ joue _____ .

LES SPORTS ET LES RÉCRÉATIONS (Sans Faire et Sans Jouer)

Some popular sports provide the action by supplying their own verbs.

1. aller à la pêche/pêcher- to go fishing (Think of a perch 'to hook' this one!)

2. boxer- to box (The translation is simple, even for featherweights.)

3. monter à cheval- to horseback ride: Its literal translation is "to get up on a horse."

4. patiner (à glace)/faire du patin (à glace)- to ice skate: Performed with or without a partner, this sport can be coated *à glace*- **with ice to distinguish it from #5.**

5. patiner à roulettes- to roller skate: *La roulette*- **the wheel is on the bottom of a skate and in a casino.** (A good balance is advised for both activities.)

6. patiner à planche à roulettes- to skateboard: *Une planche*- **a board, and perhaps** *un casque*- **a helmet, have been added to #5.**

7. plonger- to dive: Use plunge **or even** a plunger **to access this verb.**

8. plonger sous-marine- to scuba dive, to snorkel. The actual meaning is "to dive under water." (The French use the same term for both sports unless they want 'to get into it deeper.')

'An All Sports Bulletin'- Put the letters beside the numbers of the phrases to form sentences.

_____ 1. M. et Mme Congé sont sur la Seine

_____ 2. Ma cousine patine à glace

_____ 3. Il y a deux équipes

_____ 4. Les hommes qui boxent ou luttent

_____ 5. Le petit gagne le jeu,

_____ 6. Pour faire du jogging

_____ 7. Tu restes à la plage,

_____ 8. David a une raquette, mais

_____ 9. Les joueurs portent toujours les casques

_____ 10. M. et Mme Dubois apportent **des cartes-f. (some maps)**

A. il ne joue pas au tennis

B. montent à cheval très bien.

C. font un tour à bicyclette.

D. l'une pour le soccer est **ronde (round.)**

E. quand ils jouent au hockey.

F. pour un jeu de base-ball ou basket.

G. quand elle joue au golf.

H. plonger dans une piscine.

I. portent des culottes.

J. où ils font une promenade en bateau.

_____ 11. Après les classes, les élèves   K. quand nous jouons aux dames.

_____ 12. J'ai peur de   L. jouent aux échecs.

_____ 13. La balle pour le football américain est   M. et il rentre avec beaucoup de billes.
        ovale;

_____ 14. Quand il plonge sous-marine,   N. le parc est un endroit populaire.

_____ 15. Mon père et mon oncle sont à l'étang   O. et danse **à la fois (at the same time).**

_____ 16. Ma sœur a les rouges, et j'ai les noirs   P. parce qu'il fait du ski très bien

_____ 17. Mme Vert marche beaucoup   Q. M. Profond trouve **des trésors-m. (some
                                                     treasures.)**

_____ 18. M. Sommet va aux hautes montagnes   R. mais je fais de la natation dans l'océan.

_____ 19. Les cow-boys et les cow-girls   S. quand ils font de la randonner.

_____ 20. Deux hommes sérieux à cette table-là   T. où ils vont à la pêche.

JOUER AUX INSTRUMENTS - Playing Instruments

To talk about playing musical instruments, the French compose their sentences with forms of
jouer **+ partitives. They have a medley of ways to express themselves through music.**

1. jouer du bois- to play woodwind instruments including *la clarinette* **and** *le saxophone* (Those
two can really 'jazz up' a party.)

2. jouer des cuivres- to play brass instruments such as *le clairon-* **the bugle,** *le cor d'harmonie-*
the French horn and *la trompette* (Playing them well requires a special 'brass polish.')

3. jouer de la guitare- to play the guitar (You can 'string on' the word *électrique* after it.)

4. jouer du piano- to play the piano (*Du* is the only key needed for this one.)

5. jouer des tambours- to play the drums (Use the base of tambourine 'to snare' the meaning!)

6. jouer du violon- to play the violin (The instruments sound similar after 'fiddling around' with
the last vowel.)

'On a Last Note'- Complete the sentences with forms of *jouer* **+ a partitive and an instrument.**

1. The soldier wakes up when someone _____.

2. Several rock stars sing and _____ at the same time.

3. The standing performer at the symphony _____.

4. A few people who march in a parade also _____.

5. In New Orleans musicians often _____ ou

_____.

6. Do you think that Elton John sings as well as he _____?

7. During the Middle Ages one used _____ to announce events.

UNE REVUE - A Review

Les Adjectifs Possessifs, Les Adjectifs Démonstratifs, Le Vocabulaire de la Famille (Part Two), Aller, Locations, Les Contractions Françaises, Le Futur Proche, Les Partitifs Français, Faire (avec le Temps et les Sports), Les Saisons, Jouer (avec les Sports et les Instruments)

'Ring Toss'- Circle the letters of the words and phrases that do not belong with the others.

1. a. l'étang	b. la planche	c. le lac	d. le fleuve
2. a. l'institut	b. le lycée	c. le collège	d. le lieu
3. a. le printemps	b. l'été	c. le parapluie	d. l'hiver
4. a. le gratte-ciel	b. le champ	c. la campagne	d. la ferme
5. a. la banlieue	b. le quartier	c. l'arrondissement	d. l'édifice
6. a. la piscine	b. la mer	c. l'équipe	d. la rivière
7. a. des cuivres	b. des trésors	c. des tambours	d. des bois
8. a. lutter	b. plonger	c. nager	d. aller à la pêche
9. a. l'alpinisme	b. la randonnée	c. les billes	d. le jogging
10. a. le ping-pong	b. les boules	c. le golf	d. la chasse
11. a. le soleil	b. la glace	c. la neige	d. la pluie
12. a. Il fait chaud	b. Il fait du soleil	c. Il fait mauvais	d. Il fait beau
13. a. salue	b. rencontrer	c. faire la connaissance de	d. faire une valise
14. a. faire des achats	b. faire des progrès	c. faire des emplettes	d. faire des magasins
15. a. faire de son mieux	b. visiter	c. faire un tour	d. faire une promenade
16. a. faire la vaisselle	b. faire la cuisine	c. faire la lessive	d. faire la natation

----

'Fitting Responses'- Select the appropriate phrases from the following list, and put them in the correct forms to complete the sentences: aimer écouter, aimer faire des exercices, aller avoir, aller faire la voile/faire une promenade en bateau à voile, aller faire un feu, aller neiger, faire attention, aller faire du cyclisme, faire la connaissance de, faire du ski, faire une faveur, faire un voyage, jouer au basket, jouer du bois, jouer au football américain

1. Il y a des nuages, et il fait très froid. Je pense qu'il _____.

2. Je _____ le temps de _____ pour ma copine.

3. Travers Lesvilles a un vélo très cher. Il _____ dans le Tour de France.

4. Il y a deux équipes de joueurs et des **pom-poms (cheerleaders.)** De jeunes hommes _____
_____ ou _____.

5. Tu _____ le jazz à un club où on _____?

6. Voici une invitation de nos amis à passer le jour à la mer. Nous _____
_____.

7. Astrid et son petit ami restent dans un chalet dans les montagnes. Cet après-midi ils _____
_____, et ce soir ils _____ dans **la cheminée**
(the chimney, the fireplace).

8. M. Bonneforme reste dans un hôtel où il y a un gymnase. Il _____
_____ quand il _____.

9. M. et Mme Poli _____ toujours au nom quand ils _____

_____ d'une personne.

As You Were Saying- Translate the following sentences.

1. Justin Case keeps a raincoat and an umbrella in his car. _____
_____ .

2. Those blue flowers are from my niece and (my) nephew. _____
_____ .

3. The train from Nice is not going to arrive at that station. _____
_____ .

4. My stepsister and (my) stepbrother love to play in the snow. _____
_____ .

5. Paige Turner goes from the library to her dormitory each evening. _____
_____ .

6. Where are his mother-in-law's suitcases? _____
_____ ?

7. Are you (*tu*) going to do your homework and watch (the) television at the same time? _____
_____ ?

8. There is (some) bread and (some) cheese in the kitchen, but we do not have any wine. _____
_____ .

9. Your (formal form) son-in-law's job is in a Paris suburb. What does he do? _____
_____ ?

10. Are those people going to take a boat ride? They do not have (any) tickets. _____
_____
_____ .

CARDINAL NUMBERS 70 -1,000,000

When you worked at telling time, you retired in the '60s. Now, you will go back to work in the '70s and learn how to make millions.

70- soixante-dix: This number might have originated because the French didn't have anything left to 'ante' after *quarante, cinquante and soixante.*

71- soixante-onze: Being 60 and 11 at the same time, a septuagenarian can return to his youth.

72-79- soixante-douze through soixante-dix-neuf: 12 through 19 are added to the 60 base. The hyphens should be thought of as a plus rather than a minus.

80- quatre-vingts: Notice that this number is comprised of four twenties!

81- quatre-vingt-un: The s on *vingt* and the *et* before *un* have disappeared.

82-89- quatre-vingt-deux through quatre-vingt-neuf: The '80s 'shuffle along' accompanied by 'single numbers.' (Old age has its advantages.)

90- quatre-vingt-dix: For this decade, one continues the program started in the '80s.

91-99- quatre-vingt-onze through quatre-vingt-dix-neuf: 97, 98 and 99 show a little extra dash. (Perhaps adrenaline is kicking in.)

100- cent: <u>Century</u> and 100 pennies in a dollar make perfect 'cents.' Notice that there is no *un* before *cent*!

101- cent un (une): Because they are also definite articles, *un* and *une* agree in gender with any following noun.

(Ex. cent une anneés)

200, 300, 400, etc.- deux cents, trois cents, quatre cents: As rounded off numbers, the '00s end with an <u>s</u>.

Ex. 300 croissants = trois cent<u>s</u> croissants. (You're 'on a roll.' Continue the pattern up to 900!)

1.000- mille: <u>Millennium</u> comes around to help with this number. Like *cent*, *mille* is not preceded by *un*.

1.000.000- un million: Notice the *un* in front of <u>a</u> million!

<u>A Number of Explanations</u>

1. The drop the <u>s</u> from *vingt* and *cent* trick occurs whenever another number follows.
Quatre-vingt-cinq = 85, *deux cent huit* = 208, *sept cent seize* = 716.

2. Just as we do not say six thousands, no <u>s</u> is added to *mille* in French.
Ex. trois mille **noms d'écrans** = 3,000 **screen names**

3. *Mille* becomes *mil* in dates.
Ex. 1945 = mil neuf cent quarante-cinq

4. *Et* appears only in 21, 31, 41, 51 and 61 (Or in a movie classic.)

5. *Million*, being a noun, calls for an <u>s</u> if plural.

5a. When *million* is followed by another noun, *de* or *d'* goes after it. (So does the IRS!)
(Exs. douze millions de dollars, cinq millions d'**étoiles (stars).**

6. Periods are used with numerals and decimals in English, while commas make their points in French.
Ex. 2,500 = 2.500 (The switch from a period to a comma amounts to small change.)

7. *Font*, the equivalent of <u>equals</u>, is used in French arithmetical operations.

Exs. Neuf et sept font seize. Huit multiplié par trois font vingt-quatre.

Exchanging Information- **Write these phone numbers as numerals.**
1. trente-cinq. soixante. quatre-vingt-douze. cinquante-neuf _____
2. trente-trois. soixante-onze. quarante-neuf. soixante-quatre _____
3. quarante-deux. quatre-vingts. trente-six. quatre-vingt-dix-sept _____
4. soixante-quinze. quatre-vingt-deux. trente-huit. soixante-sept _____
5. quatre-vingt-dix-neuf. cinquante-trois. vingt et un. quarante-six _____
6. vingt-quatre. quatre-vingt-huit. soixante-cinq. quatre-vingt-treize _____
7. soixante-dix-neuf. quatre-vingt-dix. cinquante-six. quatre-vingt-cinq _____

Taking Short Cuts- **Write these addresses as numerals.**
1. cent vingt-trois Avenue des Ponts _____
2. cinq cent quatre-vingt-deux Rue Saint-Paul _____
3. sept cent soixante-trois Rue Wagram _____
4. mil neuf cent quarante-cinq Avenue du Maine _____
5. deux mil quatre cent quatre-vingt-onze Boulevard Saint-Cyr _____
6. six mil huit cent soixante-quatorze Rue de Sèvres _____
7. neuf mil trois cent trente et un Avenue des Écoles _____

Figuring It Out- **Write the French words for the numerals in parentheses.**
1. (50) _____ états
2. (72) _____ personnes
3. (76) _____ drapeaux
4. (80) _____ quartiers
5. (84) _____ grands magasins
6. (87) _____ statues de Napoléon
7. (90) _____ cartes de la France
8. (91) _____ messages sur le répondeur téléphonique
9. (95) _____ routes au Canada
10. (100) _____ ans dans **un siècle (a century)**
11. (101) _____ petits amis
12. (121) _____ **choix-m. (choices)**
13. (150) _____ feuilles de papier
14. (313) _____ euros
15. (500) _____ **ouvriers-m. (workers)** dans l'usine
16. (742) _____ noms d'écrans
17. (1.000) _____ verbes irréguliers
18. (2.010) _____ étoiles dans le ciel
19. 3.000.000 _____ de mots français
20. 8.900.099 _____ de personnes

ORDINAL NUMBERS

Cardinal numbers are the foundation of ordinal numbers in both languages. Ordinal numbers end with -st, -nd, -rd and -th in English. It delights students to the 'nth' degree that French has fewer options.

The Order of Ordinals
First = premier/première: The first ordinal has an è and a final e to show agreement with any feminine noun that follows it. First is the last one to do that.
Ex. la première petite amie- the first girlfriend
Second = deuxième: There used to be a second choice when *second(e)* referred to the second of two, and *deuxième* meant the second in a series. Today, that distinction is not necessary.
Exs. le deuxième mari- the second husband, la deuxième partie- the second part
Third = troisième: Excluding *premier,* the suffix -ième fits all numbers.
Exs. le troisième enfant- the third child, la vingtième réunion- the twentieth meeting

---

Out of the Ordinal
1. The final e of a cardinal number is dropped before -ième is added. (It's 'the cardinal rule' for ordinals.)
Exs. le trentième roi- the thirtieth king, la douzième nuit- the twelfth night.
2. As in English, q is followed by u.
3. While we change v to f (five > fifth), the reverse applies in French. Cardinal *neuf* turns into ordinal *neuvième.*
4. Vowels are not dropped from definite articles before *huitième* and *onzième.*
Exs. le huitième étage- the eighth floor, la onzième fois- the eleventh time
5. *Premier* is the only ordinal number used with the titles of rulers. (Ex. François Premier)
Otherwise, a cardinal number is used. (Ex. Pape Jean Six- Pope John the Sixth)
The definite article is omitted in both cases above before the name of a ruler.
(It is fitting that 'a cardinal' number be used when speaking of a pope. 'A Roman numeral' ought to be acceptable too.)
6. The ordinal abbreviation for *premier* is 1er; for *première*, it's 1ère. The other ordinals indicate their standing with an elevated e. (Ex. cinquantième = 50^{e})
7. Cardinal numbers precede ordinals in French.
Ex. les trois premières semaines > the first three weeks. (It puts a new twist on the expression "turn-around time.")

'Going for a Degree'- Write the French words for the following numerals.

1. 3e _____	6. 18e _____
2. 5e _____	7. 21e _____
3. 9e _____	8. 36e _____
4. 10e _____	9. 47e _____
5. 14^{e} _____	10. 60^{e} _____

'Qualifying for a Position'- Translate the following phrases.

1. the first love _____
2. her second impression _____
3. their fourth season _____
4. the fifth time _____
5. that eighth meeting _____
6. the ninth state _____
7. the eleventh floor _____
8. my sixteenth trip _____
9. the twentieth century _____
10. Charles VII _____
11. Louis XIV _____
12. our thirtieth anniversary _____
13. the seventieth person _____
14. the hundredth day _____

_____

les Escaliers de Montmartre par Brassaï (Paris)

LES ADVERBES DE QUANTITÉ - Adverbs of Quantity

How much do you want to know about adverbs of quantity? A lot? A little? Enough? In order to master them, students just need to learn a short vocabulary list and a twist of grammar. Regardless of the gender or plurality of the next word, adverbs of quantity are followed by *de* or *d'* without definite articles. (It does not involve *beaucoup de travail* > a lot of work.)

Common Adverbs of Quantity
1. **assez de/d'- enough of:** Ex. assez d'assiettes- enough plates
2. **autant de/d'- as much of, as many of:** Ex. autant d'**auteurs**- as many **authors**
3. **beaucoup de/d'- much, many, a lot of:** You have seen *beaucoup de traductions*- many translations *beaucoup de fois*- many times.
4. **combien de/d'- how much, how many:** <u>Combine</u> things to arrive at the total amount.
Ex. Combien de **réveillons du nouvel an** sont dans un siècle? > How many **New Year's eves** are in a century? (That's 10 'Times Squared.')
5. **moins de/d'- fewer, less of:** With its similarity to <u>minus</u>, there are *moins de questions*.
6. **peu de/d'- little, few of:** It is fitting for this little adverb to have *peu de lettres*.
7. **plus de/d'- more of:** The close translations are a plus in themselves.
Ex. Le médecin impatient **a besoin de** plus de patients. > The impatient doctor **needs** more patients.
8. **tant de/d'- so much of, so many of:** Ex. tant de tantes- so many aunts
9. **trop de/d'- too much of, too many of:** Pronouncing the <u>p</u> is one letter too many.
Ex. There is no such thing as spending *trop de temps* in St. Tropez.

Information You Need More of
1. **Adverbs of quantity can go in front of possessive and demonstrative adjectives.**
Exs. beaucoup de mes choix- many of my choices, plus de ces questions-là- more of those questions
2. *Assez* without *de/d'* means <u>rather</u> and precedes adjectives. (That is *assez intéressant*.)
3. **Sets of antonyms on the above list are *beaucoup de* vs. *peu de* and *plus de* vs. *moins de*.**
4. **To distinguish *autant de* from *tant de*, consider this: The first adverb begins with <u>a</u>, and so do its meanings- as much of, as many of. (So much for *tant de*!)**
5. **With no nouns to lean on, adverbs of quantity convert to simple adverbs.**
Exs. Elle parle trop. > She talks too much. C'est assez. > That's enough. Merci beaucoup!

A Little Work- Choose from the following adverbs of quantity to complete the sentences below. If there are multiple blanks, write all the possible answers: assez de/d', autant de/d', beaucoup de/d', combien de/d', moins de/d', peu de/d', plus de/d', tant de/d', trop de/d'

1. _____ adverbes de quantité sont sur la liste?
2. Guy a cent euros. Guillaume a deux cents euros. Guy a _____ argent.
3. Allons Z. et Allons O. n'ont pas _____ temps de faire leurs lits.
4. Les hommes n'ont pas _____ **chaussures-f. (shoes)** que les femmes.
5. La petite demande, " _____ couleurs sont dans un arc-en-ciel?"
6. Robert surfe sur le net. Rochelle cherche un boulot. Roland fait ses devoirs. Cette famille a besoin de (d') _____ un ordinateur.

7. Madame Achètetout fait toujours des magasins. Elle pense qu'elle n'a pas _____ ou _____ vêtements.

8. Mes cinq cousins n'habitent plus avec ma tante. Elle a _____ ou _____ réponsibilités ces jours-ci.

9. Justin Saison joue au soccer en automne. Il fait du ski en hiver. **C'est tout! > That's all!** Ce jeune homme-là n'aime pas _____ ou _____ ou _____ sports.

10. Mme Courir-Partout a quatre petits enfants. Elle fait la cuisine, elle fait la vaisselle, et elle fait la lessive. Elle a _____ ou _____ ou _____ **choses-f. (things)** à faire.

LES NOMS DE QUANTITÉ - Nouns of Quantity

Nouns of quantity identify things in measured portions. Like adverbs of quantity, these nouns are followed by *de* or *d'* without definite articles.
Here are a few handfuls of such short phrases:

'A Table of Contents'
1. une boîte de/d'- a box of
Ex. une boîte de chocolats- a box of chocolates (The s on *de* has been devoured.)
2. un bol de/d'- a bowl of (Just take out the w and the Cheerios!)
3. une bouteille de/d'- a bottle of
Ex. quatre-vingt-dix-neuf bouteilles de **bière** sur **le mur** > ninety-nine bottles of **beer** on **the wall** (*La* before *bière* has already fallen.)
4. une carafe de/d'- a carafe of, a decanter of: Most people don't 'care if' *le vin* is served *dans une bouteille* or *dans une carafe*.
5. une corbeille de/d', un panier de/d'- a basket of
Ex. une corbeille d'œufs et un panier d'œufs (You should not 'put all your eggs in one basket.')
6. une cuiller/une cuillère de/d'- a spoonful of: This rare noun offers two possible endings. (But that does not constitute 'a spoonerism.')
7. une douzaine de/d'- a dozen of: The French phrase has the same sound as a dozen eggs- *une douzaine d'œufs.* (They are included in the mix.)
8. un goût de/d'- a taste of
Ex. un goût de Gouda- a taste of Gouda
9. un kilo de/d', un kilogramme de/d'- a kilo of (The longer French measure is pronounced like a message informing someone of a murder.)
10. une livre de/d'- a pound of: *Une* differentiates this noun from *un livre.* (The only items sold by books are matches.)
11. un mètre de/d'- a meter of: The French measurement is almost equivalent to an American yard. Although only a shepherd would want a yard of sheep, a seamstress might be interested in *un mètre de laine-* **a meter of wool.**
12. un morceau de/d'- a piece of: Relating the noun to <u>morsel</u> will help you remember it <u>more so</u> than any other word.
13. un pot de/d', une marmite de/d'- a pot of, a jar of

Ex. Maman fait une marmite de marmelade et un pot de **potage**. > Maman makes a jar of marmalade and a pot of **soup**.
14. un sac de/d'- a sack of: Tired French campers 'sack out' in their *sacs de couchage*- **sleeping bags.**
15. un tas de/d'- a pile of (Owen Lotz would love to say "ta ta" to his pile of bills.)
16. une tasse de/d'- a cup of: Students who pull all-nighters are familiar with *un tas de tasses de café*- **a pile of cups of coffee.**
17. une tranche de/d'- a slice of: Even those who do not see a resemblance between the French noun and trench **should have no difficulty digging into** *une tranche de gâteau.*
18. un vase de/d'- a vase of (Just add water and flowers to this one!)
19. un verre de/d'- a glass of: Here's a French tongue-twister!: *Le vers vert va vers le verre vert.* > **The** green **worm** goes toward the green glass.

<u>Facts 'for Good Measure'</u>
1. Nouns of quantity can precede or be followed by possessive and demonstrative adjectives.
Exs. *mon verre de vin*- my glass of wine, *leur bouteille de vin*- their bottle of wine
      un bol de ce lait-ci- a bowl of this milk, *une tasse de ce lait-la*- a cup of that milk
2. Multiple translations for a can include *une boîte, un pot* **and** *un broc.* (We all know the French "Can Can.")

<u>'Quantitative Analysis'</u>- **Circle the letters of the correct answers to complete the sentences.**
1. Ce Noël M. Stingie donne _____ stylos à son secrétaire.
a. un bol de   b. une boîte de   c. un kilo de   d. un pot de
2. Vous apportez _____ fleurs à votre voisine qui est dans l'hôpital.
a. un goût de   b. une cuillère de   c. une carafe de   d. un vase de
3. On a besoin de deux _____ pain pour faire un sandwich.
a. paniers de   b. tasses de   c. tranches de   d. sacs de
4. En automne les petits aiment jouer dans _____.
a. des verres d'eau   b. les tas de feuilles   c. des pots de potages   d. des goûts de sucre
5. Quand Blaise ne va pas bien, sa mère prépare _____.
a. une marmite de soupe   b. un plat de viande   c. un mètre de coton   d. une bouteille de bière
6. Eric aime Hélène. Il apporte toujours _____ à sa petite amie.
a. un kilo de glace   b. une corbeille de vêtements   c. un bouquet de roses   d. une paire de patins
7. Mme Singer fait un manteau d'hiver. Elle va à un grand magasin, et elle demande _____.
a. deux douzaines d'œufs   b. un goût de vers   c. quatre mètres de laine   d. une boîte de bonbons
8. M. Comprendtout travaille aux Nations Unies où il fait _____.
a. un morceau de bois   b. des pages de traductions   c. des sacs de couchage   d. un broc de potage

----

<u>'The Facts of the Matter'</u>- **Label the statements** *vrai* **or** *faux.*
_____ 1. Moins de = trop de.
_____ 2. Peu de est le contraire de beaucoup de.
_____ 3. Assez de = avoir besoin de plus.
_____ 4. Autant de = **l'égalité-f. (equality)**.
_____ 5. Une corbeille est un panier.

_____ 6. Un kilo = une livre.

_____ 7. Un tas est une grande quantité.

_____ 8. Une carafe est comme une bouteille.

_____ 9. Un verre est une tasse.

_____ 10. Un goût est une grande tranche.

_____ 11. Un pot est une marmite.

_____ 12. Normalement, on mange le gâteau avec une cuillère.

Windsurfing on Lake Clairvaux (the Jura Region)

LES VÊTEMENTS - Clothing

Several articles of clothing have been scattered on previous pages, but until now, the topic was not fully 'ad-dress-ed.'
Here are *les mots de mode*- fashion words for every season and every reason.

The Women's Department

1. le tailleur- the woman's suit (In their closets or in their cars, ladies often have a spare *tailleur*.)
1a. le tailleur-pantalon and l'ensemble-pantalon- the women's pantsuit
An important note: *La taille* means the waist and the size of the garment.
2. la robe- the dress (Don't confuse it with the robe which is listed under 'un-dress!')
2a. la robe du soir- the evening gown
3. la jupe- the skirt: *Les jupons*- the petticoats can spread *les jupes* into the 'out-skirts.'
4. le chemisier- the blouse: Ironically, this noun is masculine while *la chemise*- the shirt is typically found in the men's department.
4a. *La blouse* and *le blouson* refer to unfitted tops. *-Lous* provides a loose association.
5. le maillot de bain- the swimsuit: Women wear *un maillot une pièce, un maillot deux pièces* or *un bikini*. (The model sometimes depends upon the model.)
5a. *Le bikini français* refers to a different type of one-piece swim wear. (Pay for the bottom, and the top is 'free'!)
6. la chemise de nuit- the nightgown: If thought of as the nightshirt, it will not be confused with *la robe du soir*. (A woman puts on the latter to wear out for the evening and the former when she is 'worn out' for the night.)
7. les talons (m.)- the heels: The first three letters indicate that this footwear makes one appear 'tal-ler.'
8. le sac à main- the handbag, the pocketbook, the purse: The word-for-word translation is "a sack for the hand." *Le sac à bandolière* is the shoulder bag. (It may be 'strapped for cash.')
9. le porte-monnaie- the coin/change purse: The term says "carry-change."

Les Sous-Vêtements de Femme- Women's Underwear
1. les bas (m.)- the stockings (the nylons) cover the *plus bas*- the lower part of the body.
2. les pantihose (m.)- the pantyhose: Different vowels 'run' inside the nouns. The French term is rather outmoded today and is covered by …
2a. les collants (m.)- the tights: Both this item and *le collage*- the wall hanging are derived from *coller*- to stick.
3. le slip- the panties: The French word seems to denote a different article of lingerie, but *le slip* is 'brief-er' and is a synonym for *la petite culotte*.
4. le soutien-gorge- the bra: Its precise translation is "the throat-supporter." Nevertheless, the French are bound to use the term *le soutien-gorge* more often than *la brassière*.
5. la combinaison- the slip (Women might wear this item under clingy or see-through fabrics 'to be on the safe side.')

Mentioning Menswear

Since many items of clothing can be worn by both sexes, the list of men's only attire is skimpy. Nevertheless, it is usually the man who wears ....

1. le pardessus- the overcoat: The consecutive prepositions *par* **and** *dessus* **mean** <u>by</u> **and** <u>over</u>, **respectively.** (Nothing tops *le pardessus*.)

2. le smoking- the tuxedo: (Some men 'look hot' wearing them.)

3. le costume- the man's suit: The same word fits <u>a costume</u>. *Le complet* **is its synonym.** A pair of pants and perhaps a vest make the suit <u>complete</u>.

4. le bleu de travail- the overalls: The "work blue" is readily distinguished from 'white collar' clothing. Overalls are also referred to as *la salopette*. **Be sure to pronounce the last syllable!** The first two form *un gros mot*- a bad word.

5. le maillot de corps- the undershirt (A good looking man wearing one might prompt a 'maillot my!') *Le tricot de corps*- the knit of the body is 'a take-off' of *le maillot de corps*.

6. le caleçon- the boxer shorts: They expand to *le caleçon de bain* **to become** <u>the bathing trunks</u>. *Le slip* **and** *la culotte* **are also labels for men's briefs.** (That 'gets to the bottom of' the subject.)

7. la cravate- the tie: With the gender of articles exchanged so frequently, it shouldn't seem 'loopy' that this noun is feminine.

8. les bretelles (f.)- the suspenders (Stretch your imagination to secure this one!)

<u>**'Dressing to Suit the Occasion'**</u>- **Fill in the blanks with 'the most fitting' responses. Answers should include definite or indefinite articles. The items can be 'worn' only once.**

1. Le costume et _____ sont les synonymes.

2. Il y a _____ dans son sac à main.

3. Les collants sont plus longs que _____.

4. _____ sont à la mode, mais ils ne sont pas toujours confortables.

5. M. Shiver porte toujours _____ quand il fait très froid.

6. À la plage ou à la piscine, ma grand-mère porte _____, et mon grand-père porte _____.

7. Le vieux McDonald porte _____ ou _____ quand il travaille dans les champs.

8. M. et Mme Bienhabilés **assistent à (attend)** un bal. Il porte _____. Elle porte _____.

9. Des femmes portent souvent _____ sous leurs robes et **presque (almost)** toujours _____ sous leurs chemisiers.

10. Luke Sharp porte _____ et _____ avec son complet.

11. Jim Ware fait ses exercices dans sa maison. Il porte **seulement (only)** _____ / _____ et _____.

12. Les femmes élégantes portent _____ ou _____ quand elles vont à l'église.

The Unisex Garment District

Men's and women's clothing styles vary, but several items share one name.

1. le chapeau- the hat: Chaps and ladies can 'top off' their attire with this accessory.

2. la casquette- the cap: Unlike the synonym for a coffin, similar sounding *la casquette* could be placed six feet above the ground. The French are 'straight forward' with *la casquette*, but they 'play all the angles' with *le beret.*

3. le manteau- the coat: The same word means a <u>fireplace mantel</u> and should 'wrap this up.'

4. l'imperméable (m.)- the raincoat: The name of this outerwear means that water can not get through. (No 'slicker' clues are necessary.)

5. le veston- the jacket: One puts *le veston* over the vest.

6. le gilet- the vest: This item 'is covered by' #5.

7. le pull, le pull-over- the pullover: (Both French versions 'are neck and neck' in popularity.)

8. le tricot- the sweater: As this word refers to anything knit, pinning it down to one article of clothing is 'tric-ky.'

9. le chandail- the sweater: It has a plain front or includes buttons or a zipper. *Le cardigan (le cardie)* always has a closing. (But the choice can 'be left open.')

10. l'ensemble (m.)- the outfit: This word, meaning <u>go together</u>, offers one a chance to show his or her sense of fashion coordination.

11. le pantalon- the pants: The French and English words look quite similar, but ours has been 'shortened.'

12. le(s) blue-jean(s)- the blue jeans: (There is a slight difference with the French cut.)

<u>An interesting aside</u>: Story has it that <u>denim</u> got its name because the fabric was first made in **Nîmes, France. So, its origin is** *de Nîmes.* (It's a fascinating tidbit for anyone into 'jeaneology.')

13. le short- the shorts: The French version is even more abbreviated.

14. le tee-shirt- the tee-shirt, the T-shirt: (The writing can vary in English.)

15. le peignoir- the bathrobe: Sometimes thought of as feminine lingerie, *le peignoir* is a unisex garment, but *la robe de chambre*- the dressing gown is usually worn by a woman. (That should explain 'disrobe' from 'dat robe.')

16. le pyjama- the pajamas: Change the first vowel, remove the <u>s</u>, and take 'a few zs.'

17. les chaussures (f.)- the shoes: *Chausser* is best translated as "to shoe size."
Ex. Elle chausse un 40.
Les chaussures can be 'paired' with their synonym *les souliers* in which <u>soles</u> is spelled out.

17a. les chaussures de sport, les tennis, les baskets- the sneakers (Some French people 'are game for' all of them.)

18. les bottes (f.)- the boots: The French style 'boots out' an <u>o</u> and adds a <u>t</u> and an <u>e</u>.

19. les pantoufles (f.)- the slippers (With their 'fluffy' sound, *les pantoufles* should fit comfortably into your vocabulary.)

20. les chaussettes (f.)- the socks: Even those who are not Red Sox fans could prefix *chaussettes* with <u>Massa</u> to remember its translation and not confuse it with *les chaussures*. (That the team is located in Boston 'does not mean beans' in this case.)

21. l'écharpe (f.)- the scarf, the sash: Pronounced similar to "A sharp" in music, this accessory 'is tied to' its synonym, *le foulard.*

22. la ceinture- the belt ('Ceint-ure' going to tuck in your shirt, why not wear a belt?) *La ceinture* *de sécurité*, the seat belt, is an item that we put on and then 'take off.'

23. le tablier- the apron: It is worn while preparing food to be taken to the <u>table</u>.

24. le mouchoir- the handkerchief (This indispensable accessory can add color to drab attire.)

25. le parapluie- the umbrella: The French translation could 'be watered down' to *par-* by and *pluie-* rain.)

26. les gants- the gloves: Related to medievel <u>gauntlets</u>, they are most often worn today only in cold weather. (However, some women still consider them as 'ele-gant (k)nightwear.')

27. le portefeuille- the billfold, the wallet: Literally, the noun means "carry a leaf." (The French realize how easy it is 'to blow money.')

Les Bijoux - The Jewelry

1. la montre- the watch: Identical to singular forms of *montrer*, you might look at *la montre* as an object for <u>showing</u> the time.

2. le collier- the necklace: Picture it worn around the collar for your good luck charm!

3. le bracelet- the bracelet- The articles are exchanged without additional adornments.

3. la bague- the ring: *Baguettes* are the smaller stones on a ring. Of course, *une baguette* is also a loaf of French bread. (The way the first pieces are cut is far more important.)

3a. l'alliance (f.)- the wedding band (That is <u>Lord of the Rings</u>.)

4. les boucles d'oreille- the earrings: Their actual meaning is "buckles/ curls of the ear." (They can now be visualized with a new 'twist.')

5. l'épingle (f.)- the pin: Notice that the translation is 'fastened' inside the French noun!

<u>**'Coordinating a Wardrobe'**</u>- Put the letters of the items beside the numbers of the translations.

_____ 1. les pantoufles	A. the cap
_____ 2. les chaussettes	B. the shoes
_____ 3. le chandail	C. the bathrobe
_____ 4. le gilet	D. the scarf
_____ 5. la ceinture	E. the underpants
_____ 6. l'imperméable	F. the umbrella
_____ 7. le mouchoir	G. the gloves
_____ 8. la casquette	H. the coat
_____ 9. les sous-vêtements	I. the belt
_____ 10. les gants	J. the wedding band
_____ 11. les chaussures, les souliers	K. the apron
_____ 12. les boucles d'oreille	L. the vest
_____ 13. le manteau	M. the socks
_____ 14. le peignoir	N. the wallet
_____ 15. l'alliance	O. the raincoat
_____ 16. la culotte, le slip	P. the jacket
_____ 17. le tablier	Q. the ring
_____ 18. le veston	R. the slippers

_____ 19. le parapluie

_____ 20. l'écharpe, le foulard

_____ 21. la bague

_____ 22. le portefeuille

S. the earrings

T. the underwear

U. the handkerchief

V. the sweater

What Should Be Donated? - Circle the letter of the item that does not belong in the group.

1. a. les bas   b. les bijoux   c. les chaussettes   d. les collants
2. a. la salopette   b. le blue-jean   c. le bleu de travail   d. le jupon
3. a. le collier   b. le parapluie   c. l'imperméable   d. les bottes
4. a. le smoking   b. le complet   c. le chapeau   d. le costume
5. a. l'écharpe   b. le foulard   c. le mouchoir   d. le maillot
6. a. la ceinture   b. la chemise de nuit   c. le pyjama   d. le peignoir
7. a. le chandail   b. la cravate   c. le pull-over   d. le tricot
8. a. le manteau   b. le pardessus   c. la casquette   d. le veston
9. a. le sac à main   b. le portefeuille   c. le porte-monnaie   d. l'ensemble
10. a. le caleçon   b. la robe   c. la jupe   d. le soutien-gorge
11. a. les souliers   b. les bretelles   c. les talons   d. les chaussures
12. a. le slip   b. la combinaison   c. la petite culotte   d. la montre
13. a. les gants   b. les pantoufles   c. les chaussettes   les bottines
14. a. la chemise   b. le chemisier   c. la bague   la blouse
15. a. le gilet   b. l'alliance   c. le tablier   le pardessus

---

'A Choice of Dressings'- From the following list, select three items that fit each scenario and write them in the blanks provided: les bijoux, des bikinis, un bleu de travail, un blue-jean, les bottes, les caleçons de bain, un chapeau, des chaussures de sport, une chemise, un complet, une cravate, les écharpes, les gants, un gilet, les maillots, un pantalon, un pyjama, rien (nothing), une robe du soir, une salopette, un short, les shorts, des sous-vêtements, des talons, un tailleur, un tee-shirt, un tricot de corps, un veston, les vestons

1. Le costume de M. Classique a trois pièces- _____, _____ et

_____.

2. Les enfants en vacances à la plage portent _____, _____

et _____.

3. Bob fait du jogging. Il porte _____, _____ et _____.

4. Madame Lacroix assiste à **une messe (a mass)** à son église. Elle porte _____,

_____ et _____.

5. M. Beau Champs travaille dans la ferme aujourd'hui. Porte-t-il _____ ou

_____ ou _____?

6. Quand Ben Habillé est dans son bureau dans un gratte-ciel, il porte _____,

_____ et _____.

7. Les petits jouent dans la neige. Ils portent _____, _____ et

_____.

8. Mme Chichi va porter _____, _____ et _____

à **la soirée (the evening party)** élégante.

9. Tu restes au lit. Tu portes _____ ou _____ ou _____.

LES ÉTOFFES et LES MÉTAUX - Materials and Metals

Although silk ties are not for sale in France, a shopper could be 'up to his neck in' *cravates de/ en soie*- ties of silk. To avoid consecutive nouns, *en* or *de/d'* (without an article) links the object to its contents. This French configuration is *apropos* as students are given the topic before they learn the material.

Inside Information

L'étoffe (f.) is a general heading that means <u>the material</u>. Because it does not identity a specific fabric such as *une toile*- a cloth or *un tissu*- a tissue, *l'étoffe* isn't followed by *de/d'* or *en*. 'In the other hand,' you might see *un mouchoir de/en toile*- a cloth handkerchief or *un mouchoir de/en papier*- a paper handkerchief (a tissue).

The Assembly Line

1. le coton- the cotton: This fabric goes into *les maillots de corps*- T-shirts.

2. le cuir- the leather: Pronounced like <u>queer</u>, *le cuir* can still be genuine.

3. la dentelle- the lace

Ex. La Bretagne est célèbre pour **sa** belle **broderie** de/en dentelle. > Brittany is known for **its** beautiful lace **embroidery**. (It's a far cry from dental work.)

4. la fourrure- the fur: Referring to the article of clothing and to the material, the noun has <u>fur</u> wrapped inside.

5. la laine- the wool: The French word starts like lamb, but then it strays.

6. le lin- the linen: English leaves a line in linen, but French cleverly irons it out.

7. le nylon- the nylon

Ex. On trouve la lingerie de/en nylon **partout**. > We find nylon lingerie **everywhere**. (It could give intimate clothing a bad name.)

8. le polyester- the polyester (The material is a combination of fabrics and two female names, Polly and Esther.)

9. la soie- the silk

Ex. Solange a soixante robes du soir de/en soie. > Solange has sixty silk evening gowns. (She is very 'materialistic.')

10. le suède- the suede: For the French, this fabric applies only to gloves.

Ex. les gants de/en suède

10 a. Le daim- the deer/buckskin is used for shoes and handbags.

Ex. les chaussures et les sacs à main de/en daim. (The pocketbook cannot be 'purse-sueded.')

11. le velours- the velvet: *L'ours*- the bear inside the noun makes the fabric cuddly.

Vocabulary with Substance

1. l'acier (m.)- the steel: Fine steelwork looks <u>lacier</u> than other metals.

2. l'argent (m.)- the silver, the money

Ex. Olympia préfère ce collier d'/en argent-ci. > Olympia prefers this silver necklace. (She does not 'go for the gold.')

3. le béton- the concrete: One can 'bet-on' its solid foundation.

4. le bois- the wood, the woods

Ex. M. Dubois **coupe** trois boîtes de/en bois dans les bois. > Mr. Dubois **cuts** three wooden boxes in the woods.

An interesting note: *Un chèque de/en bois* **is a wooden check.** (However, it can still 'bounce.')

5. le caoutchouc- the rubber: Several decades ago, people wore rubbers as <u>coats for shoes</u>.

6. le cuivre- the copper; le cuivre jaune- the brass: Both are found in *la cuisine*. **The latter is an 'instru-metal' part of** *le clairon*- **the bugle and** *la trompette*- **the trumpet.**

7. l'étain (m.)- the tin, the pewter: Putting an <u>r</u> **in front of** *étain* **indicates one function of a tin.**

8. le fer- the iron: Pronounced like *faire, le fer* **is also the object used for pressing.**

Ex. le fer de/en fer- the iron iron

9. l'or (m.)- the gold: Leave the <u>e</u> **'in reserve' for the English word** <u>ore</u>!

10. la paille- the straw: In both languages, this noun names the material and the slender drinking tube. (With no alternate word, the English and the French were 'clutching at straws.')

11. la plastique- the plastic: The material is easy to see through without any surgery.

12. le plomb- the lead: Related to <u>plumbing</u>, **this heavy metal landed on the bottom of the list.** (It was not possible 'to get the lead out' sooner.)

'Manufacturing Answers'- Choose the best responses from the following list to complete the sentences. *De/d'* **or** *en* **must precede the material or the metal: l'acier, l'argent, le caoutchouc, le coton, le cuir, le cuivre, le daim, la dentelle, la fourrure, la laine, le nylon, l'or, la paille, la plastique, le polyester, la soie, le velours**

1. Les cartes de crédit sont toujours _____.
2. J'ai plus de dix tee-shirts _____.
3. Dick, Jane et Sally portent leurs bottes _____ quand il pleut.
4. Les tables et les chaises _____ dans le palais sont très chères.
5. La première maison des trois petits **cochons-m. (pigs)** est _____.
6. Les ballerines portent les collants _____.
7. La Bretagne est célèbre pour sa broderie _____.
8. Dans les cuisines des restaurants, il y a souvent des marmites _____.
9. Elvis chante de ses chaussures _____ bleu.
10. Je n'ai pas besoin de **repasser au fer (to iron)** ses pantalons _____.
11. Les montres _____ sont moins chères que les montres _____.
12. **Comme (As)** il fait froid, nous portons nos pardessus et nos chandails _____.
13. Chez Harley Davidson, Helmut trouve des vestons et des casquettes _____.
14. Des rois dans les fables portent des vêtements _____, et ils portent les épées

_____.

15. La vedette porte une robe du soir _____ et un manteau _____.

PRESENT TENSE CONJUGATION - REGULAR -IR VERBS

Mastering the forms of regular -<u>ir</u> verbs entails attaching the correct endings to specific stems. Why not begin by filling yourself in on the conjugation of *remplir*?

Remplir - To Fill

<u>Singular</u>	<u>Plural</u>
je remp<u>lis</u>- I fill, do fill, am filling	nous remp<u>lissons</u>- we fill, do fill, are filling
tu remp<u>lis</u>- you fill, do fill, are filling	vous remp<u>lissez</u>- you fill, do fill, are filling
il remp<u>lit</u>- he//it fills, does fill, is filling	ils remp<u>lissent</u>- they fill, do fill, are filling
elle remp<u>lit</u>- she/it fills, does fill, is filling	elles remp<u>lissent</u>- they fill, do fill, are filling

----

Surprise Endings

1. Regular verbs with -<u>ir</u> infinitive endings are also known as <u>second conjugation verbs</u>. After those two letters are taken off, the endings are added to the stem.
2. All singular forms of regular -<u>ir</u> verbs are pronounced the same. Listeners can tell from the subject pronouns who or what is being discussed. So, although the endings spell "Is it?" twice, no questions have to be asked.
3. For the plural forms, -<u>iss</u> + regular -<u>er</u> endings are added to the stem.
3a. -<u>Ent</u> is not a nasal combination in verb endings. The <u>e</u> with no accent mark is a reminder to pronounce the preceding consonant.

Verbs from 'Ir to Ir'

1. agir- to act: Being so short, this verb can be thought of as a one-act play.
2. bâtir- to build: The word is closely related to *le bâtiment*- <u>the building</u>.
3. blanchir- to bleach, to whiten: *Blanc* is ' poured into' the French verb.
4. choisir- to choose: Its English cognate and *le choix* offer options for remembering it.
5. finir- to finish: Close in spelling to its counterpart, the French verb contains two endings. It has a fin (*la fin*- the end) with an -<u>ir</u> tail attached to it.
6. grandir- to grow, to become larger: *Grand*- big, large, great spreads to form this word.
7. grossir- to gain weight: It is a possible result of going to the 'gross-ery' store too often.
8. guérir- to cure, to heal (Its pronunciation is a synonym for 'a happy backside.')
9. maigrir- to lose weight: The verb stem took a little off from *maigre*- thin.
10. obéir à- to obey (to): The cognates are close in spelling. However, *obéir* is followed by *à* or a contraction because one must obey <u>to</u> someone or something.
Ex. Luke Skywalker obéit à Obi-Wan Kenobi. > Luke Skywalker obeys Obi-Wan Kenobi.
11. punir- to punish (One might do this to someone who does not do #10.)
12. réfléchir à- to think (about), to reflect (on): *Penser à* and *réfléchir à* are synonyms.
13. remplir- to fill, to replenish: Three letters of <u>empty</u> are inside *remplir*. (So, is the French verb half-full or half-empty?) Forms of *remplir* take *de* or a partitive to express fill/filled <u>with</u>.
14. réussir à- to succeed: Every plural form has a quadruple <u>s</u>. The entire conjugation touts its success with an *à* or even an *à* + (for contractions.)
Ex. Ils réussissent à **cloner** un mouton. > They succeed **at cloning** a sheep. (Success does not, in this case, breed success.)

15. rougir- to blush: Most of the adjective *rouge* is showing through this verb.

<u>Giving -IR Verbs a 'Wh-ir-l'</u>- Replace the blanks with the correct forms of the verbs in parentheses. Then translate the completed sentences.

<u>Helpful Words and Constructions</u>
1. aller bien- to go well, to fit, to look good on
Ex. Cet ensemble cher-là va bien à Cher. > That expensive outfit looks good on Cher.
2. faire + an infinitive- to have something done, to make something happen: The subject of the sentence does not do the action.
Ex. Otto Nettoyer fait laver sa voiture. > Otto Nettoyer has his car washed.
3. verser- to pour

1. (remplir) Les serveurs _____ les carafes de l'eau.
_____.

2. (blanchir) Nous _____ des sous-vêtements.
_____.

3. (maigrir) Manges-tu moins de bonbons? Je pense que tu _____.
_____.

4. (rougir) Les petites _____ quand elles ont honte.
_____.

5. (grossir) Mme Potelée _____, et ses vêtements ne **vont** pas **bien**.
_____.

6. (choisir) Qui va _____ les joueurs pour cette équipe-ci?
_____?

7. (réussir) M. Motivé _____ parce qu'il fait de son mieux.
_____.

8. (guérir) Les médecins _____ autant de gens que possible.
_____.

9. (bâtir) On qui prépare à _____ un immeuble d'habitation **verse** le béton. _____
_____.

10. (agir) Quel âge Sophie Stiquée a-t-elle? Elle _____ comme un adulte. _____
_____.

11. (finir) Si tu _____ tes devoirs à l'heure, vas-tu aller au spectacle? _____
_____?

12. (obéir à, punir) Quand ils n'_____ pas ___ leurs maîtresses, est-ce que M. et Mme Soyezsage _____ leurs enfants? _____
_____?

13. (faire bâtir) E. Nuff et sa femme ne _____ pas _____ une quatrième maison.
_____
_____.

14. (réfléchir à) Je _____ _____ la forme du verbe pour cette réponse. _____
_____.

91

<u>**Filling Orders**</u>- **Choose the correct forms of the following verbs to complete the sentences: agir, bâtir, blanchir, choisir, finir, grandir, grossir, guérir, maigrir, obéir à, punir, remplir, réussir à, rougir**

1. Je fais toujours la gymnastique, mais je ne _____ pas.
2. La banlieue _____ parce que la vie dans les villes est très chère.
3. Que faites-vous quand vous _____ votre travail?
4. Ma mère fait la lessive. Elle _____ les chemises que mon père porte au bureau.
5. On _____ un centre commercial deux kilomètres de ma maison.
6. Bea Zare porte un imperméable à la plage. Elle _____ **étrangement (strangely)**.
7. Les souris mangent toujours, mais elles ne _____ pas.
8. C'est **facile (easy)**! Tu _____ les verbes que tu _____.
9. On _____ les criminels qui n'_____ pas ____ **lois-f. (laws)**.
10. Ils parlent seulement le bon français avec Prudence. Elle _____ s'il y a de gros mots dans la conversation.
11. Comment vas-tu _____ ____ tes examens si tu n'étudies pas?
12. Je pense qu'un pot de soupe au **poulet (chicken)** va _____ ma grand-mère.

le Chenonceau (the Loire Valley)

PRESENT TENSE CONJUGATION - REGULAR -RE VERBS

All aboard for a cruise through the conjugation of -re verbs on the SS Nothing! Check out the singular endings on *perdre* to see how this boat got its name! Its significance will keep you from getting lost while you navigate regular <u>third conjugation verbs</u>.

Perdre - To Lose

Singular	Plural
je perd<u>s</u>- I lose, do lose, am losing	nous perd<u>ons</u>- we lose, do lose, are losing
tu perd<u>s</u>- you lose, do lose, are losing	vous perd<u>ez</u>- you lose, do lose, are losing
il perd_ - he/it loses, does lose, is losing	ils perd<u>ent</u>- they lose, do lose, are losing
elle perd_ - she/it loses, does lose, is losing	elles perd<u>ent</u>- they lose, do lose, are losing

----

'Anchoring -RE Verbs'
1. All singular -<u>re</u> verb forms have the same pronunciation.
2. The plural endings of -<u>er</u> and -<u>re</u> verbs are identical.
3. The infinitive stems of regular -<u>re</u> verbs usually end with <u>d</u>. However, *rompre*- to break (off) and *interrompre*- to interrupt do just that with a <u>t</u> in the third person singular.
Ex. **Une publicité** interrompt leur **émission de télévision** préférée. > A **commercial/advertisement** interrupts their favorite **television program**.
4. The <u>d</u> in the third persons has a <u>t</u> sound when the subject and the verb are inverted.
Ex. Sally, vend-elle ses **coquillages au bord de la mer?** > Does Sally sell her **seashells at the seashore?** (Do her customers hear 'the sound of the <u>t</u>'?)

The Captain's Log
1. attendre- to wait for: <u>For</u> is waiting inside *attendre*.
2. défendre- to defend (No outside support is necessary.)
3. descendre- to descend (What the SS Nothing should not do.)
4. entendre- to hear, to understand: As in English, the French versions of "I hear you," and "I understand you" can be used with the same verb. (Yet, it's not a double entendre.)
5. perdre- to lose, to waste: *Perdre* is lost without its antonym *trouver*.
6. rendre- to give back, to return, to yield: Rendering -<u>re</u> for -<u>er</u> yields one of its translations.
6a. rendre visite à- to call on, to visit (a) person(s) vs. *visiter*- to visit a place

Ex. Elle rend visite à M. Toll. > She visits Mr. Toll. (And literally 'pays a visit.')
Ex. Elle visite des musées à Paris. > She visits some museums in Paris.

7. rompre- to break, to break off: *Casser*- to break can be seen and heard.

Ex. Christelle **pleure** quand Chrétien rompt **leurs fiançailles**. > Crystal **cries** when Christian breaks **their engagement**. (Crystal is 'shattered.')

8. répondre à- to answer to, to respond: The first letter of the verb is the <u>r</u> in RSVP- *Répondez, s'il vous plaît!*- Answer, please! Even if one does nothing inappropriate, he/she must answer <u>to</u> someone.

Ex. **Votre explication** ne répond pas à ma question, Marc. > **Your explanation** does not answer my question, Marc.

9. vendre- to sell: A <u>vending machine</u> helps 'to dispense' the meaning of this verb.

<u>'On Board Activities'</u>- **Using the correct forms of** *attendre, défendre, descendre, entendre, interrompre, perdre, rendre, rompre, répondre à* **and** *vendre*, **complete the sentences. A few verbs can be used more than once.**

1. _____-vous des voix étranges?
2. Suzette _____ des vêtements au Bon Marché cet après-midi.
3. Combien de temps _____-ils le métro?
4. Je ne _____ pas ___ mon téléphone cellulaire quand je suis au bureau.
5. Mlle Gardepeu _____ les cadeaux qu'elle n'aime pas bien.
6. Nous avons peur souvent de _____ d'hauts lieux.
7. Ma voisine _____ **les jouets-m. (the toys)** de ses enfants sur E-Bay.
8. Qui _____ les animaux innocents dans la forêt?
9. La mère gronde son fils quand Rudy _____ une conversation.
10. _____-tu la musique qui joue dans ce magasin-ci?
11. Si vous maigrissez, vous _____ des kilos.
12. Nous _____ ou nous _____ ___ **un courrier électronique (an e-mail)** important.
13. Mon copain ne _____ pas sa promesse.
14. Ma tante Seule a cinquante ans, et elle n'a pas de mari. Elle _____ **encore (still)** Le Prince Charmant.

<u>Three Conjugations Come Into Play</u>- **Translate the following sentences.**
1. The priest pours the wine at the mass. _____.
2. Ray Ception does not hear well on his cell phone. _____
_____.
3. The wolf (**Le loup**) pays a visit to the three little pigs. _____
_____.
4. Notta Wird does not answer her father when he asks for an explanation. _____
_____.
5. We do not have any e-mails because our computer is not working. _____
_____.
6. At the evening party, some glasses fall off the table, and the pot breaks. _____

7. Mom's outfit is too small because she is gaining weight. _____
_____.

8. Their father is having their screen names changed. _____
_____.

9. If he succeeds in selling the car, he is going to give the money back to his mother. _____
_____.

10. You (*tu*) do not lose any time. You watch your favorite program while you iron. _____
_____
_____
_____.

Paris from the Arc de Triomphe

LES ADJECTIFS INTERROGATIFS - Interrogative Adjectives
QUEL, QUELLE, QUELS, QUELLES - What, Which, What A!

Quel, quelle, quels and *quelles* are interrogative adjectives. Their meanings are <u>what</u>, <u>what a(n)</u> and <u>which</u>. The four forms precede the nouns they modify and agree with them in gender and in number. (Since every member of the quartet sounds the same, you might wonder, "What the *quel* is the difference?")

Interrogative Adjectives

Singular	Plural
quel (masculine) - what, what a(n), which	quels (masculine) - what, which
quelle (feminine) - what, what a(n), which	quelles (feminine) - what, which

----

WHAT You Need to Know

1. *Quel* goes before masculine singular nouns. *Quel jour est-ce aujourd'hui?*, and *Quel temps-il?* should look very familiar. *Quel dommage!* > **What a pity!** if they don't.

2. *Quelle* precedes feminine singular nouns. As you have seen *Quelle heure est-il?* time and time again you cannot say, *"Quelle surprise!"*

3. *Quels* is used in front of masculine plural nouns. *Le Petit Chaperon Rouge*- <u>Little Red Riding Hood</u> exclaimed, *"Quels grands yeux tu as!"* > **"What big eyes you have!"** (As she was trying 'to quell' her fear.)

4. *Quelles* goes before feminine plural nouns. *Le Petit Chaperon Rouge* said fearfully, **"Quelles grandes dents tu as!"** > **"What big teeth you have!"** (Nobody accused her of "crying wolf.")

5. *Quel* and Associates can be found in front of any form of *être*. *Quels sont les mois de l'année?* will never go out of date, and *Quelles sont les saisons de l'année?* requires an answer that is not subject to change. An interrogative adjective agrees with the first noun after the verb.

6. *Quel* and Associates are translated by <u>which</u> when a choice is involved.
Ex. Quels petits ont **les autocollants** sur leurs devoirs? > Which little children have **stickers** on their homework? (Probably those with 'happy faces.')

7. Because the *quel* quartet means <u>what a/an</u> as well as <u>what</u> and <u>which</u>, there's no *un* or *une* in the translation. *Quel soulagement!* > **What a relief!**

<u>What an Answer</u>! - Complete the scenarios by replacing the blanks with *quel, quelle, quels* or *quelles* and the following nouns: l'affaire (f.)- the bargain, la blague- the joke, la chance, le château, le choix, le dommage, la famille, le film, le fouillis- the jumble/the hodgepodge, l'histoire, le jeu, la salutation, le soulagement, le vol- the flight, la vue- the view. Nouns may be used more than once, and two answers may be possible.
Ex. Je voyage de Paris à New York City. Il pleut, et des enfants pleurent dans l'avion.
Quel vol! > What a flight!

1. Louis visite la résidence d'un roi français. _____!
2. Carver, Peggy, Woody et Twiggy _____!
3. On fête les acteurs et les actrices célèbres à Cannes. _____!
4. Chaleureuse donne cinq bisous à son petit-fils. _____!
5. Les Alpes de France, les lacs d'Italie, les îles de Grèce _____!

6. Après un match de quatre heures, notre équipe gagne. _____!
7. M. Jongleur, qui habite avec sa femme, aime Lille. _____!
8. J'adore écouter les plaisanteries d'Alain. _____ il raconte!
9. Huit heures en l'air et deux heures pour chercher nos valises. _____!
10. Rabais trouve un tailleur par Versace pour 100 euros. _____!
11. J'étudie sept heures. L'examen est facile. _____!
12. L'Hôtel Ritz ou Les Quatre Saisons? _____!
13. Il y a des livres, des cahiers et des papiers partout. _____!
14. Ta famille passe une semaine **gratuite (free)** à la Côte d'Azur. _____!
Il fait mauvais six jours. _____!

TEL, TELLE, TELS, TELLES - Such, Such A

It is very easy to 'tel' that these four adjectives look like and rhyme with the *Quel* family. **Such** members of the *tel* group also agree in gender and in number with the nouns they precede. Yet, each set has unique features. The *Quel* family welcomes questions, while the *Tel* family engages in the middle of conversations. In addition, although **a** is included in the translation of *quel* and *quelle*, *un* precedes *tel*, and *une* precedes *telle*. An invariable *de* goes in front of *tels* and *telles*. *Pareil* parallels *tel* in meaning. Their eight possible forms could all be referred to as "such and such" in English.
Ex. J'ai de telles bonnes mémoires de mon voyage à Paris. C'est une telle belle ville. > I have such good memories of my trip to Paris. It is such a beautiful city.

Such a Short Exercise! - Fill in the blanks with *un tel, une telle, de tels* or *de telles*.

1.	_____ plaisir	8.	_____ merveilleuse famille
2.	_____ vue	9.	_____ date importante
3.	_____ couleurs	10.	_____ bons prix
4.	_____ erreur	11.	_____ belle dentelle
5.	_____ affaires	12.	_____ examen difficile
6.	_____ idée	13.	_____ bonnes blagues
7.	_____ quartier intéressant	14.	_____ bijoux chers

LES PRONOMS INTERROGATIFS - Interrogative Pronouns

Who is ready to read some good news? "What's that?," you might ask. *Qui* and *que* have made several cameo appearances. Now it's time for a front-face view of "Who's who?," and "What's what?"

	Who? Whom? (Persons)	What? (Things)
Subject	Qui, Qui est-ce qui	Qu'est-ce qui
Object Pronoun	qui	que (qu'), qu'est-ce que
Object of a Preposition	qui	quoi

Since You Asked

1. With only a quick glance, *qui est-ce qui* and *qu'est-ce qui* might seem identical. A closer look reveals that the person has two i's. <u>What</u> is the cyclops with one <u>i</u>.

Ex. Qui est-ce qui a peur de grand **méchant** loup? > Who is afraid of the big **bad** wolf?

Ex. Qu'est-ce qui arrive à minuit le 31 décembre? What happens at midnight December, 31?

<u>A helpful hint</u>: **Because *qui* means and is used exactly the same as *qui est-ce qui*, take the short cut!** (Consider that as *qui* advice!)

2. *Qui* serves three French functions and has two English translations. Object pronouns as well as objects of prepositions are <u>whom</u>. (Just ask a well-spoken owl!)

Ex. Qui le président n'invite-t-il pas à sa soirée? > Whom is the president not inviting to his evening party? (Possibly those who have 'an out-of-office reply.')

2a. Short phrases with *qui* include *à qui*- to whom, *avec qui*- with whom, *de qui*- of/from whom and *pour qui*- for whom. (The last one is also the name of a Looney Tune pig.)

Ex. À qui vont-ils **louer la cabane** dans les bois? > To whom are they going to **rent the cabin** in the woods? (Probably to anyone 'hunting.')

3. French offers two ways to express <u>whose</u>.

3a. *À qui* is used to show <u>possession</u>.

Ex. À qui est cette montre d'or-ci? > Whose gold watch is this? (The owner can provide 'the missing link.')

3b. *De qui* is used to show <u>relationship</u>.

Ex. De qui la petite **Orpheline** Annie est-elle l'enfant? Whose child is Little **Orphan** Annie?

Notice that the word order *À qui* and *de qui* + a verb + a noun is different from English!

4. *Que/qu'* and *qu'est-ce que/qu'est-ce qu'* are direct object pronouns meaning <u>what</u>. Either can be used if the question has a subject.

4a. *Que/qu'* are used if the subject and the verb are inverted; *Qu'est-ce que/qu'est-ce qu'* apply if the word order is not switched.

Ex. Que faites-vous avec les décorations après le Noël? > What do you do with the decorations after Christmas?

Ex. Qu'est-ce que vous faites avec les décorations après le Noël? > What do you do with the decorations after Christmas? (Are they left 'hanging around the house'?)

4b. <u>E</u>s dropping with *qu'* and *qu'est-ce qu'* is French protocol.

Ex. Qu'est-ce qu'Oprah pense de l'opéra? > What does Oprah think of the opera?

However, <u>I</u> cannot be dropped from *qui, qui est-ce qui* and *qu'est-ce qui*. (The best place to find 'i drops' is at your local pharmacy.)

5. French sentences do not end with prepositions. They go in front of interrogative phrases and take *quoi* as their objects.

Ex. Avec quoi coupe-t-il **le fil métallique**? > With what is he cutting **the wire**? (We know that it is not correct to say, "What is he cutting the wire with?," but we 'mangle' it anyway.)

5a. *Pourquoi* is a combination of <u>for</u> and <u>what</u>.

Ex. Pourquoi **empruntes**-tu **mon marteau**? > Why are you **borrowing my hammer**?/What are you borrowing my hammer for? (The first translation should 'strike' you as grammatically correct.)

6. *Qu'est-ce que c'est?* > What is it? literally says, "What is it that it is?" When a noun or *cela/ça* is added to the question, the phrase reads, *qu'est-ce que c'est qu'un(e)* _____?

Ex. Qu'est-ce que c'est qu'**un kiosque**? > What is **a kiosque**? (It's a free-standing, tube-shaped pole covered with advertisements.)

If somebody points to one and asks, *"Qu'est-ce que c'est que cela?"* > "What is that?," you can knowingly respond, *"C'est un kiosque."* (*Le kiosque* offers more information.)

<u>**A very important note**</u>**:** *Qui* and *que* **are also relative pronouns and are used in statements.** *Qui* **provides a clause with a subject;** *que* **is needed if the clause has one.**

Ex. **Le mec inamical** <u>qui</u> loue cette maison-là est en vacances. > **The unfriendly guy** who rents that house is on vacation.

Ex. Nous **remarquons** <u>que</u> le mec inamical est en vacances. We **notice** that the unfriendly guy is on vacation. (He is welcome to stay away.)

<u>**'Q-ing up' for the Empty Spaces**</u>**- Complete the questions by using** *qui, qu'est-ce qui, qu'est-ce que/qu'est-ce qu', que/qu', quoi, à qui, de qui, qu'est-ce que c'est* **or** *qu'est-ce que c'est que cela.*

1. _____ est-il le neveu?
2. _____ qu'un boum? C'est une fête pour les jeunes.
3. Il y a tant d'ambulances dans la rue? _____ arrive?
4. _____ Ben emprunte de Franklin?
5. Nicolas rougit. De _____ a-t-il honte?
6. _____ rencontres-tu à la gare d'Austerlitz?
7. _____ on porte pour plonger sous-marine?
8. L'enfant curieux demande, " _____ fait tourner le monde?"
9. _____ vendez-vous aujourd'hui, M. Marchand?
10. De _____ a-t-on besoin pour couper un fil métallique?
11. _____ qu'un TGV? C'est un train à grande **vitesse (speed)**.
12. _____ sont ces **I-Cosses (I-Pods)?**
13. Barnum demande à Bailey, "Avec _____ vas-tu au cirque?"
14. _____ Gaëlle et Léo remarquent quand ils regardent le ciel?
15. Quelle mauvaise odeur dans la cuisine! _____?

Question the Answers!- Using *qui* (with or without a prep.), *qu'est-ce qui, qu'est-ce que, qu'est-ce qu', quoi* or *qu'est-ce que c'est qu'un(e)*, write the questions that prompted the responses. The words and phrases to be replaced are underlined.
Ex. Son grand-père écoute <u>le jazz</u>. > <u>Qu'est-ce que</u> son grand-père écoute?

1. <u>Grégoire</u> gagne toujours quand nous luttons.

_____?

2. Il finit <u>ses devoirs</u> en classe.

_____?

3. Ce bateau à voile-là est <u>à M. Bonvent</u>.

_____?

4. <u>Le vol de Toulouse</u> va arriver bientôt.

_____?

5. <u>Un truc</u> est une chose qu'on ne nomme pas.

_____?

6. <u>L'astronaute</u> a le nom d'écran "Missiletoe."

_____?

7. Mlle Lacaisse n'a pas de <u>cartes de crédit</u>.

_____?

8. Elle pense <u>à son petit ami</u> de matin jusqu'à nuit.

_____?

9. <u>Les sœurs Sueur</u> ne jouent pas au tennis quand il fait très chaud.

_____?

10. Faye Lemieux réussit <u>à son examen de biologie</u>.

_____?

11. Les voyageurs <u>ont sommeil, et ils ont faim</u>.

_____?

12. <u>Ses fourrures</u> coûtent deux cent mille euros.

_____?

13. <u>La Bête</u> rend visite à La Belle.

_____?

14. **<u>La barbe à papa</u> (cotton candy)** est un grand bonbon très **doux (soft, sweet.)**

_____?

_____

UNE REVUE - A Review

Cardinal Numbers, Ordinal Numbers, Les Adverbes et Les Noms de Quantité, Les Vêtements, Les Étoffes et Les Métaux, Present Tense Conjugation of Regular -IR Verbs, Present Tense Conjugation of Regular -RE Verbs, Les Pronoms et Les Adjectifs Interrogatifs

'Split Decisions'- **Label the statements** *vrai* **or** *faux*.

_____ 1. There is no s on *vingt* or on *cent* if another number follows them.

_____ 2. The French numbers for seventy, eighty and ninety end with -ante.

_____ 3. *Cent* and *mille* are not preceded by *un*.

_____ 4. *Million* takes *de* or *d'* when another number follows it.

_____ 5. *Sont* precedes the answers in French mathematical calculations.

_____ 6. *Tant de* and *autant de* are synonyms.

_____ 7. *Trop, assez* and *beaucoup*, when not followed by *de* or *d'*, can end a sentence.

_____ 8. Adverbs and nouns of quantity are followed by definite articles.

_____ 9. *Un morceau de* and *une tranche de* are close in meaning.

_____ 10. *Un tas de* and *une tasse de* are synonyms.

_____ 11. Le caleçon, le slip et la culotte sont les sous-vêtements.

_____ 12. Les bretelles, les ceintures et les cravates sont les accessoires.

_____ 13. On porte un porte-monnaie et un portefeuille dans une casquette.

_____ 14. *Dans* links the noun to what it is made of.

_____ 15. *Le suède* and *le daim* describe the same wearing apparel.

_____ 16. *Le lin* and *la laine* are synonyms.

_____ 17. L'acier, le cuivre et le fer sont des métaux.

_____ 18. Regular -ir verbs have -iss throughout their plural forms.

_____ 19. No regular -ir verbs are followed by *à*.

_____ 20. Forms of *faire* followed by infinitives express to have something done.

_____ 21. Regular -er and -re verbs do not have the same plural endings.

_____ 22. The stems of all -re verbs end with a d.

_____ 23. The four members of the *Quel* family are pronounced identically.

_____ 24. *Tel* and its family are interrogative adjectives.

_____ 25. *Qui est-ce qui* and *qu'est-ce qui* are interchangeable.

_____ 26. *Qu'est-ce que* and *que* refer to things.

_____ 27. *Qui* and *quoi* are used after prepositions.

_____ 28. Who and whom are both translated by *qui*.

'Uninvited Guests'- **Circle the letters of the terms that do not belong.**

1. a. beaucoup de	b. tant de	c. peu de	d. trop de
2. a. un verre de	b. une bouteille de	c. une carafe de	d. un mètre de
3. a. la cravate	b. la combinaison	c. l'écharpe	d. le foulard
4. a. la chemise de nuit	b. le peignoir	c. les pantoufles	d. le bleu de travail
5. a. les boucles d'oreille	b. les talons	c. les chaussures	d. les souliers
6. a. le chaperon	b. le veston	c. les chaussures	d. le manteau
7. a. le tailleur	b. la jupe	c. le chemisier	d. le smoking

8. a. les chaussettes	b. les gants	c. les bas	d. les collants
9. a. la paille	b. le plomb	c. l'or	d. l'argent
10. a. la dentelle	b. la soie	c. l'étain	d. le cuir
11. a. le pardessus	b. le velours	c. le caoutchouc	d. le fer
12. a. seulement	b. sous	c. encore	d. partout
13. a. -is	b. -s	c. -it	d. -issent
14. a. qu'est-ce qui	b. qu'est-ce que	c. que	d. quoi
15. a. le nom d'écran	b. le courrier électronique	c. le téléphone cellulaire	d. le poulet

----

'Both Sides of the Story'- Match the letters to the numbers of the phrases to form sentences.

_____ 1. La robe n'est pas sa taille,

_____ 2. Quand on voyage par avion

_____ 3. Normalement, on coupe la laine des moutons

_____ 4. Mon fils verse un bol de lait

_____ 5. Cent multiplié par dix

_____ 6. Jennie Reuse emprunte un stylo,

_____ 7. Le monsieur qui vend les souliers demande à Piet,

_____ 8. Les jouets de mes petits-enfants remplissent ma maison.

_____ 9. Je ne rends pas visite à Giselle

_____ 10. M. Achat est au grand magasin

_____ 11. Il y a une deuxième explication

_____ 12. Un ours ne maigrit pas

_____ 13. Les touristes regardent les publicités

_____ 14. Patience attend à la gare une heure

_____ 15. M. Augment bâtit une grande maison

_____ 16. Il y a un message de ton oncle

_____ 17. Le loup n'agit pas comme sa grand-mère,

_____ 18. Quand Mlle Bloom travaille dans son jardin en été,

_____ 19. Dorée Diamant a tant de bijoux.

_____ 20. Madame Joie regarde toujours son alliance.

A. et le Petit Chaperon Rouge a peur.

B. parce que je n'ai pas son adresse.

C. parce que le train est en retard.

D. Elle n'en a pas besoin de plus.

E. quand il ne mange pas en hiver.

F. parce que sa famille grandit.

G. sur ton répondeur de téléphone.

H. et elle en rend deux.

I. et elle ne va pas bien à la femme.

J. elle porte un short et un tee-shirt.

K. Quel fouillis!

L. "Quelle pointure chaussez-vous?"

M. une fois par an.

N. font mille.

O. C'est l'amour!

P. ou il choisit un complet et des chemises.

Q. qui sont sur les kiosques.

R. on attache une ceinture de sécurité.

S. pour notre chat.

T. si tu n'entends pas la première.

LES ADJECTIFS FRANÇAIS - French Adjectives

AGREEMENT OF TYPES OF ADJECTIVES

Singular		Plural		Meaning
Masculine	Feminine	Masculine	Feminine	
sage	sage	sages	sages	wise, well-behaved
lourd	lourde	lourdes	lourdes	heavy
enchanté	enchantée	enchantés	enchantées	enchanted, delighted
fier	fière	fiers	fières	proud
bon	bonne	bons	bonnes	good
neuf	neuve	neufs	neuves	new
égal	égale	égaux	égales	equal
précieux	précieuse	précieux	précieuses	precious

LES ADJECTIFS FRANÇAIS
'In-Formation' (1)

Tucked away in your 'gray matter' is a list of French colors and their forms. The first spin on the color-memory wheel should land on those ending with an e, such as *beige, jaune, turquoise, rose, rouge and orange.* Their masculine and feminine singular forms are the same. Adding an s makes them plural. The following adjectives blend in perfectly with that scheme.

1. difficile- difficult: It is smooth sailing after the cult is transferred to an *île*.
Ex. **un métier** difficile- **a** difficult **trade, job**
2. drôle- amusing, funny: *Drôle* plays a comic role.
Ex. **une pièce** drôle- **a** funny **play**
3. facile- easy: The cognate facilitate is most helpful.
4. faible- weak: There is a strong resemblance to feeble.
5. fantastique- fantastic: Many English words that end with -ic appear like *magique* with *-ique* in French.
6. gauche- left, awkward: A person whose actions are *gauche* is often left out.
7. inutile- useless: In French as in English, -in and -im mean not. With the prefix removed, the adjective is *utile*- useful.
Ex. **un renseignement** utile- **a** useful **piece of information**
8. large- broad, wide: The translations do not come across the same way.
Ex. **un fauteuil** large- **a** wide **armchair**
9. libre- free: Feel free to associate this word with liberty!
10. maigre- lean, thin: Related to meager, *maigre* has slimmed down from *maigrir. Maigre* and *mince* are synonyms. (There's 'a pinch less than an inch' inside *mince*.)
11. malade- ill, sick: The prefix *mal* means bad, but it would not hurt to remember *malade* via malignant and malady.
12. sage- wise, sensible, well-behaved: A glimpse inside the adjective confirms the adage, "With

age comes wisdom."

<u>A note</u>: A mainstay of a French parent's repertoire is *Sois sage!*- Be well behaved!

13. **sympathique**- nice, congenial, likeable: *Sympathique* is *un faux ami*- a false friend. Its short form, *sympa*, is used in colloquial French, and that's nice.

Ex. **une foule** sympathique- **a** nice **crowd**

14. **timide**- timid: The cognate is one letter 'shy' of the French word.

15. **vide**- empty (This is a vacancy listing.)

Ex. **un gazomètre** vide- **an** empty **gas tank** (The expression is "running on empty," but in this case, the driver will be walking.)

LES ADJECTIFS FRANÇAIS
'In-Formation' (2)

Like *bleu, brun, noir* and *vert*, these adjectives attach an <u>e</u> to the masculine singular to become feminine singular. An <u>s</u> added to both genders makes them plural. These are 'follow-the-noun' modifiers.

1. **charmant**- charming, pleasing: It is *intéressant* that many French adjectives that end in -<u>ant</u>, -<u>ante</u>, -<u>ants</u> and -<u>antes</u> have cognates with an -<u>ing</u> suffix.

Exs. un prince charmant, une princesse charmante, des princes charmants, des princesses charmantes

Additional -<u>ant</u> adjectives include *amusant*- entertaining, amusing, *brûlant*- burning, *fascinant*- fascinating, *obéissant*- obedient **and** *pleurant*- crying

2. **clair**- bright, clear, light: <u>Clear</u> is lightly reflected in the French word.

3. **content**- content, satisfied, pleased: The translations provide 'a table of contents.'

Exs. **une vache** contente- **a** contented **cow**, **des touristes** contents- some satisfied tourists

4. **diligent**- diligent: This is a bilingual description of someone who does not dilly-dally.

Exs. **un savant** diligent- **a** diligent **scientist**, **des dilettantes** diligentes- **some** diligent **dabbler**s (in a cultural subject)

5. **droit**- right, straight: 'Rite' is found inside *droite* and *à droite*- to the right. But beware! *Tout droit* means straight ahead.

Exs. **la main** droite- **the** right **hand**, **la route** tout droit- **the road** straight ahead

6. **étroit**- narrow

Exs. **un esprit** étroit- **a** narrow **mind**, des rues étroites- some narrow streets

<u>An interesting note</u>: French explorers named the Michigan city Detroit because of its location on the narrow part of The Great Lakes.

7. **fort**- strong, sturdy: This adjective is lodged in <u>fortify</u> and <u>fortitude</u>.

Exs. **un corps** fort- **a** strong **body**, des odeurs fortes- some strong odors

8. **lourd**- heavy, awkward

Exs. **des paquets** lourds- **some** heavy **packages**, des valises lourdes- some heavy suitcases

<u>An interesting note</u>: Patients travel to Lourdes, France, hoping to be cured by the holy waters from its famous sanctuary. (An appropriate opening for their prayers would be, "Oh, Lourdes.")

9. **parfait**- perfect, splendid: As an edible noun, *le parfait* is a treat for the palate; as a complimentary adjective, it is a treat for the ears.

Exs. un choix parfait- a perfect choice, **une forme** parfaite- **a** perfect **forme/figure** (The latter is not the result of eating too many *parfaits*.)

10. poli- polite, polished: Although two letters have been removed from the English translation, the trait does not 'rub off' easily. *Impoli*- impolite is its antonym.
Exs. **un invité** poli- **a** polite **guest, des meubles** polis- **some** polished **furniture**

11. prêt- prepared, ready: When a magician announces "presto," he is not pulling that s from nowhere. The circumflex indicates that the next letter is an English s in hiding.
Exs. **un plan** prêt- **a** ready **plan**, des chambres prêtes- some prepared rooms

----

LES ADJECTIFS FRANÇAIS
'In-Formation' (3)

Adjectives that end with an é in the masculine singular add an e to become feminine singular. Their plural forms have an s. All four adjectives are pronounced the same. The second e gets 'the silent treatment.' Their cognates typically end with -ed and are past participles.
Exs. un homme bien habillé- a well-dressed man, une femme bien habillée- a well-dressed woman
Notice the accessory on the feminine form!

1. caché- concealed, hidden: As a noun without an accent, the stash is hidden cash.
2. étonné- amazed, astonished: The French word and <u>astonished</u> both carry a <u>ton</u>, and anyone *étonné* is close to being <u>stunned</u>.
Exs. une foule étonnée- an astonished crowd, des gens étonnés- some amazed/astonished people
3. fatigué- fatigued, tired: The exhausted d 'dropped off.'
3a. *Avoir sommeil* and *être fatigué* are close in meaning, but the latter is more often a result of emotional issues or physical exertion. (For the former, it's neither necessary 'to get worked up' nor to work out.)
4. occupé- busy, in use, occupied: Those who travel internationally see this word 'in use.'
Exs. **un castor** occupé- a busy **beaver, une abeille** occupée- a busy **bee** (Both of them are involved in 'the construction business.')
5. passé- bygone, outmoded, past: The Art-Deco revival and the popularity of vintage clothing prove that we have not seen the last of the past.
Ex. **L'horlogerie** est un métier passé. > **Clock making** is an outmoded trade. (The clockmaker now 'has time on his hands.')

The Other Way Around- Match the letters of the adjectives to the numbers of their antonyms.

_____ 1. fantastique	A. large	
_____ 2. utile	B. malcontent	
_____ 3. clair	C. libre	
_____ 4. difficile	D. faible	
_____ 5. occupé	E. inutile	
_____ 6. passé	F. stupide	
_____ 7. étroit	G. parfait	
_____ 8. fatigué	H. impoli	

____ 9. fort	I. horrible
____ 10. content	J. droit
____ 11. poli	K. facile
____ 12. terrible	L. moderne
____ 13. gauche	M. obscur
____ 14. sage	N. énergique

LES ADJECTIFS FRANÇAIS
'In-Formation' (4)

Adjectives ending in -er in the masculine singular attach an e at the end of the word and put an accent *grave* over the preceding e to form the feminine singular. -Er modifiers generally follow nouns, but true to its name, *premier* goes first.

1. entier- entire, complete, whole: The cognates are written almost identically. *Complet*, a rogue adjective with variations in spelling just like *entier*, is its synonym.
Exs. **la vérité** entière/complète- **the** entire/whole **truth**, **les faits** complets- **the** complete **facts**
2. étranger- foreign: This modifier is pleased to introduce the noun *l'étranger*- the stranger, the foreigner. Without the final r, the adjective is just plain strange.
Exs. un film étranger- a foreign film, des affaires étrangères- some foreign affaires
3. fier- proud, haughty: Associate this adjective with fiercely proud to recall its meaning.
Exs. une famille fière- a proud family, **des paons** fiers- **some** proud **peacocks** (They generally 'open up' with little encouragement.)
4. familier- familiar: Having exchanged 'vow-els,' these two modifiers belong together.
Exs. une expression familière- a colloquialism, **des visages** familiers- **some** familiar **faces**
5. léger- light, flimsy, slight: An accent *aigu* is planted over the first e, and an accent *grave* goes over the second one in the feminine forms. Like its antonym *lourd*, *léger* applies only to things.
Exs. un bateau léger- a light boat, une bière légère- a light beer (Both include 'a slight tip.')

'A Permit to Add On'- Pay special attention to noun-adjective agreement when translating the following phrases.
1. a free bee _____
2. the right hand _____
3. the amusing faces _____
4. some busy mothers _____
5. the proud parents _____
6. the fantastic magic _____
7. some diligent beavers _____
8. an enchanted forest _____
9. the content peacocks _____
10. a hidden truth _____
11. the first films _____
12. some tired people _____

13. the familiar facts _____

14. a reserved table _____

15. the outmoded clothing _____

16. a light fabric _____

17. the entire world _____

18. some perfect vacations _____

19. the foreign nations _____

20. some heavy metals _____

LES ADJECTIFS FRANÇAIS
'In-Formation' (5)

Many French adjectives ending in <u>s</u>, <u>l</u>, <u>n</u> and <u>t</u> feature a unique <u>slant</u> for spelling their feminine forms: They double those four final consonants before adding an <u>e</u>. *Violet,* **which 'blossoms' in-to** *violette,* **is 'of the same bent.' Likewise, the** *quel* **and** *tel* **families 'double up' to accommodate the feminine adjectives among them.**

1. actuel- present: Notice that this *faux ami* **does not mean actual!** (Even the word has a different slant.)
Ex. à l'heure actuelle- at the present time
The translation for <u>actual</u> is *réel.* **Its synonym is** *vrai.*
2. bas- low, deep: This adjective has its foundation in <u>the basement</u>.
Exs. **un salaire** bas- a low **salary**, une voix basse- a low or deep voice
3. cruel- cruel: There is no need to explain its 'mean-ing.'
4. canadien- Canadian, européen- European, italien- Italian and parisien do a final consonant 'double take' in the presence of feminine nouns.
Exs. **la mode de vie** européenne - **the** European **lifestyle**, les montagnes canadiennes - the Canadian mountains
5. épais- thick (You are on your own to find a trick for thick.)
Exs. **un brouillard** épais- **a** thick **fog**, une tranche épaisse de gâteau- a thick slice of cake (It is a lot easier to see your way through the second one.)
<u>A reminder</u>: **Like nouns that end with -<u>s</u>, -<u>x</u> and -<u>z</u>, adjectives with those final consonants are identical in their masculine singular and plural forms.**
Exs. le prix bas- the low price, les prix bas- the low prices
6. mignon- cute, dainty, delicate, nice, sweet: Although the adjective ends with *non*, **it has only positive things to say about the noun.**
Exs. un filet mignon- a sweet loin of beef, des princesses mignonnes- some sweet princesses (They are equally nice to serve.)
7. net- clean, pure: (But net pay starts out as 'gross.')
Exs. **avoir des idées nettes- to be clear-headed,** un cheval net- a clean horse (The masculine form of the adjective and the horse's response sound very similar.)
8. sot- silly, foolish, stupid: The same word means <u>a drunkard</u> in English. (His actions might be worse than *sot sot*.)

Exs. une décision sotte- a foolish decision, **des regards** sots- **some** stupid **expressions/looks**

<u>**And in Addition**</u>- **Circle the letters of the correct responses.**
1. Les pilotes remarquent qu'il y a beaucoup de brouillard. Le ciel n'est pas _____.
a. facile   b. charmant   c. clair   d. gauche
2. Comme on cherche tout sur le net, les encyclopédies sont presque _____.
a. drôles   b. larges   c. vides   d. inutiles
3. Kurt Ossy n'interrompt pas **lorsque (while)** ses parents parlent. Quel garçon _____!
a. poli   b. épais   c. difficile   d. timide
4. Le peuple américain est _____. Les gens choisissent leurs modes de vie.
a. maigre   b. libre   c. fantastique   d. prêt
5. La foule amusée pense que cette pièce-là est _____.
a. basse   b. droite   c. drôle   d. cruelle
6. Les étudiants intelligents n'ont pas d'esprits _____.
a. étroits   b. mignons   c. utiles   d. parfaits
7. Nous écoutons **les conseils-m. (the advice)** de Salomon parce qu'il est très _____.
a. mince   b. fort   c. léger   d. sage
8. Ta grand-mère passe les soirs seul dans son fauteuil confortable. Est-elle _____?
a. lourde   b. contente   c. sympathique   d. actuelle
9. La pièce est nette et les meubles sont _____.
a. cachés   b. fiers   c. polis   d. amusants
10. Après la maladie de Mme Patraque, son corps est _____.
a. diligente   b. faible   c. étrange   d. sotte

<u>**'Let's Hear the Details!'**</u>- **Put the correct forms of the adjectives in parentheses in the blanks.**
1. le paquet _____ (vide)   11. une surface _____ (net)
2. les regards _____ (cruel)   12. une idée _____ (sage)
3. la taille _____ (mince)   13. des potages _____ (épais)
4. les lignes _____ (étroit)   14. un métier _____ (facile)
5. le touriste _____ (gauche)   15. une place _____ (occupé)
6. l'invitée _____ (charmant)   16. une vache _____ (maigre)
7. la voisine _____ (canadien)   17. des meubles _____ (lourd)
8. les savants _____ (diligent)   18. des personnes _____ (mignon)
9. les langues _____ (européen)   19. des desserts (m.) _____ (prêt)
10. les renseignements _____ (utile)   20. des vins _____ (léger)

108

LES ADJECTIFS FRANÇAIS
'In-Formation' (6)

Adjectives that end with <u>f</u> in the masculine singular exchange that consonant for <u>ve</u> to form the feminine singular. An <u>s</u> added to modifiers of either gender makes them plural. A similar letter switch occurs in English where singular nouns ending in <u>fe</u> have <u>ves</u> for plural endings. (Wives can verify their equality as halves of relationships.)
'F(i)VE' adjectives are listed below.

1. actif- active:The feminine singular activates the same adjective in both languages.
Exs. une mode de vie active- an active lifestyle, **des volcanoes** actifs- **some** active **volcanoes** (They both get people out of the house.)
2. attentif- attentive: This <u>f</u> to <u>ve</u> modifier is also identical to English in the feminine singular.
Exs. **un commissaire** attentif- **an** attentive **auditor**, des spectatrices attentives- some attentive spectators (They attach different meanings to 'show time.')
3. naïf- naïve: The dieresis (*le tréma*) indicates that the word is separated into syllables between the two vowels.
4. neuf- new, unused: As an adjective, *neuf* is <u>new</u> to you. It is heard in the expression *Quoi de neuf?*- What's new?
Ex. neuf chambres à coucher neuves- nine new/unused bedrooms (*Neuf* before the noun and *neuves* after it leave a space to accommodate guests.)
5. vif- lively, sharp, deep: Its synonym with the same root is *vivant*.
Ex. Anne Imée montre **un penchant** pour les couleurs vives. > Anne Imée shows a **strong liking** for lively colors.

LES ADJECTIFS FRANÇAIS
'In-Formation' (7)

Adjectives and nouns that end with <u>al</u> in the masculine singular change to <u>aux</u> in the masculine plural. *Un cheval loyal*- a loyal horse is one of *des chevaux loyaux*- some loyal horses. The feminine breeds add <u>e/es</u> to the masculine singular.
Say 'Al-Aux' to the adjectives below!

1. égal- equal: The two words are close in spelling, all things being equal.
Exs. **un revenu** égal- an equal **income**, des salaires égaux- some equal salaries/wages (The two sets of words are almost equal sequels.)
2. général- general: The French *général* is decorated with accent *aigus* over both *é*s.
Exs. une éducation générale- a general education, une connaissance générale- a general knowledge
3. mondial- world, world-wide: This derivative was given to the French by *le monde*.
Exs. un sport mondial- a world-wide sport, **les guerres** mondiales- **the** world **wars**
4. national- national, international- international: Their masculine singular forms are at home in both languages.
5. social- social: These adjectives travel in the same social circle.

Ex. **L'arriviste** n'a pas encore **d'aide sociale. The social climber** doesn't have **social security** yet. (First, he/she has 'to reach' the right age.)

6. spécial- special: The addition of the accent *aigu* makes it *spécial*.

Exs. un arrangement spécial- a special arrangement, **des comptes** spéciaux- **some** special **accounts**

<u>An interesting note</u>: *Il est très spécial* **is a diplomatic way of saying "He is very peculiar."**

7. total- total: *Total, complet* **and** *entier* **are synonyms which add up to the same thing.** *Totaux* **registers an identical pronunciation with the dog, Toto, in the** <u>Wizard of Oz</u>.

Exs. **l'effet** total- **the** total **effect**, **une perte** totale- a total loss

---

LES ADJECTIFS FRANÇAIS
'In-Formation' (8)

A *généreux* number of French adjectives come with -ous in English. These modifiers cross out the <u>x</u> from the masculine forms and readdress themselves with <u>-se/ses</u> endings when feminine.

1. curieux- curious: Three possible endings show how this one turns out.

Exs. une foule curieuse- a curious crowd, des regards curieux- some curious looks

2. dangereux- dangerous: A warning is posted inside both adjectives.

Exs. un endroit dangereux- a dangerous place, une affaire dangereuse- a dangerous affair (The first is labeled risky; the second risqué.)

3. délicieux- delicious: There is 'a deli' on the left corner of each of them.

Exs. **un déjeuner** délicieux- **a** delicious **lunch**, des viandes délicieuses- some delicious meats

4. fameux- famous, celebrated: Though it usually has a positive connotation, *fameux* **can have a pejorative sense. Become acquainted with** *célèbre,* **and you will get along famously!**

Ex. Quand l'événement fameux va-t-il **avoir lieu**? > When is the famous event going **to take place?**

5. furieux- furious, raging: (Ironically, furious often follows the phrase 'engaged in.')

Exs. une discussion furieuse- a furious discussion, **des batailles** furieuses- **some** raging **battles**

6. joyeux- joyous, cheerful: This adjective spreads itself around and is found before or after a noun.

Exs. Joyeux Noël!- Merry Christmas!, Joyeuse**s Pâques!**- Happy **Easter!**, être d'humeur joyeux- **to be in a joyful mood**

7. sérieux- serious: (The look doesn't vary much between the two languages.) **Its synonym,** *grave,* **does not have an accent mark.**

Ex. **des doutes** sérieux- **some** serious **doubts** (The French *doute* gives us an <u>out</u>.)

<u>-Eux Adjectives That Do Not Include -Ous</u>

1. affreux- awful, dreadful: The French and English words aren't related nor would they want to be.

Exs. le temps affreux- the awful/dreadful weather, les vêtements affreux- the awful/dreadful clothing (People should not go out in either.)

2. heureux- happy: Happy Hour is the same in both languages, but if the French were to trans-late that phrase, it would be *heure heureuse. Heureux* **and** *content* **are almost synonymous. On the downside,** *malheueux* **is** <u>unfortunate</u> **and** <u>unhappy</u>.

Exs. **un cocktail** heureux- **a** happy **cocktail party**, **une** chanson **heureuse**- **a** happy **song** (They can both end on 'a high note.')

3. ennuyeux- boring: *Amusant* and *intéressant* keep their distance from this adjective.

4. paresseux- lazy, idle: The French adjective cannot be bothered to offer any helpful clues.

Exs. une ouvrière paresseuse- a lazy worker, des étudiants paresseux- some lazy students

----

'Gender Benders'- **Write the following adjectives in the gender and plurality indicated.**

1. magique (f.p.) _____
2. malade (m.p.) _____
3. charmant (f.s.) _____
4. clair (f.s.) _____
5. parfait (f.p.) _____
6. âgé (m.p.) _____
7. étonné (m.p.) _____
8. frustré (f.s.) _____
9. entier (f.p.) _____
10. factuel (m.p.) _____

11. haïtien (f.s.) _____
12. muet (mute) (f.p.) _____
13. actif (m.p.) _____
14. descriptif (f.p.) _____
15. pensif (f.s.) _____
16. principal (f.s.) _____
17. social (m.p.) _____
18. précieux (f.s.) _____
19. nombreux (m.p.) _____
20. délicieux (f.p.) _____

'Being Choosy'- **Select the appropriate adjectives from the following list and put them into the correct forms in the spaces provided. Each modifier should be used once.**

actif, actuel, affreux, attentif, caché, dangereux, drôle, ennuyeux, étranger, faible, familier, fort, heureux, imaginatif, lourd, naïf, paresseux, passé, réel, romantique, sérieux, social, vide

1. Les plongeurs trouve des trésors _____ dans les bateaux d'une époque _____.
2. Des élèves _____ font souvent des erreurs. Ils ne sont pas _____.
3. Atlas, un homme très _____, va porter des paquets _____.
4. Pour un visiteur _____, les quartiers parisiens ne sont pas _____.
5. Ma grand-mère est vive. Sa vie _____ n'est pas _____.
6. **Les** jeunes **amoureux (the lovers)** _____ passent une semaine parfaite sur une île _____.
7. Les histoires qu'Hugh Meur raconte sont _____ quand il a un regard _____ sur son visage.
8. Polyanna est _____. Elle pense que les prisons (f.) ne sont pas _____ et qu'on ne fait pas de choses _____ là.
9. Mme Aulit ne va pas bien. Elle est trop _____ pour avoir une vie _____ à l'heure _____.
10. Paul et Paula, deux petits très _____, pensent qu'une boîte _____ est une maison _____.

"BANGS"- ADJECTIVES THAT PRECEDE NOUNS

The title was aimed to grab your attention. "Bangs" is an acronym that stands for <u>beauty</u>, <u>age</u>, <u>numbers</u>, <u>goodness</u>, and <u>size</u>. The unique set of 20 modifiers usually precedes nouns. However, some can be placed on either side of a noun, and a subcategory of those changes both meanings and locations. "Bangs" adjectives have a full rang of forms. (Are you ready 'to fire away'?)

Beauty	Age	Numbers	Goodness	Size
*beau	jeune		bon	court
joli	*nouveau		faux	grand
laid	*vieux		gentil	gros
			mauvais	haut
			méchant	long
			merveilleux	petit
			vilain	
			vrai	

"Bangs"- Target Practice
Adjectives That Describe Beauty or Lack of It
1. *beau- handsome, pretty, good looking: Its 'beau-tiful' face is seen in *Il fait beau*. (Nouns follow it because of its attractive appearance.)
Ex. **un** beau **pays-** a beautiful/pretty **country**
2. joli- pretty: This adjective should not be confused with <u>jolly</u>- *gai*. (With *Joli* for a last name, it is understandable why Angelina was in no hurry to change it to Pitt.)
Ex. **un** joli **tableau-** a pretty **picture**
3. laid- ugly: The nice features have been 'laid to rest.'
Ex. un laid monstre- an ugly monster

Adjectives That Describe Age
1. jeune- young: This is the only "bangs" adjective ending with an <u>e</u> in the masculine singular. Consequently, its singular forms are the same, and its plural forms are identical. (They are indeed fortunate to stay young.)
2. *nouveau- another, new: This modifier translates <u>another</u> before the noun and <u>new</u> after it.
Ex. un nouveau centre commercial nouveau- another new shopping center (Store owners know how important it is 'to get the word out.')
3. *vieux- former, old: The flip-side of *jeune* used to specify <u>former</u> before a noun and <u>old</u> after it. That distinction is a bit *vieux* nowadays, and the adjective with either sense usually precedes nouns.
Ex. Deux vieux présidents des États-Unis ont les noms des voitures. > Two former presidents of the United States have the names of cars.

Numbers Precede the Nouns That They Modify
Ex. les dix premières années de ma vie- the first ten year of my life

----

Adjectives That Describe Goodness or a Lack of It

1. bon- good: *C'est très bon* to see this adjective again after *bonjour, bonsoir* and *bonne nuit.*

Ex. Les bonnes bonnes mangent trop de bonbons. > The good maids eat too much candy.

2. faux- false, fake, forged: This French word reveals itself in *vrai ou faux* exercises and in *faux ami(s)*. The feminine singular of *faux* is *fausse*, qualifying it as a "false slant" adjective.

Exs. **une** fausse **pièce**- a forged **coin**, de fausses dents- some false teeth

<u>An important aside</u>: To piece together all the meanings of *la pièce*, picture this: At the entrance to *une pièce*- a room, you give the cashier *plusieurs pièces*- several coins that are *dans la poche de votre deux pièces*- in the pocket of your two-piece outfit, and you pay for *quelques pièces de bonbons*- a few pieces of candy. Then you watch *une pièce*- a play or just *une pièce d'une pièce*- a part of a play in which the actor has *une pièce dans sa main*- a gun in his hand.

3. gentil- nice: Although this adjective looks similar to gentle, that word is translated by *doux*. But yet, a gentleman is still *un gentil homme.* (That's nice to know.)

4. mauvais- bad: This modifier was forecasted in *Il fait mauvais (temps.)*

5. méchant- naughty or wicked/evil: Naughty before a noun, *méchant* changes into wicked/evil after it. Its synonyms are *mauvais* and *vilain*.

Exs. le méchant garçon- the naughty boy, **le diable** méchant- the wicked **devil** (If the two meet each other, "all hell will break loose.")

6. merveilleux- marvelous, wonderful: Altering a few letters makes the words look more alike, but they are wonderful as they are.

Exs. **de** merveilleux **cours**- some marvelous/wonderful **courses**, **de** merveilleuses **nouvelles**- some marvelous/wonderful **news**

7. vilain- ugly, wicked: Very close to <u>villain</u>, *vilain* gets away with one <u>l</u> and takes the synonyms *laid* and *méchant* with it.

8. vrai- real, true, genuine: Verify and veritable could possibly be considered cognates of *vrai.* (But that might be stretching the truth.)

Exs. **un** vrai **génie**- **a** true **genius, a** real **genie**, une vraie blonde- a real blond (None of them actually comes out of a bottle.)

Adjectives That Designate Size

1. court- short: This adjective refers only to things.

Ex. un court **roman**- a short **novel**

2. grand- great, big/tall: Like *méchant*, *grand* is two-sided. Before a noun, it signifies <u>great</u>, but after it, *grand* stands for <u>big</u> or <u>tall</u>. Charles de Gaulle, a former French president, was six feet, four inches. One might refer to him as *un grand homme grand.*

3. gros- overweight: This is a 'reduced' form of *grossir*- to gain weight. *Les gros mots*- **the curse words was previously mentioned.** (Just the phrase!)

Ex. Victoria est une grosse femme qui porte de très jolis sous-vêtements. > Victoria is a stout woman who wears very pretty underwear. (Now everyone knows "Victoria's Secret.")

4. haut- high, tall, lofty: While *grand* describes a person's size, *haut* refers to attitude, to public standing and to the height of a non-living thing. Although <u>haughty</u> has a negative connotation, *la haute couture*- **high fashion is favored worldwide.**

Ex. Son bébé dans **son lit d'enfant crie** à haute voix. > Her baby in **his crib is screaming** in a high voice. (The mother might be thinking, "What can I do for crying out loud?")

5. long- long, tedious, drawn out: Like its antonym *court*, *long* applies only to things. However, *court* precedes nouns exclusively, and *long* goes on either side elusively. Ending with a rare **-ue** in the feminine singular, *long* is 'a long shot.' (The names of Donald Duck's three nephews might come to the 'resc-__ue__.')
Exs. de longue date- long ago, la version longue- the uncut version
Longtemps, an adverb, is a combination of words to be used for <u>a long time.</u>
6. petit- small, little: Describing people and things, *petit* has a large order to fill. *Le Petit Prince* **is the king of French short stories.**

"Bangs"- Loads of Ammunition
1. The majority of adjectives on the list end with consonants. Adding an _e_ to *court, grand, haut, méchant, petit* **and** *vilain* **makes them feminine singular.** *Bon, gros* **and** *gentil* **are "slant" words. They double the final consonant of the masculine singular and attach an _e_ to become feminine singular. The plural forms of both types end with an _s_.** *Gros, mauvais, faux* **and** *vieux* **are "sxz" adjectives that retain that spelling in the masculine plural.**
Exs. de faux billets- some counterfeit bills, de mauvais gens- some bad people (They can be difficult to change.')
2. *Des* **usually becomes** *de* **or** *d'* **in front of plural "bangs" adjectives. The _s_ on** *des* **is omitted if the adjective and the noun do not make a two word unit. That explains the previous examples; In** *de jolis sous-vêtements,* **the _s_ was 'washed,' and in** *de faux billets,* **the _s_ was not 'accepted.'**
<u>Important exceptions</u>: *Des grands magasins, des jeunes filles* and *des petits pois* have plural partitives because all department stores are large, all girls are young, and all peas are small.
3. For 'two-lane' modifiers that 'drive' one meaning before a noun and a different one after it, go by these directions:
3a. If the trait is not visible (abstract), put the adjective in front of the noun.
Exs. une grande idée- a great idea, un nouveau plan- another plan
3b. If the characteristic is visible (literal), put the adjective after the noun.
Exs. **une fenêtre** grande- **a** big/large **window, des lunettes** nouvelles- **some** new **glasses** (You can actually 'see the difference.')
<u>An important note</u>: The examples and exercises in this book often take a puristic approach for forms of *grand, nouveau and vieux* so that the adjectives highlight their original meanings and positions in relation to the nouns.
4. When an adjective describes people or things of both genders, the masculine form is used.
Ex. Ma cousine, Heloïse, et son frère, Hellion, sont méchants. > My cousin, Heloïse, and her brother, Hellion, are naughty.
5. When plural adjectives describe a noun, each modifier is placed in its regular position. Two adjectives preceding or following a noun are joined by *et.*
Ex. une jolie femme sympathique- a pretty and nice lady (She's much more popular than one who is 'pretty nice.')
Ex. de bonnes et de mauvaises nouvelles- some good and some bad news ("Bangs" adjectives 'brace themselves' before the news.)
Ex. des étudiants attentifs et intelligents- some attentive and intelligent students (They also 'follow' *le professeur*.)

<u>*An Opportunity to Interview the Stars</u>
Beau, nouveau and *vieux* include a fifth form. It is placed in front of a masculine singular noun beginning with a vowel or a mute <u>h</u>. The concept is identical to the use of *cet.*
1a. The essence of beauty is *beau, bel, belle, beaux and belles.* (It is seen in Bel-Air, California.)
Exs. un beau garçon- a handsome boy, un bel homme- a handsome man, une belle famille- a beautiful family, de beaux enfants- some beautiful/handsome children, de belles femmes- some beautiful women
1b. Forms of *nouveau* rhyme with those of *beau.* The fifth member, *nouvel*, provides a novelty.
Exs. un nouvel étudiant- another student, un étudiant nouveau- a new student (Notice the difference in how new is used!)
1c. Being the oldest member of the trio, *vieux* has even more to say. Its masculine singular and plural forms are identical. The feminine members turn <u>ux</u> into <u>ille(s)</u>. 'For old times sake,' the complete line up is *vieux, vieil, vieille, vieux* and *vieilles.*
Vieil, vieille and *vieilles* are pronounced similar to <u>V.A.</u>, which stands for Veterans Administration. (With that hint, what is old should not be forgotten.)
Exs. **une** vieille **amitié**- a former/longstanding **friendship**, un ami vieux- an aged friend
2. Each starred "bangs" adjective has the same pronunciation for its feminine and fifth forms. In addition, their masculine singular and plurals are said identically. Therefore, all "five form" adjectives have only two oral presentations. (There is something to be said for that.)
Exs. un bel arbre- a beautiful tree, une belle voix- a beautiful voice, de belles robes- some beautiful dresses
Exs. un nouveau plan- another plan, des maisons nouvelles- some new houses

----

<u>NON-"BANGS" ADJECTIVES THAT PRECEDE NOUNS</u>

Though not of the typical "bangs" caliber, this unique group of adjectives also precedes nouns. Frequently invited to join in conversations, they offer plenty of general information.

<u>'Another Shot'</u>
1. autre- other: Aside from the <u>s</u> before plural nouns, *Il n'y a pas d'autre changement.* > There is no other change.
Exs. un autre auteur- an other author, d'autres faits- some other facts
2. chaque- each, every: It has two translations but one invariable singular form.
Ex. Jacques, **un je-sais-tout**, n'assiste pas à chaque cours. > Jacques, **a know-it-all**, does not attend each/every class. (Maybe that is why he claims, "The professors don't know Jack.")
3. quelque- some: The singular form *quelque* has <u>some</u> followers which include *quelque chose*-something and *quelque part*- somewhere. The plural, *quelques*- a few, can also be translated as <u>some</u> in limited quantities.
Ex. Rhea Lee Phar et moi remarquons quelque chose inconnue dans le brouillard. > Rhea Lee Phar and I notice something unfamiliar in the fog. (She asks me, "Is there a stranger in our 'mist?'")
Ex. Monsieur Ditrien donne un million de dollars à quelques **organisations caritatives** secrètes. > Mr. Ditrien gives a million dollars to a few secret **charities**. (He doesn't give away everything.)
4. plusieurs- several: The beginning of the adjective leaves a reminder that it is always plural.

Ex. Pourquoi y a-t-il plusieurs publicités tous les jours à la télévision pour la **même** chose? > Why are there several advertisements/commercials every day on television for the **same** thing? (Maybe people 'are just not getting it.')

Opposites Attract- **Match the letters to the numbers of the words that are antonyms.**

_____ 1. épais	A. fort
_____ 2. large	B. familier
_____ 3. mauvais	C. impoli
_____ 4. diligent	D. méchant
_____ 5. jeune	E. nouveau
_____ 6. vrai	F. mince
_____ 7. difficile	G. malheureux
_____ 8. étrange	H. sot
_____ 9. lourd	I. droit
_____ 10. petit	J. inutile
_____ 11. amusant	K. vieux
_____ 12. différent	L. bas
_____ 13. gentil	M. grand
_____ 14. utile	N. paresseux
_____ 15. court	O. laid
_____ 16. faible	P. facile
_____ 17. haut	Q. même
_____ 18. sage	R. étroit
_____ 19. joyeux	S. faux
_____ 20. poli	T. affreux
_____ 21. gauche	U. ennuyeux
_____ 22. beau	V. bon
_____ 23. passé	W. léger
_____ 24. merveilleux	X. long

Some 'Straight Talk' Is Needed- **Unscramble the phrases to form complete sentences.**

1. démodés/ Qu'est-ce qu'/ avec ces vêtements/ on va faire? _____
_____?

2. mauvaises notes/ Les étudiants paresseux/ de leurs/ ne sont pas fiers. _____
_____.

3. est court/ mais il a/ Son nom réel/ nom d'écran/ un long. _____
_____.

4. et larges-là/ à cette petite fille-ci/ Ces lunettes/ ne vont pas bien/ grandes. _____
_____.

5. les romans/ le même/ sont/ Est-ce que/ auteur célèbre/ par/ historiques? _____
_____?

6. de l'homme/ Plusieurs gens/ les mots sages/ très intelligent/ écoutent. _____
_____.

7. et sa voix/ familiers/ après longtemps/ Son beau visage/ basse/ sont toujours. _____

8. de la jolie vedette/ les bijoux énormes/ remarquent/ parfait/ Les jeunes hommes/ et le corps.

_____

9. Quelques invités/ de la cuisine/ une autre pièce/ parce que les odeurs/ vont à/ sont très fortes.

_____

10. voyagent/ les pensées sages/ studieux/ aux hautes montagnes/ Les dilettantes/ de théologie/ des maîtres/ pour entendre. _____

_____

11. chaque repas délicieux/ mais je préfère/ spéciaux/ prépare/ J'aime bien/ que ma gentille tante/ ses déjeuners. _____

_____

12. les belles couleurs/ la petite/ elle compte/ claires/ La première fois que/ regarde un arc-en-ciel.

_____
_____

ADJECTIVES THAT PRECEDE and FOLLOW NOUNS
Group #1

Some French adjectives project the same sense whether they are placed before or after nouns. The optional word order proves that in a few instances, "You can have it both ways."

<u>Adjectives on the Move</u>
1. gras- fat, obese: This adjective does not lose anything when it moves to either side of a noun. Masculine singular and plural *gras* 'carry the same weight.' The <u>s</u> is doubled before an <u>e</u> is added for the feminine forms.
Ex. After celebrating *le Mardi Gras* all night, one might *faire la grasse matinée*- sleep all morning/ get up very late.
<u>An interesting aside</u>: **Grasse, France is known for its perfume industry.**
2. plein- full: Related to <u>plenty</u>, *plein* 'takes full advantage' of its status to 'pop up' wherever it wants.
Exs. **en plein air- in the open air, la marée pleine- the full tide**
<u>An important note</u>: *Plein* **describes a pregnant animal. So, a woman who has had enough to eat should not say, "*Je suis pleine,*" unless she is expecting a pregnant pause in the conversation. A pregnant woman is** *enceinte.*
3. prochain- next: Links on a <u>chain</u> are next to each other.
Exs. la prochaine fois- the next time, le mois prochain- the next month
4. profond- deep, profound: This French adjective can surface on either side of a noun, but it's more commonly brought up after it.
Exs. **une profonde révérence- a** deep **bow/curtsy, un puits** profond- a deep **well** (Both are effective for granting someone's wishes.)
<u>A reminder</u>: *Joyeux* and *long*, **previously mentioned, belong in this two-sided category.**

117

ADJECTIVES THAT PRECEDE and FOLLOW NOUNS
Group #2

Many frequently used adjectives change their identities as they move around the nouns. *Grand, méchant, nouveau* and *vieux* on the "bangs" list are mobile modifiers which belong to this club where nouns can only 'get a word in edgewise.'

Adjectives That Put in Their 'Two Sense' Worth

1. ancien- former vs. old: Like its synonym *vieux*, this cognate for <u>ancient</u> means <u>former</u> before the noun but <u>old</u> after it.
Ex. Dina Saur et vous êtes d'anciennes amis anciennes. > Dina Saur and you are former, old friends. (They may have gone to Jurassic Park High together.)

2. brave- fine/worthy vs. brave: Bravo to the first meaning for depicting one's character and to the second for connoting courageous action.
Ex. Le brave Shining Exemple aide les familles sur **leur réserve** indienne. > Brave Shining Example helps the families on **their** Indian **reservation**.
Ex. **Le soldat** brave défend son pays en Irak. > **The** brave **soldier** defends his country in Iraq.

3. cher- dear vs. costly/expensive: Its four forms are pronounced identically. However, *cher* + a noun is <u>priceless</u>, while a noun + *cher* is <u>pricey</u>. *Bon marché*- inexpensive is an invariable antonym of post-noun *cher*.
Ex. Ma chère amie Nicole a des billets chers. > My dear friend Nicole has some expensive tickets.

4. dernier- last vs. most recent: Before a noun, *dernier* refers to the final one in a series; after a noun, it is 'given last rites' as the one that just passed/the most current.
Exs. avoir le dernier mot- to have the last/final word, les courriers électroniques derniers- the most recent e-mails. (The first example requires no response.)

5. différent- diverse/various vs. différent/alternate: The different differences are also expressed in English, where they are always in front of nouns. With the first phrase below, the directions are mapped out, but with the second, one can chart his own course.
Exs. de différentes routes- some (of several) routes, **des chemins** différents- **some** different/alternate paths, ways

6. pauvre- pitiable vs. poor: Although it is <u>pitiable</u> to see *pauvre* before a noun, this adjective is not any 'better off' after one where it is <u>financially challenged</u>.
Ex. Le pauvre **mendiant** pauvre habite à la rue. > **The** wretched, poor **beggar** lives on the street.

7. propre- own vs. clean: The owner stakes his claim before the noun and tidies up after it.
Ex. M. Passepartout, qui voyage souvent, a besoin de sa propre chambre propre. > Mr. Passepartout, who travels often, needs his own clean room.

8. riche- abundant/plentiful vs. rich/wealthy: <u>Lush</u> before the noun, it turns into <u>plush</u> after it. (Rich with meanings, this adjective is able to afford different views.)
Exs. les riches champs- the verdant/abundant fields, les nouveaux-riches- the recently wealthy

9. sale- disgusting vs. dirty: Neither the pre- nor the post-noun meaning offers 'a bargain.'
Exs. **un** sale **tour**- **a** dirty/disgusting **trick**, une fenêtre sale- a dirty window (It is not always easy to see through either.)

10. seul- lone, only, unique vs. alone, single, unaccompanied: Ironically, the lone French word is accompanied by an entourage of English translations.

Exs. mon seul ordinateur- my only computer, la femme seule- the single/unaccompanied woman
11. triste- wretched vs. sorrowful, sad: The twist with *triste* involves a feeling as opposed to a look. Placed before or after the noun, *triste* is not 'in a good place.'
Exs. une triste situation- a wretched situation, un visage triste- a sad face
<u>A note</u>: As their pre- and post-noun meanings do not vary greatly, placing *différent, riche, sale,* and *triste* incorrectly in conversation does not constitute *un grand faux pas grand.*

THE MOST IRREGULAR FRENCH ADJECTIVES

Some stray, French adjectives usually follow nouns and do not belong in groups. Nevertheless, these novel modifiers are popular enough to be included in conversations.

<u>'Tying up the Loose Ends'</u>
1. doux- gentle, mild, soft, sweet: This multimeaning adjective has a feminine form when the <u>x</u> is replaced by <u>ce</u>. It keeps the <u>x</u> in the masculine plural. (That's all that you need to do to *doux*.)
Exs. du temps doux- some mild weather, **une senteur** douce- **a sweet smell**
2. fou- crazy: This adjective starts out looking foolish and ends up being crazy. That should be expected as it is related to *la folie*- the insanity. Its five forms are *fou, fol, folle, fous* and *folles.* Notice that the masculine plural does not end with <u>x!</u>
Exs. être fou/folle de quelqu'un(e)- to be totally in love with someone, **gagner un argent fou- to earn loads of money** (Maybe this adjective isn't so crazy after all!)
3. mou- soft: This is the fifth adjective with a fifth form. *Mol, molle and molles* are cognates of <u>mollify</u>, but the resemblance of *mous,* the masculine plural form, to *la mousse* might provide a 'smoother' way to remember the word.
Exs. un tissu mou- a soft texture, **une moule** molle- a soft **mussel**
4. frais- cool, fresh: This adjective appears in *Il fait frais.* > It is cool. The masculine forms are cool as *frais,* but conditions change when the feminines, *fraîche* and *fraîches,* complete with circumflexes, are around.
Exs. du pain frais- some fresh bread, **des fraises** fraîches- **some** fresh **strawberries**
5. sec- dry, arid: Like *blanc,* this adjective adds an -<u>he</u> for its feminine forms where *les accents graves* over the first <u>è</u>s 'hang out' together. *Mouillé-* wet, damp is the antonym of *sec.*
Exs. du vin blanc sec- some dry white wine, **une gorge** sèche- **a** dry **throat**
6. *franc*- free, exempt, frank: This adjective, which mirrors *blanc* and *sec,* is more 'outspoken' about attaching -<u>he</u> to change the masculine into the feminine gender.
Exs. **du conseil** franc- **some** frank **advice**, une boutique franche- a duty-free shop
<u>An interesting aside</u>: Before the euro was introduced as standard European currency, *le franc* was the unit of monetary exchange in France, Belgium and Switzerland. (It's 'frankly' ironical that its translations include <u>free</u> and <u>exempt</u>.)

'Close Calls'- Circle the letters of the words most similar in meaning to those on the left.

1. gentil   a. jeune   b. sympathique   c. haut   d. sale
2. maigre   a. bon marché   b. petit   c. mince   d. gauche
3. vieux   a. seul   b. actuel   c. vrai   d. ancien
4. quelques   a. plusieurs   b. des   c. autres   d. quels
5. étrange   a. bizarre   b. formidable   c. timide   d. droit
6. triste   a. affreux   b. sec   c. malheureux   d. clair
7. parfait   a. prêt   b. merveilleux   c. paresseux   d. utile
8. dernier   a. faux   b. prochain   c. caché   d. passé
9. nouveau   a. étonné   b. profond   c. neuf   d. chaque
10. méchant   a. vilain   b. bas   c. léger   d. pensif
11. propre   a. fier   b. net   c. vif   d. fort
12. franc   a. mondial   b. actif   c. muet   d. sincère
13. drôle   a. pauvre   b. amusant   c. frais   d. faible
14. heureux   a. égal   b. joli   c. joyeux   d. vide
15. mignon   a. doux   b. entier   c. sot   d. fou
16. poli   a. bon marché   b. mouillé   c. plein   d. sage

'Casting a Spell'- Put the adjectives in parentheses into their correct forms and positions.
Exs. (the wonderful) amitié > la merveilleuse amitié, (the dry) vin > le vin sec

1. (a lively) conversation _____
2. (some unhappy) nouvelles _____
3. (the last/final) bataille _____
4. (some brave/courageous) pompiers _____
5. (a crazy) foule _____
6. (a deep) affection _____
7. (a narrow) ligne _____
8. (a few) faits _____
9. (next) jeudi _____
10. (the low) marée _____
11. (the true) histoire _____
12. (the dry) puits _____
13. (the poor/impoverished) pays _____
14. (each, expensive) billet _____
15. (those dreadful) ensembles-là _____
16. (their own) métiers _____

Distinguishing the Characteristics- Translate the following sentences.
1. Fresh strawberries are not inexpensive. _____
_____.

2. **The company (L'entreprise-f.)** does not pay equal salaries. _____
_____.

3. Naomi is giving beautiful yellow and blue flowers to her mother. _____

_____.

4. There are some new socks in the small drawer. _____

_____.

5. Why are the naughty children eating the delicious desserts? _____

_____?

6. The dear old (longtime) friends (f.) speak on the telephone often. _____

_____.

7. The poor woman's hands are full of dirty clothes. _____

_____.

8. Our gray cat likes to stay in the soft, wide armchair. _____

_____.

9. Why does the rich woman wear false furs but real jewelry? _____

_____?

10. That handsome man plays very good music on this heavy instrument. _____

_____.

11. Elle Même is the only single woman who lives in the apartment building. _____

_____.

12. The weather is dreadful in Montreal in the winter, but young children there are content to spend several hours in the deep snow. _____

_____.

_____

An Aqueduct (Nîmes)

TOUT, TOUTE, TOUS, TOUTES - ALL

Tout, toute, tous and *toutes* said consecutively seem to signal an approaching train. Each form of *tout* totes an article with it.
Take this 'train of thought' one stop further!

Singular	**Plural**
tout + le (masc.) - all the	tous + les (masc.) - all the
toute + la (fem.) - all the	toutes + les (fem.) - all the

"All Aboard"
1. The Tout Line precedes definite articles as well as possessive and demonstrative adjectives. They all agree with the nouns following them. (It's a long haul.)
Exs. tous mes espoirs- all my hopes, toutes ces pièces-là- all those plays
2. Pulling *le, la* and *l'*, the meanings of *tout* and *toute* are <u>all the</u>, <u>the whole</u> and <u>the entire</u>. The plural forms share the limited translations of <u>all the</u> and <u>every</u>. *Tout* is a synonym for *entier*.
Exs. **tout le monde**- everyone/everybody (all the whole/the entire world, the whole world)
      toute l'équipe- the whole team/the entire team
      tous les jours- all the days, every day, toutes les modes- all the fashions/every fashion

----

'Switching Tracks'- Put the correct forms of *tout* before the nouns and the translations for the phrases after them.
Ex. <u>tous</u> les timbres- all the stamps, every stamp

1. _____ les vaches _____
2. _____ la vérité _____
3. _____ le déjeuner _____
4. _____ les abeilles _____
5. _____ cet après-midi-ci _____
6. _____ ces cahiers-là _____
7. _____ ces fenêtres-ci _____
8. _____ mon cœur _____
9. _____ ton revenu _____
10. _____ les romans classiques _____
11. _____ les gratte-ciel en acier _____
12. _____ les belles plages _____

_____

LES ADVERBES FRANÇAIS - French Adverbs

Adverbs are the tattle-tales of a language. They willingly report how, when, where and to what extent verbs, adjectives and other adverbs are performing. Even though these modifiers have a lot to say, they are invariable with only one way to express themselves.

Various Varieties of Invariables

1. **Many French adverbs come from the masculine singular forms of corresponding adjectives. If the modifier ends with a vowel, -ment is added as the suffix. -Ment is the equivalent of -ly in English.**
Exs. absolument- absolutely, facilement- easily, vraiment- truly
Two exceptions: The adverbial form of *fou* **is** *follement,* **and** *gai* **is** *gaiement.* (Each goes merrily on its own way.)

2. **When the masculine singular form of an adjective ends with a consonant, -ment is typically attached to the feminine singular.**
Exs. également > equally, fier > fièrement > proudly, vif > vivement > lively
An exception: *Amablement* **will do** **nicely** **if you can't think of its irregular synonym** *gentiment.*

3. **An adverb's stem does not bend to agree in gender or in number.** (And the students cheered *collectivement.*)

4. **When the masculine singular form of an adjective ends with either -ant or -ent, those letters are dropped, and -amment or -emment is added to compose the related adverb. Some of those used** *fréquemment*- **frequently include** *constamment*- **constantly,** *couramment*- **fluently,** *évidemment*- **evidently and** *récemment*- **recently.**
An exception: *Lentement*- **slowly is made up of the feminine singular form of the adjective plus -ment.** (It is not 'up to speed' with the others in the -ent group.)
Ex. Art Iculer parle anglais lentement et **soigneusement** parce qu'il a peur de faire des fautes. > Art Iculer speaks English slowly and **carefully** because he is afraid of making mistakes.

5. **In simple French tenses, adverbs can go directly after the verbs they modify.**
Ex. Il embrasse souvent sa tante (souvent). > He hugs his aunt often. (The English word order could suggest that the aunt is named "Often.")

5a. **Short adverbs such as** *bien, mal, plus, trop* **and** *mieux*- **better sometimes precede infinitives.**
Ex. Les joueurs du football américain vont plus étudier ce semestre-ci. > The football players are going to study more this semester. (They understand the dual sense of "tackle.")

5b. **As in English, French adverbs can precede adjectives and other adverbs they modify.**
Exs. très **tranquille**- very calm, trop **vite**- too fast, too **quickly**

6. *Bien, fort* **and** *tout* **are used in front of adjectives as synonyms for** *très.*
Ex. **Les poissons** qu'il **attrape** sont tout petits. > **The fish** that he **catches** are very small. (They are not much larger than 'a bite.')

7. **Modifiers including** *chaque, gauche, tout* **and** *jeune* **prove that not all adjectives can be made into adverbs.** (However, while you're in a Chinese neighborhood, you might run into 'Yung Lee.')

8. *D'une façon*- **in a fashion/in a way and** *d'une manière*- **in a manner/in a way are followed by adjectives when no related adverb exists.**
Ex. La femme **désolée** marche d'une façon fatiguée. > The **desolate/devastated** woman walks in a tired fashion. (One should not misconstrue that to mean that her clothes look worn out.)

Important notes

a. Do not add a suffix to *vite!* It moves quickly as is.

b. *Vachement,* literally translated as "cowly," is rather popular in French conversation. (When you hear it used, it should 'ring a bell.')

c. *Très très-* very very, *extrêmement-* extremely and *incroyablement-* incredibly are more formal than *vachement.*

d. autrement- otherwise. The form of this adverb is standard, but its meaning shows <u>otherwise</u> and not 'otherly.'

How It Is 'Ment' to Be- Change the adjectives into adverbs, and translate those words.

1. unique _____ _____
2. libre _____ _____
3. probable _____ _____
4. poli _____ _____
5. complet _____ _____
6. général _____ _____
7. généreux _____ _____
8. curieux _____ _____
9. attentif _____ _____
10. naïf _____ _____
11. entier _____ _____
12. léger _____ _____
13. doux _____ _____
14. franc _____ _____
15. lent _____ _____
16. prudent _____ _____

ADVERBS WITHOUT SUFFIXES

Many common adverbs do not end with -<u>ment</u>. How many have you *déjà vu*?

1. alors- so, then, well: This 'pause word' is as indispensable to the French language as *le vin* is to their meals. *Alors* precedes comments, prompts listeners to offer their opinions or is added if the speaker has nothing more to say. (Alors!)

2. aussi- also, too: Both meanings should be included.

Ex. Vous ne pouvez pas avoir votre gâteau et le manger aussi. > You can't have your cake and eat it too. (Some might ask, "Then what good is it to have a cake?")

3. d'abord- at first, first: Not counting *d'*, <u>ab</u> are the <u>first</u> letters of this word.

4. demain- tomorrow: *(La) main-* the hand inside *demain* will be 'raised' in the future.

Ex. Elles vont donner une montre à leur père demain. > They are going to give a watch to their father tomorrow. (There's no present like the time.)

5. d'habitude- usually: Related to <u>habit</u> and <u>habitual</u>, its meaning is close to *normalement.*

6. encore- again, still, yet: This adverb is still around, making its *encore* performance yet, once

again. *De nouveau* is 'a stand in' if *encore* needs a break.

Ex. Sa fiancée, qui fait le whisky, est encore en prison. > His fiancée, who makes whiskey, is in prison again. (Does he love her 'still'?)

7. ensemble- together: This adverb 'gets it together' as a noun meaning an <u>outfit</u> and a <u>musical group</u>.

Ex. Des femmes ne sont pas bien ensemble **lorsqu'**elles portent le même ensemble. > Some women are not on good terms/do not get along **when/while** they are wearing the same outfit.

8. enfin- at last, finally: *Fin* **comes in last in this word, but the adverb can begin a sentence.**

Ex. Enfin, M. Hare va laver et polir cette voiture-là. > Finally, Mr. Hare is going to wash and polish that car. (Will he use 'turtle wax'?)

9. ensuite- afterwards, next: <u>To ensue</u> and *ensuite* **are related. The latter shares a suite with the phrases** *tout de suite-* **immediately/right away,** *par la suite-* **afterwards,** *et ainsi de suite-* **and so forth.** (*Suite* has a very large 'following.')

10. hier- yesterday: This adverb is a mainstay of the past tense. (It will seem like only yesterday when you see it again.)

11. jamais- ever, never: Used in affirmative sentences, *jamais* **means <u>ever</u>. Surrounding a verb,** *ne + jamais* **is <u>never</u>. This concept is identical to <u>never</u> with or without the <u>n</u>.**

Ex. La Princesse Jasmine porte jamais un pyjama? > Does Princess Jasmine ever wear pajamas? (Or does she just 'stick to' the carpet?)

12. loin- far, a long way: Followed by *de/d'* **plus a noun or pronoun,** *loin* **is a preposition.**

Ex. La femme aux lunettes est très loin derrière. > The woman in glasses is very far behind. (She is not 'near-sighted.')

13. maintenant- now (As you are acquainted with this adverb, it doesn't require high maintenance.)

14. partout- everywhere: This adverb, literally "by all," and *surtout-* **above all/especially are on 'a** *tout*-**do' list.**

Ex. Barker accompagne son maître partout, mais le chien aime surtout les tours en voitures. > Barker accompanies his master everywhere, but the dog especially likes car rides. (Everybody is very thankful that it prefers 'to go' outdoors.)

15. près- close, near, nearby: Like its antonym *loin,* *près* **is a preposition when it is followed by** *de/d'* **plus a noun or a pronoun.**

Ex. Plusieurs châteaux de la Loire sont près. > Several castles of the Loire are nearby. (They might be listed under 'turret' attractions.)

16. presque/presqu'- almost, nearly: *Que/qu'* **at the end puts this adverb even closer than** *près.* *Presque* **and** *presqu'* **precede adjectives and nouns.**

Ex. Le prix pour l'autobus et pour le métro est presqu'égal. > The price for the bus and for the subway is almost equal.

17. quelquefois- sometimes: Comprised of *quelque-* **some and** *fois-* **time, it is a synonym for** *de temps en temps-* **from time to time.** (*Quelquefois,* use one and *de temps en temps,* the other!)

<u>**Match a Pair That's** *Au Contraire*</u>- **Put the letters beside the numbers of the antonyms.**

_____ 1. toujours	A. vite
_____ 2. moins de	B. pas encore
_____ 3. tristement	C. bien
_____ 4. de bonne heure	D. également

_____ 5. ici   E. faiblement

_____ 6. rarement   F. franchement

_____ 7. déjà   G. ne ... jamais

_____ 8. différemment   H. en retard

_____ 9. loin   I. peu de

_____ 10. sérieusement   J. faussement

_____ 11. lentement   K. plus de

_____ 12. d'abord   L. exclusivement

_____ 13. secrètement   M. là

_____ 14. mal   N. enfin

_____ 15. parfaitement   O. sottement

_____ 16. beaucoup de   P. soigneusement

_____ 17. totalement   Q. près

_____ 18. fortement   R. affreusement

_____ 19. dangereusement   S. souvent

_____ 20. sincèrement   T. heureusement

'Getting the Word Out'- **Complete the sentences by selecting the correct adverbs from the following list and putting them in the spaces: assez, aussi, autrement, demain, de temps en temps, d'habitude, enfin, ensemble, ensuite, hier, loin, maintenant, ne ... jamais, partout, presque, tout de suite, quelquefois, très**

1. Il est douze heures moins cinq. Il est _____ midi.

2. Anne Ordre va finir ses devoirs. _____, elle va rencontrer ses copains au parc.

3. Que fais-tu à ce moment? Je réponds à ces questions _____.

4. C'est aujourd'hui le seize septembre. C'était _____ le quinze du mois.

5. Je pense que le vert et le jaune vont bien _____.

6. Comme la mère n'a pas le temps de **ranger (straighten up, tidy up)**, les jouets de ses petits sont _____.

7. Bernard adore Bernice, mais il habite à Douai, et elle habite à Vence. Malheureusement, les deux villes sont très _____.

8. Sandy va aller à la plage _____ matin passer le week-end.

9. Gaspille Tout dépense tous les euros qu'il gagne. Pour cette raison, il ____ a _____ _____ d'argent.

10. C'est urgent! J'ai besoin de ta réponse _____. _____, je vais téléphoner à quelqu'un d'autre dans dix minutes.

11. La tante Espérance attend son neveu longtemps. _____, il arrive à sa maison, et elle est _____ soulagée.

12. _____, Mme Lacroix n'aime pas assister seul à la messe. _____ ou _____ son mari va à l'église _____.

'In a Manner of Speaking'- **Translate the following sentences.**

1. Our pets play well together. _____.

2. They never stay here more than three days. _____
_____.

3. Obviously, bees and beavers do not succeed at their work easily. _____
_____.

4. When we arrive, we like to take a walk in the streets nearby. _____
_____.

5. The rich woman acts disagreeably when she is not well. _____
_____.

6. All the extremely handsome men do not have girlfriends? Really? _____
_____?

7. The professor looks at Anne Surqui suspiciously because she always has the answers too quickly.
_____
_____.
_____

Young Girls at the Piano by Auguste Renoir (le Musée d'Orsay, Paris)

127

LES COMPLÉMENTS DES OBJETS DIRECTS - Direct Objects

Anyone who did not understand direct objects in English class might have better luck learning them *à la française*. Even if <u>what</u> and <u>whom</u> are no mystery to you, it will be helpful to review the case directly and objectively.

Direct Object Pronouns

Singular	Plural
me (m') - me	**nous - us**
te (t') - you	**vous - you**
le (l') - him, it	**les - them**
la (l') - her, it	

The model sentences
Mes amis aiment bien la pizza. > My friends like pizza.

'Slicing It up'
1. From the sentence above, take the subject, *Mes amis*, and the verb, *aiment*, and ask, "<u>what?</u>" The answer, "*la pizza*," is the direct object. It is also found by asking the subject and the verb, "<u>whom?</u>"
Ex. Le Père Noël choisit Rodolphe. > Santa Claus chooses Rudolph.
Santa Claus chooses whom?/Whom does Santa Claus choose? The answer, (the direct object), that 'flashes' is Rudolph.
1a. Going back to 'triangle one' and substituting pizza with a pronoun, the correct choice is <u>it</u>. Santa would prefer not to replace Rudolph, but if he had to, Saint Nick would refer to his loyal reindeer as <u>him</u>.
2. French direct object pronouns usually precede verbs.
Ex. Le docteur Gary les guérit. > Doctor Gary cures them.
Ex. Mercedes la lave-t-elle chaque mercredi? > Does Mercedes wash it every Wednesday?
3. *Le, la, l'* and *les* replace nouns preceded by the same named definite articles. In those instances, the direct objects are 'a given.'
Exs. Le pronom **remplace** le nom. > The pronoun **replaces** the noun.
 Le pronom le remplace. > The pronoun replaces it.
4. As direct object pronouns, *vous* again means <u>you</u>, but *nous* now translates as <u>us</u>.
Ex. Jean nous rencontre à **la foire**. > John is meeting us at **the fair**. (It's a 'midway' location.)
5. Direct object pronouns often substitute for nouns preceded by demonstrative and possessive adjectives.
Exs. Ruby ne **prête** pas ses bagues. > Ruby does not **lend** her rings.
 Ruby ne les prête pas. > Ruby does not lend them. (They are not leaving her hands.)
6. *Me* and *te* change to *m'* and *t'* in front of a vowel or a mute <u>h</u>.
Ex. Si tu n'es pas à **l'arrêt de bus** à l'heure, **le chauffeur d'autobus** ne t'attend pas. > If you aren't at **the bus stop** on time, **the bus driver** does not wait for you. (The other passengers come first.)
7. *Le/L'* can express the idea of a previous sentence.
Ex. Faith Fullie rend tout de suite les vêtements qu'elle emprunte de Lenda. > Faith Fullie promptly

returns the clothing that she borrows from Lenda.

    Lenda l'apprécie. > Lenda appreciates it. (The girls like each other's 'style.')

8. Although they are placed between subjects and verbs, direct object pronouns do not have a relationship with either of them.

Ex. Ray Sherche nous cherche à la bibliothèque. > Ray Sherche is looking for us at the library.

Ray Sherche and *cherche* are filed together. *Nous* belongs in a separate folder.

9. Object pronouns go between conjugated verbs and infinitives.

Ex. Nous allons vous inviter à la soirée. > We are going to invite you to the party. (Does *vous* make it a formal invitation?)

'In a Word'- Replace the words and phrases with *le, la, nous, vous* or *les*.

1. Jacques _____
2. la Maison Blanche _____
3. les copains _____
4. le problème _____
5. l'avion _____
6. Babar et vous _____
7. Fifi et moi _____
8. le ciel clair _____
9. la crise mondiale _____
10. les billets gratuits _____

11. tout le monde _____
12. toutes les rues vides _____
13. ce diable méchant _____
14. ces siècles passés _____
15. mon lama et moi _____
16. votre hôtel bon marché _____
17. sa chère mère _____
18. Manon et sa jolie fille _____
19. ses idées sottes _____
20. toi et ton **ombre-f. (shadow)** _____

'Taking Advantage of the Substitute'- Change the underlined noun phrases into pronouns, and rewrite the sentences.

Ex. Quand est-ce que Effie va visiter <u>la tour Eiffel</u>? > Quand est-ce que Effie va <u>la</u> visiter?

1. Taylor coupe <u>la belle toile</u>. _____.
2. Le serveur verse <u>le vin sec</u>. _____.
3. Demandez-vous <u>mes conseils</u>? _____?
4. Sofia ne vend pas <u>ses meubles</u>. _____.
5. Écoutes-tu <u>la musique classique</u>? _____?
6. Ma copine emprunte <u>mes bottes de cuir</u>. _____.
7. Anne Core fait <u>la même faute souvent</u>? _____?
8. Il ne prête jamais <u>son téléphone cellulaire</u>. _____.
9. Quelle entreprise bâtit <u>ces centres commerciaux</u>? _____?
10. Nous attendons <u>vous deux</u> à l'arrêt d'autobus. _____.
11. Renée ferme <u>ces fenêtres-la</u> quand elle entend <u>la pluie</u>. _____

_____.

12. Le Comte Von Count ne garde pas <u>tout son argent</u> dans une banque. _____

_____.

13. Le Petit Chaperon Rouge apporte <u>une corbeille de fruits</u> à sa grand-mère. _____

_____.

14. Allez-vous blanchir <u>ces chemises-ci</u> quand vous faites <u>la lessive</u>? _____

_____.

VOIR - TO SEE and CROIRE - TO BELIEVE

Although *voir* ends with -**ir**, it is not a regular second conjugation verb. (In spite of that, *grossir, maigrir* and *voir* grouped together do share a 'weight and see' theme.) **Besides, though *croire* ends with -re, it is not a regular third conjugation (SS *Nothing*) verb. As you study these two verbs, exchange the y in *voir* for the cr in *croire*. Yes, "Seeing is believing!"**

Voir - To See

Singular	Plural
je vois- I see, do see, am seeing	nous voyons- we see, do see, are seeing
tu vois- you see, do see, are seeing	vous voyez- you see, do see, are seeing
il/elle voit- he/she sees, does see, is seeing	ils/elles voient- they see, do see, are seeing

---

Croire - To Believe

Singular	Plural
je crois- I believe, do believe, am believing	nous croyons- we believe, do believe,
tu crois- you believe, do believe, are believing	vous croyez- you believe, do believe, are believing
il/elle croit- he/she believes, does believe, is believing	ils/elles croient- they believe, do believe, are believing

---

A View of the Credits
1. *Voir* and *croire* are "boot verbs." By outlining the entire singular and the third person plural forms, you make an elongated boot. The included verbs share a similar spelling pattern and an identical pronunciation.
2. The *nous* and *vous* form endings for both verbs are prefaced by a y. The vowel switch from i does not alter the **wa** sound.
3. *Le clairvoyant* who looks into the future precariously and *le voyeur* who peers into strangers' windows vicariously are French words related to *voir*. Credit, credo and credible are indebted to *croire* for believing in them.
4. Two very common phrases are *Je crois que oui.* > I believe so, and *Je crois que non.* > I don't believe so. Could one substitute a form of *penser* to express the same thing? *Je pense que oui.*

Two very interesting asides
a. *l'avoir*- to have it and *la voir*- to see her/it are said identically. The meaning is determined by the content of the previous sentence.
Ex. Devila? Nous allons la voir demain. > Devila? We are going to see her tomorrow. (Nobody can have her because she is already 'possessed.')
b. Because *revoir* means <u>to see again</u>, *au revoir* does not express finality.

Notes from the 'Oir' Choir- Write the correct forms of the verbs in parentheses in the spaces.
1. (croire) Tout le monde les _____.
2. (voir) _____-vous ce que je _____?
3. (croire) Honoré et moi _____ que oui.

4. (voir) Quelle pièce vas-tu _____ ce soir?
5. (croire) Vous ne nous _____ pas toujours.
6. (croire) Qui _____ les histoires étranges que Bea Zarr raconte?
7. (voir) Si je ne les _____ pas souvent, je suis triste.
8. (croire) Nous ne sommes pas naïfs. Nous ne _____ pas tout.
9. (croire, voir) Ils le _____ s'ils le _____ de leurs propres yeux.
10. (croire, voir) Elle _____ que tu _____ Victoire quelquefois.

From Your Point of View- Translate the following sentences.
1. I see them every month. _____.
2. Do you (*tu*) believe the good news? _____?
3. We are very happy when we see her. _____

_____.
4. Mr. and Mrs. Longtemps are going to see their old (former) friends tomorrow. _____

_____.
5. I am sure that my parents do not believe us. _____

_____.
6. Lorgnette does not see far **without (sans)** her glasses. _____

_____.
7. Mr. Mirage sees it, but he does not believe it. _____

_____.
8. Their daughter who lives in another city rarely sees them. _____

_____.
9. Do you (*vous*) ever see her in church? _____

_____.
10. Why don't you (*tu*) believe me? _____?

_____

SAVOIR - TO KNOW and CONNAÎTRE - TO KNOW (TO BE ACQUAINTED WITH)

Being irregular verbs with very similar translations, *savoir* and *connaître* should be presented together. However, the two must also be pulled apart to distinguish between their French uses and to put you 'in the know.'

Savoir - To Know (A Fact)

Singular	Plural
je sais- I know, do know	nous savons- we know, do know
tu sais- you know, do know	vous savez- you know, do know
il/elle sait- he/she knows, does know	ils/elles savent- they know, do know

----

Connaître - To Know (To Be Acquainted With)

Singular	Plural
je connais- I know, do know, I am acquainted with	nous connaissons- we know, do know, we are acquainted with
tu connais- you know, do know, you are acquainted with	vous connaissez- you know, do know, you are acquainted with
il/elle connaît- he/she knows, does know, he/she is acquainted with	ils/elles connaissent- they know, do know, they are acquainted with

----

No Know Differences
In addition to meaning <u>to know</u>, *savoir* and *connaître* have other points in common.
1. The singular forms of each verb have the same pronunciation. Their irregular -ais, -ais, -<u>ait</u> endings are reminiscent of *faire*.
2. Like *voir* and *croire*, *savoir* and *connaître* take direct objects. They are therefore referred to as <u>transitive verbs</u>.
<u>A note</u>: Most French speakers say, *"Je ne sais pas,"* but the short colloquial phrase, *sais pas,* is also commonly used.

Knowing *Savoir* for a Fact
1. <u>How</u> in <u>know how</u> is not translated. It is included in the verb.
Ex. Mon petit frère sait faire du ski nautique. > My little brother knows how to water ski. (He 'stays up on' things like that.)
2. *Savoir* and its plural forms have a <u>v</u>.
2a. The soaps- *les savons* and the *nous* form of *savoir* are spelled the same. Moreover, *savent* is pronounced like <u>suave</u>, the synonym for an ointment. ('Apply them' to remember the verbs!)
3. An often used French-English term is *savoir-faire*- know-how/expertise. Its abridged form is "savvy." *Savoir-vivre*, literally "to know how to live," is also a popular French-English phrase. *Un idiot savant*- 'an idiot scientist' refers to someone extremely gifted in one area but devoid of ability in all others. Now, you are *au courant*- in the know.

Becoming Acquainted with *Connaître*

1. *Connaître* expresses familiarity with people, places, things and ideas.
Ex. Les arrondissements de Paris? M. Maville les connaît très bien. > The Parisian arrondissements? Mr. Maville knows them very well. (He travels in those 'circles.')

2. When <u>to be acquainted with</u> can replace <u>to know</u>, use a form of *connaître*.
Ex. Connais-tu Passepartout? Je ne sais pas son vrai nom. > Do you know (Are you acquainted with) Passepartout? I do not know his real name. (Maybe, he just 'goes by' that.)

3. Though *tu reconnais*- you <u>recognize</u> -<u>ir</u> endings on this verb and on *connaître*, notice that the infinitives end with -<u>re</u>! Things aren't always as *ils paraissent*- they <u>seem</u> or as *ils apparaissent*- they <u>appear</u>.

4. A circumflex is found over the <u>i</u> in *connaître*, on its related infinitives and on their third person singular forms. There is no <u>s</u> in those instances.

5. Unlike *savoir*, conjugated forms of *connaître* are not followed by infinitives.
Ex. Je sais faire une imitation parfaite de cet anglais-là, mais je ne le connais pas personnellement. > I know how to do a perfect imitation of that Englishman, but I don't know him personally. (He might agree that it's 'spot-on.')

6. *Faire la connaissance de*- to make the acquaintance of; *être enchanté(e)(s) de faire votre connaissance*- to be delighted to make your acquaintance. The latter is sometimes watered down to *enchanté(e)(s)*. (When the speaker 'goes light on the delighted.')

'Know' Two Ways about It- **Choose the correct forms of *savoir* and *connaître* and their related expressions, and put them in the spaces provided.**

1. _____-vous faire les crêpes?
2. Mona St. Michel _____ la Bretagne et la Normandie très bien.
3. Nous allons _____ les résultats de nos examens bientôt.
4. Quels voisins _____-vous?
5. Quand tu rencontres quelqu'un pour la première fois, tu fais _____.
6. Comment _____-vous qu'ils ont raison?
7. Je crois que tu _____ quelque chose de cette matière-ci.
8. "Mme Chignon, _____-vous une bonne coiffeuse?"
9. Nous _____ assez bien le Marais, mais nous ne _____ pas arriver là par métro.
10. On reconnaît tout de suite que l'homme poli a du _____.
11. Je _____de ton regard que tu ne _____ pas ce que tu fais.
12. _____-tu M. Modem et M. Écran? Ils sont vachement forts dans **l'informatique (computing)**. Ils _____ faire tout avec les ordinateurs.

Extra 'Sentensory' Perception- **Circle the letters of the responses that complete the sentences.**

1. Hyme Lemieux est un égoïste. Nous l'appelons _____.
a. un vol de reconnaissance   b. un copain sage   c. un je-sais-tout   d. un savoir-vivre

2. Lorsque Stella regarde le ciel par nuit, _____.
a. elle reconnaît d'anciens amis   b. elle voit la lune et des étoiles
c. elle fait ma connaissance   d. on fait un feu dans la cheminée

3. Je vais rendre visite à mes voisins nouveaux pour me présenter parce que _____.
a. je ne crois pas leurs enfants
b. le couple ne va jamais me voir
c. le monsieur est un idiot savant
d. je ne les connais pas encore

4. Si on a une question d'informatique, on la demande à mon père qui _____.
a. rentre de temps en temps
b. n'est pas au courant
c. sait toujours de quoi il parle
d. a tort fréquemment

5. Enfin, le médecin de Mme Porte de Mort sait la guérir, et _____.
a. on n'est pas enchanté de faire sa connaissance
b. elle paraît être malade
c. tout le monde connaît ces **drogues-f. (drugs)**
d. sa famille croit aux miracles

6. On n'a pas besoin de beaucoup d'argent pour avoir _____.
a. du savoir-faire et des manières
b. des vêtements à la mode
c. tous les parfums et tant de savons chers
d. son propre avion

7. Labby et moi allons réussir à la chimie. Nous **posons (ask)** des questions si _____.
a. nous ne savons pas ce que nous faisons
b. la vérité est évidente
c. les profs ne nous croient pas autrement
d. nous ne le voyons pas d'abord

8. Je vais faire des magasins avec vous. Vous reconnaissez les bonnes affaires _____.
a. si les prix ne sont pas assez bas
b. si vous connaissez bien les clercs
c. le moment où vous les voyez
d. et vous avez l'intention de les payer

l'Opéra/le Palais Garnier (Paris)

MLLE ESPOIR ET LA BONNE FÉE - Ms Espoir and The Fairy Godmother
La Première Partie - Part 1

Du Vocabulaire du Conte

1. l'espoir (m.)- the hope
2. les cheveux (m.)- the hair
3. pendant- during
4. l'avenir (m.)- the future

5. le rêve- the dream
6. le vœu- the wish
7. jeter- to throw, to toss

Mlle Espoir a vingt-cinq ans. Elle a un joli visage, **les** longs **cheveux** blonds et les yeux bleus. Cette jeune femme est aussi en bonne forme. On la considère très belle. **Pendant** la semaine, Mlle Espoir travaille dans une maison de haute couture. Tous les samedi après-midi on la voit dans le Jardin du Luxembourg. Lorsqu'elle est là, elle réfléchit à **son avenir** et à l'homme de **ses rêves**. Il n'existe pas encore dans sa vie, mais Mlle Espoir le connaît déjà. Son prince charmant est très beau, très gentil, très intelligent et assez riche. Comment va-t-elle rencontrer cet homme parfait?

La jeune femme fait **un vœu,** et elle **jette** de la monnaie dans la fontaine où les enfants jouent avec leurs petits bateaux à voile.

Write complete answers in French to the following questions.

1. Quel âge Mlle Espoir a-t-elle? _____.

2. Comment est-elle? _____
_____.

3. Où travaille-t-elle? _____.

4. Que fait-elle chaque samedi après-midi? _____
_____.

5. À quoi réfléchit-elle? _____
_____.

6. Comment est l'homme de ses rêves? _____
_____.

7. Que fait-elle **avant de (before)** jeter des pièces dans l'eau? _____
_____.

8. Qu'est-ce que les enfants font dans la fontaine? _____
_____.

135

MLLE ESPOIR ET LA BONNE FÉE - Ms Espoir and The Fairy Godmother
La Deuxième Partie - Part 2

Du Vocabulaire du Conte
1. tout d'un coup- suddenly
2. la bonne fée- the fairy godmother
3. la prière- the prayer
4. la feuille de papier- the piece of paper

5. Puis-je- May I?
6. remercier- to thank
7. Pense à moi!- Think about me!

On trouve Mlle Espoir l'année prochaine en même endroit. Elle n'a pas encore de petit ami. Cette jeune femme assiste souvent aux soirées, et elle rencontre fréquemment de jeunes hommes sympathiques, mais M. Spécial n'est pas dans sa vie.
Tout d'un coup une bonne fée apparaît. Mlle Espoir ne croit pas ses yeux.

La bonne fée: Bonjour mademoiselle. Tu n'as pas besoin de jeter plus de pièces dans la fontaine.
Mlle Espoir: Je ne crois pas aux bonnes fées.
La bonne fée: Si tu me reconnais, tu sais que les bonnes fées existent. J'ai la réponse à **tes prières**.
Mlle Espoir: Vous ne me connaissez pas. Comment savez-vous mes vœux?
La bonne fée: Les bonnes fées savent tout. L'homme que tu cherches t'attend aussi.
Mlle Espoir: Combien coûtent vos services?
La bonne fée: Mes services sont gratuits, mademoiselle.
(La bonne fée montre **une feuille de papier** à Mlle Espoir.)
La bonne fée: Voici une description complète de ton prince charmant et des instructions pour faire sa connaissance.
(Mlle Espoir regarde tout soigneusement. D'abord, elle rougit et ensuite, elle pleure de joie. Enfin, elle parle à la bonne fée.)
Mlle Espoir: Comment **puis-je** vous **remercier**?
La bonne fée: **Pense à moi** le jour de ton mariage!
Mlle Espoir: Merci mille fois!
(Elle donne un baiser à la bonne fée!)

Write complete answers in French to the following questions.
1. Est-ce que Mlle Espoir a un petit ami au commencement de la deuxième partie? _____

_____.
2. Qui apparaît **soudainement (suddenly)**? _____.
3. Qu'est-ce que Mlle Espoir n'a plus besoin de faire? _____

_____.
4. Comment la bonne fée répond-elle à la phrase, "Je ne crois pas aux bonnes fées?" _____

_____.
5. À quoi la bonne fée a-t-elle la réponse? _____

_____.
6. Comment sait-elle les vœux de Mlle Espoir? _____

_____.
7. Qu'est-ce que l'homme de ses rêves fait maintenant? _____

136

8. La jeune femme va payer les services de la bonne fée? _____
_____.
9. Qu'est-ce qu'il y a sur la feuille de papier? _____
_____.
10. Comment Mlle Espoir réagit-elle? _____
_____.
11. Quelle suggestion la bonne fée offre-t-elle? _____
_____.
12. Que Mlle Espoir fait-elle à la fin du conte? _____
_____.
_____

A Dance in the City by Auguste Renoir (le Musée d'Orsay, Paris)

UNE REVUE - A Review

Les Adjectifs Français, Les Adverbes Français, Les Compléments des Objets Directs, Voir, Croire, Savoir, Connaître, Idiomatic Expressions, Mlle Espoir et la Bonne Fée

'To Tell the Truth'- Label the statements *vrai* or *faux.*

_____ 1. Most French adjectives precede nouns.

_____ 2. Adjectives ending with an é are typically past participles of verbs.

_____ 3. Adjectives that end with an f in the masculine singular change that consonant to ve to form the feminine singular.

_____ 4. *Sympathique* and *gentil* are *faux amis.*

_____ 5. Adjectives and nouns ending with s, x and z change in the masculine plural.

_____ 6. Masculine singular adjectives and nouns ending with al have aux plural endings.

_____ 7. *Heureux*, *ravi* and *joyeux* could be considered synonyms.

_____ 8. *Malheureux, triste* and *désolé* could be considered antonyms.

_____ 9. Some "bangs" adjectives can both precede and follow nouns.

_____ 10. All adjectives with five forms end with an x in the masculine plural.

_____ 11. The fifth form of adjectives precedes feminine singular nouns that begin with a vowel or a mute h.

_____ 12. All "bangs" adjectives with five forms have -lle in their feminine endings.

_____ 13. *Des* typically precedes plural "bangs" adjectives to express some.

_____ 14. Adjectives may have a literal meaning before nouns but an abstract sense after them.

_____ 15. Adjectives in the *tout* family are followed only by definite articles.

_____ 16. The -ment suffix corresponds to -ly in English.

_____ 17. The root of many French adverbs is the feminine singular form of the adjective.

_____ 18. Adverbs agree with the verbs they modify.

_____ 19. Adverbs ending with -amment and -emment come from adjectives that end with -ant and -ent.

_____ 20. Placed before adjectives, *bien* and *tout* mean very.

_____ 21. Object pronouns have the same word order in French and in English.

_____ 22. Definite articles and some direct object pronouns are the same French words.

_____ 23. The subject of the sentence agrees with the direct object pronoun.

_____ 24. Direct object pronouns precede infinitives.

'Slots to Consider'- Use *le, la, l' les, te* and *vous* and the correct forms of *voir, croire, savoir* and *connaître* to complete the following sentences.

Ex. Le français? Je sais le parler un peu. > French? I know how to speak it a little.

1. Farrah Wai habite à Montréal, et je _____ _____ rarement.

2. Ce n'est pas vrai, mais tout le monde _____ _____.

3. Quels sont les noms des planètes? Gale Acsie et moi _____ _____.

4. Es-tu familier avec les deux aéroports à Paris? Oui, je _____ _____ bien.

5. Paul ne vous distingue pas de votre frère s'il ne _____ _____ pas ensemble.

6. Aida fait ces exercices avec moi parce qu'elle _____ _____ faire vite.

7. Gigi aime parler de ces vedettes, mais elle ne _____ _____ pas.

8. Mlle Espoir reconnaît-elle son prince charmant quand elle _____ _____?

9. Pourquoi donnes-tu ton numéro à Anne Cloude? Elle _____ _____.

10. Elles continuent à raconter l'histoire étrange, mais on ne va jamais _____ _____.

11. Je visite souvent cette cathédrale célèbre. Je _____ _____ maintenant.

12. Ta mère pense que ton explication est vraie. Heureusement, elle _____ _____.

'Making the Rounds'- Circle the letters of the best responses to complete the scenarios.

1. Salomon est très sage. Il fait rarement _____.
a. des connaissances riches   b. des décisions sottes   c. son propre lit   d. des devoirs faciles

2. Une voisine ou une autre rend visite à la malade chaque jour.
a. Elles ne savent pas qu'elle est vraiment paresseuse.   b. Elle est presque prête maintenant.
c. Les individus vilains ne sont pas loin.   d. Elle a de la chance de connaître de tels gentils gens.

3. Lorsque la petite est au jardin zoologique, elle adore regarder les animaux qui _____.
a. font du travail utile   b. croient aux fées   c. agissent très drôles   d. ont des corps faibles

4. "Chérie, je ne te vois pas **depuis (since)** longtemps. Comment ça va?"
a. "Tu marches seul sur ces chemins dangereux?"   b. "Quel brouillard épais!"
c. "Tu passes encore ton temps avec des mendiants?"   d. "Quoi de neuf?"

5. Le chauffeur d'autobus est en route au centre de Paris. Pour arriver là, il tourne _____.
a. à droite à l'Ile de la Cité   b. lentement pour parler aux jeunes passagers
c. tout droit près du Boulevard St. Germain   d. très vite sur une rue étroite

6. Toutes ces fleurs-ci donnent une senteur très douce.
a. Les murs sont tout mouillés à cause de la pluie.   b. Qui le remplace si on verse tout?
c. La pièce a l'odeur d'une parfumerie.   d. Les souvenirs des batailles sont partout.

7. Si tu demandes à Mme Svelte comment elle garde sa bonne forme, elle répond, _____.
a. "Je suis au courant des affaires mondiales."   b. "Le verre est toujours demi-plein."
c. "Je mange des repas légers, et je suis sportive."   d. "Je sais ce qui cache dans les ombres."

8. Est-ce que ces étudiants-là qui ne font jamais attention en classe _____?
a. ont des peurs profondes   b. pensent à leurs petites amies
c. parlent de nos espoirs librement   d. rêvent de leurs tristes avenirs

VOULOIR - TO WANT, TO WISH

Related to <u>voluntary</u> and <u>volunteer</u> and a synonym for *désirer*, *vouloir* is 'a most wanted' verb. Were it not for the <u>l</u>s in the plural forms, *vouloir* could fit as "a boot verb," and its strategically placed <u>x</u>s could be thought of as laces.

Singular	Plural
je veux- I want, do want,	nous voulons- we want, do want,
I wish, do wish, am wishing	we wish, do wish, are wishing
tu veux- you want, do want	vous voulez- you want, do want
you wish, do wish, are wishing	you wish, do wish, are wishing
il/elle veut- he/she/it wants, does want	ils/elles veulent- they want, do want
he/she/it wishes, does wish, is wishing	they wish, do wish, are wishing

----

'A Wish List'

1. <u>Eu</u> appears throughout the singular and in the third person plural. The <u>l</u>, found in the infinitive, is seen in all the plural forms.
2. The singular verbs are pronounced identically. *Veulent* is enunciated by placing your tongue behind your upper teeth.
3. Forms of *vouloir* take direct object pronouns.
Exs. Samson veut voir Dalila constamment. > Samson wants to see Delilah constantly.

    Samson veut la voir constamment. > Samson wants to see her constantly. (Delilah is 'the object of his desire' grammatically and literally.)
4. *Vouloir* means <u>to want</u> and <u>to wish</u>. *Désirer* is synonymous with the first verb; *souhaiter* with the second. So, when you hear the phrase, "*Nous vous souhaitons un Joyeux Noël*" > "We wish you a Merry Christmas," you can consider yourself 'seasoned.'
5. It is more courteous to use the conditional tense to ask for something. The first person singular of that conjugation is *je voudrais* > I would want/like. Your request will likely be granted *de bon gré*- willingly.
6. *Avoir envie de*- to feel like is a synonym for *désirer*.
Ex. Mme Epuisée n'a pas envie de discipliner ses enfants aujourd'hui. > Mrs. Epuisée does not feel like disciplining her children today. (She can be sure that 'they won't mind.')

Expressing Wants and Desires

1. sans le vouloir- unintentionally: Its one-word antonym is *exprès*- on purpose.
Ex. Maline prétend à téléphoner à son ancien petit ami sans le vouloir. > Maline claims to phone her former boyfriend unintentionally. (She certainly knows 'which buttons to push.')
2. vouloir bien- to really want/to be happy to: Its synonym is *être heureux de*.
Ex. Nita Maid ne veut pas bien **accueillir** d'invités à son appartement parce que c'est **en désordre**. > Nita Maid doesn't really want to **welcome** any guests to their apartment because it is **messy**. (Would they just 'pick up and leave'?)
3. "Vouloir, c'est pouvoir." "Quand on veut, on peut." The former proverb means, "To want is to be able." The latter says, "When one wants, one can." Both of them are more familiar to us as "Where there's a will, there's a way." (Quite possibly, there is also a deceased.)

4. vouloir dire- to mean: If taken apart, the phrase reads "to want to say." C'est ce que vouloir dire veut dire. > It's what <u>to mean</u> means.

<u>'Want Ads'</u>- Correct forms of *vouloir* and its related idioms are needed to fill these vacancies. (The conditional tense applies for two of the positions.)

1. M. Pesant _____ maigrir, mais il ne _____ pas faire d'exercices.

2. _____-tu écouter la chanson que je sais jouer du piano?

3. Pendant un examen, le prof donne une réponse aux étudiants _____.

4. Anne et Antoine ne _____ pas assister à mon boum, et je ne _____ pas les inviter.

5. Margaux et moi _____ faire des emplettes ensemble. Nous _____ bien aller aux magasins moins chers.

6. Les Fautfaire vendent leurs **objets d'époque-m. (antiques)** pour louer une petite maison à la Côte d'Azur. "_____, on peut."

7. Ann Ergie _____ pas rester chez elle. Elle cherche des amis qui _____ faire un tour à bicyclette.

8. "Cher Père Noël, Je _____ cent cadeaux." Cet enfant _____ trop.

9. Pepin demande à son frère plus âgé, "Que _____ "Facebook?"

10. M. Bienélevé parle au serveur. "Je _____ la soupe à l'oignon et la salade niçoise, s'il vous plaît."

POUVOIR - TO BE ABLE, CAN

Can is a helping/auxiliary verb in English. *Pouvoir* is an independent verb in French where <u>to be able</u> and <u>can</u> are translated the same. So, even though forms of *pouvoir* have two meanings, they share one conjugation. *Pouvoir* is introduced directly after *vouloir* because they rhyme in their singular forms and have similar spelling changes.

Let's see what you can do with the power of *pouvoir*!

<u>Singular</u>	<u>Plural</u>
je peux- I am able, I can	nous pouvons- we are able, we can
tu peux- you are able, you can	vous pouvez- you are able, you can
il/elle peut- he/she/it is able, he/she/it can	ils/elles peuvent- they are able, they can

---

<u>Can and Able- The Non-Biblical Version</u>

1. Excluding the <u>v</u> to <u>p</u> switch, the singular forms of *vouloir* and *pouvoir* are identical. (Vouloir c'est pouvoir!)

2. The <u>v</u> originating in *pouvoir* and seen throughout its plural mirrors the <u>l</u> in *vouloir*. Because of those additional consonants, the two verbs are not considered genuine "boot verbs." (Nevertheless, *vouloir* and *pouvoir* leave 'their imprints' in the same spots.)

Ex. Nous ne pouvons pas faire toujours ce que nous voulons. > We cannot always do what we want. (But we can go to the *vous* form for 'a second person's opinion.')

3. Conjugated forms of *pouvoir* are followed by infinitives. ('Cans' are stacked with other verbs.)
Ex. M. Ensemble peut **frotter** l'estomac et **tapoter** la tête en même temps. > Mr. Ensemble can **rub** his stomach and **pat** his head at the same time.
4. Direct objects go between conjugated forms of *pouvoir* and infinitives. The pronoun belongs to the second verb.
Ex. Sophia Loren a plus de quatre-vingts ans? Je ne peux pas le croire. > Sophia Loren is more than eighty years old? I cannot believe it. (She is well preserved even without 'canning.')
5. A form of *pouvoir* plus an infinitive is used when asking permission.
Ex. Est-ce que je pourrais emprunter **ton aspirateur**? May I borrow **your vacuum**? (I asked without being 'pushy.')
5a. *Je peux* via inversion is *Puis-je?* Its pronunciation rhymes with the English noun siege. (For which permission is never requested.)
Ex. "Maman, puis-je jouer 'Maman, Puis-je' avec toi?" > "Mom, may I play "Mother May I?" with you?" (It's difficult to refuse a child who asks so 'twicely.')
6. *Peut-être* is <u>maybe/perhaps</u>. When it begins a sentence, the subject pronoun and the verb are inverted.
Ex. Il est peut-être **d'humeur changeante**./Peut-être est-il **d'humeur changeante**. > Perhaps, he is **moody**. (It can 'go either way' with him.)

<u>For *Vouloir* of a Better Verb, There's *Pouvoir*-</u> **Put the correct forms of *vouloir* and *pouvoir* in the blanks. (#2 requires an expression.)**

1. Dorothée _____ voir **le Magicien (The Wizard) d'Oz**, mais elle ne connaît pas la route.
2. M. Clandestin mentionne son revenu _____.
3. Vous ne _____ pas être dans deux villes à la fois.
4. Je _____ faire la différence entre le Pepsi et le Coca.
5. Si tu ne _____ pas aller à la gare seul, nous _____ t'accompagner.
6. Désirée et moi _____ rencontrer les hommes de nos rêves.
7. "_____ -on poser une question à un étranger, Papa?"
8. Kay Nyne aime tes chiens. Elle _____ les garder lorsque tu es à Dordogne.
9. Les petits ne _____ pas toujours expliquer ce qu'ils _____ dire.
10. Il n'y a pas de voitures dans leur **allée-f. (driveway)**. _____ sont-ils en vacances.
11. "Monsieur, je _____ une chambre spacieuse avec deux lits."
12. Sonny Burns et moi ne _____ pas aller à la plage, mais nous _____ nager dans la piscine de nos voisins.

<u>Can with a Plan-</u> **Put the correct forms of *pouvoir* in the blanks, and write a question for each statement. The required interrogatives are in parentheses.**
Ex. Mimi <u>peut</u> voler à Montréal avec Maurice. > Mimi can fly to Montreal with Maurice.
(Avec qui) Avec qui Mimi peut-elle voler à Montréal?

1. Une princesse ne _____ pas assister au bal sans une robe du soir élégante.
(Qui) _____?
2. Dumas et moi _____ visiter le Château d'If à Marseille.

142

(Qu'est-ce que) _____?
3. Nous _____ faire la vaisselle pour aider l'hôtesse.
(Pour qui) _____?
4. Vous _____ voyager de l'Angleterre en France en **aéroglisseur-m. (hovercraft.)**
(Comment) _____?
5. Les fleurs ne _____ pas **pousser (to grow, to push)** sans soleil.
(Qu'est-ce qui) _____?
6. Einstein _____ expliquer la théorie de relativité.
(Qu'est-ce qu') _____?
7. Tu _____ trouver des timbres pour ta collection **en ligne (on line.)**
(Que)_____?
8. Des avions comme l'ancien Concorde _____ aller extrêmement vite.
(Qu'est-ce qui) _____?

_____

DEVOIR - MUST, SHOULD, OUGHT TO, HAVE TO, TO OWE

Like the noun *les devoirs,* the verb *devoir* expresses something that has to be done. It makes its point with five motivating meanings. Knowing how to wield this verb is 'a must.'

Singular	Plural
je dois- I must, should, ought to, have to, owe, do owe, am owing	nous devons- we must, should, ought to, have to, owe, do owe, are owing
tu dois- you must, should, ought to, have to, owe, do owe, are owing	vous devez- you must, should, ought to, have to, owe, do owe, are owing
il/elle doit- he/she/it must, should, ought to, has to, owes, does owe, is owing	ils/elles doivent- they must, should, ought to, have to, owe, do owe, are owing

----

The Persuasive Edge
1. The conjugation of *devoir* **should remind you of the layouts of** *vouloir* **and** *pouvoir.* **Although -oi fits in all the right places, the v in the third person plural keeps** *devoir* **from being a genuine "boot verb." The** *nous* **and** *vous* **forms stay tied to the infinitive.**
2. Because *devoir* **is an independent verb, its conjugated forms are followed by infinitives.**
Ex. "Cendrillon, tu dois rentrer chez toi à minuit." > "Cinderella, you must/ought to/have to be home at midnight." (With 'a personal coach,' she has no excuse for being late.)
An exception: When *devoir* **expresses** **to owe, no verb comes after it.**
Ex. The Lone Ranger doit de l'argent à son cheval blanc. > The Lone Ranger owes some money to his white horse. (But the masked cowboy is known for saying "Hi Ho, Silver," not "I owe Silver.")
3. Direct object pronouns are placed between conjugated forms of *devoir* **and infinitives.**
Ex. Leur chambre à coucher est en désordre. Ils doivent la **nettoyer** maintenant. > Their bedroom is a mess. They have to **clean** it now. (That could easily be 'arranged.')
4. Interesting notes
a. The translation "should" should be reserved for the conditional tense. *Devoir* **ought to, must,**

has to have enough present tense meanings without it.

b. When a credit card is used, *croire* is the collateral. However, a debit card has only *devoir* for a backing. One owes on the spot. (The card and the money are 'swiped' simultaneously.)

c. *Le devoir* is both a written essay and a duty.

A 'Form-er's' Market- Write the correct forms of *vouloir*, *pouvoir* or *devoir* in the spaces.

1. Mlle Sansdoute répond, "Oui de bon gré," parce qu'elle _____ bien le faire.

2. Mollie et moi _____, _____ aller au centre commercial avec vous.

3. Il est très tard. Le petit ne _____-il pas être au lit maintenant?

4. **Le gérant (the manager)** demande, "Je _____ vous aider, Madame?"

5. Vous n'avez pas de choix. Vous _____ manger chez elle dimanche soir.

6. Je fais un voyage en France. Qu'est-ce que vous _____ de Paris?

7. Si tu empruntes mes disques compacts, tu _____ les rendre en bon état.

8. Anne Ziety a peur de voler. Elle _____, _____, _____ faire ses vacances tout près.

9. Je ne _____ pas le répéter, mais je ne _____ pas garder ce secret.

10. Si nous _____ réussir, nous _____ faire de notre mieux.

'Fulfilling Obligations'- Circle the letters of the correct responses to complete the sentences.

1. Polly Tesse a de telles bonnes manières. Elle pense qu'elle doit ____.
a. remercier tout le monde pour tout   b. être d'humeur changeante
c. faire la connaissance des mendiants   d. faire nettoyer tout

2. Si vous ne pouvez pas lever cette boîte lourde, vous devez ____.
a. la goûter   b. emprunter un aspirateur   c. trouver une autre en ligne   d. la pousser

3. On qui ne veut pas avoir de problèmes avec la police doit ____.
a. frotter les yeux doucement   b. obéir à toutes les lois   c. garder ses objets d'époque
d. rester dans sa propre allée

4. Dan Gereux et ses copins patinent à planche à roulettes dans la rue. Ils doivent ____.
a. jouer aux boules là   b. savoir leur adresse   c. faire attention aux autos
d. donner le journal au voisin

5. Mme Mains-Pleines fait trop à la fois. Ne doit-elle pas ____?
a. croire à ses rêves   b. rendre grâce à quelqu'un   c. être à l'heure pour son vol
d. finir une chose avant de commencer une autre

6. Je n'ai pas l'intention de le voir encore, mais je dois à M. Tenace ____.
a. l'espoir d'une vie pleine   b. **la courtoisie (the courtesy)** d'une réponse
c. de bons vœux pour l'avenir   d. tout l'argent dans mon compte

7. Les adolescents doivent passer les fêtes d'hiver avec des gens ennuyeux, et ____.
a. ce n'est pas leur devoir de les attendre   b. ils préfèrent jouer aux billes dans la neige
c. les jeunes ne veulent pas avoir cent ans   d. ils n'ont pas envie de le faire

8. Qu'est-ce que la jeune femme doit faire pour **attirer (to attract)** l'attention des hommes qui ____?
a. sont toujours autrement occupés   b. veulent tapoter leurs estomacs
c. n'ont jamais l'intention de travailler   d. savent pourquoi elles sont seules

LES COMPLÉMENTS DES OBJETS INDIRECTS - Indirect Objects

Indirect objects relate <u>to whom</u> or <u>to what</u> something is done. English uses the same words for both direct and indirect object pronouns. Consequently, we end up us buying her, offering you and cooking them. With their more defined method for handling indirect object pronouns, the French have a solution for such awkward encounters.

Indirect Object Pronouns

<u>Singular</u>	<u>Plural</u>
me (m') - to me	nous - to us
te (t') - to you	vous - to you
lui - to him, to her, to it	leur - to them

The Direct Route to Indirect Object Pronouns

1. The direct object pronouns *me, te, nous* **and** *vous* **reappear on the above list. However, since they are indirect object pronouns,** <u>to</u> **precedes their translations.**
Ex. Le vendeur d'autos **d'occasion** te vend **de la vraie camelote**. > The **used** car salesman is selling **a real piece of junk** <u>to you</u>. (If he can sell you, the car and his reputation will only 'go downhill.')
Ex. Thierry est **contrarié**, mais il nous prête une valise **de toute façon**. > Thierry is **annoyed,** but he is lending a suitcase <u>to us</u> **anyway**. (He is eager 'to send them packing.')

2. *Lui* **means** <u>to him</u>, <u>to her</u> **and** <u>to it</u>. **The last translation refers to animals.**
Ex. Anne Formatique veut lui rendre l'ordinateur. > Anne Formatique wants to return the computer <u>to him/to her</u>.

3. *Leur***, the possessive adjective** <u>their</u>**, is dually an indirect object pronoun meaning** <u>to them</u>**. It applies to people and to animals.**
Ex. Que leur donnez-vous pour le Noël? > What are you giving <u>to them</u> for Christmas?

4. Even with the option of gender for *lui* **and** *leur***, a listener can correctly identify the sex of the individual(s) being discussed. As pronouns replace nouns, the gender was previously assigned.** (The *lui* and *leur* unisex attire is 'a cover-up.')
Exs. Pierre montre **la jolie affiche** à Emmanuelle. > Pierre shows **the** pretty **poster** to Emmanuelle.
    Pierre <u>lui</u> montre **la jolie affiche**. > Pierre shows **the** pretty **poster** <u>to her</u>.
In the second set of sentences, the pretty poster remains, but Emmanuelle is replaced.

5. Indirect object pronouns usually precede conjugated verbs as well as infinitives.
Exs. Le cow-boy chante seulement une chanson aux chevaux. > The cowboy sings only one song to the horses.
    Le cow-boy <u>leur</u> chantent seulement une chanson. > The cowboy sings only one song <u>to them</u>. (Others may not be within his 'range.')
Exs. Pourquoi ce cyclops-là ne veut-il pas parler à l'autre? > Why doesn't that cyclops want to speak to the other one?
    Pourquoi ce cyclops-la ne veut-il pas <u>lui</u> parler? > Why doesn't this cyclops want to speak <u>to it</u>? (They may not 'see eye to eye.')

6. Indirect objects refer only to people, characters and animals. However, direct objects, which apply to living and nonliving nouns and pronouns, are 'wanted dead or alive.'

7a. A select group of verbs including *avoir, entendre, étudier, fermer, guérir, voir, croire, vouloir,* and *pouvoir* are accompanied only by direct objects. One who finds someone "to close for him" has opened up an idiom.

7b. Verbs with <u>to</u> and <u>for</u> in their translations also take only direct objects. Some examples are *attendre, chercher, écouter, payer* **and** *regarder*.

Ex. Rocky les attend pour longtemps à **la falaise**. > Rocky waits for them for a longtime on **the cliff**. (He is probably 'on edge.')

7c. Verbs followed by *à* **such as** *obéir à, désobéir à-* **to disobey,** *répondre à, ressembler à-* **to look like/to resemble and** *téléphoner à* **require indirect objects.**

Exs. Le pauvre Slash ressemble à **un tueur** bien-connu. > Poor Slash looks like **a well-known killer**.
    Le pauvre Slash lui ressemble. > Poor Slash looks like him. (And has no girls 'to take out.')

8. When <u>for</u> means <u>on behalf of</u>, *pour* **+ an object of a preposition is used.**

Ex. Qu'est-ce que Mme Defarge **tricote** pour vous? > What is Mrs. Defarge **knitting** for you? (Her famous 'yarn' is revealed in British and in French history.)

Ex. Je ne sais pas si tu dois choisir un téléphone cellulaire pour lui. > I do not know if you ought to choose a cell phone for him. (He will have 'to make the call.')

9. The majority of verbs take direct and indirect object pronouns. With both types in the same sentence, the former is inanimate; the latter is living.

<u>A note</u>: **You will soon learn how to put French direct and indirect object pronouns together in one sentence.** (It is not necessary to show <u>it to you</u> now.)

Impersonal Expressions with Indirect Object Pronouns

Impersonal expressions have <u>it</u> as subjects and third person singular verb forms. Two familiar ones are *Il neige.* **> It snows, does snow, is snowing and** *Il pleut.* **> It rains, does rain, is raining.** (A person can 'reign' only if he/she is a king or a queen.)

Indirect Object Pronouns and Impersonal Relationships

1. *S'il te plaît* **and** *s'il vous plaît* **translate literally as "If it is pleasing to you." The speaker uses an indirect approach to make the request.**

2. Il faut- It is necessary. The subject of the English sentence becomes the indirect object of the French one.

Ex. Il nous faut changer nos coiffeurs fréquemment. > We need (It is necessary for us) to change our hairstyles frequently. ('Permanent' ones are so passé.)

3. Il reste- It remains. When it is conjugated, *rester* **means to stay/to remain. As an impersonal verb, it is preceded by an indirect object pronoun and 'left' in the third person singular.**

Ex. Il nous reste seulement **les os** de **la dinde**. > We have only **turkey bones** left. ('Its remains to be seen.')

4. *Manquer-* **to miss, to be missing/to be lacking can be conjugated or have only an impersonal form. Interpreted as "to miss/not to get to," its synonym is** *rater*.

Ex. Jay Z et Kanye manquent beaucoup d'argent parce qu'ils ratent leur concert. > Jay Z and Kanye 'are out a lot of money' because they are missing their concert.

4a. Third person forms of *manquer* **can follow indirect object pronouns.**

Ex. Il lui manque **les moyens** de ... > He/She is lacking **the means** to ...

146

4b. Possibly the two most confusing French phrases that native English speakers encounter are *Je te manque.* **> You miss me., and** *Tu me manques.* **> I miss you.** (It seems to be a case of mixed emotions.) **Yet, if they're translated as "You are missing to me," and "I am missing to you," the order seems more logical.** (It just involves a little indirect *manquer* business.)

Direct, Indirect or Reject- Label the statements *vrai* **or** *faux.*

_____ 1. Direct and indirect object pronouns are not the same in English.

_____ 2. *Nous* and *vous* are subject as well as direct and indirect object pronouns.

_____ 3. To can always be translated before indirect object pronouns.

_____ 4. Direct and indirect object pronouns cannot precede infinitives.

_____ 5. Direct and indirect object pronouns do not agree with subjects and verbs.

_____ 6. All verbs can take both direct and indirect object pronouns.

_____ 7. French indirect object pronouns refer only to things.

_____ 8. Verbs followed by *à* require indirect object pronouns.

_____ 9. *Il faut* and *avoir besoin de* are close in meaning.

_____ 10. Forms of *rester* and *manquer* cannot follow indirect object pronouns.

_____ 11. *Je te manque* translates as "I miss you."

_____ 12. In an impersonal expression, the subject of the English sentence is the indirect object of the French one.

'To Whom It May Concern'- Replace the underlined phrases with indirect object pronouns, and rewrite the sentences.
Ex. Cela fait égal <u>à Igor</u>. > (That is all the same to Igor.) > Cela <u>lui</u> fait égal.

1. Je pense que mon petit ami ressemble <u>à Robert Pattinson</u>. _____
_____.

2. Donnes-tu ces vêtements-ci <u>aux pauvres</u>? _____
_____?

3. La grand-mère chante <u>au bébé</u> quand il pleure. _____
_____.

4. M. Jettison vend de la vraie camelote <u>aux gens naïfs</u>. _____
_____.

5. Le client contrarié va parler <u>au gérant</u>. _____
_____.

6. Quelquefois, il faut parler <u>aux étrangers</u>. _____
_____.

7. Les Aufour veulent bien rendre visite <u>à M. Dindon</u>. _____
_____.

8. On doit montrer de la courtoisie surtout **<u>aux vieillards-m. (to the elderly)</u>**. _____
_____.

9. Il reste <u>à Gaspiller</u> cinquante euros. _____.
10. Combien d'argent manque <u>aux étudiants</u> pour payer **le loyer (the rent)**? _____
_____?

147

'Being Indirectly Involved'- Use the correct forms of the verbs from the following list to translate the exercise below: aller, avoir, devoir, donner, être, expliquer, manquer, montrer, parler, prêter, rester, répondre à, téléphoner à, vouloir

1. The Frenchmen speaks to me slowly. _____.

2. Who gives you (informal form) so many unique gifts? _____
_____?

3. Her son phones her almost every day. _____
_____.

4. Odette owes me so much money. _____.

5. We have two days left in Paris. _____.

6. Why isn't he answering you (formal form)? _____?

7. I am going to explain the homework to him. _____
_____.

8. Rie Skai is ashamed to show the photos to us. _____
_____.

9. Ruby and Opal do not want to lend their jewelry to her. _____
_____.

10. We miss them when they are not here. _____
_____.

Revermont (the Jura Region)

DIRE - TO SAY, TO TELL

Dire is the first in a group of popular verbs that has been waiting for you. It has so much to say and so much to tell directly and indirectly. Once you are familiar with this verb, you'll be able to ask, "How do you say ___?" You won't have 'to hunt for *dire*.'

Singular	Plural
je dis- I say, do say, am saying, I tell, do tell, am telling	nous disons- we say, do say, are saying, we tell, do tell, are telling
tu dis- you say, do say, are saying, you tell, do tell, are telling	vous dites- you say, do say, are saying, you tell, do tell, are telling,
il/elle dit- he/she/it says, does say, is saying, he/she/it tells, does tell, is telling	ils/elles disent- they say, so say, are saying, they tell, do tell, are telling

----

'Targeting *Dire*'

1. All singular forms of *dire* sound the same. -<u>Is</u>, -<u>is</u>, -<u>it</u>, -<u>it</u> a coincidence that *faire, voir, croire, savoir, connaître, devoir* and *dire* form 'a single file'?
2. *Dire* is the third verb mentioned that does not end with -<u>ez</u> in the *vous* form. If you recall the others, *vous <u>êtes</u> très intelligent, et vous <u>faites</u> attention.*
3. Because the infinitive means <u>to say</u> and <u>to tell</u>, each conjugated form has six translations.
Ex. Les pauses dans son explication nous disent beaucoup. > The pauses in his explanation tell us/do tell us/are telling us/say to us, do say to us/are saying to us a lot. (Truer words were never broken.)
4. Forms of *dire* can take direct and indirect objects.
Ex. Pouvez-vous me dire la route à la Rue Sésame? > Can you tell (to) me the way to Sesame Street? (Would you like the directions spelled out?)

What *Dire* Has to Say for Itself

1. **Comment dit-on en français .....?** > How does one say in French ....?
2. **Ce nom me dit quelque chose.** > That name 'rings a bell.' (Is it, by any chance, Quasimodo?)
3. **dire des bêtises**- to talk nonsense (The speaker might 'be-teased' about doing so.)
4. **Cela va sans dire.** > That goes without saying. (Too late! It has already been mentioned.)
5. **pour tout dire:** This phrase is our equivalent of <u>frankly speaking</u>.
6. **C'est-à-dire**- "That is to say" is closely related to *vouloir dire*- to mean. "Take your choice!," *comme on dit*- as one says.

'*Dire*, Could I Have a Word with You?'- Fill in the blanks with the correct forms of *dire*.

1. "C'est si bon! Les amoureux le _____ en France."
2. Pourquoi me _____-tu **ces rumeurs-f. (these/those rumors)**?
3. Comment le _____-vous en français?
4. Quand Betty nous _____ des bêtises, nous ne lui répondons pas.
5. Il est plus facile de le _____ que le faire!
6. Vous ne devez pas croire tout ce qu'ils vous _____.
7. Pour tout _____, nous lui _____ la même chose constamment.
8. Washington _____, "Je ne peux pas _____**un mensonge (a lie)**."

9. Monsieur Franc _____ franchement ce qu'il veut _____.

10. On _____, "Cela va sans _____," si on est d'accord avec vous.

LIRE - TO READ

It is not necessary *lire* between the lines to know why this verb is placed directly after *dire*. The two are very closely related in form and in function. But like all family members, they do have their differences.

Here's an accurate reading of *lire*:

<u>Singular</u>	<u>Plural</u>
je lis- I read, do read, am reading	**nous lisons- we read, do read, are reading**
tu lis- you read, do read, are reading	**vous lisez- you read, do read, are reading**
il/elle lit- he/ she reads, does read,	**ils/elles lisent- they read, do read,**
is reading	**are reading**

<u>**'For Your Reading Enjoyment'**</u>

1. When the first letters of *dire* and *lire* are exchanged, their conjugations look almost identical. <u>Almost</u> is the key word; the *vous* form of *lire* ends with -<u>ez</u>. Besides, *lire* books an <u>s</u> throughout the plural. While conjugated forms of *lire* have three meanings, those of *dire* have six.

2. The third person singular, *lit*, can be read in <u>literature</u>.

Ex. Lise lit au lit. > Lise reads in bed.

3. The *Lire* family accepts both direct and indirect objects.

Ex. Lisez-vous **les comptines de Mère Oie** aux enfants? > Do you read **the Mother Goose nursery rhymes** to the children? Oui, je les lis. > Yes, I read them., Oui, je leur lis. > Yes, I read to them.

<u>**Interesting notes**</u>

a. *La fleur-de-lis*, the lily flower, was originally a symbol of French royalty. Seen worldwide, it is the main feature of Quebec's flag.

b. *La lecture* is the reading. *Le lecture* and *la lectrice* are the readers.

Ex. Un lecture lit les lignes d'un roman. **Un diseur/une diseuse de bonne aventure** lit les lignes de vos **paumes**. > A reader reads the lines of a novel. **A fortune teller** reads the lines of your **palms**.

'A Good Read'- Circle the letters of the correct answers to complete the sentences.

1. Il ne faut pas croire tout ce que (qu') _____.

a. je vous dis   b. on veut dire   c. vous lisez   d. vous avez dans les mains

2. Colin reconnaît les lettres de l'alphabet, mais _____.

a. sa mère connaît plusieurs comptines   b. il aime dire des mensonges

c. ses livres manquent des pages   d. il ne peut pas lire encore

3. La lecture, le jardinage et **la peinture (the painting)** sont des activités _____.

a. qui attirent des tueurs
                                              b. que les gens seuls aiment faire

c. qui doivent payer le loyer
                                          d. qu'on voit toujours sur les affiches

4. Lowen Cash emprunte des livres de la bibliothèque ou il _____.

a. les lit de toute façon
                                         b. les trouve dans une librairie d'occasion

c. fait des collages des journaux
                                d. remarque qu'ils manquent des chapitres

5. Comment peut-on lui donner **un abonnement (a subscription)** si on ne sait pas _____?

a. quelle sorte de lecture lui intéresse
                      b. attirer l'attention de quelqu'un

c. pourquoi son nom nous dit quelque chose
               d. si elle dit des bêtises

6. Cristelle Balle veut savoir son avenir. Ainsi, elle _____.

a. pose des questions aux étoiles dans le ciel
         b. assiste aux cours de l'informatique

c. rend visite chez la diseuse de la bonne aventure
      d. lit un tas de revues de science-fiction

ÉCRIRE - TO WRITE

Écrire, the final 'communication verb,' enables us to express our points of view creatively. See how the conjugated forms of *écrire* 'correspond' to one another and to other verbs!

<u>Singular</u>	<u>Plural</u>
j'écris- I write, do write, am writing	nous écrivons- we write, do write, are writing
tu écris- you write, do write, are writing	vous écrivez- you write, do write, are writing
il/elle écrit- he/she writes, does write, is writing	ils/elles écrivent- they write, do write, are writing

---

'Written Confirmation'

1. Like *dire, lire* and several other irregular verbs, *écrire* includes <u>-is</u>, <u>-is</u> and <u>-it</u> at the end of its singular forms. Along with *devoir, pouvoir and savoir*, *écrire* has a <u>v</u> throughout the plural. However, that consonant is not present in its infinitive. (The <u>v</u> checks in later.)

2. By replacing the <u>é</u> of *écrire* with an <u>s</u>, you see the relationship to <u>scribble</u> and <u>scribe</u>. The é to s switch makes most French-English cognates seem less *étrange*.

3. *Écrire* takes both direct and indirect objects.

Ex. Pourquoi ta cousine de Philadelphie ne t'écrit-elle pas en stylo? > Why doesn't your cousin from Philadelphia write to you in pen? (Maybe, none are available in 'Pencilvania.')

4. Although <u>to write</u> and <u>to describe</u> do not look alike, *écrire* and *décrire* and their conjugations are only one letter apart.

Ex. L'étudiante pauvre écrit un poème à ses copains. Elle décrit pourquoi elle ne peut pas encore les **rembourser**. > The poor student writes a poem to her pals. She describes why she can not **pay** them **back** yet. (She titled it "Money Ode.")

5. *Écrire un petit mot à quelqu'un*- **to write a note to someone** (The indirect object preceded by *à* helps 'spread the news.')

6. *L'écriture*- **the handwriting** is related to <u>scripture</u>.

7. *L'écrivain* is the male writer; *la femme écrivain* is the female writer. (In the second translation, the feminine gender is noted, but the 'male' still gets through.)

'Open Communication'- Complete the sentences with the correct forms of *dire, lire* or *écrire*.

1. M. et Mme Branchés _____ le Monde tous les dimanches.
2. Sol Ésable _____ toujours des cartes postales lorsqu'il est en vacances.
3. Comment _____-vous en français "I-Pod?"
4. Tout le monde _____ les fables de La Fontaine.
5. Tu peux _____ un petit mot à ton prof si tu as peur de lui parler.
6. Comme on _____ en français, "C'est la vie!"
7. Je sais bien qu'ils ne nous _____ pas la vérité.
8. Jeanne Tille a du temps libre. Elle va à l'hôpital _____ aux malades.
9. Ses enfants lui manquent. Malheureusement, ils ne lui _____ pas.
10. Nous pouvons _____ les phrases que Claire Ment _____.
11. Di Rien ne _____ pas qui t' _____ **les étiquettes-f. (the notes)**.
12. _____-vous simplement "merci" à une hôtesse, ou lui _____-vous **une carte de remerciements (a thank you note)** aussi?

'Don't Miss the Connection!'- Match the letters to the numbers to form complete sentences.

_____ 1. Le petit ami d'Aimée

_____ 2. Ton étiquette manque des mots

_____ 3. Ma mère a un abonnement à Vogue

_____ 4. Nous disons que tu as tort,

_____ 5. Dans sa lettre romantique à Thérèse,

_____ 6. Beauregard sait où sa sœur cache **la clé (the key)**,

_____ 7. Je vais leur écrire aujourd'hui

_____ 8. Tu peux lire les mots,

_____ 9. Quand ma petite nièce dit "un livre,"

_____ 10. Anne Formée écoute les nouvelles,

_____ 11. On ne peut pas croire quelqu'un

_____ 12. L'élève écrit avec un crayon

_____ 13. Lis-tu mes courriers électroniques?

_____ 14. Sleuth lit des romans **d'espion (spy)**

_____ 15. On doit faire attention avant de signer un contrat.

_____ 16. Vous écrivez un petit mot

_____ 17. Tu dois avoir mon numéro de téléphone

_____ 18. Le petit garçon est très fier.

_____ 19. On ne dit pas en français

_____ 20. Mai Tresse dit à la mère que son fils lit assez bien,

A. mais sais-tu ce qu'ils veulent dire?

B. parce qu'il fait tant de fautes.

C. Il sait écrire son nom.

D. et elle lit le New York Times aussi.

E. Il faut lire entre les lignes.

F. "French toast."

G. Ainsi, je ne peux pas le lire entièrement.

H. ou des mystères par Agathe Christie.

I. lui dit toujours qu'il l'aime.

J. sur chaque carte de Noël.

K. je lui lis un conte.

L. et le méchant garçon lit **son journal intime (her diary)**

M. parce que tu m'appelles souvent.

N. mais évidemment, tu n'es pas d'accord.

O. parce qu'ils attendent des nouvelles pour longtemps.

P. qui dit souvent les mensonges.

Q. et qu'il va arriver à écrire mieux bientôt.

R. Je n'ai jamais de réponses.

S. Nous aimons lire cette revue ensemble.

T. Claude écrit qu'elle lui manque.

LES IMPÉRATIFS - COMMANDS

Read this please! Consider these first two sentence as previews of coming attractions! Though the subject <u>you</u> is not expressed, it is understood via the imperative form of the verb. Concisely stated, grammar's 'command performances' are brief.
See how *parler* **speaks for itself!**

Parler à l'Impératif

tu **form - Parle français! > Speak French!**
nous **form - Parlons français! > Let's speak French!**
vous **form - Parlez français! > Speak French!**

The Order of Commands

1. The <u>s</u> is dropped from the *tu* **forms of all regular -<u>er</u> verbs and** *aller***. Furthermore, irregular verbs including** *accueillir*- **to welcome,** *couvrir*- **to cover,** *offrir*- **to offer and** *ouvrir*- **to open are conjugated like regular -<u>er</u> verbs and are without an <u>s</u> in their** *tu* **forms.**
Ex. Reese, accueille les invités! > Greet the guests!
Ex. Joue une chanson sur le piano! > Play a song on the piano!
Ex. Offre un bonbon à chaque invité! > Offer a candy to each guest!
Ex. Va à ta chambre! > Go to your room!
(One of 'Reese's pieces' was all they could take!)
<u>An exception</u>: **When followed by a pronoun, the imperative** *tu* **form of** *aller* **is** *vas.*
2. Most regular and irregular -<u>ir</u> and -<u>re</u> verbs keep the <u>s</u> in their *tu* **form commands. They are the same as the conjugated forms but with the subjects understood.** (You can take advantage of not having to explain <u>yourself</u>.)
Ex. Remplis les mots qui manquent! > Fill in the words that are missing!
Ex. Vois ce film-là avec moi, s'il te plaît! > See that film with me, please!
Ex. Attends ta sœur ici! > Wait for your sister here!
Ex. Fais de ton mieux, Tante Tente! > Do your best Aunt Tente!
3. First person plural imperatives end with -<u>ons</u>. Translated as "let's" plus a verb, they are the *nous* **forms without that subject pronoun.** (Just a 'we' bit of a change.)
Ex. Alain, allons au Centre Pompidou! > Alain, let's go to the Pompidou Center!
Ex. Achetons des affiches à ce musée-là! > Let's buy some posters at that museum!
Ex. Disons à Art quelle heure nous allons! > Let's tell Art what time we are going! (Alain does not want 'to leave Art hanging.')
4. The *vous* **form, used when speaking to one or more individuals, is typically recognized by its -<u>ez</u> ending.**
Ex. Madame, montrez les appartements **disponibles** à ma fille, s'il vous plaît! > Madame, show the **available** apartments to my daughter, please! (After that, she is 'on her own.")
Ex. S'il vous plaît monsieur, vendez ces livres anciens-ci pour moi! > Please sir, sell these old books for me! (The deal might include 'a binding agreement.')
5. Adding *s'il te plaît/s'il vous plaît* **at the beginning or end of imperatives shows** *politesse.* (And gives the speaker's request less of a commanding tone.)
6. *Donc* **with multiple meanings is sometimes added for emphasis.**

Ex. Pensez donc! > (Just) think!

Ex. Dis donc, comment vas-tu le payer? > Say (now), how are you going to pay for it?

7. A negative imperative includes *ne (n')* before the verb and *pas* or an alternate negation after it. ("Thou shall not" in the Ten Commandments is not an imperative. The subject was included because Moses did not trust that 'you understood.')

Ex. N'**oubliez** pas **le point d'exclamation** après chaque impératif! > Don't **forget the exclamation mark** after each command!

Ex. Ne fais jamais des affaires avec M. Escroquer! > Never do business with Mr. Escroquer!

8. Direct and indirect object pronouns follow verbs in affirmative commands.

Ex. Coupons-les! > Let's cut them! (The French verb has a 'redeeming' feature.)

Ex. Poussez la porte pour l'ouvrir et **tirez**-la pour la fermer. > Push the door to open it, and **pull** it to close it!

Ex. Prêtez-nous vos oreilles! > Lend us your ears! (We never hear what happens after that.)

<u>An important note</u>: In affirmative commands, *me* becomes *moi*, and *te* changes to *toi*.

Ex. Rencontre-moi à St. Louis, Louis! > Meet me in St. Louis, Louis!

9. Object pronouns go in front of verbs in negative commands. (French sentences are accustomed 'to following' this order.')

Ex. Ne me pose pas de questions! > Don't ask me any questions!

Ex. Ne lui faisons pas une offre pour cette voiture d'occasion! > Let's not make him an offer for that used car! (They might 'be stuck with it.')

Ex. **Le gâteau** pour les chiens? Ne leur donnez jamais de sucre! > **Cake** for dogs? Never give sugar to them!

10. Most imperative forms of *avoir* and *être* reappear in their present subjunctive conjugations. <u>Let's have</u> them now, and <u>let's be</u> prepared!

<u>Avoir</u>	<u>Être</u>
aie	sois
ayons	soyons
ayez	soyez

10a. Each *avoir* command form contains a clipped long <u>a</u> sound.

Ex. Ayez **l'appoint** quand vous montez dans un autobus! > Have the **exact change** when you get on a bus! (Or you won't 'sit well with' the other passengers.)

10b. *Sois* has the same pronunciation as *la soie*- the silk. (If you would like more material, put an <u>r</u> in front of *ayons*!)

10c. Plural imperative forms of *avoir* and *être* end with -<u>yons</u> and -<u>yez</u>.

Ex. **Ayez la bonté** de répondre, s'il vous plaît! > **Kindly** answer, please! **It literally says, "Have the goodness to answer, please!"** (The request is seen in French 'sign' language.)

Ex. Ne soyons pas les derniers arriver au match de base-ball! > Let's not be the last ones to arrive at the baseball game! (They might miss the first ones 'out.')

Ex. Sois/soyez **le bienvenu!** > Feel **welcome!** (That applies to <u>you</u> and to <u>you</u>.)

'Command Posts'- Label the statements *vrai* or *faux*.

_____ 1. Subjects are reflected in the verb endings of imperative sentences.

_____ 2. The final s is dropped in the *tu* form of -er, -ir and -re verbs.

_____ 3. There is no s in the imperative *tu* form of verbs conjugated like -er verbs.

_____ 4. The *vous* command form is always directed toward plural listeners.

_____ 5. All *vous* form commands end with -ez.

_____ 6. The -ons imperative ending translates as "let's."

_____ 7. All *nous* form commands end with -ons.

_____ 8. *Donc* precedes an imperative to add emphasis to the verb.

_____ 9. Object pronouns precede verbs in affirmative and in negative commands.

_____ 10. Plural imperative forms of *avoir* and *être* contain a y.

'Taking Orders'- Put the verbs in the forms indicated! Then, translate the commands!

1. déjeuner (nous) _____ dans un restaurant japonais aujourd'hui!

_____!

2. goûter (tu) Piet, _____ un petit morceau avant de couper une tranche!

_____!

3. blanchir (vous) Ne _____ pas les chaussettes dans l'eau tiède, s'il vous plaît!

_____!

4. rendre (tu) _____ les vêtements que tu empruntes, s'il te plaît!

_____!

5. aller (nous) _____ chercher des affaires à Bon Marché!

_____!

6. faire (vous) _____ un feu dans la cheminée M. Bûche, s'il vous plaît!

_____!

7. offrir (tu) _____ l'appoint au passager qui le cherche, Monet!

_____!

8. décrire (vous) " _____ le tueur!" le détective leur dit.

_____!

9. tomber (tu) Ne _____ pas de la falaise, Cliff!

_____!

10. tirer (tu) Ne _____ pas les cheveux de ta sœur, Harry!

_____!

11. interrompre (tu) Rudy, ne m'_____ pas lorsque je te parle!

_____!

12. ouvrir (vous) N'_____ jamais le courrier de quelqu'un d'autre!

_____!

13. avoir (vous) _____ la bonté de me trouver une chaise disponible, mon bon homme!

_____!

14. être, avoir (tu) _____ comme le lion brave et _____ du courage!

Write It Right!- Translate the following commands!

1. Don't cry my little one! _____ !
2. Wear them (vous) to the dance! _____ !
3. Let's go to Montmartre by subway! _____ !
4. Don't stay (*vous*) at the mall the whole afternoon! _____

_____ !
5. Carrie, pack (*tu*) your bags now! _____ !
6. It is raining. Let's go home right away! _____

_____ !
7. Cut (*tu*) it carefully! _____ !
8. Don't **touch (toucher)** (*vous*) them, please! _____

_____ !
9. Don't write (*tu*) on the walls, Marc! _____ !
10. Be here *(vous)* on time, please! _____ !
11. Pay attention (*vous*) to the wet **tile floors (les sols-m.)**! _____

_____ !
12. Daddy, read some nursery rhymes to us, please! _____

_____ !
13. Don't **teach (enseigner)** (*tu*) any bad words to her! _____

_____ !
14. Don't forget (*vous*) to say, "Please, Thank you, and You're welcome! " _____

_____ !

_____

LES NÉGATIFS FRANÇAIS - French Negatives

As *ne ... pas* is no stranger, *ne ... plus* no longer poses a problem, and *ne ... jamais* is not a term you have never seen, you have 'a heads up' on French negatives. *Ne* plus an adverb of negation is considered a unit. Double negatives result in a positive. (Of that you can be sure.)

Negative Forms

ne ... pas- not
ne ... pas du tout- not at all
ne ... point- not, not at all
ne ... guère- hardly, scarcely
ne ... jamais- never

ne ... ni ... ni- neither nor
ne ... personne- nobody, no one
ne ... plus- no more, no longer
ne ... que- only
ne ... rien- nothing

'Negative Influences'
1. A single word is almost always enough to make an English sentence negative. That is *ne pas* so in French. With few exceptions, each part of a negation surrounds a conjugated verb.
Ex. Don Moitout ne remercie jamais Jénée Reuse pour sa bonté. > Don Moitout never thanks Jénée Reuse for her kindness. (What does he 'take her for'?)
2. Most negative terms are adverbs. They express the limited or non-existent action of verbs.
Ex. Mmes **Additionner** et **Soustraire** ne veulent plus enseigner les mathématiques. > Mrs. **Add** and Mrs. **Substract** do not want to teach mathematics any more/any longer. (The experience 'has done a number on' them.)

Getting Something Positive from Negatives
1. ne ... guère- hardly, scarcely: Pronounced like *la guerre*- the war, *ne ... guère* is synonym for *à peine*.
Ex. Il y a encore des tranches de Camembert et de Brie, mais il n'y a guère de Gruyère. > There are still some slices of Camembert and Brie, but there is hardly any Gruyère.
2. ne ... jamais- never (The *mais* inside *jamais* does not allow for an exception.)
Ex. Il ne faut jamais dire jamais! > "Never say never!" (Yet, the proverbs state it twice.)
3. ne ... ni ... ni- neither ... nor: *Ne/N'* precedes the verb, and *ni* goes before each noun or adjective. Speakers are concerned neither with separate translations for *ni* nor with the order of the words after it.
Ex. Pourquoi son bébé pleure-t-il? Il n'a ni faim ni sommeil. > Why is her baby crying? He's neither hungry nor sleepy? (She'll find out 'in the end.')
4. *Ne ... pas du tout* and *ne ... point*, both translated as "not at all," are stronger than *ne ... pas*.
Ex. Leur absence ne la **gêne** pas du tout. > Their absence does not **bother** her at all. ("Let bye gones be bye-gones!")
5. ne ... personne- nobody, no one: Notice that the negation starts and ends with *ne!*
Ex. Ne dites à personne que son appartement est en désordre! > Don't tell anyone that his/her apartment is a mess! (He/She might just want 'to let it go.')
6. ne ... que- only: With *seulement* for a synonym, *ne ... que* is not the only translation for only.
Ex. Notre mère dit qu'elle n'a que deux mains. > Our mother says that she has only two hands. (But there is always one 'left.')

7. ne ... rien- nothing, not anything: Used so often, there is 'much ado about nothing.' A prime example is *de rien* as a reply to *merci beaucoup*.

Ex. "Qui ne risque rien gagne rien." > "Nothing ventured nothing gained." (Nothing is not lost with either translation.)

A very important note: *Personne ne* and *Rien ne* are subjects of sentences. Notice the switched word order! The negative phrases take the third person singular of verbs.

Ex. Personne ne peut disputer **le juge,** et rien ne va changer son opinion. > Nobody can dispute **the judge**, and nothing is going to change his opinion. (The order of the 'sentences' can't be 'reversed.')

8. A negative phrase usually precedes an infinitive. *Ne personne,* **which surrounds the verb, is an exception.**

Ex. **Cette commère** décide de ne rien dire. **That gossip** decides to say nothing/not to say anything. (Well, isn't that something?)

Ex. **Cette commère** décide de ne dire à personne. > **That gossip** decides not to tell anyone. (Usually, nobody is an exception for the busybody!')

Another Side of Negatives

1. As a one-word response, *jamais* **means never.**

Ex. Est-ce que Patience **crie après les gosses**? Jamais! > Does Patience **scream at the kids**? Never! (Since the French expression translates as "to scream after," the kids can yell first.)

2. When not preceded by *ne* **in a sentence,** *jamais* **is ever.**

Ex. Si tu as jamais l'occasion, tu dois le faire. > If you ever have the opportunity, you ought to do it! (And if opportunity knocks unexpectedly on your door, you should check out 'the opening.')

3. As a one-word response, *personne* **means nobody/no one.**

Ex. Qui connaît ce peintre **ermite**? Personne. > Who knows that **hermit** painter? Nobody. (Even so, he may have 'a good self-image.')

4. *Pas* **is used without** *ne* **in short phrases such as** *pas encore*- **not yet,** *pas moi*- **not me,** *pas vrai*- **not true and** *pas possible*.

Ex. Pas de **circulation** à Paris? Pas possible! > No **traffic** in Paris. Not possible! (People sometimes take this 'alternate route.')

An interesting aside: *Le pas* **is the step. A bilingual term is** *un faux pas*- **a mistake (a false step).**

Au Contraire, Mon Frère- **Put the letter beside the number of its antonym.**

_____ 1. presque jamais	A. plaire
_____ 2. tout le monde	B. ne ... jamais
_____ 3. tout neuf	C. pas du tout
_____ 4. tous les deux	D. moins de
_____ 5. plus qu'il est nécessaire	E. vendre
_____ 6. ajouter	F. souvent
_____ 7. toutes les choses	G. pas encore
_____ 8. plus de	H. ne ... personne
_____ 9. déjà	I. à peine assez
_____ 10. tout le temps	J. fermer

_____ 11. pousser
_____ 12. ouvrir
_____ 13. gêner
_____ 14. acheter
_____ 15. extrêmement

K. ne ... rien
L. d'occasion
M. tirer
N. ni l'un ni l'autre
O. soustraire

'Say It Isn't So!'- Using the underlined words and phrases as a reference, rewrite the sentences *au négatif.* They will include *ne … guère, ne … jamais, ne ... ni … ni, ne … que, ne … personne, ne ... rien, pas encore, Personne ne* and *Rien ne*

Ex. Si nous parlons à voix basse, est-ce que Turner Tupp entend <u>tout</u>? > Si nous parlons à voix basse, est-ce que Turner Tupp <u>n</u>'entend <u>rien</u>?

1. M. Gomme fait des faux pas <u>fréquemment</u>. _____

_____ .

2. <u>Tout le monde</u> sait tout. _____ .

3. Tu penses que <u>tout</u> est impossible! _____ .

4. Est-ce que Bonnie et Ben font <u>toujours</u> de leur mieux? _____

_____ ?

5. Des invités sont <u>déjà</u> ici. _____ .

6. Il y a <u>une foule</u> devant le Planète Hollywood. _____

_____ .

7. Fabrice <u>et</u> moi savons tricoter et **coudre (to sew)**. _____

_____ .

8. <u>Quelqu'un</u> a la clé à la maison de l'ermite. _____

_____ .

9. Cette commère te gêne <u>jamais</u>? _____ ?

10. Lavez les sols <u>et</u> **les plafonds-m. (the ceilings)**! _____

_____ !

11. Ècris <u>quelque chose</u> dans mon journal particulier! _____

_____ !

12. C'est incroyable! Les petits qui ont <u>quatre ans</u> peuvent lire. _____

_____ .

'Catch the Second Act!'- Circle the letters of the responses that best complete the scenarios.

1. Notre gendre paresseux ne veut pas nettoyer le garage, mais _____.
a. il doit verser la peinture
b. son bleu de travail ne lui va pas
c. le toit et les pas sont sales
d. il ne faut que deux heures de le faire

2. Ces maîtresses-là n'enseignent plus l'écriture parce que (qu') _____.
a. on utilise tant les ordinateurs
b. les élèves préfèrent les murs vides
c. on n'a jamais ni crayons ni sylos
d. elles ne regardent plus les jeux en plein air

3. M. Poche-Vides doit trouver un deuxième boulot parce qu'il _____.
a. ne rêve pas d'une bonne mode de vie
b. tourne tout ce qu'il touche en or
c. ne peut guère payer son loyer
d. a assez de savoir-faire

4. Mary n'habite plus ici, et elle ne nous rend jamais viste. Pour ça, _____.

a. elle nous manque à peine
b. personne n'a plus de faits disponibles
c. on ne doit pas croire les nouvelles
d. elle assiste à ses classes avec son agneau
5. Comme nous avons peur d'avoir tort, nous _____.
a. voulons leur offrir tout
b. faisons seulement des bêtises
c. préférons ne pas parler
d. décidons de ne jamais l'ouvrir
6. Personne ne considère les blagues d'Anne Ouieuse amusantes, mais _____.
a. on accueille les étrangers à ce pays
b. c'est un soulagement qu'elles sont drôles
c. elle ne frotte ni l'estomac ni la tête
d. elle les dit de toute façon
7. M. Inconscient ne fait jamais attention à ce que sa femme porte. Si c'est une robe du soir ou un bikini français, _____.
a. il n'a pas la bonté de lui remercier
b. cela lui fait toujours égal
c. il coupe trop de toile
d. personne ne regarde les dernières modes
8. Quand ses bébés pleurent ou crient pendant la journée, personne ne les entend parce que _____.
a. rien n'est plus doux que leurs voix
b. les planchers et les plafonds ne sont pas épais.
c. tout le monde est à l'extérieur de la maison
d. les voisins ne sont ni près ni loin

'Developing the Negatives'- Translate the following sentences.

1. Never say (*vous*) "never!" _____!

2. Who feels like swimming in the winter? Nobody! _____
_____!

3. No credit? No problem! I have a wallet full of money. _____
_____.

4. The fireman intends to never **smoke (fumer).** _____
_____.

5. Don't forget (*tu*) to give them kisses! _____
_____!

6. Several students know Payne, but nobody wants to talk to him. _____
_____.

7. Nothing is more important than **your health-f. (votre santé).** _____
_____.

8. Listen (*vous*) to her if she says, "Don't touch it!" _____
_____!

9. What beautiful weather! There are hardly any clouds, and there is only a little wind. _____
_____.

10. Neither snow nor rain **prevents (empêcher)** him from **delivering (distribuer)** the mail. _____
_____.

11. I do not know anyone who never tells a lie. _____
_____.

12. Why can't he answer the questions (that) the judge asks him? _____
_____?
_____

TENIR - TO HOLD and VENIR - TO COME

The double feature presentation of *tenir-venir* provides a very popular set. Flip the <u>t</u> to a <u>v</u> for simultaneous viewing!

Tenir -To Hold

Singular	Plural
je tiens- I hold, do hold, am holding	nous tenons- we hold, do hold, are holding
tu tiens- you hold, do hold, are holding	vous tenez- you hold, do hold, are holding
il/elle tient- he/she/it holds, does hold, is holding	ils/elles tiennent- they hold, do hold, are holding

----

Venir -To Come

Singular	Plural
je viens- I come, do come, am coming	nous venons- we come, do come are coming
tu viens- you come, do come, are coming	vous venez- you come, do come, are coming
il/elle vient- he/she/it comes, does come, is coming	ils/elles viennent- they come, do come, are coming

----

<u>Basic Programming</u>- Fill in the blanks with the correct forms of *tenir* and *venir*.

1. Arrriver et _____ sont les synonymes.
2. _____-vous ici souvent?
3. **Nos malles-f. (trunks)** _____ plus que nos valises.
4. Les grands-parents de Lauren Tien _____ du Canada.
5. Lassie _____ toujours quand tu l'appelles.
6. Joie et moi sommes heureuses quand nous _____ un beau bébé.
7. Dis-moi à quelle heure tu _____ ce soir!
8. Qu'est-ce que le magicien _____ dans sa main?
9. Nous ne pouvons pas _____ tout en même temps.
10. Le petit ne sait pas quel numéro _____ après dix.

<u>'Getting a Hold on'</u> *Tenir* and Its Offspring
1. *Tenir* is a quasi "boot verb." The entire singular and the third person plural have an <u>i</u> before the <u>e</u>. The double <u>n</u> in the toe keeps the verb from fitting like a perfect boot.
2. In addition to its primary meaning <u>to hold</u>, *tenir* has its hands full with to keep, to last and to take up.
Ex. Le café le tient **éveilé**. > The coffee keeps him **awake**. (He is 'up and running.')
Ex. Leur mariage tient toujours. > Their marriage is still lasting. (The couple is holding on.)
Ex. Tes animaux **en peluche** tiennent trop de place. > Your **stuffed** animals take up too much space. (They are 'too full to move.')
2a. **More translations include to control** *(tenir une classe),* **to cope** *(tenir l'alcool)* **and to respect** *(tenir une promesse).* **With all those interpretations and as a synonym for** *garder,* *tenir* **is a very 'tenacious' verb.**

3. Constructions with forms of *tenir*: (There are others 'on hold.')

3a. Tiens!- Here it is!, Here you are! Said consecutively, the term means Well, well!

Ex. "Tiens! Voici le paquet que vous attendez. Tiens, tiens! Il est enfin ici." > "Here it is! Here is the package that you have been waiting for. Well, well! It is finally here." (By then, it probably does not matter what 'tied it up.')

3b. Followed by *à*, forms of *tenir* express an attachment to someone or to something.

Ex. Nous tenons beaucoup à vous rencontrer. > We are really looking forward to meeting you. Anyone questioning the speaker's sincerity might curtly ask, **"À quoi ça tient?" > "Why is that?"**

3c. Followed by *de*, *tenir* is a synonym for *ressembler à*- to resemble.

Ex. **Ces jumeaux** tiennent de leur père. > **Those twins** take after their father. (The odds are 'two to one' that they will catch him.)

Prefixed Verbs with *Tenir* in 'a Holding Pattern'

1. contenir- to contain, to hold

Ex. Ils contiennent contient quatre <u>n</u>s. > They contain contains four <u>n</u>s.

2. détenir- to hold (up), to delay, to detain

Ex. Un agent de police détient **les voleurs. >** A policeman is detaining the **thieves.** (But only one of them needs information about 'the hold up.')

3. maintenir- to keep up, to maintain: The <u>maintenance</u> department takes responsibility for the upkeep of a building.

Ex. Si Sol Idité le dit, il le maintient. > If Sol Idité says it, he sticks to it. (He won't pull out.)

4. retenir- to hold back, to restrain, to retain

Ex. **Les barrages (m.)** retiennent l'eau. > **The dams** hold back the water. (So that people are able to 'conserve their energy.')

5. soutenir- to support, to defend, to sustain

Ex. **Les jambes** de M. Wobbles peuvent à peine le soutenir. > Mr. Wobbles' **legs** can hardly support him. (He will soon 'have to get out from under.')

<u>An interesting note</u>: **The translations for *contenir*, *détenir*, *maintenir*, *obtenir* (to obtain), *retenir* and *soutenir* all end with -<u>tain</u>.**

Venir and Phrases That Come with It

1. Because *tenir* and *venir* function as one TV set, the latter also has 'a wandering <u>i</u>' throughout the singular and in the third person plural. That form highlights their way of 'double <u>n</u> up.'

Ex. L'eau vient **jusqu'à nos genoux.** > The water comes **up to our knees.** (It is about a foot deep.)

Ex. Leurs gosses impolis viennent ici seulement parce qu'ils veulent quelque chose. > Their impolite kids come here only because they want something. (If their parents taught them a lesson in manners, would they 'come around'?)

2. The two verb groups offer one difference in programming. Unlike *tenir*, *venir* is intransitive, meaning that it cannot take a direct object. That applies as well to its synonym, *arriver*, and to its antonym, *aller*.

3. *Venir de (d')* has three meanings:

3a. Translated as "to come from," *de/d'* is tucked neatly into French sentences.

Ex. D'où venez-vous? > Where do you come from?

Ex. La foule ne sait pas d'où vient leur vol. > The crowd does not know where their flight is coming from. (It doesn't really matter 'when it comes down to it.')

3b. Followed by an infinitive, *venir de (d')* means <u>to have just</u>. Someone who <u>comes from</u> doing something has just done it.

Ex. M. Storm vient de laver sa voiture. Malheureusement, il commence à **pleuvoir**. > Mr. Storm just washed his car. Unfortunately, it is starting **to rain**. (No problem! He should put it in the garage, and that will 'cover it.')

3c. In interrogative sentences, forms of *venir de* are synonyms for *comment* and *pourquoi*.

Ex. D'où viennent leurs moyens de faire un safari africain? > How do they have the means to go on an African safari? (Maybe it's a 'plain' tour with one 'flat' fee.)

4. venir chercher- to call for, to come to get

Ex. Mme Gâtée dit à son chauffeur, "Venez me chercher au spa tout de suite!" > Mrs. Gâtée says to her chauffeur, "Come get me at the spa right away!" (Did someone 'rub her the wrong way'?)

Ex. Les parents de Randée Vous ne connaissent pas **son flirt**, Rusé Foxx, parce qu'il ne vient jamais la chercher à leur maison. > Randée Vous' parents do not know **her boyfriend**, Rusé Foxx, because he never comes to get her at their home. (They meet 'on the sly.')

5. faire venir- to call for, to send for

5a. A conjugated form of *faire* plus any infinitive means <u>to have something done/made</u>.

Ex. Ces français-là font venir du vin de la France. > Those French people have some wine sent from France. (They may be nostalgic for their 'stomping grounds.')

6. venir à + an infinitive- to happen to: In this construction, the sentences start with *si*- if.

Ex. Si tu viens à louer un yacht cet été, invite-nous **à bord**! > If you happen to rent a yacht this summer, invite us **on board**! ('Being tied up' for a while is not an excuse to refuse the request.)

<u>**Prefixed Verbs That Come Out like *Venir***</u>

1. devenir- to become: This verb should not be confused with *deviner*- to guess.

Ex. Sylvan devient **un** peintre **paysagiste** comme son père et son grand-père. > Sylvan is becoming **a landscape** painter like his father and his grandfather. (They share 'a common background.')

<u>**An important note:**</u> **Indefinite articles are not used before unmodified nouns after forms of *être* and *devenir*.**

2. prévenir- to alert, to warn: Notified in advance, one might <u>prevent</u> the outcome. *Avertir* is a cognate of <u>advertise</u> and a synonym for *prévenir*. (Whoever coined the phrase, "An ounce of prevention is worth a pound of cure," was using preventative measures.)

3. revenir- to come again, to come back

Ex. Des gens croient que vos bonnes actions vous reviennent. > Some people believe that your good deeds come back to you. (Are they stamped "Return to Sender"?)

<u>**An important reminder:**</u> ***Rentrer,* also translated as <u>to come back</u>, means to return to a familiar location.**

<u>**'Switching Channels'**</u>- **Arrange the phrases below in the correct sequence to form sentences.**

1. les avertit/ les tenir/ mais il ne peut pas / Le juge _____

_____.

2. du cinéma/ venir chercher/ mes enfants / Ils doivent _____

_____.

3. détient/ à l'aéroport/ Est-ce qu'/ l'espion/ on _____

_____?

4. si elle/ coudre/ à Betsy/ Georges demande/ vient à _____

_____.

5. de Mme Crevée/ du calme/ Tiens, tiens/ gardent/ Les gosses _____

_____!

6. vient/ à un accent/ son flirt/ intéressant/ D'où _____

_____?

7. tant de/ Comment/ circulation / le vieux pont/ soutient-il _____

_____?

8. à ses animaux/ douze ans/ Addie Laisense/ tient encore/ en peluche/ qui a _____

_____.

9. et il n'a pas/ un jardinier/ Herb/ faire venir/ son jardin/ les moyens de/ ne maintient pas _____

_____

10. renouveler mon abonnement/ des renseignements utiles/ parce que des articles/ à cette revue-là/ Je viens de/ contiennent _____

_____.

'The TV Connections'- Put the correct forms of the verbs in parentheses in the blanks.
1. (devenir) Quelques jeunes femmes rêvent de _____ vedettes.
2. (tenir) **Ces mômes-là (Those brats)** sont affreux. Personne ne peut les _____.
3. (venir de) Fabio et Fabrizio sont italiens. Ils _____ l'Italie.
4. (soutenir) Les prêtres disent que la religion les _____.
5. (contenir) Combien d'organes **vitaux (vital)** le corps humain _____-il?
6. (venir de) Hannah fait un voyage au Montana. Elle _____ ____ faire sa valise.
7. (revenir) Après mes visites chez elle, ma grand-mère me dit toujours "_____ me voir bientôt!"
8. (tenir) Avant de **traverser (cross)** la rue, Mme Soigneuse _____ leurs mains.
9. (venir de) Est-ce que tu _____ ____ passer par **le douanier (the customs official)** sans rien déclarer?
10. (faire venir) Fay D'or a les moyens de _____ les dernières modes de Paris.
11. (tenir de) Parcelle de Chou, qui est adoptée, _____ exactement ____ sa gardienne.
12. (tenir, contenir) Le Prince Charmant _____ une très petite boîte. Devine ce qu'elle _____!
13. (venir, tenir à) _____ l'après-midi lorsque les petits sont éveillés, s'il vous plaît! Ils _____ beaucoup ___ vous voir.
14. (venir d', soutenir) M. Cane _____ ____ avoir une opération. Quand il marche, une infirmière doit le _____.

Being Held Accountable- Translate the following sentences.
1. Guadeloupe and Martinique do not come from France. _____

_____.

2. Annie Versaire is holding a few gifts. _____.
3. I look like neither my mother nor my father. _____

4. It takes very little money to sustain him. _____
_____ .

5. The little children want to know where babies come from. _____
_____ .

6. Those plants retain very little water. Why is that? _____
_____ ?

7. We have chocolates sent from Belgium before Christmas. _____
_____ .

8. Ann Atomy is keeping her promise to her parents. She is becoming a doctor. _____
_____ .

9. If you (*vous*) happen to be in town, don't forget to call me! _____
_____ !

10. A magician makes a joke about the women who are no longer there. He says, "I just saw them."
_____
_____ .
_____

SORTIR - TO GO OUT, TO COME OUT and PARTIR - TO GO AWAY, TO LEAVE

Sortir and *partir* have similar translations, but the difference in meaning always comes back to this: *Sortir* offers a faster return than *partir*. The models below show that the conjugations travel on parallel tracks. (The helping verbs have gone away.)

Sortir - To Go Out, To Come Out

Singular	Plural
je sors- I go out, I come out	nous sortons- we go out, we come out
tu sors- you go out, you come out	vous sortez- you go out, you come out
il/elle sort- he/she/it goes out, he/she/it comes out	ils/elles sortent- they go out, they come out

----

Partir - To Go Away, To Leave

Singular	Plural
je pars- I go away, I leave	nous partons- we go away, we leave
tu pars- you go away, you leave	vous partez- you go away, you leave
il/elle part- he/she/it goes away, he/she/it leaves	ils/elles partent- they go away, they leave

----

Sorting out Facts about *Sortir* and *Partir*

1. The singular forms of *sortir* and *partir* each have one pronunciation. A t is seen in the infinitive, in the third person singular and throughout the plural of both verbs.

2. Conjugated forms of *sortir* and *partir* are followed by *de/d'* + a noun to clarify that one leaves from a location. (These French verbs are chaperoned, but the English ones leave alone.)

Ex. **Le public** sort du théâtre après le spectacle. > **The audience** leaves/comes out (from) the theater after the show.

Ex. **Un navire de croisière** part du quai maintenant. > **A cruise ship** is leaving (from) the dock now.

3. *Sortir de* and *venir de* are synonyms. *Entrer dans* is the antonym of *sortir de*.

Ex. La malade sort de sortir du lit. > The sick lady just got out of bed. (That woman does not appear 'to be out of sorts.')

Ex. D'où sortent toutes ces chaussettes-ci? > Where do all these socks come from? (Most likely from more than 'two feet away.')

4. In addition to *de* or a partitive, forms of *partir* leave with *avec, en* and *pour*.

Ex. L'épouse part pour les montagnes avec son petit ami, et son époux part en vacances à la plage. > The wife is leaving for the mountains with her boyfriend, and her husband is leaving for a vacation at the beach. (No further 'background information' is needed.)

An interesting aside: A popular Country Western singer's family is identified in the *nous* form of *partir*.

Sortir Expressions to Come out with

1. sortir par les oreilles- to come out of one's ears/to have it up to here

Ex. Les excuses de Bea Cause sortent par mes oreilles. > Bea Cause's excuses are coming out of my ears. (Does her voice have a 'piercing' quality?)

2. Est-ce que je peux sortir? > May I be excused? (If yes, one can just leave it at that.)

3. sortir avec- to go out with

Ex. Avec qui Sophie sort-elle **actuellement**? > With whom is Sophie going out **currently**? (She has quite an 'as-sort-ment' of men.)

4. sortir- to be made public, to be released

Ex. Leur dernier film va sortir bientôt . > Their latest film is going to be released soon. (Then, their audiences might 'be held captive.')

5. sortir du placard- to come out of the closet: The exact translation is "to come out of the cupboard." (It's the first step toward 'getting things aired out.')

6. sortir + a direct object- to extract, to remove, to take out

Ex. Un fou sort son fusil devant un kiosque à journaux. > A crazy guy takes out his gun in front of a newspaper stand. (He was intrigued by the contents of 'a magazine.')

A Partial List of Idioms with *Partir*

1. partir de rien- to start from nothing

Ex. Tant d'artistes qui partent de rien deviennent célébrités. > So many **entertainers** who start from nothing become celebrities. (But still, people 'walk all over the stars' in Hollywood.)

2. partir de l'hypothèse que- to assume that

Ex. Partons de l'hypothèse que sortir et partir ont de différents usages! > Let's assume that *sortir* and *partir* have different usages!

3. partir d'un bon sentiment- to be well meant. The English equivalent is "It's the thought that counts."

Ex. Bernice, une cuisinière épouvantable, m'invite à dîner. Cela part d'un bon sentiment. > Bernice, a terrible cook, invites me to dinner. It's the thought that counts. (Partez de l'hypothèse que je mange **en route**! > Assume that I eat **on the way**!)

4. partir bien/mal- to get off to a good/bad start

Ex. Leur cheval part bien, et il est de l'avance sur les autres. > Their horse is off to a good start, and it is ahead of the others. (If it stays on that track, they'll have 'a whinny.')

5. partir tout seul- to go off by itself

Ex. On est **coupable** d'**un meurtre** si son revolver part tout seul? > Is one **guilty** of **a murder** if his pistol goes off by itself? (The killer didn't 'give it his best shot.')

6. faire partir- to remove, to make disappear

Ex. **Le vinaigre** fait partir l'odeur de **fumée**. > **Vinegar** makes **smoke** odor disappear. (That household tip continues 'to circulate.')

<u>**'Phrases On Leave'**</u>- Circle the letters of the correct responses.

1. On admire surtout les riches qui _____.
a. sortent seulement avec les pauvres   b. ne partent jamais en navire de croisière
c. partent du rien et réussissent   d. sortent peu d'argent de leurs comptes
2. Le moment où M. et Mme Toux voient la fumée, ils _____.
a. partent en vacances   b. sortent du bâtiment   c. n'avertissent pas le public
d. savent que le film sort
3. **L'avocat-m. (the lawyer)** _____ que son client n'est pas coupable.
a. traverse la rue pour exprimer   b. tue les gens qui pensent   c. part de l'hypothèse
d. sort du placard pour montrer
4. L'herbe est encore mouillée parce qu'il _____.
a. sort de pleuvoir   b. vient de faire chaud   c. fait partir tout l'eau   d. y a des nuages
5. Anne Discrète, qui ne connaît guère Mme Fossile, lui demande son âge. La première _____.
a. sort un mouchoir de sa poche   b. sort sans le vouloir   c. ne peut pas l'attraper
d. part mal dans leur conversation
6. **Les informations-f. (the news)** à la télévision de tous les meurtres et les vols _____.
a. partent d'un bon sentiment   b. sortent par nos oreilles   c. nous donnent de **la foi (the faith)**
d. sont bienvenues chez nous
7. Courtoisie et moi savons que ce n'est pas poli de parler aux téléphones cellulaires pendant **le discours (the speech)**. Nous posons cette question-ci "_____?"
a. Pourquoi sortez-vous ce truc-là?   b. Pourrions-nous sortir?   c. Cela part tout seul?
d. Devons-nous revenir tout de suite?

LAISSER - To Leave Behind, To Allow and QUITTER - To Leave, To Abandon

French speakers cannot 'get away with' just *sortir* **and** *partir*. **Used in different contexts,** *laisser* **and** *quitter* **also include** <u>leave</u> **in their translations.** (Their language has 'a large pile of leaves.')

<u>**'Raking the Remaining Leaves'**</u>

1. *Laisser***- to leave behind, to allow, to drop off has a regular -<u>er</u> conjugation.**

Ex. Laisse-moi! > Leave me alone! (The presence of "alone" is not requested either in French.)

2. With forms of *laisser*, <u>behind</u> **is left behind, and** <u>off</u> **is dropped off.**

Ex. Si Pete laisse quelque chose, garde-le pour lui, s'il te plaît! > If Pete leaves something (behind), keep it for him, please! (That's not much to ask, "for Pete's sake!")

Ex. Laisse-moi au centre commercial où je peux laisser mon salaire de la semaine! > Drop me (off) at the mall where I can leave (behind) my week's salary.

3. The literal translation of *laissez-faire* **is "allow to do," but it typically means "Leave it alone" or "Let it Be!"** (The Beatles preferred the last interpretation.)

4. laisser tomber- to drop: Because it actually says "to allow to fall," the French translation of to drop ironically necessitates adding a verb.

Ex. Chez Cartier, Shard laisse tomber un vase très cher, et il **fracasse**. > At Cartier's, Shard drops a very expensive vase, and it **shatters**. (Now, no one is interested in what 'it is cracked up to be.')

'Calling It Quits'
1. *Quitter*- **to leave, to quit, to abandon is also a regular -er verb.**

Ex. Si votre voiture est **en panne**, ne la quittez pas sur **l'autoroute**! > If your car **breaks down**, do not leave/abandon it on **the highway**! (Police suggest that drivers find 'a shoulder' to cry on.)

2. *Quitter* **leaves us with two useful expressions:**
2a. Ne quitte pas!/Ne quittez pas!- Don't hang up!
2b. quitter ce monde- a euphemism for to die. (The caller in 2a. couldn't 'hold on any longer.')

Which Leaves Should Stay?- Label the statements *vrai* or *faux*.
_____ 1. *Sortir* and *partir* have regular -ir verb conjugations.
_____ 2. *Entrer dans* and *sortir de* are antonyms.
_____ 3. One translation of *sortir avec* is "to date."
_____ 4. *Sortir* and *partir* can be used interchangeably.
_____ 5. A form of *sortir* is used in the translation of "It's the thought that counts."
_____ 6. *Laisser* and *quitter* have regular -er verb conjugations.
_____ 7. Appropriate translations of *laisser* are "to leave behind" and "to let/permit."
_____ 8. *Laisser* and *quitter* cannot take direct objects.
_____ 9. A form of *laisser* is used in the translation of "Don't hang up!"
_____ 10. *Quitter* means to quit and to abandon.

'Leaving It Up to You'- Fill in the blanks with the correct forms of *sortir, partir, laisser, quitter* and idioms that include those verbs. Some sentences are open to two possible answers.
Ex. Le son des cloches est affreux. Il sort par nos oreilles. > The sound of the bells is awful. It is coming out of our ears.

Du Vocabulaire de l'Exercice
1. **le lutin- the elf**   5. **la miette- the crumb**
2. **l'échantillon (m.)- the sample**   6. **renverser- to dump over**
3. **le miel- the honey**   7. **le pupitre- the desk**
4. **le fantôme- the ghost**

1. **Les lutins** ne _____ pas avec Père Noël à la fin de décembre.
2. Matrushka n'est pas bien habillée quand elle _____ le soir.
3. Après notre jour de mariage, nous _____ pour l'Europe.

4. _____-moi une étiquette, s'il te plaît!

5. Le castor ne _____ / _____ jamais son projet. Il le finit.

6. On qui dépense tout aujourd'hui ne _____ rien pour l'avenir.

7. Les animaux _____ / _____ ____ l'arche deux par deux.

8. Ma petite fille me donne **des échantillons** d'un parfum comme un cadeau. _____

_____.

9. Winnie l'Ourson ne peut pas _____ / _____ son pot de **miel**.

10. Crois-tu qu'**un fantôme** est l'esprit de quelqu'un qui ne _____ / _____ jamais?

11. Quelques gens qui _____ et qui deviennent riches sont très généreux.

12. M. et Mme Sanshoraire ont envie de _____ ____ Rome pour visiter Athènes.

13. Quand les petits _____ / _____ ____ leur maison, Hansel et Gretel _____ **des miettes**.

14. Les mômes ne _____ pas tranquilles les autres, et ils **renversent les pupitres**. La maîtresse les faire _____ ____ la salle de classe.

'Parting Words'- Translate the following sentences.

1. Tinker never goes out without her bell. _____

_____.

2. That plane leaves from Dakar at noon. _____

_____.

3. My dog does not leave any crumbs on the floor. _____

_____.

4. Don't leave (*vous*) your children alone in the car! _____

_____!

5. Mr. and Mrs. Claus leave presents in the cupboard for the elves. _____

_____.

6. Let's not assume that his speech is going to be boring! _____

_____!

7. Some people believe that when one leaves this world, his spirit remains here. _____

_____.

8. "Mrs. Grasse, don't leave without a few perfume samples!" _____

_____!

9. Is the lawyer leaving his wife to go out with Miss Take? _____

_____?

10. Don't (*tu*) hang up! I just dropped my pen! _____

_____!

_____

UNE REVUE - A Review

Vouloir, Pouvoir, Devoir, Les Pronoms Indirects, Impersonal Expressions, Dire, Lire, Écrire, Les Impératifs, Les Négatifs Français, Tenir, Venir, Sortir, Partir, Laisser, Quitter

A Verbal Exchange- Match the letters to the numbers of their synonyms.

_____ 1. prévenir	A. permettre
_____ 2. sortir de	B. garder
_____ 3. accueillir	C. tenir de
_____ 4. désirer	D. avoir une obligation de
_____ 5. laisser	E. faire plus fort
_____ 6. pouvoir	F. venir de
_____ 7. devoir	G. expliquer en détail
_____ 8. falloir	H. être originaire de
_____ 9. rentrer	I. avoir envie de
_____ 10. faire regarder	J. donner de bon gré
_____ 11. ressembler à	K. abandonner
_____ 12. rembourser	L. laisser quelque chose par erreur
_____ 13. décrire	M. avertir
_____ 14. offrir	N. aller à l'autre **côté (m.)- the side**
_____ 15. empêcher	O. retourner habituellement
_____ 16. manquer	P. rendre ce qu'on doit
_____ 17. tenir	Q. rencontrer à la porte
_____ 18. quitter	R. ne pas permettre
_____ 19. soutenir	S. attirer l'attention de
_____ 20. traverser	T. être capable de
_____ 21. venir de	U. rater
_____ 22. oublier	V. être nécessaire de

'Applying a Finish'- Circle the letters of the responses that best complete the scenarios.

1. On qui part du rien sait que/qu' _____.

a. on fait tout exprès   b. on peut demander un échantillon   c. vouloir c'est pouvoir

d. on dit ce qu'on veut dire, et on veut dire ce qu'on dit

2. Si Mme Rappelletout ne laisse pas une étiquette avant de sortir, son fils _____.

a. la lit le soir   b. ne sait pas où elle est   c. part en vacances   d. fait venir un voisin

3. Mme Douleur ne sort pas de sa chambre, et elle mange à peine.

a. Faites venir un médecin!   b. Laissez-la quitter ce monde!   c. Elle veut faire la lessive

d. Ne passe jamais l'aspirateur lorsqu'elle pleure!

4. Owen doit 100 euros à Don Louis. Le premier demande, "_____?"

a. Puis-je laisser un appoint dans ton allée?   b. Tu laisses tomber de l'argent partout?

c. Tu prêtes ton argent à tout le monde?   d. Puis-je te rembourser la semaine prochaine?

5. Mme Étonnée reconnaît un tueur d'une affiche à la poste.

a. C'est son devoir d'avertir la police.   b. Personne ne la souhaite un bon voyage.

c. Il lui reste des vêtements d'occasion.   d. Elle le veut quand elle le voit en ligne.

6. Sydney est en Australie. Elle ne peut pas rentrer pour passer le Noël avec sa famille.

a. Son nom lui dit quelque chose.
b. Ils tricotent et disent des bêtises.
c. Sa mère dit, "Tu vas me manquer."
d. Il faut couper la dinde à l'heure.

7. "Madame, vous permettez que je fume?" La femme répond, "____."

a. Écoutez mon discours, s'il vous plaît!
b. Ne me dites jamais de mensonges!
c. Cela ne me dérange pas du tout.
d. Cela va sans dire qu'elles sont d'accord.

8. Connais-tu la peinture de la fille en jaune qui tient un livre dans la main?

a. Oui, j'ai une clé pour l'ouvrir.
b. Comme on dit, elle sort du placard.
c. Tiens! C'est une comptine de la Mère Oie.
d. Tu veux dire la Lectrice par Fragonard.

9. La commère n'est pas bienvenue ici, et nous ne tenons pas à la voir.

a. Personne ne la vient chercher.
b. Sortons avant son arrivée!
c. Rien ne l'empêche de faire un faux pas.
d. Elle veut distribuer ses abonnements.

10. Le petit rêve d'une vie **audacieuse (adventurous)**. Il veut devenir espion, et ____.

a. le garçon vient de décrire un voleur
b. heureusement, le gosse ne rentre jamais
c. un douanier va le retenir
d. ses parents le laissent parler de son idée

11. Bella fait tomber une cloche, et elle la fracasse. Le gentil gérant lui dit, "____."

a. Il ne faut pas la payer.
b. Les lutins te font renverser des choses.
c. Tu laisses des miettes sur le sol.
d. Quelqu'un est en panne sur l'autoroute.

12. La secrétaire employée récemment ne peut guère lire l'écriture de son **patron (boss)**.

a. L'avis de son avocat part d'un bon sentiment.
b. Évidemment, elle ne part pas bien.
c. C'est à dire qu'elle quitte son boulot.
d. Des esprits traversent à l'autre côté.

Responses Needed- 'Write' Away!- Translate the following sentences.

1. Where do her grandparents come from? _____?

2. Travers must know his flight number. _____.

3. "I would like" is preferable to "I want." _____
_____.

4. We want to wish you (*vous*) a Merry Christmas. _____
_____.

5. One sees "push" and "pull" on several doors. _____
_____.

6. Tell me (*tu*) that you miss me! _____!

7. Don't open (*tu*) it before your birthday! _____
_____!

8. Pay attention (*vous*) when you cut the meat, Chopin! _____
_____!

9. Doctor Vital, I have only two questions about my health. _____
_____.

10. No traffic? Nobody wants to go out when it rains. _____
_____.

11. Justine wants to go out with Justin, but he never talks to her. _____
_____.

12. Guess (*tu*) who is coming to dinner this evening! _____
_____.

171

LES PRÉPOSITIONS FRANÇAISES - French Prepositions

Prepositions are location indicators. By coincidence, since these direction signals do not budge from their posts as the first words of phrases, they themselves are easy to spot. You have seen numerous prepositions <u>in</u> sentences and <u>on</u> several pages <u>throughout</u> the book. <u>With</u> that good background, you are better prepared <u>for</u> this chapter.

Prepositions We Have Gotten Around To

1. à- to, in, at: This lone letter goes between nouns, follows verbs and blends into contractions.
Ex. Rip tient à porter son sweat-shirt **aux trous**. > Rip insists on wearing his sweatshirt **with holes**. (It might be fine around 'the hood.')

<u>A very important note</u>: When *à* plus a noun or an infinitive expresses the purpose of an object, the preposition can be translated as <u>for</u>. However, preceding the names of food, the contraction means <u>with</u>.
Ex. le rouge à lèvres- the lipstick, la crême à raser- the shaving cream
Ex. la soupe à l'oignon- the onion soup, le gâteau aux fraises- the cake with strawberries

2. dans- in vs. en- in: The first one applies to something visible (*à l' intérieur de*); the second to something abstract.
2a. *Dedans*- inside is an adverb. *Dans* is inside <u>inside</u>.
Ex. Les étudiants universitaires ne sont pas bienvenus dans son hôtel en avril. > College students are not welcome in his hotel in April. (Has he had too many 'spring breakers'?)

3. de/d'- from, of: As a multipurpose preposition, it connects two verbs, precedes the names of materials and metals and follows adverbs and nouns of quantity. Substituting for 's, *de/d'* also shows possession. With definite articles added, it morphs into *du, de la, de l'* and *des*.
Ex. La patronne de votre mère vient de faire venir des douzaines de boîtes de kilts d'**un entrepôt** en Écosse. > Your mother's boss just had dozens of boxes of kilts sent from **a warehouse** in Scotland. (Hopefully, the stock will not be 'de-pleat-ed.')

Pairs on Opposing Teams

1. avec- with vs. sans- without: When <u>with</u> means <u>accompanied by</u>, *avec* is used.
1a. Contractions can express <u>with</u> at the beginning of descriptive phrases.
Ex. La femme **à la perruque** ne sort plus avec l'homme **au postiche**. > The woman with **the wig** no longer goes out with the man with **the toupee**. (Did they accuse each other of 'putting on 'hairs'?)
1b. S*ans* is frequently followed by a noun *sans partitif* or by an infinitive.
Ex. Ces pauvres mendiants-là passent un autre jour sans argent et sans manger. > Those pitiable beggars are spending another day without money and without eating. (Unfortunately, there has not been 'any change' recently.)

2. avant- before vs. après- after: Both prepositions precede nouns, pronouns and expressions of time.
Ex. Nous sortons ce soir, et tu n'as pas un clé. Tu vas arriver avant ou après minuit? > We are going out this evening, and you don't have a key. Are you going to arrive before or after midnight? (Maybe they should just 'leave it open.')
<u>An important note</u>: *Avant* takes *de* before an infinitive.
Ex. avant de devenir écrivain > before becoming a writer

3. pour- in favor of, in order to, considering, in the direction of vs. contre- against (*Pour* 'over-flows' with meanings as opposed to *contre* with only one.)

3a. Meaning <u>in order to</u>, *pour* is followed by an infinitive.

Ex. M. Dove n'est pas pour la guerre, mais il sait qu'on doit défendre son pays pour avoir la paix. > Mr. Dove isn't in favor of the war, but he knows that one must defend one's country in order to have peace.

Ex. Je suis **en colère** contre M. Brouillé. > I am **angry** with Mr. Brouillé. (Considering the scenario, against makes more sense than with.)

3b. par contre- on the other hand: (There are also four fingers and a thumb.)

4. devant- in front of, before vs. derrière- in back of, behind, after: *En face de* is a synonym for *devant*. **The three French prepositions refer to location as opposed to time.**

Ex. **Quel culot!** Quelques gens qui arrivent après nous sont devant nous maintenant! > **What nerve!** Some people who arrive after us are in front of us now. (They definitely should 'be put in line.')

Ex. On peut voir **le dos** de la vache de derrière **la grange**. > One can see **the back** of the cow from behind **the barn**. (The 'dairy air' shows the advantage of hind-sight.)

<u>**Multiple-Word Locators Ending with *de/d'***</u>

1. au-dessus de- above: Its synonym is *en haut de*. Grab *un pardessus*- an overcoat and keep the first preposition warm!

Ex. L'avion vole au-dessus de la pluie. > The airplane is flying above the rain. (But some passengers might still feel a few 'drops.')

2. au-dessous de- below: Only the <u>o</u> differentiates this term from its antonym *au dessus de*. Pull up *les sous-vêtements*- the <u>under</u>wear to tell them apart! *Au-dessous de* **is very close in meaning to *au fond de*- at/on the bottom of.**

Ex. Ils racontent des histoires des trésors cachés au-dessous de la mer. > They tell stories of treasures hidden below the sea. (It's amazing 'what they come up with.')

2a. *Dessus*- on top and *dessous*- underneath, not followed by *de/d'*, are adverbs.

3. autour de- around: One taking <u>a tour</u> of a city goes around it.

Ex. Deux mains vont autour de **l'horloge** de droite à gauche. > Two hands go around **the clock** from right to left. (A third one 'seconds the motion.')

4. à côté de- beside: The similar looking noun, *la côte*- the coast, is beside the land.

Ex. M. et Mme Richelieu habitent à côté de leurs fils à la côte d'Azur. > Mr. and Mrs. Richelieu live beside their sons on the French Riviera. (And obviously not 'on next to nothing.')

5. en dehors de/d'- outside of: Its synonym is *à l'extérieur de*. Connect *dehors de/d'* to its translation by relating outside to out 'do-ors!'

Ex. M. Deuxvies ne fait pas d'affaires en dehors **des heures ouvrables**. > Mr. Deuxvies does not do any business outside of **business hours**. (He must have made 'a previous deal' with his family.)

5a. *Dehors*, not followed by *de/d'*, is an adverb. (It's outside by itself.)

6. loin de/d'- far from vs. près de/d'- near

Ex. Les fils qui habitent près de Chicago sont loin de leur mère en Floride. Ils lui rendent des visites séparées. > The sons who live near Chicago are far from their mother in Florida. They visit her separately. ('A time share' does not interest them.)

6a. The antonyms, *loin* and *près*, not followed by *de/d'*, are adverbs.

Taking Turns- Put the letters beside the numbers of the antonyms.

_____ 1. avant   A. dedans
_____ 2. au-dessus de   B. sans
_____ 3. loin de   C. en haut de
_____ 4. dehors   D. contre
_____ 5. à   E. près de
_____ 6. au fond de   F. à l'intérieur de
_____ 7. devant   G. après
_____ 8. avec   H. derrière
_____ 9. à l'extérieur de   I. de
_____ 10. pour   J. au-dessous de

Prepositions That Go off on Their Own

1. à travers- across, through: The related verb is _traverser_- to cross.
Ex. Ma tante croit que les fantômes peuvent passer à travers un mur. > My aunt believes that ghosts can pass through walls. (Does she have 'concrete evidence'?)

2. chez- at the home of, 's _____ place
Ex. Lou rencontre Lois chez elle la première fois qu'il sort avec elle. > Lou meets Lois at her home the first time that he goes out with her. (Another location would be 'out of place.')

3. entre- between: Its cognate is the prefix -_inter_.
Ex. Nos ouvriers pas motivés aiment dire qu'ils sont entre les vacances. > Our unmotivated workers like to say that they are between vacations. (That could explain 'the faraway look in their eyes.')

4. par- by, through: The French preposition is 'by all means' useful to tell how one arrives at a destination.
Ex. **Le propriétaire** va offrir des tours bon marché par **montgolfière**. > **The owner** is going to offer inexpensive tours by **hot-air balloon**. (They will probably 'be filled to capacity.')

5. parmi- among: _Entre_ is used for two people or two things; _parmi_ serves three or more.
Ex. Delly voit du pastrami parmi le corned-beef, **le rosbif** et **le jambon**. > Delly sees some pastrami among the corned beef, **the roast beef** and **the ham**. (They also serve three or more.)

6. pendant- during, through: Its related adverb, _pendant que,_ begins a clause and means <u>while</u>.
Ex. Les dindes mangent bien pendant le printemps et l'été. > Turkeys eat well during the spring and the summer. (In anticipation of 'their fall.')

7. sauf- except: Its synonym is _à part_. Its translation includes <u>for</u>.
Ex. Tout le monde est bienvenu chez moi sauf les Omis. > Everyone is welcome to my home except the Omis. (If they turn up, they will be turned down.)

8. sur- on: Place a circumflex over the <u>u</u>, and bet on this word for <u>sure</u>!
Ex. Nous sommes sûrs que la clé de voiture est sur **le comptoir**. > We are sure that the car key is on **the counter**. (Why would anyone 'walk off with' it?)

9. vers- toward: This preposition shares its pronunciation with _le verre_ and _vert_.
Ex. Louis XVI et Marie Antoinette, **en chemin** de Paris, voyagent vers Versailles. > Louis XVI and Marie Antoinette, on their way from Paris, are traveling toward Versailles. (They would have chosen "traveling toward" over "be-headed.")

'Having One up on' French Prepositions

1. Because prepositions cannot end French sentences, they are found *à l'intérieur d'une phrase.*
Ex. Tipsy ne sait pas encore pour qui elle va voter. > Tipsy does not know yet for whom she is going to vote. (She likes going from 'party to party.')

2. Consecutive prepositions are not used in French. It is something that the speakers are never 'up against.'

'These Arrows Have a Point'- Choose from the following prepositions to identify the location or destination of the arrows in relation to the circles: à côté du, au-dessous du, au-dessus du, à travers, autour du, dans, contre, entre, loin du, près du, sur, vers

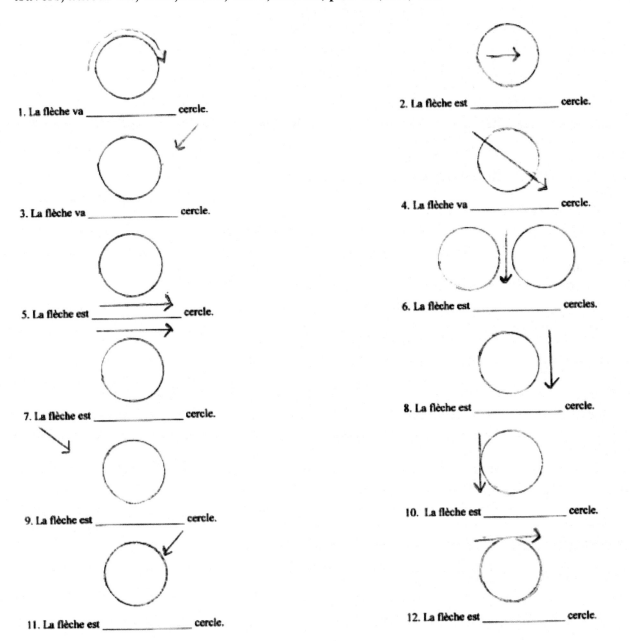

1. La flèche va _____ cercle.

2. La flèche est _____ cercle.

3. La flèche va _____ cercle.

4. La flèche va _____ cercle.

5. La flèche est _____ cercle.

6. La flèche est _____ cercles.

7. La flèche est _____ cercle.

8. La flèche est _____ cercle.

9. La flèche est _____ cercle.

10. La flèche est _____ cercle.

11. La flèche est _____ cercle.

12. La flèche est _____ cercle.

Propositions for the Prepositions- Label the statements *vrai* or *faux*.

_____ 1. *Dans* and *en* are interchangeable.
_____ 2. *Sauf* and *à part* are synonyms.
_____ 3. *Avant* and *après* signify locations.
_____ 4. *Devant* and *en face de* are antonyms.
_____ 5. *À* before a noun or an infinitive expresses the use of an object.
_____ 6. Without *de/d'*, many prepositions are adjectives.
_____ 7. *Entre* and *parmi* are interchangeable.
_____ 8. *À* (with or without contractions) and *vers* express <u>in the direction of</u>.
_____ 9. *Derrière* and *devant* are related to time.
_____ 10. *Par* and *à travers* can both be translated by <u>through</u>.
_____ 11. When followed by an infinitive, *pour* means <u>in order to</u>.
_____ 12. *Pendant* and *pendant que* have the same meaning.
_____ 13. *Autour de* and *à côté de* refer to locations that are close-by.
_____ 14. French sentences sometimes end with prepositions.

'A Good Sense of Direction'- Circle the letters of the answers that best complete the sentences.

1. Les très pauvres _____ vêtements sales nous demandent de la monnaie.
a. sur   b. sans   c. dans   d. des

2. Les canards ont soif, et ils marchent _____ l'étang.
a. loin de   b. vers   c. au-dessous de   d. parmi

3. Combien de l'air chaud y a-t-il _____ une montgolfière?
a. à travers   b. pour   c. derrière   d. à l'intérieur d'

4. M. Postiche et Mme Perruque ne passent pas beaucoup de temps _____ le coiffeur.
a. pendant   b. chez   c. entre   d. en

5. L'endroit préféré des cochons est _____ la grange du vieux McDonald.
a. à côté de   b. au-dessus de   c. au fond de   d. avant

6. Casper dit que les fantômes apparaissent _____ corps distincts.
a. après   b. devant   c. sans   d. par

7. Puis-je toucher les plantes _____ soie qui sont _____ comptoir?
a. à la .... à côté du   b. avec .... au-dessus du c. en .... sur le   d. à part .... près du

8. Lorsque ces trois filles-là sont _____ colère, il n'y a jamais de conversation _____ elles.
a. dans .... d'   b. de .... pour   c. en face de .... entre d. en .... parmi

9. Comme il n'y a pas assez d'**espace-m. (space)** _____ cet entrepôt, des camions doivent **stationner (to park)** _____.
a. en dehors de .... dedans   b. devant .... à l'arrière   c. sous .... contre   d. avant .... après

10. On n'arrive pas _____ Venise _____ gondole.
a.. à .... par   b. vers .... à l'extérieur d'une   c. autour de .... avec une   d. chez .... sur une

----

'Meeting Half-Way'- Translate the underlined phrases.

1. Le méchant gosse fracasse tous les objets <u>on the counter</u>. _____.

2. Où Pat Iner va-t-elle <u>during her winter vacation</u>? _____
_____?

3. Faites-nous savoir si vous êtes <u>for or against the idea</u>! _____!

4. M. Enpanne laisse sa voiture <u>on the side of the highway</u>. _____

_____.

5. Rencontre-moi <u>in front of the clock before noon!</u> _____

_____!

6. Est-ce que ton chien cache <u>underneath the bed when you are angry?</u> _____

_____?

7. Rien ne change jamais <u>in that little village which is far from a city.</u> _____

_____.

8. Nous pouvons stationner <u>near the restaurant or at Maxim's.</u> _____

_____.

9. Les touristes <u>with the heavy suitcases do not want to go around Paris.</u> _____

_____.

10. <u>Except for mathematics,</u> Addie Scion ne réussit pas <u>without studying often.</u> _____

_____.

_____

l'Arc de Triomphe (Paris)

LES EXPRESSIONS GÉOGRAPHIQUES - Geographical Expressions

Assume that you are French and have taken a trip! Checking into your room and writing brief postcards are almost simultaneous actions. Voici une carte postale de vous!

Chère Giselle,
Salutations de l'Afrique! Je suis à Marrakesh au Maroc, un pays extraordinaire.
Gros bisous,

Prepositions Preceding Place Names

TO, IN
À- Before Cities
En- Before Feminine Countries, Continents and Provinces
Au, Aux- Before Masculine Countries and Provinces
FROM
De- Before Cities
De la, De l'- Before Feminine Countries, Continents and Provinces
Du, De l', Des- Before Masculine Countries and Provinces

'Getting to a Point'
1. *À* is used before the names of most cities to express **to** or **in**.
Exs. à New York, à Londres, à Madrid
Ex. Nous achetons du chocolat à Bruxelles. > We buy some chocolate in Brussels.
An exception: If a definite article is part of the name, a contraction translates to and in.
Exs. le Caire- au Caire (Cairo), la Havane- à la Havane, le Havre- au Havre, la Nouvelle-Orléans- à la Nouvelle-Orléans
Those familiar with the five boroughs of New York City know how to get *au Bronx*- to the Bronx.

Feminine Countries

1. l'Allemagne- Germany
2. l'Angleterre- England (*la terre* = the land)
3. l'Autriche- Austria
4. la Belgique- Belgium
5. l'Écosse- Scotland (*écossais* = plaid)
6. l'Espagne- Spain
7. la France- France

12. l'Irlande- Ireland
13. l'Inde- India
14. l'Italie- Italy
15. la Norvège- Norway
16. la Nouvelle-Zélande- New Zealand
17. la Pologne- Poland
18. la Roumanie- Rumania

8. la Grande-Bretagne- Great Britain
9. la Grèce- Greece
10. la Hongrie- Hungary (Notice the article *la*)
11. l'Icelande- Iceland

19. la Russie- Russia
20. la Suède- Sweden
21. la Suisse- Switzerland
22. la Turquie- Turkey

---

1. *En,* meaning <u>to</u> or <u>in,</u> precedes the names of most feminine countries. The majority of European countries are feminine.

Ex. Gyro aime la nourriture en Grèce mais pas **la graisse** dans la nourriture. > Gyro likes the food in Greece but not **the grease** in the food.

2. **Feminine countries not located in Europe include *l'Algérie, la Chine, l'Égypte, l'Éthiopie* and *l'Argentine.*** (*L'argent*- silver, money is found inside *l'Argentine.*)

Ex. Les pyramides en Égypte sont parmi les Sept Merveilles du Monde. > The pyramids in Egypt are among The Seven Wonders of the World. (They might be judged the winner because they have 'the most points.')

3. **Many feminine countries that are near each other start with vowels.**

Exs. l'Allemagne, l'Angleterre, l'Espagne, l'Italie

4. *En,* without an article, expresses <u>to</u> or <u>in</u> before the names of continents. (Ex. en Europe)

1. l'Afrique- Africa
2. l'Antarctique- Antarctica*
3. l'Asie- Asia
4. l'Australie- Australia

5. l'Europe- Europe
6. l'Amérique du Nord- North America
7. l'Amérique du Sud- South America/
   l'Amérique Latine

<u>An important note:</u> **Six of the seven continents are feminine. *L'Antarctique* > Antarctica is the exception.** (It is 'left out in the cold.')

4a. **The names of continents in French begin with vowels.** (That is a 'global warning.')

Ex. On peut dire que Lima est en Amérique du Sud ou en Amérique Latine. > We can say that Lima is in South America or in Latin America.

Ex. Il y a beaucoup de crimes qui **impliquent** la jeunesse en Asie? > Are there many crimes that **involve** the youth in Asia? (Some believe that 'euthanasia' is a crime in itself.)

5. *En* translates <u>to</u> or <u>in</u> before feminine provinces including:

l'Alsace which is near la Lorraine
la Bretagne which is near la Normandie
la Bourgogne (Burgundy) and la Champagne (Two of the 'vinest' provinces in France)
la Provence- France's playground

Ex. Je demande une quiche Lorraine et une bouteille de Bourgogne quand je déjeune en Provence. > I order a quiche Lorraine and a bottle of Burgundy when I lunch in Provence.

6. *En* will also get you <u>to</u> or <u>on</u> a feminine island such as *la Corse* > Corsica, *la Guadeloupe* and *la Martinique.*

Masculine Countries

1. l'Afghanistan- Afghanistan*
2. le Brésil- Brazil
3. le Canada- Canada

11. le Japon- Japan
12. le Koweït- Kuwait
13. le Liban- Lebanon

4. le Chili- Chile	**14. le Luxembourg- Luxembourg**
5. le Danemark- Denmark	**15. le Maroc- Morocc**
6. l'Équateur- Ecuador (the equator)*	**16. le Mexique- Mexico**
7. Haïti- Haiti*	**17. le Pakistan- Pakistan**
8. l'Iran- Iran*	**18. le Pays de Galles- Wales**
9. l'Irak- Iraq*	**19. le Pérou- Peru**
10. Israël- Israel*	**20. le Portugal- Portugal**

----

1. *Au* translates <u>to</u> or <u>in</u> before the names of most masculine countries.

Ex. En quelle saison fait-il très frais au Chili? > In which season is it chilly in Chile?

Ex. Luxembourg est la seule ville au Luxembourg. > Luxembourg is the only city in Luxembourg.

1a. Our northern and southern neighbors, *le Canada* **and** *le Mexique,* **are masculine nouns.**

1b. Several South American countries including *le Brésil, le Chili, l'Équateur* **and** *le Pérou* **are masculine.**

1c. Most Middle Eastern countries are masculine 'as a rule.' Some examples are *l'Iran, l'Irak, Israël, le Koweït* **and** *le Liban. La Jordanie-* **Jordan and** *La Syrie-* **Syria have 'a different view.'**

1d. The French names of African countries such as *le Congo-* **The Congo,** *le Niger-* **Nigeria,** *le Sénégal-* **Senegal et** *le Zaïre-* **Zaire are masculine nouns.**

2. *Aux* **expresses <u>to the</u> and <u>in the</u> preceding plural names of places.** *Les États-Unis-* **the United States and** *les Pays-Bas* **(the low countries)- the Netherlands are two examples.**

Ex. **Le Moulin** Rouge n'est pas aux Pays Bas. > **The** Red **Windmill** is not in the Netherlands.

Getting There in a Roundabout Way

1. Rather than trying to remember the genders for compound state names, put *dans l'état de* **in front of them.**

Ex. dans l'état de New York

2. Contractions are en-'compass'-ed in the four directions. By going *au nord* **> to the north,** *au sud* **> to the south,** *à l'est* **> to the east and** *à l'ouest* **> to the west, you can't go wrong.**

'A One-Way Ticket'- Translate these geographical phrases.

1. to Calais in the North _____

2. to Santa Fe in the West _____

3. to Pau in the South _____

4. to Madrid in Spain _____

5. to Cairo in Egypt _____

6. to Montreal in Canada _____

7. to Dakar in Senegal _____

8. to London in England _____

9. to Japan in Asia _____

10. to Vence in Provence _____

11. to Warsaw (Varsovie) in Poland _____

12. to Brazil in South America _____

13. to Fort-de-France in Martinique _____

14. to Aukland in New Zealand _____

'From-mer's' Guide

1. *De (d')* **takes us <u>from</u> most cities.**
Exs. de Boston, de Lyon, d'Amiens
<u>An exception</u>: **If a definite article is part of the name, <u>from</u> is translated by a partitive.**
Exs. le Caire- du Caire, le Havre- du Havre, la Nouvelle Orléans- de la Nouvelle-Orléans
2. *De (d')* **expresses <u>from</u> before feminine singular locations used as adjectives. Otherwise,** *de la (de l')* **translates <u>from</u>.**
Ex. Tous les parfums d'Europe ne viennent pas de la France. > All perfumes from Europe (European perfumes) do not come from France. (For example, Cologne is found in Germany.)
Customs officials in feminine named countries, continents, provinces and islands have to check your passport when you 'en-ter' and require seeing it again before you 'de-part.'
Ex. Cette croisière des Canaries en Turquie n'est pas une bonne idée. > That cruise from the Canary Islands to Turkey isn't a good idea. (It's really 'for the birds.') **Cependant,** un voyage de la Sicile en Italie m'intéresse. > **However,** a trip from Sicily to Italy interests me.
Ex. Combien d'heures faut-il par avion pour voyager en Europe de l'Asie? > How many hours does it take by plane to travel to Europe from Asia? (Is one 'dis-oriented' when he lands?)
<u>An interesting note</u>: **The feminine markers** *en* **and** *de* **also precede fabrics and metals.** (What do you 'make of that'?)
3. *Du* **and** *de l'* **are used before the names of masculine singular locations to express <u>from</u>.**
Ex. Du monde part du Brésil en été. > Some people leave (from) Brazil in the summer. (Things 'cool down' after the Carnival.)
Ex. Des avions peuvent voler de l'océan Pacifique à l'océan Atlantique en six heures. > Some planes can fly from the Pacific Ocean to the Atlantic Ocean in six hours. (But the return trip can be made in only three hours, counting 'the time you take off.')
4. *Des* **means <u>from</u> in front of plural locations.**
Ex. Quand ils sont en France, des gens leur demandent, "Venez-vous des États Unis?" > When they is in France, some people ask them, "Do you come from the United States?"

<u>Sticky and Tricky</u>
1. Asterisks placed after *l'Afghanistan, l'Antarctique, l'Équateur, l'Iran* **and** *l'Irak* **indicate that because they begin with vowels, those nouns are preceded by the feminine locators** *de l'* **and** *en*.
Ex. Les **citoyens** peuvent-ils traverser de l'Irak en Iran pendant une guerre? > Can the **citizens** cross from Iraq into Iran during a war? (They would have 'to be up in arms' to try it.)
2. *Haïti* **and** *Israël,* **each with** *un tréma* **and no definite article, are on the masculine list. But, as they begin with either a vowel or a mute <u>h</u>, the feminine markers give them direction.**
Ex. Très peu de gens voyagent de Haïti en Israël. > Very few people travel from Haiti to Israel. (Yet, according to the explanation above, both have many unique features.)
3. Generally, geographical names that end with an <u>e</u> are feminine. Exceptions are *le Cambodge-* Cambodia, *le Mexique, le Thaïland* **and** *le Zaïre.*
Ex. Aller du Cambodge en Asie au Zaïre en Afrique, nous observons plusieurs **mœurs** différentes. > Going from Cambodia in Asia to Zaire in Africa, we notice several different **customs**.

French Mountains
Of the four major mountain chains in France, three have feminine plural names. They are *Les Alpes* in Eastern France *Les Pyrénées*, along the border of France and Spain and *Les Vosges* in Eastern France. *Le Jura*, north of the Alps, is a masculine singular noun.

Ex. Le Mont-Blanc est aux Alpes. > Mont Blanc is in the Alps.

Ex. Le lieu de naissance de Victor Hugo est près du Jura. > Victor Hugo's birthplace is near *le Jura*.

French Waterways
These bodies of water are split between masculine and feminine. Navigating the correct gender is a matter of memorization.

1. *la Manche*- the English Channel spans twenty-six miles from the southernmost tip of Great Britain to the northernmost spot in France. The common noun, *la manche,* means <u>the sleeve</u>. (Its arm reaches two countries.)

2. *la mer Méditerranée*- the Mediterranean Sea is so-named because when it was discovered, it was 'the middle of the earth.'

3. *la Loire*- the Loire River is famous for the *châteaux* that dot its valley.

4. *le Rhin*- the Rhine runs between France and Germany. (Both countries could claim, "The fine, Rhine wine is mine.")

5. *la Seine*- the Seine flows through Paris. (Anyone who jumps off one of its bridges is 'in Seine.')

6. *le Rhône*- the Rhone passes through Avignon in southeastern France.

7. *le Saône*- the Saone crosses Lyon as does *le Rhône*. (Accompanied by the Rhone, the Saone is not alone in Lyon.)

Ex. M. Fleuve regarde son hôtel du Rhône, et Madame Rivière regarde son appartement du Saône. > Mr. Fleuve is looking at his hotel from the Rhone, and Mrs. Rivière is looking at her apartment from the Saone. (Maybe they will 'run into each other.')

'Going Back on Your Word'- Translate the geographical phrases.
1. from La Paz to Quito _____
2. from Le Havre in France _____
3. from Nantes in the west _____
4. from the Jura to the Vosges _____
5. from Syria to Algeria _____
6. from Guadeloupe to Haiti _____
7. from Jerusalem in Israel _____
8. from Cambodia to Thailand _____
9. from Beirut (Beyrouth) in Lebanon _____
10. from Buenos Aires in Argentina _____
11. from Acapulco in Mexico _____
12. from Cherbourg to the Mediterranean Sea _____

13. from Germany to the Alps in Switzerland _____

14. from the English Channel to the Atlantic Ocean _____

Spaces and Places- Use the correct prepositions and nouns to fill in the blanks with the names of the cities, states, provinces, countries and continents described.
Ex. (un pays) Deepa fait un tour en autobus, et elle voit le Taj Mahal <u>en Inde</u>.

1. (un continent) Cuba est une île _____.
2. (un pays) Takashi a une maison près du Mont Fujiyama. Il habite _____.
3. (une ville) _____ nous voyons des pièces dans des théâtres de Broadway.
4. (un continent) L'Algérie et la Tunisie sont deux pays _____.
5. (un état) Nous visitons le Mont Rushmore _____.
6. (un pays) La maison de Shakespeare est à Stratford-sur-Avon _____.
7. (un continent) Le Cambodge, la Chine et la Corée sont _____.
8. (un pays) Nous faisons un pique-nique près du Lac Genève _____.
9. (un continent) Il y a beaucoup de kangourous et koalas _____.
10. (un pays) M. Moscou peut voir le Kremlin de son bureau. Il est _____.
11. (un état) Tu passes ton **jour de congé (day off)** au Grand Canyon _____.
12. (une ville, un pays) Corinne visite le Musée Smithsonian pendant son voyage _____
_____.
13. (une ville, un pays, un pays) La Tour Eiffel est _____. La Tour de
Pisa est _____.
14. (un pays, un continent) Fatima et Niles montent à **chameau (camel)** _____ lorsqu'ils visitent les pyramides. Ils ont l'intention de partir en safari _____ aussi.
15. (une ville, un continent) Un touriste passe par le Palais Buckingham _____. C'est
la première fois qu'il est _____.
16. (une ville, un pays) M. et Mme Baklava vont faire un tour de l'Acropolis et le Parthénon pendant
leur voyage _____.

'The Ins and Outs of Travel'- Choosing among *à, au, à la, aux, de, d', du, de la, des* and *en*, put the correct prepositions on the lines provided.
1. (to) _____ Marseille (from) _____ Port-au-Prince
2. (from) _____ Manhattan (to the) _____ Bronx
3. (from) _____ Havane (to) _____ Miami
4. (to) _____ Irlande (from) _____ Écosse
5. (from) _____ Pologne (to) _____ Hongrie
6. (to) _____ Congo (from) _____ Zaïre
7. (from) _____ Équateur (in) _____ Amérique du Sud
8. (to) _____ Melbourne (in) _____ Australie
9. (from) _____ Bretagne (to) _____ Normandie
10. (to) _____ Martinique (from) _____ Guadeloupe
11. (to) _____ Corse (from) _____ Suisse
12. (from) _____ Mexique (to) _____ Canada
13. (to) _____ Allemagne (from the) _____ Pays-Bas
14. (to) _____ Lima (in) _____ Pérou (to) _____ Lisbon (in) _____ Portugal
15. (to) _____ Reykjavik (in) _____ Islande (from) _____ Copenhague _____ Danemark
16. (from) _____ Nouvelle-Orléans (in the) _____ États-Unis (to) _____ Orléans (in) _____ France

To and Fro- Translate the following sentences.

1. Alsace is not far from Lorraine. _____.

2. Rafi from Lebanon works with Latif in Kuwait. _____
_____.

3. One ought to visit Austria and Hungary in the spring. _____
_____.

4. They know several inns from the Pyrenees to the Alps. _____
_____.

5. Mazda from Brazil is going out with Rodrigo from Portugal. _____
_____.

6. The Borge family from Denmark is on vacation in the Netherlands. _____
_____.

7. Many people who live in Great Britain come from Australia. _____
_____.

8. Mr. and Mrs. Fjord are going from Stockholm in Sweden to Oslo in Norway to see her. _____
_____.

9. The accents in Ireland and in Wales are not the same. _____
_____.

10. There is a difference in French customs between Louisiana (la Louisiane) and Canada. _____
_____.

11. Look (*tu*) at **the schedule (l'horaire-m.)**! The last train from Avignon to Lyon leaves at 18:30.
_____
_____.

12. Paris is neither far from the English Channel nor from Belgium. _____
_____
_____.

LES PRONOMS Y et EN

Being miniature in size, *y* and *en* could be considered 'the jewels of French pronouns.' *Y*, most often translated as <u>there</u>, is a 'brilliant' substitute for prepositional phrases that tell locations. *En*, 'multifaceted' in meanings, replaces partitive phrases. Like many French pronouns, these 'gems' are typically set in front of verbs.

Read the 'Y' Mail

1. Unlike its synonym *là*, *y* precedes verbs except in affirmative commands. The literal translation for *il y a*- there is/there are is "It has there."

Ex. Trois états aux États-Unis n'ont que quatre lettres. Il y a une carte dans ce tiroir-là. Pourquoi n'y cherches-tu pas? > Three states in the U.S. have only four letters. There's a map in that drawer. Why don't you look there?

2. The adverb *là* is used if the location has not been specified.

3. *Y* replaces prepositional phrases that indicate locations. Its generic meaning is <u>there</u>.

Exs. Amman te téléphone quand il arrive en Jordanie! > Amman calls you when he arrives in Jordan.
    Amman te téléphone quand il y arrive. (With the short cut, he arrives faster.)

Ex. A French childrens' song starts, "Sur le pont d'Avignon, on y danse, on y danse."

Y* takes the place of *"Sur le pont d'Avignon." If that were not so, the round , as well as the dancers, would go around and around forever.

4. *Y* can substitute for words and phrases not expressed in English.

Exs. Est-ce que vos vaches, Chocolat et Vanille, sont derrière la grange? > Are your cows, Chocolate and Vanilla, behind the barn?
    Oui, elles y sont. Yes, they are (there.)

Exs. Crois-tu à la vie extraterrestre? > Do you believe in extraterrestrial life?
    Non, je n'y crois pas. > No, I don't (believe in it.) (Yet, there's a far out possibility.)

5. The final <u>s</u> on a verb is <u>not</u> dropped before *y* in affirmative *tu* form commands.

Ex. Restes-y! > Stay there!

Ex. Vas-y! > Go there!

6. *Y* is placed between a conjugated verb and an infinitive.

Exs. Après son petit voyage à Little Rock, Fred va rencontrer Wilma à Boulder. > After his short trip to Little Rock, Fred is going to meet Wilma in Boulder.
    Après son petit voyage à Little Rock, Fred va y rencontrer Wilma. > After his short trip to Little Rock, Fred is going to meet Wilma there. (Not 'to leave any stone unturned,' they might eat at Hard Rock Café.)

The Answers Are THERE. - Change the underlined phrases to *y*, and rewrite the sentences.
Ex. Est-ce qu'on porte toujours un parapluie <u>à Cherbourg</u>? > Est-ce qu'on <u>y</u> porte toujours un parapluie? > Does one always carry an umbrella there?

1. Les Frères Ringling sont <u>au cirque</u>. _____.
2. Nous n'allons pas <u>à la plage</u> en hiver. _____.
3. Ça va bien <u>chez vous</u>, n'est-ce pas? _____?
4. Alice n'habite plus <u>dans mon voisinage</u>. _____.

5. Auvergne est <u>au sud de la France</u>. _____.
6. Ne laissez pas vos livres <u>par terre</u>! _____!
7. Sue Titre voit des films étrangers <u>à Soho</u>. _____

_____.
8. Le spectacle a-t-il lieu <u>devant la fontaine</u>? _____?
9. Nous allons passer l'après-midi <u>en ville</u>. _____

_____.
10. Tes amis ne veulent pas attendre <u>devant la gare</u>? _____

_____.
11. Ni Mona ni Lisa ne travaille <u>loin du Louvre</u>. _____.
12. Loue un appartement <u>près de l'université</u>! _____!

En and Its Entourage

1. Formerly labeled a preposition, *en* doubles as a pronoun that replaces already named places and things.

2. The pronoun *en* precedes verbs except in affirmative commands.
Exs. La police ordonne aux Hookah de sortir de la Turquie. > The police order the Hookahs to leave/ to get out of Turkey.

La police ordonne aux Hookah d'en sortir. > The police order the Hookahs to leave/to get out of there. (The couple then realized that 'hookahs' were not welcome everywhere in that country.)

3. *En* takes the place of partitive phrases. Its translations are <u>some</u>, <u>any</u>, <u>of it</u>, <u>of them</u>, <u>about it</u>, <u>about them</u>, <u>from it</u>, <u>from them</u>, and <u>from there</u>. (The meanings 'go *en* and *en*.')
Exs. M. Bossu donne de l'eau à son chameau. > Mr. Bossu gives some water to his camel.

M. Bossu en donne à son chameau. > Mr. Bossu gives some to his camel. (He does not want the animal 'to leave high and dry.')

4. English sentences ending with numbers include *en* in the French translations.
Exs. Combien de couleurs sont dans un arc-en-ciel? > How many colors are in a rainbow?

Il y en a sept. > There are seven (of them.) (Unless I am 'a shade off.')

5. *En* replaces *de* + noun phrases not expressed in English.
Exs. Azita, a-t-elle de la musique iranienne? > Does Azita have any Iranian music?

Non, elle n'en a pas. > No, she doesn't (have any.)

6. The final <u>s</u> on a verb is <u>not</u> dropped before *en* in affirmative *tu* form commands.
Ex. Cherches-en! > Look for some!
Ex. Laisses-en! > Leave some!

7. *En*, like *y*, is placed between a conjugated verb and an infinitive.
Ex. Si vous voulez en parler, vous devez en sortir. > If you want to talk about it, you must come out from there. (Otherwise, they will have a 'panel' discussion.)

Very important notes

1. The preposition *en* is replaced by *y*.
Exs. Beaucoup de citoyens en Roumanie parlent français. > Many citizens in Rumania speak French.
Beaucoup de citoyens y parlent français. > Many citizens speak French there.

2. *Y* precedes *en* when both are in a sentence. They are placed together in front of verbs except in affirmative commands.

Ex. On voit des animaux au Cirque du Soleil? > Do you see animals at the Cirque du Soleil?
  Non, d'habitude on n'y en voit pas. > No, usually you do not see any there.
Ex. Parlons-en! > Let's talk about it!

Enforcing _En_- Change the underlined phrases to _en_, and rewrite the sentences.
Ex. Il y a un tas _de linge sale_ dans ta chambre. > Il y _en_ a un tas dans ta chambre. (There is a pile of it in your room.)

1. Tu lis des œuvres-f. (works) de fiction? _____?
2. Starbucks vend une variété de cafés. _____.
3. Melody écoute de vielles chansons sur son I-Cosse. _____
_____.
4. Dee Rien ne parle pas de sa vie personnelle. _____.
5. Nous n'avons pas de bonne chance. _____.
6. Elle va donner du gâteau au petit. _____.
7. Racontez des plaisanteries, s'il vous plaît! _____!
8. Cherche de la monnaie, s'il te plaît! _____!
9. Jette ne veut pas garder des cartes postales? _____.
10. Ne peux-tu pas trouver du papier blanc? _____?

'Briefly Stated'- Rewrite the sentences by replacing the phrases in bold type with _y_ or _en_.
Ex. Nous allons rencontrer un prince d'Éthiopie **chez Addas**. > **Nous allons y rencontrer un prince d'Éthiopie.**

1. Il parle avec ses parents **de son avenir**. _____
_____.
2. Je sais ce que tu caches **au-dessous du lit**. _____
_____.
3. La reine d'Angleterre ne porte pas toujours sa couronne **dans le palais**. _____
_____.
4. Quelle femme dit, "J'ai trop **de vêtements**?" _____
_____?
5. Cette affiche annonce **des pièces de Molière**. _____.
6. Pour aller **en Europe**, nous avons besoin **de passeports**. _____
_____.
7. "Je dois sortir **du bureau**. Réponds **au téléphone**, s'il te plaît!"_____
_____!
8. Mlle Presqueprise attend **des nouvelles** de son fiancé qui est **en Martinique**. _____
_____.
9. Que penses-tu **de mon idée**? Je songe longtemps à étudier **à l'étranger**. _____
_____.
10. Mme Tremblante devient anxieuse **dans la cour**. Elle a peur **de faire une faute**. _____
_____.

187

On a Fast Track with _Y_- Translate the short sentences below. Assume that the locations have already been mentioned.

1. It is there. _____. It is not there. _____.
2. Let's go there! _____!
3. Don't go there! (_tu_ and _vous_) _____! _____!
4. Answer it! (_tu_) _____!
5. I am thinking about it. _____.
6. We don't believe in it. _____.
7. Stay there! (_tu_ and _vous_) _____! _____!
8. Wait there a minute! (_tu_) _____!

On a Fast Track with _En_- Translate the sentences below.

1. I don't have any. _____.
2. Are you (_vous_) sure of it? _____?
3. I am leaving some for you (_vous_)._____.
4. She does not need any. _____.
5. Do you (_tu_) want some? _____?
6. There are two (of them). _____.
7. There isn't enough of it. _____.
8. What do you (_tu_) think of it? _____?

_____

Garden at Sainte-Adresse by Claude Monet (le Musée d'Orsay, Paris)

LES PRONOMS INVARIABLES - CECI, CELA (ÇA) - Invariable Pronouns - This, That

The endings of these invariable pronouns were introduced in the adverbs *ci*-here and *là*- there. Besides, *ci* is the tail of *ici*- here, and *là* is the nose of *là-bas*- over there. *Voici!* > Here it is! and *Voilà!* > There it is! are your confirmations.

Making the Connection- Adverbs and Their Related Pronouns
1. Being indefinite pronouns, *ceci* and *cela (ça)* refer to unnamed objects, ideas or facts.
Ex. Que pensez-vous de ceci? > What do you think of this?
Ex. Je n'aime pas bien cela. > I don't like that.
2. *Ceci* and *cela* can be subjects, direct objects and objects of prepositions.
Ex. Lourdes, loue ceci pour porter tes valises! > Lourdes, rent this to carry your suitcases! (It is easy to unload nouns by using pronouns.)
Ex. Où est **ta carte d'embarquement**? Tu ne vas pas **monter à bord de l'avion** sans cela. > Where is **your boarding pass**? You are not going **to board the plane** without that.
3. *Cela* is the full-scale model of *ça*.
Ex. Ça va comme ci, comme ça. > It is going so-so./Things are OK.
3a. *Ça* often replaces *cela* in conversations.
Ex. La mère de Pryde le félicite de ses bonnes notes. Elle lui dit, "Ça me plaît beaucoup." > Pryde's mother congratulates him for his good grades. She says, "That pleases me very much."
A note: *Qu'est-ce que c'est que cela (ça)?* > **What is that? flies a bit faster if *ça* replaces *cela*.**
4. As parallels to *-ci* and *-là*, *ceci* refers to a nearby object or idea; *cela* to one further away.
Exs. Je te donne ceci parce que je n'en ai plus besoin. > I am giving you this because I do not need it anymore.
    Merci mille fois! J'aime bien cela > Thanks a thousand times! I really like that.

'Doing This and That'- Fill in the blanks with c*eci* or *cela (ça)*, and translate the completed sentences.
1. Il pleut, mais _____ ne fait rien. _____

2. _____ va te faire plaisir. Ton professeur d'anglais est absent. _____

3. Le dernier train du jour part à 20 heures. _____ ne te donne pas assez de temps. _____

4. Un paquet dans sa main, Fred Ex me dit, "_____" est pour vous. _____

5. Écoute _____! Il y a une rumeur que Paul tombe amoureux de Pauline. _____

6. Madame Spinit dit nous qu'elle adore jouer à la roulette. _____ ne va jamais la rendre riche. _____

7. Pourrais-tu m'aider à écrire ce conte? _____ est vachement difficile. _____

8. Mon beau-père tient une revue sentimentale qu'íl vient de trouver sur **ma commode (my dresser/**

chest of drawers. Il me demande, "Tu lis _____ à l'école?" _____

_____

_____?

_____

CE (C') - AN INVARIABLE SUBJECT PRONOUN

Il, elle, ils and *elles* were among the first pronouns that you met. Could a different subject pronoun replace them? Give a military salute, and answer, "Yes *Ce!*"

How *Ce (C')* Serves
1. *Ce/C'* **has eight translations. They are <u>he, she, it, this, that, they, these</u> and <u>those</u>.**
Ex. C'est la vie. > That's/It's life.
Ex. Ce sont mes cousins de Québec. > They are my cousins from Quebec.
2. Unlike *il, elle, ils* **and** *elles,* *ce/c'* **is used only with third person forms of** *être.* (Otherwise, it is out of 'ce-vice.')
Ex. Ce et c' sont vraiment le même pronom. > *Ce* and *c'* are really the same pronoun.
3. *Ce/C'* **has a pass to replace** *il, elle, ils* **and** *elles* **in the following instances:**
3a. Before a modified noun
Ex. C'est notre bateau à voile. > It is (This is/That is) our sailboat.
Ex. Ce sont/Ils sont des enfants **doués**. > They are **gifted** children.
However, with an unmodified noun, *il, elle, ils* **or** *elles* **is always 'called up.'**
Ex. Il est soldat. > He is a soldier.
Ex. Elles ne sont pas catholiques. > They are not Catholic(s).
3b. Before a proper noun (If that makes common nouns 'improper,' they need to be modified.)
Ex. Nommez une ville en France qui n'a que trois lettres C'est Pau. > Name a city in France that has only three letters? It's/That's Pau.
Ex. Nommez deux villes françaises (à part Paris) connues pour leurs cathédrales! Ce sont Chartres et Reims. > Name two French cities (except for Paris) known for their cathedrals. They're Chartres and Reims.
3c. Before a pronoun
Ex. C'est le téléphone de Marc par terre? Oui, c'est à lui. > Is this/that Mark's phone on the ground? Yes, it's his.
Ex. C'est la sœur de Marc à la ligne? Oui, c'est elle. > Is that Mark's sister on the line? Yes, it is she. (She called to tell Mark 'to pick up' his phone.)
3d. Before a superlative
Ex. <u>Bon Anniversaire</u>, c'est la chanson la plus populaire du monde. > <u>Happy Birthday</u>, that's/it's the most popular song in the world. (Or possibly just the best known one 'on record.')
Ex. C'est le plus grand et le plus intelligent de la classe. > He is the tallest and the most intelligent in the class. (Plus he gives a new meaning to' high grades.')
3e. Before dates
Ex. C'est aujourd'hui le 14 juillet. > Today is July 14th. (No 'storms' have been predicted.)
3f. Before a masculine singular adjective to refer to a previously mentioned idea.
Ex. Ce garçon gâté a toujours tout ce qu'il veut. C'est vrai. > That spoiled boy always has everything

that he wants. That's true.

However, when referring to (a) preceding noun(s), *il* or *elle* **is used.**

Ex. "Regarde cette chambre à coucher! Elle est **indescriptible**." > "Look at this bedroom! It is indescribable." (In all that mess, the speaker can't even find another adjective.)

'A Letter of Reference'- Fill in the second blanks with *Ce, C', Il, Elle, Ils* or *Elles*. **If the correct answer is** *Ce* or *C'*, **put the letter of the rule from the previous explanations on the first blank. If** *Il, Elle, Ils,* **or** *Elles* **is the answer, that line will remain blank.**

Ex. <u>c</u> **Ce sont eux, Charles et Camilia.**

____ 1. _____ est huit heures et demie du matin.

____ 2. Françoise et Francine, _____ sont françaises.

____ 3. _____ sont les chocolats les plus délicieux.

____ 4. _____ est médecin. Il travaille avec les Médecins Sans Frontières.

____ 5. _____ est le Musée D'Orsay.

____ 6. Ils vont à la synagogue le samedi. _____ sont **juifs (Jewish)**.

____ 7. Ne réponds pas au téléphone! _____ est lui encore.

____ 8. M. Donnetout est très généreux. _____ est évident.

____ 9. _____ est le 20 janvier, un jour spécial pour lui.

____ 10. Des vins français? _____ sont Beaujolais, Chardonnay et Merlot.

____ 11. Ivan Ay étudie très peu, et il réussit toujours à ses examens. _____ est vraiment doué.

____ 12. _____ n'est pas à moi de prédire l'avenir.

____ 13. Larmette pleure si ses parents lui disent "non." _____ est gâtée.

____ 14. Deux villes françaises avec les noms de femmes? _____ sont Lille et Nancy.

____ 15. _____ est **le moindre (the least)** de ses problèmes.

Pronouns on Parade- Use *ce, c', ceci, cela, il, elle, ils, elles* and *on* to translate these sentences.

1. It's **a bird (un oiseau)**. It's a plane. It's Superman. _____

_____.

2. What is that? Where does that come from? _____

_____?

3. It is bad weather today. That does not please me. _____

_____.

4. They have a good life. They do a little of this and a little of that. _____

_____.

5. It's Ray Ponse on the computer. I am going to say "Hi" to him. _____

_____.

6. There's Celeste! She is the woman of his dreams. Unfortunately, he is the man of her nightmares.

_____

_____.

7. It is wonderful news. Nobody is going to believe it, but it is true. _____

_____.

_____

DISJUNCTIVE (ACCENTUATED, EMPHATIC, STRESS) PRONOUNS

Because it is easier to recognize unattached pronouns than accentuated or emphatic ones, and since there are no requests for stress, this set is referred to as <u>disjunctive</u>.

<u>Singular</u>	<u>Plural</u>
moi - me	**nous** - us
toi - you	**vous** - you
lui - him, it	**eux** - them (masc.)
elle - her, it	**elles** - them (fem.)

<u>In Name Only</u> (A Brief Review)
1. *Moi* and *toi* are used in affirmative commands.
Ex. Une mère dit à son fils, "Réponds-moi quand je te parle!" > A mother says to her son, "Answer me when I speak to you!" (Won't he then be in more trouble for interrupting?)
2. *Lui*, the third person singular indirect object pronoun, means <u>to him</u> and <u>to her</u>.
Ex. Elle lui offre un tour en montgolfière. > She is offering him a ride in a hot air balloon. (He might 'take her up on it.')
3. *Elle* and *elles* were previously labeled as third person feminine subject pronouns.
Ex. Les jeunes femmes vont à **la station** rencontrer **des célibataires**. > The young women are going to **the resort** to meet **some bachelors**. (They plan to check out 'the pool.')
4. *Nous* and *vous* have been very busy being subject, direct and indirect pronouns.
Ex. **Une éclaireuse du Moyen-Orient** nous explique les mœurs de ces pays-là. > **A guide from the Middle East** explains the customs of those countries to us. (She 'covers' almost everything.)
5. *Eux*, which is in the third person masculine plural slot, is the lone disjunctive-only pronoun.
(The explanations and examples below explain 'what is with <u>them</u>.')

<u>Getting Used to the Uses</u>
<u>Disjunctives function:</u>
1. As a one word response
Ex. Qui pense que sa petite amie est laide? Moi. > Who thinks that his girlfriend is ugly? Me. (That certainly 'cuts to the quick.')
2. For emphasis: As the first words in sentences, *moi* and *toi* are followed by commas before *je* or *tu* is added.
Ex. Toi, tu fais les magasins tout le temps. > You, you shop all the time. (Maybe, she would like to find another 'outlet.')
3. After a comparative (following *que/qu'*): A disjunctive pronoun is the subject of a verb that is not expressed.
Ex. Simian a **un singe** parce que d'autres animaux ne sont pas si intelligents qu'eux. > Simian has **a monkey** because other animals are not as intelligent as they (are).
4. Following *C'est* and *Ce sont*
Ex. Don Louie Bail et Anne O'Cent ne sont pas coupables. **Néanmoins**, ce sont eux qu'on punit. > Don Louie Bail and Anne O'Cent are not guilty. **Nevertheless**, it is they whom one punishes. (The one to blame is "Scott Free.")

4a. *Ce sont,* rather than *C'est,* goes before *eux* and *elles.*
Ex. Ce n'est pas Alli Bye qui **vole** l'argent de ton porte-feuille. Ce sont elles. > It's not Alli Bye who **is stealing** the money from your wallet. It is they. (She didn't even 'have a hand in it.')

5. As a compound subject or object
Ex. **Pour le moment,** Dulcinea et lui rencontrent en secret à un moulin. > **For now,** Dulcinea and he meet secretly at a windmill. (Perhaps things will 'turn around for them.')

6. After a preposition
Ex. Comme l'enfant **a l'habitude de** voir Mickey et Minnie Mouse à leurs costumes typiques, il ne reconnaît pas les deux sans eux. > Because the child **is used to** seeing Mickey and Minnie Mouse in their typical costumes, he doesn't recognize the two without them. (It is 'out of character' for them.)

Verbs followed by *à* and those related to motion take disjunctive pronouns. An abbreviated list includes: *aller, venir, être à-* **to belong to,** *faire attention à, penser à* **and** *songer à.*
Ex. Ces plantes sèches-là sont à elle, mais tu peux les avoir. > Those dry plants are hers, but you can have them. (Their appearance makes them 'a dead giveaway.')

'Dis-stress' Signals- **Refer to the previous list, and write the number of the reason that explains why a disjunctive pronoun is needed. Then, translate the pronouns in parentheses.**
Ex. 4a. (They are the ones) Ce sont <u>eux</u> qui méritent les bonnes notes. > They are the ones who deserve the good grades.

1. _____ Une carafe de vin ordinaire pour (us) _____, s'il vous plaît!
2. _____ Blanche et (he) _____ vont faire du ski à Chamonix.
3. _____ La petite Debbie? Qui fait plus de gâteaux qu'(she) _____?
4. _____ (You) _____, _____ vas choisir qui va être sur quelle équipe.
5. _____ Il ne reconnaît pas ta voix au téléphone. Dis ton nom au lieu de dire, "C'est (I) _____!"
6. _____ Faites comme chez (you) _____! (Make yourself at home!)
7. _____ Qui passe les vacances à une station? Pas (us) _____.
8. _____ (Me) _____, _____ préfère sortir avec de beaux célibataires.
9. _____ Ces deux personnes riches-là sont M. et Mme Rothchild? Oui, ce sont (they) _____.
10. _____ "Ma fille, personne n'a un singe comme un animal de compagnie sauf (you) _____."

Outstanding Replacements- **Rewrite the sentences by substituting the correct disjunctive pronouns for the underlined terms.**
Ex. Mlle Espoir songe-t-elle à <u>M. Spécial</u>? > Mlle Espoir songe-t-elle à <u>lui</u>?

1. Ce sont <u>Maire et Claire</u> qui vont à une maison de haute couture. _____
_____.
2. On trouve tant de marteaux et **clous-m. (nails)** chez <u>M. Charpentier</u>. _____
_____.
3. Les États-Unis sont plus jeunes que <u>la France</u>. _____
_____.
4. Ce yacht-ci est à <u>tes parents</u>? _____?
5. C'est <u>Lady Gaga</u> qui porte les costumes si extravagants. _____

193

6. Nicolas et <u>Chrétien</u> assistent à un festival de film à Cannes. _____.

7. <u>Vous et vos amis</u> avez l'habitude de partir en croisières. _____.

8. Ce sont <u>Monet et Manet</u> qui font de bonnes impressions. _____.

9. <u>Parker et moi</u> pouvons stationner le camion dans votre allée. Pas <u>Charles</u>! _____!

10. Fais attention à <u>la petite</u> quand elle te parle de ses cauchemars! _____.

Strasbourg (the lower Rhine River)

COMPARER LES ADJECTIFS FRANÇAIS - Comparing French Adjectives

Are you more or less interested in knowing how to compare French adjectives? The concept is similar to English, but in some instances here, it is even easier.

The bodies of the phrases have been dissected to show how they function.

Plus + Adjective + Que/Qu' ---------------- More + Adjective + Than
Moins + Adjective + Que/Qu' ------------- Less + Adjective + Than
Aussi + Adjective + Que/Qu' -------------- As + Adjective + As
(Pas) Si + Adjective +Que/Qu' ------------ Not As + Adjective + As

----

'Comparative Anatomy'

1. *Plus, moins, aussi* and *si* precede adjectives: <u>Than</u> is translated by *que/qu'*.

Ex. Superman est plus fort qu'une locomotive. > Superman is more powerful than a locomotive. (He is also a master of 'da-skies.')

Ex. Les dents de Flossie sont plus claires que les étoiles. > Flossie's teeth are brighter than the stars. (Do they come out at night?)

Ex. Ton chien semble moins **amical** aujourd'hui qu'hier. > Your dog seems less **friendly** today than yesterday. (He might not feel like 'putting himself out.')

1a. *Plus* and *moins* followed by opposing adjectives relay the same messages.

Ex. Qu'est-ce qui est plus léger qu'une feuille? > What is lighter than a leaf? carries the same weight as Qu'est-ce qui est moins lourd qu'une feuille? > What is less heavy than a leaf?

1b. The French formula for the balanced comparative <u>as + adjective + as</u> reads *aussi + adjectif + que*. (*Aussi* is also <u>also</u>.)

Ex. Les oranges sont aussi rondes que les pommes? > Are the oranges as round as the apples? (Talk about comparing apples and oranges!)

1c. <u>Not as</u> is expressed by a verb in the negative + *si + adjectif + que*.

Ex. Ses deux premières plaisanteries ne sont pas si drôles que sa troisième. > Her first two jokes are not as funny as her third. (She got 'the last laugh' after all.)

2. A comparative phrase can be followed by a noun, a disjunctive pronoun, an adjective, an adverb or a clause.

Ex. Personne n'est moins généreux que lui. > No one is less generous than he. (That's one thing that he can't keep to himself.)

Some French adjectives are outcasts that do not fit into the typical comparative mold.

Irregular Adjectival Comparisons

Positive Forms		Comparative Forms
1. Bon(ne)(s)(nes)- Good	---	Meilleur(e)(s)(es)- Better
2. Mauvais(e)(es)- Bad	---	Plus Mauvais(e)(es)- Worse
	or	
Mauvais(e)(es)- Bad	---	Pire(s)- Worse
3. Petit(e)(s)(es)- Small	---	Plus Petit(e)(s)(es)- Smaller
	vs.	
Petit(e)(s)(es)- Small	---	Moindre(s)- Less

'For Better or for Worse, Etc.'

1. The four forms of *meilleur* are pronounced the same. (That is 'an across the board' response to "What could be better?")
Ex. Le silence est meilleur qu'un mauvais choix de mots. (And that's not saying much.)

2. When things go from bad to worse, French speakers have an option. *Plus mauvais* with three possible endings can be replaced by *pire* with one singular and one plural spelling. (Because the adjectives are interchangeable, there is no '*pire*' pressure.)
Ex. Les hivers au Maine sont-ils plus mauvais/pires que les étés en Floride? > Are winters in Maine worse than summers in Florida? (Both are acceptable 'to some degree.')

3a. *Plus petit(e)(s)(es)* is used when smaller refers to (a) visible noun(s) or pronoun(s).
Ex. Les lutins de Père Noël sont-ils plus petits que **les nains** de Blanche Neige? > Are Santa's elves smaller than Snow White's **dwarfs**? (It only matters to those interested in 'small talk.')

3b. *Moindre(s)*- less precedes (a) nonvisible noun(s) and expresses lower quality or importance. This comparative is neither preceded by *plus* nor followed by *que*.
Ex. La santé ou **la richesse**? Celle-ci est de moindre importance. > Health or **wealth**? The latter is of less importance. (Providing that there is 'a list of inexpensive medical providers.')

A reminder: *Moins + adjectif + que* means <u>less + adjective + than</u> before (a) visible noun(s).

<u>An Equal Sequel</u>?- Fill in the blanks by using *plus + adjectif + que, moins + adjectif + que, aussi + adjectif + que, si + adjectif + que* and comparative forms of *bon, mauvais* and *petit*.
Ex. Abe et Georges disent toujours la vérité. Un est <u>aussi</u> honnête <u>que</u> l'autre.

1. Booker étudie cinq heures par jour et nous seulement trois. Nous sommes _____ diligents _____ lui.
2. Mes neveux sont de vrais jumeaux. Pierre est _____ grand _____ Pierrot.
3. Un mouton n'est pas _____ timide _____un agneau.
4. Belle gagne plus de **concours de beauté-m. (beauty contests)** parce qu'elle est _____jolie _____ sa sœur.
5. La Tour Eiffel est presque _____ vieille _____ la Statue de la Liberté.
6. Mon chat bouge très peu ce soir. Il **a l'air (seems)** _____ énergique _____ d'habitude.
7. Il y a des touristes qui disent qu'en général, les villageois sont _____aimables _____ les habitantes des grandes villes.

8. Les pieds des belles/demi-sœurs ne sont pas _____ étroits _____ la chaussure de verre.

9. M. Parier perd très souvent au casino, mais il y va de toute façon. Pour lui, gagner est _____ important _____ jouer.

10. Les croissants beurrés sont délicieux, mais les pains au chocolat sont _____.

11. Leurs fils sont méchants. Cependant, Lucifer, qui n'obéit jamais, est _____ _____/ _____ _____ son frère.

12. Le Peugeot et le Citroën sont _____ _____ _____ nos voitures américaines.

'Comparison Shopping'- Translate the phrases in parentheses, and put them in the sentences.

1. (less lively) Ma grand-mère paraît _____ cette année-ci.

2. (as hot) Fait-il _____ à Paris en été qu'à Manhattan?

3. (lazier than) M. Faitrien est _____ son vieux chien.

4. (longer than) Est-ce que la Loire est _____ la Seine?

5. (as crazy as) Lou Nee est _____ vous.

6. (higher than) Yodel demande, "Est-ce que les Alpes sont _____ les Pyrénées?"

7. (less handsome than) Ann Gagée croit que les autres types sont _____ _____ son fiancé.

8. (more interesting than) Lisette pense que les romans sont _____ _____ **les quotidiens-m. (the daily newspapers).**

9. (as precise as) Une horloge n'est pas pas _____'une autre.

10. (more powerful), (friendlier) Les rois _____ ne sont pas d'habitude _____.

11. (as fresh) Les fruits aux marchés ne sont pas _____ à la fin du jour.

12. (a comparative form of *bon*) Quel musée est _____ que le Louvre?

13. (a comparative form of *mauvais*) Cette idée-ci est _____ que l'autre.

14. (a form of *pire*) Les notes de Faye Lieu sont _____ ce semestre.

15. (a comparative form of *petit*) Dans tant de maisons, **les salles à manger (the dining rooms)** sont _____ que **les salons (the living rooms).**

16. (a form of *moindre*) Ne considère pas les faits d'être de _____ **valeur (value)!**

COMPARER LES ADVERBES FRANÇAIS - Comparing French Adverbs

Here's your chance to reinforce the adverbs you have studied and to see how easily they adapt to comparative forms. This special offer requires no written and no verbal agreements.

Read the Fine Print!

1. Since adverbs do not show agreement, the warranty for the original spelling is in effect. The comparative forms typically consist of *plus, moins, aussi* **or** *si* **followed by an adverb +** *que*.

Ex. Le champagne **coule** moins librement que la bière chez moi. > Champagne **flows** less freely than beer at my home. (Just to give people 'a heads up.')

2. Adjectives ending with consonants generally use their feminine singular forms before adding -ment and becoming adverbs.

Ex. Le pirate doit regarder **son équipage** plus attentivement qu'avant. > The pirate has to watch **his crew** more attentively than before. (He knows not 'to turn a blind eye.')

3. Adjectives ending with -<u>ant</u> and -<u>ent</u> in the masculine singular generally have -<u>amment</u> and -<u>emment</u> respectively as adverbial suffixes.

Ex. M. et Mme Concorde ont l'intention de voler avec **leur chiot** aussi fréquemment que possible. > Mr. and Mrs. Concorde intend to fly with **their puppy** as frequently as possible. (They hope 'to get away with it.')

The adverbial comparison contract is not without exceptions. The irregularities are related to their rebel adjectival counterparts.

Irregular Adverbial Comparisons

Positive Forms	**Comparative Forms**
1. Bien- Well --	**Mieux- Better**
2. Mal- Badly --	**Plus Mal- Worse**
<div align="center">**or**</div>	
Mal- Badly ---	**Pis- Worse**
3. Beaucoup- Much --	**Plus- More**
4. Peu- Little ---	**Moins- Less**

<u>**The Shifty Deal**</u>

1. *Mieux* and *pis* **cannot be preceded by** *plus*. (You can't make better better and would not want to make worse worse.) **However,** *plus* **strengthens** *mal* **by making it <u>more badly</u>.**

Ex. M. Ay enseigne mieux que M. Cee qui n'a pas un **corrigé** > Mr. Ay teaches better than Mr. Cee who doesn't have an **answer key**. (That explains everything.)

Ex. Poêle Aufeu dit que M. Méchant la **traite** plus mal/pis que M. Mauvais. > Poêle Aufeu says that Mr. Méchant **treats** her worse than Mr. Mauvais. (He is 'the lesser of two evils.')

2. *Plus* **and** *moins*, **components of comparative phrases themselves, are the adverbial comparative forms of** *beaucoup* **and** *peu* **respectively.**

Ex. L'essence coûte plus en ville qu'en banlieue, n'est-ce pas? > **Gas** costs more in town than in the suburbs, doesn't it?

Ex. Le gérant m'entend lorsque je dis à des amis que j'aime **les marchandises** moins dans ce magasin que dans un autre. > The manager hears me while I tell some friends that I like **the merchandise** less in this store than in another. (The speaker might want 'to take it back.')

3. *De* **translates <u>than</u> before numerals.**

Ex. L'écureuil cache plus de cinq *noix* dans l'arbre. > **The squirrel** hides more than five **nuts** in the tree. (It is keeping them on lay away.)

4. <u>Popular Expressions with</u> *Mieux* <u>and</u> *Pis*

a. tant mieux- so much the better, even better

b. tant pis- so much the worse, too bad

c. Mieux vaut tard que jamais!- Better late than never!

Ex. Si on arrive **au marché aux puces** de grand matin, tant mieux! Si on arrive tard, tant pis! Il n'y a pas autant d'affaires. Mais mieux vaut tard que jamais! > If we arrive at/get to **the flea market** early in the morning, so much the better! If we get there late, too bad! There aren't as many bargains. But better late than never!

Pumping Up the Adverbs- Using the signs in parentheses as a reference, rewrite the sentences in comparative forms.
Ex. (+) Parlez doucement à Thierry ou il va pleurer! > Parlez plus doucement à Thierry ou il va pleurer!

1. (+) Je peux le faire facilement maintenant. _____
_____.

2. (+) Tu dois couper le papier soigneusement. _____
_____.

3. (-) Ray Alistique le dit gentiment. _____
_____.

4. (=) Pourquoi ne parlent-ils pas cette langue couramment? _____
_____?

5. (-) Eddie Torial lit les quotidiens souvent. _____
_____.

6. (=) Est-ce qu'il agit impoliment en classe? _____
_____?

7. (+) Vos médecins croient que vous allez bien aujourd'hui. _____
_____.

8. (- deux choix) Luc Itup répond mal sans son corrigé. _____
_____/_____.

9. (+) Mme Aurabais dépense beaucoup au marché aux puces que moi. _____
_____.

10. (-) Ces marchandises qui n'ont pas de valeur coûtent peu. _____
_____.

How Do the Translations Compare?- Write these adverbial phrases in French.
1. less politely than his sister _____
2. as quickly as a squirrel _____
3. sooner than this evening _____
4. as frequently as possible _____
5. more happily than you (*vous*) _____
6. not as late as tomorrow _____
7. as slowly as **a snail (un escargot)** _____
8. not as far as China _____
9. better than yesterday _____
10. worse than us _____, _____
11. more than ever _____
12. less than last month _____
13. more than fifty euros _____
14. less than a hundred years _____

LES FORMES SUPERLATIVES DES ADJECTIFS FRANÇAIS
The Superlative Forms of French Adjectives

Those who don't understand what the title means should just 'give it their <u>best</u> shot.' Concisely stated, the superlatives of French adjectives are formed by inserting definite articles in front of comparative forms.
The following explanations and examples are <u>most</u> helpful.

Superlative Formulas

Le (L', La, Les) + Plus + Adjectif (-e, -s, -es) + De (Du, De l', De La, Des)
or
Le (L', La, Les) + Moins + Adjectif (-e, -s, -es) + De (Du, De l', De la, Des)

<u>Acquiring Superlative Status</u>
1. As in their positive and comparative modes, the superlatives of French adjectives agree both in gender and in number with the nouns they describe. The definite articles preceding *plus* and *moins* put superlatives at the top of the ladder.
Exs. le pompier le plus courageux > the most courageous fireman, l'infirmière la plus travailleuse > the hardest working nurse, les maîtresses les moins impatientes > the least impatient schoolteachers (Most of them do a superlative job of going above and beyond the call of duty.)
2. Adjectives in superlative forms keep their positive positions.
2a. When an adjective follows a noun, a coordinating definite article goes before *plus* or *moins*.
Ex. Doucette a une façon la plus **apaisante** avec leur bébé pleurant. > Doucette has a most **soothing** manner with their crying baby. (They 'have to hand it to her.')
Ex. **Un chasseur** achète les balles les moins chères. > **A hunter** buys the cheapest bullets. (He hopes 'to get a lot of bang for his buck.')
2b. When an adjective precedes a noun, the superlative phrase can begin with a definite article, a demonstrative or a possessive adjective. The familiar sound of "bangs" signals adjectives that identify beauty, age, numbers, goodness and size. Those modifiers keep their prenoun positions in superlative phrases.
Ex. Voici une photo de mon plus beau cousin. > Here is a photo of my most handsome cousin. (Possibly 'taken' a while ago.)
Ex. Remarque que les plus méchants élèves admirent cette maîtresse-là! > Notice that the naughtiest pupils admire that schoolteacher! (She is always 'up front with them.')
2c. Not every positive form modifier that can either precede or follow a noun is able to wander as a superlative. For example, *propre* means <u>own</u> before a noun but <u>clean</u> after it. Someone can have *la voiture la plus propre* > the cleanest car, but he cannot claim the 'ownest' one.
3. <u>In</u> and <u>of</u> are translated by *de, du, de l', de la* and *des* in superlative phrases.
Ex. Ces hôtels-là ont les lits les plus confortables de Paris. > Those hotels have the most comfortable beds in Paris. (Who would 'turn them down'?)
Ex. Gill achète le poisson le plus frais du marché. > Gill buys the freshest fish in the market. (Is it 'a big-mouthed bass'?)

When definite articles precede the irregular comparative forms of these adjectives, they have superlative status.

Irregular Adjectival Superlatives

Comparative Forms	**Superlative Forms**
1. Meilleur(e)(s)(es)- Better ------------------------	Le (La)(Les) Meilleur(e)(s)(es)- The Best
2. Plus Mauvais(e)(es)- Worse --------------------	Le (La)(Les) Plus Mauvais(e)(es)- The Worst
or	
Pire(s)- Worse ------------------------------------	Le (La)(Les) Pire(s)- The Worst
3. Plus Petit(e)(s)(es)- Smaller ----------------------	Le (La)(Les) Plus Petit(e)(s)(es)- The Smallest
vs.	
Moindre(s)- Less ---------------------------------	Le (La)(Les) Moindre(s)- The Least

----

'Going to Extremes'

1. With a definite article, <u>better</u> is upgraded to <u>best</u>.

Ex. C'est le meilleur maire. > He is the best mayor.

Ex. Beau Vine est fier de ses meilleures vaches. > Beau Vine is proud of his best cows. (He refers to them as *la crème de la crème*.)

2. Preceded by definite articles, *plus mauvais* and *pire* become <u>worst</u>.

Ex. Savez-vous pourquoi les cinémas montrent les plus mauvais/les pires films de l'année? > Do you know why movie theaters show the worst films of the year? (It's part of 'a screening process.')

3. When *le, la* or *les* is placed before *plus petit(e)(s)(es)*, <u>smaller</u> shrinks to <u>the smallest</u>.

Ex. La plus petite de la classe est aussi la plus intelligente. > The smallest girl in the class is also the most intelligent. (Her classmates 'look up to' her.)

3a. Following a definite article, *moindre(s)* means <u>the least</u>.

Ex. Pendant un concours de beauté, les juges voient que Passi Douée a le moindre talent. > During a beauty contest, the judges see that Passi Douée has the least talent. (She will be eliminated 'without any question.')

'Giving Adjectives the Third Degree'- Put the letters beside the numbers to form sentences.

____ 1. Rhode Island est	A. le plus beau célibataire
____ 2. C'est un fait que _____ sont en hiver.	B. la plus haute montagne du monde.
____ 3. Les gens en bonne santé ont	C. le plus riche des États-Unis?
____ 4. Le dimanche mes voisins portent	D. le plus mauvais tueur de l'histoire.
____ 5. Le lion dans le Magicien d'Oz est	E. les pommes les plus délicieuses.
____ 6. Qui est ____ des films français?	F. le plus petit état des États-Unis.
____ 7. Quels profs n'aiment pas	G. le plus long fleuve du monde.
____ 8. **Les ouragans (the hurricanes)** ____ sont en août et en septembre.	H. les villes les plus chères.
____ 9. Everest est le nom de	I. les vies les plus actives.
____ 10. Quelquefois les gens qui ont la plupart d'argent sont	J. les plus forts
____ 11. Jack the Ripper n'est pas	K. les détails les plus ennuyeux.
____ 12. Bozo n'est pas l'homme	L. la plus vieille femme du monde
____ 13. L'Amazone en Amérique du Sud est	M. leurs meilleurs vêtements.

_____ 14. On dit que les singes sont les animaux   N. les plus courts jours de l'année

_____ 15. En automne on vend   O. les moins paresseux des animaux?

_____ 16. Penses-tu que les roses sont   P. les plus pauvres individus.

_____ 17. New York et Paris sont parmi   Q. les plus modernes.

_____ 18. Les édifices les plus intéressants ne   R. les plus intelligents.
          sont pas toujours

_____ 19. On n'écoute pas quand Drone raconte   S. le plus heureux du cirque.

_____ 20. Est-ce que les castors sont   T. les meilleurs étudiants de la classe?

_____ 21. Je lis de _____ qui a 112 ans.   U. le caractère le moins courageux.

_____ 22. Est-ce que Bill Gates est l'homme   V. les plus jolies fleurs?

Access to the Top and Bottom Levels- **Put the listed adjectives in the correct superlative forms to complete the sentences: bon, cher, clair, compliqué, dangereux, fort, généreux, heureux, incroyable, mauvais, moins, occupé, petit, profond, propre, sec, tranquille, triste**

Ex. C'est l'émission <u>la plus populaire</u> chez moi. > It's <u>the most popular</u> TV show in my home.

1. Les chameaux habitent dans les climats _____.

2. Beaucoup de familles sont presque toujours dans **la salle de séjour (the family room)**. Ces jours-ci, le salon est la pièce _____ de la maison.

3. Les histoires imaginatives de Figment sont _____.

4. Les questions _____ sont souvent à la fin de l'examen.

5. Les bonnes de cette station-là travaillent toute la journée. On y trouve les chambres _____
_____.

6. Tous les petits ne sont pas d'accord. Demandez-leur, "Qui est **le héros (the hero)** _____
_____ / _____ héros?"

7. Qu'est-ce que Mme Cheap va faire avec toute sa richesse? On dit qu'elle est la femme _____
_____ de la ville.

8. Un roman dans ses mains, Lisa ne bouge pas de sa chaise près du lac. C'est l'ambiance _____
_____ pour elle.

9. Pourquoi **des présentateurs de journal télévisé-m. (some newscasters)** vont-ils à une plage pendant un ouragan? C'est l'endroit _____.

10. Des vieillards qui ont peu d'argent ont l'habitude de faire leurs emplettes aux marchés _____
_____.

11. Le merveilleux ange a _____ rêves, mais le diable épouvantable
a _____ _____ / _____ cauchemars.

12. Le roi ne traite pas tous les citoyens également. Certains d'entre eux ont les vies _____
_____; d'autres ont les vies _____.

13. Jack et Jill portent l'eau du puits _____ ou de **la source (the spring)** _____?

14. Le chien a besoin seulement de _____ / _____
indication-f. (the clue) pour trouver même _____ os.

LES FORMES SUPERLATIVES DES ADVERBES FRANÇAIS
The Superlative Forms of French Adverbs

The superlative forms of adverbs relate the strongest and the weakest performances of verbs. Consider their comparative status as the second degree while mastering the superlative level!

The PhD of Adverbs
1. Adverbs attain a superlative status when *le* precedes their comparative forms. Because they modify verbs, neither gender nor number agreement is included in the curriculum.
Ex. Ces caddies-là écoutent le plus attentivement **les demandes** des joueurs de golf. > Those caddies listen the most attentively to **the requests** of the golfers. (And 'follow them to a tee.')
Ex. Le môme habite le plus proche au voisin très hostile. > The brat lives the closest to the very hostile neighbor. (They are only 'a stone's throw away' from each other.)
2. Like their adjectival counterparts, <u>in</u> and <u>of</u> are translated by *de, du, de l', de la* or *des* after superlative adverbial phrases.
Ex. Gerrie Atric agit le plus vivement **des personnes du troisième âge**. > Gerrie Atric acts the liveliest **of the senior citizens**. (She doesn't need anyone 'to push' her.)

When *le* precedes their irregular comparative forms, these adverbs have a superlative status.

Irregular Adverbial Superlatives

Comparative Forms	Superlative Forms
1. Mieux- Better	Le Mieux- The Best
2. Plus Mal- Worse	Le Plus Mal- The Worst
or	
Pis- Worse	Le Pis- The Worst
3. Plus- More	Le Plus- The Most
4. Moins- Less	Le Moins- The Least

Of Definite Use
1. *Le* before irregular comparative forms gives those adverbs a superlative makeover. (With *le mieux* as a superlative adverb, you save the best for last.)
Ex. La boîte la plus lourde est **emballée** le mieux. > The heaviest box is **wrapped** the best. (It seems that someone 'put a lot into it.')
2. Both *le plus mal* and *le pis* bring out <u>the worst</u>.
Ex. De toutes les femmes, Mme Ruenne cuisine le plus mal/le pis. > Of all the women, Mrs. Ruenne cooks the worst. (Friends have 'reservations' before going to her home to eat.)
3. *Le* preceding *plus* offers <u>the most</u> while *le* before *moins* makes it an easy superlative to form, <u>to say the least</u>.
Ex. Rhea Flux hésite à dire au médecin que l'indigestion l'**inquiète** le plus. > Rhea Flux hesitates to tell the doctor that indigestion **bothers** her the most. (She really did not want 'to bring it up.')
Ex. Plusieurs gens dépensent le moins **en épicerie** après les fêtes d'hiver. > Several people spend the least **on groceries** after the winter holidays. (They may find that 'things are tight.')

'Quality Control'- Circle the letters of the correct responses to complete the sentences.

1. M. O. Pinion donne ses conseils ____.
a. le plus sincèrement   b. le plus élégamment   c. le moins souvent   d. le plus librement
2. Un escargot marche ____ de tous les mollusques, n'est-ce pas?
a. le plus régulièrement   b. le moins   c. le plus lentement   d. le plus légèrement
3. Al Lergie réagit ____ de tout le monde si quelqu'un fume près de lui.
a. le plus curieusement   b. le pis   c. le plus bravement   d. le moins constamment
4. Les profs les plus âgés **devancent (anticipate)** nos questions ____.
a. le moins clairement   b. le plus honnêtement   c. le plus mal   d. le plus instinctivement
5. Tu emballes le cristal le plus soigneusement parce qu'il fracasse ____.
a. le plus loin   b. le plus facilement   c. le plus gentiment   d. le plus rarement
6. Raiza Hand est vraiment perceptive. Avec peu d'indications, elle sait les réponses ____.
a. le plus vite   b. le plus fièrement   c. le plus récemment   d. le plus mauvais
7. Les personnes sages du troisième âge ne jugent pas tout ____.
a. le plus objectivement   b. le moins complètement   c. le plus naïvement   d. le plus tard
8. Un conducteur en panne à l'autoroute ne pense pas toujours à son problème ____.
a. le plus   b. le plus également   c. le moins sincèrement   d. le plus logiquement
9. Quels enfants dans les contes de fées sont traités ____?
a. le plus cruellement   b. le moins directement   c. le plus furieusement   d. le plus proche
10. Au fond des cartes de Noël, on voit la phrase, "____!"
a. le cadet de **mes soucis-m. (my worries)**   b. le pis de l'affaire   c. mes meilleurs vœux
d. le mieux pour la fin

Giving Adverbs Their Final Grades- Translate the following sentences.

1. I speak English the most fluently. _____
_____.

2. Cora Spondance writes to him the least often. _____
_____.

3. American tourists visit London and Paris the most frequently. _____
_____.

4. Mr. Weiner expresses his ideas the most frankly. _____
_____.

5. We lose weight the fastest in the summer. _____
_____.

6. Justin Foniques reads the worst in the class. _____
_____.

7. Arthur and Catherine dance the best of everybody. _____
_____.

8. He calls me the most often of my four children. _____
_____.

9. Do you (*tu*) accomplish the least in the evening? _____
_____?

10. Always do your (*vous*) best! _____
_____!

UN JOUR AU CARNAVAL - A Day at the Carnival

Du Vocabulaire du Conte

1. à une faible distance- a short distance away
2. l'humeur (f.)- the mood
3. l'escale (f.)- the stop
4. se passer- to go on, to happen
5. éclairé- lit up
6. il y a à parier- the odds are
7. l'avaleur de sabres (m.)- the sword swallower
8. la galerie de jeux- the amusement arcade
9. tenter- to try
10. énervé- irritated
11. gaspiller- to waste money
12. C'est facile comme tout!- There's nothing to it!
13. sonner- to ring
14. le maillet- the mallet
15. manier- to wield
16. le sommet- the top
17. l'auto tamponneuse- the bumper car
18. en ce cas- in this/that case
19. plutôt- instead, rather
20. le casse-croûte- the snack
21. répugnant- disgusting
22. la prévision- the prediction
23. suit- follows
24. le titre- the title
25. la grande roue- the ferris wheel
26. les montagnes russes- the roller coaster
27. le manège de chevaux de bois- the carousel

C'est samedi. Blaise et sa petite amie, Colette, ont des plans de passer toute la journée à un carnaval. Malheureusement, Colette a de mauvaises nouvelles quand elle lui téléphone tôt le matin. Elle ne va pas bien, et elle n'a pas envie de sortir. Comme Blaise ne veut ni rester chez lui ni aller là seul, il décide de demander à son copain, Guy, de l'accompagner.

Blaise: Allô Guy?

Guy: Oui, ça va?

Blaise: Ça ne va pas si bien. Colette vient de me dire qu'elle est malade, et pour ça, elle ne peut pas aller au carnaval avec moi. Voudrais-tu m'y rencontrer?

Guy: Qui a envie d'étudier le week-end? J'aime mieux ton idée.

Blaise: C'est bien. Je vais être au guichet près du parking à onze heures.

(**Malgré** une foule énorme, Blaise arrive à voir Guy **à une faible distance**.)

Guy: Salut Blaise! Ton deuxième choix est ici.

Blaise: Tu es amusant, mais je ne suis pas de **la** meilleure **humeur** maintenant.

Guy: Alors, un jour au carnaval peut te guérir.

Blaise: Tu as raison. Voici cent billets! Tu peux me rembourser plus tard.

Guy: Merci beaucoup! Quelle est notre première **escale**?

Blaise: Voyons ce qui **se passe** à cette tente **éclairée**!

Le premier homme: Venez par ici voir l'homme le plus grand du monde!

Blaise: Je sais qui c'est. Il joue au basket pour une équipe américaine.

Le deuxième homme: Mesdames et Messieurs, entrez et voyez la plus grasse femme de l'Europe!

Blaise: Pourquoi ne pouvons-nous pas la voir d'ici?

Le troisième homme: Mesdames et Messieurs, ne ratez pas l'occasion de voir une très belle femme coupée en deux!

Blaise: Après cela, devient-elle la plus petite dame du monde?

Guy: Sais pas, mais **il y a à parier** que ce monsieur-là connaît **l'avaleur de sabres**.
Blaise: Ces spectacles ne nous intéressent pas. Allons à **la galerie de jeux**!
Guy: Et gagner un prix pour Colette, peut-être.
Blaise: J'espère bien que oui.

D'abord, Blaise perd quelques billets au jeu où on tire aux canards nageants. Il n'est pas content. Ensuite, il jette des balles pour renverser trois bouteilles. Pas de chance encore! Le pauvre type a moins de billets, et il est même plus malheureux. Enfin, il **tente** sa chance à couvrir un cercle des trois plus petits rangés en ordre spécifique. Il n'y réussit pas. Quel jeune homme **énervé**!

Guy: Ne **gaspille** plus de billets, Blaise! Achète un petit cadeau pour Colette!
Blaise: Absolument pas! Je suis très déterminé à rentrer avec un bon prix pour elle. Je veux visiter le strand devant nous où on utilise ses muscles.
Guy: D'accord, Atlas. Allons-y!
Blaise: **C'est facile comme tout**. Je frappe un morceau de bois. Le truc monte très haut, et la cloche **sonne**. On me donne un animal en peluche.

Blaise donne vingt billets au ouvrier. La première fois, Blaise ne fait pas si mal, mais il ne frappe pas **le maillet** assez fortement. La deuxième fois, il **manie** le maillet avec toutes ses forces. Les copains regardent très anxieusement pour voir si ce truc va monter **au sommet** de la colonne. Heureusement, la cloche sonne, et le fier Blaise gagne un ours en peluche.

Guy: Félicitations! Quelle performance extraordinaire! Nous déjeunons avant ou après notre escale **aux autos tamponneuses**?
Blaise: Allons-y d'abord! Cette attraction est tout près.
Guy: **En ce cas**, je vais prendre une glace en route. J'ai vraiment faim. Tu en voudrais une?
Blaise: Non, mais **plutôt** un hot-dog.
(Blaise paie **les casse-croûte**, et il goûte son hot-dog.)
Blaise: Quelle viande **répugnante**! On fait ces hot-dogs dans la maison de reptiles? Goûte-le!
Guy: Non merci. Personne ne peut dire que tu n'es pas extrêmement généreux.
Blaise: Je ne vais pas avoir d'appétit jusqu'au dîner. Allons aux autos tamponneuses!
(Ils descendent de cette attraction-là, et Guy offre une suggestion.)
Guy: Allons consulter une diseuse de bonne aventure!
Blaise: Après ce hot-dog, je ne peux pas traiter plus de mauvaises nouvelles.
Guy: Tu ne veux pas le faire?
Blaise: Pourquoi pas? J'ai un ours en peluche pour me protéger.
(Blaise et Guy entrent dans la tente de Madame Saittout.)
Guy: Bonjour Madame. Pourrions-nous écouter **vos prévisions** ensemble?
Mme Saittout: Mais certainement. Trente billets les deux.
(Chaque jeune homme lui donne quinze billets.)
Mme Saittout: Je vois clairement de ma boule de cristal que vous allez avoir la malchance. Mais je peux changer cela. Il faut me payer seulement cent euros.
(Les amis amusés remercient Mme Saittout, et ils sortent de sa tente. Néanmoins, elle les **suit** dehors en criant, "Tant pis pour vous, mes jeunes hommes!")

Blaise: Les diseurs de bonne aventure ont jamais raison?

Guy: On va voir. Mais en tout cas, "bonne" ne devrait pas être une partie de leur **titre**.

Blaise: Remarque qu'il faut payer avant d'entendre les prévisions!

Guy: Tous ses clients ne veulent pas payer après.

Blaise: Que veux-tu faire maintenant? **La grande roue** ou cette attraction-là?

Guy: Tu ne veux pas dire **les montagnes russes**? Es-tu totalement fou? Cela voyage aussi vite qu'un TGV (un train à grande vitesse).

Blaise: Tu préfères peut-être **le manège de chevaux de bois**?

Guy: D'accord! Allons-y! Mais n'oublie pas les mots de Mme Saittout!

(Chaque ami paie trente billets pour monter aux montagnes russes.)

Blaise: Regarde-nous! Toi, tu as peur de cette attraction et moi, je tiens un ours en peluche aux bras.

(Les copains trouvent que la scène est très drôle. Quelle grande fin pour leur jour au carnaval!)

Écrivez les réponses complètes en français aux questions suivantes.

1. Qu'est-ce que Colette et Blaise ont l'intention de faire samedi? _____
_____.

2. Pourquoi Colette lui téléphone-t-elle? _____
_____.

3. Où et à quelle heure Blaise rencontre-t-il son copain? _____
_____.

4. Qu'est-ce que Blaise donne à Guy quand il arrive? _____
_____.

5. Qui sont trois personnes dans la tente éclairée? _____
_____.

6. Quels conseils Guy offre-t-il à Blaise? _____
_____.

7. Qu'est-ce que Blaise espère faire dans la galerie de jeux? _____
_____.

8. Qu'est-ce qu'il faut faire pour gagner un prix au stand? _____
_____.

9. Que Blaise choisit-il pour son prix? _____.
10. Que mangent-ils en route aux autos tamponneuses? _____
_____.

11. Quelle question Guy pose-t-il à Madame Saittout? _____
_____.

12. Qu'est-ce qu'elle raconte de leur avenir? _____
_____.

13. Qu'est-ce que la diseuse de bonne aventure crie quand Blaise et Guy sortent de sa tente? _____
_____.

14. À quoi Guy compare-t-il les montagnes russes? _____
_____.

15. Pourquoi les copains sont-ils amusés avant de monter cette attraction-là? _____
_____
_____.

UNE REVUE - A Review

Les Prépositions Françaises, Les Expressions Géographiques, Y et En, Ceci et Cela (Ça), Ce (C'), Les Pronoms Disjonctifs, Comparer les Adjectifs et les Adverbes Français, Les Formes Superlatives des Adjectifs et des Adverbes Français, Un Jour au Carnaval

Fact or Fictitious?- Label the statements *vrai* or *faux*.

_____ 1. All French prepositions end with *de*.

_____ 2. *Avant* and *après* are antonyms.

_____ 3. The majority of French prepositions are related to location.

_____ 4. *Au* and *à la* precede the names of most French cities to express <u>to</u>, <u>in</u> or <u>at</u>.

_____ 5. The French names of most Middle Eastern countries are preceded by *le*.

_____ 6. The names of all countries and continents ending with <u>e</u> are feminine.

_____ 7. *Aux* is used before the names of masculine plural countries to express <u>from</u>.

_____ 8. *Y* replaces prepositional phrases referring to location.

_____ 9. *En* replaces partitive phrases.

_____ 10. Both *y* and *en* have one translation.

_____ 11. *Y* and *en* do not always precede verbs.

_____ 12. *Ceci* and *Cela* have one location in a sentence.

_____ 13. *Ce/C'* can precede any conjugated verb.

_____ 14. *Ce/C'* and other subject pronouns are not always interchangeable.

_____ 15. Disjunctive pronouns are used after *que/qu'* in comparative phrases.

_____ 16. Disjunctive pronouns are not used after prepositions.

_____ 17. A disjunctive pronoun can stand alone as a response.

_____ 18. French comparative phrases can begin with *plus de* and *moins de*.

_____ 19. *Aussi + adjectif + que* expresses equality.

_____ 20. *Petit(e)(s)(es)* and *moindre(s)* have the same meaning.

_____ 21. Adverbs agree in gender and in number with the verbs they modify.

_____ 22. *Mieux* and *pis* cannot be preceded by *plus* or *moins*.

_____ 23. Superlative adjectival terms begin only with definite articles.

_____ 24. <u>In</u> is expressed by *dans* in superlative phrases.

_____ 25. Irregular adverbs have *le* in front of their superlative forms.

'Fair Assumptions'- Circle the letters of the responses that best complete the scenarios from Un Jour au Carnaval.

1. Blaise est de mauvaise humeur parce que/qu' _____.

a. il n'a pas assez de billets

b. Colette ne peut pas l'accompagner

c. il est un type malheureux

d. Guy n'arrive pas à l'heure

2. Les deux copains n'entrent pas dans la la tente éclairée parce que/qu' _____.

a. ils ne connaissent pas les gens dedans

b. Blaise préfère manger un casse-croûte

c. les jeunes hommes ont peur de spectacles

d. ces attractions ne leur intéressent pas

3. Blaise _____ dans la galerie des jeux.

a. perd un tas de billets   b. gagne trois prix   c. parie tous ses euros   d. achète un hot-dog

4. Le truc monte au sommet de la colonne, et la cloche sonne. Blaise _____.

a. est prêt à rentrer chez lui   b. frappe sa tête à l'auto tamponneuse   c. choisit un ours en peluche
d. va à la maison de reptiles

5. Madame Saittout dit qu'elle peut empêcher leur malchance si les deux amis ____.
a. regardent la balle en cristal avec elle   b. passent le jour dans sa tente
c. n'écoutent pas ses prévisions   d. lui donnent cent euros

6. Guy ne veut pas monter aux montagnes russes _____.
a. à cause de la grande vitesse   b. parce qu'il préfère aller à la grande roue
c. parce que la diseuse de bonne aventure le suit   d. à cause du mauvais temps

7. Les amis pensent que leur réaction aux montagnes russes est drôle parce que/qu' ____.
a. le manège de chevaux de bois ne marche pas   b. ils n'agissent pas bravement
c. c'est leur dernière escale   d. Blaise sait bien manier un maillet

----

'There's More to It'- Translate the underlined phrases, and rewrite the full sentences.
Ex. Portia porte <u>her prettiest dresses there</u>. > Portia y porte ses plus belles/jolies robes.

1. Susan Boyle? Qui chante <u>sweeter than she</u>? _____
_____?

2. Il n'est pas <u>as friendly as the guy beside him</u>. _____
_____.

3. Pourquoi ne fait-elle pas d'emplettes <u>there with them</u>? _____
_____?

4. Elle n'a pas <u>any near her apartment building</u>. _____
_____.

5. Parmi toutes les villes en Europe, Val Ise goes <u>to Madrid the most</u>. _____
_____.

6. Jay Desfaits est sûr que <u>the richest countries in the world have the least crimes</u>. _____
_____.

7. **Ce SMS (this text message)** de Ciu Soon dit qu'il vient <u>here by the fastest route</u>. _____
_____.

8. Elsée D'où pense que <u>the best leather purses come from Argentina and from Italy</u>. _____
_____.

9. Mes copines veulent visiter le Mexique cet été. <u>Me, I prefer to vacation in Canada</u>. _____
_____
_____.

10. <u>The most extraordinary hosts</u> devancent toutes les demandes de leurs invités. _____
_____
_____.

ORTHOGRAPHIC/STEM CHANGING VERBS

Isn't orthographic an impressive synonym for spelling? These verbs are sometimes referred to as stem-changing, root-changing, and if one goes to extremes, 'radical changing.' Regardless of their label, most are "boot verbs" with regular -er endings.
One style is displayed in the box below.

VERBS WITH È

Acheter - To Buy, To Purchase

Singular	Plural
j'achète- I buy, do buy, am buying	nous achetons- we buy, do buy, are buying
tu achètes- you buy, do buy, are buying	vous achetez- you buy, do buy, are buying
il/elle achète- he/she/it buys, does buy, is buying	ils/elles achètent- they buy, do buy, are buying

----

Buying Power and More

1. For this category of orthographic changing verbs, knowing where to add an accent is a *grave* decision. The accented forms create a boot, outlined by the entire singular and the third person plural.
A helpful hint: If you don't hear the final e, the preceding one gets a *grave*.
2. The infinitive and the *vous* form endings have a clipped long a sound. The *nous* form has no final e. So, in those three cases, no accent mark is required.

Verbs Conjugated Like *Acheter*

1. achever- to complete: Its synonyms are *finir* and *terminer*. Completing a task can be thought of as an achievement. *Achever* also means to finish off, to fatigue.
Ex. Le dix-huitième trou les achèvent. > The eighteenth hole finishes them off. (They were 'running themselves ragged.')
2. lever- to lift, to raise: This verb is one of a related set. They all should be 'taken up' together because their meanings and forms are so similar.
2a. élever- to bring up, to raise (a child or an animal): *Un élève* is on hand to offer help.
2b. enlever- to remove, to take away: *enlever à quelqu'un*- to take away from someone: Notice that the verb is followed by *à* (not *de*)!
Ex. Après que le père enlève la voiture à sa fille, il doit la **conduire** partout. > After the father takes the car away from his daughter, he must **drive** her everywhere. (Hopefully, she's discreet about telling him where to go.)
A very important note: The prefixes listed above and below, a, e, em, en and pro, do not affect the orthographic changes in the main part of the verb.
3. mener- to lead: Its synonym is *conduire*. Verbs that include men refer to humans or animals leading or being led. *Apporter* means to bring things.
3a. amener- to bring, to lead: Consider the *a* as indicating to!
3b. emmener- to lead away, to take away: An emigrant leaves a county.
3c. promener- to walk someone or something, to show around: This verb is an additional step

to *la promenade.*

Ex. La petite femme promène son chien énorme, ou il la promène? > Is the little woman walking her huge dog, or is he walking her? (It's difficult to tell heads from tails.)

4. geler- to freeze, to gel: *La gelée* is Jello. *Le congélateur* is **the freezer.** (That's just 'frozen food for thought.')

5. peser- to weigh: (There are no English cognates to balance this verb.)

Expressions That Vitalize Verbs 'in Grave Condition'

1. acheter quelque chose de quelqu'un- to buy something <u>from</u> someone, acheter quelque chose à/pour quelqu'un- to buy something <u>for</u> someone: Notice the choice of prepositions!

Ex. N'achète pas les meubles de tes parents! > Never buy furniture from your relatives! (That should should be 'a given.')

2. lever le pied (to lift the foot) = <u>ralentir</u>- to slow down

Ex. Lève le pied de l'accélérateur! > Lift your foot from the accelerator! (It is a warning for drivers who mistake I-95 for the speed limit.)

3. emmener déjeuner quelqu'un- to take someone (out) to lunch

Ex. M. Essaye emmène déjeuner sa femme malheureuse. > Mr. Essaye takes his unhappy wife (out) to lunch. (It gives a new twist to 'whining' and dining.)

Detecting an Accent- Change everything in the sentences from the singular into the plural and vice versa.

Ex. Nous promenons nos chiens trois fois par jour. > Je promène mon chien trois fois par jour.

1. Le paresseux n'achève rien. _____.

2. Quelle route mène de Paris à Alfortville? _____
_____?

3. Combien ces boîtes pèsent-elles? _____?

4. Le riche emmène déjeuner la pauvre. _____
_____.

5. Le lac ne gèle pas dans ce village. _____
_____.

6. Nous amenons nos chevaux aux champs. _____
_____.

7. Les américains achètent plus de vêtements que les français. _____
_____.

8. J'achète cette fleur pour ma mère. _____
_____.

9. Elles élèvent leurs enfants être polis, n'est-ce pas? _____
_____?

10. Levez les pieds! Nous ne faisons pas **de course (a race)!** _____
_____!

DOUBLE FINAL CONSONANT VERBS

Verbs like *appeler*- to call, *jeter*- to throw/to throw away and their derivatives double their last consonants in a "boot" form before the final mute <u>e</u>.
Conjugated verbs look like this on the "Double L Double T Ranch."

Jeter - To Throw, To Throw Away

<u>Singular</u>	<u>Plural</u>
je jette- I throw, do throw, am throwing	nous jetons- we throw, do throw, are throwing
tu jettes- you throw, do throw, are throwing	vous jetez- you throw, do throw, are throwing
Il/elle jette- he/she/it throws, does throw, is throwing	ils/elles jettent- they throw, do throw, are throwing

----

1. appeler- to call: Je m'appelle > I call myself/My name is. If you call a person, an animal or a thing, the verb is conjugated without a reflexive pronoun.
Ex. Il appelle un chat un chat. > He calls a spade a spade.
a. appeler à l'aide- to call (out) for help
Ex. Ta mère appelle **"au secours!"** Le dîner vient de **prendre feu.** > Your mother is calling **"help!"** Dinner just **caught on fire.** (Now she can call out for Chinese.)
2. jeter- to throw, to throw away: Its cognate is <u>to jettison</u>.
<u>An interesting aside:</u> People used to purchase *des jetons* before making a call in a phone booth. The false coins were inserted into a pay phone slot. The idea has been jettisoned.

VERBS WITH ACCENTS THAT CHANGE DIRECTIONS

An infinitive with an <u>é</u> over the next to last <u>e</u> keeps the quick long <u>a</u> sound in the *nous* and *vous* forms only. For the rest of the conjugation, an accent *grave* replaces the accent *aigu* in a "boot" form. Concisely stated, if you don't hear the final <u>e</u>, the preceding <u>é</u> changes to <u>è</u>.

Espérer- To Hope

<u>Singular</u>	<u>Plural</u>
j'espère- I hope, do hope, am hoping	nous espérons- we hope, do hope, are hoping
tu espères- you hope, do hope, are hoping	vous espérez- you hope, do hope, are hoping
il/elle espère- he/she/it hopes, does hope, is hoping	ils/elles espèrent- they hope, do hope, are hoping

----

<u>Verbs That Fluctuate with 'Es'</u>
1. célébrer- to celebrate: It's not easy to celebrate when four forms are in *grave* condition.
2. espérer- to hope: <u>To aspire</u> may be 'reaching for' a related verb. *Désespéré*- desperate leaves one *sans espoir*- without hope.

3. posséder- to own, to possess: Swap the <u>d</u> for a double <u>s</u>, and claim this verb!

4. préférer- to prefer: There is no choice but to leave the first <u>e</u> with an <u>é</u>.

5. protéger- to protect: Maneuvering the last letters of the French infinitive helps to secure its meaning. The bilingual word, *protégé*, offers further protection.

6. répéter- to rehearse, to repeat: The reminder not to change the first <u>é</u> is a 'stress' rehearsal.

7. sécher- to dry: You can whet your appetite with a glass of *vin sec*.

Expressions for É to È Verbs

1. espérer bien- to truly hope

Ex. Un homme offre un verre à une belle femme. Il lui dit, "J'espère bien te revoir." > A man offers a drink to a beautiful woman. He says to her, "I truly hope to see you again." (Was it just 'a one shot deal?')

2. posséder quelqu'un = duper- to take someone in, to take someone for a ride

Ex. Un beau gigolo possède **une veuve** riche. > A handsome gigolo dupes **a rich widow.** (She gives him the benefit of the doubt, and he does not doubt the benefit.)

You Can Have It Both Ways- Put the correct forms of the verbs in parentheses in the blanks.

1. (espérer) J' _____ que des types sympathiques viennent à mon boum.
2. (posséder) Nous _____ deux voitures, et nous vous en offrons une.
3. (célébrer) La famille Drapeau _____ tous **les jours fériés (holidays)** ensemble.
4. (préférer) Décida veut acheter un pull. Elle me demande, "Tu _____ le rouge ou le bleu?"
5. (protéger) Rien n'est plus important que _____ votre santé.
6. (préférer) M. et Mme D'Or _____ fêter leur cinquantième anniversaire là.
7. (espérer) _____-tu devenir riche ou célèbre ou tous les deux?
8. (répéter) Si je ne **comprends (understand)** pas le parleur, je lui dis, "_____, s'il vous plait!"
9. (préférer) Madame Campagne habite loin de Paris. Elle _____ avoir plus d'espace.
10. (protéger) Connaissez-vous cette expression-ci? "Le bon Dieu _____ les enfants et les vieillards."

'Perfecting Your Swing'- Write the correct forms of *acheter, achever, élever, enlever, lever, emmener, mener, geler, peser, appeler, jeter, espérer, posséder, préférer, protéger* and *répéter* in the blanks. (*Acheter* is used more than once.)

1. Quand l'eau _____, elle devient la glace.
2. Oreille _____ les conjugaisons trois fois, et elle les sait parfaitement.
3. La traduction d'un proverbe anglais est "Tous les chemins _____ à Rome."
4. Son prénom est Jeffroi, mais je le/l' _____ **Schtroumpf (Smurf).**
5. _____ cette valise pour moi, s'il vous plaît! Elle est très lourde.
6. Y a-t-il une femme qui _____ seulement ce dont elle a besoin?
7. Les petits de la veuve sont tellement polis. Elle les _____ bien.
8. Il y a tant de trous dans son manteau. Rien ne le _____ du froid.
9. Slim et toi êtes au gymnase presque tous les jours. Penses-tu que vous _____ trop?

10. Son père va _____ à lui son téléphone cellulaire parce qu'elle ne fait pas bien à ses études.

11. Mlle Naïve croit que tout le monde dit la vérité. On peut la _____ très facilement.

12. Ne _____ pas les livres si tu ne les veux plus!

13. Il y a des gens qui ne commandent rien en ligne parce qu'ils _____ voir ce qu'ils _____ d'abord.

14. Ces quatorze exemples-ci vous _____? Je/J' _____ bien que non.

Heading in the Correct Direction- Write the correct forms and translations for the verbs listed.
Ex. mener- third person sing. (il) --------- il mène- he leads, does lead, is leading

1. lever- second person sing. _____, _____
2. jeter- first person sing. _____, _____
3. enlever- third person sing. (il) _____, _____
4. peser- third person pl. (ils) _____, _____
5. préférer- second person pl. _____, _____
6. geler- third person pl. (ils) _____, _____
7. élever- first person sing. _____, _____
8. posséder- first person pl. _____, _____
9. protéger- third person pl. (elles) _____, _____
10. espérer- second person sing. _____, _____
11. appeler- second person pl. _____, _____
12. célébrer- third person sing. (on) _____, _____
13. achever- second person pl. _____, _____
14. emmener- first person pl. _____, _____

-CER VERBS

It's all about we. The *nous* forms of -cer verbs have a little twist. A cedilla under the c gives the consonant a soft sound and is found in French words with ça, co or cu combinations.

Verbs Hooked under the 'Ç'

Commencer is 'just for starters.' Associate the c with cedilla in the *nous* forms of:

1. annoncer- to announce: Even without a u in the first verb, the very close resemblance speaks for itself.

Ex. Jim Shorts et moi annonçons tous les matches de boxe. > Jim Shorts and I announce all the boxing matches.

2. avancer- to advance: Drop the d from the English version, and keep moving!

3. effacer = enlever- to efface, to erase, to rub out: If you're unfamiliar with the cognate efface, use another 'tip' to erase.

4. lancer- to launch, to throw: The English verb and noun are 'offshoots.' (Like King Arthur, we see 'Lance a lot.')

5. menacer- to menace, to threaten: The translations follow closely enough to be menacing.

6. placer- to place, to set: No clues are necessary. This one is right in front of you.

7. prononcer- to pronounce: Nobody sees nor hears from <u>u</u> in the French version.

8. remplacer- to replace: The prefixes <u>re</u> and <u>rem</u> replace <u>again</u>.

Ex. Nous remplaçons **le canapé déglingué** dans la salle de séjour. > We are replacing the **beaten-up sofa** in the family room. (Was it the scene of too many pillow fights?)

9. renoncer à- to give up, to renounce: The second translation equals the French infinitive with <u>u</u> given up and *à* added.

<u>Undercurrents of the 'Ç'</u>

1. annoncer = prédire- to forecast, to predict

Ex. **Des météorologistes** annoncent le brouillard pour demain. > **Some weathermen** forecast fog for tomorrow.

2. avancer une pendule, un horloge, une montre- to set a clock/a watch forward

Ex. Le petit-fils avance l'horloge de sa grand-mère une heure au printemps. > The grandson sets his grandmother's clock one hour ahead in the spring. (It's 'a hands me down.')

3. commencer- to take up

Ex. Quelques étudiants très motivés vont commencer l'astronomie. > A few very motivated students are going to take up astronomy. (Others should not 'take up space.')

4. effacer- to delete, to erase

Ex. Nous effaçons plus de courriers électroniques que nous lisons. > We delete more e-mails than we read. (Unfortunately, some of the senders don't take "delete" for an answer.)

5. mal prononcer un mot- to mispronounce a word.

Ex. Un type américain mal prononce le mot quand il demande à une française de le rencontrer à une brassière et pas à une brasserie. > An American guy mispronounces the word when he asks a French woman to meet him at a *brassière* and not at a *brasserie*.

-GER VERBS

Anybody who wants to buy a vowel for the *nous* form of -<u>ger</u> verbs should make it an <u>e</u>. Just as a cedilla enables a soft <u>ç</u>, an <u>e</u> before -<u>ons</u> prompts a soft <u>g</u>. The resulting sound is similar to the <u>i</u> in *je*.

<u>We and "the Add an E Verbs"</u>

1. bouger- to move, to shake, to change a position: It made a motion to be placed as #1.

2. changer- to change: The only change is the token <u>e</u> in the slot before -<u>ons</u>.

3. charger- to load, to charge (a battery or a purchase), to give someone the responsibility to do something (Its usage has a large 'turnover.')

4. corriger- to correct, to grade: Pairing the French verb with <u>incorrigible</u> might be beneficial.

Ex. Corrigeons ces erreurs avant de regarder le corrigé! > Let's correct these errors before looking at the answer key! (There's nothing wrong in that.)

5. déménager- to move, to move out: The first <u>e</u> stays put; the second goes into a "boot" box.

6. déranger- to bother, to disrupt, to disturb, to inconvenience: The prefix <u>de</u> is the equivalent of <u>un</u> and <u>not</u>. Ex. *Ne pas déranger!* > Do not disturb!

Ex. Il ne dérange pas Ann Grie que **le commerce de proximité** dans son voisinage va fermer **définitivement**. > It does not bother Ann Grie that **the convenience store** in her neighborhood is going to close **for good**. (She had 'a run-in' with them.)

7. manger- to eat: Bring out the <u>e</u> for <u>eat</u> before <u>-ons</u>!

8. mélanger- to mix, to mingle: This verb 'blends' an <u>e</u> into the *nous* form.

9. ménager- to handle carefully, to show consideration: <u>To manage</u> has only a 'fragile' association with the French verb. So, handle with care! *Le ménage* is both <u>housework</u> and <u>household</u>.
Ex. Il faut ménager cette fille **sensible**. > It is necessary to handle this **sensitive** girl carefully. (Her feelings are easily hurt.)

10. nager = faire la natation- to float, to swim: The verb is familiar, but the <u>e</u> in front of <u>-ons</u> is something '*nous*.'

11. partager- to divide up, to share: By dividing something up, each person gets <u>a part</u>.
Ex. Les parents de Pierre partagent plusieurs bouteilles de Partager à Paris avant de partir. > Pierre's parents/relatives share several bottles of Partager in Paris before leaving.

12. plonger- to dive, to swoop down: The French verb is a cognate of <u>to plunge</u>. It 'surfaces' in *plonger sous-marin*- to scuba dive.

13. protéger- to protect: The é changes to è in the form of a boot.

14. ranger- to arrange, to put in order, to tidy up
Ex. **Le garde forestier** qui habite seul range sa cabane. > **The forest warden** who lives alone tidies up his cabin. (Some folks call him 'The Lone Arranger.')

15. songer à = penser à = considérer = réflechir à- to think about: (The French certainly put a lot of thought into their conversations.)

16. voyager- to travel: Though other forms of this verb have been around, until now, <u>we</u> never **traveled.**
Ex. Nos gosses apportent plus quand nous voyageons en voiture que par avion. Our kids bring more when we travel by car than by plane. (Where they tend 'to carry on' less.)

<u>**An important note:**</u> -**Ger** verbs often have English cognates that end with -**ect.** Learn *corriger*, *diriger*- to direct/to lead, *négliger*- to neglect and *protéger* together!

<u>**Germane -Ger Idioms**</u>
1. changer = déplacer- to move someone/something from place to place
Ex. **Des agents immobiliers** changent les meubles fréquemment pour donner un air différent à leurs maisons. > **Some real estate agents** move furniture frequently to give their homes a different look. (Relocation is their specialty.)

2. changer en = transformer en- to change someone/something into
Ex. Le bon Spiderman peut changer en mauvais Spiderman. > Good Spiderman can change into bad Spiderman. (Do they have separate web sites?)

3. corriger quelqu'un de- to cure someone of
Ex. Ray Médie pense qu'il peut corriger sa femme **des jeux d'argent.** Elle lui demande d'y parier. > Ray Médie thinks that he can cure his wife of **gambling.** She asks him to bet on it.

4. Ça déménage!- It's awesome! (It's as cool as 'all get out.')

5. être déménagé- to be off one's rocker, to be crazy (The person may have 'lost it' in the move.)

6. donner à manger = nourrir- to feed someone
Ex. Mme Purée donne à manger au bébé les légumes. > Mrs. Purée gives the baby vegetables to eat.

(And hopes that she doesn't get any 'feed back.')

7. ménager ses forces- to save one's strength

Ex. Notre fils paresseux ménage ses forces jusqu'au jour du déménagement. > Our lazy son is saving his strength until moving day. (Until then, he is not 'lifting even a finger.')

8. nager dans le bonheur- to be overjoyed: It actually says "to swim in happiness."

Ex. Diva nage dans le bonheur de son mariage récent. > Diva is overjoyed about her recent marriage. (She is really just 'getting her feet wet.')

9. nager complètement- to be totally lost

Ex. Moi, je nage complètement coudre à la main. > Me, I am completely lost sewing by hand. (I end up 'knitting my brows.')

10. plonger quelqu'un dans- to put someone into a certain position

Ex. Ne lui pose pas de telles questions personnelles! Tu la plonges dans **l'embarras.** > Don't ask her such personal questions! You're putting her in **a difficult position.** (She might have 'to wrestle with her conscience.')

What Are WE Going to Do?- Circle the letters of the answers that go with the initial sentences.

1. Nous aimons passer nos vacances en Angleterre. Nous _____.
a. les ménageons proprement   b. y voyageons encore cet été   c. ne montons pas à bord de l'avion
d. le traitons bien

2. Les espèces menacées ne nous dérangent pas. Pourquoi _____?
a. les menaçons-nous?   b. protégeons-nous les bêtes?   c. levez-vous vos épées?
d. ne songeons-nous pas au dérangement?

3. Travers Lamer et moi ne partons pas tout simplement de ce voisinage. Nous _____.
a. protégeons les enfants que nous élevons   b. appelons un chat un chat
c. déménageons des États-Unis   d. ménageons nos forces

4. Cela fait **sourire (to smile)** des étrangers _____.
a. lorsque vous effacez ce qu'ils écrivent   b. si des touristes les menacent
c. quand tu ménages bien leurs sensibles   d. quand nous mal prononçons des mots

5. Les pompiers annoncent, "Nous _____."
a. partageons tout ce que nous avons   b. nageons complètement
c. ne négligeons personne qui crie "au secours!"   d. rangeons tout au commerce de proximité

6. Quand la marée est trop basse, je ne nage pas dans l'océan. Je _____.
a. sais effacer toutes les indications   b. jette des coquillages dans l'air
c. voyage sans carte d'embarquement   d. donne à manger aux oiseaux

7. M. Poumon et ses fils ne renoncent pas à fumer. Nous _____.
a. n'enlevons pas le congélateur   b. ne pouvons pas les en corriger
c. plongeons dans le bonheur   d. chargeons ces types-là

8. Les parents disent aux enfants, "Restez-là!" Les petits répondent, " Nous _____."
a. possédons l'agent immobilier   b. vous plongeons dans l'embarras   c. les lançons partout
d. ne bougeons pas

9. Les week-ends mon père préfère être seul pendant quelques heures. Pour ça, je _____.
a. ne le dérange pas   b. ne veux pas le bouger   c. ne range pas le garage
d. remplace ce qu'il ne veut plus

10. Les enfants vont y patiner à glace **aussitôt que (as soon as)** nous _____.

a. les emmenons déjeuner   b. sommes déménagés   c. commençons le projet
d. annonçons que le lac est gelé

'A Second Coat with Detailing'- Put the letters beside the numbers of the synonyms.

____ 1. lever le pied	A. penser à
____ 2. guérir	B. être extrêmement heureux
____ 3. charger	C. transformer en
____ 4. voyager	D. faire peur à
____ 5. songer à	E. donner à manger à
____ 6. lancer	F. abandonner
____ 7. appeler à l'aide	G. jeter
____ 8. nager dans le bonheur	H. duper
____ 9. nourrir	I. corriger quelqu'un de
____ 10. Ça déménage!	J. crier "au secours"
____ 11. déplacer	K. organiser
____ 12. annoncer	L. ne rien comprendre
____ 13. changer en	M. donner à quelqu'un la responsabilité de
____ 14. effacer	N. changer le lieu de
____ 15. renoncer à	O. aller d'un lieu à un autre
____ 16. corriger	P. ralentir
____ 17. ranger	Q. enlever
____ 18. menacer	R. faire mieux
____ 19. nager complètement	S. C'est magnifique
____ 20. posséder quelqu'un	T. informer de

-YER VERBS

French infinitives with -yer endings have many consecutive vowels in their conjugations. The y changes to i to fit like a boot. Taking after the infinitives, the *nous* and *vous* form endings with -yons and -yez 'can not be kicked around.'
Here's the model to use!

Employer- To Employ, To Use

Singular	Plural
j'emploie- I use, do use, am using	nous employons- we use, do use, are using
tu emploies- you use, do use, are using	vous employez- you use, do use, are using
il/elle emploie- he/she/it uses, does use, is using	ils/elles emploient- they use, do use, are using

-----

For '-Yer' Information
The plural endings of -oyer verbs are identical to those of *voir*.
In addition to *employer*, which is used less frequently than *utiliser*, -oyer "boot verbs" include:
1. envoyer- to send: The English noun envoy is on a mission inside.
Ex. Les étudiants motivés emploient leur temps sagement. > The motivated students use/spend their

time wisely. (They should get credit for that.)

2. nettoyer = faire le ménage- to clean: It is 'neat' when you see *net* related to this verb.

Ex. Carri Ère n'a pas le temps de **prendre soin de** ses tailleurs. Ainsi, elle les fait **nettoyer à sec.** > Carri Ère doesn't have time **to take care of** her suits. So, she has them **dry cleaned.** (She has other 'pressing engagements.')

3. renvoyer- to dismiss, to expel, to fire, to send back (This verb has multiple ways to get back at someone.)

'U and I' Together
-**Uyer** verbs change **y** to **i** as they slip into a boot.

1. ennuyer- to bore, to annoy, to bother: The bilingual noun *ennui* (boredom) is related to this verb.

Ex. Personne n'ennuie les pessimistes plus que les optimistes. > Nobody annoys/bothers pessimists more than optimists. (A positive outlook irks those who 'frown around.')

2. essuyer- to wipe: If the u is changed to an a, *essuyer* becomes *essayer*. Try to remember that!

-Ayer Verbs- Have it Your Way!
-**Ayer** verbs offer a choice: Keep the **y** or switch it to an **i** in "boot" form. Common -**ayer** verbs include: *balayer*- to sweep, *essayer*- to try (on) and *payer*- to pay (for).

Ex. La belle Cendrillon balaie **le plancher** avant le bal. Le jour **suivant,** elle essaie la chaussure de verre. > Beautiful Cinderella sweeps **the wooden floor** before the ball. The **following** day, she tries on the glass shoe. (Alas! Her man's home will be her castle.)

A helpful hint: Since -oyer and -uyer verbs involve a y to i change in "boot" form, it might be easier to file -ayer verbs with them. Then, it will not be necessary to remember which set has an optional vowel switch.

-Yer Verbs and Their 'I' Expressions
1. essayer de faire quelque chose- to try to do something: Notice that *essayer* is followed by *de*.

Ex. C'est la troisième fois que Toulouse essaie de **faire un bénéfice** de **la Bourse.** > This is the third time that Toulouse is trying **to make a profit** from **the stock market.** (When at first he did not succeed, he tried and tried 'a gain.')

2. payer par chèque- to pay by check; payer en espèces/payer comptant- to pay in cash

A note: Les espèces means both species and cash.

Ex. Comme **le marchand** ne connaît pas tous les clients, ils doivent lui payer en espèces. > Because **the merchant** does not know all the customers, they have to pay him in cash. (It's his idea of 'taking things at face value.')

3. payer quelque chose à/pour quelqu'un- to pay for/to buy something for someone. This idiom can be exchanged for *acheter quelque chose à/pour quelqu'un*.

Ex. Ma bonne amie paie à la masseuse pour nos massages. > My good friend is paying the masseuse for our massages. (She enjoys having her 'palm greased.')

4. envoyer quelqu'un sur les roses- to send someone packing

Ex. Le propriétaire envoie Eve Icte sur les roses parce qu'elle ne paie jamais le loyer. > The owner/ the landlord sends Eve Icte packing because she never pays the rent. (It was an appropriate solution since she was 'a thorn in his side.')

5. faire du nettoyage- to clean out completely

Ex. Dunn va **faire du nettoyage** dans son entreprise. Il renvoie **les salariés** moins diligents. > Dunn is going to clean out his company completely. He is dismissing (firing) **the** less diligent **employees.** (He is ready for an overall overhaul.)

6. renvoyer l'ascenseur- to return the favor: Its actual meaning is "to send back the elevator."

Ex. Mireille me demande d'emprunter mes talons. Je lui dis, "Bien sur, si tu renvoies l'ascenseur." > Mireille asks to borrow my high heels. I tell/say to her, "Of course, if you return the favor." (I'm not 'letting her off' that easily.)

7. renvoyer dans son foyer- to send home: It literally says "to send back to his hearth/home."

Ex. Le chiot de notre voisin vient de **mâcher** les pantoufles de mon frère. Il va le renvoyer dans son foyer. > Our neighbor's puppy just **chewed** my brother's slippers. He is going to send it home. (It's 'in the doghouse' now!)

An Interesting Observation: Many orthographic changing verbs and their related expressions have meanings directly or indirectly associated with housework.

Some examples are: *balayer, enlever, essuyer, faire du nettoyage, faire le ménage, jeter, nettoyer, ranger and sécher.* (That's quite 'a laundry list.')

'Y's Choices- Put the correct forms of *balayer, employer, ennuyer, envoyer, essayer de, essuyer, nettoyer* and *payer* on the lines provided. *(On peut utiliser des verbes plus d'une fois.)*

1. Ma belle-sœur me (m') _____ une surprise.
2. Les vieillards banals _____ la veuve vivante.
3. Je lave et je repasse mes vêtements au lieu de les _____ à sec.
4. Quelques **cinéastes (filmmakers)** _____ faire tous les genres de film.
5. La mère _____ la glace de la bouche de sa petite.
6. Je préfère _____ la phrase "sans espoir" au mot "désespéré."
7. Mon petit ami va _____ pour mon billet d'avion.
8. La carte postale dit, "Nous t' _____ des bisous de la Belgique."
9. Les élèves _____ coudre à main des costumes indiens.
10. Ne/N' (*vous*) _____ pas la gelée du plancher! _____-la!

Answer '-Yer' Way- Use the correct forms of *envoyer, nettoyer, ennuyer, essuyer, essaye*r, *payer* and *renvoyer* to write answers to the questions.

Ex. La Petite Locomotive fait-elle de son mieux? > Does the Little Engine do her best? > Oui, elle essaie autant que possible. > Yes, she tries as much as possible.

1. Que fait-on s'il n'a pas de carte de crédit? _____
_____.
2. Pourquoi sa maison est-elle toujours très propre? _____
_____.
3. Qu'est-ce qu'on fait avant de pour payer les vêtements neufs? _____
_____.
4. Qu'est-ce qui arrive aux salariés paresseux à cette usine-là? _____
_____.

5. Qu'est-ce que M. Franchement dit à l'homme qui le gêne? _____
_____.

6. Qu'est-ce que vos invités **prévenants (considerate)** font avant d'entrer chez vous? _____
_____.

7. Comment remerciez-vous quelqu'un de vous rendre service? _____
_____.
_____

la Cathédrale de Reims

USES OF THE DEFINITE ARTICLES - LE, LA, L', LES

THE is not always used in French as it is in English. While we might promptly toss out unused articles, the French find <u>definite</u> uses for them.

<u>**Putting THE Articles in Place**</u>
1AI. Nouns used in a general sense are usually preceded by definite articles.
Ex. Les pommes et les oranges sont les fruits préférés des américains. > Apples and oranges are the favorite fruits of Americans. (In a recent survey, they picked both.)
Ex. Reid Lotz dit souvent que l'intelligence est plus importante que la beauté. > Reid Lotz often says that intelligence is more important than beauty. (But not everyone values books over looks.)
2AI. Definite articles are used before the names of languages.
Ex. Plusieurs linguistes en Suède étudient le suédois, le norvégien, le français et l'anglais. > Several linguists in Sweden study Swedish, Norwegian, French and English. (What a smorgasbord!)
<u>**An exception:**</u> **No articles are used after *parler*, *en* and *de(d')*.**
Ex. Par la fin de l'année scolaire, tous les étrangers dans la classe de Mme Helsinki parlent finnois. > By the end of the school year, all the foreigners in Mrs. Helsinki's class speak Finnish. (Being non-natives, they cannot consider themselves 'Finnished' products.)
3A1. Definite articles are used before titles (ranks and professions) followed by a name.
Ex. La reine Élisabeth a un rapport assez unique avec le docteur Heathrow. > Queen Elizabeth has a rather unique rapport with Dr. Heathrow. (She would like to take off a few pounds; he wants to add a few to her bill.)
<u>**An exception:**</u> **No articles are used with titles of direct address.**
Ex. "M. Edison, je voudrais vous présenter à Général Électrique." > "Mr. Edison, I would like to in-troduce you to General Electric." (They were 'de-light-ed' to meet each other.)
4AI. Definite articles usually precede the names of body parts.
Ex. La mère dit à son petit, "Donne-moi la main." L'enfant répond, "Mais Maman, j'en ai besoin." > The mother says to her little boy, "Give me your hand!" The child answers, "But Mommy, I need it."
Ex. Kaye Nyne a les oreilles pointues. > Kaye Nyne has pointed ears.
<u>**An exception:**</u> **If the owner of the body part needs to be clarified, a possessive adjective is used as an ID tag.**
Ex. Elle n'aime pas bien **sa coupe de cheveux**. > She doesn't like **her haircut**. (Given enough time, 'it will grow on her.')
5AI. A definite article is used when a proper name follows an adjective.
Ex. Vous pouvez reconnaître le méchant Damien des trois six à la tête. > You can recognize naughty Damien by the three sixes on his head. (What a calculating devil!)
6AI. *Le* precedes a day of the week when it is used in a general sense. The preposition <u>on</u> is not translated.
Ex. Jean et Janine **jonglent** le jeudi en juin et en juillet. > John and Janine **juggle** Thursdays in June and in July. (Toss that French sentence around a couple times!)
7AI. *Le/L'* precede the names of seasons.
Ex. Le printemps est la plus mauvaise saison pour Frosty **le bonhomme de neige**. > (The) Spring is the worst season for Frosty **the snowman**. (We see only condensed versions of him 'in the spring.')
<u>**A reminder:**</u> ***En* means <u>in the</u> before the names of three seasons. *Au printemps* is the exception.**

8AI. Definite articles replace <u>a/an</u> and <u>per</u> before nouns of weight and measure.
Ex. Les clous coûtent $5.00 la livre. > Nails cost $5.00 a pound. (However, hammers are not sold by 'the pound.')
<u>An exception:</u> *Par* **is used without an article to indicate frequency of time.**
Ex. Elle fait couper les cheveux quatre fois par année. > She has her hair cut four times a year. (But more often if 'she can't stand it any longer.')
9AI. Definite articles precede dates.
Ex. C'est aujourd'hui le 15 avril. C'est aujourd'hui le 26 décembre. ("Many Happy Returns" applies to both days.)
10AI. Definite articles express <u>the</u> before the names of geographical locations.
Ex. La France est presque aussi grande que le Texas. > France is almost as large as Texas. (They can both claim that Spanish is the first language South of the Border.)
11AI. <u>Common Expressions with Definite Articles</u>

1. à/dans l'école- to, in, at school
2. à/dans l'église- to, in, at church
3. à la maison- at home, to the home
  at the house, to the house
4. le matin- in the morning

5. l'après-midi- in the afternoon
6. le soir- in the evening
7. la semaine prochaine- (the) next week
8. le mois dernier- (the) last month
9. l'année dernière- l'année passée- (the) last year

Ex. La plupart des étudiants assistent **aux cours** à l'université le matin. > Most of the students attend **classes** at the university in the morning. (If they 'are up for it.')
12. A definite article plus an adjective can replace a noun. This exchange just requires 'pulling a grammatical switch.'
Ex. Le gentil fantôme leur rend visite au milieu de la nuit. > The nice ghost visits them in the middle of the night. > Le gentil leur rend visite au milieu de la nuit. > The nice one visits them in the middle of the night. (See how quickly the ghost disappeared!)

<u>Is That a Definite Answer?</u>- Circle the letters of the correct answers to complete the sentences.
1. Est-ce qu'on parle _____ français au Luxembourg?
a. le   b. ___
2. _____ professeur Hawkins habite en Angleterre.
a. Le   b. ___
3. Mes frères **taquinent (tease)** _____ petit Charles.
a. ___   b. le
4. "Michelle, je voudrais vous présenter à _____ reine Élizabeth."
a. ___   b. la
5. J'aime Paris _____ printemps.
a. le   b. au
6. L'anniversaire de naissance de Noëmi est _____ 22 juillet.
a. ___   b. le
7. Midas paie cinq euros _____ kilo d'or.
a. le   b. pour un
8. À qui sont les bottes que Lou Boutin tient _____ mains?

a. à ses   b. dans les
9. ____ fruits et ____ **légumes (vegetables)** sont bons pour votre santé.
a. ___ .... ___   b. Les .... les
10. Mlle Pompeii lit bien ____ latin.
a. le   b. ___
11. L'homme et la femme vont à Deauville une fois ____ semaine.
a. par   b. la
12. ____ adjectifs peuvent remplacer ____ noms.
a. Les .... les   b. ___ .... ____
13. On trouve Madeleine ____ église ____ dimanche.
a. dans .... sur   b. à l'/dans l' ... le
14. ____ empereur César dit, "Prêtez-moi ____ oreilles!"
a. L' ... vos   b. ___ .... des

Deciding on THE Use- Check **THE** rules above and translate the following sentences.
1. English is her second language. _____.
2. Is your (informal form) birthday August 8? _____
_____?
3. Nothing is sweeter than sugar. _____.
4. If you (*vous*) know the answer, raise your hand! _____
_____!
5. My aunts have a picnic in the park in the afternoon. _____
_____.
6. Is there snow on Mt. Sinai? _____
_____?
7. Today is September 20. Is it fall yet? _____
_____?
8. Time and tide wait for nobody. _____.
9. Raoul lives in Northern Spain. He speaks Spanish and French. _____
_____.
10. That box of chocolates costs $10.00 per pound. _____
_____.
11. Beautiful Belle dances with the nice beast. _____
_____.
12. "Good morning, Dr. Deviner. Is Dr. Saitplus here today?"_____
_____?
13. What can the little one do in the winter that he can not do in the spring? _____
_____?
14. Gifted children are going to attend a meeting Wednesday. _____
_____
_____.

OMISSION OF DEFINITE and INDEFINITE ARTICLES

As for using French articles in the following instances, "Just forget it!" Some things are better left unsaid.

1AO. Definite articles are not used with numerical titles.
Ex. Henri VIII et ses huit épouses > Henry VIII and his eight wives (There was never a shortage of 'ladies-in-waiting.')

2AO. Indefinite articles are omitted before unmodified predicate nouns of nationality, occupation, profession and religion.
Ex. Ahmed est égyptien. Il vient du Caire. Fatima est égyptienne. Elle vient d'Alexandrie. > Ahmed is (an) Egyptian. He comes from Cairo. Fatima is (an) Egyptian. She comes from Alexandria. (They have 'Tut-an-khamun.')
Ex. M. Volesauf veut devenir pilote. > Mr. Volesauf wants to become a pilot. (Hopefully, he will be able 'to land the job.')

An important note: An indefinite article is used if the predicate noun is modified.
Ex. Monah et Gronah sont les infirmières **empathiques.** > Monah and Gronah are **empathic** nurses. (They 'take pains with' their patients.)

3AO. Indefinite articles are not used after forms of _quel_.
Ex. Quelle **saleté** quelques animaux font au cirque! > What a **filthy mess** some animals make at the circus! (No one can make them 'clean up their act.')

4AO. Indefinite articles are not used with _cent_ and _mille_.
Ex. **Mon professeur particulier** prend cent dollars par heure. > **My tutor** charges a hundred dollars per hour. (He certainly doesn't accept 'poor' students.)

Sorting Out the Articles- Write the number-letter codes of the previous explanations + exc. for exception (if applicable) on the lines. (AI = article included; AO = article omitted)
Ex. __3AI exc.__ **"Président Hollande, nous sommes enchantés de faire votre connaissance."**

_____ 1. Tahitia a les yeux très exotiques.
_____ 2. L'anniversaire de naissance des jumeaux est le 9 mars.
_____ 3. La soie est plus chère le mètre que le coton.
_____ 4. Est-ce que Gesny parle Créole chez lui?
_____ 5. Le Professeur Congé-Sabbatique n'enseigne pas ce semestre.
_____ 6. M. Scintillant lave sa voiture deux fois par semaine.
_____ 7. L'acier et le fer sont deux métaux très forts.
_____ 8. D'habitude, M. et Mme Repos restent à la maison.
_____ 9. On offre l'hébreu à votre université?
_____ 10. La Caroline du Nord a des montagnes très pittoresques.
_____ 11. Les œufs coûtent deux dollars la douzaine.

_____ 12. Quel soulagement! Henri VIII n'est plus roi.

_____

Definite, Indefinite or Omit?- Translate the following sentences.

1. Mr. Matière is a very good teacher. _____

_____.

2. Little Olga, who is Russian, knows how to read and write in English. _____

_____.

3. Her daughters are never in school. What a pity! _____

_____.

4. Handsome Beauregard has yellow teeth. _____

_____.

5. It is necessary to pay **taxes (les impôts-m.)** by April 15. _____

_____.

6. Is Sophia teaching Italian to the youngest ones? _____

_____?

7. One thousand priests no longer speak Latin in church. _____

_____.

8. How can he become a writer? He attends the class only once a month. _____

_____.

_____

l'Arc de Triomphe du Carrousel (Paris)

UNE REVUE - A Review

Orthographic/Stem Changing Verbs, Uses of Definite Articles, Omission of Definite and Indefinite Articles

'Watering Down' Root-Changing Expressions- Match the letter to the number of its synonym.

_____ 1. posséder quelqu'un	A. faire un achat
_____ 2. donner à manger à quelqu'un	B. être fou
_____ 3. enlever à quelqu'un	C. acheter comme un cadeau
_____ 4. nager dans le bonheur	D. prendre une forme différente
_____ 5. espérer bien	E. rendre une faveur
_____ 6. achever quelqu'un	F. duper
_____ 7. être déménagé	G. montrer de la considération
_____ 8. lever le pied	H. informer de
_____ 9. payer quelque chose à quelqu'un	I. crier "au secours
_____ 10. songer à	J. faire sortir/partir quelqu'un
_____ 11. acheter quelque chose	K. prendre quelque chose d'une personne
_____ 12. annoncer	L. réfléchir à
_____ 13. corriger quelqu'un de	M. faire rentrer
_____ 14. renvoyer l'ascenseur	N. vouloir sincèrement
_____ 15. appeler à l'aide	O. aller moins vite
_____ 16. renvoyer dans son foyer	P. guérir une personne de
_____ 17. envoyer quelqu'un sur les roses	Q. nourrir
_____ 18. ménager quelqu'un	R. n'avoir aucune idée
_____ 19. changer en	S. être très heureux
_____ 20. nager complètement	T. faire très fatigué

Sewing Up Verbs with Minor Alterations- Choose the letters of the correct infinitives, and put them in their proper forms in the spaces provided.

Ex. Tu es heureux à l'université? J'_espère_ bien que oui.

a. emmener   **b. espérer**   **c. essuyer**   **d. effacer**

1. En Égypte on monte à un chameau, ou on le (l') _____ à travers le désert.
a. élever   b. mener   c. taquiner   d. lancer
2. Est-ce que que tu vas _____? Qui achète ta maison?
a. jeter   b. posséder   c. déménager   d. renvoyer
3. On entend cette expression: "Il faut un village pour _____ un enfant."
a. amener   b. enlever   c. emmener   d. élever
4. On doit _____ ou _____ aux chiots qui ont faim.
a. nourrir .... donner à manger   b. protéger .... charger   c. plonger .... sécher
d. posséder .... emmener déjeuner
5. Aide-moi à _____ ces boîtes! Elles _____ beaucoup.
a. geler .... partager   b. appeler .... renoncer   c. avancer .... songer   d. lever .... peser
6. Ne (N') _____ pas les choses avant de les _____!

a. acheter .... déplacer   b. jeter .... remplacer   c. prononcer .... changer   d. renvoyer .... ranger

7. J'espère que je ne vous _____ pas veut dire la même chose que je ne veux pas vous

_____ .

a. essayer .... achever   b. inquiéter .... déranger   c. menacer .... bouger   d. employer .... corriger

8. Ton essai original contient de merveilleuses idées. _____ les erreurs grammaticales

au lieu de (d') _____ les pages complètement!

a. Placer .... répéter   b. Ménager tes forces .... nager   c. Corriger .... effacer

d. Balayer .... essuyer

9. L'agent immobilier explique qu'on _____ parce

que cet édifice n'a pas de (d') _____ .

a. payer moins pour l'appartement .... ascenseur   b. acheter tout pour le propriétaire .... impôts

c. lever le prix .... commerce de proximité   d. devoir nettoyer constamment ... bonne fée

10. Charlotte et ses trois meilleures amies _____ le loyer. Comme les jeunes femmes

n'ont pas de comptes en banque, elles _____ .

a. ménager .... n'y songer pas   b. partager .... payer comptant   c. envoyer .... être déménagées

d. emmener .... faire du nettoyage

Added Comments- **Translate the underlined phrases to complete the sentences.**

1. Pourquoi les fantômes sortent-ils <u>only at night</u>? _____ ?

2. <u>Coffee from South America</u> est le meilleur. _____

_____ .

3. Stu Dieux voudrait <u>to meet Professor Génie</u>. _____

_____ .

4. Des deux femmes, Claire Awl <u>has prettier hair</u>. _____ .

5. <u>Summer has the longest days</u> de l'année. _____

_____ .

6. <u>A hundred hours in Paris.</u> <u>What a</u> visite brève! _____

_____ !

7. Mlle LeCœur pense que <u>French and Italian are the most romantic languages.</u> _____

_____ .

8. <u>Young MaCaulay is the only one at home</u> quand sa famille part pour les vacances. _____

_____ .

9. La mère de Preston lui dit, "<u>Don't wipe your dirty hands on my clean clothes!</u>" _____

_____ !

10. Allez-vous assister au service <u>Sunday, February 18, Dr. Chapel</u>? _____

_____ ?

_____

FALSE -IR VERBS

**COURIR- To Race, To Run, To Rush, DORMIR- To Sleep, MENTIR- To Lie,
SENTIR- To Feel, To Sense, To Smell, SERVIR- To Serve**

With singular endings consistent in their irregularity and plural forms that could be taken for regular -<u>er</u> or -<u>re</u> verbs gone astray, these five verbs parallel *sortir* and *partir*.
Give *courir* a run through!

Courir - To Run, To Rush, To Race

<u>Singular</u>	<u>Plural</u>
je cours- I run, do run, am running	nous courons- we run, do run, are running
tu cours- you run, do run, are running	vous courez- you run, do run, are running
il/elle court- he/she/it runs, does run, is running	ils/elles courent- they run, do run, are running

---

<u>'Birds of a Feather'</u>
Aside from different meanings, the false -<u>ir</u> quints are identical. Their irregular endings are -<u>s</u>, -<u>s</u>, -<u>t</u>, -<u>ons</u>, -<u>ez</u>, -<u>ent</u>.
<u>An exception</u>: *Courir* is the only verb in the set that keeps its entire stem throughout the conjugation.

<u>Real Idioms with False -IR Verbs</u>
1. courir- to run, to rush, to race: This verb is related to *un courant*- <u>a current of water</u> and to *un coursier*- <u>a courier</u> who rushes with the mail.
<u>Current Expressions with *Courir*</u>
a. entrer sortir en courant- to run in and out
Ex. Des hommes entrent et sortent des magasins en courant au lieu d'y passer du temps. > Some men run in and out of stores instead of spending time there. (A quick "hello" and 'a good buy' suffice.)
b. courir à l'échec = courir à sa perte- to be on the road to ruin, to be headed for failure: *Échec* is French chess without an <u>s</u> at the end.
Ex. La pauvre Jeanne D'arc court à sa perte en Normandie. > Poor Joan of Arc is headed for failure in Normandy. (She is 'on the road to 'Rouen.")
c. courir sur le système = courir le haricot (the green bean) a quelqu'un- to get on one's nerves
Ex. Mme Pasvrai court leurs haricots quand elle ment. > Mrs. Pasvrai gets on their nerves when she lies. (They fight the urge 'to snap' at her.)
d. laisser courir- to leave things alone
Ex. Des personnes veulent nettoyer **les ruisseaux**, mais d'autres préfèrent les laisser courir. > Some people want to clean up **the streams**, but others prefer to leave them alone. (And let them 'run their course.')
e. Le bruit (the noise) court que ... Rumor has it that ...
Ex. Le bruit court que M. Deuxvies a une maîtresse mariée. > Rumor has it that Mr. Deuxvies has a married mistress. (Most likely, their spouses would find no humor in the rumor.)
f. courir sa chance- to try one's luck
Ex. Vanessa court sa chance sur la Roue de la Fortune. > Vanessa is trying her luck on *the Wheel of*

Fortune.

g. courir les filles- to chase the girls

Ex. La plupart des types qui courent les filles ont des relations brèves. > Most guys who chase girls have brief relationships. (Judging from the verb, they might even be 'racy.')

h. tenir (quelqu'un) au courant- to keep someone informed (Run it by him!)

Ex. Tiens-moi au courant de tes plans! > Keep me informed of your plans!

----

2. dormir- to sleep: <u>Dormant</u> and <u>dormitory</u> are derived from the French verb.

<u>'A Doze' of Expressions with *Dormir*</u>

a. n'en pas dormir- to lose sleep over it

Ex. Quand Barbara réfléchit à tous les invités qui vont venir ce week-end, elle n'en dort pas. > When Barbara thinks about all the guests who are going to come this weekend, she loses sleep over it. (For her, 'the rest is yet to come.')

b. dormir debout- to be asleep on one's feet: The actual translation is "to sleep standing."

Ex. Nous sommes tellement fatigués que nous dormons debout. > We're so tired that we're asleep on our feet. (Will they wake 'up right'?)

c. une histoire à dormir debout- a "bs" story (The French can stand for it.)

Ex. Le vendeur de voitures dit à Noah Scam qu'il peut vendre un Ferrari pour huit mille euros. C'est une histoire à dormir debout. > The car salesman tells Noah Scam that he can sell a Ferrari for eight thousand euros. It's a "bs" story.

d. dormir aux poings fermés- to be sound asleep: It is literally "to sleep with closed fists."

Ex. Noah Scam dort aux poings fermés. > Noah Scam is sound asleep. (And very possibly dreaming of getting even with the Ferrari salesman.)

e. dormir comme un loir- to sleep like a dormouse and dormir comme une souche- to sleep like a log

Ex. Ichabod Crane dort comme une souche chaque nuit à Sleepy Hollow, mais il est sans sommeil à Seattle. > Ichabod Crane sleeps like a log every night in Sleepy Hollow, but he's *Sleepless in Seattle.*

----

3. mentir- to lie: If one aug<u>ments</u> the truth, it is considered lying. (The underlined segment is admittedly 'a stretch.')

<u>Dishonorable Mention with *Mentir*</u>

a. mentir sur- to lie about

Ex. Mme Wrinkles connaît beaucoup de femmes qui mentent sur leurs âges. > Mrs. Wrinkles knows many women who lie about their ages. (But most people can 'read between the lines.')

b. sans mentir- honestly

Ex. Prenez garde à ces gens qui disent "sans mentir" trop souvent. > Beware of those people who say "honestly" too often.

c. mentir comme on respire- to be a compulsive liar: Its word-for-word translation is "to lie as one breathes."

Ex. Il est évident de **son langage du corps** que M. Masquerade ment comme il respire. > It is obvious from **his body language** that Mr. Masquerade is a compulsive liar.

----

4. sentir- to feel, to sense, to smell: Its cognates include <u>sense</u>, <u>sensation</u>, <u>sensual</u>, <u>sensitive</u> and <u>sentiment</u>. (It puts in far more than its 'two sense worth.')

Expressions That Make Sense
a. sentir la différence- to tell the difference

Ex. Sentir la différence entre leurs jumelles identiques n'est pas **un défi**. > Telling the difference be-between their identical twin girls is not **a challenge**. (They share the same 'make-up.')

b. sentir la rose- to smell good

Ex. Whiff sait que ses chaussures de sport ne sentent pas la rose. > Whiff knows that his sport shoes do not smell good. (His nose smells better.)

c. sentir- to look as though, to appear to be: With these translations, forms of *sentir* need direct objects to complete the sentences.

Ex. Ça sent l'automne. > It looks as though autumn is on its way. (Its cover 'has been blown.')

----

5. servir- to serve: Its closely related cognates are 'at your service.'

Idioms That Serve You Well
a. servir quelqu'un- to wait on someone

Ex. **La jeune-mariée va** servir son mari. > **The newlywed** is going to wait on her husband. (She just needs 'the proper setting.')

b. servir le déjeuner, servir le dîner à quelqu'un- to serve lunch/dinner to someone

Ex. La Grenouille sert le déjeuner de midi jusqu'à deux heures et demie. > La Grenouille (The Frog) serves lunch from noon until 2:30 p.m.. (Later in the afternoon, it 'gets a jump on' dinner.)

c. servir à quelqu'un- to be useful to/for someone

Ex. La chambre supplémentaire ne sert pas à Madame Pourrien > The extra room is not useful to/for Mrs. Pourrien. (She 'picks it up' but has no other place to put it.)

d. servir de- to act as

Ex. L'actrice sert d'une serveuse lorsqu'elle cherche des rôles. > The actress works as a server while she is looking for roles. (Her regular customers know what 'she is waiting for.')

e. À quoi sert-il? -What is this used for?/What is the use for this?

Ex. **Un chevalier** demande au roi, "À quoi cette épée-là sert-elle?" Le roi lui répond, "Cela ne sert à rien." > **A knight** asks the king, "What is that sword used for?" The king answers, "That is not used for anything." (A sharper response would have been "It has no point.")

'Turn Around Time' for False -IR Verbs- Change the singular subjects and verbs into plural forms and vice versa. Then rewrite the sentences.
Ex. Le coursier aux jambes courtes court très vite? > Les coursiers aux jambes courtes courent très vite?

1. Tu sors du bureau maintenant. _____.

2. Les fleurs sentent bonnes. _____.

3. Cet étudiant ne dort pas dans le dortoir. _____
_____.

4. Le serveur n'y sert pas le déjeuner. _____
_____.

5. Une personne diligente ne court jamais d'un défi. _____
_____.

6. Les trains partent-ils de ce quai-ci? _____?

7. À quoi ces édifices servent-ils? _____ ?
8. Pourquoi les filles mentent-elles? _____ ?
9. Ne pars pas aujourd'hui, s'il te plaît! _____

_____!
10. Ne me servez pas cela, s'il vous plaît! _____

_____!

'Choice Expressions'- Circle the letters of the answers that best complete the sentences.
1. Le matin de Noël l'enfant _____ au salon aussi vite que possible pour voir ses cadeaux.
a. ment   b. dort   c. court   d. sent
2. Dans la petite chanson française, on demande au Frère Jacques, _____?
a. "Courez-vous?"   b. "Dormez-vous?"   c. "Mentez-vous?"   d. "Servez-vous?"
3. M. et Mme Saute _____ à leur médecin chaque fois que leur enfant **éternue (sneezes)**.
a. servent   b. dorment   c. sentent   d. courent
4. Il fait si froid que tu ne peux pas _____.
a. dormir comme un loir   b sentir tes mains   c. mentir sur le temps   d. sentir la différence
5. Il fait beau, et des oiseaux chantent. Ma tante me remarque, _____
a. "Ça sent le printemps!" b. "On le laisse courir." c. "N'en dors pas!" d. "Ça te sert bien!"
6. Les parents donnent un bisou à leur enfant, et ils lui disent, " _____, mon petit!"
a. Cours ta chance   b. Dors bien   c. C'est à toi de servir   d. Dors debout
7. Mlle Plastique utilise ses cartes de crédit constamment. Elle _____.
a. dort aux poings fermés   b. ment comme elle respire   c. court à l'échec   d. sert des clients
8. Ma mère me dit, "Le café est prêt, et il y a des croissants dans le micro-ondes. "Vas-y et _____!"
a. sers-toi!   b. sers d'une cuisine!   c. cours à ta perte!   d. laisse-les courir!
9. Le Georges Curieux regarde un truc au marché aux puces. Il demande au vendeur, _____?
a. "C'est à moi?"   b. "À quoi sert-il?"   c. "sans mentir?"   d. "Dormez-vous debout?"
10. Sa bonne mémoire et son bon sens de l'humour _____.
a. sentent la rose   b. sont une histoire à dormir debout   c. mentent sur tout   d. le servent bien

----

A Reality Check for False -IR Verbs- Translate the following sentences.
1. Does Spot run faster than Puff? _____

_____?
2. My grandmother's perfume smells good. _____

_____.
3. Keep (*vous*) us informed, OK? _____ ?
4. How many hours does Wee Willie Winkie sleep each night? _____

_____?
5. The child speaks softly because the babies are sleeping. _____

_____.
6. Dee LaVérité scolds me when I lie. _____.

_____
7. I can't tell the difference. _____.
8. What are those rooms used for? _____?

_____

FALSE -RE VERBS (SET 1)

PRENDRE- To Take, APPRENDRE- To Learn, COMPRENDRE- To Understand, ENTREPRENDRE- To Undertake, SURPRENDRE- To Surprise

This group begins its journey like regular -re verbs on the *SS Nothing*, but its irregular plural forms show that these false -re verbs have chartered their own boat.

Prendre - To Take

Singular	Plural
je prends- I take, do take, am taking	nous prenons- we take, do take, are taking
tu prends- you take, do take, are taking	vous prenez- you take, do take, are taking
il/elle prend- he/she/it takes, does take, is taking	ils/elles prennent- they take, do take, are taking

----

'Yours for the Taking'
1. Three facts re: the *prendre* set
a. They are conjugated like regular -re verbs in the singular.
b. They are done with the d in the plural. (It has been taken away.)
c. The third person plural forms double the n before adding -ent. Did it 'come to you' that the *venir/tenir* group does likewise?

Prendre Expressions That Can Be Taken at Their Word
a. prendre un train/un avion/un taxi/un métro- to take a plane, a train, a taxi, a subway
Ex. Prenez-vous un taxi quand vous n'avez pas le temps de marcher? > Do you take a taxi when you do not have time to walk? (Sometimes the 'weight' is taken into consideration.)
b. prendre des choses comme elles sont = prendre la vie comme elle vient- to take things as they are, to take life as it comes
Ex. Sereine ne prend pas de **médicament pour l'hypertension**. Elle prend la vie comme elle vient. > Sereine does not take any **medication for high blood pressure**. She takes life as it comes.
c. prendre = duper- to fool, to dupe
Ex. Une fois **suffit!** Il ne va pas me prendre une deuxième fois. > Once **is enough!** He's not going to fool me a second time. (But if he does, is he "super duper"?)
d. prendre = considérer
Ex. Ils prennent M. Jester pour un idiot. > They take Mr. Jester for an idiot. (The bells on his hat and slippers give him 'a certain ring.')
e. prendre = réagir à- to react to
Ex. Nous ne savons pas prendre les nouvelles de leur mariage. > We do not know how to react to the news of their marriage. (Is the couple planning a 'cool' reception?)
f. prendre- to deal with, to handle
Ex. Comment la maîtresse prend-elle ses méchants élèves? > How does the schoolteacher handle her naughty students? (Maybe she talks about 'the room for improvement.')
g. prendre- to take down, to note
Ex. Le médecin prend notre température, **notre pouls** et **notre sang**. > The doctor takes our tempera-

ture, **our pulse** and **our blood**. (We feel 'listless' when we leave.)

h. prendre- to accept

Ex. Le lycée ne prend plus d'élèves cette saison. > The lycée is not taking more students this season. (The school might find it 'difficult to take' some who are already enrolled.)

Important notes

a. When to take means to bring, use *apporter*.

Ex. Ça sent la pluie. Apporte un parapluie! > It feels like rain. Bring an umbrella!

b. Here's a retake: passer un examen = to take an exam

Ex. Tu passes un examen, et tu espéres que tu y réussis. > You take an exam, and you hope that you succeed (on it.)

Prendre Expressions That Take on Different Meanings

a. C'est à prendre ou à laisser!- Take it or leave it!

Ex. La propriétairc de l'appartement leur dit, "C'est à prendre ou à laisser!" Ils lui répondent, "Non, merci." > The apartment owner says to them, "Take it or leave it!" They answer, "No, thanks." (She can take it that they're leaving it.)

b. Il faut en prendre y en laisser- to believe half of what one says. Its word-for-word translation is "It is necessary to take some and leave some."

Ex. Mme Fausse ment si souvent qu'il faut en prendre y en laisser. > Mrs. Fausse lies so often that it is necessary to believe half of what she says. (Is the right half what is left?)

c. passer prendre = aller chercher- to get, to pick up

Ex. Sois prêt! Nous passons te prendre bientôt. > Be ready! We are picking you up soon. (Is that why it is called "getting a lift?")

d. prendre quelqu'un sur le fait- to catch someone in the act: The precise translation is "to take someone on the fact."

Ex. La sécurité est excellente sur Broadway. La police peut prendre un voleur sur le fait. > The security is excellent on Broadway. The police can catch a thief in the act. (Especially one who's trying 'to steal lines.')

e. prendre = manger- to eat; prendre = boire- to drink

Ex.Thurston te dit fréquemment pourquoi il prend huit verres d'eau chaque jour. > Thurston tells you frequently why he drinks eight glasses of water each day. (He may need 'to get it out of his system.')

A very important note: In French, a person can take food or a drink, but he can't have it.

f. prendre = faire payer- to charge

Ex. Des bonnes prennent 150 euros par heure. > Some maids charge 150 euros an hour. (They reall 'clean up!')

g. à tout prendre- on the whole

Ex. À tout prendre, ces expressions avec prendre ne sont pas difficiles à apprendre. > On the whole, these expressions with *prendre* are not difficult to learn.

234

A Match Made in Columns- **Put the letters beside the numbers of the phrases that complete the thoughts.**

_____ 1. Voici vos deux choix.

_____ 2. Allons aux Deux Magots ensemble!

_____ 3. Il oublie toujours la route à Nantes.

_____ 4. La femme riche quitte ce monde.

_____ 5. Les frères ne répondent guère quand nous leur parlons.

_____ 6. Tes sœurs semblent tristes récemment.

_____ 7. Milan est malin. Je l'attrape chaque fois qu'il cherche dans mon sac à main.

_____ 8. À quelle heure mangez-vous le soir veut dire

_____ 9. Le film ne commence pas jusqu'à 20 heures.

_____ 10. Vous n'allez pas le déranger facilement.

_____ 11. Beaucoup de gens qui habitent à Paris n'ont pas de voitures.

_____ 12. Personne ne croit pas toutes ses histoires.

_____ 13. Quels sont les renseignements sur la bouteille de médicaments?

_____ 14. Ton ami est impoli. On va le faire sortir?

_____ 15. Arielle agit comme une jeune femme de 20 ans, mais elle est plus jeune que ça.

A. Il prend des choses comme elles sont.

B. Absolument pas! On le prend avec bon humeur.

C. Je le prends sur le fait.

D. Pourquoi ne prend-il des directions?

E. On prend les autobus ou les taxis.

F. Pourrais-tu passer me prendre?

G. Il faut en prendre y en laisser.

H. Prends ton temps!

I. Elle ne peut pas le prendre avec elle.

J. **Son comportement (her behavior)** ne me prend pas.

K. À prendre avant les repas!

L. C'est à prendre ou à laisser!

M. Quand prenez-vous le dîner?

N. Qu'est-ce qui les prend?

O. Nous les prenons pour deux muets.

Four Take-Offs of _Prendre_

1. apprendre- to learn: Since this verb is a cognate of <u>apprentice</u>, the meaning is easy to grasp. The conjugated forms of _apprendre_ are followed by _à_ before an infinitive.

Ex. Il veut apprendre **à sauter en chute libre**. > He wants to learn **to skydive**. (Hopefully, his parachute will 'be open to the idea.')

Expressions Worth Learning

a. apprendre à- to hear of: If you consider _à_ as <u>about</u>, the terms are used the same bilingually.

Ex. Skipper vient d'apprendre à une croisière bon marché. > Skipper just heard about an inexpensive cruise. (He's not one 'to go overboard.')

b. apprendre à connaître quelqu'un- to get to know someone

Ex. "Le plus que j'apprends à connaître des personnes, le plus que j'aime mon chien." > "The more I get to know some people, the more I love my dog."

c. apprendre à quelqu'un à faire quelque chose = enseigner à quelqu'un à faire quelque chose- to teach someone to do something

<u>An important note</u>: <u>To teach</u> and <u>to learn</u> can have the same meaning in French.

d. apprendre à = dire à quelqu'un quelque chose, annoncer- to tell someone something

Ex. Elle apprend à tous ses amis qu'elle est enceinte encore. > She is telling all her friends that she is pregnant again. (Someone could reply, "Baby One More Time.")

---

2. comprendre- to understand, to include
This verb has 'a mutual understanding' with <u>comprehend</u>, but be sure to include <u>include</u> as the second meaning because *comprendre* is <u>comprised</u> of both.
Ex.**Ton addition** ne comprend pas le pourboire. > **Your bill** does not include the tip. (It is subtracted from *l'addition totale*.)
<u>**Misunderstood Expressions**</u>
a. ne comprendre rien- not to understand at all
Ex. Paul ne comprend rien de la littérature russe. Il pense que <u>La Guerre et La Paix</u> sont deux romans séparés. > Paul understands nothing at all about Russian literature. He thinks that <u>War and Peace</u> are two separate novels.
b. se faire comprendre- to make oneself understood
Ex. Un bébé essaie de se faire comprendre. > A baby tries to make himself /herself understood. (And is very happy 'to share a few pointers.')

---

3. entreprendre- to start, to set out, to undertake: *<u>Entrepreneur</u>* **is one cognate. The conjugated forms of** *entreprendre* **are followed by** *de* **before an infinitive.**
Ex. Quelle idée **formidable**! L'entreprise de Dulce entreprend de **fabriquer** le chewing-gum de chocolat. > What a **fantastic** idea! Dulce's company is starting **to manufacture** chocolate chewing gum. (Translating *entreprendre* in that example as "to undertake" could forecast 'a dying business.')
A note: le monde de l'entreprise = the business world

---

4. surprendre- to surprise
Ex. Elle va les surprendre avec un cadeau d'Au Printemps. > She's going to surprise them with a gift from Au Printemps. (It has been 'in store for them' for a while.)

<u>**Re: False -RE Verbs**</u> **- Using the correct forms of** *prendre, apprendre, comprendre, entreprendre* **and** *surprendre*, **translate the sentences.**
1. I take lunch at 12:30. _____.
2. When you (*vous*) teach, you also learn. _____
_____.
3. Who takes a bus or a subway to get to (to arrive at) the office? _____
_____?
4. That's enough! We're not taking it anymore. _____
_____.
5. The Foggs do not understand anything that we are telling them. _____
_____.
6. How can one take one's time when one is taking an exam? _____
_____?
7. Are you (*tu*) ready to learn to speak French? _____
_____?
8. She understands that she is undertaking a great challenge. _____
_____.
9. Miss Take speaks it well enough to make herself understood. _____
_____.

10. They think that they are going to surprise us. _____

_____ .

'Take It from There'- Circle the letters of the responses that best complete the sentences.

1. Kaye Sera n'est pas une femme anxieuse. Elle prend _____.
a. des notes   b. la vie comme elle vient   c. un bon repas   d. mal les nouvelles

2. L'addition totale ne (n') _____ pas ni le vin ni le dessert.
a. prend   b. accepte   c. comprend   d. annonce

3. Ses enfants ont un rendez-vous chez le dentiste cet après-midi. Leur mère _____ à l'école.
a. les prend   b. les apporte   c. passe les prendre   d. ne comprend rien

4. À mon avis, des hôtels exclusifs ne (n') _____ pas trop pour les services qu'ils offrent aux invités.
a. apprennent   b. comprennent   c. surprennent   d. prennent

5. Je travaille avec une femme qui ne dit pas toujours la vérité. Est-ce que je dois informer aux autres que (qu') _____ ?
a. c'est à prendre ou à laisser   b. il faut en prendre y en laisser   c. elle le prend comme cela
d. elle ne sait pas ce qu'elle prend

6. _____ nous le trouvons moins cher acheter un nouveau que réparer le vieux.
a. À tout prendre   b. Apprendre par cœur   c. Ne rien entreprendre   d. Prendre sur le fait

7. Pierrot a un boulot au cirque où il apprend _____.
a. aux enfants à jongler   b. à jouer aux billes   c. à duper son patron   d. à coudre à la main

8. En général, les gens dans le monde d'affaires doivent _____.
a. le prendre avant les repas   b. prendre soin des impôts   c. déranger les clients qui dorment
d. se faire comprendre

9. Comme David et Douglas n'ont pas l'air content, leur mère leur demande, _____ ?
a. Je vous surprends, n'est-ce pas?   b. Apprenez-vous à conduire notre voisine enceinte?
c. Qu'est-ce qui vous prenez?   d. L'enseignez-vous à vos amis ?

10. Un professeur doit _____ une matière très bien avant de la (l') _____ à ses étudiants.
a. prendre .... entreprendre   b. sentir .... servir   c. enseigner .... se faire comprendre
d. comprendre .... apprendre

FALSE -RE VERBS (SET 2)

CONDUIRE- To Conduct, To Drive, To Lead, CONSTRUIRE- To Build, To Construct, DÉTRUIRE- To Destroy, To Ruin, INTRODUIRE- To Introduce, To Launch, To Show In, PRODUIRE- To Cause, To Produce, To Yield, TRADUIRE- To Convey, To Translate

On first impression, these six infinitives with strange stems might look 'uired'(weird). Yet, like those in False -RE Set #1, these verbs wear 'uniform' conjugations under their outer coverings. Get comfortable driving around *conduire* before navigating the others in this group!

Conduire - To Conduct, To Drive, To Lead

Singular	Plural
je conduis- I conduct, drive, lead, run	nous conduisons- we conduct, drive, lead, run
tu conduis- you conduct, drive, lead, run	vous conduisez- you conduct, drive, lead, run
il/elle conduit- he/she/it conducts, drives, leads, runs	ils/elles conduisent- they conduct, drive, lead, run

---

We're Going to Analyze -Uire Conjugations

1. The singular forms of *conduire* and 'its passengers' have regular -**ir** verb endings after -**ire** is dropped off. (**U** can stay.)

2. The pronunciation is identical for the singular forms of each verb.

3. The plural forms have regular -**er/-re** endings. However, they're attached to the first/second person singular forms. ('Uired' verbs are wired together.)

---

1. conduire- to conduct, to drive, to lead, to run: Conduct, **conduit** and **conductive** lead back to *conduire*. Its synonym is *rouler*.

Ex. Il va perdre **son permis de conduire** s'il continue à conduire comme ça. > He's going to lose his driver's license if he continues to drive like that. (A 'wreck-less' highway trumps a reckless driver.)

Expressions with *Conduire* in the Leading Role

a. conduire quelqu'un quelque part- to drive somebody somewhere

Ex. Payne, qui est difficile à prendre, va la conduire à un bar ce soir. > Payne who is difficult to take, is going to drive her to a bar this evening. (If 'he drives her to drink,' he should drive her home.)

b. conduire = guider- to guide

Ex. Prenez-vous le tour qui vous conduit par **les égouts** de Paris? > Are you taking the tour that leads you through **the sewers** of Paris? (It's lowest on the list of attractions.)

c. conduire = mener- to lead

Ex. "Tous les chemins mènent à Rome." > "All roads lead to Rome." (Somebody coined the phrase when the Atlantic and Pacific Oceans were only a chariot ride away from each other.)

d. conduire- to run, to supervise

Ex. Tu as l'impression que nous conduisons une entreprise lucrative. > You have the impression that we run a lucrative business. ('By all accounts,' it looks that way.)

e. conduire- to conduct

Ex. Ils font **les expériences** pour comprendre comment les fils métalliques conduisent l'électricité. > They do **experiments** to understand how metal wires conduct electricity. (It 'sparks their interest.')

---

2. construire- to build, to construct, to start: Its synonym is *bâtir*.

Phrases under Construction

Ex. Trop de **critique** ne construit pas de **confiance en soi**. > Too much **criticism** does not build **self-confidence**. (It could even result in a building block.)

An important note: *Faire construire* means to have something built. This phrase is constructed like *faire venir*- to have something sent and *faire payer*- to charge.

Ex. Jacques fait construire une maison. > Jack is having a house built. (Nobody claims that 'This is the house that Jack built.')

---

3. détruire- to destroy, to ruin: *Construire* is its antonym.
Taking Apart *Détruire*
Ex. La force de **la Dame Nature** détruit les maisons **au hasard**. > The force of **Mother Nature** destroys homes **at random**. (Nothing is worse than 'her level best.')
Ex. Olivette n'est jamais sans une bouteille de vodka. Elle détruit sa santé et sa réputation. > Olivette is never without a bottle of vodka. > She is destroying/ruining her health and her reputation. (Might Olivette be playing Russian roulette?)

----

4. introduire- to introduce (to present), to launch, to show in
How *Introduire* Presents Itself
Ex. **L'entremetteuse** introduit une jeune femme à de vieux célibataires riches, mais elle ne veut pas sortir avec eux. > **The matchmaker** introduces a young woman to some old rich bachelors, but she doesn't want to go out with them. (She prefers in alone to 'out-dated.')
Ex. Ces entreprises introduisent de nouveaux produits constamment. > Those companies launch new products constantly. (Some of them must 'get off the ground.')

----

5. produire- to cause, to produce, to yield
A Short Production Line
Ex. La plaisanterie dans l'exemple prochain va produire **un petit rire**. > The joke in the next example is going to produce **a chuckle.**
Ex. Le pirate prend trop pour **le maïs** qu'il produit. > The pirate charges too much for **the corn** that he produces. (It's from 'a-buck-an-ear.')
Ex. Leurs comptes bancaires produisent très peu d'intérêt. > Their bank accounts yield very little interest. (So little that they hardly care about them.)

----

6. traduire- to convey, to translate
Getting the Point Across
Ex. Sa peinture traduit un sentiment de tranquillité. > Her painting translates a feeling of tranquility. (Maybe it's 'a still life.')
Ex. Comment peut-elle traduire en anglais si vite? > How can she translate into English so quickly?

Checking the 'Uire-ing'- Fill in the blanks with the correct forms of the verbs in parentheses.
1. (détruire) Ses mensonges _____ ma confiance en lui.
2. (construire) Pourquoi _____-vous une maison près de la plage en Floride?
3. (produire) Cette entreprise-là à Toledo _____ des épées.
4. (introduire) Je vous _____ à un mec doué de Douai.
5. (traduire) _____ d'une langue à une autre sans une faute est un défi.
6. (produire) Je suis étonné. Les égouts de Paris ne _____ pas une mauvaise odeur.
7. (introduire) La société décide d'_____ l'assurance maladie pour ses ouvriers.
8. (conduire) M. et Mme Einstein ne découragent jamais leur fils quand il _____ ses expériences.
9. (traduire) Bea Lang et moi _____ les annonces pour les étrangers qui montent à bord de l'avion.
10. (détruire, faire construire) **Un incendie (a fire)** _____ la très belle maison que

239

les jeunes-mariés viennent de _____.

'Ui're' Set- Fill in the blanks with the correct forms of *conduire, construire, détruire, introduire, produire* and *traduire,* and write the translations in the spaces preceding the sentences.
Ex. <u>conducts</u>- La créateur de Frankenstein <u>conduit</u> des expériences dans un laboratoire.

1. _____ L'antonyme de contruire est _____.
2. _____ Chantal, je voudrais vous _____ à mes parents.
3. _____ Ne _____ pas mot pour mot d'une langue lorsque tu parles une autre!
4. _____ François passe tout son temps libre avec de mauvais mecs. À cause de cela, il _____ sa réputation.
5. _____ Les vaches du vieux McDonald ne _____ pas assez de lait.
6. _____ Je viens de lire que Gucci _____ une nouvelle ligne de parfum cette semaine.
7. _____ Un copain va _____ Walker à l'université parce qu'il n'a pas une voiture.
8. _____ Polly Glott travaille aux Nations Unies. Elle peut _____ plusieurs langues.
9. _____ À présent, **leur logement-m. (their housing)** est un petit appartement cher en ville, mais ils _____ _____ une maison en banlieue.
10. _____, _____ Quand l'entremetteuse _____ un célibataire à une femme enceinte, cela _____ un petit rire.

FALSE -RE VERBS (SET 3)

POURSUIVRE- To Continue, To Hound, To Prosecute, To Pursue, SUIVRE- To Attend, To Follow, To Keep Up With, To Understand, SURVIVRE- To Survive, VIVRE- To Live

Even though these false -re verbs end with -*ivre* which means <u>drunk</u>, they start out by walking their own straight line. But then, they need the support of -<u>uire</u> verbs.

Suivre - To Attend, To Follow, To Keep up with

Singular	Plural
je suis- I follow, do follow, am following	nous suivons- we follow, do follow, are following
tu suis- you follow, do follow, are following	vous suivez- you follow, do follow, are following
il/elle suit- he/she/it follows, does follow, is following	ils/elles suivent- they follow, do follow, are following

----

<u>Tips Regarding the Tipsy Verbs</u>
1. The same sounding, singular forms are conjugated by removing -<u>vre</u> from the infinitive and adding -s, -s and -t to the remaining stem.
2. In the plural forms, the <u>v</u> 'checks in' again. The -<u>re</u> is deleted from the infinitive and regular -er/-re endings are added.
Ex. M. et Mme Curie suivent une classe de cuisine indienne. > Mr. and Mrs. Curie attend an Indian cooking class. (It 'adds spice to their lives.')
3. Ironically, *je suis*- I follow is identical to *je suis*- I am. (It is admirable to follow God, but a person who claims to be God 'is high on himself.')

<u>*Suivre* Is behind the Following Expressions</u>
a. suivre- to keep up with, to follow: The bilingual translations are in step with each other.
Ex. Ralentissez lorsque vous roulez dans **une tempête de neige,** ou personne ne peut vous suivre! > Slow down while you drive **in a snowstorm,** or no one can follow you! (But someone might 'catch the drift.')
b. suivre = comprendre- to understand: The verbs grasp the same sense in both languages.
Ex. Jill dit à Jacques qu'elle suit ce qu'il lui explique. > Jill tells Jack that she understands what he is explaining to her. (Jill leads Jack to believe that she is following him.)
c. suivre- to do well/poorly in
Ex. Les Suisses suivent bien pendant les auditions de **la tyrolienne.** > The Swiss do well during the **yodeling** auditions. (They always get 'call-backs.')
d. suivre un régime- to be on (to follow) a diet
Ex. Mlle Cochonette n'a pas d'intention de suivre un régime. > Miss Piggy has no intention of being on a diet. (Even though the singular forms *suis, suis* should motivate her.)
e. suivre- to be behind someone, to back someone up
Ex. Mme Holdon **conteste la facture** pour **son déambulateur,** et une voisine la suit. > Mrs. Holdon **disputes the bill** for **her walker,** and a neighbor backs her up. (She can certainly use 'the support.')
f. faire suivre quelqu'un- to have someone followed
Ex. Comme Mme Soupçonne croit que son mari a une liaison avec son amie, elle va le fait suivre. > As Mrs. Soupçonne believes that her husband is having an affair with her friend, she is going to have him followed. (If only he were 'up front with her!')
g. faire suivre le courrier- to have the mail forwarded
Ex. **Votre facteur** n'apporte pas de factures chez vous quand vous faites suivre le courrier. > **Your postman** does not bring any bills to your home when you have the mail forwarded.
It's a fact. *La facture* = the bill and *le facteur* = the postman.

<u>Short Backup Expressions with *Suivre*</u>
a. Lisez la suite!- Read on!
b. et ainsi de suite- and so forth
c. à suite- to be continued
d. à la suite- one after the other (Suites are adjoining rooms.)
e. suivant- following (adjective): Its synonym is *prochain*.
f. tout de suite- right away (It is pronounced somewhat like a synonym for an excess of sugar.)

Keeping Up with *Suivre*- Circle the letters of the answers that best complete the sentences.

1. Suivre bien est l'antonyme de (d') ____.
a. ne rien comprendre   b. prendre feu   c. apprendre à connaître quelqu'un   d. à tout prendre

2. ____ est le synonyme pour et cetera.
a. Tout de suite   b. À la suite   c. Lisez la suite!   d. Et ainsi de suite

3. Esau Itall sait que vous dites la vérité, et il va ____.
a. partager votre logement   b. rouler autour de la ville   c. vous suivre cent pour cent
d. suivre un cours difficile

4. Faye Laqueue n'attend pas longtemps parce que le salarié ____.
a. la détruit au hasard   b. l'appelle tout de suite   c. construit la confiance en soi
d. conteste la facture

5. La jeunesse apprend l'informatique à l'école. Pour ça ____.
a. on lui offre l'assurance maladie   b. elle nage complètement   c. elle la suit facilement
d. on lui demande de lire la suite

6. M. Hawk et moi **embauchons (hire)** un détective privé. Nous espérons ____.
a. suivre un régime loyalement   b. les conduire quelque part à grande vitesse
c. leur apprendre à faire quelque chose   d. prendre les gens sur le fait

----

Verbs That Take after *Suivre*

1. poursuivre- to continue, to hound, to prosecute, to pursue

Ex. Malgré les protestations de ses parents, Upton va poursuivre les leçons de sauter en chute libre. > Despite his parents' protests, Upton is going to pursue sky-diving lessons. (His parents could decide to 'ground him.')

Ex. Chaque fois que Pinocchio ment, Jiminy Cricket le poursuit. > Whenever Pinocchio lies, Jiminy Cricket hounds him. (Maybe Pinocchio did not realize that 'there were strings attached.')

Ex. Pouvez-vous poursuivre en justice quelqu'un qui vole votre identité? > Can you prosecute (sue) someone who steals your identity? (Would you be 'pressing false charges'?)

Ex. Mon oncle et ma tante poursuivent leur rêve d'**une retraite** en Europe. > My uncle and my aunt are pursuing their dream of **a retirement** in Europe. (That's no trivial pursuit.)

----

2. survivre- to outlive, to survive: Forms of this verb are followed by *à* or a contraction in front of a noun or pronoun.

Ex. Owen Lotz survit à **ses épargnes**. Il doit trouver un boulot ou devenir mendiant. > Owen Lotz is outliving **his savings**. He must find a job or become a beggar. (His previous 'foot in the door' might turn into 'a hand out' on the street.)

Ex. Mme Bonnevue ne peut pas survivre sans sa télévision. > Mrs. Bonnevue cannot survive without her television. (It will be bad news if someone 'pulls the plug.')

----

3. vivre- to live, to exist: Its antonym is *mourir*- to die.
Habiter and *demeurer*, **both meaning to reside, are not synonymous with *vivre*.**

Ex. Ceux qui vivent à l'âge de cent ans doivent offrir **leurs bougies** de naissance au musée de **cire**. > Those who live to the age of one hundred ought to offer their **birthday** candles to the **wax** museum.

Expressions That *Vivre* Brings to Life

a. vivre bien- to live well: It has the same usage in English.
Ex. Une femme divorcée dit à son ex-mari, "J'espère que tu vis bien **ailleurs**." > A divorced woman says to her ex-husband, "I hope that you live well **somewhere else**."

b. vivre dans le passé- to live in the past: The expression lives on in both languages.
Ex. Au milieu de la nuit, le vieil homme lit les histoires des guerres mondiales. Il vit dans le passé. > In the middle of the night, the old man reads stories about the world wars. He lives in the past. (If he read a newspaper, he might be up with the Times.)

c. difficile/facile à vivre avec- difficult/easy to live with: Notice the connecting *à*!
Ex. Un médecin demande à Madame Hertz s'il est difficile à vivre avec **la douleur**. > A doctor asks Mrs. Hertz if it is difficult to live with **the pain**. (She might wonder how the doctor knows what she calls her husband.)

d. _____ pour vivre: A verb form naming an occupation goes in the blank = _____ for a living
Ex. Mlle G. String **se déshabille** pour vivre. > Ms G. String **strips** for a living. (Hopefully, she earns enough to cover 'the bare necessities.')

e. vivre de jour en jour- to live from day to day
Ex. Walter et Mitty vivent de jour en jour. Ils ont des vies ennuyeuses. > Walter and Mitty live from day to day. They have boring lives. (If they met Mlle G. String, they could live from night to night.)

f. vivre d'amour et d'eau fraîche- to live on love alone: Its word-for-word translation is "to live from love and from fresh water."
Ex. Gérard et Géraldine vivent d'amour et d'eau fraîche. > Gerard and Geraldine live on love. (Their equity is 'in trust for each other.')

g. *C'est la vie!*- That's life!, said *le bon vivant*- one who lives well.

h. *Vive la France!*- Long live France!

A note: The verb form *vive* will be explained later. *Vive la langue française!*

Selecting 'the Following Verbs'- Put the correct forms of *poursuivre*, *suivre*, *survivre* and *vivre* in the spaces provided.

1. Mme Vogue et moi _____ les dernières modes.
2. J'ai un bon professeur particulier, mais je _____ mal en mathématiques.
3. Les souris _____ dans les champs, dans les greniers, dans les restaurants et ainsi de suite.
4. Quand des très malades _____ aux opérations, ils ne rentrent pas tout de suite.
5. Ne mens pas à tes parents! Je ne vais pas te _____.
6. Tu le _____ en justice. Combien paies-tu pour un avocat?
7. Le logement sur les îles ne _____ pas toujours aux pires tempêtes.
8. Un couple va à la station de taxi. Un porteur avec un chariot de bagages le _____.
9. Si elle ne lui donne pas son numéro de téléphone, ce type ne peut pas la _____.
10. Raggedy Ann ne veut plus _____ avec Andy. Il mendie pour _____.

The Many Faces of *Ivre*- Circle the letters of the best responses to complete the sentences.

1. Malgré peu d'économies, des personnes en retraite ___ bien.
   a. comptent   b. vivent   c. sonnent   d. surprennent
2. Des individus ne ___ pas les carrières qui sont les meilleures pour eux.

a. jonglent   b. poursuivent   c. parient   d. prennent

3. Les soldats qui ____ guerres peuvent nous raconter des histoires fascinantes.

a. survivent aux   b. vivent bien aux   c. ne savent rien des   d. font suivre quelqu'un aux

4. Lorsque nous sommes en vacances, nous ne ____ .

a. vivons pas dans le passé   b. traduisons pas pour vivre   c. faisons pas suivre le courrier

d. poursuivons personne en justice

5. Si tu ne comprends pas tout dans le premier paragraphe, ____ !

a. suis un régime   b. lis le suivant   c. vis de jour en jour   d. vive la différence

6. Antoine et Cléopâtre sont les fiancés sans argent. Ils ____ .

a. suivent mal en géographie   b. suivent la route à Rome   c. ont des affaires souvent

d. vivent d'amour et d'eau fraîche

7. Pour voler à l'étranger, il faut montrer un billet, un passeport, une carte d'embarquement ____ .

a. de jours en jour   b. et ainsi de suite   c. au moins une fois   d. au hasard

8. Si la cire de la bougie brûle Jack Be Nimble, va-t-il ____ ?

a. vivre dans le passé   b. survivre à la douleur   c. suivre un régime   d. sauter pour vivre

----

FALSE -RE VERBS (SET 4)

RIRE - To Laugh, SOURIRE - To Smile

As *rire* is at the rear of *sourire*, it's very easy for a smile to break into laughter. How ironic that **ire** is a synonym for angry! Nevertheless, the speaker's happy face while pronouncing the verb forms shows otherwise.

Rire - To Laugh

Singular	**Plural**
je ris- I laugh, do laugh, am laughing	nous rions- we laugh, do laugh, are laughing
tu ris- you laugh, do laugh, are laughing	vous riez- you laugh, do laugh, are laughing

il/elle rit- he/she/it laughs, does laugh
      is laughing
	ils/elles rient- they laugh, do laugh,
	          are laughing

Laughing Matters

1. If you picture the stems of *rire* and *sourire* as *ri* and *souri,* the one letter singular endings are -**s**, -**s** and -**t**.

2. For the plural forms (the last laughs), regular -**er/-re** plural endings are added.

3. The first and the second persons singular of *rire* are *ris. Le ris de veau* is **calf's brain** which is considered a delicacy. (Many diners choose *le bifteck* rather than 'pick their brains.')

4. The first two singular forms of *sourire* are *souris. La souris* is **the mouse**, a great office pet.

Laugh Lines

a. rire aux éclats- to roar with laughter: The exact translation is "to laugh with sparkles." *Rire bruyamment-* **to laugh loudly is almost its synonym.**

Ex. Les hyènes pensent que les lions qui rient aux éclats sont **les copieurs**. > Hyenas think that lions who roar with laughter are **copycats**.

b. C'est à mourir de rire- It's hilarious. It literally means "It's to die from laughing." (You can also find <u>fun</u> in the word <u>funeral</u>.)

Ex. Regarde ce film de Charlie Chaplain! C'est à mourir de rire. > Watch this Charlie Chaplain film! It's hilarious.

c. Il vaut mieux en rire qu'en pleurer- It is better to laugh from it than to cry from it. (It is said when 'an issue isn't worth a tissue.')

d. rire aux larmes- to laugh until one cries: Word-for-word, it's "to laugh with tears." (It's said when 'funny turns to runny.')

e. Il n'y a pas de quoi rire- It is no laughing matter/There is nothing to laugh about

Ex. Il n'y a pas de quoi rire si on vole la plume de Yankee Doodle. > It's no laughing matter if someone steals Yankee Doodle's feather. (It doesn't 'tickle' him at all.)

f. rire de- to laugh at: Notice the switch in prepositions!

Ex. La mère rit de la plaisanterie de son fils. Lorsqu'elle prépare le dîner, il cherche **un extincteur**. > The mother laughs at her son's joke. While she is preparing dinner, he looks for **a fire extinguisher**.

<u>Some Happy Face Expressions with *Sourire*</u>

a. sourire à quelqu'un- to smile at someone. It 'turns up' with the same usage in English.

Ex. Personne ne sait si **la Joconde** sourit au peintre. > Nobody knows whether **Mona Lisa** is smiling at the painter. (That was Da Vinci's 'stroke of genius.')

b. sourire aux anges- to have a vacant grin: It actually says "to smile at the angels."

Ex. Ces jeunes femmes sourient aux anges lorsqu'elles regardent la statue de David. > Those young women have a vacant grin while they are looking at the statue of David. (Could they be pondering 'a heavenly body'?)

c. sourire à- to appeal to

Ex. Son sourire magnétique nous sourit. > His magnetic smile appeals to us. (The attraction is easily explained.)

<u>'Happy Talk'</u>- Use the correct forms of *rire* and *sourire* and the related idioms to translate the sentences.

1. I always smile when I am with her. _____
_____.

2. A month in Europe appeals to me. _____.

3. We are not laughing at his bad luck. _____.

4. Do you (*vous*) think that <u>Mona Lisa</u> is smiling? _____
_____?

5. Some strangers smile when they see her baby. _____
_____.

6. Do you (*tu*) roar with laughter when you watch those movies? _____
_____?

7. Evan Lee has a vacant grin because he has a secret. _____
_____.

8. A person who takes life as it comes says, "It's better to laugh than to cry from it." _____
_____.

245

True Confessions for False -RE Verbs- Put the letters beside the numbers of the corresponding sentences.

_____ 1. Rita suit une classe de yoga.

_____ 2. Pour survivre à leur critique, le fils leur dit toujours "d'accord."

_____ 3. Nos grands-parents suivent les modes courantes.

_____ 4. Une vieille dame veut vivre à l'âge de cent ans.

_____ 5. Les étudiants ne peuvent pas suivre ce que le prof leur dit.

_____ 6. Céleste sourit souvent aux anges.

_____ 7. Madame Delacrime est presque certaine qu'elle reconnaît le voleur.

_____ 8. Les voisins hostiles ne vont plus vous crier.

_____ 9. L'enfant rit aux éclats quand il jette ses jouets partout.

_____ 10. Je demande au fermier, "Est-il difficile à vivre avec le son des coqs le matin?"

_____ 11. Nous ne savons pas leur adresse d'été.

_____ 12. Quelquefois la jeunesse ne comprend pas que la vie coûte cher.

_____ 13. L'expression est "poursuivre des moulins à vent."

_____ 14. Les soldats survivent à cette guerre.

_____ 15. Vous allez dire à la réunion que les impôts sont trop hauts.

_____ 16. Notre chien suit le facteur, mais cela ne le dérange pas.

_____ 17. Il ne peut pas survivre.

_____ 18. Mme Hanches ne suit pas un régime.

_____ 19. Mireille et Marc acceptent le fait qu'ils ne suivent pas bien en physique.

_____ 20. Un jour à la campagne me sourit.

A. On ne vit pas toujours d'amour et d'eau fraîche.

B. Il doit ralentir un peu et exprimer mieux ses idées.

C. Il en rit, et il dit, "Je n'aime pas travailler seul."

D. Allons-y ce dimanche!

E. Il y a toujours des chocolats dans son sac à main.

F. Ensuite, il fait ce qu'il veut.

G. Il répond, "Mais non, je suis près d'eux lorsqu'ils chantent."

H. Nous allons vous suivre.

I. Cela veut dire ne pas faire face à la réalité.

J. Elle donne l'impression qu'elle n'a pas de soucis.

K. Il perd trop de sang.

L. Votre père sait les prendre.

M. Elle y assiste trois fois par semaine.

N. Elle pense à le faire suivre.

O. Ils disent, "Ils vaut mieux en rire qu'en pleurer."

P. Ils ne vivent pas dans le passé.

Q. Sa mère pense, "Il n'y a pas de quoi rire."

R. Ils font suivre leur courrier.

S. Ils ne veulent pas rester après cela dans ce pays.

T. La recommandation de son médecin est "Attendez!"

UNE REVUE - A Review

'In Other Words'- **Match the letters to the numbers of the synonyms.**

____ 1. apprendre à	A. accepter
____ 2. dormir debout	B. ne pas changer
____ 3. construire	C. ruiner
____ 4. survivre	D. assister à
____ 5. rire aux éclats	E. aller vite
____ 6. servir à	F. bâtir
____ 7. laisser courir	G. dire les mensonges constamment
____ 8. sentir	H. être utile pour
____ 9. prendre pour	I. enseigner à
____ 10. courir	J. aller chercher
____ 11. introduire	K. étonner (pas fortement)
____ 12. suivre	L. courir le haricot à quelqu'un
____ 13. sans mentir	M. considérer comme
____ 14. passer prendre	N. rouler
____ 15. produire	O. trouver quelque chose très amusante
____ 16. prendre le dîner	P. être extrêmement fatigué
____ 17. prendre	Q. présent
____ 18. courir sur le système	R. paraître/sembler être
____ 19. mentir comme on respire	S. vivre après
____ 20. conduire	T. manger le repas du soir
____ 21. surprendre	U. vraiment
____ 22. détruire	V. faire passer

'Choosing Your Words Carefully'- **Circle the letters of the answers to complete the scenarios.**

1. Chantal dit, "Je ne peux pas le faire mieux." Je vais ____.
a. dormir aux poings fermés   b. le laisser tomber   c. sentir la différence   d. courir les garçons

2. M. Sansfoyer ne cherche pas le travail, et il passe sa vie à la rue. Il ____.
a. entre et sort en courant   b. dort debout   c. sent la rose   d. court à l'échec

3. Je ne reconnais pas le truc à sa main. Je demande à mon père, ____,
a. "C'est à moi de servir?"   b. "Est-ce que je cours ma chance?"   c. "À quoi sert-il?"
d. "Tu ris aux larmes?"

4. La fille dit qu'elle sort toujours en groupe. En réalité, elle sort avec son petit ami.
a. Les garçons en prennent beaucoup.   b. Elle sert d'une danseuse exotique.
c. Ses parents courent sur son système.   d. Elle raconte une histoire de dormir debout.

5. On remarque "Nous ne savons pas prendre ce que vous nous dites" avant de dire ____.
a. Comment devons-nous y réagir?   b. Pouvons-nous prendre la vie comme elle vient?
c. Faut-il en prendre y en laisser?   d. Passons-nous vous prendre?

6. Au lieu de dire "si on considère tout," on peut utiliser l'expression "____."
a. prendre quelqu'un sur un fait   b. faire payer trop   c. à tout prendre   d. C'est à mourir de rire

7. Avant de commencer la scène prochaine, le directeur dit aux acteurs, ____!
a. "Ne me dérangez pas!"   b. "Repos!"   c. "Servez-vous!"   d. "Tenez-moi au courant!"

8. Angélique montre à sa petite sœur comment jouer de la harpe. La grande sœur ____.
a. apprend à la connaître   b. ne comprend rien   c. lui apprend à le faire   d. se fait comprendre
9. Tu voudrais habiter au Tibet. Tu dois ____.
a. surprendre des gens   b. savoir ce qui te prend   c. servir quelqu'un   d. l'apprendre à tes parents
10. Quelqu'un vous montre la ville de Londres?
a. Oui, un chauffeur nous conduit.   b. Oui, nous le faisons construire à ce moment.
c. Non, nous n'en apprenons pas l'histoire.   d. Oui, nos hôtes nous font entrer.
11. Écoutez le bruit devant cette usine-là!
a. Personne ne peut le traduire.   b. Qu'est-ce qu'on y produit?   c. Pourquoi les détruisent-ils?
d. Où est-ce qu'on l'introduit?
12. Les frères assistent aux messes au Mont St. Michel, n'est-ce pas?
a. Non, ils n'y conduisent pas d'entreprises.   b. Non, ils ne rient pas aux éclats.
c. Oui, ils vont poursuivre des religieuses en justice.   d. Oui, ils les suivent tous les jours.
13. Je peux vérifier que je ne mens pas sur cela.
a. Je ne le suis pas du tout.   b. Mes amis vont me suivre.   c. On peut me faire suivre.
d. Je vais y survivre.
14. Dans des endroits loin de la civilisation, il y a des gens qui ____.
a. sont bons vivants   b. ont du savoir-vivre   c. chassent pour vivre
d. vivent d'amour et d'eau fraîche
15. Malgré ses dettes et sa mauvaise santé, Mme Çava n'est pas découragée. A son avis, ____.
a. C'est à mourir de rire.   b. On doit sourire aux anges.   c. Il n'y a pas de quoi rire.
d. Il vaut mieux en rire qu'en pleurer.

PREPOSITIONS THAT PRECEDE INFINITIVES

The following terms were 'addressed' previously. Their uses before verbs is 'stamped' below.

Prepositions Delivered before Infinitives
1. à- about, in, to
Ex. Le fils ne peut pas emprunter la voiture parce qu'il continue à conduire trop vite. > The son can't borrow the car because he continues to drive too fast. (Now, a parent 'is putting his/her foot down.')
2. au lieu de- in place of, instead of
Ex. Au lieu de payer le prix plus élevé aux États-Unis, des personnes font envoyer leur médicament du Canada. > Instead of paying the higher price in the United States, some people have their medication sent from Canada. (Our Northern neighbors don't charge us 'top dollar.')
3. avant de- before
Ex. Avant de laver leurs sols, la jeune-mariée balaie pendant que son époux cherche **la serpillière.** > Before washing their floors, the bride sweeps while her husband looks for **the mop.** (The broom and the glide make a coordinated team.)
An important reminder: As a preposition, *avant* precedes nouns and expressions of time.
Ex. Le jockey va avoir une fête de célibataire avant sa cérémonie de mariage. > The jockey is going to have a bachelor bash before his wedding. (It's his version of a 'bridle' party.)
4. de- about, for, of, to
Ex. Comme essayer de et **tâcher de** sont les synonymes, on tâche d'utiliser un pour l'autre. > As try and **try** are synonyms, one tries to use one for the other.
5. pour- in order to: Often omitted after verbs of motion, *pour* is a synonym for *afin de.*
Ex. Pour empêcher **les caries**, ne mange pas trop de **sucreries**! > In order to prevent **cavities,** do not eat too many **sweets**! (That advice comes 'by word of mouth.')
Ex. La dame malade monte en haut chercher quelque chose. > The sick lady goes upstairs to look for something. (One might wonder 'what she came down with.')
6. sans- without
Ex. L'agricultrice/la fèrmière quitte son mari sans l'avertir. > The woman farmer leaves her husband without warning him. (Did he find a 'John Deere' letter?)

Sticking with the Prepositions- Use the prepositions in parentheses to form single sentences.
Ex. (avant d') Gigi gronde la petite. Elle n'écoute pas son explication. > Gigi gronde la petite avant d'écouter son explication. (Gigi scolds the little girl before listening to her explanation.)

1. (pour) Nous attendons longtemps. Nous te voyons. _____
_____.

2. (au lieu d') Je gaspille tout mon argent. Je n'en épargne pas un peu. _____
_____.

3. (sans) Est-ce que tu sors de la maison? Tu me dis "au revoir"? _____
_____?

4. (avant d') Noëlle crie de joie. Elle ouvre ses cadeaux. _____
_____.

5. (pour) Babette fait la cuisine nuit et jour. Elle prépare une fête magnifique. _____

6. (pour) Brad et Angelina sont chez Spago. Ils célèbrent leurs films populaires. _____ .

7. (au lieu de) Mon grand-père boit le chocolat chaud. Il ne prend pas le café. _____ .

8. (avant de) Justin Nower regarde son émission de télé préférée. Il fait ses devoirs. _____ .

9. (sans) Anne Formée est-elle pas au courant? Elle lit le Monde chaque jour. _____ ?

10. (avant de) Ann Arrière passe l'aspirateur. Elle range le salon et les chambres à coucher. _____

_____

_____ .

Colmar (The Upper Rhine River)

250

LES PARTICIPES PRÉSENTS - PRESENT PARTICIPLES

With their -ing endings, present participles are easily recognized in English. Examples include doing, reading, studying, telling and working. *Les participes présents* with a distinctive, trailing -ant are the French equivalent.
Here's how 'the little bugger' works:

'Trapping the -Ant'
1. *Le participe présent* of most verbs is found by deleting -ons from the present tense *nous* form and replacing it with -ant. The translations for the present participles above are *faisant, lisant, étudiant, disant* and *travaillant.*
2. The invariable present participle refers to the subject of the sentence.
3. Verbs with irregular present participles include *avoir- ayant* (having), *être- étant* (being) and *savoir- sachant* (knowing)
Ex. Pas sachant la route en Amérique, M. Colomb demande les directions. > Not knowing the way to America, Mr. Colombus asks for directions. (People told him 'flat out.')
4. **Although a present participle can start an English sentence, an infinitive serves that purpose in French.**
Ex. Avoir un avis est bon, mais savoir quand l'exprimer est encore meilleur. > Having an opinion is good, but knowing when to express it is even better.
5. *En,* **translated as <u>while</u> or <u>upon</u>, often precedes** *un participe présent.*
Ex. En écoutant la radio, Hoover passe l'aspirateur. > While listening to the radio, Hoover vacuums. (Sometimes he only picks up static.)
An important reminder: -<u>Ant</u>, -<u>ante</u>, -<u>ants</u> and -<u>antes</u> are also adjectival endings.
As a present participle
Ex. En attendant une toilette libre sur un bateau de croisière, des femmes parlent du voyage. > While waiting for an unoccupied toilet on a cruise ship, some women talk about the trip. (Perhaps, they are discussing who has the first and who has the second 'seating.')
As an adjective
Ex. Des femmes, attendantes une toilette libre sur un bateau de croisière, parlent du voyage. > Some women, waiting for an available toilet on a cruise ship, talk about their trip.
Attendantes **agrees with** *les femmes. En,* **from the first example, 'had to be flushed.'**
6. *Tout* **precedes** *en* **to emphasize that an action is ongoing. The translation for such phrases is "while still _____ ing."**
Ex. Tout en écrivant le premier roman, Paige commence à écrire un deuxième. > While still writing the first novel, Paige starts to write a second one. (Talk about 'a fully booked schedule!')

A 'Prep' Rally- Translate the following sentences.
1. Mlle Gomme efface les réponses entièrement au lieu de corriger les erreurs. _____

_____.

2. En nageant une heure chaque jour, le vieillard tient sa bonne forme. _____

_____.

3. Avant de prendre un médicament, vérifiez la date d'expiration! _____

_____!

251

4. La petite Fleurette commence à comprendre tout ce que nous lui disons. _____

_____.

5. Au lieu d'échanger des cadeaux cette année, nous allons faire une croisière. _____

_____.

6. Les belles-sœurs de Cendrillon lui commandent de balayer le plancher. _____

_____.

7. Chez moi, on ne discute pas les régimes en mangeant les sucreries. _____

_____.

8. Pensez-vous à payer vos dettes tout en achetant des choses inutiles? _____

_____?

Going through 'a Phrase'- Use **à**, *de, en, pour, sans, au lieu de, avant de* or *en* + **a present participle to translate the following phrases.**

1. before answering the telephone _____
2. to succeed in earning a living _____
3. without being there _____
4. while spending the winter with them _____
5. to have just learned _____
6. in order to follow the route _____
7. instead of spending so much money _____
8. upon seeing you (*vous*) today _____
9. before tasting the meal _____
10. without knowing the reason _____
11. while being on vacation _____
12. instead of sending it by e-mail _____
13. before being 21 years old _____
14. while traveling around the world _____

_____

LE VIDE-GRENIER DE M. ET MME PARTIR
Mr. and Mrs. Partir's Garage Sale
La Première Partie

Du Vocabulaire du Conte

1. le vide-grenier- the garage sale, the empty attic
2. les frais d'expédition- the shipping costs
3. mettre une annonce- to place an ad
4. les provisions- the supplies
5. mettre ensemble les rangs- to put the racks together
6. déplier- to unfold
7. la nappe- the tablecloth
8. le canapé, le sofa- the sofa
9. les rideaux- the curtains
10. rigoler- to kid, to joke
11. le brimborion- the knick-knack
12. la boîte de musique- the music box
13. les serre-livres- the bookends
14. le cadre- the picture frame
15. le bougeoir en faïence- the ceramic candle holder
16. le bric-à-brac- the junk
17. au fait- by the way
18. être engagé- to be involved
19. faire le tri dans- to sort through
20. la quincaillerie- the hardware, the hardware store
21. la penderie- the closet
22. le drap- the sheet
23. la taie d'oreiller- the pillowcase
24. le dessus-de-lit- the bedspread
25. l'édredon (m.)- the comforter
26. étaler- to display
27. le livre de poche- the paperback
28. le livre relié- the hard cover book
29. le magnétoscope- the VCR
30. quànt à- as for
31. le couvert- the tableware
32. le service- the set of dishes
33. la batterie de cuisine- the pots and pans
34. l'argenterie (f.)- the silverware
35. à condition que- as long as
36. la recette- the recipe

M. et Mme Partir, un couple français qui habite dans l'état de New York, va déménager. Ils vont rentrer en France le mois prochain. Les vide-greniers n'y sont pas populaires. Comme ils ne veulent pas payer **les frais d'expédition** pour les choses qu'ils n'utilisent plus, le couple décide de tenir **un vide-grenier** chez eux avant leur départ.

Il y a tant de choses à faire avant cet événement qui va avoir lieu le 15 et le 16 avril de huit heures du matin jusqu'à une heure de l'après-midi. Tout d'abord, Mme Partir doit téléphoner pour **mettre une annonce** dans le journal local. Elle espère que les deux ne vont pas travailler deux jours entiers pour payer pour cette publicité chère.

Pendant que Madame Partir est à Walmart pour acheter **des provisions** pour faire des panneaux, son mari mari balaie le garage et **met ensemble des rangs**. Après cela, il **déplie** et essuie des tables, et il les couvre de vieilles **nappes.**

Aussitôt que sa femme arrive chez eux, ils parlent de ce qu'ils veulent vendre.

Mme Partir: Il y a **un canapé** fleuri dans le salon. Achetons un plus neutre en France!
M. Partir: Pas possible de le montrer, Sylvie. Nous ne pouvons pas le porter au garage, et si nous le

laissons dedans, les gens qui entrent voudront regarder tout.

Mme Partir: Tu as raison. Que penses-tu de vendre **les rideaux** des chambres à coucher? Ils ne vont pas aller aux fenêtres de notre nouvelle maison.

M. Partir: Alors, vendons-les si nous en pouvons obtenir un bon prix.

Mme Partir: Tu **rigoles**? Les bleus en dentelle sont de la Bretagne. Les roses en soie sont de Lyon.

M. Partir: Ce projet devient très difficile.

Mme Partir: N'y perds pas espoir encore! Il y a tant de **brimborions** à vendre. **Boîtes de musique, serre-livres** en cuir, **cadres** en toile, **bougeoirs en faïence**

M. Partir: Quelle est l'expression? Les camelotes d'un homme sont les trésors d'un autre?

Mme Partir: Tu considères ces objets décoratifs comme le **bric-à-brac**?

M. Partir: D'accord, mais n'oublie pas qu'à un vide-grenier on dépense très peu.

Mme Partir: Je le sais bien. **Au fait**, des vêtements de bonne qualité que nous ne portons plus sont déjà dans une boutique à revendre. Je vais séparer par prix le tas qui reste.

M. Partir: Lorsque tu es **engagée** avec cela, je vais **faire le tri dans ma quincaillerie.**

(Clément appelle Sylvie qui est dans la cuisine maintenant.)

M. Partir: Ne vendons pas tous les bons jeans! Ils coûtent quatre fois le prix en France.

Mme Partir: Seulement les vieux. Tu peux en être sûr.

(Un peu plus tard, Clément trouve Sylvie occupée dans **sa penderie.**)

Mme Partir: Tu sais ce qui est un best-seller?

M. Partir: Bien sur! C'est un livre très populaire.

Mme Partir: C'est vrai, mais je veux dire à un vide-grenier. C'est le linge. **Draps, taies d'oreillers, édredons, dessus-de-lit** et serviettes. Je vais en **étaler** beaucoup.

M. Partir: Comment sais-tu ça, Sylvie? Tu consultes avec Marthe Stewart?

Mme Partir: Non, de temps en temps, je vais aux ventes juste regarder.

M. Partir: Et tu n'achètes rien?

Mme Partir: Quelques articles que je vends ce week-end.

M. Partir: Quelle entrepreneuse. Parlant des best-sellers, gardons-nous tous nos romans américains?

Mme Partir: À part tes préférés, distribuons autant que possible! Ils pèsent tant, et ça coûte cher de les expédier. Notre bibliothèque en ville peut prendre ceux que nous ne vendons pas. Mais bien sur, **mes livres de poche** par Danielle Steel vont en France.

M. Partir: Tu dois t'assurer qu'elle reste une célébrité internationale.

Mme Partir: Clément, j'apprécie ton bon sens de l'humour. Ça fait plus facile ce travail sans fin.

M. Partir: Merci chérie. Si nous vendons ces volumes d'encyclopédies? On les lit toujours?

Mme Partir: Je crois que non. On trouve tous les renseignements sur un ordinateur ces jours-ci.

M. Partir: On ne sait jamais. Plaçons-les dans une boîte avec **les** autres **livres reliés.**

(En route au garage pour ranger les livres, Clément se tourne vers Sylvie.)

M. Partir: Le mot "volume" me fait penser aux électroniques. Si le prix est assez bas, il y une possibilité de dire "au revoir" au stéréo et même **au magnétoscope.**

Mme Partir: Et les disques? Sont-elles des pièces de collection?

M. Partir: Je ne crois pas qu'elles valent pas beaucoup aujourd'hui, mais peut-être elles auront plus de valeur à l'avenir.

Mme Partir: **Quant à** l'avenir immédiat, prenons du déjeuner!

M. Partir: Une bonne idée pendant que nous avons toujours des assiettes et **des couverts.**

Mme Partir: Espérons que nous en avons moins après demain. **Un service, une batterie de cuisine**

et de **l'argenterie** vont être en vente. Tu peux m'emmener déjeuner lundi.

M. Partir: Mon plaisir, **à condition que** tu gardes **tes recettes**.

Which Ones Are for Keeps?- **Circle the letters of the correct choices to complete the sentences.**

1. La traduction pour *a garage sale* est ___.

a. une maison à vendre   b. un garage à louer   c. un vide-grenier   d. un marché aux puces

2. Pour faire la publicité pour leur vente, Mme Partir ___.

a. achète des rangs   b. balaie le garage   c. déplie des tables   d. met une annonce dans le journal

3. Sylvie veut vendre le canapé fleuri et ___.

a. laisser entrer tout le monde   b. acheter un autre en France   c. le porter au garage

d. garder les rideaux des chambres à coucher

4. Des brimborions qui peuvent attirer l'affaire sont ___.

a. les rideaux en dentelle et en soie   b. les boîtes de musique, les serre-livres et les cadres

c. les vêtements de bonne qualité   d. la quincaillerie que M. Partir n'utilise plus

5. Sylvie a l'intention de vendre seulement les vieux parce que ___.

a. les blue-jeans sont beaucoup plus chers en France   b. son mari est dans sa penderie

c. les nouveaux sont dans un tas de linge   d. Clément fait un tri dans les camelotes

6. Mme Partir sait qu'on va acheter le linge parce que (qu') ___.

a. tout le monde préfère l'étaler   b. Danielle Steel lui parle

c. elle a tant de draps et taies d'oreillers   d. elle va aux ventes quelquefois

7. M. et Mme Partir vont essayer de vendre autant de romans que possible parce qu'ils ___.

a. pensent que les deux pèsent trop   b. ne veulent pas payer les frais d'expédition

c. ne vont pas à la bibliothèque en ville   d. gardent tous les livres de poche

8. Comme ils ne veulent plus leurs encyclopédies, le couple va ___.

a. trouver les renseignements sur l'ordinateur   b. avoir un bon sens de l'humour

c. retourner au garage pour les arranger   d. les placer avec les autres livres reliés

9. Si leur prix est assez bas, il y a une possibilité de (d') ___.

a. jeter des choses de valeur   b. reconnaître des pièces de collection

c. vendre le stéréo et le magnétoscope   d. jouer leurs disques à l'avenir

10. M. Partir va emmener déjeuner sa femme parce que (qu') ___.

a. ils ont toujours des assiettes et des couverts   b. Mme Partir n'a plus de recettes

c. M. Partir n'aime pas leur argenterie   d. ils vendent le service et la batterie de cuisine

----

Écrivez des réponses complètes en français aux questions suivantes.

1. Quand M. et Mme Partir vont-ils rentrer en France? _____

_____.

2. Pourquoi tiennent-ils un vide-grenier avant leur départ? _____

_____.

3. Quelles sont les dates du vide-grenier? _____·

4. Que M. Partir fait-il quand sa femme n'est pas à la maison? _____

_____.

5. Quelle est la première chose que Sylvie pense à vendre? _____

_____.

6. Pourquoi son mari dit-il que c'est une mauvaise idée? _____

7. Quels brimborions Sylvie va-t-elle étaler? _____

8. Quelle suggestion Clément fait-il des jeans? Pourquoi? _____

9. Quels articles de linge Sylvie va-t-elle étaler? _____

10. Comment sait-elle que le linge vend vite aux vide-greniers? _____

11. **Selon (according to)** Mme Partir, pourquoi doivent-ils vendre tant de romans? _____

12. Quels livres de poche va-t-elle prendre en France? _____

13. Pourquoi Sylvie croit-elle que personne ne va acheter les volumes d'encyclopédie? _____

14. Quels objets de cuisine vont-ils essayer de vendre? _____
_____

LE VIDE-GRENIER DE M. ET MME PARTIR
Mr. and Mrs. Partir's Garage Sale
La Deuxième Partie

Du Vocabulaire du Conte
1. en train de- in the middle of
2. le coin- the corner
3. le courant- the current (of electricity)
4. l'appareil électroménager de cuisine (m.)- the kitchen appliance
5. le four à micro-ondes- the microwave oven
6. le robot de cuisine- the food processor
7. la cafetière- the coffee maker
8. l'ouvre-boîtes (m.)- the can opener
9. le grille-pain- the toaster
10. peiné- distressed
11. la prise- the plug
12. Zut!- darn, damn!
13. la tondeuse à gazon- the lawn mower
14. le coussin- the cushion
15. le râteau- the rake
16. l'accessoire de cheminée (m.)- the fireplace accessory

19. le berceau- the cradle
20. la chaise à bascule- the rocking chair
21. faire le paquet-cadeau- to gift wrap
22. liquidé- sold out
23. le torchon- the dishtowel
24. le set de table- the place mat
25. marchander- to bargain
26. le casse-tête/le puzzle- the puzzle
27. la poupée- the doll
28. le jeu de societé- the board game
29. convaincre- to convince
30. le numéro de comédie- the comedy routine
31. faire livrer- to have delivered

C'est aujourd'hui vendredi, le quinze avril. Il est six heures et demie du matin. M. Partir est **en train de** placer des panneaux dans son voisinage. Il va **de coin** en coin avec des signes, un marteau et des clous dans ses mains.

Mme Partir est dans la cuisine où elle prépare le petit déjeuner en comptant les billets et les pièces. Il faut faire de la monnaie pour les premiers clients. Mais, quelque chose plus importante la préoccupe. Le courant électrique n'est pas le même en France qu'aux États-Unis. Ils doivent acheter un truc spécial pour convertir tous leurs **appareils électroménagers de cuisine** … **four à micro-ondes**, **robot de cuisine, cafetière, ouvre-boîtes** et **grille-pain**? Ça va coûter cher s'il faut les remplacer. Sylvie se pose cette question, "Où est Clément quand j'ai besoin de lui?"
(Comme si son mari entend son nom, il apparaît.)

M. Partir: Sylvie, tu as un air **peiné.**
Mme Partir: Oui, je réfléchis à nos gadgets. Nous ne pouvons pas utiliser **ces prises** en France.
M. Partir: C'est le cadet de nos soucis. Cependant, changer le temps n'est pas ma spécialité.
Mme Partir: Il pleut maintenant?
M. Partir: Non, mais ça sent la pluie.
Mme Partir: Zut alors!
M. Partir: Viens avec moi au garage! Ne laissons pas tout dehors!
(Ils déplacent le stéréo, le magnétoscope et **les coussins** des meubles de patio.)
M. Partir: La tondeuse à gazon, le râteau et **les accessoires de cheminée** peuvent y rester.
Mme Partir: Nous n'avons que quarante minutes jusqu'à **l'ouverture** officielle.
M. Partir: Moins que ça! Des personnes aiment arriver de bonne heure pour de ne pas manquer les meilleures affaires.
Mme Partir: Tu ne parles pas trop bientôt. Je vois nos premiers clients d'ici.
M. Partir: N'oublions pas de parler anglais avec eux!
(However, the couple has translated the dialogue for you from English into French.)

M. Partir: Bonjour Madame, Monsieur.
La femme #1: Par hasard, vendez-vous des meubles de bébé? **Un berceau** ou une chaise-haute?
Mme Partir: Malheureusement, vous êtes vingt-cinq ans trop tard. Nos enfants sont grandis.
La femme #1: Notre fils et notre grand-fils vont nous rendre visite la semaine prochaine.
L'homme #1: (parlant à sa femme) Nous pouvons louer ces choses.
Mme Partir: Je viens d'avoir une idée. Est-ce qu'**une chaise à bascule** vous intéresse?
La femme #1: Pourquoi pas? Où est-elle, et combien en demandez-vous?
Mme Partir: C'est là-bas. Trente dollars.
L'homme #1: Vous prenez vingt-cinq pour cela?
M. Partir: Bien sûr, mais nous ne **faisons** pas **un paquet-cadeau.**
La femme #1: (parlant à Mme Partir) Votre mari est humoristique.
Mme Partir: C'est une raison qu'il n'est pas à vendre.

La femme paie pour la chaise à bascule pendant que les deux hommes la mettent dans le camion des clients. De huit heures du matin jusqu'à midi, Sylvie et Clément sont vraiment occupés. Ils vendent tant de vêtements et accessoires. De plus, la prévision de Mme Partir devient une réalité. Le linge est presque **liquidé,** même **les torchons** et **les sets de table**. Finalement, à leur surprise, des clients leur font de bonnes offres pour les encyclopédies et les rideaux.

Mme Partir: Nous faisons très bien, et heureusement il fait encore beau.
M. Partir: Il y a une autre bonne chose. Nous ne gaspillons pas notre temps mettant les prix sur les articles. On adore **marchander**.
Mme Partir: Absolument! Et ce qui est dix dollars aujourd'hui va coûter moins demain.
M. Partir: D'autres clients arrivent.
Mme Partir: Bonjour tout le monde.
L'homme #2: Combien demandez-vous **ces casse-têtes**?
M. Partir: Un dollar pour les petits et deux dollars pour les grands.
La femme #2: Avez- vous **des poupées** à vendre? Je les collectionne.
Mme Partir: Non madame. Je n'en ai pas.
L'homme #2: (tenant un animal en peluche dans ses bras) C'est un ou deux dollars aussi?
Le fils: Non Papa. C'est un singe.
La femme #2: (riant) Quels sont les prix de ces vêtements sur le rang?
Mme Partir: Deux dollars.
Le fils: Chacun Maman, pas tous.
La femme #2: (souriant) Bobby, tu es amusant, mais ça suffit.
Le fils: (tenant le Monopoly et le Clue dans ses mains) Ceux-ci sont bon marché?
Mme Partir: Non, ceux-là sont **des jeux de société.**
L'homme #2: (riant) Bobby, tu viens de rencontrer ton match.
La femme #2: N'essaie pas de la **convaincre** de **faire un numéro de comédie** avec toi!
(La famille paie pour leurs achats, et elle part. Il est une heure de l'après-midi.)
M. Partir: Je pense que nous n'allons pas voir plus de clients aujourd'hui. Nous pouvons fermer la porte de garage.
Mme Partir: D'accord, mais regarde ce fouillis! Il faut l'arranger avant demain.
M. Partir: Plus tard. **Faisons livrer** une pizza!
Mme Partir: Cette idée-là et **une sieste** semblent parfaites.

Real Deal?- Label the statements *vrai* or *faux*.

_____ 1. M. Partir pense à vendre le marteau et les clous qu'il a dans ses mains.
_____ 2. Le robot de cuisine et l'ouvre-boîtes sont deux appareils électroménagers.
_____ 3. Clément considère la différence entre les courants électriques être un problème.
_____ 4. On laisse dehors la tondeuse à gazon, le râteau et les accessoires de cheminée.
_____ 5. Clément dit que des gens vont arriver tôt le matin à cause du mauvais temps.
_____ 6. Avant l'ouverture, Clément dit à sa femme de ne pas parler aux clients.
_____ 7. Les Partir n'ont ni un berceau ni une chaise-haute à vendre.
_____ 8. Les enfants de Clément et Sylvie sont encore petits.
_____ 9. L'homme #1 paie vingt-cinq dollars pour la chaise à bascule.
_____ 10. Sylvie fait un paquet-cadeau, et elle met l'achat dans le camion.
_____ 11 Les deux ne collent pas les prix sur les articles.

_____ 12. L'homme #2 veut savoir combien coûte l'animal en peluche.
_____ 13. Le prix de tous les vêtements sur le rang est deux dollars.
_____ 14. Bobby cherche quelqu'un pour jouer le Monopoly et le Clue avec lui.
_____ 15. M. Partir veut faire livrer une pizza avant d'arranger le fouillis.

Écrivez des réponses complètes en français aux questions suivantes.

1. Où est M. Partir à six heures et demie du matin? _____
_____.

2. Quelle préoccupation importante Sylvie a-t-elle à ce moment? _____
_____.

3. Qu'est-ce qu'ils déplacent? _____
_____.

4. Qu'est-ce que le couple #1 cherche? _____
_____.

5. Que Sylvie dit-elle quand la femme #1 remarque que Clément est humoristique? _____
_____.

6. Comment savez-vous que la prévision de Sylvie devient une réalité? _____
_____.

7. Pour quelles choses fait-on de bonnes offres? _____
_____.

8. Selon M. et Mme Partir, pourquoi ne faut-il pas mettre de prix sur les articles? _____
_____.

9. Qu'est-ce qui intéresse l'homme #2? _____.
10. Qu'est-ce que la femme #2 collectionne? _____.
11. Qu'est-ce que le fils dit quand son père demande si l'animal en peluche est un ou deux dollars?
_____.

12. Quelle question Bobby pose-t-il du Monopoly et Clue? _____
_____.

13. Comment Sylvie y répond? _____.
14. Quelle est la suggestion de M. Partir? _____
_____

LE VIDE-GRENIER DE M. ET MME PARTIR
Mr. and Mrs. Partir's Garage Sale
La Troisième Partie

Du Vocabulaire du Conte
1. C'est reparti!- Here we go again!   **23. la somme- the amount**
2. être perdu dans ses pensées- to be lost in one's thoughts
3. la salle à manger- the dining room   **24. être disposé à- to be willing to**

4. la bibliothèque- the bookcase/the library
5. la table basse- the coffee table
6. la vente aux enchères (f.)- the auction
7. porter malheur- to bring bad luck
8. l'antiquaire- the antique dealer
9. la balançoire- the swing
10. la bascule- the see-saw
11. la glissade- the slide
12. d'ailleurs- besides, moreover
13. divertir- to entertain
14. le tapis- the rug
15. le ton- the tone
16. la salle de bain(s)- the bathroom
17. le rideau à douche- the shower curtain
18. la balance- the scale
19. le fric- the money (slang)
20. sans arrêt- non-stop
21. l'abat-jour (m.)- the lamp-shade
22. l'appareil-photo (m.)- the camera

25. le matelas- the mattress
26. bavarder- to chat
27. epuisé- exhausted
28. la perceuse- the drill
29. la scie- the saw (A play on words and words to play on)
30. les pinces (f.)- the pliers
31. la clef- the wrench
32. le tournevis- the screwdriver
33. le reveille-matin- the alarm clock
34. nous serons- we will be
35. le maquillage- the make-up
36. échanger un contre l'autre- to exchange one for the other
37. l'avertissement (m.)- the warning
38. s'attendre à- to expect
39. n'importe quel- any, no matter what
40. Marché conclu!- It's a deal!

Samedi, le seize avril est le deuxième jour du vide-grenier de M. et Mme Partir. Il est sept heures du matin. Clémemt conduit autour de son voisinage pour faire certain que les panneaux sont toujours en place. Sylvie arrange ce qui reste à vendre, et il y en a beaucoup.
M. Partir entre dans le garage.

M. Partir: C'est reparti! Aujourd'hui il n'y a pas de nuages dans le ciel.
Mme Partir: Quelles bonnes nouvelles! Prenons du café et des croissants avant que les premiers clients arrivent. Clément, tu **es perdu dans tes pensées**.
M. Partir: Oui, c'est vrai. Je réfléchis aux meubles que nous n'expédions pas en France. Si nous ne les montrons pas, nous ne pouvons pas les vendre.
Mme Partir: Tu parles du canapé fleuri et de **l'ensemble de salle à manger**?
M. Partir: Oui, il y en a plus?
Mme Partir: Dans le salon il y a **une bibliothèque** et **une table basse**.
M. Partir: Et pas d'espace pour ces meubles chez nous en France.
Mme Partir: Affichons un signe avec une description des meubles et leurs prix! Les clients peuvent nous en demander.
M. Partir: Nous prenons des rendez-vous pour les montrer?
Mme Partir: Voilà! Si ça ne marche pas, il y a **des ventes aux enchères.** Je vais faire ce panneau-là tout de suite.
M. Partir: Tiens! Tiens! Je crois que nous avons déjà un visiteur.
M. Partir: Bonjour monsieur. Vous cherchez un truc en particulier?
L'homme #3: Vendez-vous des objets d'époque en or? Des alliances qui vous **portent malheur**?
M. Partir: (souriant) Non, mais des bijoux de bonne qualité sont à vendre. Je peux vous montrer des broches, des colliers et des boucles d'oreille.

L'homme #3: Non, merci de toute façon.

Mme Partir: (entrant dans le garage) Quelqu'un était ici?

M. Partir: Un antiquaire cherchant des bijoux anciens. Je viens de parler de toi.

Mme Partir: Comment tu adores me taquiner!

M. Partir: Puis-je t'aider avec ce signe-là?

Mme Partir: Pas à ce moment. Des clients sortent de leur voiture.

M. et Mme Partir: Bonjour madame! Bonjour les enfants!

La femme #3: Bonjour. Je vois ce que je voudrais. Combien **ces clochettes** coûtent-elles?

Mme Partir: L'une en or est sept dollars. Je demande trois dollars la petite.

Le petit fils: (interrompant) Maman, demande à la femme si elle a **une balançoire, une bascule** ou **une glissade!**

La petite fille: (interrompant) Maman, demande-lui si elle a des jeux de vidéo!

La femme #3: (deux clochettes à sa main) Vous acceptez huit dollars pour tous les deux?

M. Partir: Vous voulez dire les clochettes ou les enfants?

(Les deux femmes rient ensemble. La femme #3 paie huit dollars, et la famille part.)

Mme Partir: J'espère que ces étrangers ne pensent pas que nous sommes fous.

M. Partir: Nous ne les reverrons pas. **D'ailleurs**, tout le monde est amusé.

Mme Partir: Voici ton occasion de **divertir** un autre couple.

M. Partir: Bonjour madame! Bonjour monsieur!

L'homme #4: Bonjour. Avez-vous des romans historiques à vendre?

M. Partir: Bien sur. Je vais vous montrer où ils sont.

La femme #4: Moi, je cherche des accessoires pour une chambre d'amis, comme un petit **tapis** clair, des animaux en porcelaine, des tableaux **au ton** pastel.

Mme Partir: Il n'y a rien comme vous décrivez, mais s'il y a **une salle de bain** voisine, peut-être **ce rideau à douche** ou **cette balance** vous intéresse.

M. Partir: Ma femme veut la vendre parce qu'elle marche trop bien.

L'homme #4: (souriant et parlant à sa femme) Combien de **fric** as-tu dans ton sac à main?

La femme #4: (parlant à Mme Partir) Faut-il payer comptant?

Mme Partir: Oui, s'il vous plaît.

La femme #4: En ce cas, nous voulons ces cinq livres, ces deux bougies et ce cadre en toile.

Pour les quatre heures suivantes, les clients arrivent **sans arrêt**. Ils demandent tout **des abat-jours** à un zoom pour **un appareil-photo**. Les choses qu'on cherche et **la petite somme** qu'on est **disposés à** payer surprennent Sylvie et Clément. Néanmoins, ils vendent une plante en soie, un tas de vêtements d'hiver, un ensemble de corbeilles et même **un** vieux **matelas**. De plus, cinq personnes prennent des rendez-vous pour voir les meubles.

Quand il y a moins de clients, leur voisin, Jim, vient pour **bavarder** avec eux.

Jim: Sylvie et Clément, comment ça va?

M. Partir: Nous sommes **épuisés,** et toi?

Jim: Pas mal, merci.

M. Partir: Il me semble qu'à un vide-grenier, le jeu de marchander est aussi important que le prix.

Jim: Je le sais bien. Christine et moi tenons un vide-grenier de temps en temps, mais aujourd'hui, je fais du shopping. Vends-tu **une perceuse** ou **une scie**?

M. Partir: Non, Jim. Quant aux outils, j'ai seulement **des pinces, des clés et des tournevis**. Il n'y a rien d'autre qui attire ton attention?

Jim: Oui, **ce réveille-matin** en cuivre. Sylvie et toi ne le voulez plus?

M. Partir: Pas du tout. **Nous serons** en retraite en France.

Jim: Bon pour vous. Au fait, Christine a besoin du **maquillage** et du parfum.

M. Partir: Tu ne dis pas de bien de ta femme.

Mme Partir: (riant) Jim, prends cette bouteille de Chanel pour elle.

Jim: (rigolant) Ah bon! J'**échange une contre l'autre**.

M. Partir: Et prends ce réveille-matin comme un souvenir de nous.

Jim: Merci mille fois. Nous allons vous inviter à dîner. C'est une promesse et **un avertissement**.

Mme Partir: (taquinant) Fais attention Jim! Christine est ma bonne amie.

Jim: (souriant) À tout à l'heure!

M. et Mme Partir: À bientôt, Jim!

Mme Partir: Clément, il est midi et demi. Nous pouvons fermer ou non?

M. Partir: En quelques minutes. Je pense que nous allons voir encore du monde.

Mme Partir: On **s'attend aux** prix même plus bas au dernier moment.

M. Partir: À cette heure prenons-nous **n'importe quelle** offre?

Mme Partir: On va voir. Est-ce que tu acceptes mon offre de payer pour le dîner ce soir?

M. Partir: Marché conclu!

'Making Ends Meet'- Match the letters to the numbers to form complete sentences.

_____ 1. Les enfants vont en haut et en bas	A. les objets d'époque.
_____ 2. Mme Partir place un bouquet de fleurs et des livres d'art	B. à payer une grande somme.
_____ 3. La famille passe plus d'heures	C. des prix très bas après les jours fériés.
_____ 4. Les antiquaires cherchent	D. pour savoir si elle grossit ou maigrit.
_____ 5. Une clochette est un brimborion	E. nous allons le faire encore.
_____ 6. Un tapis couvre un petit espace	F. elle prend le temps pour bavarder.
_____ 7. Mme Partir utilise sa balance	G. n'a pas besoin d'un réveille-matin.
_____ 8. Les belles bougies donnent	H. sur la table basse.
_____ 9. Le monsieur n'est pas disposé	I. aiment monter à une balançoire.
_____ 10. Les épuisés croient que	J. sur toutes nos lampes.
_____ 11. M. Partir emprunte les pinces	K. qui sonne doucement.
_____ 12. C'est reparti veut dire	L. pour plier les fils métalliques.
_____ 13. Il n'y a pas d'abat-jours	M. une ambiance tranquille.
_____ 14. Il faut une scie	N. fait un trou avec son tournevis.
_____ 15. Des grands magasins offrent	O. mais **une moquette (a carpet)** va de mur en mur.
_____ 16. On qui ne dort pas bien	P. pour couper le bois.
_____ 17. Sylvie, qui n'a pas de perceuse,	Q. sur une bascule.
_____ 18. Ne dérangez pas	R. n'importe quel matelas est confortable.
_____ 19. Les gens de tous âges	S. dans la salle de séjour que dans le salon.
_____ 20. Mme Partir est occupée, mais	T. est un avertissement.

Écrivez des réponses complètes en français aux questions suivantes.

1. Pourquoi M. Partir conduit-il autour de son voisinage à sept heures du matin? _____
_____.

2. Qu'est-ce que Mme Partir fait lorsque son mari n'est pas là? _____
_____.

3. Quels meubles veulent-ils vendre? _____
_____.

4. Quelle est la première suggestion de Sylvie? _____
_____.

5. Qu'est-ce que l'homme #3 (l'antiquaire) cherche? _____
_____.

6. Quelle plaisanterie Clément fait-il quand la femme #3 lui dit, "Vous acceptez huit dollars pour les deux?" _____
_____.

7. Qu'est-ce qui intéresse l'homme #4? _____.

8. Quels articles la femme #4 cherche-t-elle? _____
_____.

9. Pourquoi Clément dit-il que sa femme ne veut plus la balance? _____
_____.

10. Quelle question la femme #4 pose-t-elle à Sylvie? _____
_____?

11. Quels deux faits surprennent les Partir? _____
_____.

12. Qu'est-ce que Jim voudrait acheter? _____
_____.

13. Quels outils Clément vend-il? _____
_____.

14. De quoi Christine a-t-elle besoin? _____.

15. Qu'est-ce que Sylvie donne à Jim comme un cadeau pour sa femme, et qu'est-ce que Clément lui offre comme un souvenir? _____
_____.

16. Quelle offre Sylvie fait-elle à son mari? _____
_____.

Une Revue du Vide-Grenier de M. et Mme Partir

Discarding Items- Circle the letters of the answers that do not belong with the others.

1. a. la salle de bain	b. la salle à manger	c. la salle de séjour	d. la salle de ventes
2. a. le drap	b. le dessus-de-lit	c. la sieste	d. l'édredon
3. a. la penderie	b. l'annonce	c. le signe	d. le panneau
4. a. la nappe	b. la serviette	c. la taie d'oreiller	d. le cadre
5. a. rigoler	b. déplier	c. taquiner	d. plaisanter
6. a. le brimborion	b. la camelote	c. la recette	d. le bric-à-brac

7. a. l'assiette   b. le service   c. les vaisselles   d. le grille-pain

8. a. la peine   b. le matelas   c. le travail   d. le souci

9. a. l'argenterie   b. le robot de cuisine   c. l'ouvre-boîtes   d. la cafetière

10. a. les serre-livres   b. les boîtes à musique   c. les bougeoirs   d. les singes

11. a. les coussins   b. les rideaux   c. les coins   d. les tapis

12. a. le berceau   b. le fouillis   c. la chaise-haute   d. la chaise à bascule

13. a. divertir   b. coller   c. placer   d. afficher

14. a. le jeu   b. le casse-tête   c. la tondeuse à gazon   d. la poupée

15. a. la balançoire   b. la prise   c. la bascule   d. la glissade

16. a. les pinces   b. la clé   c. le marteau   d. la bougie

17. a. l'abat-jour   b. le réveille-matin   c. le râteau   d. la clochette

18. a. le fric   b. la perceuse   c. la scie   d. le tournevis

----

See Anything That You Can Use?- Circle the letters of the responses that complete the phrases. If none apply, circle **e**.

1. À un vide-grenier il faut ____ des rangs et des boîtes pour trouver les meilleurs achats.
a. étaler   b. faire le tri dans   c. faire livrer   d. porter malheur   e.

2. Quand le client n'est pas disposé à accepter le prix le plus bas, le vendeur fâché dit: "____"
a. C'est reparti!   b. Déplions-le!   c. C'est à prendre ou à laisser!   d. Marché conclu!   e.

3. ____ la possibilité du mauvais temps, les Partir déplacent des articles qui sont dehors.
a. À cause de   b. En train de   c. À condition que   d. Par hasard   e.

4. À une quincaillerie on trouve des outils tel que (qu')____
a. des poupées   b. du maquillage   c. un objet d'époque   d. une vente aux enchères   e.

5. La boîte à musique qui sourit à Évelyne ____.
a. appelle à son aide   b. la possède   c. attire son attention   d. l'envoie sur les roses   e.

6. Comme il ne peut pas conduire la vente et faire entrer du monde en même temps, le couple ____.
a. marchande pour vivre   b. ménage ses forces   c. jette ses possessions
d. prend des rendez-vous   e.

7. Les antiquaires disent que les bijoux de bonne qualité ne les intéressent pas, et ils ajoutent "Merci de toute façon." Ils veulent dire, "Merci ____."
a. au fait   b. sans arrêt   c. quand même   d. de rien   e.

8. Lorsqu'on ne les regarde pas soigneusement, des clients malhonnêtes ____.
a. avancent les pendules   b. enlèvent ce qui est en vente   c. nagent dans le bonheur
d. n'ont pas l'intention de voler   e.

9. Quand Jim dit que sa femme et lui vont inviter les Partir à dîner, il ____.
a. fait un paquet-cadeau   b. appelle un chat un chat   c. doit payer comptant
d. attire des affaires   e.

10. Jim suit Clément qui dit que des clients aiment marchander parce que Jim ____.
a. prend la même somme   b. construit des garages   c. va chercher des provisions
d. tient des vide-greniers aussi   e.

METTRE - TO PUT (ON), TO PLACE, TO SET

The phrase, "The Mets are in first place," provides a direct access to one meaning of this verb. (If you are not a Mets fan, or if you are a stickler for statistics, bring in a substitute for "first!") **The players on the *mettre* team include *admettre*, *commettre*, *omettre*, *permettre*, *remettre*, *soumettre* and *transmettre*. Their respective 'batting order' is admit, commit, omit, permit, remit, submit and transmit. They wear a -<u>mit</u> suffix in their translations. *Compromettre*- to compromise and *promettre*- to promise are exceptions.** (Consider them 'out in left field!')

Mettre - To Put (On), To Place, To Set

Singular	Plural
je mets- I put, do put, am putting	nous mettons- we put, do put, are putting
I place, do place, am placing	we place, do place, are placing
I set, do set, am setting	we set, do set, are setting
tu mets- you put, do put, are putting	vous mettez- you put, do put, are putting
you place, do place, are placing	you place, do place, are placing
you set, do set, are setting	you set, do set, are setting
il/elle met- he/she/it puts, does put,	ils/elles mettent- they put, do put, are putting
is putting	they place, do place, are placing
he/she/it places, does place, is placing	they set, do set, are setting
he/she/it sets, does set, is setting	

The Line-Up for *Mettre* and Its Teammates
1. The singular forms of *mettre* and its related verbs 'throw a curve ball.' Only one <u>t</u> is assigned per person. True to normal -<u>re</u> verb sequence, the *il/elle* form drops the <u>s</u>. In fact, this set is the truest of the false -<u>re</u> verbs. Coincidentally, *mets*, *met*, *mais* and *mai* share the same sound.
2. The *mettre* group has regular -<u>er</u>/-<u>re</u> plural endings.

Mettre Has Other Ways of Putting It
1. mettre- to keep: In this sense, the verb is used the same in both languages.
Ex. Ils connaissent quelqu'un qui met son argent au-dessous de son matelas. > They know somebody who keeps his money under his mattress. (It assures him of 'financial comfort.')
2. mettre quelque chose à + un infinitif- to put something on/out + an infinitive: The additional *à* disqualifies it as a word-for-word translation.
Ex. Mme Démodé et ses sœurs mettent leur linge à sécher. > Mrs. Démodé and her sisters hang their laundry out to dry. (And 'put themselves out' at the same time.)
3. mettre = revêtir- to put on, to apply
Ex. Des actrices mettent les lunettes de soleil au lieu de mettre du maquillage. > Some actresses put on sunglasses instead of applying make-up. (It allows them to play' hide and peek.')
4. mettre = faire fonctionner- to set something
Ex. L'étudiant paresseux ne met jamais son réveille-matin, et il **sèche** toujours ses cours du matin. > The lazy student never sets his alarm clock, and he always **skips (cuts)** his morning classes. (Someone should give him 'a wake-up call.')
5. mettre = installer- to put up, to lay, to hang

Ex. Un frère sait mettre les moquettes; l'autre sait mettre le **papier peint**. > One brother knows how to lay carpets; the other knows how to hang **wallpaper**. (They are known for being 'flexible.')

6. mettre = supposer = dire comme exemple- to say for example

Ex. Deux avocats opposés, mettons M. Oui et M. Non, sont au milieu d'**un procès**. > Two opposing attorneys, let's say for example, Mr. Oui and Mr. Non, are in the middle of **a trial**. (The judge called a recess and told them not 'to take a swing at each other.')

7. *Mettre le couvert*, to set the table, is literally "to put on the cover."

Ex. Quand ma mère met le couvert dans la salle à manger, elle sort la bonne porcelaine, mais si nous mangeons dans la cuisine, elle utilise la vaisselle de tous les jours. > When my mother sets the table in the dining room, she brings out the good china, but if we eat in the kitchen, she uses her everyday dishes. (The setting determines the setting.)

A *Mettre* Meter- Put the correct forms of *mettre* in the spaces provided.

1. Arranger et _____ en ordre sont les synonymes.
2. Robin _____ des miettes à nourrir les oiseaux.
3. _____ le tableau dans le foyer, s'il te plaît!
4. _____-vous le couvert après chaque repas?
5. Shelly et moi ne _____ pas tous les œufs dans un panier.
6. Les commères _____ leurs nez partout.
7. Comment _____-tu la température à un four à micro-onde?
8. En _____ de l'argent dans son compte bancaire chaque mois, M. Écureuil épargne pour son avenir.
9. Quand sa mère ne la voit pas, Rose _____ du rouge à lèvres.
10. Comme leurs penderies et leurs armoires sont pleines, **les camarades de chambre (roommates)** _____ des vêtements sur les chaises.

Replacements and a String of Expressions for the *Mettre* Team

1. admettre- to admit

a. admettre = faire quelqu'un réussir à- to make someone succeed at/in

Ex. Jean réussit à un examen, et on lui **fait crédit**, mais il remercie le prof qui l'admet. > John passes an exam, and one **gives** him **credit**, but he thanks the teacher who makes him succeed. (Who gets the credit for the credits, and does the one who passes have the passive role?)

b. admettre = tolérer- to allow: Both verbs are synonyms for *permettre*.

Ex. **La règle d'or** n'admet **aucune** exception. > **The Golden Rule** allows **no** exceptions. (However, even exchanges are encouraged.)

----

2. commettre- to commit

a. commettre = faire- to make

Ex. **L'officier de l'état civil** commet une erreur quand il omet l'année sur **l'acte de naissance** de la nouvelle-née. > **The registrar** commits an error when he omits the year on the newborn girl's **birth certificate**. (Thereby enabling the grown woman to have 'a wide range of dates.')

----

3. permettre- to allow, to permit, to mind

Ex. Vous permettez que je fume? > Do you mind if I smoke? (Smokers who don't ask for permission 'burn some people up.')

---

4. promettre- to promise

a. promettre de faire quelque chose- to promise to do something. Note that *de* is the connecting preposition.

Ex. Si Mme Abacus promet de faire quelque chose, nous pouvons compter sur elle. > If Mrs. Abacus promises to do something, we can count on her. (She has 'a long line' of references.)

b. *Ça promet.*- That's a good start./That's promising.

Ex. Les météorologistes ne prévoient pas d'ouragans pour juillet. Ça promet. > The weathermen predict no hurricanes for July. That's a good start. (No one wants to be an 'eye'witness.)

---

5. remettre = to put back: This verb is used for repeated actions.

a. remettre ensemble- to put together again

Ex. Selon une comptine anglaise, tous les chevaux du roi et tous les hommes du roi ne pouvaient pas remettre Humpty Dumpty ensemble. > According to an English nursery rhyme, all the king's horses and all the king's men couldn't put Humpty Dumpty together again. (His great 'fall' led to a nonexistent winter.)

b. remettre quelque chose droit- to set something straight again/restraighten

Ex. M. Framer remet droit les peintures qui restent. > Mr. Framer restraightens the paintings that are left. (And hopes that his customers 'buy the works.')

c. remettre en marche (une machine, un moteur)- to restart, to switch on again (a machine or a motor)

Ex. M. Otto Sitts ne sait pas pourquoi sa voiture ne fonctionne pas. Il essaie de remettre en marche le moteur. > Mr. Otto Sitts does not know why his car is not running. He tries to restart the engine. (He doesn't have 'fine motor skills.')

d. remettre = confier- to entrust

Ex. Les passagers remettent leurs vies entre les mains des pilotes. > The passengers put their lives in the pilots' hands. (They, if need be, rely 'on their manuals.')

e. remettre- to deliver, to hand in, to hand over

Ex. **Des locataires** ne remettent pas les clés à la porte quand ils partent. > **Some tenants** do not hand in the door keys when they leave. (They just 'make a bolt for it.')

f. remettre- to postpone (a date, a decision, a meeting)

Ex. "Remettez pas à demain ce que vous pouvez faire aujourd'hui." > "Don't put off until tomorrow what you can do today." (One can always procrastinate later.)

g. remettre + un nom- to add more, to put on more of something

Ex. Paul Bunyan dit, "Remettez **des bûches**! Je peux en couper un tas." > Paul Bunyan says, "Put on more **logs**! I can chop a pile of them." (As he proudly 'adds a notch.')

h. remettre = recommencer = faire encore la même chose- to start again, to redo something

Ex. C'est la quatrième fois que Lee Cœur dit au serveur, "Remettez-moi, ça!" > It is the fourth time that Lee Cœur says to the bartender, "The same, again." (When he was asked if he could handle one more round, the customer said "he'd plead the fifth.")

'It Doesn't Stay Put'- Fill in the blanks with the correct forms of the verbs in parentheses, and translate the completed sentences.
Ex. (mettre) Est-ce que quelques français <u>mettent</u> le drapeau tricolore le 14 juillet? > Do some French people <u>put up/hang</u> the tricolored flag July 14th?

1. (mettre) M. Noir et M. Decker _____ leurs outils dans leurs camions. _____

_____.

2. (mettre) Maxine _____ une robe de chambre avant le de nettoyer. _____

_____.

3. (mettre) Les tableaux que ce locataire _____ sur ses murs sont affreux. _____

_____.

4. (mettre) Il ne faut pas _____ **un minuteur (a timer)** quand vous cuisinez les œufs.

_____

5. (mettre) Est-ce que vous _____ le couvert avant de préparer la salade? _____

_____?

6. (admettre) Acette et moi sommes les meilleurs étudiants de la classe à cause de l'influence de nos mères. Elles nous _____. _____

_____.

7. (permettre) Je vous _____ de stationner dans mon allée. _____

_____.

8. (promettre) Mme Ronde perd cinq kilos par mois. Ça _____! _____

_____!

9. (remettre) Le vent fait tomber les rangs. Nous devons les _____ droit. _____

10. (remettre) Le titre d'une chanson country et western est " _____ une Bûche sur le Feu!" _____

_____!

From Place to Place- Match the letters to the numbers to form complete sentences.

____ 1. Si ses enfants **jurent (swear)**, leur mère
____ 2. Mme Plusforte veut aller au gymnase aujourd'hui,
____ 3. M. Campbell met de la soupe
____ 4. Faye Bien n'a pas de mauvaises notes
____ 5. Mettre du papier peint n'est pas une activité
____ 6. Mes parents ne vont pas être prêts à déménager ce week-end,
____ 7. Il faut continuer à mettre debout
____ 8. Quand nous avons très froid, nous remettons des couvertures
____ 9. Le technicien me demande: "Voyez-vous un écran noir
____ 10. Est-ce qu'il y a un procès

A. et nous devons remettre la date.
B. ou la mettez-vous dans une machine à laver la vaisselle?
C. si on admet qu'il est coupable?
D. mais son horaire ne le permet pas.
E. Est-ce que ça veut dire que j'ai tort?
F. parce qu'elle ne veut pas savoir si elle grossit.
G. pour quelqu'un **pressé (hurried)**.
H. parce que nous admettons que nous ne disons pas toujours la vérité.
I. pour mettre tous ces miroirs.
J. dans le four à micro-ondes à chauffer.

_____ 11. Paul montre l'identification fausse,

_____ 12. Mettons que vous avez un point

_____ 13. Le propriétaire donne cet avertissement à ses locataires:

_____ 14. Est-ce que vous lavez la bonne porcelaine à main

_____ 15. Ma tante ne permet pas une balance chez elle

_____ 16. Nous n'avons pas assez de fil

_____ 17. Mlle Pasmenteuse et moi méritons du crédit

_____ 18. Bunny met ses pantoufles confortables

K. "Ne remettez pas haut la musique!"

L. quand vous le remettez en marche?"

M. un bébé qui apprend à marcher.

N. met du savon dans leurs bouches.

O. et le propriétaire ne lui permet pas d'entrer dans le club.

P. parce que sa mère ne les admet pas.

Q. quand elle reste à la maison.

R. au lieu de remettre en marche le chauffage

BATTRE - TO BEAT (UP), TO ABUSE, TO CONQUER

Battre and its teammates are conjugated like *mettre*. (The Mets 'go to bat for you.') **Nevertheless, because *battre* means <u>to beat up</u>, you'll have to bring in *gagner*- to win. The *battre* league drafts *combattre*- to combat, to fight, *débattre*- to debate, to haggle and *rebattre*- to beat again. The best known of the series is conjugated below.**

Battre - To Beat (up), To Abuse, To Conquer

Singular	Plural
je bats- I beat, do beat, am beating	nous battons- we beat, do beat, are beating
tu bats- you beat, do beat, are beating	vous battez- you beat, do beat, are beating
il/elle bat- he/she/it beats, does beat, is beating	ils battent- they beat, do beat, are beating

---

Marching to the Beat of *Battre*

1. M*ettre* and *battre* follow the same drummer with conjugations in step with one another. The lone <u>t</u> in the singular forms is doubled throughout the plural. Like *mettre*, *battre* has regular -<u>re</u> verb endings. ("Pronounce the singular forms of *battre* aloud!" she said with 'a sheepish grin.')

2. *Battre* refers to beating or striking a person; *frapper* applies to beating, knocking or striking a thing.

Ex. Big Bird surprend Burt et Ernie quand il frappe à leur porte. > Big Bird surprises Burt and Ernie when he raps on their door. (He could have 'knocked them over with a feather.')

3. *Battre* and <u>battle</u> are cognates. It's less obvious that *combattre* is both <u>to combat</u> and <u>to fight.</u>

Ex. Lorsque les pompiers combattent un incendie dans son immeuble d'habitation, M. Bonarien bat sa femme. > While the firemen are fighting a fire in his apartment building, Mr. Bonarien is beating his wife. (Good advice for both situations is "Get out!")

4. Even though *combattre* and *lutter* both mean <u>to combat</u>, <u>to fight</u> and <u>to struggle</u>, they are not used the same way. (One would expect these verbs to show their differences.)

4a. Forms of *combattre* are followed by a direct object.

Ex. M. Toux prend les médicaments pour combattre **son rhume**. > Mr. Toux is taking drugs to fight

his cold. (They will win if they 'knock him out.')
4b. Forms of *lutter* are followed by a preposition.
Ex. Les explorateurs luttent contre le froid dans l'Antarctique. > The explorers fight against the cold in the Antarctic. (But they are already 'under the weather.')

Battre Idioms with a Striking Apprearance
a. battre un tapis- to beat a rug
Ex. Plutôt que battre les tapis de nos jours, la plupart des gens passent les aspirateurs. > Rather than beating rugs nowadays, most people vacuum. (While 'putting in a plug for' modern technology.)
b. battre la mesure- to beat time
Ex. **Un chef d'un orchestre** bat la mesure, et un **meurtrier** tue le temps. > **An orchestra conductor** beats time, and **a murderer** kills time. (They both must 'face the music.')
c. battre son plein- to be in full swing
Ex. Arrive vers 21 heures quand leur fête bat son plein! > Arrive around 9 pm. when their party is in full swing! (Will they be playing music from the '30s then?)

---

rebattre- to beat again
a. rebattre les oreilles avec- to keep harping about
Ex. Le professeur d'histoire rebat les oreilles avec **le Far West**. > The history teacher keeps harping about **the Wild West**. (If that's not 'beating a dead horse!')

'Bagging' Verbs with One or More 'Ts'- Circle the letters of the phrases that best complete the sentences.
1. **Les commerçants-m. (the shopkeepers)** surprennent le voleur quand ils _____.
a. sèchent un cours   b. sonnent une alarme   c. mettent du rouge à lèvres   d. mettent le couvert
2. En janvier et en février, la saison touristique en Floride _____.
a. met du bric-à-brac à vendre   b. permet tout le monde à dormir   c. bat son plein
d. lutte pour ses droits
3. En l'honneur de ton anniversaire de naissance, _____.
a. Remettons-nous du champagne!   b. Confions nos vies entre tes mains!
c. Tolérons ton camarade de chambre impoli!   d. Battons nos femmes!
4. Le locataire dit qu'il augmente le loyer parce qu'il _____.
a. ne va pas commettre une erreur   b. doit frapper à chaque porte
c. bat des tapis tous les jours   d. met de nouvelles moquettes
5. "Shiva, même avec deux couvertures sur ton lit, tu as froid. Je vais _____ tout de suite."
a. battre la mesure avec le chef d'orchestre   b. te rebattre les oreilles avec ta maladie
c. remettre en marche le chauffage   d. mettre le minuteur
6. Les fiancés remettent la cérémonie à la semaine prochaine car l'officier de l'état civil _____.
a. remet les alliances   b. jure pendant le procès   c. doit les remettre debout
d. ne va pas être disponible jusqu'au ce temps-là

How Would You Put It?- **Use the correct forms of the verbs in parentheses to translate these sentences.**

1. (mettre) What are you (*tu*) putting in that drawer? _____
_____?

2. (admettre) I admit that I cut classes from time to time. _____
_____.

3. (combattre) Stay (*tu*) home! You are fighting a cold. _____
_____.

4. (battre) Summer is in full swing after July 1. _____
_____.

5. (mettre) Pat Terne and I do not know how to put up (to hang) wallpaper. _____
_____.

6. (remettre) Are you (*vous*) and Gigi postponing the party because of the bad weather? _____
_____?

7. (débattre) The customers and the sellers debate the prices at a garage sale. _____
_____.

8. (permettre) My father does not allow any curse words in our home. _____
_____.

9. (rebattre) Chase, please don't (*tu*) keep harping me about my finances! _____
_____!

10. (mettre, combattre) The firemen put on their coats and their boots, and they go to fight the fires.
_____
_____.
_____

une Montgolfière

BOIRE - TO DRINK

If it were not for the irregular plural forms, you would have been offered *boire* many chapters ago. Verbs with <u>v</u>s in just their plurals have dropped in before, but these unfamiliar <u>u</u>s in the *nous* and *vous* forms warrant checking their IDs.

<table>
<tr><td colspan="2"><u>Singular</u></td><td colspan="2"><u>Plural</u></td></tr>
<tr><td>je bois- I drink, do drink, am drinking</td><td></td><td>nous buvons- we drink, do drink, are drinking</td></tr>
<tr><td>tu bois- you drink, do drink, are drinking</td><td></td><td>vous buvez- you drink, do drink, are drinking</td></tr>
<tr><td>il/elle/on boit- he/she/it/one drinks, does drink
    is drinking</td><td></td><td>ils/elles boivent- they drink, do drink,
    are drinking</td></tr>
</table>

'Drinking It In'

1. Though not attached to a regular stem, the singular forms of *boire* have familiar -<u>ir</u> endings. The verbs in the first half of the conjugation share the same pronunciation.

2. A <u>v</u> is 'on tap' throughout the plural. The conjugation of *devoir* is identical to *boire* if the <u>d</u> is changed to a <u>b</u> throughout, and the <u>e</u> is switched to a <u>u</u> in the *nous* and *vous* forms.

Ex. Vous buvez **un boisson** dans les bois. > You drink **a drink** in the woods. (You could have it 'on the rocks.')

3. *Boire* is not "a boot verb" because the <u>v</u> is not present when the conjugation kicks off.

Refreshing Expressions with *Boire*

a. offrir à boire à quelqu'un- to offer somebody a drink: The French offer <u>à</u> twice.

Ex. Son patron lui offre une bière à boire quand il l'emmène déjeuner. > Her boss offers her a beer to drink when he takes her to lunch. (She might answer, "Just one, since it's light.")

b. boire à la santé de quelqu'un- to drink to someone's health: Note that the word order for the ends of these idioms is transposed.

Ex. Buvons à la santé de notre famille! > Let's drink to our family's health!

c. boire- to absorb, to soak up: The 'full' sense of the verb is used in both languages.

Ex. **Le lave-linge** de Mme Flood vient de tomber en panne. Elle ne peut pas boire toute l'eau avec sa serpillière. > Mrs. Flood's **washing machine** just broke down. She cannot soak up all the water with her mop. (Maybe she should just 'throw in the towel.')

d. Il y a à boire et à manger là-dedans. > You shouldn't believe all of it: Word-for-word it says, "There's to eat and to drink inside there."

Ex. Des entreprises **prétendent** qu'en suivant leurs régimes **prescrits**, on maigrit vite. Il y a à boire et à manger là-dedans. > Some companies **claim** that by following their **prescribed** diets, one loses weight quickly. You should not believe all of it. (Their prescriptions should read, "To be taken with a grain of salt.")

e. boire comme un trou- to drink like a fish: The actual translation is "to drink like a hole."

Ex. Mme Lafin quitte son mari parce qu'il boit comme un trou. > Mrs. Lafin is leaving her husband because he drinks like a fish. (He wasn't such 'a great catch.')

RECEVOIR - TO RECEIVE
APERCEVOIR- To Notice, To Catch a Glimpse of, DÉCEVOIR- To Disappoint
PERCEVOIR- To Perceive, To Detect

Though these four verbs have *voir* as suffixes, their plural conjugations are not 'seen' like that. Moreover, *décevoir* <u>disappoints,</u> but it does not deceive. As you are going *apercevoir*, the conjugations of these *boire* related verbs also keep <u>vs</u> throughout their plurals.

Recevoir - To Receive

<u>Singular</u>	<u>Plural</u>
je reçois- I receive, do receive, am receiving	nous recevons- we receive, do receive, are receiving
tu reçois- you receive, do receive, are receiving	vous recevez- you receive, do receive,
il/elle reçoit- he/she/it receives, does receive, is receiving	ils reçoivent- they receive, do receive, are receiving

----

The Reception Line
1. *Apercevoir, décevoir, percevoir* and *recevoir* have one pronunciation for their singular forms.
2. Only the *nous* and *vous* forms have the infinitive stem.
3. *Une cedille* is inserted under the <u>c</u> with a boot outline, but these verbs are knock offs because the <u>v</u> is found just in the plurals.
4. *Apercevoir* and *percevoir* are as close in meaning as they are in spelling. The subtle difference is <u>noticed</u> in the first verb and <u>detected</u> in the second one.
<u>A helpful hint</u>: Consider the similarity between the conjugations of this quartet and *devoir*!

Acceptable Expressions with *Recevoir*
a. recevoir- to hear
Ex. Nous vous recevons **cinq sur cinq**. > We hear you **loud and clear.** (French speakers can 'put in their twenty-five cents worth.')
b. *Recevez Monsieur (Madame, Mademoiselle) l'expression de mes sentiments distingués* is a long phrase meaning "Yours truly."
Ex. À la fin d'une lettre Bic écrit, "Recevez Monsieur, l'expression de mes sentiments distingués." > At the end of a letter Bic writes, "Yours truly." (French 'sign language' is often very expressive.)
c. recevoir = accueilir- to welcome
Ex. Wright rencontre les parents de **sa correspondante**, et ils le reçoivent **à bras ouverts**. > Wright meets **his pen pal's** parents, and they welcome him **with open arms.** (He might not be sure how 'to address' them.)
d. recevoir quelqu'un à dîner- to have someone to dinner
Ex. Ta tante reçoit deux étudiants de l'université à dîner. > Your aunt has two students from the university to dinner. (Were the guests pleased with 'their courses'?)

An important note: To get has several French translations.
a. passer prendre- to get/to call for someone or something
b. arriver- to get somewhere

c. arriver + à + an infinitive- to get/to understand something
Recevoir or *obtenir* is used only when one <u>receives</u> someone or something. (Get it?)

<u>Verbs with a Take on Recevoir</u>
1. apercevoir- to notice, to catch a glimpse of: Its synonym is *remarquer*.
Ex. Pendant leur tour de Hollywood, des touristes essaient d'apercevoir des vedettes. > During their tour of Hollywood, some tourists try to catch a glimpse of the stars. (Who may appear and disappear 'in the twinkling of an eye.')
a. *Un aperçu* is a general idea.
Ex. Après sa visite à **une école maternelle,** la dame enceinte a un aperçu de quoi s'attendre. > After her visit to **a nursery school**, the pregnant lady has a general idea of what to expect.

----

2. décevoir- to disappoint
a. *décevoir les espoirs de quelqu'un*- to disappoint someone's hopes
Ex. L'équipe du basket d'un autre lycée gagne **le match de qualifications** contre notre équipe. Cela déçoit les espoirs de mon école. > The basketball team from another lycée wins **the play-offs** against our team. That disappoints the hopes of my school. (They could keep their 'hoops up' for next year.)

----

3. percevoir- to perceive, to detect: Its synonym is *ressentir*.
Ex. Ils perçoivent de l'hésitation dans ma voix. > They detect some hesitation in my voice. (But they stop themselves before saying anything.)

<u>Checking the Verbs with Vs</u>- **Put the correct forms of *boire, apercevoir, décevoir, percevoir* and *recevoir* in the blanks. Two responses are possible for some sentences.**

1. Penny _____ du courrier souvent de sa correspondante.
2. Un enfant de treize mois _____ d'une bouteille ou d'une tasse?
3. Selon le proverbe: "Il est meilleur de donner que _____."
4. Les canadiens _____ des chinois aux Jeux Olympiques.
5. La plupart des professeurs _____ que des étudiants sèchent leurs cours.
6. Je préfère dire "peut-être" que dire "oui." Je ne voudrais pas te _____.
7. On _____ des monuments de l'air avant d'**atterrir (to land).**
8. Ma grand-mère dit, "Tu me _____ quand tu jures."
9. M. Levin, _____-vous l'odeur du pain frais de cette boulangerie-là?
10. Mon médecin me demande, "Combien d'eau _____-tu chaque jour?"
11. Même si le garçon n'aime pas le cadeau qu'il _____, il doit dire "Merci beaucoup."
12. Anne Vitée ne vient pas à ma soirée ce samedi. Cela me _____.
13. On _____ des soucoupes volantes seulement à la campagne.
14. Qu'est-ce que les détectives _____ de **sa déclaration (his/her statement)**?
15. Ne riez pas lorsque vous _____!

'Meetings Called to Order'- Put the phrases in the correct sequences to form sentences.

1. une moto/ Elle veut/ comme un cadeau/ recevoir _____
_____.

2. offre/ un whisky/ Jack Daniels/ à boire/ à l'invité _____
_____.

3. cinq sur cinq/ de ce que/ mais j'ai un aperçu/ tu me racontes/ Je ne te reçois pas _____
_____.

4. mais/ des automobilistes/ Al Erte / il aperçoit/ en panne/ toujours/ roule rapidement _____
_____.

5. à dîner/ M.Thon/ comme un trou/ parce qu'il boit/ Ils ne reçoivent pas _____
_____.

6. pas prescrits/ déçoivent mes espoirs/ quand/ des drogues/ Mes joueurs préférés/ ils prennent
_____
_____.

7. reçoit son correspondant/ de Pinot Noir/ Avec une bouteille/ Guy/ chaleureusement/ dans sa main
_____
_____.

a Vineyard in Bordeaux

METTONS LE COUVERT! - Let's Set the Table!

With no verbs to conjugate, no rules to apply and no idioms to learn, this chapter has to be "a set up." That puts it perfectly. A vocabulary review and a few additional 'terms of service' are all that is required.

1. <u>Indispensable items are as follows:</u>
a. la nappe- the tablecloth: Think of taking a long *'nappe'* so as not to confuse it with b.
b. la serviette- the napkin, the towel: Two English nouns are 'folded' into one French word.
c. le set de table/le napperon- the place mat: It goes by two 'undercover' names.
2. <u>To get full-service, one needs:</u>
a. la soupière- the tureen: Pronounced like *sous pierre*- under stone, this large bowl might coincidentally be earthenware.
b. l'assiette creuse- the soup bowl/the soup dish: *Creux* means <u>hollowed out</u>, but soup fills that that empty spot. *Le bol de potage* is the 'watered down' version of *l'assiette creuse*.
c. l'assiette- the plate or the dish
d. le plat- the platter: *Plat(e)*, an adjective, means <u>flat</u>. (*Le plat du jour* is usually not.)
e. le plateau- the tray (It is typically flatter than the platter.)
f. le bol- the bowl: *La coupe* is <u>the fruit bowl</u>.
g. le saladier- the salad bowl: Just add -<u>ier</u> to the salad 'endive' right in.
h. la tasse- the cup; la soucoupe- the saucer (*La soucoupe volante*, the flying saucer, needs its own setting.)
3. <u>Placing *l'argenterie*- the silverware</u>
a. la fourchette- the fork: It has <u>four</u> prongs.
b. le couteau (de cuisine)- the kitchen knife: *Le couteau à beurre* is <u>the butter knife</u>, and *le couteau à pain* is <u>the bread knife</u>. (Many knives applied for the job, but only three 'made the cut.')
c. la cuillère- the spoon: Its multiple choices are: *la cuillère à soupe*- the soupspoon, *la cuillère à bouche*- the tablespoon, *la cuillère à café*- the teaspoon, *la cuillère à dessert*- the dessert spoon. (You have just been spoon-fed.)
4. <u>Space must be set aside for:</u>
a. la louche- the ladle (It's much too large to fit into one's *bouche*.): **It serves the expression, *C'est louche*. > It's highly suspicious.** (It's just not 'ration-al.')
b. le dessous-de-plat- the trivet/the tuit: (These scorch-proof plaques come in all shapes. However, those who finally purchased a circular one are glad that they got 'a round tuit.')
c. le dessous-de-verre, le dessous-de-bouteille- the coaster (The small mat keeps a glass or a bottle from 'making a bad impression.')
d. la salière- the salt shaker: It contains *le sel*- the salt. Notice how the vowel shifted!
e. la poivrière- the pepper shaker: It contains *le poivre*- <u>the pepper</u>. ('Sultan Pepper Shakers' sits at the head, not in the middle, of the royal table.)
<u>A helpful hint</u>: **There are two 'patterns' in a complete table setting. Nouns trimmed with -<u>ette</u> are *l'assiette, la fourchette* and *la serviette*. Those that have -<u>er</u> or -<u>ère</u> borders are *la cuillère, le saladier, la poivrière, la salière* and *la soupière*.**

'A Placement Test'- Match the nouns listed to the corresponding numbers on the picture:
l'assiette, l'assiette creuse, le bol, la carafe, la coupe, le couteau de cuisine, la cuillère à thé, la cuillère à bouche, le dessous-de-bouteille, le dessous-de-plat, la fourchette, la louche, la nappe, le plat, le plateau, la poivrière, le saladier, la salière, la serviette, le set de table/le napperon, la soucoupe, la soupière, la tasse, le verre

----

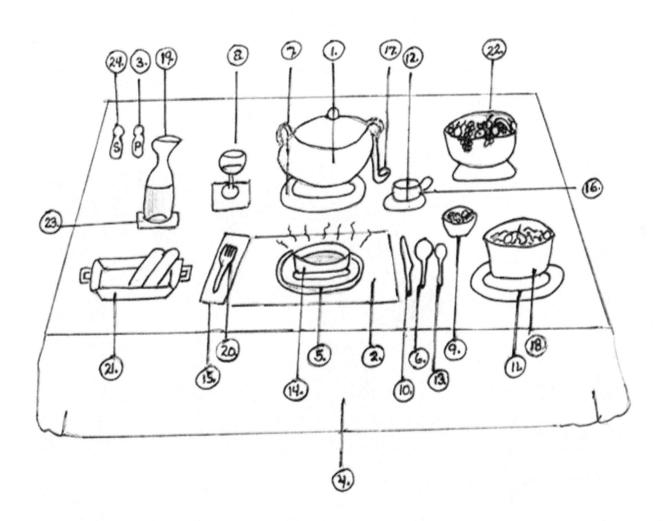

'Laying It on the Table'- Circle the letters of the answers that best complete the phrases.

1. Quand on met le couvert correctement, on place la fourchette sur _____.
a. le couteau   b. la serviette   c. le saladier   d. le dessous-de-verre

2. Pour servir la soupe d'une soupière, on utilise _____.
a. une salière   b. une cuillère   c. une soucoupe   d. une louche

3. Dans la comptine, l'assiette part en courant avec _____.
a. la cuillère   b. le plat   c. la poivrière   d. le verre

4. Il est très facile de couper une baguette avec _____.
a. une assiette creuse   b. un couteau à beurre   c. un couteau à pain   d. une tondeuse à gazon

5. Mlle Sanschichis met les sets de table/les napperons au lieu _____ si on prend des sandwichs.
a. d'un plateau   b. d'une nappe   c. d'un édredon   d. d'une batterie de cuisine

6. Des invités vont venir chez moi cet après-midi. Pour ça, il y a ____ au milieu de la table.
a. un ouvre-boîtes   b. un dessous-de-plat   c. une tasse   d. une coupe

7. Arrangeons des tranches de rosbif, du jambon et du corned-beef ____!
a. sous l'argenterie   b. loin de la porcelaine   c. autour du plateau   d. à côté de la vaisselle

8. Les serveurs mettent ____ sur le dessous-de-bouteille.
a. des carafes de vin et des verres   b. des draps et des taies d'oreillers
c. un grille-pain et de petites assiettes   d. des casseroles et des cuillères à dessert

UNE REVUE - A Review

Mettre, Admettre, Commettre, Permettre, Remettre, Battre, Rebattre, Boire, Recevoir, Apercevoir, Décevoir, Percevoir and Mettons le Couvert!

Getting the Maximum out of the Maxims- Circle the letters of the answers that best explain or complete the initial phrases.

1. La fille loyale promet d'aller au supermarché pour sa mère.
a. Elle a d'autres choses à faire.   b. Sa mère fait la même promesse.
c. On peut compter sur elle.   d. On ne sait pas où ils sont maintenant.
2. Mettons que vous n'avez pas de boulot!
a. Prenons tout ce que vous avez!   b. Ne lui offrons rien!
c. Devinons ce que vous faites avec ça!   d. Disons, par exemple, que vous ne travaillez pas!
3. Le vent fait tomber le pot de fleurs à l'entrée. Il faut _____.
a. le remettre droit   b. l'acheter de nouveau   c. battre la mesure   d. avoir un aperçu
4. La bonne hôtesse accueille ses invités, et elle _____.
a. déçoit leurs espoirs   b. remet en marche leurs moteurs   c. bat le blanc d'un œuf
d. leur offre à boire
5. Les personnes qui combattent leurs ennemis _____.
a. n'accueillent jamais les étrangers   b. luttent contre les individus qui les attaquent
c. **décollent (take off)** et atterrissent en même temps   d. arrivent à les comprendre
6. M. et Mme Partir montrent leurs marchandises sur les rangs et sur les tables.
a. Ils permettent aux clients de les prendre.   b. Ils remettent le vide-grenier à demain.
c. Ils les mettent à vendre.   d. Les choses ont une mauvaise odeur.
7. Comme tant de gens vendent leurs maisons à cause de l'économie, _____.
a. on aperçoit que les voisinages changent   b. nous recevons à dîner des locataires
c. on paie **nos emprunts logement (our mortgages)**   d. on le reçoit cinq sur cinq
8. Une heure en avant au printemps; une heure en retard en automne. N'oubliez pas de (d') ____!
a. installer des moquettes nouvelles partout   b. admettre la règle d'or
c. remettre vos horloges et vos montres   d. remettre des bûches dans la cheminée
9. Soo Yung n'a que 25 ans, et il a déjà sa propre entreprise.
a. Cela bat un tapis.   b. Cela m'est égal.   c. Faites-le fonctionner!   d. Ça promet.
10. Je dis cinq fois par jour, "Nagette, l'idée ne m'intéresse pas." Néanmoins, elle _____.
a. déçoit mes espoirs   b. me rebat les oreilles avec ça   c. ne frappe guère à ma porte
d. passe prendre mes amis
11. Pas tout le monde remet l'éducation de leurs petits entre les mains des maîtresses dans les écoles maternelles. Des mères et des pères _____.
a. pensent qu'il y a à boire et à manger là-dedans   b. apprennent à leurs enfants chez eux
c. boivent comme des trous   d. lisent seulement des comptines
12. Quand le chauffage tombe en panne, des locataires froids _____.
a. boivent à la santé de Père Noël   b. demandent le permis de fumer   c. battent leur plein
d. remettent des vêtements

279

'Tabling a Motion?'- Label the statements *vrai* or *faux*.

_____ 1. Une nappe est plus grande qu'une serviette.

_____ 2. On boit la soupe directement d'une soupière.

_____ 3. On met les fruits dans une coupe.

_____ 4. Quand on met le couvert, on place la soucoupe sur la tasse.

_____ 5. Le couteau et la cuillère vont à gauche de l'assiette.

_____ 6. Le set de table et le napperon sont des synonymes.

_____ 7. On met la salière et la poivrière au milieu de la table.

_____ 8. Le dessous-de-verre et le dessous-de-bouteille ne sont pas plats.

Une Revue des Verbes

A Congregation of Conjugations- Write the correct pronouns and forms of the verbs indicated.

Ex. combattre- third person sing. -------------------- <u>il/elle/on combat</u>

Ex. conduire- third person plural ------------------- <u>ils/elles conduisent</u>

1. sentir- second person sing. _____

2. servir- third person plural _____

3. dormir- first person sing. _____

4. courir- first person sing. _____

5. mentir- second person plural _____

6. apprendre- first person plural _____

7. comprendre- first person sing. _____

8. prendre- third person sing. _____

9. prendre- third person plural _____

10. surprendre- second person plural _____

11. battre- second person sing. _____

12. mettre- third person sing. _____

13. permettre- first person sing. _____

14. promettre- second person plural _____

15. apercevoir- first person sing. _____

16. recevoir- first person plural _____

17. recevoir- third person plural _____

18. boire- first person plural _____

19. boire- third person plural _____

20. construire- second person sing. _____

21. introduire- first person plural _____

22. traduire- first person sing. _____

23. survivre- second person sing. _____

24. vivre- third person sing. _____

25. rire- first person sing. _____

26. sourire- second person plural command _____

LA CUISINE FRANÇAISE et LA NOURRITURE FRANÇAISE
French Cooking and French Food

You have recently set the table and absorbed the verb to drink. The next logical topic is French food, the epitome of culinary delights. Though the most complicated recipes may be the secrets of world renowned chefs, recognizing the choices listed on French menus is available to everyone. Just blend the ingredients presented in this chapter together to prepare or order *plusieurs repas délicieux* > several delicious meals! *Bon appétit!*

LE DÉJEUNER - Breakfast

Le petit déjeuner is literally "the small/little lunch." Compared to our plentiful first meal of the day, the French edition is abridged.

Un Choix de Boissons- A Choice of Beverages/Drinks
1. le café noir ou le café au lait- black coffee or coffee with milk (The *olé* sound at the end doesn't qualify it as a Spanish drink.)
2. le thé- the thé: The silent <u>h</u> leaves room to squeeze in *du citron* > some lemon.
3. le chocolat chaud- the hot chocolate (It might be wearing 'a coat of marshmallows.')

Une Variété de Pains- A Variety of Breads
1. le croissant- This international favorite is available both as *le croissant nature* > natural and as *le croissant au beurre* > made with butter.
2. la brioche- the bun with high egg and butter content
3. le pain au chocolat- the roll with chocolate inside
4. le pain aux raisins- the roll with raisins inside: But, *un raisin* is <u>a grape</u>, and *un raisin sec* is <u>a raisin</u>.
5. la tartine à la confiture- the slice of *baguette* (French bread) with jam.
<u>An interesting note</u>: *Le pain perdu*- French toast is typically sprinkled with powered sugar and served as a dessert. (Maple syrup is not found on "the lost bread.")

In recent years, French breakfast options, but not necessarily their waistlines, have expanded to include:
1. le yaourt- the yogurt (As many French women consider this dairy product to be their diet secret, others should 'get to the bottom of it.')
2. les céréales- the cereals: Natural grain cereals are gaining in popularity. (But the French still plan to keep Captain Crunch on our side of the Atlantic and Count Chocula in Transylvania.)

In addition to *le petit déjeuner français*, large French hotels and resorts often offer:

1. le jus d'orange- orange juice and perhaps even *le jus de carotte*- carrot juice (The latter is for travelers who prefer vitamin As 'over Cs' (overseas).

2. le beignet- the doughnut: The deep-fried version sprinkled with sugar is a popular breakfast treat in New Orleans.

3. les œufs avec bacon- eggs with bacon: (But asking for for biscuits, gravy and grits might prompt the French translation for, "Y'all go back home, ya hear!"

4. la gaufre- the waffle: The Belgium variety laced with powdered sugar beats the competition 'from square one.'

LE DÉJEUNER - Lunch

In France, noon until 2 pm. was formerly reserved for the largest meal of the day. Now, busier schedules push many midday diners away from the table faster. Consequently, the traditional 'noon dinner' is often postponed until after work hours. The soups and *entrées* listed are eaten at *le déjeuner* and *le dîner*. A loaf of French bread, a bottle of wine and a pitcher of water normally accompany those meals.

When a Fast-Food Restaurant Doesn't 'Cut *le Dijon*'

Deux Soupes Très Populaires- Two Very Popular Soups

1. la soupe à l'oignon gratinée: Onion soup topped with melted cheese is a most popular warm-up preceding lunch or dinner.

2. la vichyssoise: Served cold, this well known soup consists of cream, potatoes, onions, puréed leeks and chicken stock.

Des Entrées- Some *Entrées*

1. le pâté de foie gras- goose liver pate (This is a famous delicacy even though it sounds 'fowl.')

2. le pâté de lapin- rabbit pâté (If it weren't tasty, it would have 'flopped' years ago.)

3. la saucisse en pâté feuilleté- small sausage in a layered *pâté*: *Le saucisson* is a larger, cooked sausage that can be sliced.

4. la mousse de foies de volaille- chicken liver mousse

5. la mousse de saumon et câpres- salmon mousse with capers (Eating it is an adventure.)

6. les coquilles St. Jacques- scallops on the half-shell (Don't they sound 'divine'?)

7. les escargots au beurre- snails in butter (These morsels are to be savored at a slow pace.)

8. l'avocat et œufs à la mousse de crabe- avocado and eggs with crab mousse

Note: *Un avocat* means <u>an attorney</u> and <u>an avocado</u>.

Quelques Déjeuners Légers - A Few Light Lunches

1. la salade niçoise: Greens, *les anchois*- anchovies, *le thon*- tuna and *les œufs durs*- hard boiled eggs are tossed in *l'huile d'olive*- olive oil.

2. la quiche Lorraine: This popular mixture of eggs, cheese and bacon is served in a pie shell.

3. l'omelette aux fines herbes: This omelet can be enhanced with *les champignons*- mushrooms, *les épinards*- spinach or any other vegetable of choice. (It's a chance 'to have your fill.')

4. le soufflé au fromage- cheese soufflé (It 'goes down' easily.)

Souffler means <u>to blow (up)/to puff (up)</u>, and that's 'eggs-actly' what happens to the mixture of egg yolks and beaten egg whites. When chocolate, lemon or banana is put into the basic recipe, it becomes *un dessert soufflé.*

5. les crêpes- thin pancakes made with flour, eggs, milk and butter: Though available in many French restaurants, these favorites are the specialty of *les crêperies.*

5a. Unsweetened ones consisting of buckwheat are *les crêpes salées/les galettes.* Before they are folded, *fromage, asperges-* asparagus, *épinards, champignons,* etc. are added.

5b. Like *les soufflés, les crêpes* are listed on dessert menus. Sweet crêpes, *les crêpes sucrées,* are made from wheat flour. They are typically filled with strawberry sauce, then rolled and topped with whipped cream. (They are found under 'the diet starts tomorrow column.')

5c. *Les Crêpes Suzettes,* consisting of caramelized sugar, orange juice and orange peel (*l'écorce d'orange),* include *Grand Marnier. Les crêpes,* as well as the guests, are then 'lit.'

<u>Des Sandwichs Typiques</u>

1. le sandwich de jambon au fromage: Served in a *baguette,* this ham and cheese sandwich has a French flair.

2. le croque-monsieur- a toasted sandwich filled with ham and cheese

<u>An interesting note:</u> Tourists who crave *un déjeuner américain* can stop at McDonald's, Burger King or Quick for *un hamburger* or *un cheeseburger.* However, they have to pass on having the meal passed to them through an open window.

<u>Describably Delicious</u>- **Match the letters of the descriptions to the numbers of the items.**

_____ 1. le yaourt	A. ce qu'on met sur la tartine au lieu du beurre
_____ 2. la vichyssoise	B. ce qu'on trouve dans une mousse de crabe
_____ 3. la quiche Lorraine	C. deux poissons qui sont dans une salade niçoise
_____ 4. la crêpe Suzette	D. une pâtisserie qu'on prend pour le petit déjeuner; une spécialité de la Nouvelle-Orléans
_____ 5. le saucisson	E. se voit à la carte des petits déjeuners américains
_____ 6. les anchois et le thon	F. le deuxième repas du jour
_____ 7. le petit déjeuner	G. plus grand qu'une saucisse; on le coupe en tranches
_____ 8. le boisson	H. un type de pain fait avec œufs et beurre
_____ 9. le plat principal	I. une tourte faite avec œufs, fromage et bacon
_____ 10. le pâté	J. un produit laitier qui est bon pour un régime
_____ 11. le soufflé	K. servie comme une entrée ou pour le déjeuner
_____ 12. la gaufre	L. le premier repas du jour
_____ 13. la confiture	M. deux poissons dans une mousse
_____ 14. le croque-monsieur	N. ce qu'on sert après l'entrée
_____ 15. le déjeuner	O. une soupe froide
_____ 16. l'avocat et les œufs	P. une entrée faite avec fromage ou un dessert fait avec chocolat, citron ou banane

_____ 17. la brioche   Q. ce qu'on boit
_____ 18. le saumon et les câpres   R. un sandwich grillé et plein de jambon et fromage
_____ 19. la crêpe salée/la galette   S. une entrée fait du foie d'un oiseau
_____ 20. le beignet   T. un dessert avec l'écorce d'orange et la liqueur

----

LES LÉGUMES - Vegetables

Les légumes listed here are found in *une salade mixte,* served as side dishes and added to flavor *les entrées* and *les plats principaux.*

The Garden of 'Eating'
1. la laitue: Lettuce 'heads the list' as the most popular uncooked green vegetable.
2. le chou- the cabbage: The French word provides 'the stem' of *le chou-fleur-* the cauliflower, *les choux de Bruxelles-* the Brussels sprouts and *la choucroute-* the sauerkraut.
Popular Expressions in the Cabbage Patch
a. *Mon petit chou,* my little cabbage, is a term of endearment equivalent to "my darling."
b. chouette- neat, great, cool
c. faire un chou blanc- to draw a blank
Ex. Henri pense que Gaëlle est chouette. Il l'appelle "mon petit chou" parce qu'il fait un chou blanc, et il oublie son nom. > Henry thinks that Gaëlle is great. He calls her "my little cabbage" because he draws a blank, and he forgets her name. (Will Gaëlle tell Henry to find 'a fill in'?)
3. la tomate- the tomato: Because tomatoes and cucumbers contain seeds, some people consider them as fruits. (That makes for a 'ripe' argument.)
4. le concombre- the cucumber: Two nasal sounds are 'peeled off' consecutively.
5. le céleri- the celery (Dieters often munch a bunch at lunch.)
6. la carotte- the carrot: The French spelling 'chops off' an <u>r</u> and adds a <u>t</u>.
7. le champignon- the mushroom: Possibly *le champion des légumes français,* they are always a safe pick for *sauces, soupes, salades, crêpes et omelettes.*
8. le poivron vert/rouge- the green/red pepper: The name of the vegetable sounds similar to the spice, *le poivre,* a pepper-upper!
9. l'oignon (m.)- the onion: This is one of very few French words in which <u>oi</u> is not pronounced like <u>wa</u> in English. (Maybe the onion just wanted to be 'separated.')
A related expression is: *Occupe-toi de tes oignons!* > Take care of your onions! A more familiar translation is "Mind your own business!"
10. la betterave- the beet: *Le radis* is <u>the radish</u>. Both the word stems and the vegetables are 'on common ground.'
11. l'asperge (f.)- the asparagus: Oddly enough, *une grande asperge* translates as "a beanpole."
12. le brocoli- the broccoli (Is the deleted <u>c</u> in French 'a broccoli cut'?)
13. les épinards- the spinach: It has 'a pumped up' masculine plural form. Change the <u>é</u> to an <u>s</u> to remember its meaning.
14. l'haricot vert- the green bean/the string bean: It might be served 'straight' or in *les haricots verts amandine-* green beans with almonds.
15. les petits pois- the peas: "These little dots" are found in 'P-pods' but not in I-Pods.

16. **l'aubergine (f.)- the eggplant:** It could be available at *une auberge.*

17. **la courge- the squash:** This vegetable shares its stem with *la courgette*- the zucchini. (French squash is squished inside it.)

When Vegetables Get Together

1. *Une salade,* which consists of just lettuce, is eaten before, with or after the main course. *Une salade mixte* is the American equivalent of lettuce plus one or more vegetables.

2. *Les crudités* is an appetizer of raw vegetables in a vinaigrette dressing. It looks like our party tray assortment with carrots, celery and pepper slices, but a 'pointed' difference is their addition of asparagus spears.

3. *La ratatouille* is a stewed vegetable compote with *courgettes, tomates, poivrons rouges et verts, oignons et ail*- garlic. The combination is mixed in *l'huile d'olive.* Served as a meal, it is accompanied by rice or bread. *Touiller* means to (purposefully) <u>toss food</u>.

LES FÉCULENTS - Carbohydrates

Requests for Light Starch

1. **le maïs- the corn:** <u>Maize</u> is derived from le *maïs.* It's 'popped' into two syllables by *un tréma.* This *féculent* feels equally at home in the vegetable field.

2. **les pâtes- the pasta:** Unlike le *pâté, les pâtes* is a feminine plural noun. *Les nouilles* is its synonym. (That answers the question, "What's '*nouilles*?'")

3. **la pomme de terre- the potato:** Literally meaning "the apple of the earth," this staple can be prepared *au four*- in the oven/baked, *purée*- mashed or *frit*- fried.
<u>An interesting note:</u> *Les pommes frites*- French fries refers to how they are prepared. The past participle of *frire*- to fry is *frit.*

4. **le riz- the rice:** *Le riz blanc, brun, sauvage* (wild) and *cantonais* (fried) can go into, beside or under *les plats principaux.* (It is easily 'converted.')

5. **The term *les croûtons* comes from *la croûte*- the crust.** These sautéed or rebaked bread cubes are a garnish for soups and salads. (They could be entitled to their own 'scattergory.')

'Discarding Leftovers'- Circle the letters of the answers that do not belong in the groups.

1. a. les épinards	b. le champignon	c. le chou	d. la laitue
2. a. la courge	b. l'aubergine	c. l'huile	d. la courgette
3. a. les petits pois	b. l'asperge	c. l'haricot vert	d. la choucroute
4. a. le céleri	b. le riz	c. le radis	d. la carotte
5. a. la pomme de terre	b. la tomate	c. le poivron	d. le concombre
6. a. les pâtes	b. les nouilles	c. les légumes	d. les spaghettis
7. a. brun	b. sauvage	c. cantonais	d. niçoise
8. a. au four	b. puré	c. amandine	d. frit
9. a. l'aubergine	b. la ratatouille	c. la salade mixte	d. la crudité
10. a. l'oignon	b. l'ail	c. le poivre	d. la betterave

LA VIANDE - Meat, LA VOLAILLE - Poultry, LES POISSONS - Fish
LES FRUITS DE MER - Shellfish

Because space is unavailable for a complete menu of all four-legged, two-legged and no-legged creatures that make their way to the table in edible form, they appear here *au naturel*.

Les Viandes- Meats

1. le bifteck = le steak- the steak: Would you like to have it prepared *sanglant*- rare (bloody), *à point*- medium or *bien cuit*- well-cooked?

2. le bœuf- the beef: It is ironic that *le bœuf* has *œuf* inside it but *la poule*- the hen does not.

3. le rosbif- the roast beef (The French word has been cut into, but it is still recognizable.)

4. le veau- the veal: Some animal rights' activists are opposed to eating this meat. (They would rather pull 'a hamstring' than 'a calf muscle.')

5. l'agneau- the lamb: The British sacrifice our English word for <u>mutton</u>, which is similar to *le mouton*- the sheep.

6. le porc- the pork and le jambon- the ham: *Le cochon*- the pig knows that the two cuts aren't made with 'pinking shears.')

7. les côtelettes- the ribs: Whether you ask for *les côtelettes d'agneau*- the lamb ribs, *les côtelettes de bœuf*- the beef ribs, *les côtelettes de porc*- the pork ribs or *les côtelettes de veau*- the veal ribs, you could be accused of 'choosing sides.'

8. le bœuf haché- the ground beef (If it is lean, the 'steaks' are raised to a higher level.)

9. la boulette- the meatball (Formed from any type of meat, *les boulettes* 'make the rounds.')

La Volaille- Poultry

Although you are very familiar with *le poulet* (<u>poultry</u> was 'plucked' from it), you have not yet been formally introduced to:

1. le canard- the duck (If you hunt, you will find the duck 'Pe-king' through previous pages.)

2. l'oie (f.)- the goose (This bird tries to pronounce its French name when it squawks.)

3. la poule- the hen: She adores the endearing term *ma petite poule*.

4. la dinde- the female turkey and le dindon- the male (tom) turkey: Thanksgiving is translated as *le jour de graces*- the day of thanks. (But 'Dindon Day' sounds much cuter.)

5. la caille- the quail, le faisan/la poule faisane- the pheasant: The French often give these birds 'a shot' for Christmas when they or *l'oie* are 'dressed' and at the table.

<u>An important note</u>: Undomesticated, edible animals and birds such as *la caille* and *le faisan/la poule faisane* are referred to as *le gibier*. *Le lapin*- the rabbit is also 'fair game' and is listed on menus in upscale French restaurants. (You should not expect to see it offered at I-Hop.)

Les Poissons- Fish

Le thon- **the tuna and** *le saumon*- **the salmon were 'brought up' previously as ingredients in** *les entrées*. **Other 'cast members' are** *le flétan*- **the halibut,** *la sole*- **the sole and** *la truite*- **the trout.**

<u>An interesting aside</u>: *Un poisson* **is referred to as** *une pêche* **before it is caught.** (The concept is not unlike a woman changing her name once she has been 'hooked.')

Les Fruits de Mer = Fruits of the Sea- Shellfish

1. la coquille- the scallop is also <u>the shell</u>. (The same word covers both.) *Les coquilles St. Jacques* is 'just for openers.'

2. la crabe- the crab: The French variety extends itself with an <u>e</u>.

3. la crevette- the shrimp, the prawn (*La Corvette* and *la crevette* sound similar, but the latter has a top that is peeled off and not rolled back.)

4. l'huître (f.)- the oyster

Ex. La serveuse sert ton thon et huit huîtres. > The waitress serves your tuna and eight oysters. (This French selection is ordered 'repeatedly.')

Le monde est à lui. > **The world is his oyster.** (It certainly applies if the name is Rockefeller.)

5. le homard/la langouste- the lobster: **Aspirate the <u>h</u>, and throw away the <u>d</u> to get the most out of** *le homard.*

6. la moule- the mussel (Vendors selling these crustaceans proudly show off their 'mussels.')

7. la palourde- the clam: **Notice that** *lourde-* **heavy is inside.** (That might be why clams are often 'stuffed.')

Ways to Cook *Les Plats Principaux*

au four- baked, *grillé-* broiled/grilled, *frit-* fried, *rôti-* roasted, *cuit au barbecue-* barbecued and *cuit à la vapeur-* steamed. **Of course, not all methods apply to all foods. Steamed steak would be 'rare,' and fried lobster would not be a 'Maine' dish.**

'Leather, Feather' or Neither- Circle the letters of the answers that complete the sentences.

1. La viande qui vient d'une petite vache est ____.
a. le rosbif   b. l'agneau   c. le veau   d. le steak

2. Tous ces plats principaux sont des spécialités de Noël sauf ____.
a. l'oie   b. la caille   c. le faisan   d. les boulettes

3. Le bifteck ne peut pas être préparé ____.
a. sanglant   b. dans une coquille   c. à point   d. bien cuit

4. La dinde, le dindon, le poulet et la poule sont les noms ____.
a. de gibier   b. de bœuf   c. de volaille   d. de fruits de mer

5. Tous les suivants sont des noms de poisson sauf ____.
a. le thon   b. le canard   c. le flétan   d. la truite

6. Le porc, le jambon et le bacon viennent d'un(e) ____.
a. cochon   b. lapin   c. pêche   d. agneau

7. Une langouste est un synonyme pour un(e) ____.
a. crabe   b. palourde   c. moule   d. homard

8. On qui a de la chance trouve **une perle (a pearl)** dans un(e) ____.
a. bifteck   b. huître   c. crevette   d. saumon

9. Tous les suivants sont le gibier sauf ____.
a. la caille   b. le faisan   c. la coquille   d. le lapin

10. On ne cuit pas au barbecue le ____.
a. poisson   b. poulet   c. porc   d. bœuf haché

LES SAUCES FRANÇAISES - French Sauces

La sauce makes food more appetizing. Though French chefs may know more than 57 varieties, dilettantes and diners are usually content to prepare and/or taste the most popular ones. They can be spread over four categories: white, brown, tomato and mayonnaise/hollandaise.

Les Sauces Blanches - White Sauces

A mixture of butter and flour forms the base for white *roux*, a popular sauce that accompanies poultry, fish, veal and vegetables. Perhaps, the best known is *la sauce béchamel*. When poultry or veal stock- *le bouillon de poulet* or *de veau* is added to *le roux*, the result is *la sauce veloutée/ la sauce blonde*. *Béchamel* plus cheese and seasonings equals *la sauce mornay*, while *béchamel à la crème* becomes *la sauce suprême*. (The phrase *béchamel à la crème est une sauce suprême* seems to just roll off one's tongue.)

Les Sauces Brunes - Brown Sauces

La sauce brune, served with red meat, chicken, veal and game, is prepared by simmering meat stock- *le bouillon de bœuf* for hours and mixing it with *le roux*. If bone trimmings are added, *la sauce brune* becomes *la sauce ragoût*. Sprinkled with *beaucoup de poivre*, the sauce is known as *la sauce diable*- devil sauce. (The name may come from it being 'as hot as hell.')
La sauce Robert is a brown sauce with *la moutarde*- mustard. *La sauce piquante*, tart sauce, has *des cornichons*- pickles et *des câpres*. *La sauce chasseur*- hunting sauce has *les champignons, les echalotes*- shallots and *le vin blanc* and is usually served on game.

Les Sauces Tomates - Tomato Sauces

The best known *des sauces tomates*, typically served with *les boulettes* and *les pâtes/les nouilles*, is *la sauce Bolognaise*. *Les oignons, l'ail* and *les feuilles de basilic*- basil leaves give added flavor to this tomato sauce. *La sauce aurore*, which is normally reserved for poultry, is a combination of *béchamel* and tomato sauces.

Les Sauces Hollandaises/Les Sauces Mayonnaises - Hollandaise/Mayonnaise Sauces

Both types of sauces are made by flavoring *les jaunes d'œuf chauds*- warm egg yolks with *le jus de citron* and melted butter. To prepare *la sauce mousseline*, *la creme fouettée*- whipped cream is added. (Does beating eggs and whipping cream constitute 'Julia Child abuse'?)
Les sauces hollandaises can befriend fish, chicken or vegetables. *La hollandaise, le vin blanc, le bouillon de poisson* and a little luck render *la sauce vin blanc*. *La sauce béarnaise* consists of an egg and butter base, *l'estragon*- tarragon, *les echalotes, le vinaigre* and *le vin*. For *la rémoulade*, cooks blend *l'anchois* or *le pâté d'anchois, la moutarde, les câpres* and *les cornichons fines* with

la mayonnaise froide. Since *la rémoulade* goes well with cold meats, poultry and seafood, every-one can 'have a picnic' with it.

Just as *la salade niçoise* is so named because it originated near Nice, sauces are also labeled for their derivations. Besides *la sauce bolognaise* (of Italian heritage), there is *la sauce bordelaise*, a brown sauce enhanced with red Bordeaux wine. It's most at home on steak and game. *La sauce lyonnaise*, made with *les oignons fines, le persil-* parsley and *le vin blanc*, normally accompanies beef and poultry. (With wine added so frequently to these recipes, it is not just the main course that 'gets sauced.')

'Get Cookin'- Match the letters of the ingredients to the names of the sauces.

_____ 1. la sauce veloutée/la sauce blonde	A. une sauce aux tomates, oignons, ail et feuilles de basilic
_____ 2. la sauce piquante	B. le roux brun aux morceaux de viande
_____ 3. la sauce béarnaise	C. le roux brun au vin rouge
_____ 4. la sauce suprême	D. la combinaison d'une sauce béchamel et une sauce tomate
_____ 5. la sauce bolognaise	E. le roux brun aux oignons, persil et vin blanc
_____ 6. la rémoulade	F. le roux blanc au bouillon de poulet ou au veau
_____ 7. la sauce béchamel	G. le roux brun au poivre
_____ 8. la sauce lyonnaise	H. une sauce béchamel au fromage et épices
_____ 9. la sauce diable	I. une sauce hollandaise à la crème fouettée
_____ 10. la sauce mousseline	J. une sauce béchamel à la crème
_____ 11. la sauce ragoût	K. une sauce hollandaise au bouillon de poisson et vin blanc
_____ 12. la sauce mornay	L. le roux brun aux champignons, echalotes et vin blanc
_____ 13. la sauce aurore	M. le roux blanc
_____ 14. la sauce vin blanc	N. le roux brun aux cornichons et câpres
_____ 15. la sauce Robert	O. la mayonnaise fraîche aux anchois, moutarde, câpres et cornichons fines
_____ 16. la sauce bordelaise	P. le roux brun à la moutarde
_____ 17. la sauce chausseur	Q. une sauce hollandaise à l'estragon, echalotes, vin ou vinaigre

----

LES APÉRITIFS - Predinner Drinks, LES CANAPÉS - Appetizers
LES SOUPES - Soups and LES ENTRÉES - Introductory Dishes

Picture yourself at dinnertime seated in a French restaurant, *une carte/un menu* in your hands! Before the main attraction is presented, familiarize yourself with these show starters!

Les Apéritifs- Wines and Liquors
1. un kir- a Burgundy white wine with *crème de cassis-* a black currant, flavored liquor
2. un pastis- a liquor enhanced with *anise-* a licorice-tasting herb

Des apéritifs familiers are whiskey, martini, Muscadet and Porto.
Le champagne is offered not only on special occasions but also as an after dinner drink.

Les Amuse-Gueule, Les Canapés, Hors-d'œuvre - French Appetizers

The salty and/or spicy contents of the appetizers could prompt people to drink more. (With delicious tidbits in one hand and continual refills in the other, it becomes increasingly difficult 'to hold one's liquor.')

Finger Foods Honoring 'The No-Drinking Alone Policy'

1. les vol-au-vent: Translated as "windblown," these appetizers 'go topless' until prawns, fruit, cheese or mushrooms are put inside. Then they are ready for a recap.

2. les barquettes- "little boats": These filled, puffed pastries are baked or broiled.

3. les biscuits salés/les crackers: The small pieces of bread or toast are topped with fish, cheese, meat, *foie gras* **or caviar (fish roe).** (It would be interesting to see fish 'roe' in a *barquette*.)

A reminder: *Un canapé* is also a sofa. (The spread on that is much larger.)

'Don't Can the Soup!'

In addition to *la soupe à l'oignon gratinée*, **diners 'warm up to':**

1. les bouillons/les consommés- the broths/the clear soups: A particular favorite is *le consommé de poulet*, **chicken broth.**

2. les potages- the soups: *Les potages* **and** *les soupes* **are often interchangeable terms. You may want 'to take a pot shot,' and use either of them with any qualifying ingredient!**

Ex. *un potage aux légumes*- a vegetable soup (The categories 'spill over' onto one other.)

3. les crèmes/les bisques- broth thickened with cream soups: These could be dually listed as *les potages*. **When cream and wine are added to** *la soupe à l'oignon*, **it becomes** *une crème*. (Its taste could result in tipping the bowl as well as the waiter.)

While *la soupe de jus d'asperges verte* **is asparagus soup,** *la purée de céleri* **is celery soup. Moreover, we refer to** *le potage aux champignons* **as mushroom soup and label** *la crème d'artichauts* **as artichoke soup.** (No matter 'how you slice it,' they are all vegetable soups.)

However, any creamy soup with crustaceans is *une bisque*. *La bisque de homard*- **lobster bisque fits the description.**

4. les veloutés- thick velvety soups: With their creamy bases, most *veloutés* **could be considered as** *des crèmes*. *Le velouté de tomates* **is creamy tomato soup. Additional 'souper stars'include** *le velouté de châtaignes et bacon*- **chestnut soup with bacon and** *le velouté d'épinards aux moules*- **spinach soup with mussels.** (The 'flex' of green are noticeable.)

5. Two popular soups should not 'be put on the back burner': *le potage parmentier*, **also known as** *la soupe au poireau et pommes de terre*- **potato leek soup (a warm version of vichyssoise) and** *la soupe à l'ail gratiné*- **creamy garlic soup with grated cheese.**

6. la panade- bread soup: This at-home staple is fed to infants and served to young children in the morning. *(La panade* gives a unique meaning to the phrase 'born and bread.') **The basic recipe plus eggs makes** *la panade à la reine. La soupe à l'oseille blanchie*- **white sorrel soup is an all-in-the-family favorite** *panade*.

7. la garbure- vegetable soup with ham: A popular choice is *la soupe à l'oseille au jambon*.

Two subcategories of French soups

a. *Une gratinée* refers to a soup covered with melted cheese. *La soupe à l'oignon gratinée*, onion soup topped with *gruyère*, is an example.

b. *Un tourain* typically has garlic as an ingredient.

<u>A note</u>: *La marmite* is <u>the soup</u> and <u>the pot</u> in which it is cooked. The dual meaning is similar to the English use of the word <u>casserole</u>.

'Taking Stock'- Label the statements *vrai* or *faux*.

_____ 1. Le champagne n'est pas un apéritif.

_____ 2. Whiskey, Muscadet et Porto ne sont pas les apéritifs.

_____ 3. Un kir, un pastis et un martini sont des apéritifs.

_____ 4. Un amuse-gueule, un canapé et un hors-d'œuvre sont des synonymes.

_____ 5. Il n'y a rien à l'intérieur des vol-au-vent ou des barquettes.

_____ 6. Des bouillons sont aussi des consommés.

_____ 7. Un potage n'est pas une soupe.

_____ 8. Il y a des fruits de mer dans une bisque.

_____ 9. Un potage parmentier chaud est comme une vichyssoise froide.

_____ 10. Un tourain contient toujours du fromage.

_____ 11. Il y a des légumes et du jambon dans une garbure.

_____ 12. Le velouté de châtaignes et bacon est une panade.

_____ 13. Des soupes aux légumes peuvent être purées, crèmes et veloutés.

_____ 14. D'habitude, on ne prend pas la soupe à l'oseille blanchie dans un restaurant.

_____ 15. Les poireaux et les pommes de terre sont dans une panade à la reine.

UN DÎNER CHEZ DIDIER

Du Vocabulaire du Conte

1. **le prix fixe**- the multicourse meal at a fixed price
2. **à la carte**- individually priced menu items
3. **les œufs au diable**- deviled eggs
4. **en matière de nourriture**- when it comes to food
5. **la carte blanche**- the complete authority to act
6. **le filet mignon**- the tenderloin cut of steak (*le Châteaubriand*)
7. **le steak pommes frites**- steak with French fries
8. **non plus**- either
9. **le poulpe**- octopus
10. **le calmar**- squid
11. **la bouillabaisse**- fish and seafood stew
12. **oser**- to dare
13. **le canard à l'orange**- duck in orange sauce
14. **le coq au vin**- chicken (not rooster) in red wine with mushrooms
15. **la poule au pot**- chicken (not hen) stuffed with sausage, mushrooms and rice and served in a pot
16. **le bœuf Bourguignon**- pot roast cooked in red wine
17. **les aliments**- the foods
18. **le ragoût**- stew made with lamb or rabbit
19. **le gigot d'agneau**- leg of lamb
20. **les cuisses de grenouille**- frog's legs (thighs)
21. **faisant une grimace**- giving a look of disgust
22. **les cervelles de veau**- calves' brains
23. **le front**- the forehead
24. **la truite meunière**- trout with butter and lemon sauce
25. **le pot au feu**- braised meat and vegetables prepared in a stockpot
26. **les rognons**- beef kidneys
27. **la blanquette de veau**- veal in white sauce
28. **Ça y est!**- That's it!

Tiffany et Brad, qui viennent de St. Louis, célèbrent leur dixième anniversaire à Paris. Ils vont dîner Chez Didier, un restaurant très exclusif près de leur hôtel. Manger **au prix fixe** est moins cher qu'**à la carte,** mais ils sont contents de payer plus pour avoir plus de choix. Brad sait lire le français plutôt bien, et il reconnaît les noms de quelques potages et entrées.

Tiffany commande **les œufs au diable** et la soupe à l'oignon gratinée. Brad n'est pas si conservateur **en matière de nourriture**, et il choisit une mousse de foies de volaille et un potage parmentier. Les deux sont ravis de leurs choix.

Le mari suggère que sa femme commande un plat principal typiquement français. Tiffany est un peu hésitante, mais enfin, elle est d'accord.

(Although their conversation was in English, they gave their **carte blanche** to have it translated into French.)

Tiffany: Tu as raison, Brad. Si on est dans un pays étranger, on doit goûter ses spécialités. Qu'est-ce que tu recommandes?

Brad: Ni **le filet mignon** ni **le steak pommes frites.** Nous pouvons les manger chez nous.

Tiffany: Et pas la fondue **non plus**. Je ne suis pas en France pour cuisiner.

Brad: Selon cette description-ci, il y a **du poulpe** et **du calmar** dans **la bouillabaisse**.

Tiffany: Tu sais que je n'**ose** pas l'essayer.

Brad: Le canard à l'orange te plaît?

Tiffany: Je crois que non. Après ça, je ne pourrai pas manger de dessert.

Brad: Tiens! **Le coq au vin** ou **la poule au pot**? En réalité, les deux sont faits des poulets.

Tiffany: Le bœuf Bourguignon, c'est une possibilité.

Brad: Mais tu me dis toujours qu'il y a trop de vin aux plats principaux.

Tiffany: Tu reconnais ces autres sélections?

Brad: Pas vraiment. Demandons à notre serveur de nous conseiller!

(Le serveur arrive à leur table.)

Brad: Aidez-nous à traduire **des aliments** sur le menu, s'il vous plaît!

Le serveur: Á votre service, Monsieur.

Brad: Merci beaucoup. Qu'est-ce que c'est qu'**un ragoût?**

Le serveur: Chez Didier, c'est une soupe épaisse faite d'agneau et avec des légumes.

Brad: Et **le gigot d'agneau** est la jambe de l'animal, n'est-ce pas?

Le serveur: Exactement! Et **les cuisses de grenouilles** sont les jambes aussi.

Tiffany: Brad, que veut-dire une grenouille?

Brad: un Kermit français.

Tiffany: (faisant une grimace en l'entendant) Et **les cervelles de veau**?

(Il ne faut pas lui dire. Tiffany comprend le sens de la phrase quand le serveur touche **son front**.)

Tiffany: Je pense que je vais attendre le dessert.

Brad: La truite meunière pour ma femme.

Le serveur: Et pour vous, monsieur?

Brad: Je décide parmi **le pot au feu, les rognons** et **la blanquette de veau**.

Le serveur: Tous les trois sont des spécialités délicieuses, mais à mon opinion, vous devez choisir la blanquette de veau. Un vin blanc va bien avec ça aussi bien qu'avec la truite.

Brad: Ça y est. La blanquette de veau.

Le serveur: Bien sûr, Monsieur. Je vais apporter votre vin et plus de pain tout de suite.

Écrivez des réponses complètes en français aux questions suivantes.

1. Pourquoi Tiffany et Brad sont-ils à Paris? _____
_____.

2. Décrivez Chez Didier! _____
_____.

3. Pourquoi préfèrent-ils payer à la carte au lieu du prix fixe? _____
_____.

4. Qu'est-ce qu'ils commandent comme des entrées? _____
_____.

5. Qu'est-ce que Brad suggère à sa femme? _____
_____.

6. Pourquoi ne veulent-ils pas commander ni le filet mignon ni le steak pommes frites? _____
_____.

7. Qu'est-ce que Brad dit du coq au vin et de la poule au pot? _____
_____.

8. Pourquoi demandent-ils au serveur de leur conseiller? _____
_____.

9. Selon le serveur, comment cuisine-t-on le ragoût chez Didier? _____

10. Comment le gigot d'agneau ressemble-t-il aux cuisses de grenouilles? _____.

_____

11. Qu'est-ce que Tiffany dit quand elle comprend le sens de la phrase "cervelles de veau"? _____.

_____

12. Quel plat pricipal Brad commande-t-il pour sa femme? _____.

_____

13. Parmi quels plats principaux Brad choisit-il? _____.

_____

14. Pourquoi le serveur suggère-t-il la blanquette de veau? _____.

_____

15. Pourquoi le serveur va-t-il retourner très bientôt?_____.

_____

_____

l'Hôtel Matignon (Paris)

LES FRUITS - Fruits

After *le plat principal* and before *le dessert*, more food is served at a multicourse French dinner. The feast includes a presentation of cheeses and fruits. Help yourself to the spread!

Fruitful Words Bunched Together

1. **la pêche**- the peach, **la poire**- the pear, **la pomme**- the apple and **la prune**- the plum: **You can put them into the same basket because they are all five-letter, feminine nouns starting with a p and ending with an e.**
A note: *Une prune* is <u>a plum</u>; *un pruneau* is <u>a prune</u>.

2. **le pamplemousse**- the grapefruit and **la pastèque**- the watermelon: **Both feminine nouns also begin with a p and end with an e.** (Perhaps they need more than five letters because of their size.)

3. **le raisin**- the grape*: It makes sense that the* **le raisin sec**- the dry grape is the raisin, but there is no logic in finding *eau* in *le pruneau.*

4. **la fraise**- the strawberry and **la cerise**- the cherry: **Small, red and eaten by the handful, they can be 'picked' to go together.** *Les cerises* resemble <u>cherries</u> if a few letters are 'pitted.'

5. **la framb<u>oise</u>**- the raspberry: **This fruit conveniently grows in** *les bois.* **A couple other 'berry' healthy fruits are** *la myrtille*- **the blueberry and** *la mûre*- **the blackberry. When the blackberry is ripe, it is** *une mûre mûre.* (The blueberry can't 'call on' a Blackberry if 'it's in a jam.')

6. **la baie**- the berry: *L'air<u>elle</u>* is the cranberry. **Think of the cranberry in 'rel-ish' form!**

7. **l'ananas (m.)**- the pineapple: **This symbol of hospitality does not welcome the last letter of its name being pronounced. The 'core' of** *l'ananas* **is found inside la** *banane.*

8. **la noix de coco**- the coconut: **This fruit grows on the coconut palm tree.** (After 'a shakedown,' its nut, meat, milk and water are revealed.)

9. **la mangue**- the mango: The longer this tropical fruit is in the sun, the redder it gets. (That should give you the hang of *la mangue.*)

10. **l'orange (f.)**- the orange: **This citrus fruit touts universal 'ap-peel.'** *La mandarine* is the tangerine. (Which one you choose is up to 'hue.')

11. **le citron**- the lemon: *Le citron vert* is <u>the lime</u>.

12. **le brugnon/la nectarine**- the nectarine: **Not considered as a citrus fruit,** *le brugnon* **is a cross between** *une pêche* **and** *une prune.*

13. **la datte**- the date and **la figue**- the fig: **These Middle Eastern specialties are foreign to very few people.** (And their popularity is not 'shriveling.')

14. **la citrouille**- the pumpkin: (It is 'cut out' to be on its own.)

<u>An important note</u>: **Many fruits share their names with colors and shades of colors. Examples are orange, cherry, strawberry, lemon and lime. As adjectives, fruit colors are invariable.**
Ex. Les lampes orange qu'ils viennent d'acheter ne marchent pas. > The orange lamps that they just bought don't work. (They turned out to be 'lemons.')

LES NOIX - Nuts

Exposed or in their shells, nuts can be found everywhere. (They are an interesting addition to our diets and to our society.)

A Handful of Nuts
1. **l'amande- the almond: Whether used in pastes or eaten as a snack, *l'amande* is in demand.**
2. **la cacahuète- the peanut** (People can joke about the French pronunciation, but to them it 'means peanuts.')
3. **la châtaigne/le marron- the chestnut: This variety offers dual translations and adds its taste to ingredients in soups and sauces.**
4. **la noix- the walnut: The French word for this kind of nut and its generic name are the same.** (The other types are not 'just plain nuts.')

Picking Fruits and 'Chew-sing' Nuts- Circle the letters of the choices that do not belong.

1. a. la fraise	b. le marron	c. la framboise	d. la myrtille
2. a. la noix de coco	b. la citrouille	c. l'orange	d. la mandarine
3. a. le raisin sec	b. le pruneau	c. la nectarine	d. la datte
4. a. la mandarine	b. la figue	c. le pamplemousse	d. l'orange
5. a. le citron vert	b. le citron	c. l'ananas	d. la banane
6. a. la cacahuète	b. l'amande	c. la mangue	d. la châtaigne
7. a. la pomme	b. la pêche	c. le brugnon	d. la mûre
8. a. le raisin	b. la noix	c. la prune	d. le citron
9. a. la cerise	b. la poire	c. la pomme	d. l'airelle
10. a. la pastèque	b. le pamplemousse	c. la citrouille	d. la cacahuète

----

LES BOISSONS SANS ALCOOL - Nonalcoholic Drinks

Imbibing without Inhibitions
1. **l'eau minérale- mineral water: Évian, Perrier and Vittel are three well-known brands. Long before they met with acclaim here, these bottled waters were a mainstay of European diets.** (It gives them leverage on the beverage.)
2. **le Coca- Coke is popular, but the French usually 'dispense with'** *Coca Light-* **Diet Coke.**
3. **l'Orangina- the carbonated, soft drink made from oranges, lime and orange pulp**
4. **le citron pressé- freshly squeezed lemon juice** (The French term suggests that any wrinkles from puckering have been ironed out.)
5. **le limonade- lemonade: But** *le citron* **is the actual translation for** <u>the lemon.</u>
6. **les jus de fruits- fruit juices:** *La pomme, l'orange, le raisin* **and** *l'ananas* **are a few 'extracted' from the list.** (They'll never know the difference because they are 'drunk' all day.)

LES BIÈRES FRANÇAISES - French Beers

Many who prefer no wine to a cheap one often opt for beer. In addition, the French have taken a greater interest in it since 'drink and drive laws' have become more restrictive. (Even though wine 'reigns' in France, beer 'pours' there.)

Something is always brewing in Alsace-Lorraine where 80 percent of French beer is produced. That region's blond lagers are generally sweeter and lighter than those of their German neighbors. (Drinker there are less likely to show off their 'six packs.') *Le Pêcheur*, **an Alsatian brewery, recently launched** *Bire Amoureuse*. **The golden lager which contains ginseng is advertised as an aphrodisiac.** (Carried in a paper bag, this beer could be renamed 'Hops in the Sack.')

Sweet, brown beers are the specialties of Nord-Pas de Calais where the most popular label is *la bière de Garde*. **Originally brewed by local farmers, it is referred to as "a farmhouse ale."** (That could explain why the *La Vache qui Rit*, The Laughing Cow, is so happy.) **Three well-known** *bières de garde, Castelain, la Choulette* **and** *Ch'ti,* **are sold in blond, amber and brown.** (Are 'the heads' on those beers different?)

Brittany *(la Bretagne),* **a peninsula in Northwestern France, is the most recent province 'to tap in to' high volume beer production.** *Coreff,* **the region's specialty, is pumped by hand.** (Bartenders there don't need 'to avoid the draft.')

No Booze and Some Brews- Circle the letters of the responses that best complete the sentences.

1. World popular mineral waters do not include _____.
a. Évian   b. Perrier   c. Moët   d. Vittel

2. Orangina contains all of the following except _____.
a. oranges   b. orange pulp   c. lime   d. lemon

3. The popular drink made from freshly-squeezed lemon juice is _____.
a. le jus de citron   b. le citron pressé   c. l'eau de limon   d. le limon pressé

4. Eighty percent of French beer is produced in _____.
a. Germany   b. Belgium   c. Nord-Pas de Calais   d. Alsace-Lorraine

5. A well-known French lager containing ginseng is called _____.
a. le Pêcheur   b. la bière blonde   c. la Bire Amoureuse   d. le champagne noir

6. All of the following are *bières de garde* except _____.
a. Castelain   b. Coreff   c. la Choulette   d. Ch'ti

LES VINS FRANÇAIS - French Wines

Ah! French wine! It is time for the long awaited French toast: "Here's to France, its people, its culture, its language and its vineyards!"
Educated consumers do not overlook the basic facts before looking over the wine list.

What Is Not Heard through the Grapevine
1. **Seven to eight billion bottles of French wine are produced every year from two million acres of vineyards.** (Fortunately, the people don't have to worry about their 'plants' shutting down.)
2. **Italy and France are currently competing to claim the world's largest wine production.**
3. **French wines are usually mixtures of grape varieties. For example, *Merlot* might be blended with *Cabernet Sauvignon*, another red wine grape. Yet, varietal white wines are more common than varietal red ones.** (One could interpret that to mean that drinking 'clearly' has its advantages.)
4. **Whether they are red, rosé, white, table variety or luxury priced, all French wines have one thing in common: There is a mutual attraction between them and meals. They are as welcome with lunch at a sidewalk café as with a full-course dinner at Maxim's.**
5. **In the past forty years, France's wine consumption has dropped off. However, its profitable, world-wide distribution puts *un bouchon-* a cork into that data.**

Where the Best Wine 'Sell-ers' Are Located
1. ***L'Alsace* in the eastern part of France is predominantly a white wine region.**
2. **Bordeaux on the Atlantic coast is red wine territory.**
3. **The Rhone Valley in the South gets credit for *Beaujolais*, a popular red wine.** (It touts a most attractive label as it is both handsome and pretty.)
4. **Burgundy *(la Bourgogne)* in East Central France is the birthplace of red and white wines. It is the home of *Chardonnay*. The heart of this province, *la Côte d'Or*, yields some of the world's priciest selections including *Pinot*.** (Although it is inland, *la Côte d'Or* is "The Gold Coast.")
5. **Chablis, a well-known white wine, is cultivated between *La Côte d'Or* and Paris.** (Obviously, Chablis' upbringing is not shabby.)
6. **Champagne 'bubbles' in *la Champagne,* the province bordering Belgium and Luxembourg. That is France's coldest, wine growing region.** (Thus making it the best place 'to chill.')
An important note: Though *la Champagne* is feminine, the sparkling wine is *un vin*. Therefore, *le champagne* is a masculine noun. (It gives new meaning to 'a split of champagne.')
7. ***Le Languedoc-Roussillon,* which covers five departments in South Central France, produces the country's least expensive wines. Its bottles are typically marked *Vin du pays d'Oc*.** (Because it is so reasonably priced, some view *Vin du pays d'Oc* wine as the undisputed 'liter.')
8. **The Loire Valley, found beside the river of the same name, spreads from Central to Western France and is a white wine region. While *Sauvignon Blanc* is made near Bordeaux, *Muscadet* is produced far away in *Pays Nantois*.** (Imagine being the mouth of *la Loire!*)

9. *La Provence* in Southeastern France and very near the Mediterranean Sea is known for rosé and red wines. (It is nice 'to get some color' while relaxing on the beaches of Nice and St. Tropez.)

LES FROMAGES FRANÇAIS - French Cheeses

France's President, Charles de Gaulle, stated that it was almost impossible to rule in a country that had (at that time) 246 cheeses. What resistance he would have encountered if he had tried to rule out some!

Select Members of 'the Cheeseboard'
1. *Boursin* is a newcomer to the cheese world. It has a cream cheese texture and is available in a variety of flavors. Packaged in small boxes, *Boursin* is sold throughout the United States.
2. *Brie* is a soft white cheese with a grayish tinge, a white rind and a hint of ammonia. (The last feature might be the result of a cow mating with a 'Clor-ox.')
3. *Camembert* is soft and creamy. It has the notorious di-'stinc'-tion of being the world's worst smelling cheese.
4. *Gruyère* is hard and yellow. As a melting cheese, it is often used in quiches and sauces.
5. *Munster*, light yellow with a shiny rind, is matured in caves. Seventh century monks deserve the credit for its origin. (This is one aged cheese.)
6. *Neufchâtel* is a dry cheese with a white rind and a grainy texture. Even though it dates back to the sixth century, *neuf* is ironically part of its name.
7. *Port Salut*, semisoft with an orange crust, has a mild flavor but a strong smell. ('Past-eur-ize' is no guarantee of 'past your nose.')
8. *Reblochon* has a creamy, springy texture. Consisting of milk from three breeds of cows, this cheese is aged in mountain cellars. (The animals must 'have a field day' in the basements.)
9. *Roquefort*, made from ewe's milk, is also known as "blue cheese." White and crumbly, it has distinctive veins of blue mold. (If the veins are 'stripped,' it is probably 'dressing.')
10. *Valençay* is a goat's milk cheese with a blue-gray color. It has a citric taste and a pyramidal shape. (Not unlike an inverted 'goat-ee.')
11. *La Vache Qui Rit*- Laughing Cow Cheese is mentioned 'just for the fun of it.' The semisoft, spreadable wedges are sold in ninety countries and are a favorite at French picnics. (If the cows knew that they were back on home turf, they could have the last laugh.)
An important note: Except for *la Vache Qui Rit*, the names of French cheeses are masculine because the general category is *le fromage*. *Le* applies even if the origin is a feminine province. (Ex. Le Brie vient de la Brie.)

Selections Aged to Perfection- Label the statements *vrai* or *faux*.

1. _____ Les États-Unis et la Grèce sont les plus grands producteurs de vin du monde.
2. _____ On met des variétés de raisins ensemble pour faire des vins.
3. _____ En Bourgogne, on produit les vins rouges et les vins blancs.
4. _____ Les vins les moins chers viennent de la Côte d'Or.
5. _____ On produit le champagne dans une région chaude près de l'Espagne.
6. _____ Le Chablis est cultivé en Bordeaux.
7. _____ Le vin rosé est une spécialité de la Provence.
8. _____ Le Muscadet et le Sauvignon Blanc sont faits dans la Vallée de la Loire.
9. _____ Le Beaujolais et le Chardonnay sont cultivés dans le même endroit.
10. _____ Le Gruyère et le Munster sont deux fromages jaunes.
11. _____ Le Port Salut est fait du lait des **brebis (ewes)**.
12. _____ On vend la Vache Qui Rit seulement en France et aux États-Unis.
13. _____ Le Camembert et le Port Salut ont les odeurs très fortes.
14. _____ Le Boursin est un des plus vieux fromages français.
15. _____ Le Valençay a la forme d'une pyramide.
16. _____ Le Brie et le Gruyère ont les croûtes orange.
17. _____ Nous appelons le Roquefort "un fromage bleu."

Ball at le Moulin de la Galette by Auguste Renoir (le Musée d'Orsay, Paris)

LES DESSERTS FRANÇAIS - French Desserts

Nothing tops the bottom of a French menu. The word "dessert" may signal the finale of a meal, but the list of mouth-watering treats is endless. Since there couldn't possibly be room for all of them, the categories include the best-known nonpastry and *pâtisserie* desserts. You may fall in love 'at first bite.'

Just Plain Delicious

1. le gâteau- the cake: There's *le gâteau au chocolat, le gâteau à la vanille, le gâteau aux fraises,* etc. (French cakes are not usually 'package deals.')
2. le gâteau sec- the cookie: Although it actually means "the dry cake," it ironically 'whets one's appetite' for seconds.
3. la tarte- the tart: Made of fruit and sugar, it could endearingly be called "a sweet tart."
4. la tourte- the pie: This can be a main course or a dessert pastry. Examples include *un pâté de croûte-* a pork pie and *une tourte aux pommes-* an apple pie. Both have a round form. (There is no 'pi' squared.)
5. la glace- the ice cream, the ice, the mirror: One word fits all. Moreover, *le parfum* means the perfume and the flavor. Considering that smell and taste are related, a double translation does make 'scents.'
6. le sorbet- the sherbet: Almost any fruit is available as a sherbet flavor.
Exs. le sorbet au citron- lemon sherbet, le sorbet à la framboise- raspberry sherbet (Many more 'ice picks' are available.)

No Slice French Desserts

1. le clafouti- a custard-like dessert made with cherries: It 'stems from' the Limousin region in South Central France.
2. la crème caramel- baked custard with a caramel sauce: *La crème brûlée,* which means burnt cream, shares its ingredients with *la crème caramel* but has a hardened, caramel topping. (Not all burnt offerings are sacrifices.) *Le flan* is a variation of *la crème caramel.*
3. le gratin des fruits rouges- a soufflé-type dessert with cherries and raspberries: It tastes half-sweet and half-sour. (But it is not always shared fifty-fifty.)
4. la mousse au chocolat- chocolate mousse: This chilled confection consists of eggs and cream blended with chocolate. (The ingredients 'take a beating' before everything is 'smoothed over.')
5. l'omelette norvégienne- Norwegian omelet (Baked Alaska): Made with meringue and vanilla ice cream and served with flaming *Grand Marnier,* it is simultaneously a hot and cold dessert.
6. la poire Belle-Hélène- the beautiful Helen pear: Pre-'pear'-ed with poached fruit halves and filled with vanilla ice cream, the fruit is coated with chocolate sauce.
7. la teurgoule- cinnamon-laced, rice pudding: "Twisted mouth" possibly got its French name because of the facial expression that Normands made while tasting its spiciness.
8. *Les soufflés,* previously mentioned on the lunch menu, are sweetened desserts as well. With chocolate, lemon or banana added to the basic recipe, they're a wonderful way 'to blow a diet.'

Les Pâtisseries Françaises- French Pastries

1. **le canelé- a small pastry with a spongy, custard center and a caramelized crust: This dessert resembles a minibundt cake.** (The repeated <u>m</u> shape gives a clue to its taste.)

2. **la Charlotte- a chilled, sponge cake filled with a fruit purée:** *La Charlotte russe,* **a lady finger with custard inside, is a treat that you might want 'to get your hands on.'**

3. **le congolais- the coconut biscuit: It is soft on the inside and crunchy on the outside.** (They are quickly consumed without even 'a shred of evidence.')

4. **les crêpes sucrées- sweetened crepes: Here is your second helping of the thin pancakes rolled in strawberry sauce and topped with whipped cream.** *La crème Chantilly,* **sweet vanilla cream, is** *la crème de la crème.*

Les Crêpes Suzette **are made with caramelized sugar, orange juice, orange peel and** *Grand Marrnier.* **Then, the ingredients are set aflame.** (Among Hélène, Charlotte and Suzette, the last one is by far 'the hottest number' at the dinner table.)

5. **l'éclair au chocolat- the chocolate eclair: This very popular pastry is filled with custard and glazed with chocolate.** *L'éclair,* <u>the lightning,</u> **describes the speed at which they might be eaten.**

6. **le financier- the muffin-shaped dessert with almonds** (Based on its name, it should be 'richer.')

7. **les Madeleines- small, shell-shaped cakes with a butter-lemon taste** (The consistency is similar to pound cake, but it's not that heavy.)

8. **le millefeuille- the thousand sheets is better known to us as "a Napoleon."** (That is the general name.) **Consisting of several layers of puff pastry alternating with cream and/or jam, it is drizzled with chocolate stripes.** (That explains how the sheets are folded.)

9. **le pain d'épice- spice bread/gingerbread: There is plenty of honey, a fair amount of aniseed and 'a snap' of ginger inside. In Reims and in Dijon, it is 'the specialty of the house.'**

10. **les petits fours- "the small ovens:" These minitreats feature alternating tiers of sponge cake and butter cream finished off with a glaze and sugared designs.** (As well as by all who see them.)

11. **la profiterole- the cream puff: Filled with vanilla ice cream, this pastry is coated with warm chocolate sauce.** (Drizzling is predicted.)

12. **la tarte Tatin: This upside-down dessert combines apples, caramelized butter and sugar.** (It corresponds to pineapple upside-down cake, but they are not 'pan pals.')

----

la bûche de Noël- the Yule log: Not listed on menus, it is likely to be seen on the table when the family returns home from Christmas Eve Mass. Shaped like a log, this sponge cake has chocolate butter cream inside and outside and might be decorated with berries and powdered sugar. (Why would Santa want a cookie?)

Bilingual Baking Basics

1. **la couche- the coating: The same word means** <u>the diaper.</u> (The first is placed on top of a baked item; the second has 'bottom' priority.)

2. **la crème renversée- the custard: Its literal translation is "upside-down cream."**

3. **sucré(e)- sweet, sugared: It 'supplements' the noun,** *le sucre.*

4. **aigre- sour:** *Le vinaigre* **is vinegar.** *Le vin aigre* **is sour wine.**

5. **flambé(e)- burning/flaming** (Adding a 5th to a dessert creates fireworks like the 4th.)

6. **le pâté feuilleté- the puffed pastry:** *La feuille* **is both** <u>the sheet of paper</u> **and** <u>the leaf.</u>

'Putting the Words in Your Mouth'- Match the letter with the description to the number of its name.

_____ 1. une poire Belle-Hélène

_____ 2. un millefeuille

_____ 3. un pain d'épice

_____ 4. une Charlotte

_____ 5. une tourte

_____ 6. un sorbet

_____ 7. un gratin des fruits rouges

_____ 8. une Madeleine

_____ 9. un clafouti

_____ 10. un canelé

_____ 11. une profiterole

_____ 12. une omelette norvégienne

_____ 13. une mousse

_____ 14. une bûche de Noël

_____ 15. une teurgoule

_____ 16. une crème caramel

_____ 17. une tarte tatin

_____ 18. un congolais

A. une crème renversée aux cerises

B. un pudding au riz et **à la cannelle (f.)- cinnamon**

C. un dessert fait des œufs, crème et chocolat

D. une soufflé aux cerises et aux framboises

E. un dessert flambé fait de meringue, glace et Grand Marnier

F. une pâtisserie feuilletée et glaceé aux couches de crème ou confiture

G. une pâtisserie remplie et couverte du chocolat

H. un dessert à l'envers aux pommes caramélisées

I. un fruit coupé, rempli de glace et couvert d'une sauce au chocolat

J. une crème renversée à une sauce caramélisée

K. un dessert froid au parfum de fruit

L. une petite pâtisserie à la crème dans le centre

M. un gâteau fait du miel et **gingembre (m.)- ginger**

N. un biscuit fait avec le noix de coco

O. un plat principal ou un dessert sucré

P. un gâteau à la crème de chocolat servi pour le Noël

Q. un petit gâteau rempli de purée de fruits ou crème renversée

R. un petit gâteau au beurre dans la forme d'une coquille

LES DIGESTIFS - After Dinner Drinks

If American after dinner drinks were not named "cordials," they could be called "polites." Sipping *un digestif* after a multicourse French meal enables people to enjoy each other's company and the ambiance for a few more minutes. Several well known cordials in the United States are *digestifs* in France. They include the coffee liqueurs, Kahlua and Tia Maria, as well as almond-flavored Amaretto and Bailey's Irish Cream. If any *Grand Marnier* is left after having flavored *le canard à l'orange* and *les crêpes Suzette*, this would be the perfect setting for guests 'to finish it off.' (Or vice versa.)

Brandies and cognacs distilled from fruits are *les eaux de vie*- the waters of life. A French favorite is *Guinettes*- cherries in brandy.

No food is served with *un digestif*, but it is an ideal time to pass around (or pass on) a cigar.

An honorable mention goes to French chocolates. *Les bonbons* let us save the best for last.

UNE REVUE DE LA NOURRITURE FRANÇAISE

'Picking at the Food'- Circle the letters of the choices that do not belong with the others.

1. a. la brioche	b. la confiture	c. le croissant	d. la tartine
2. a. le chou-fleur	b. le chou de Bruxelles	c. la choucroute	d. la chouette
3. a. les épinards	b. les pâtes	c. les nouilles	d. les spaghettis
4. a. la boulette	b. le bœuf haché	c. la dinde	d. le rosbif
5. a. le canard	b. le saucisson	c. l'oie	d. la poule
6. a. l'escargot au beurre	b. le saumon fumé	c. le flétan au citron	d. la truite meunière
7. a. la crevette	b. la langouste	c. la palourde	d. les côtelettes
8. a. au four	b. cuit à la vapeur	c. feuilleté	d. rôti
9. a. la viande	b. la volaille	c. le poisson	d. le pâté
10. a. l'apéritif	b. l'entrée	c. le repas	d. le plat principal
11. a. la sauce béarnaise	b. la sauce béchamel	c. la sauce Mornay	d. la sauce suprême
12. a. le potage parmentier	b. la crème d'artichauts	c. le velouté de châtaigne	d. le ragoût
13. a. la carte blanche	b. le bœuf bourguignon	c. les cuisses de grenouille	d. la bouillabaisse
14. a. le brugnon	b. la pastèque	c. la cacahuète	d. l'ananas
15. a. la citrouille	b. le flan	c. le pamplemousse	d. la cerise
16. a. la Choulette	b. l'Orangina	c. le Castelain	d. le Coreff
17. a. le champagne	b. le Beaujolais	c. le Chardonnay	d. le Pinot Noir
18. a. le Neufchâtel	b. le Châteaubriand	c. le Boursin	d. le Brie
19. a. le gâteau sec	b. le sorbet	c. la tarte	d. la tourte
20. a. la mousse	b. le clafouti	c. la teurgoule	d. le congolais
21. a. le financier	b. la Madeleine	c. la crème brûlée	d. le pain d'épice
22. a. la crème Chantilly	b. le millefeuille	c. les petits fours	d. les profiteroles

----

'Wrapping up the Food'- Label the statements *vrai* or *faux*.

_____ 1. Le pain perdu est la traduction pour "French toast."

_____ 2. Les gaufres sont les spécialités de la Nouvelle-Orléans.

_____ 3. La vichyssoise est une sauce française.

_____ 4. Une quiche est une tourte aux œufs et fromage.

_____ 5. On sert les crêpes sucrées comme un dessert.

_____ 6. Les crudités contiennent du thon, des anchois et des œufs.

_____ 7. L'aubergine et la courge sont deux légumes verts.

_____ 8. Le riz et le maïs sont deux féculents.

_____ 9. Le persil, l'estragon et l'ail sont les épices.

_____ 10. L'agneau, le veau et le bifteck sont le gibier.

_____ 11. La caille, le faisan et le lapin sont la volaille.

_____ 12. Les fruits de mer ont des coquilles.

_____ 13. Sanglant, à point et bien cuit sont des façons de préparer les pommes de terre.

_____ 14. La ratatouille est un sandwich fait avec du jambon et du fromage grillé.

_____ 15. Les sauces blanches et brunes contiennent du roux.

_____ 16. Le kir et le pastis sont deux vins rouges.

_____ 17. Les vols-au-vent et les barquettes sont les hors-d'œuvre.

_____ 18. Il y a des fruits de mer dans une bisque.
_____ 19. Les panades et les garbures sont des soupes claires.
_____ 20. Manger le prix fixe est plus cher que manger à la carte.
_____ 21. Le coq au vin et la poule au pot ne sont pas les entrées.
_____ 22. Les framboises, les myrtilles et les mûres sont les types de noix.
_____ 23. On produit la plupart des bières françaises près de l'Allemagne et la Belgique.
_____ 24. Le Muscadet et le Chablis sont deux vins rouges.
_____ 25. Le Roquefort et le Valençay ne sont pas faits du lait de vache.
_____ 26. D'habitude, une salade française n'est pas comme la nôtre.
_____ 27. L'omelette norvégienne, le clafouti et la teurgoule sont les pâtisseries françaises.
_____ 28. Les canelés et les éclairs au chocolat contiennent de la crème renversée.
_____ 29. Les eaux de vie sont les digestifs.
_____ 30. Les Guinettes sont faites des raisins.

LES PARTIES DU CORPS - Parts of the Body

This chapter covers and uncovers every feature of human anatomy. The idioms and comments related to the vocabulary insure that learning the terms will be a painless experience.

The Top of the 'Corps-orate' Ladder

1. la tête- the head: The first e has 'a roof over its head.'
Catchy 'Head-Lines'
a. risquer la tête- to risk one's head: The English version is "to risk one's neck." (The stakes are higher in French.)
b. gagner d'une tête- to win from (not by) a head (Either way, one is not looking at 'da-feet.')
c. avoir la tête dure- to have a hard head: A synonym is *être têtu*- to be stubborn. (Notice that it is not *tête têtue*.)
d. avoir une petite tête- to be dim-witted (The French give 'little' credit to such a person.)
e. agir sur un coup de tête- The actual translation is "to act on a blow to the head": The idea is similar to "to act on impulse." (The French person might get some 'sense knocked into' him/her.)
f. la tête-à-tête- the French/English face-to-face conversation

---

2. le visage/la figure- the face (Take the location of the French *figure* at face value!)
A Facial Expression
a. montrer son vrai visage- to show one's true colors (or to reveal what has been 'made up.')
An important note: *La figure* can also refer to a person.
Ex. George Washington et Abraham Lincoln sont deux grandes figures dans l'histoire américaine. > George Washington and Abraham Lincoln are two great figures in American history.

---

3. les cheveux- the hair: One strand is *un cheveu*. As in English, the French noun is rarely used in its singular form. (That would be 'splitting hairs.')
Sayings Adorning *les Cheveux*
a. tirer par les cheveux- to pull by the hair: The English equivalent is "to pull somebody's leg." Both idioms mean to attempt to make a far-fetched story believable.
b. arriver comme un cheveu sur la soupe- The literal translation is "to arrive like a hair on the soup." (It 'boils down to' showing up at the worst time.)

---

4. le front- the forehead (Most people must 'con-front' at least a few wrinkles on their *fronts*.)
A One-Liner with *le Front*
a. faire front aux difficultés- to face up to difficulties (Bilingually, the idioms mean that problems are dealt with 'head on.')

---

5. les yeux- the eyes: The two French words together sound much like our description of someone who is more apathetic (lazier.) *L'œil* is the singular form. (It has one i.)
Idioms Seen with *les Yeux*
a. attirer l'œil de quelqu'un- to attract one's attention, to catch someone's eye (The first step is 'to throw a glance.')

b. ne pas avoir les yeux dans la poche- not to miss a thing: The word-for-word meanng is "not to have one's eyes in the pocket."

c. à mes yeux- in my opinion: Its synonym is à *mon avis*. (A favorable impression can usually be judged from the 'ayes.')

d. coûter les yeux de la tête: "To cost the eyes from the head" is equal to our "to steal someone blind."

----

6. le nez- the nose: A person turning up his nose at an idea might vote "nay."

<u>Short 'Nasal Passages'</u>

a. rire au nez de quelqu'un- to laugh in someone's face ("Laughing in/at somebody's nose" could increase the chance that his/her temper will 'flare.')

b. fermer la porte au nez de quelqu'un- to shut the door in somebody's face

c. On a du nez- One has good instincts (Does that give him less chance of 'blowing it'?)

d. montrer le bout de son nez- to make an appearance: The real translation is "to show the end of one's nose." (Those who have been waiting will 'get the point.')

e. raccrocher au nez de quelqu'un- "to hang up on someone's nose" can be rephrased to read: "to slam the phone down on somebody" (There's a different 'tone' at the end of the conversation.)

----

7. la bouche- the mouth (It tells us what is tasteful and others what is tasteless.)

<u>Oral Presentations with *la Bouche*</u>

a. fermer la bouche- to close one's mouth: That's French for "Shut up!" (Nothing more needs to be said.)

b. parler la bouche pleine- to talk with one's mouth full (While the speaker chews what he wants to say, the others choose if they want to listen.)

c. n'avoir que ce mot à la bouche- to be all that one talks about: The exact meaning is "to have only this word in the mouth." (The speaker does not even 'give lip service' to another topic.)

d. faire la fine bouche- to turn up one's nose

e. La bouche cousue!- Don't breathe a word of it! ("The mouth sewn" does not guarantee that the listener won't share, at least, 'the thread of the conversation.')

----

8. les dents- the teeth: *La dent* is the singular form. The 'root' is exposed in <u>dentist</u>, <u>dental</u> and <u>dentures</u>.

<u>'Pearls of Wisdom' Extracted from *les Dents*</u>

a. avoir la dent- to be hungry (Said when 'a good bite' just isn't enough)

b. garder une dent contre quelqu'un- to hold a grudge against someone (It could be followed by 'chewing that person out.')

c. avoir les dents longues- to be very ambitious (That person gets 'points' for being motivated.)

d. être sur les dents- to be keyed up/to be under great pressure ("Being on one's teeth" could explain why that person feels great pressure.)

e. n'avoir rien à se mettre sous la dent = n'avoir rien à manger- "to have nothing to put under the tooth" (Hunger can't be satified by 'chewing gums.')

f. "Oeil pour œil, dent pour dent": "An eye for an eye, a tooth for a tooth:" (The wording of the proverbs 'comes out' almost the same in both languages.)

----

9. la langue- the tongue, the language: One's native tongue is one's first language. The English and French words both end with **-ngue**. (They are 'tongue-tied.')

Flavorful Idioms with _la Langue_

a. tirer la langue- to stick out one's tongue (Most people do not approve of this means of showing disapproval.)

b. avoir la langue bien pendue- to be a gossip: The word-for-word translation is "to have a well hung tongue." (The positive words with a negative connotation do not constitute a tongue twister.)

c. n'avoir pas la langue dans la poche- not to be at a loss for words: This idiom and _n'avoir pas les yeux dans la poche_- **not to miss anything have an identical form but different meanings.**

d. donner la langue au chat- to give up: The person who stops guessing 'gives his tongue to the cat.' (Neither has much to say, but the cat might have 'a scratch pad.')

e. avaler la langue- to swallow one's tongue, not to say anything (Swallowing your tongue keeps you from having 'to eat your words.')

----

10. les lèvres- the lips: _La lèvre_ is the singular form. Note the similarity in spelling and in function to **a lever.** (With that mnemonic, the word for 'lip sticks.')

Phrases Put Together with _les Lèvres_

a. la sourire aux lèvres- with a smile on one's lips (Sour is not associated with _sourire_.)

b. Son nom est sur toutes les lèvres. > His/her name is on everyone's lips. (Both phrases 'smack' of pros and cons.)

----

11. la joue- the cheek: It is related to jowls. The singular form of this noun is the first and third person singular of _jouer_; **its plural is the second person singular of the verb.** (That's a little word play for the word "play.")

A Pinch of Expressions with _les Joues_

a. joue contre joue- cheek to cheek (A 'touching' phrase in both languages.)

b. tendre l'autre joue- to turn the other cheek: _Tendre_ **means to tighten/to tense. That is exactly what someone does while maintaining a stiff upper lip.**

----

12. l'oreille (f.)- the ear: It is related to _l'oreiller_- **the pillow and** _les oreillons_- **the mumps.**

Sound Sayings with _les Oreilles_

a. tirer les oreilles à quelqu'un- to really tell someone off: The literal meaning is "to pull someone's ears." (The recipient may have also 'pulled' something.)

b. ouvrir bien les oreilles- to listen carefully (It is frequently recommended that people close their mouths while opening their ears.)

c. venir aux oreilles de quelqu'un- to come to somebody's attention (What "comes to someone's ears" will probably go further.)

d. dire quelque chose à l'oreille de quelqu'un- to speak in someone's ear: The synonym for this idiom is _chuchoter_- **to whisper.** (Things said in a low tone can reach a high volume of people.)

----

13. le sourcil- the eyebrow: The French noun shares its pronunciation with our description of a shiny, black, bruised mammal (a sore seal).

14. la paupière- the eyelid (There are no clues for the word, but it is not 'an oversight.')

15. le cil (m.)- the eyelash: The biological term for little hairs is cilia.

16. la mâchoire- the jaw: Even those who missed the action in the movie <u>Jaws</u> will feel it while pronouncing this French word.

17. le menton- the chin: The Southeastern-most city in France is Menton. If you picture a map of the country as a facial profile, Menton resembles the chin. (The name fitting the location gives it 'a double chin.')

<u>A 'Features' Presentation</u>- **Using the correct nouns from the following list, fill in the blanks: la figure/le visage, les cheveux, le front, les sourcils, le cil, l'œil, les yeux, le nez, la bouche, les lèvres, les dents, les joues, les oreilles, la mâchoire, le menton**

<u>Getting a Head Start</u>

1. la coutume- the custom

2. la fièvre- the fever

3. carré- square

4. raide- straight (for hair)

5. le cache- the eyepatch

6. épiler les poils (pincer)- to pluck little hairs

1. _____ Mlle Fatiguée les ferme avant de dormir.
2. _____ On les bouge lorsqu'on parle.
3. _____ C'est ici qu'on voit la barbe d'un homme.
4. _____ Les adultes qui en prennent soin en ont vingt-neuf.
5. _____ C'est **une coutume** de faire un vœu quand on en perd un.
6. _____ Anne Quiètée le touche pour voir si son fils a **une fièvre.**
7. _____ Nous en avons besoin pour entendre.
8. _____ Deux mots décrivent ce trait qui est rond, ovale, **carré**, etc.

9. _____ La langue et les dents sont à l'intérieur.
10. _____ On peut les avoir longs, courts, bouclés ou **raides.**
11. _____ C'est entre les yeux et la bouche. On l'utilise pour sentir.
12. _____ Cette partie du visage bouge quand on mange.
13. _____ Les pirates qui portent **un cache** en ont seulement un.
14. _____ Des femmes **épilent (pincent) ces poils** au-dessus des paupières.
15. _____ Elles deviennent rouges quand on a froid ou si on rougit.

<u>'About Face'</u>- **Circle the letters of the answers that best complete the scenarios.**

1. Mon fils vient de choisir une bague de fiançailles pour Martine. Avec les mots suivants, il me conseille de ne lui rien dire:

a. "Joue contre contre!"   b. 'Tire la langue!"   c. "Bouche cousue!"   d. "Fais un vœu!"

2. M. Passûr n'a aucune idée pourquoi son patron veut lui parler. Est-ce que le salarié va entendre de bonnes ou de mauvaises nouvelles? Il _____.

a. est sur les dents   b. rit à son nez   c. a une sourire aux lèvres   d. va lui chuchoter

3. Je suis prêt à aller à l'aéroport faire un vol. Une amie du lointain frappe à ma porte pour me rendre visite. Elle _____.

a. parle la bouche pleine   b. arrive comme un cheveu à la soupe   c. a une petite tête

d. dit quelque chose à mon oreille

4. Delphine parle constamment de Thierry, son petit ami. Elle _____.

a. fait la fine bouche   b. a du nez   c. n'a que ce mot à la bouche   d. lui tire les oreilles

5. Pour avancer dans le monde d'entreprise aujourd'hui, il faut _____.

a. tirer quelqu'un par les cheveux   b. agir sur un coup de tête   c. avaler la langue
d. avoir les dents longues

6. Si je ne veux pas répondre à mon téléphone cellulaire, je le laisse sur le comptoir. Je ne _____.

a. fais pas front aux difficultés   b. raccroche pas au nez de quelqu'un
c. ferme jamais ma bouche   d. tends plus l'autre joue

7. Uri n'a pas le temps de prendre le déjeuner aujourd'hui. Par cinq heures de l'après-midi, il _____.

a. attire l'œil de quelqu'un   b. a la langue dans la poche   c. a la dent   d. a une petite tête

8. On ne peut pas changer l'avis de quelqu'un qui a une tête dure.

a. À ses yeux, il a raison.   b. Il ferme la porte au nez de quelqu'un.   c. Il ouvre bien les oreilles.
d. Son nom est sur toutes les lèvres.

9. Alors, dites-moi! Combien de provinces y a-t-il en France?

a. Cela vient aux oreilles de quelqu'un?   b. Avez-vous la langue bien pendue?
c. Vous avez les cils bouclés?   d. Donnez-vous votre langue au chat?

10. Tu ne comprends pas comment M. Houdini fait ses tours? Tu _____.

a. risques ta tête   b. as les yeux dans ta poche   c. montres le bout de ton nez
d. as une mâchoire carrée

The Body - A Cover Story without Headlines

1. le cou- the neck: If you say the French noun twice, you get <u>crazy</u>.
<u>Expressions with 'Neck Ties'</u>
a. être en dette jusqu'au cou- to be in debt up to one's eyes/eyeballs (The French idiom enables a person to see his way out of the dilemma.)
b. être impliqué jusqu'au cou- to be in it up to one's neck (The collars are inscribed identically.)

----

2. la gorge- the throat: Our use of gorge as a small canyon 'echoes' the French view of _la gorge_.
<u>Terms Voiced with _la Gorge_</u>
a. prendre quelqu'un à la gorge- to put a gun to someone's head (Despite the lowered target, the victim can still be silenced.)
b. rester en travers de la gorge- to be hard to take, to be difficult to swallow (Things might "stay across the throat" if they don't 'go down the right way.')

----

3. l'épaule (f.)- the shoulder: _L'épaulette_, the military style shoulder tab, comes from _l'épaule_.
<u>Phrases with Shoulder Padding</u>
a. Tout repose sur vos épaules. > Everything rests on your shoulders. (The translations 'balance' one another.)
b. n'avoir pas d'épaules assez larges/solides- not to be in a strong enough financial position (If you do not have broad enough shoulders, 'extra backing' is helpful.)

----

4. le dos- the back: The related anatomical term is <u>dorsal</u>.

Idioms Supported by *le Dos*

a. avoir les cheveux dans le dos- to wear one's hair loose (Or not to engage 'the locks.')

b. y aller avec le dos de la cuiller- to do things halfway: "Going there with the back of the spoon" 'doesn't hold any water.'

c. l'avoir dans le dos- to have had it, to be fed up with something (But the French have 'the backbone' to retaliate.)

d. tomber sur le dos de quelqu'un- to drop in on somebody (If an unexpected visitor "falls on the back of someone," the unprepared host may not be 'head over heels' with the idea.)

---

5. la poitrine- the chest: This term applies to male and female anatomies. *Les seins,* the bust/the breasts, is/are a feminine feature with a masculine gender.

An Unexpanded List of Chest Expressions

a. *Elle n'a pas de poitrine*- She is flat-chested. (A nice 'booty' is not always found with 'a treasure chest.')

---

6. la taille- the waist: You could 'tie' a sash around your waist. A second meaning is <u>the height</u>. Its synonym is *la hauteur*. A third translation is <u>the size</u>. (It seems that one *taille* fits all.)

Idioms 'for Good Measure'

a. être de la même taille- to be of the same height (By deleting a couple of vowels from *taille*, you make both adjectives equally <u>tall</u>.)

b. à la taille de- to be a match for (The French score a few 'points' in the middle of the noun.)

c. avoir la taille mannequin- to have a perfect figure (Women who achieve it are no 'dummies.')

An interesting note: *Le mannequin français* is living; *le modèle* is not.

---

7. la hanche- the hip: The <u>h</u> is aspirated. (With no apostrophe, it's a 'broader' term.)

---

8. la jambe- the leg: The words *la jambe* and *le jambon* look similar. However, the first one is a gam, and the second is a ham.

Sayings That Dangle from *la Jambe*

a. faire une belle jambe!- To do a lot of good!: Both expressions have a sarcastic sense.

b. traîner la jambe- to drag one's feet: In the French version, one pulls the entire extremity but only one of them. (Each leg has 'a personal trainer.')

c. prendre ses jambes à son cou- to rush off (A person who constantly "takes his legs to his neck" becomes 'permanently pressed.')

---

9. la cuisse- the thigh: *Les cuisses de grenouille* help 'pad' this term.

---

10. le genou- the knee: <u>Genuflect</u> is a cognate. Putting an <u>x</u> on the French noun makes it plural and 'crosses its knees.'

Phrases That 'Cap-ture' *le Genou*

a. prendre quelqu'un sur les genoux- to take somebody on one's lap: Since your lap disappears when you stand, the French keep it translated as *genoux*.

b. faire du genou à quelqu'un- to play footsie with someone (The French consider this as 'a joint action' while Americans might just 'get a kick out of it.')

c. être à genoux devant quelqu'un- to idolize (In that position, it's harder 'to look up to someone.')

d. être sur les genoux- to be ready to drop (The feeling often precedes 'nightfall.')

----

11. la cheville- the ankle: The French word sounds like Ford's competitor, 'Che-vy.'

A Saying with a Twist _à la Cheville_

a. être en cheville avec quelqu'un pour faire quelque chose- to be in cahoots with somebody to do something (The French infer that what they are doing is 'lowdown.')

----

12. le pied- the foot: The French word is a cognate of <u>pedal</u>, <u>pedestrian</u> and <u>podiatrist</u>.

Idioms Based on _le Pied_

a. un coup de pied- a kick: This is an unwelcome "knock" on the foot.

b. à pied- on foot, aller à pied- to walk

c. Ce n'est pas le pied!- It's no picnic! (Both expressions infer that 'the grass could be greener.')

d. un pied noir- a French person born in Algeria

e. un pied-à-terre- a small living space away from one's primary residence (Its square footage is inconsequential.)

f. avoir bon pied bon œil- to be fit as a fiddle (The foot and the eye 'are in tune with each other.')

g. avoir les pieds sur terre- to have one's feet firmly on the ground

h. partir du bon pied- to get off to a good start, to get off on a good foot (It's probably the 'right' one.)

i. faire des pieds et des mains pour obtenir quelque chose- to move heaven and earth in order to get something (Said when 'the sky is the limit.')

----

13. le talon- the heel: As a parallel to English, the French noun refers to <u>the end of a loaf</u> and to <u>the bottom of a loafer</u>.

An Expression Heightened by _le Talon_

a. être sur les talons de quelqu'un- to be hot on the heels of someone (Catching the person would help the 'elevated' crime rate.)

----

14. l'orteil (m.)- the toe: So as not to confuse this word with _l'oreille_, remember that <u>t</u> is for <u>toe</u>.

----

15. le bras- the arm: Think of <u>embrace</u> to join the two nouns!

Phrases Linked by _les Bras_

a. bras dessus, bras dessous- arm in arm: The exact meaning, "arm over, arm under," explains how _les bras_ are 'hooked.'

b. en bras de chemise- in shirt sleeves (The trunk is covered, but the limbs are half bare.)

c. lever les bras au ciel- to throw up one's arms to heaven (The English version is really tough on the digestive tract.)

----

16. le coude- the elbow: This word needs more 'elbow room' than _le cou_.

Phrases that Rest on _les Coudes_

a. donner un coup de coude à quelqu'un- to nudge somebody. As the <u>p</u> is not pronounced, _coup de_ and _coude_ sound the same.

b. avoir/garder quelque chose sous le coude- to have/to keep something handy (This expression might strike English speakers as 'humer-us.')

---

17. le poignet- the wrist and part of *la poignée de porte*- the doorknob share the same pronunciation. (The two meanings 'take turns.')

---

18. la main- the hand: <u>Manicure</u>, <u>manual</u> and <u>manufacture</u> are hand-me-downs from *la main*.
<u>Idioms with 'a Show of Hands'</u>
a. donner la main à quelqu'un- to hold someone's hand: Notice that the French meaning is neither to applaud nor to help!
b. être adroit de ses mains- to be clever with one's hands: The French idiom includes <u>of</u> rather than <u>with</u>. (The *de* is for dexterity.)
c. porter la main sur quelqu'un- to lay a hand on someone (*Porter* implies that the act 'leaves an impression.')
d. Les mains en l'air!- Hands up! (Its dual warning is to put 'the arms' down.)
e. demander la main de quelqu'une- to ask for someone's hand in marriage (Several other body parts are included in the deal.)
f. avoir la main heureuse- to be lucky: Its synonym is *avoir de la chance*. (You may have 'a happy hand' because Lady Luck has a smiling face.)
g. avoir la main verte- to have a green thumb (The French do not 'weed out' just the thumb to do the gardening.)
h. à la main- by hand: This phrase is part of *écrit à la main*- handwritten, *fait à la main*- handmade and *cousu à la main*- handsewn. (They all feature 'a hands on' activity but not necessarily a 'handsome' reward.)
i. avoir un tour de main/un don pour faire quelque chose- to have a knack for doing something

---

19. le doigt- the finger: The French noun is related to <u>digit</u>. *L'orteil* and *le doigt de pied* are <u>the toe</u>. ('Count on' *les doigts* for being versatile!)
<u>Expressions Tapped from *le Doigt*</u>
a. montrer quelqu'un du doigt- to blame someone: The precise translation is "to show someone <u>some</u> finger." (You get 'the point.')
b. être à un/deux doigt(s) de faire quelque chose- to be very close to doing something (Success is a matter of extending oneself a bit more.)
c. gagner les doigts dans le nez- to win hands down (A person might "win the fingers in the nose," but who wants the prize?)

---

20. le pouce- the thumb
<u>An interesting fact:</u> *Un pouce* is also <u>an inch</u>. The measurement is taken from the middle to the the top of the thumb. (Give someone an inch, and he'll take a thumb.)

---

21. l'ongle (m.)- the nail: *L'ongle du pied* is <u>the toenail</u>. *Le clou*- <u>the carpentry nail</u> shouldn't be confused with *l'ongle* even if one has 'hammer toes.'

'Available Transplants'- **Put the nouns from the following list beside the correct numbers on the picture: la cheville, le cœur, le cou, le coude, la cuisse, le doigt, l'épaule, le front, le genou, la gorge, la hanche, la jambe, la joue, la langue, les lèvres, la main, le menton, l'œil, l'oreille, l'orteil, le pied, le poignet, le pouce, le poumon, la taille, le talon**

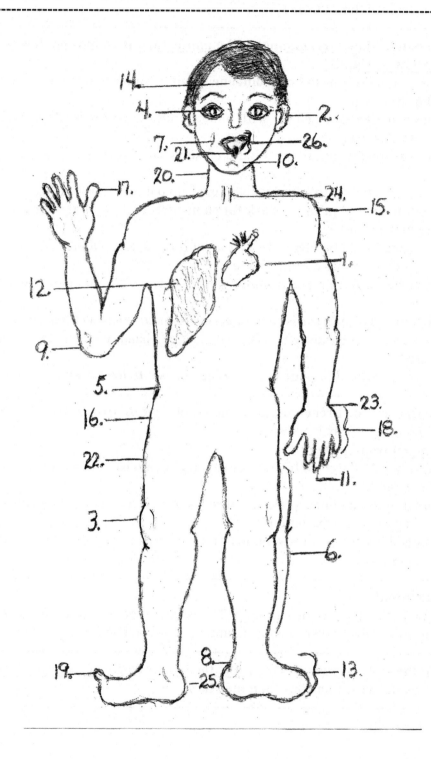

'Body Parts- The Assembly Line'- Match the letters to the numbers to make full sentences.

_____ 1. le cou	A. est entre la gorge et la taille
_____ 2. la gorge	B. sont à l'arrière des pieds et au-dessous des chevilles
_____ 3. les épaules	C. est en haut de la jambe
_____ 4. le dos	D. est où on porte une montre ou un bracelet
_____ 5. la poitrine	E. est au milieu de la jambe entre la cuisse et la cheville
_____ 6. les seins	F. sont nécessaires pour jouer des instruments
_____ 7. la taille	G. a une colonne vertébrale dedans
_____ 8. la hanche	H. sont coupés de temps en temps
_____ 9. les jambes	I. sont où on porte les chaussettes et les chaussures
_____ 10. le genou	J. est où on porte un col ou une cravate
_____ 11. les chevilles	K. sont à côté des doigts
_____ 12. les pieds	L. sont d'habitude plus larges sur des hommes
_____ 13. les talons	M. sont où les femmes portent des soutien-gorge
_____ 14. les orteils	N. est une partie du bras entre l'épaule et le poignet
_____ 15. le coude	O. sont en haut des pieds
_____ 16. le poignet	P. sont utiles pour tenir des choses
_____ 17. les mains	Q. est entre la bouche et la poitrine
_____ 18. les doigts	R. sont longues et nécessaires pour marcher et courir
_____ 19. les pouces	S. est où on porte une ceinture
_____ 20. les ongles	T. sont aussi les doigts de pieds

'Using Body Language'- Circle the letters of the answers that best complete the scenarios.

Du Vocabulaire de l'Exercice
1. en couverture- on the cover
2. la carrière- the career
3. tailler- to sharpen, to trim

4. les bulletins scolaires (m.)- the report cards
5. le but- the goal

1. Madame Seplaint dit à son mari, "Tu es paresseux. C'est moi qui fais tout le travail, et ____.
a. j'ai les cheveux dans le dos."
b. nous ne sommes pas de la même taille."
c. tout repose sur mes épaules."
d. tu es à genoux devant moi."

2. Aussitôt qu'il ne pleut plus, le fils ferme les fenêtres de sa voiture. Sa mère répond, ____!
a. "Tu as les pieds sur terre."
b. "Cela fait une belle jambe!"
c. "Tu es sur les talons de quelqu'un."
d. "Les mains en l'air!"

3. Ma tante rend visite à son médecin. Il lui annonce, ____.
a. "Vous êtes en dette jusqu'au cou."
b. "Il me reste en travers de la gorge."
c. "Vous êtes adroite de vos mains."
d. "Vous avez bon pied bon œil."

4. Les jeunes femmes que nous voyons **en couverture** de Vogue font des exercices, et elles suivent des régimes. Pour ça, elles ____.
a. l'ont dans le dos
b. sont en cheville avec quelqu'un
c. ont la taille mannequin
d. prennent quelqu'un à la gorge

5. Gabby n'entre pas même dans sa salle de bain sans son téléphone cellulaire. Cette femme ____.
a. le garde toujours sous le coude
b. a un tour de main pour le faire
c. me montre du doigt

d. est impliquée jusqu'au cou

6. M. et Mme Pasassez veulent acheter une maison, mais le banquier leur dit, ____.
   a. "Madame, vous n'avez pas de poitrine."   b. "Vous n'avez pas d'épaules assez larges."
   c. "Vous êtes des pieds noirs."   d. "N'y allez pas avec le dos de la cuiller."

7. Je demande à ma voisine comment elle arrive à jongler son temps entre **sa carrière** et sa famille. Elle me répond, ____.
   a. "Je tombe sur le dos de tout le monde."   b. "Je traîne la jambe."   c. "Ce n'est pas le pied."
   d. "Je **taille** souvent mes crayons."

8. Qui n'adore pas voir les amoureux qui promènent par la Seine? Ils sont toujours ____.
   a. avec un coup de pied   b. bras dessus, bras dessous   c. à un doigt de faire quelque chose
   d. en bras de chemise

9. Mlle Pressée prépare tout à l'avance pour le jour suivant. Le matin elle doit ____.
   a. être sur les genoux   b. lever les bras au ciel   c. prendre les jambes au cou
   d. gagner les doigts dans le nez

10. Pour aider une personne très occupée, on peut dire simplement ____.
    a. "Je porte la main sur quelqu'un?"   b. "Avez-vous la main verte?"
    c. "Je vous prends sur mes genoux?"   d. "Puis-je faire quelque chose pour vous?"

11. Anne et son frère sont très fiers. Ils viennent de recevoir leurs premiers **bulletins scolaires**, et ils ont des notes supérieures. Ces élèves-là ____.
    a. font du genou à quelqu'un   b. partent du bon pied   c. ont des bras croisés
    d. donnent les mains à leurs parents

12. L'ambition est une qualité admirable. Quand un tel individu a **un but**, il ____.
    a. a la main heureuse   b. est à la taille de l'autre   c. fait tout à la main
    d. fait des pieds et des mains pour l'obtenir

The Inside Story - Vital Organs and More

1. le crâne- the skull: Most of this word is encased inside <u>cranium</u>.
<u>An interesting note</u>: *La tête de mort*- "the head of death" is <u>the skull and crossbones.</u> (Ironically, the insignia indicates 'a no crossing zone.')

----

2. le cerveau- the brain (The CEO of the body is on top because of 'the right connections.')
<u>An Expression with 'a Brain Stem'</u>
a. faire travailler votre cerveau- to use your brain (It entails taking 'the nap' out of synapse.)

----

3. le cœur- the heart (Only surgeons and those in love are allowed into its 'chambers.')
<u>Sayings That Come from</u> *le Cœur*
a. connaître par cœur- to know by heart (And not to skip a beat)
b. de bon cœur- heartily, willingly (Without any high pressure)
c. de tout cœur- from the bottom of one's heart (Is that the location of deep feelings?)
d. avoir un cœur d'or- to have a heart of gold (Both sayings reflect a 'shining' quality.)
e. en avoir le cœur net- to be clear about it in one's mind (French and English thought processes function at different junctions.)

f. avoir quelque chose sur le cœur- to have something on one's mind (This would be a good time to have 'a heart to mind' talk.)

g. "Loin des yeux, loin du cœur"- "Out of sight, out of mind": The actual French translation is "Far from the eyes, far from the heart." (Neither proverb is very far off.)

h. avoir un coup de cœur pour quelqu'un- to fall in love with someone (If a lover inflicts "a blow to the heart," are there grounds for 'cardiac arrest'?) *Tomber amoureux(se) de quelqu'un(e)* **has the same meaning.**

----

4. le poumon- the lung: <u>Pulmonary</u> is derived from this word.
<u>An Idiom That Airs Out</u> *les Poumons*
4a. Votre région est le poumon économique du pays. > Your region is the economic heart of the country. Just as French exchanges a heart for a lung, *économique* can be replaced by *financier*-financial, *agricole*- agricultural, etc. (The expression leaves 'breathing room' for other adjectives.)

----

5. la rate- the spleen (Does a quick tempered person have 'a mean spleen'?)
6. l'abdomen (m.)- the abdomen (The French and English nouns have a 'tight' connection.)

----

7. l'estomac (m.)- the stomach: The <u>c</u> in *estomac* is uncustomarily silent. (However, when you're very hungry, you can hear it gurgle.)
8. le ventre- the abdomen, the stomach, the tummy (*Le ventre* is 'full' of translations.)
<u>Tummy Phrases That Stick out</u>
a. avoir mal au ventre- to have a stomach ache (It is unrelated to 'a gut reaction.')
b. avoir quelque chose dans le ventre- to have something on one's mind (In both of these idioms, 'food for thought' is being tossed around.) **Its synonym is *avoir quelque chose sur le cœur*.**

----

9. l'intestin (m.)- the intestine: The English word has 'a loop' at the end.
10. le foie- the liver: *Le pâté de foie* was served in the preceding chapter. (This is not *la première fois* that you have seen *le foie*.)

----

11. le rein- the kidney: This word is similar in spelling to both *la reine* and *rien*.
Ex. La reine aux mauvais reins ne fait rien sauf s'asseoir sur **le trône.** > The queen with bad kidneys does nothing but sit on **the throne.**
<u>A Pair of Kidney Expressions</u>
a. *Ses cheveux tombent sur les reins.* > Her hair comes down to her waist. (When she 'looks back on it,' she probably wishes that she had pinned it up.)
b. n'avoir pas les reins assez solides- not to be in a strong financial position (Could the lender be 'a kidney donor'?) *N'avoir pas les épaules assez solides* **is synonymous with this idiom.**

----

12. la vessie- the bladder: Associate the French word with <u>vessel</u>, and ask yourself whether it is half-full or half-empty!
13. les organes génitaux- the genitals (The French and English nouns are on 'intimate' terms.)
14. le squelette- the skeleton: "A skeleton in the closet" is closely connected to *un cadavre dans le placard*- a cadaver in the cabinet. ('Bone china' might be found there.)

----

15. le(s) os- the bone(s). <u>Osteopath</u> and <u>osteoporosis</u> are two of its cognates. Notice *os* in *le dos!*
<u>Sayings with Unburied Bones</u>
a. trempé jusqu'aux os- soaked to the skin (It's the result of 'pelting' rain)
b. Il y a un os- There's a snag/problem (Could it be referred to as 'a bone spur'?)

---

16. la côte- the rib (Liver with ribs on the side is found on an anatomical menu.)

---

17. la peau- the skin: *L'eau* and *la peau* are rare feminine gender words ending with *-eau.*
<u>Idioms Found under *la Peau*</u>
a. faire peau neuve- to adapt a new image (One must shed the old one first.)
b. être bien dans sa peau- to be happy with oneself: If an individual is "well in his skin," things are going smoothly. But a person *mal dans sa peau* needs to make adjustments.
c. se mettre dans la peau de quelqu'un- to put oneself in someone else's place/shoes (French requests a soul transfer; English asks for a sole exchange.)

---

18. la chair- the flesh: The French noun shows its reserved seating on *les os.*
<u>Expressions That Reveal *la Chair*</u>
a. avoir la chair de poule- to have goose bumps (Although hen and the goose feathers are 'on the rise,' the swan's is 'down.')
b. bien en chair- plump: Those who are *bien en chair* aren't necessarily *bien dans leur peau*. (It is not always a 'fitting' conclusion.)

---

19. l'artère (f.)- the artery (It is for 'northbound traffic' only.) *La grande artère* **is the main road.**

---

20. la veine- the vein: As opposed to *les artères, les veines* are southbound. (You cannot speak of both 'in the same vein.')
<u>An Idiom Carried by *les Veines*</u>
a. être en veine- to be "on a roll" (This surprising translation comes from 'out of the blue.')

---

21. le muscle- the muscle (The nouns 'work out' the same; the pronunciation has a different 'tone.'

---

22. le nerf- the nerve, the tendon: Bilingually, the terms often touch on psychological strength.
<u>A Small Bundle of Axioms Containing *les Nerfs*</u>
a. une attaque de nerfs- a nervous attack (One symptom is 'a-fraid' nerve.)
b. avoir les nerfs fragiles- to be high-strung (Such a person is 'tightly wired.')
c. être sur les nerfs- to be all keyed up (The cure might be 'to let it all out.')
Être sur les dents and *être sur les nerfs* **are synonyms.** (A root canal is a painful reminder.)
d. donner/porter/taper sur les nerfs de quelqu'un- to get on someone's nerves. *Taper* **is** <u>to tap</u>**,** <u>to knock</u>**,** <u>to slap</u>**.**

---

23. le sang- the blood (Is Sangria Dracula's favorite drink?)
<u>Sayings from Which *du Sang* Can Be Taken</u>
a. le sang froid- the calm/the cold blood: Used in both languages, the phrase connotes nerve or courage in 'a positive vein.' One who *garde son sang froid*, **keeps his cool. Conversely, a person**

who *perd son sang froid* loses it. The worst is *faire quelque chose de sang froid-* **to do something in cold blood.**

b. avoir du sang dans les veines- to have courage (The description fits someone who does not just 'go with the flow.')

c. avoir quelque chose dans le sang- to have something in one's blood (The sayings can be 'transfused' from one language to another.)

----

24. la sueur- the sweat (Since this noun is feminine, a more appropriate translation might be 'beads of perspiration.')

25. la larme- the tear: *L'alarme-* **the distress signal** is more alarming than *les larmes.*

Very important notes

1. A form of *avoir* + *mal/une douleur* + a contraction + a body part expresses what hurts, pains or aches. The literal translation is "to have hurt/pain in the ____."

Ex. Andy Hertz ne fait pas attention en classe aujourd'hui parce qu'il a mal au ventre. > Andy Hertz is not paying attention in class today because he has a stomach ache.

2. Qu'as-tu?, Qu'est-ce que tu as?, Qu'avez-vous?, and Qu'est-ce que vous avez? are four ways to ask, "What do you have?" and "What is the matter with you?"

2a. A medical problem prompts the response, "J'ai mal + a contraction + a body part."

Ex. J'ai mal à la gorge. > I have a sore throat.

'A Delicate Operation'- Remove the letters of the answers that do not fit in the groups.

1. a. l'abdomen	b. la peau	c. l'estomac	d. le ventre
2. a. la gorge	b. le dos	c. la poitrine	d. les seins
3. a. les cheveux	b. les cils	c. les sourcils	d. les lèvres
4. a. les reins	b. le foie	c. les neufs	d. les poumons
5. a. la vessie	b. le crâne	c. la côte	d. le squelette
6. a. le sang	b. la larme	c. la chair	d. la sueur
7. a. le genou	b. la rate	c. le poignet	d. le coude
8. a. la veine	b. le cœur	c. la paupière	d. l'artère
9. a. les mains	b. les jambes	c. les pieds	d. les joues
10. a. les clous	b. les cheveux	c. les dents	d. les ongles

Are These Sentences Anatomically Correct? - Label the statements *vrai* or *faux.*

_____ 1. Le cerveau est à l'intérieur du crâne.

_____ 2. Il y a des os dans le cœur.

_____ 3. Les intestins sont une partie de la vessie.

_____ 4. Il n'y a pas de chair sur les poumons.

_____ 5. Les artères et les veines sont partout dans le corps.

_____ 6. Le foie et les reins ne sont pas des organes vitaux.

_____ 7. On a des muscles dans l'estomac.

_____ 8. Il y a du sang dans les nerfs.

_____ 9. Les organes génitaux contiennent des larmes.

_____ 10. La sueur ne vient pas des yeux.

_____ 11. La rate est dans l'arrière partie du corps.
_____ 12. Les artères portent le sang au cœur, et les veines le portent du cœur.
_____ 13. Le cerveau a seulement une partie.
_____ 14. Les animaux n'ont pas de côtes.
_____ 15. Tout le monde a un squelette.
_____ 16. L'abdomen et le ventre sont des synonymes.

'Every Body's Business'- **Circle the letters of the correct answers to complete the scenarios.**

1. Quand Mme Cœur d'Or entend que quelqu'un dans le voisinage ne va pas bien, elle lui apporte de la soupe. Elle ____.

a. attire l'œil de quelqu'un
b. arrive comme un cheveu sur la soupe
c. est très attentionnée aux autres
d. sait précisément ce qu'elle fait

2. L'élève demande à sa maîtresse, "Que veut dire connaître par cœur?" Elle lui explique, "C'est une façon de dire qu'on ____."

a. a mal au ventre
b. montre son vrai visage
c. n'a pas la bonne circulation
d. apprend quelque chose mot pour mot

3. Quand Maurice n'arrive pas à répondre aux questions faciles, sa mère lui suggère, "Fais travailler ton cerveau." Elle veut dire ____!

a. Tombe amoureux de quelqu'un!
b. Utilise ton intelligence!
c. Montre le bout de ton nez!
d. Tire ta langue!

4. M. Cranquebille va de banque en banque emprunter de l'argent. On lui répète ces phrases, "Vous n'avez pas les épaules assez solides," et "Vous n'avez pas les reins assez solides." Ces personnes-là veulent dire que ____.

a. son compte financier n'est pas bon
b. M. Cranquebille porte sur leurs nerfs
c. cet homme doit remplacer sa vessie
d. le prêteur a mal à la rate

5. La pauvre Iseult! Son petit ami déménage à une autre ville, et elle n'a pas de nouvelles de lui. Ses amis mentionnent cette phrase, "Loin des yeux, loin du cœur" parce que (qu') ____.

a. son flirt lui offre une tête de mort
b. Iseult n'a pas de poitrine.
c. on oublie quelqu'un qui n'est pas proche.
d. le jeune homme est très têtu.

6. Les Rainier portent leurs imperméables pendant **l'orage (m.)- the thunderstorm**. Néanmoins, ils sont trempés jusqu'aux os. Ces gens ____.

a. pleurent des larmes de crocodile
b. finissent ce qu'ils sont en train de faire
c. font peau neuve
d. sont très mouillés à cause de la pluie

7. Des petits enfants n'ont pas la chair de poule quand ils voient des étrangers déguisés le 31 octobre. Pourquoi ces très jeunes ____?

a. sont-ils sur les talons de quelqu'un
b. n'ont-ils pas peur d'eux
c. savent-ils qu'il y a un os
d. portent-ils la main sur leurs parents

8. Comme sa tante ne fait pas attention à ce qu'il dit, Henri lui demande si elle a quelque chose sur le cœur. Elle lui explique que/qu' ____.

a. l'alarme vient de sonner
b. la grande artère en ville est fermée
c. elle a bon pied bon œil
d. elle est préoccupée

9. En parlant à sa classe de géographie, le prof Lescartes explique que Paris est le poumon gouverne-mental de la France. C'est-a-dire: ____.

a. On y fait des décisions politiques
b. Je donne ma langue au chat

c. Votre mère est bien en chair   d. Ouvrez bien les oreilles! Je vais vous chuchoter

10. Annette Honnête parle toujours de tout cœur. Tout le monde sait qu'elle _____.

a. ne dit jamais "non"   b. exprime bien ses sentiments   c. doit couvrir ses organes genitaux

d. a quelque chose dans son sang

11. Mme Prêteàcrier échange des mots très durs avec son patron, et à la fin de la journée, elle est sur les nerfs. Cette femme _____.

a. a un cadavre dans son placard   b. tue du monde de sang froid   c. n'est pas du tout calme

d. prend son patron sur ses genoux

12. Avant de juger une personne, on doit se mettre dans sa peau. Cela veut dire "_____."

a. Tirez les oreilles à cette personne!   b. Gardez une dent contre lui!

c. Ayez la langue bien pendue!   d. Essayez de comprendre l'autre individu!

le Baiser par Auguste Rodin (le Musée Rodin, Paris)

LE RIRE EST BON POUR VOUS - Laughter Is Good For You

1. **le médecin généraliste**- the general doctor/physician
2. **baisser la tension artérielle**- to lower blood pressure
3. **en outre**- furthermore
4. **l'ordonnance (f.)**- the prescription
5. **les services médicaux**- the medical services, the medical care

Le docteur Rigoler, un médecin généraliste, a un grand sens de l'humour. Même les malades rient quand il leur parle. Le docteur amusant est sûr qu'un bon rire **baisse la tension artérielle** et soulage le stress. **En outre, son ordonnance** ne coûte rien. Ce bon homme dit que ses plaisanteries sont son idée **des services médicaux** gratuits.

Rencontrez ses patients et lisez ce qu'il leur suggère!

#1
1. **supporter une injection**- to put up with/withstand a needle

Le docteur Rigoler: Bonjour, mon brave homme. Tu es ici pour passer un examen médical. Est-ce que tu as l'intention de jouer aux sports?

Le jeune homme: Bonjour Docteur Rigoler. Oui, le soccer si je peux **supporter une injection.** On va prendre mon sang?

Le docteur Rigoler: Bien sûr, et nous ne le rendons pas. Une infirmière va prendre ton pouls aussi, mais elle ne va pas le garder.

Le jeune homme: Au moins, c'est meilleur que la chirurgie dans un hôpital.

Le docteur Rigoler: Il y une opération ici. Nous t'enlevons ton argent à la fin de la visite.

#2
1. **Ça se voit**- It's obvious
2. **être enrhumé**- to have a cold
3. **les médicaments sans ordonnance**- the over-the-counter drugs
4. **tousser**-to cough

5. **avoir la grippe**- to have the flu
6. **faire une remise**- to give a discount

Le docteur Rigoler: Bonjour Madame Lapin. Il ne faut pas demander ce que vous avez. **Ça se voit** de vos yeux rouges que **vous êtes enrhumée.**

Mme Lapin: Bonjour Docteur Rigoler. **Les médicaments sans ordonnance** que je trouve dans ma pharmacie ne m'aident pas. Je **tousse** et j'éternue toute la journée.

Le docteur Rigoler: Vous y connaissez les pharmacistes, par hasard? Disons que leurs clients ont **la grippe** ou un rhume contagieux! S'ils prennent un rendez-vous ici, je peux vous **faire une remise.**

Mme Lapin: Quelle idée ingénieuse!

Le docteur Rigoler: Je vous donne une ordonnance plus forte et cette suggestion: Buvez beaucoup de liquides, et restez au lit! Je sais qu'il est difficile de faire tous les deux en même temps.

Mme Lapin: Je vais déjà mieux.

Le docteur Rigoler: Mission accomplie!

#3

1. exerçant- practicing
2. le diagnostic- the diagnosis
3. de brûlure- burning

M. Encolère: C'est ma deuxième visite cette semaine, et j'ai encore mal à la poitrine.
Le docteur Rigoler: Je suis désolé. Je suis un médecin **exerçant.** Pour ça, je ne suis toujours correct avec **mon** premier **diagnostic.**
M. Encolère: Je suis à la Comédie Française? J'ai une sensation **de brûlure** dans mes poumons.
Le docteur Rigoler: C'est parce que vous fumez trop. Buvez beaucoup d'eau pour fumer moins!
M. Encolère: Merci pour votre conseil très unique.

#4

1. prendre du poids = grossir- to gain weight
2. tricher- to cheat
3. l'horaire serré- the tight schedule
4. C'est du gâteau.- "It's a piece of cake."
5. quant à- as for

Le docteur Rigoler: Bonjour Madame Prendplus.
Mme Prendplus: Ça ne va pas bien. Je dois vous admettre que je **prends du poids.**
Le docteur Rigoler: On qui continue à **tricher** au régime passe ses examens à la clinique.
Mme Prendplus: Mais monsieur, vous savez bien que j'ai une mauvaise thyroïde. Alors, je ne perds rien sauf mes cheveux.
Le docteur Rigoler: Bien sûr, ma bonne femme. Cependant, un deuxième problème est la nourriture que vous mangez vous fait grossir. Je comprends bien qu'il est difficile de suivre un régime.
Mme Prendplus: Que faites-vous pour rester en forme?
Le docteur Rigoler: Avec **mon horaire serré, c'est du gâteau.**
Mme Prendplus: Quant à moi, cela doit être un fruit.

#5

1. le boucher- the butcher
2. autant que- as long as
3. se plaindre- to complain
4. les points de suture (m.)- the stitches
5. le groupe sanguin/le type de sang- the blood type

Le docteur Rigoler: Bonjour Frédéric. Nous avons un rendez-vous demain au Club Meds.
M. Coupertôt: Quel nom pour un hôpital!
Le docteur Rigoler: Selon ton chirurgien, **le** docteur **Boucher,** tu as des questions à me poser.
M. Coupertôt: Qu'est-ce qui va être mon état après l'opération? Un état critique?
Le docteur Rigoler: Tu vas être critique **autant que tu te plains** des repas et des infirmières.
M. Coupertôt: Ne me fais pas rire lorsque j'ai **des points de suture,** s'il te plaît! Au fait, ça me fait penser à une question. Quel est **mon groupe sanguin**?
Le docteur Rigoler: C'est O négatif, mais sois positif!

#6

1. l'arthrite- the arthritis
2. faire mal- to be painful
3. Reposez-vous les pieds!- Rest your feet!/Keep your feet up!

Le docteur Rigoler: Est-ce que Babette est prête à m'accompagner au bal?

Mme Éclopée: Tu es quarante ans trop tard, mon prince. **Mon arthrite** me **fait** très **mal**. Je ne peux plus supporter la douleur dans mes genoux et dans mes chevilles. Qu'est-ce que je dois prendre?

Le docteur Rigoler: Évidemment, ton temps.

Mme Éclopée: Mon spécialiste d'arthrite me dit si souvent, **"Reposez-vous les pieds** et faites beaucoup d'exercices!" Comment puis-je faire tous les deux?

Le docteur Rigoler: Si tu acceptes un boulot avec le Cirque du Soleil?

Mme Éclopée: Tu dois accepter un travail comme un comique.

#7

1. reculer- to turn back the clock
2. voudriez-vous?- would you like?
3. les rides (f.)- the wrinkles
4. les comprimés (m.)- the tablets
5. la salle d'attente- the waiting room
6. le lifting- the face lift
7. remonter le morale- to lift the spirits
8. confirmer- to firm up

Le docteur Rigoler: Madame Reculer, c'est un plaisir de faire votre connaissance. **Voudriez-vous** me dire la raison de votre visite aujourd'hui?

Mme Reculer: Toutes **ces rides** sur mon visage et sur mon cou me concernent.

Le docteur Rigoler: Pour ces rides-là, je recommande des **comprimés** de fer.

Mme Reculer: Je viens de rencontrer Madame Éclopée dans **la salle d'attente.** Je sais que vous êtes très amusant mais qu'il est facile de vous parler aussi.

Le docteur Rigoler: Vraiment? Voudriez-vous partager cette opinion avec ma femme?

Mme Reculer: Docteur Rigoler, je pense à **un lifting** pour **remonter mon morale.**

Le docteur Rigoler: C'est un coup sûr qu'une telle opération lève plus que cela.

Mme Reculer: Comment vous me conseillez?

Le docteur Rigoler: Ma secrétaire peut vous donner le nom d'un spécialiste. Vous devez le contacter et **confirmer** tout.

#8

1. clopiner- to hobble
2. l'entorse (f.)- the sprain
3. une radiographie- an x-ray
4. les dessous de l'histoire- the inside story
5. grimper une échelle- to climb a ladder
6. dura- will last
7. dans le plâtre- in a cast
8. l'assurance médicale- the medical coverage
9. les béquilles (f.)- the crutches

Le docteur Rigoler: Mon pauvre jeune homme, qu'as-tu?

Le jeune M. Clopiner: Je ne sais pas si c'est une fracture ou **une entorse.**

Le docteur Rigoler: Une radiographie de la jambe va nous dire **les dessous de l'histoire!**

Le jeune M. Clopiner: Grimper une échelle me porte plus de malchance que marcher sous cela.

Le docteur Rigoler: Mais, il vaut mieux casser une jambe qu'un miroir. Ta malchance ne **dura** pas sept années.

Le jeune M. Clopiner: Oui, mais ... Je vais avoir la jambe **dans le plâtre**?

Le docteur Rigoler: Certainement. Considère-le comme **assurance médicale**! Tu vas avoir besoin des **béquilles** aussi.

Le jeune M. Clopiner: Pour combien de temps?

Le docteur Rigoler: Jusqu'à ce que tu aies les pieds sur terre.

#9

1. **mal à l'aise**- uncomfortable
2. **privé**- personal, private
3. **le laisser libre cours**- to get it out of one's system
4. **le son**- the bran
5. **assis**- seated

Le docteur Rigoler: Bonjour Léon. Tu parais **mal à l'aise**.

M. Pasaller: Tu as raison Docteur. Il est nécessaire que je discute un problème **privé** avec toi.

Le docteur Rigoler: Je ne suis pas surpris. Le bruit court que toi et ma femme .....

M. Pasaller: Docteur, c'est la constipation dont je te parle.

Le docteur Rigoler: Il faut **le laisser libre cours**. Tu manges assez de fruits et légumes?

M. Pasaller: Bien sûr! Même **du son**.

Le docteur Rigoler: Alors, on peut éliminer ça. Qu'est-ce que tu fais pour l'exercice? Évidemment, tu es assis souvent.

M. Pasaller: De temps en temps, j'ai envie de courir.

Le docteur Rigoler: En ce cas là, tu vas aller mieux bientôt. Continue à prendre ton bon son Léon!

#10

1. **grâce à**- thanks to
2. **quotidien**- daily
3. **de même**- likewise
4. **l'audiophone (m.)**- the hearing aid
5. **Comment?**- What?

Le docteur Rigoler: François, comment allez-vous?

M. Tantdans: Grâce à ma bonne attitude et mon jus de pruneau **quotidien**, je vais plutôt bien. Je te rends visite juste pour dire bonjour.

Le docteur Rigoler: C'est si bon de vous revoir.

M. Tantdans: Quel dommage! Même avec mes lunettes, je ne peux pas te dire **de même**.

Le docteur Rigoler: Ça marche bien, **votre audiophone** neuf?

M. Tantdans: Comment?

Le docteur Rigoler: Vous ne changez jamais, François.

M. Tantdans: Mais si! Plusieurs fois chaque jour. Tu sais ce que je veux dire.

Le docteur Rigoler: François, n'oubliez pas que vous fêtez votre quatre-vingt-dixième anniversaire la semaine prochaine!

M. Tantdans: J'oublie tout, Docteur Plaisanterie.

'A Checkup'- <u>Écrivez des réponses complètes en français aux questions suivantes.</u>

1. Selon le docteur Rigoler, quels sont deux effets d'un bon rire? _____

_____.

2. Pourquoi dit-il qu'il contribue aux services médicaux gratuits? _____

_____.

3. **From #1.** Pourquoi le jeune homme est-il au bureau du docteur Rigoler? _____

_____.

4. De quoi le jeune homme a-t-il peur? _____

_____.

5. Quelles trois choses prend-on du jeune homme? _____

_____.

6. **From #2.** Pourquoi est-ce qu'elle s'appelle Mme Lapin? _____

_____.

7. Quelles sont deux indications qu'elle est enrhumée? _____

_____.

8. Selon le docteur Rigoler, quels sont les avantages d'une maladie contagieuse? _____

_____

_____.

9. **From #3.** Qu'est-ce que M. Encolère a? _____

_____.

10. Pourquoi le premier diagnostic du docteur Rigoler n'est-il pas toujours correct? _____

_____.

11. Que le médecin suggère-t-il pour soulager la sensation de brûlure de M. Encolère? _____

_____.

12. **From #4.** Où Mme Prendplus va-t-elle passer ses examens si elle continue à grossir? _____

_____.

13. Quels deux problèmes a-t-elle? _____

_____.

14. Pourquoi le docteur Rigoler peut-il rester en forme facilement? _____

_____.

15. **From #5.** Frédéric Coupertôt va au Club Meds demain? _____

_____.

16. Quel est le nom du chirurgien de M. Coupertôt? _____

_____.

17. Comment le docteur Rigoler répond-il quand Frédéric lui demande son type de sang? _____

_____.

18. **From #6.** Quelle est la première question que le médecin pose à Babette Éclopée? _____

_____.

19. Qu'est-ce qui lui fait mal? _____

_____.

20. Pourquoi ne peut-elle pas prendre les conseils de son spécialiste? _____

_____.

21. **From #7.** Qu'est-ce qui concerne Mme Reculer? _____

_____.

22. Que le docteur Rigoler lui recommande-t-il? _____
_____.

23. À quoi pense-t-elle et pourquoi le considère-t-elle? _____
_____.

24. **From #8.** Qu'est-ce qui va confirmer si M. Clopiner a une fracture ou une entorse? _____
_____.

25. Quelles deux choses sont nécessaires pour aider le jeune M. Clopiner? _____
_____.

26. Quand le patient va-t-il savoir que tout va bien? _____
_____.

27. **From #9.** M. Pasaller est l'amoureux de la femme du docteur Rigoler, n'est-ce pas? _____
_____.

28. Qu'est-ce que Léon prend **en plus des (in addition to)** légumes et des fruits? _____
_____.

29. Pourquoi les derniers quatre mots du docteur Rigoler sont-ils amusants? _____
_____.

30. **From #10.** Selon M. Tantdans, pourquoi va-t-il plutôt bien? _____
_____.

31. Que François dit-il quand le médecin lui demande si l'audiophone neuf marche bien? _____
_____.

32. Quel âge François va-t-il avoir la semaine prochaine? _____
_____.

33. Pourquoi la phrase finale de François est-elle drôle? _____
_____.

'On the Mend'- Switch and stitch the phrases to form sentences.
1. avec des béquilles/ append à clopiner/ Mlle Cassée/ plutôt vite _____
_____.

2. aux coudes et aux genoux/ il a mal/ a de l'arthrite/ Comme le vieillard _____
_____.

3. pour M. Bouffer/ sucrés/ n'est pas un gâteau/ Être en bonne forme/ qui mange les aliments _____
_____.

4. à ses joues et/ à son front/ considère un lifting/ les rides/ Est-ce que Mme Vaniteuse/ pour enlever
_____
_____?

5. ne sont pas toujours/ d'un médecin/ très malades/ Les patients/ dans la salle d'attente _____
_____.

6. être avec beaucoup de monde/ est contagieuse/ Si vous toussez/ parce que votre maladie/ vous ne
devez pas/ et vous éternuez _____
_____.

7. de Mme Cousue/ Le chirurgien/ et il lui dit/ comme neuf/ enlève ses points de suture/ qu'elle est
_____
_____.

8. discute/ avec une femme médecin/ à l'aise/ Mme Clandestine/ ses problèmes personnels _____
_____.

9. regarde/ la radiographie/ a une entorse / Quand le docteur Guérir/ si le patient/ il sait/ ou une fracture _____
_____.

10. et boit/ qui a quatre-vingt-six ans/ toujours/ M. Bonnevie/ fume des cigares cubains/ du vin rouge
_____
_____.

11. Votre grand-père/ mieux/ n'est-ce pas/ mais grâce à son audiophone/ est presque sourd/ il entend
_____
_____?

12. des médicaments sans ordonnance/ je reste au lit/ je prends/ mais lorsque j'ai la grippe/ Quand je suis enrhumé/ et je sors de ma maison _____
_____.

la Vénus de Milo (le Louvre, Paris)

LES VERBES RÉFLÉCHIS - REFLEXIVE VERBS

Reflexive verbs tell what subjects do to themselves. The adage "deeds come back to you," rings true in French grammar where 'the boomerang effect' is an integral component. Coordinating reflexive pronouns reinforce the subjects. Have <u>I</u> made <u>myself</u> clear?
A reflexive conjugation in statement form <u>presents itself</u> like this:

Se Laver - To Wash Oneself

<u>Singular</u>	<u>Plural</u>
je me lave- I wash, do wash, am washing myself	nous lavons- we wash, do wash, are washing ourselves
tu te laves- you wash, do wash, are washing yourself	vous vous lavez- you wash, do wash, are washing yourselves
il/elle/on se lave- he/she/one washes, does wash, is washing himself, herself, oneself, itself	ils/elles se lavent- they wash, do wash, are washing themselves

----

Looking Back and Ahead

1. With the exception of *se*, the reflexive pronouns were introduced under the headings subject, direct and indirect. Here, they require 'a double take' and denote <u>self-service.</u>

Reflexive Pronouns

<u>Singular</u>	<u>Plural</u>
me- myself	nous- ourselves
te- yourself	vous- yourselves
se- himself, herself, oneself, itself	se- themselves

----

2. Preceded by <u>se</u> or <u>s'</u>, reflexive infinitives are easy to recognize in a French dictionary.
Exs. *habiller*- to dress oneself, *se laver*-to wash oneself, *s'amuser*- to have a good time/to amuse oneself

3. Conjugated reflexive verbs include a double *nous* and a double *vous*.
Ex. **Nous nous brossons** les dents trois fois par jour. > **We brush** our teeth three times a day. (More often would really be 'squeezing' it.)

4. A reflexive pronoun precedes the verb when a sentence is affirmative, negative, interrogative or negative-interrogative.
Ex. Les petits éléphants **se baignent** dans la rivière. > The little elephants **bathe (themselves)** in the river. (And throw each other 'a baby shower.')
Ex. Ne nous levons pas avant dix heures dimanche! Let's not get up until ten o'clock Sunday! (It is our only chance for 'the rest' of the week.)
Ex. Qui ne **s'amuse** pas chez Disney? > Who doesn't **have a good time** at Disney? (Cinderella 'has a ball.')
Ex. Comment vous appelez-vous? > What is your name?/How do you call yourself?

4a. In the last example, the first *vous* is a reflexive pronoun; the second *vous* is the subject.
<u>An exception:</u> A reflexive pronoun follows the verb in an affirmative command. In this case, *te* becomes *toi.*

Ex. Lave-toi et pas le sol de la salle de bain! > Wash yourself and not the bathroom floor!

5. Following a conjugated verb, a reflexive construction is in the infinitive. The phrase includes a pronoun that mirrors the subject.

Ex. Les petites filles demandent à leur mère, "Pouvons-nous **nous maquiller**?" > The little girls ask their mother, "May we **put on makeup**?" (Mom might prefer that her daughters 'put it off.')

Ex. Il ne va pas **se coucher** sans se brosser les dents. > He's not going **to go to bed** without brushing his teeth. (He knows that he won't get any 'plaque' for it.)

Ex. "Chopin, fais attention quand tu coupes les légumes, ou tu vas **te blesser!**" > "Chopin, pay attention when you cut the vegetables, or you are going **to wound yourself!**" (It is so much easier to put 'a dressing' on a salad.)

6. The same verb can be both reflexive and nonreflexive.

Ex. La fermière s'appelle Mme Basse-Cour. > The woman farmer calls herself Mrs. Basse-Cour.

Ex. La fermière appelle un cochon. > The woman farmer calls a pig.

The first example contains the reflexive pronoun <u>herself</u>; the second includes the direct object <u>a pig</u>. Mme Basse-Cour does not call herself a pig. (It's a question of self and self-esteem.)

7. Several reflexive verbs deal with grooming or other routine activities. With those and many other reflexives, we often use <u>get</u> in the translations.

Ex. Des petits essaient de **s'habiller**. > Some little boys try **to dress themselves.**/Some little boys try try **to get dressed.**

8. After a disjunctive/stress/accentuated pronoun, -*même* means <u>self</u>. The hyphenated word can replace reflexive constructions.

Ex. L'homme **sans instruction** dit qu'il écrit son autobiographie lui-même. > The **uneducated** man says that he is writing his autobiography himself. (But that's just his story.)

8a. With or without -*même* added, *soi/soi-même* is <u>oneself</u>.

Ex. On peut compter sur soi (soi-même) faire le travail si d'autres ne sont pas disponibles. > One can count on oneself to do the work if others are not available. (The <u>elf</u> in self will help.)

<u>**'Self-Analysis'**</u>- **Label the statements *vrai* or *faux*.**

_____ 1. *Me, te, nous* and *vous* do not change their meanings whether they are reflexive, direct or indirect pronouns.

_____ 2. The third person singular and plural reflexive pronouns are not the same.

_____ 3. The infinitives of reflexive verbs include *se*.

_____ 4. Some verbs can be used with or without reflexive pronouns.

_____ 5. Reflexive pronouns usually precede verbs.

_____ 6. No reflexive pronoun changes its spelling in affirmative commands.

_____ 7. <u>Get</u> + a past participle is a translation for many reflexive verbs in French.

_____ 8. *Même* and reflexive pronouns are always used in the same sentence.

_____ 9. Not all reflexive verbs have regular conjugations.

_____ 10. Although *soi* translates as <u>oneself</u>, it is not a reflexive pronoun.

<u>Help Yourself to This Alpabetical List!</u>

1. **s'en aller = partir- to go away: When it is a reflexive verb, forms of** *aller* **are chaperoned by** *en.* (*Aller* by itself is "a no-go.")

2. **s'appeler- to call oneself, to name oneself:** (The caller is instantly connected.)

<u>A note</u>: *S'appeler* **is an orthographic/stem changing verb. Its stem is altered in a "boot" form.**

3. **s'amuser- to amuse oneself, to have a good time:** <u>Amuse</u>, <u>amusing</u> **and** <u>amusement</u> **are a few cognates for your enjoyment.**

4. **s'asseoir- to seat oneself, to sit down:** **Apologies to anyone not comfortable with the following 'seating arrangement': The first three letters of the verb make its meaning hard to forget.**

5. **se baigner- to bathe oneself, to take a bath:** *La baignoire* **means** <u>the bathtub</u>. (Drawing a dark circle around *noire* leaves 'a black ring.')

6. **se blesser- to wound oneself: The corresponding noun,** *la blessure-* **the** <u>wound</u>, **with its synonym,** *la plaie,* **are 'covered' here.**

7. **se brosser- to brush: Forms of this verb routinely precede** *les cheveux* **and** *les dents.* (It's just a matter of 'cut and paste.') *La brosse* **is** <u>the brush</u>. (Its similarity to the English word makes it easy to handle.)

8. **se casser- to break (including a body part): Abstract** *rompre* **breaks from literal** *casser.*
Ex. Plusieurs antiquités que les voleurs n'**emballent** pas bien se cassent. > Several antiques that the thieves do not **pack** well break. (Those stolen goods don't deserve 'a bad wrap.')
Ex. Quand un danseur se casse la jambe, on cherche **un remplaçant**. > When a dancer breaks a leg, they look for **a replacement**. (The original performer will be both 'in and out of the cast.')

9. **se coucher- to go to bed: It has a ready-made mnemonic with** <u>a couch</u> **folded inside.**

10. **se demander- to wonder: The meaning will come to you if you** <u>ask yourself</u>.

11. **se dépêcher- to hurry:** *La pêche-* **the peach and** *aller à la pêche-* **to go fishing look similar to part of** *se dépêcher,* **but they are not related.** (Any connection would be 'fuzzy' or 'shallow.')

12. **se doucher- to shower** (In daily routines, *se doucher* often precedes *se coucher*.) **Its synonym is** *prendre une douche-* **to take a shower.** (The penalty for the theft doesn't 'carry any water.')

13. **s'endormir- to fall asleep:** *En* **is 'tucked' in before sleep.**

14. **s'ennuyer- to be bored, to get bored:** *L'ennui* **is** <u>the boredom</u>. (The relationship between both terms keeps them busy.)

<u>A note</u>: *S'ennuyer* **is an orthographic/stem changing verb. Its root is altered in a "boot" form.**

15. **se fâcher- to become angry, to get angry: Even though there is no cognate for this verb, the expression can readily be seen on one's 'fac-e.'**

16. **s'habiller- to dress oneself, to get dressed: While a clergyman's** <u>vestments</u> **are donated from** *les vêtements,* **a nun's habit 'is cut from'** *s'habiller.*

16a. **se déshabiller- to get undressed:** *Des* **is added, not taken off, before** *habiller.*

17. **s'inquiéter- to worry:** <u>In</u>, **which means** <u>not</u>, **is cited for disturbing the peace.**

18. **se laver- to wash (oneself), to get washed:** <u>Lavatory</u> **is 'on tap' for this verb.**

19. **se lever- to get up:** <u>Levitate</u>, <u>leverage</u> **and** <u>elevator</u> **can be 'brought up' as reminders.**

<u>A note</u>: *Se lever* **is an orthographic/stem changing verb. Its** <u>è</u>s **are laced with an accent** *grave* **in "boot" form.**

20. **se maquiller- to make oneself up, to put on makeup: Think of** <u>mask</u> **to uncover a clue!** (Is an association between *se maquiller* and mascara 'extending' it?) *Le maquillage* **is** <u>the make-up</u>. (Ironically, that noun has two lines (<u>ll</u>) in the middle and <u>-age</u> at the end.)

21. se marier à/avec = to marry, to get married: *Le mari* is 'the better half' of the verb. A couple has the option of marrying <u>to</u> or <u>with</u> each other.

22. se méfier de- to mistrust, not to have confidence in: All singular forms and the third person plural are pronounced like *mes filles.*

Ex. Elles se méfient d'une de mes filles. > They mistrust one of my daughters. (One might ask 'how that girl was brought up.')

22a. se méfier de quelque chose = faire attention à- to be careful/ beware of something

Ex. Méfiez-vous de conduire dans une tempête de neige! > Be careful driving in a snowstorm! (The roads can be very 'slick.')

23. se mettre = s'habiller- to put on, **se mettre à = commencer-** to begin, **se mettre = se placer-** to situate oneself, **se mettre avec quelqu'un-** to join together (*Se mettre* 'puts on' quite a show.)

Ex. M. Récolte se met un bleu de travail, et il se met dans le champ où il se met avec des amis qui se mettent à **arroser** des légumes. > M. Récolte puts on a pair of overalls, and he 'plants himself' in the field where he joins some friends who are starting **to water** vegetables.

23e. se mettre en colère = *se fâcher-* to get angry (Just because one has a choice of terms does not mean that one can 'pick a fight.')

24. se moquer de- to make fun of: This is a most ill-fitting reflexive verb. *Se moquer de* doesn't entail grooming, doesn't have <u>get</u> in its translation and doesn't involve action done to oneself. (It 'mocks' all of the prerequisites.) *Se railler* is its synonym.

25. s'occuper de- to busy oneself with, to be involved with: The related adjective is *occupé.*

26. se peigner- to comb: *Le peigne-* the comb forms 'a part' of the verb.

27. se plaindre- to complain: The pain is plain in English and in French.

<u>A note:</u> *Plaindre* is <u>to pity</u>. (Using the reflexive form, one engages in self-pity.)

28. se préparer- to prepare oneself, to get ready (It's a very low maintenance verb.)

29. se promener = faire une promenade- to stroll, to take a walk: Both *promener* and *la promenade* have previously crossed your path.

<u>A note:</u> *Se promener,* like *promener,* is an orthographic/stem-changing verb that walks around 'in a boot' with an accent *grave* over the first <u>e</u>.

30. se rappeler- to recall, to remember: This verb is (*s'*)*appeler* preceded by an <u>r</u>. Therefore, its meaning is <u>to recall</u>. They are "boot verbs." (Don't forget to remember!)

31. se raser- to shave oneself: Its spelling is within 'a few hairs' of *le rasoir-* the razor.

32. se reposer- to rest: A body in a state of repose is at rest. (Only the eulogy can 'be moving.')

33. se rendre compte- to realize: Its literal meaning is "to give oneself an account." (A personal checking type is needed here.)

34. se réveiller- to wake up: Reveille, the bugle call at daybreak and *le réveille-matin-* the alarm clock are eye-openers.

35. se sécher- to dry oneself (off): The meaning should be 'absorbed' from *du vin sec.*

36. se sentir- to feel (physically or psychologically): *Se sentir bien/mal* mean to feel good/bad in body or in mind. Any attempts to translate the reflexive forms literally result in giving out very personal information.

<u>An important note:</u> Because forms of *sentir* express the senses, they precede adjectives (not adverbs) in English and in French. So, while someone who smells badly has a poor sense of smell, a person who smells bad should have the good sense to wash.

<u>Perceptive Observations</u>
a. Ça pue!- It smells dreadful! (The <u>pu</u> gives it away.)
b. sentir- to be aware/to be conscious of
Ex. **Les juments** sentent venir l'orage. > **The mares** feel the storm coming. (It could be attributed to their 'horse sense.')
37. se souvenir de = se rappeler- to remember: Conjugated like *venir*, this reflexive verb offers a *souvenir* as a remembrance.
38. se taire- to be quiet: Except for the -<u>ez</u> ending in the *vous* form, its conjugation is like *faire*. *Taisez-vous!* > Be quiet! is more refined than *Fermez la bouche!* > Close/Shut your mouth! (There is something to be said for that.)
39. se tromper de- to make a mistake: *Trompe l'œil* art can cause temporary double vision. (Its creators might call such illusions "tricks of the trade.")

<u>Reflecting Images from 'a Pool'</u>- **Write the verbs from the following list beside their antonyms. avoir confiance en, avoir raison, arriver, se déshabiller, divorcer, s'ennuyer, s'endormir, être satisfait de, finir, se guérir, se lever, être à l'aise, ne pas savoir, ne rien faire, se sécher, parler, prendre son temps, rester seul, être certain, se sécher, oublier**

1. se demander _____	11. s'asseoir _____
2. s'inquiéter _____	12. s'en aller _____
3. s'amuser _____	13. se méfier de _____
4. se blesser _____	14. s'occuper de _____
5. s'habiller _____	15. se rendre compte _____
6. se dépêcher _____	16. se marier à/avec _____
7. se tromper de _____	17. se laver _____
8. se taire _____	18. se plaindre de _____
9. se mettre à _____	19. se réveiller _____
10. se rappeler _____	20. se mettre avec quelqu'un _____

<u>'Self-Centered' Thinking</u>- **Circle the letters of the correct answers to complete the sentences.**
1. Comme Mme Courante n'a pas assez de temps de se baigner, elle ___.
a. se trompe du jour   b. se douche vite   c. s'ennuie pour toujours   d. se met avec son ami
2. On se réveille avant de ___.
a. se marier   b. se plaindre   c. se sentir   d. se lever
3. Tout le monde n'a pas les moyens de ___.
a. se peigner à la mode   b. se rendre compte de la vérité   c. s'en aller cet été
d. se sécher en plein air
4. Les enfants ne sont pas prêts. L'autobus scolaire va arriver dans un quart d'heure. Ils doivent ___.
a. se dépêcher   b. s'asseoir   c. se reposer   d. se fâcher
5. L'étranger ne vous répond pas quand vous lui demandez, "Comment vous appelez-vous?," mais il comprend la phrase " ___?"
a. Est-ce que vous vous brossez les dents?   b. Quel est votre nom?
c. Vous préparez-vous maintenant?   d. Pourquoi vous mettez-vous en colère?
6. Quand ils sortent ensemble le soir, mon père se rase vite, mais ma mère ___.

a. s'excuse pour jouer avec le chien   b. se maquille soigneusement   c. se met à pleurer
d. se déshabille très lentement

7. Je viens de dire à mon médecin que je travaille tous les jours. Il me demande, "___?"
a. Tu te peignes les cheveux?   b. Est-ce que tu te blesses souvent?
c. Tu te souviens de mon anniversaire, n'est-ce pas?   d. Tu te reposes un peu?

8. Comment est-ce que la jeunesse peut ___?
a. s'endormir tout en écoutant la musique forte   b. se promener lorsque nous conduisons
c. se doucher en bavardant au téléphone cellulaire   d. se baigner sans se sécher

9. M. Castor habite seul, mais il a toujours quelque chose pour le garder occupé. Il ___.
a. ne se tait pas   b. s'inquiète plus   c. ne s'ennuie jamais   d. se fâche constamment

10. Les très petits choisissent les vêtements qu'ils veulent porter, mais ils ___.
a. ne se lavent pas ensemble   b. ne savent pas s'habiller   c. se moquent de leur maîtresse
d. se trompent du chemin

11. Lorsque Heidi cache un cadeau de son petit fils, il la regarde. Elle lui dit, "___"
a. Va-t-en!   b. Assieds-toi!   c. Réveille-toi!   d. Lave-toi!

12. Nous nous couchons de bonne heure, mais nous ne ___.
a. nous asseyons pas à table en famille   b. nous moquons pas d'autres gens
c. nous rappelons rien le matin suivant   d. nous n'endormons jamais tout de suite

13. Le moment où je sens les croissants frais dans la cuisine, ___.
a. tu te tais   b. je me lève   c. je me rase les jambes   d. je me rends compte de mes erreurs

14. Avant de se déshabiller, Mme Privée tire toujours les rideaux parce qu'elle ___.
a. cherche ses lunettes   b. se casse la côte   c. se méfie des voyeurs   d. met le pyjama de son époux

----

'You Can Say That Again!'- Translate the phrases in parentheses.

1. Harry, qui n'a que seize ans, (shaves each morning) _____.
2. (I wonder why) _____ des américains ne posent pas la question, "Parlez-vous anglais?" en anglais.
3. (Does he realize) _____ qu'il se trompe du métro?
4. Avant de me coucher, (I brush my hair) _____.
5. Les Malcontent se plaignent parce qu' (they are not having a good time on vacation)._____

_____

6. Je ne vais pas te voir demain parce que (I am going away)._____.
7. (Do you (vous) get dressed) _____ dans la chambre à coucher ou dans la salle de bain?
8. Ne te moque pas d'eux! (They get angry.) _____.
9. Le pauvre M. Déprimé! (He is worried) _____ de sa santé. Pour cette raison, (he is starting to drink.) _____.
10. Maybelline ne peut pas (hurry when she is putting on make-up). _____

_____

11. Les femmes (do not want to marry) _____ les hommes qui (are involved only with) _____ leur travail.
12. La vieille femme (rests a lot) _____ parce qu'elle est fatiguée ou parce qu'(she is bored)? _____?

'A-cross' Reference- Match the letters and numbers of the phrases to form complete sentences.

____ 1. Les jumeaux se ressemblent tant

____ 2. Le soleil se lève

____ 3. Sans lire un roman romantique, ma sœur

____ 4. Nous nous dépêchons pour arriver là

____ 5. Avant chaque opération, les chirurgiens

____ 6. Quand ils vont au cinéma,

____ 7. M. Passepartout est si fatigué ce soir

____ 8. On se demande si Dee Vorcée

____ 9. **Le baigneur (the bather)** prend une serviette

____ 10. Ne moque-toi jamais d'une personne

____ 11. M. Prêteunemain va chercher ses enfants

____ 12. Ils s'inquiètent de leurs notes,

____ 13. Mlle Tropdechoix reste debout dans sa penderie

____ 14. À cause de mon horaire serré,

____ 15. Ma grand-mère se rappelle bien

____ 16. Il regarde la télévision, et il écoute la musique

____ 17. Le voisin ne reconnaît pas ma mère

____ 18. Nous nous rendons compte que M. Méchant se met en colère

____ 19. Rapunzel se brosse les longs cheveux

____ 20. Rappelez-moi laisser

A. pour se sécher.

B. et après, il faut faire la queue et attendre.

C. si elle ne se maquille pas.

D. qui fait de son mieux.

E. avant de s'habiller.

F. une clé au-dessous du **paillasson (doormat)**

G. parce qu'il crie et menace tout le monde.

H. à l'est et se couche à l'ouest.

I. comme elle a du mal à les peigner.

J. sa jeunesse en Provence.

K. ils achètent **des rafraîchessements-m. (some refreshments)**

L. va se remarier.

M. pour se reposer.

N. qu'on se trompe d'eux.

O. lorsque sa femme s'occupe de ses affaires.

P. qu'il se couche sans se déshabiller.

Q. mais ils n'étudient pas beaucoup.

R. se lavent bien les mains et les bras

S. ne peut pas s'endormir.

T. je ne m'ennuie jamais.

S'ASSEOIR - To Sit (Down)

Because neither reflexive nor nonreflexive verbs has forms like *s'asseoir*, it is like a chair out of place. With two sets of irregular stems, *s'asseoir* 'bends the rules.'

Singular
je m'assieds- I sit down, do sit down, am sitting down

tu t'assieds- you sit down, do sit down, are sitting fown

il/elle/on s'assied- he/she/it/one sits down, does sit down, is sitting down

Plural
nous nous asseyons- we sit down, do sit down, are sitting down

vous vous asseyez- you sit down, do sit down, are sitting down

ils/elles s'asseyent- they sit down, do sit down, are sitting down

---

Sit Down 'for a Spell!'- Put the correct forms of *s'asseoir* in the spaces provided.
1. Le petit _____ sur les genoux de Père Noël.
2. Je _____ lorsque je me maquille.
3. Vous _____ en regardant les nouvelles à la télé?
4. _____ (*tu*) près de moi!
5. Les étudiants préparés ne _____ pas à l'arrière de la salle de classe.
6. Se lever est l'opposé de _____.
7. Est-ce qu'Émeril _____ lorsqu'il fait la cuisine?
8. Hy Atus et moi _____ avant de prendre des rafraîchissements.
9. Ne _____ pas (*vous*) sur l'herbe trempée!
10. **Le routier (the bus driver)** demande aux passagers de _____.
11. Ben Cott a peur quand son père lui dit, " _____! Je voudrais te parler."

PLAINDRE - To Pity, SE PLAINDRE - To Complain and Associated Verbs

As verbs with -**indre** infinitive endings will be the last irregular group introduced, it calls for a celebration. (*Se plaindre* suggests a little 'whine.') *Atteindre*- to reach, *craindre*- to fear, *éteindre*- to put out, to turn off, *joindre*- to add, to contact, to join, *peindre*- to paint, to portray and *teindre*- to dye, to tint are conjugated like *plaindre* and *se plaindre*. (Misery loves company.)
These 'not so plain' verbs are conjugated like this:

Se Plaindre - To Complain

Singular	Plural
je me plains- I complain, do complain, am complaining	nous nous plaignons- we complain, do complain, are complaining
tu te plains- you complain, do complain, are complaining	vous vous plaignez- you complain, do complain, are complaining
il/elle/on se plaint- he/she/one complains, does complain, is complaining	ils/elles se plaignent- they complain, do complain, are complaining

---

-Indre Verbs Are Kindred Spirits
1. After -**dre** is removed from the infinitive, the irregular -**s**, -**s**, -**t** singular endings are added.
2. The plural forms sport an '**ign** design' before attaching -**er/-re** endings.

Indispensable -Indre Verbs
1. **atteindre- to reach:** Its cognate is **to attain.** Only an additional vowel distinguishes *atteindre* from *attendre.* (Keep an **i** on *atteindre!*)
Atteindre **Expressions within Reach**
a. atteindre son but- to reach one's goal (The done deal includes no ifs, ands or 'buts' in English.)
b. atteindre la cible- to hit the target
2. **craindre = avoir peur- to fear** (Rewording the saying to "The fear is all in your cranium" makes the spelling and the translation easier to remember.)
3. **éteindre- to put out, to turn off**

Ex. Mme Ampoule éteint toutes les lampes quand elle n'est pas chez elle. > Mrs. Ampoule turns off all the lamps when she is not home. (It helps to maintain her 'light' bill.)

4. s'éteindre- to die out, to extinguish itself: This is the reflexive form of #3.

Ex. La popularité de prendre les vacances à cet endroit s'éteint. > The popularity of taking a vacation at that place is dying out. (Some consider it as 'the last resort.')

5. joindre- to join = *ajouter*- to add and *contacter*- to get in touch with (The verb has 'joint membership.')

<u>Connected Idioms with *Joindre*</u>

a. joindre quelqu'un- to reach someone

Ex. Je peux la joindre à l'hôtel. > I can reach her at the hotel. (She will be there 'for a short stretch.')

b. joindre quelqu'un par téléphone- to contact someone by phone (And still 'keep a distance.')

c. joindre l'utile à l'agréable- to combine business with pleasure: When "the useful is joined to the pleasant," it gives a less formal meaning to an *attaché* case.

d. joindre les deux bouts- to make ends meet (Even 'loose' change comes in handy when money is 'tight.')

e. se joindre à- to join someone: Notice that the reflexive form of the verb takes *à*!

Ex. Voudrais-tu te joindre à nous? > Would you like to join us? (Has the couple recently separated?)

6. peindre- to paint, to portray (For many, art appreciation is a matter of personal taste or whatever pleases 'the palate.')

<u>An important note</u>: **The plural forms of *peindre* and *se peigner* are the same. However, because *peindre* is not often used reflexively, the verbs are easily distinguished.** (One who paints himself needs a brush and not a comb.)

7. dépeindre- to depict: It is modeled after *peindre*. The -<u>pict</u> in depict will help you to recall its meaning! (Admittedly, 'it's only part of the picture.')

a. se faire peindre- to have one's portrait painted (The result is a 'sitting' image.)

8. plaindre- to pity: The noun *la pitié* is pronounced like PTA.

<u>Compassionate Thoughts with *Plaindre*</u>

a. être bien à plaindre- to be pitied: *Bien* adds a positive note.

Ex. Les gens qui perdent tout pendant un ouragan sont bien à plaindre. > The people who lose everything during a hurricane are to be pitied. (They are in 'a sorry state.')

b. avoir pitié de quelqu'un- to have pity for/to take pity on someone: Notice the preposition *de*! You could also invite *Quel dommage*! > What a pity!/What a shame! to "the pity party."

9. se plaindre- to complain: In its reflexive form, the verb connotes <u>self-pity</u>.

<u>A Dissatisfied Expression</u>

a. se plaindre de quelque chose à quelqu'un- to complain about something to someone

10. teindre- to dye: This verb is identical to *éteindre* except that the first letter 'ran.'

a. se teindre les cheveux- to dye one's hair

<u>Interesting notes</u>: **Several English nouns derived from -<u>indre</u> verbs end with -<u>int</u>. Examples are complaint, joint, paint and tint.**

The Indre River runs through France's château country.

Intelligent Information from -Indre Infinitives- Use the correct forms of the following verbs to complete the sentences: atteindre, craindre, éteindre, s'éteindre, joindre, se joindre, peindre, dépeindre, se faire peindre, plaindre, se plaindre, teindre, se teindre

1. Ces pauvres orphelins sont bien à _____.
2. Mme Oréal a l'air plus jeune parce qu'elle _____ les cheveux.
3. Pour économiser nous _____ **la climatisation (the air conditioning)** lorsque nous ne sommes pas chez nous.
4. M. Douteux ne croit personne qui dit, "Je ne/n' _____ ricn."
5. Vous n'allez pas _____ votre but par hasard.
6. Son entreprise tient sa réunion annuelle à Euro Disney où les salariés _____ l'utile à l'agréable.
7. Au lieu de prendre une photographie, ma grand-mère _____.
8. _____ -tu tes chaussures pour aller avec ta robe du soir?
9. Vous êtes plus grand que moi. _____ cet article en haut, s'il vous plaît!
10. Les lumières chez eux _____ automatiquement à minuit.
11. Deb Itz et moi _____ les deux bouts en travaillant soixante heures par semaine.
12. Pour éviter une ambiance **fade (dull)**, je _____ les murs de chaque pièce avec une couleur différente.
13. N'essayez pas de/d' _____ Anne Ternette par téléphone! Envoyez-lui un message électronique!
14. Je n'ai aucune pitié de Visette. Elle _____ à moi de ses dettes tout en continuant à charger.
15. Jean-Marc fait un voyage en Écosse bientôt. Voudrais-tu _____ à lui?

Nothing Is Lost 'In-dre' Translation- Translate the following sentences.

1. Guillaume Tell, a hunter, always hits the target. _____
_____.

2. Pearl Buck's novels portray life in Asia very well. _____
_____.

3. Don't turn off (*tu*) the lights before **locking (fermer à clé)** the door! _____
_____!

4. Myles and Leslie are busy artists. While he is drawing, she is painting. _____
_____.

5. I reach her at home in the evening. She can't talk to me on the phone at work. _____
_____.

6. Smokey says that forest fires do not extinguish themselves. _____
_____.

7. When you (*tu*) cannot reach an item in a store, do you ask for **assistance (l'aide-f.)**? _____
_____?

8. Mr. Bouchecousue never complains about his job to anyone. _____
_____.
_____

UNE REVUE - A Review

Les Parties du Corps, Le Rire Est Bon Pour Vous, Les Verbes Réfléchis, -<u>Indre</u> Verbs and Related Idioms

'A Little Truth Serum'- Label the true statements *vrai* and the false ones *faux*.

_____ 1. Les rides ne vous font pas malades.
_____ 2. Il ne va pas bien, et il se sent mauvais sont des synonymes.
_____ 3. On qui tousse et éternue consulte un chirurgien esthétique.
_____ 4. Prendre des poids et maigrir sont des synonymes.
_____ 5. Prenez de l'eau avec les comprimés ou les pilules pour les avaler plus facilement!
_____ 6. Un médecin prend le pouls pour savoir si les poumons sont sains.
_____ 7. Pour baisser la tension artérielle, inquiétez-vous autant que possible!
_____ 8. Les médicaments sans ordonnance ne guérissent rien.
_____ 9. Des points de sutures sont nécessaires quelquefois pour fermer une blessure.
_____ 10. On peut attraper une maladie contagieuse dans une salle d'attente.
_____ 11. Tout le monde partage le même groupe sanguin.
_____ 12. Les béquilles aident un patient qui a une entorse ou une fracture.

'A Double Take'- Match the letters of the phrases to the numbers of their synonyms.

_____ 1. teindre	A. se coiffer	
_____ 2. se blesser	B. être avec quelqu'un	
_____ 3. s'habiller	C. partir	
_____ 4. se promener	D. n'avoir rien à faire pour s'occuper	
_____ 5. se méfier de	E. percevoir par l'odeur ou le goût	
_____ 6. se taire	F. devenir prêt	
_____ 7. s'ennuyer	G. mettre des vêtements	
_____ 8. se dépêcher	H. appliquer du savon et de l'eau	
_____ 9. sentir	I. prendre une place	
_____ 10. se brosser et se peigner	J. enlever des poils	
_____ 11. se plaindre	K. commencer à	
_____ 12. se fâcher	L. changer la couleur	
_____ 13. se joindre à	M. faire une faute	
_____ 14. se préparer	N. exprimer un problème	
_____ 15. se laver	O. se souvenir de	
_____ 16. se demander	P. fermer la bouche	
_____ 17. s'en aller	Q. marcher une distance	
_____ 18. se mettre à	R. se couper	
_____ 19. se rappeler	S. ne pas être sûr	
_____ 20. se raser	T. ne pas avoir la confiance en	
_____ 21. se tromper	U. se mettre en colère	
_____ 22. s'asseoir	V. aller vite	

'An Exercise to Tone the Body'- **Circle the letters of the answers that complete the sentences.**

1. On ne change pas facilement l'opinion de quelqu'un qui ___.
a. agit sur un coup de tête   b. a une tête dure   c. fait front aux difficultés
d. montre le bout de son nez

2. Mme Lapireheure n'est pas du tout bienvenue. Elle ___.
a. gagne d'une tête   b. a la dent   c. avale la langue   d. arrive comme un cheveu sur la soupe

3. J'excuse Norman pour penser seulement à lui-même, et ___.
a. je ne montre pas le vrai visage   b. je raccroche à son nez   c. je ne garde pas de dent contre lui
d. j'attire son œil

4. Nous ne faisons plus d'achats aux grands magasins. Cependant, Tati, au centre de Paris, ___.
a. a un visage rond   b. ne coûte pas les yeux de la tête   c. rit à mon nez   d. tend l'autre joue

5. Il ne faut pas vous demander ce que Bavardette pense. Elle ___.
a. n'a pas la langue dans la poche   b. ne vous tire jamais les oreilles
c. a la bouche cousue   d. parle trop la bouche pleine

6. Une personne qui est très ambitieuse ___.
a. donne la langue au chat   b. chuchote fréquemment   c. a les dents longues   d. épile tes sourcils

7. Mme Sansaide s'occupe de tout elle-même. On peut dire ___.
a. qu'elle est impliquée jusqu'au cou   b. qu'elle a les cheveux dans le dos
c. qu'elle a la langue bien pendue   d. que tout repose sur ses épaules

8. Vous pouvez reconnaître un optimiste. C'est quelqu'un qui ___.
a. est de la même taille   b. a une sourire aux lèvres souvent   c. traine la jambe
d. prend toujours des personnes à la gorge

9. Comme Les Fric reçoivent tant d'argent de leur fils riche, ils ont ___.
a. les épaules assez larges   b. les mâchoires carrées   c. les barbes bouclées   d. les mains vertes

10. Mme Pilule a mal aux hanches. De temps en temps, elle nous dit ___.
a. "Je vous prends sur mes genoux."   b. "Ne tombez pas sur le dos de quelqu'un!"
c. "Ma vie n'est pas le pied."   d. "Je n'ai pas de poitrine."

11. Il est évident de ces mères indulgentes qu'elles ___.
a. y vont avec le dos de la cuiller   b. sont à genoux devant leurs maris
c. sont sur les talons des veufs   d. se mettent en quatre pour leurs enfants

12. Si Drima n'ouvre pas les oreilles pendant le sermon du prêtre, sa sœur ___.
a. part du bon pied   b. lui donne un coup de coude   c. est en bras de chemise
d. a du vin sous le coude

13. M. Quincaillier et son fils peuvent réparer tout parce qu'ils ___.
a. l'ont dans le dos   b. se promènent bras dessus, bras dessous
c. ont le coup de main pour ce travail   d. montrent du doigt aux clients

14. Cristelle est triste parce qu'elle ne sort plus avec Christophe. Sa copine lui dit, ___
a. "Il gagne les doigts dans le nez."   b. "Tu as quelque chose sur le cœur."
c. "Pourquoi ne coupes-tu pas ton poignet?"   d. "Tu dois te raser le menton."

15. Un individu qui a du sang dans les veines ___.
a. met du maquillage sur les paupières et les cils   b. n'a pas trop de chair aux cuisses
c. montre beaucoup de courage   d. n'a pas treize côtes

16. Il ne faut pas faire peau neuve si on ___.
a. a la chair de poule   b. est bien dans sa peau   c. a une vessie et un foie   d. ne voit pas de sueur

17. Pour comprendre les sentiments d'une autre personne, ____!
a. Donnez-lui un rein!   b. Soyez trempé jusqu'aux os!   c. Gardez votre sang froid!
d. Mettez-vous dans sa peau!

18. Ses larmes de crocodile ___.
a. me donnent sur les nerfs   b. ont un doigt de pied   c. n'ont ni les orteils ni les ongles
d. font travailler son cerveau

la Victoire de Samothrace (le Louvre, Paris)

LES PRONOMS POSSESSIFS - Possessive Pronouns

Not long ago, you learned the catchy list of possessive adjectives. They are reviewed below and compared with a new label and sound track known as possessive pronouns.

Possessive Pronouns

le mien, la mienne, les miens, les miennes- mine
le tien, la tienne, les tiens, les tiennes- yours
le sien, la sienne, les siens, les siennes- his, hers, its
le nôtre, la nôtre, les nôtres, les nôtres- ours
le vôtre, la vôtre, les vôtres, les vôtres- yours
le leur, la leur, les leurs, les leurs- theirs

Handing Down Possessions

1. Possessive adjectives precede nouns and agree with them in gender and in number.
Ex. sa penderie- his/her closet; The gender of the noun takes precedence over the owner.
Ex. leurs brosses à dents- their toothbrushes; (For hygienic purposes, people sometimes label them to show possession.)
2. Possessive adjectives and possessive pronouns have something in common. The first letter of the word in each set (m, t, s, n, v, l) is the same. (Mts. are found in both, but pronouns take them to a higher level.)
3. Possessive pronouns agree in number and in gender with the nouns they replace.
With a possessive adjective: C'est ton collier de diamants. > It is your diamond necklace.
With a possessive pronoun: Le collier de diamants est le tien. > The diamond necklace is yours.
(Insurance documents would be a third way to show possession.)
4. The possessive adjectives *leur, leur* and *leurs* are identical to the related pronouns. However, the latter are adamant about keeping definite articles.
With a possessive adjective: C'est leur choix. > It is their choice.
With a possessive pronoun: Le choix est le leur. > The choice is theirs.
Both sentences convey the same meaning. (Which one they use is up to them; It's their choice.)
5. In addition to being preceded by definite articles, contractions and partitives, possessive pronouns have other ways to show their differences from the corresponding adjectives.
5a. Possessive adjectives have three forms; possessive pronouns have four. Their case is filed as *mon, ma, mes* vs. *le mien, la mienne, les miens, les miennes.*
5b. Circumflexes cap the os in *le(s) nôtre(s)* and *le(s) vôtre(s)*.
6. A possessive pronoun can replace a phrase beginning with *de*.
Ex. C'est le canapé-lit de Chantal. > It is Chantal's sofabed.
Changing Chantal's sofabed into a possessive pronoun, one 'pulls out' C'est le sien. > It's hers.
(See how easy it was 'to convert' it!)
7. *À* and *de* contract in front of possessive pronouns.
Ex. à ton appartement ou au mien > at your apartment or at mine. (The pronoun takes up less space.)
Ex. de leur point de vue ou du nôtre > from their point of view or from ours. (Phrases with pronouns have a 'narrower' perspective than those with adjectives.)

8. Disjunctive pronouns offer 'a no-frills' approach. With *à* before the pronoun, there is never a question about the gender of the replaced noun. (This method is analogous to "killing one bird with 'to' stones.")

The possessive "light" menu

à moi- mine   à nous- ours
à toi- yours   à vous- yours
à lui- his   à eux- theirs (masc.)
à elle- hers   à elles- theirs (fem.)

Ex. C'est notre tondeuse à gazon = C'est la nôtre, or C'est à nous. (Either model 'cuts it.')

The Claim Is the Same- Using *C'est* or *Ce sont* and possessive pronouns, rewrite the sentences.
Ex. Ce tailleur en laine est à elle. > C'est le sien.

1. Cet imperméable est à moi. _____.
2. Ces draps sont à eux. _____.
3. Ces serviettes en lin sont à toi. _____.
4. Cette cravate écossaise est à Ty. _____.
5. Ces chiots mignons sont à moi. _____.
6. Ces ceintures en cuir sont à lui. _____.
7. Ce cahier est à un nouvel étudiant. _____.
8. Ces bijoux sont à Goldie? _____?
9. Ces serre-livres en bois sont à nous. _____.
10. Cet **ordinateur portable (laptop)** est à vous? _____?
11. Cette cloche en étain est à Belle. _____.
12. Ce chapeau en paille est à Hattie ou à toi? _____?

'Owning Up to It'- Replace the nouns in bold type with possessive pronouns, and write the revised sentences on the lines provided.
Ex. Agathe me prête ses romans policiers. (Agatha lends me her murder mysteries.) > Agathe me prête les siens. > Agatha lends me hers.

1. Mme Bonrepas va me donner **sa recette.** _____
_____.
2. **Vos brimborions** sont chers? _____?
3. **Mon vide-grenier** a lieu ce week-end. _____.
4. Combien paies-tu **ton logement?** _____?
5. Voici **nos cartes d'embarquement!** _____!
6. **Ta retraite** te fait plaisir. _____.
7. M. et Mme Nostalgique ne remplacent pas **leurs meubles.** _____
_____.
8. Que fait-on si la ligne d'avion perd **ses valises?** _____
_____?
9. Je pense que **mon professeur particulier** enseigne bien le français. _____
_____.
10. **La chambre d'amis de mes parents** est rarement vide. _____

11. **Les vaisselles et l'argenterie de Mme Stewart** vont très bien ensemble. _____.

12. J'admets que **notre mode de vie** est très unique. _____.

<u>Locking Up Possessions</u>- **Using the correct possessive pronouns, translate the phrases in parentheses. (Check for possible contractions!)**

1. Je lui parle de mon travail, et (he talks to me about his.) _____

2. Comme sa voiture ne fonctionne pas, (she is borrowing ours.) _____.

3. Il **échoue (fail)** à ses examens, mais (I succeed on mine.) _____.

4. Je m'occupe de mes affaires, et (my neighbors are busy with theirs.) _____.

5. Nous partageons tout. Ce qui (is mine is yours- informal) _____.

6. Suivez mes conseils! (Don't follow hers!) _____!

7. Je ne me plains pas de mes problèmes, mais (you (*tu*) can complain about yours.) _____.

8. M. Passibon essaie d'oublier son **enfance (f.)- childhood**, mais (his daughter wants to remember hers.) _____.

9. Teins-toi les cheveux, mais (don't touch mine!) _____!

10. Mlle L'Amour songe seulement à son petit ami. Elle se demande (why I do not think constantly about mine.) _____.

_____

344

LES PRONOMS DÉMONSTRATIFS - CELUI, CELLE, CEUX, CELLES
The Demonstrative Pronouns -This, That, These, Those

This, that, these and those refer to both demonstrative adjectives and demonstrative pronouns in English. For precise identification, the latter have unique 'ce' names in French.

Demonstrative Pronouns

Singular	Plural
celui (masc.) - this one, that one, the one	ceux (masc.) - these, those, the ones
celle (fem.) - this one, that one, the one	celles (fem.) - these, those, the ones

----

Getting the Point
1. The demonstrative adjectives *ce, cet, cette* **and** *ces* **precede nouns and match them in gender and in number. The four demonstrative pronouns replace nouns. They agree with them in gender and plurality. Both sets include** *-ci* **and** *-là* **to differentiate this/these from that/those.**
Ex. ces fils-ci > ceux-ci (these sons here > these here)
The noun phrase kept its masculine plural status when it turned into a pronoun. ("Boys will be boys!")
Ex. ces chaussures-là > celles-là (those shoes there > those there)
The exchange of the feminine plural noun *ces chaussures* **for the corresponding pronoun** *celles* **ensures the perfect fit.**
Ex. Est-ce que tu préfères ce livre de mathématiques-ci ou celui-là? > Do you prefer this math book or that one? (They both have their 'pluses and minuses.')
2. Disjunctive pronouns are encased inside every demonstrative pronoun; c<u>elui</u>, c<u>elle</u>, c<u>eux</u> and c<u>elles</u>. (One or more women are imprisoned in 'the *celle(s)* **block.')**
3. Following a demonstrative pronoun, *-<u>ci</u>* **expresses who or what is** <u>closer</u> **while** *-<u>là</u>* **tells who or what is** <u>further away</u>**.**
Ex. Sylvie et Sylvan arrivent au concert en même temps. Celui-ci a une place très près de l'orchestre, et celle-là en a très loin. > Sylvie and Sylvan get to the concert at the same time. The latter has a seat very close to the orchestra, and the former has one very far away from it. (They might perform their own rendition of Musical Chairs.)
4. Demonstrative pronouns that introduce relative clauses refer to both people and things. The possible translations are <u>the one(s) that</u> **and** <u>those/the one(s) who</u>**.**
4a. If the clause has a subject, *que* **follows the demonstrative pronoun.**
Ex. Ceux que je cherche ne sont pas ici. > The ones that I am looking for are not here.
The items are lost, but *que* **is used because the subject** *je* **is in full view.**
4b. If the clause does not have a subject, *qui* **follows the demonstrative pronoun.**
Ex. Ceux qui conduisent à Boston ne peuvent pas rentrer chez eux vite. > Those who (the ones who) drive in Boston can't get home quickly. (Then why is it called "rush hour"?)
5. *L'un, l'une, les uns and les unes***-** <u>the one</u>**,** <u>the ones</u> **can replace demonstrative pronouns.**
Ex. "Ceux qui/Les uns qui habitent dans les maisons de verre ne devraient pas jeter de pierres." > "Those who/The ones who live in glass houses should not throw stones." (But they should close the curtains.)
6. If *de* **follows a demonstrative pronoun, the translations include** <u>the one(s) of</u> **and** <u>that (these,</u>

those) of. *De* replaces the English apostrophe.

Ex. M. Poids pense que la balance au gymnase est plus précise que celle de ses parents. > Mr. Poids thinks that the scale at the gym is more precise than the one of (that of) his parents.

The more amusing version is "Mr. Poids thinks that the scale at the gym is more precise than his parents." (One can 'weigh' both options.)

Ex. Beaucoup de gens donnent de l'argent à leurs organisations caritatives préférées. Celles de leurs amis ne les intéressent pas. > Many people give money to their favorite charities. The ones of (those of) their friends don't interest them.

Rephrasing the translation and inserting an apostrophe result in "Their friends' don't interest them." (That scenario involves different 'contributing' factors.)

'Warming Up to' Demonstrative Pronouns- Translate the following phrases and sentences.

1. ce pupitre-ci et celui-là _____

2. cet oiseau-là et celui-ci _____

3. cette vente-ci et celle-là _____

4. ces papiers-ci et ceux-là _____

5. ces poupées-là et celles-ci _____

6. Le restaurant rouge au coin est celui que nous aimons. _____

_____.

7. Ce matelas n'est pas celui que Serta vient d'acheter. _____

_____.

8. M. Vert, ne mangez pas ceux qui ne sont pas mûrs! _____

_____!

9. N'oublie pas de prendre ton billet d'avion et celui de Delta! _____

_____!

10. Odette lit la poésie par La Fontaine, mais elle ne comprend pas celle de Baudelaire. _____

_____.

11. Vous pouvez avoir mes jeux de vidéo au lieu d'emprunter ceux des enfants. _____

_____.

12. Les couleurs des peintures de Monet sont aussi claires que celles de Delacroix? _____

_____.

Demonstrative Demonstrations- Replace the underlined phrases with demonstrative pronouns, and rewrite the sentences.

Ex. <u>Ces phrases-ci</u> ne sont pas très difficiles. > <u>Celles-ci</u> ne sont pas très difficiles. (These aren't very difficult.)

1. Le bateau-mouche part de <u>cette rive-ci</u>. _____

_____.

2. Connaissez-vous <u>ces mecs-là</u>? _____?

3. <u>Ces timbres-ci</u> coûtent plus maintenant que l'année dernière. _____

_____.

4. Le swahili? Apprends-tu à parler <u>cette langue-là</u>? _____

_____?

5. Cartier n'habite plus dans cet arrondissement-là. _____.

6. Ces outils-ci ne sont pas utiles. _____.

7. M. Suisse fait construire ce châlet-là aux montagnes. _____

_____.

8. Évian préfère cette eau minérale-ci à ce jus-là. _____

_____.

9. Faut-il suivre cette route-là ou ce chemin-ci? _____?

_____?

10. Ces petits fours-ci sont plus délicieux que ces Madeleines-là. _____

_____.

Demonstrative Pronouns on Display- **Choose from the following 'models' to fill in the spaces: celui-ci, celui-là, celle-ci, celle-là, ceux-ci, ceux-là, celles-ci, celles-là, celui que (qu'), celle que (qu'), ceux que (qu'), celles que (qu'), celui qui, celle qui, ceux qui, celles qui, celui de, celle de, ceux de and celles de.** ('The showroom' took up a large space.)

1. Il y a plus de bruit à cette soirée-ci qu'à _____.

2. _____ peignent ne sont pas toujours des artistes professionnels.

3. Où pouvons-nous acheter un râteau comme _____ M. Ramasser?

4. Ces infirmières sont _____ connaissent le docteur Rigoler.

5. Les vêtements de coton sont plus légers que _____ laine.

6. **Les chandeliers (m.)- (the candlesticks)** sont dans ce paquet-ci ou dans _____?

7. Tes plaisanteries et _____ Gérard me font rire.

8. Ne lui donne pas ce parfum-là! _____ sent meilleur.

9. Ils veulent regarder trois passeports; le vôtre et _____ vos copains.

10. Elle aime regarder **les épouvantails-m. (scarecrows)** dans les revues, mais _____ sont dans les champs lui font peur.

11. Ma perceuse marche mieux que _____ M. Faituntrou utilise.

12. Ce verre de vin-ci est le mien. _____ est le tien.

13. Les livres de poches à un marché aux puces sont moins chers que _____ on vend dans une librairie.

14. Hattie Nuff ne veut pas rencontrer plus de femmes de ce club. _____ elle connaît ne sont pas très sympathiques.

15. Will Derness fait du camping en groupe. Il s'amuse plus que _____ vont seul.

LES PRONOMS INTERROGATIFS - LEQUEL, LAQUELLE, LESQUELS, LESQUELLES
Interrogative Pronouns - Which One(s)?

Quel, quelle, quels and *quelles* should "ring a bell." Those four interrogative adjectives agree in gender and in number with the nouns that follow them. *Lequel* and all its 'reverberations' are interrogative pronouns. They match the nouns that they replace in gender and in plurality. If it were not for the definite articles, the pronouns would look like "dead ringers" for the corresponding adjectives.

Interrogative Pronouns

Singular	Plural
lequel (masc.)- which one	lesquels (masc.)- which ones
laquelle (fem.)- which one	lesquelles (fem.)- which ones

The Switch from Which
1. *Lequel* and *laquelle* mean <u>which one</u>. Their plurals, *lesquels* and *lesquelles*, mean <u>which ones</u>. The latter two French pronouns are pronounced identically, but the preceding noun identifies which one of the which ones is used.
2. The prefixes <u>*le*</u>, <u>*la*</u> and <u>*les*</u> reflect the gender and the plurality of the replaced nouns.
Ex. Des trois sœurs laquelle est la plus belle? > Of the three sisters which one is the prettiest? (That does not infer that the other two are 'witch' ones.)
Ex. Lesquels vas-tu nettoyer à sec, les couvertures ou les dessus-de-lit? > Which ones are you going to dry clean, the blankets or the bedspreads? (The latter has 'top' priority.)
In the first example, *laquelle* refers to the previously mentioned noun *les sœurs*.
In the second example, *lesquels* replaces *les couvertures et les dessus-de-lit* that appear later.
2a. If interrogative pronouns substitute for nouns of both genders, the masculine forms, *lequel* and *lesquels* are used. In the second example above, *lesquels* covers both *les couvertures* (f.) and *les dessus-de-lit* (m.)
3. Interrogative pronouns take the place of people and things.
Ex. Deux locataires ne paient pas leurs loyers. Lequel est Alarue? > Two tenants don't pay their rent. Which one is Alarue? (He 'went by' his real name.)
Ex. Des cinq boîtes de musique, laquelle joue "Sainte Nuit, Douce Nuit?" > Of the five music boxes, which one plays "Silent Night?" (It is difficult to tell if you can't hear it.)

<u>An interesting note</u>: People often say <u>what</u> when <u>which</u> would be more accurate. For example, "What is your favorite color?" is perfectly translated as *"Quelle* (Which) *est votre couleur préférée?"* With an interrogative pronoun replacing the adjective, the question becomes *"Laquelle* (Which one) *est votre couleur préférée?"* (Is the difference now "as plain as black and white?")

Filling In the Fill-Ins- Replace the blanks with *lequel, laquelle, lesquels* or *lesquelles*.
1. Burger King ou MacDonald's. _____ aimes-tu mieux?
2. Des sœurs Kardashian, _____ est la plus vielle?
3. Il y a une Bourse à New York et une à Londres. _____ est plus grande?
4. Parmi tous ces restaurants-là, _____ sont près de votre maison?

5. _____ coûte plus, le chauffage en hiver ou la climatisation en été?

6. Les fleurs ou les chocolats. _____ ta mère préfère-t-elle comme un cadeau?

7. M. et Mme Partout vont en Europe avec une de leurs trois filles. _____ restent aux États-Unis?

8. Je viens de trouver deux I-Pads dans la salle de séjour. _____ est le tien?

9. Il décide entre une douzaine de roses et une écharpe de soie pour moi. _____ va-t-il choisir?

10. Toutes les jeunes femmes dans le concours annuel espèrent devenir Mlle Universe. À votre avis, _____ doit gagner le titre?

LES PRONOMS INTERROGATIFS - AUQUEL + 3 AND DUQUEL + 3

As the title suggests, the *lequel* quartet 'has strings attached.' Though they are tied to forms of that pronoun, the contractions can travel in opposite directions. Here are the points <u>to which</u> I am referring and the examples <u>from which</u> you will learn.

Prefixed Interrogative Pronouns

<u>Singular</u>	<u>Plural</u>
auquel (masc.)- at/to which one	**auxquels** (masc.)- at/to which ones
à laquelle (fem.)- at/to which one	**auxquelles** (fem.)- at/to which ones

----

duquel (masc.)- from/of which one	**desquels** (masc.)- from/of which ones
de laquelle (fem.)- from/of which one	**desquelles** (fem.)- from/of which ones

----

<u>Making the Connections To and From</u>

1. <u>At/to which one</u> is translated by the masculine singular *auquel* and by the feminine singular *à laquelle*. Their plurals, <u>at/to which ones</u>, are *auxquels* and *auxquelles*. The only one separated into two words is *à laquelle*. (She is a single female on her own.)

2. Like the *lequel* ensemble, *auquel* + 3 and *duquel* + 3 agree in gender and in number with the antecedent (the preceding noun or pronoun) and replace persons or things.

Ex. Il y a plusieurs hôtels près de l'Opéra. Auquel réserve-t-il une chambre? > There are several hotels near the Opera. At which one is he reserving a room? (There is 'a wide range' to choose from.)

Ex. Auxquels les sept nains la Blanche Neige donne-t-elle les baisers? > To which ones of the seven dwarfs does Snow White give kisses? (They must be 'Happy' and possibly, 'Bashful.')

3. Prepositions hanging loosely at the end of English sentences are neatly folded into the beginning of French ones. That is why "Which hotel is he staying at?" is 'booked' as "At which hotel is he staying?" (Welcome to France! You have just crossed the English Channel.)

4. Masculine singular *duquel* and feminine singular *de laquelle* mean <u>from/of which one</u>. Their respective plurals, *desquels* and *desquelles,* are <u>from/of which ones</u>. With its separate words, *de laquelle* is unique. (The other three form 'a sand-which.')

Ex. De laquelle des voisines M. Snob se moque-t-il? > Of which one of the neighbors does Mr. Snob make fun? (The answer is found through 'outside' sources.)

<u>A helpful hint</u>: *Auquel* + 3 digests the accompanying *à* of verb phrases; *duquel* +3 does likewise

for those followed by *de*.

'Replacement Therapy'- **Replace the underlined phrases with** *auquel, à laquelle, auxquels, aux-quelles, duquel, de laquelle, desquels* **or** *desquelles,* **and put them in the spaces provided.**

1. Je pense <u>à un voyage en Italie</u>. _____ penses-tu?
2. <u>David ou Douglas</u>? _____ apprends-tu à peindre?
3. M. Poser ne comprend pas <u>des appareils technologiques</u>. _____ réfléchit-il?
4. Frayda craint <u>des reptiles à part deux</u>. _____ n'a-t-elle pas peur?
5. Pascal Paslesdeux passe <u>deux examens aujourd'hui</u>. _____ réussit-il?
6. <u>M. Fade et son fils ou de M. Blase et son fils</u>. _____ parles-tu?
7. Françoise assiste <u>à une réception de mariage</u> pendant que ses sœurs vont <u>à une réunion de famille</u>. _____ leur mère assiste-t-elle?
8. Songette adore <u>un garçon dans son cours</u>. _____ rêve-t-elle?
9. M. et Mme Wai Ting ont <u>deux filles qui voyagent beaucoup</u>. _____ reçoivent-ils plus de cartes postales?
10. <u>Sa petite amie ou sa grand-mère</u>? _____ rend-il visite ce dimanche?
11. Les Mainspleines ont cinq petites filles. L'épouse s'en occupe <u>de trois</u>. _____ son époux s'occupe-t-il?
12. Le pied-à-terre de Fay Lechoix n'est pas assez grand pour <u>tous ses amis</u>. _____ envoie-t-elle les invitations?

The Cauldron of the 'Which'- **From the mixture of interrogative pronouns,** *lequel* + 3, *auquel* +3 **and** *duquel* +3, **extract the correct ingredients, and put them in the spaces provided.**

1. L'Allemagne ou la France? _____ fabrique plus de voitures?
2. _____ de ces chevaux-là va gagner la course?
3. À Fidgi et à Tahiti ou à Bali et à Bornéo? _____ des îles exotiques Passepartout voyage-t-il plus?
4. Mes filles ou les tiennes? _____ parles-tu?
5. **Les araignées-f. (the spiders)** ou les serpents (m.)? _____ sont plus laids?
6. L'or ou l'argent? _____ pèse plus?
7. Il y a plusieurs portes à Orly. _____ part le vol #582?
8. _____ de ces deux femmes se teint les cheveux?
9. La maîtresse s'occupe des groupes séparément. _____ lit-elle maintenant?
10. _____ de ses deux copines Sharyn dit-elle son secret?
11. Il y a au moins quatre gares de métro près de la Tour Eiffel. _____ sortent-ils?
12. Choisissez trois endroits! _____ ont les meilleures vues de Paris?
13. L'aéroport à Montréal ou l'un à Québec? _____ Giselle vole-t-elle?
14. Les Letour visitent deux pays chaque automne. _____ vont-ils cette année?

UN SOMMAIRE DES PRONOMS RELATIFS - A Summary of Relative Pronouns

As they were present for specific functions, you have met most of the relative pronouns. At this reunion, they will be reintroduced as members of one family. (It's unique to have all the relatives 'on the same page.')

Qui and *Ce Qui*- Subjects of Discussion

1. *Qui* is a subject of relative clauses. It refers to people, things, places and expressions of time. Its translations are <u>who</u>, <u>which</u> and <u>that</u>.

Ex. Tout le monde connaît la vielle femme qui habite dans une chaussure. > Everyone knows the old woman who lives in a shoe. (Considering all her children, she didn't know what not to do.)

Ex. La chaussure a un talon qui est très firme. > The shoe has a heel that is very firm. (It helps her to 'raise' the children.)

Ex. Celle-ci est la pièce qui sert de sa cuisine. > This one is the room that serves as her kitchen. (She prepares apple and peach 'cobbler' there.)

2. *Ce qui is* also a subject of relative clauses. Even though the English word combination might sound awkward to you, *ce qui* should be translated as <u>that which</u>. Attempting to label *ce qui* as <u>what</u> could easily lead to the improper choice of pronoun.

Ex. Ce qui intéresse mon frère **ne me fait rien**. > That which interests my brother **does not matter to me**. (The subject and the situation are both relative.)

Ex. Personne ne sait ce qui arrive pendant une panne d'électricité. > Nobody knows that which happens during an electrical failure. (Everyone is left 'in the dark.')

<u>An important reminder</u>: The interrogative pronoun *qui*, meaning <u>who</u> as a subject and <u>whom</u> as an object, should not be confused with the relative pronoun *qui*.

Que/Qu' and *Ce que/Ce qu'*- Objects of Discussion

1. *Que/Qu'*, relative object pronouns, are used if the clause has a subject. The translations are <u>whom</u>, <u>which</u> and <u>that</u>. Like *qui*, *que/qu'* refer to people, things, places and expressions of time.

Ex. Hansel et Gretel sont les enfants que leur belle-mère **mesquine** n'aime pas. > Hansel and Gretel are the children whom their **mean** stepmother does not love. (They started out 'on the wrong path.')

Ex. Le frère et la sœur découvrent qu'il y a une maison de pain d'épices dans la forêt. > The brother and the sister discover that there is a gingerbread house in the forest. (But it certainly wasn't "Home Sweet Home.")

2. *Ce que/ce qu'* are also object pronouns used in relative clauses. The translation "<u>that which</u>" is a repeat warning 'to close the gates' to <u>what</u>. (Hansel and Gretel had to deal with 'that witch.')

2a. Like *ce qui*, *ce que/ce qu'* can be placed at the beginning or in the middle of a sentence.

Ex. Ce que des strip-teaseuses font pendant le jour est leur secret. > That which some stripteasers do during the day is their secret. (Maybe they are 'undercover agents.')

Ex. Cette étudiante-là ne rend pas en bon état ce qu'elle emprunte. > That student does not return in good condition that which she borrows. (The owner might get the sweater 'back' but not the front.)

<u>An important reminder</u>: *Que (qu')* and *qu'est-ce que (qu')* are interrogative pronouns meaning <u>what</u>? The former is needed when the subject-verb order is inverted; the latter is used when it is not.

What to Do with *Dont*

1. *Dont* usually replaces the final *de* of verb phrases and expressions ending with that preposition. Translated as <u>whose</u>, <u>of whom</u>, <u>of which</u> and <u>from which</u>, *dont* refers to people and things. *De qui* and the *duquel* family are substitutes for *dont*.

Ex. Mlle Muffet dont la place est **un tabouret** s'assied pour son déjeuner. > Miss Muffet whose seat is **a footstool** sits down for her lunch. ('Long legs' are not an issue for her yet.)

Ex. L'araignée dont la petite fille a peur s'approche d'elle. > The spider which the little girl is afraid of approaches her. (She felt something coming over her.)

Because *avoir peur de* ends with a preposition, *dont* picks it up and places it at the beginning of the clause. (Neither spiders nor prepositions should dangle.)

Ex. L'araignée regarde le bol duquel la petite mange. > The spider looks at the bowl from which the little girl is eating. (She offered to share her lunch, but the spider said, 'No whey!')

1a. *Ce dont* includes the features of *dont* but adds <u>that</u> before its translations making them <u>that of whom</u>, <u>that of which</u> and <u>that from which</u>.

Ex. L'araignée ne veut pas parler de sa crainte des serpents. C'est ce dont elle a honte. > The spider does not want to talk about its fear of snakes. It's what (that of which) it is ashamed (of). (However, little Miss Muffet finally 'cornered it.')

Having Words with the *Lequel* Family

1. Formerly introduced as interrogative pronouns, the *lequel* + 3 group has returned to join the relatives as objects of prepositions.

1a. If a *lequel* member refers to a person or people, it is translated by <u>whom</u> and used like *qui*.

Ex. Hermione est l'amie avec laquelle Harry aime discuter la magique. > Hermione is the friend with whom Harry likes to discuss magic. (They whisper about it in the <u>Chamber of Secrets</u>.)

1b. If a *lequel* member refers to a thing or things, its translation is <u>which</u>. Which which applies depends upon the noun that is replaced. (Harry might consider it as 'which-craft' with a choice of four 'spells.')

Ex. Le numéro de la voie ferrée par laquelle Harry entre dans un nouveau monde est 9 ¾. > The train track number by which Harry enters into a new world is 9 ¾. (It was a very creative 'part.')

1c. If a *lequel* member refers to a place or an expression of time, it is translated by <u>which.</u> Used to express location, its synonym is *où*.

Ex. C'est le jardin dans lequel les ours plantent leurs fleurs. > That is the garden in which bears plant their flowers. (They are also 'Hairy Potters.')

'Black Sheep among the Relatives'- Label the statements *vrai* or *faux*.

_____ 1. *Qui* is the object of a relative clause.

_____ 2. *Qui* and *que* can both refer to people.

_____ 3. Translations of *que* as a relative pronoun are <u>who</u>, <u>which</u> and <u>that</u>.

_____ 4. As an interrogative pronoun, *que* means <u>what</u>?

_____ 5. The best translations for *ce que* and *ce qui* are <u>that which</u>.

_____ 6. *Ce qui* and *ce que* are placed only in the middle of sentences.

_____ 7. Verb phrases that include *de* are replaced by *dont*.

_____ 8. *Ce* before *dont* is translated as <u>this</u>.

_____ 9. The *lequel* + 3 family has interrogative and relative pronouns.

_____ 10. Preceded by a preposition, the *lequel* quartet can refer to a person, a location or a time.

'Putting Relatives in Their Place'- Fill in the blanks with *qui, ce qui, que (qu'), ce que (ce qu'), dont, ce dont, lequel, laquelle, lesquels* or *lesquelles* to form complete sentences.

1. L'ordonnance _____ le pharmacien prépare n'est pas la vôtre.
2. Peu de rafraîchissements au ciné? Je prends _____ est disponible.
3. M. Fracture peut-il atteindre **l'étagère-f. (the shelf)** sur _____ sa femme met ses béquilles?
4. Je ne sais pas _____ le médecin suggère pour guérir la grippe.
5. Selon M. Douteux, le diplôme _____ est dans ton bureau est faux.
6. Demandez-moi si vous ne trouvez pas tout _____ vous avez besoin!
7. Voici les cartes postales pour _____ je n'ai pas de timbres.
8. Malheureusement, _____ vous intéresse est dangereux.
9. C'est une pièce _____ joue longtemps à Broadway.
10. Ultime fait toujours de son mieux. C'est quelque chose _____ elle est fière.
11. Kidd dit _____ il a **une poubelle (a trash can)** spéciale dans _____ il met ses factures.
12. Malfait, _____ échoue à toutes ses matières scolaires, ne montre pas à personne les notes _____ il a honte.

'Relatively Speaking'- Translate the following sentences.
1. The animals he is speaking of no longer exist. _____
_____.
2. There's the hole in which the dog hides his bone. _____
_____!
3. The widow who does not pay her rent always wears diamonds. _____
_____.
4. What goes on the left and on the right of the plate is important when one sets the table. _____
_____.
5. **The piggy bank (la tirelire)** in which she keeps her change is empty. _____
_____.
6. **A CD-Rom (un cédérom)** cannot explain what you (*vous*) do not understand. _____
_____.
7. Hope and May Bea admit that they do not know what they are doing. _____
_____.
8. There are questions for which there are no answers. _____
_____.
9. Morty Fyde does not want to tell us what he is afraid of. _____
_____.
10. What one receives is not always what one deserves. _____
_____
_____.

SPECIAL USES OF THE PRESENT TENSE

DEPUIS- Since/For, DEPUIS QUAND- How Long?
(DEPUIS) COMBIEN DE TEMPS- How Long?
IL Y A _____ QUE- It Has Been _____ Since
COMBIEN DE TEMPS Y A-T-IL QUE- How Long Has It Been Since?
PENDANT- For, During

The perfect present tense, which consists of <u>has been</u> and <u>have been,</u> has no French equivalent. Its translation is in the present tense. After all, if you have been doing something, you're still in the process of doing it. As there aren't any "has beens," French women must have the formula for eternal youth. (It certainly does not include "Oil of Old Age.')

Depuis and *Depuis Quand*
1. To make a statement about an action that started in the past and is still in progress, you can use *depuis*- since/for + a present tense form of a verb.
Ex. Je pense qu'ils gardent mon secret depuis l'année dernière. > I think that they have been keeping my secret since last year. (It's really 'hard to tell.')
2. To ask a question about an ongoing action that began in the past, one option is *depuis quand*- how long + a present tense form of a verb.
Ex. Depuis quand Jennifer Lopez fait-elle des courses dans ce supermarché? > How long/since when has Jennifer Lopez been shopping in that supermarket? (Long enough for the cashier and all the cus- 'to check her out.')
Ex. Depuis quand ce vieil homme-là et la jeune femme sortent-ils ensemble? > How long/since when have that old man and the young woman been going out together? (He might have been 'taking some time off.')
<u>An important note:</u> **Although an English sentence includes <u>has been/have been</u> + a verb ending with -ing, its translation is a single verb. For example, *ils sortent quatre mois.* > They have been going out four months. (<u>Have been</u> is just an escort.)**

Combien de Temps and *Depuis Combien de Temps*?
1. *Combien de temps* means <u>how long?</u>/<u>how much time?</u>
Ex. Combien de temps faut-il pour faire un soufflé au chocolat? > How long/How much time does it take to make a chocolate soufflé? (Some can prepare it in fifteen minutes 'flat.')
2. *Depuis combien de temps* and *depuis quand* are synonymous. The present tense of the verb is used after both formats.
Ex. Depuis combien de temps Ben Dover fait-il des pilates?
Ex. Depuis quand Ben Dover fait-il des pilates? > For how long/Since when has Ben Dover been doing pilates? (Maybe twice 'weakly' and one month strong.)

Il y a + Time + *que/qu'* and *Combien de Temps y a-t-il que/qu'*?
1. *Il y a* + a time frame + *que/qu'* + a verb in the present tense also expresses an action begun in the past and still in progress.
Ex. Il y a cinq siècles que des individus cherchent la fontaine de **jouvence**. > Some individuals have

been looking for the fountain of **youth** for five centuries. (Being five hundred years old, they must have found it.)

2. *Combien de temps y a-t-il que/qu'* is the interrogative form of *Il y a* + a time frame + *que/qu'* + a verb in the present tense as well as a synonym for *depuis combien de temps*?

Ex. Combien de temps y a-t-il que/Depuis combien de temps Sue Venir garde les courriers électroniques dont elle n'a plus besoin? > How long has Sue Venir been keeping the e-mails that she does not need anymore? (Maybe for quite a while if she has 'an attachment.')

----

1. *Pendant* means <u>for</u> when it precedes a word or phrase indicating time. As in English, its use is optional. (The need for *pendant* is pending.)

Ex. M. Loser va à l'église (pendant) plusieurs heures chaque dimanche. > Mr. Loser goes to church (for) several hours each Sunday. (But he still 'doesn't have a prayer.')

2. *Pendant*, if not followed by a time reference, means <u>during/in the course of</u>. In that context, *pendant* is included <u>during</u> conversations.

Ex. Ne continuez pas à interrompre le patron pendant la réunion! > Don't continue to interrupt the boss during the meeting! (He allows 'a question and answer .... period!')

<u>'Up Until Now'</u>- Using the time periods in parentheses, answer the following questions.
Ex. Depuis quand M. Pochepleine cherche-t-il un Porsche?
(une semaine) M. Pochepleine cherche un Porsche depuis une semaine.

1. Depuis quand Bernadette habite-t-elle dans un village?
(une année) _____.
2. Depuis quand tes parents voyagent-ils en Nouvelle-Angleterre?
(deux semaines) _____.
3. Depuis quand M.et Mme Bienvenus restent-ils chez vous?
(cinq jours) _____.
4. Depuis quand apprenez-vous à parler l'arabe?
(six mois) _____.
5. Depuis quand l'ascenseur ne fonctionne-t-il pas?
(deux jours) _____.
6. Depuis quand Mme Patience fait-elle construire sa maison?
(l'automne dernier) _____
_____.
7. Combien de temps les deux hommes attendent-ils Godot?
(plus de soixante ans) _____
_____.
8. Combien de temps fais-tu cet exercice-ci?
(moins de quinze minutes) _____.
_____.

What You Have Been Learning- Translate the following sentences.

1. June travaille ici depuis mai. _____.

2. Yogi assiste à un cours de yoga depuis 2004. _____
_____.

3. Leur fils sert en Irak depuis le commencement de la guerre. _____
_____.

4. Mme Coudre fait les rideaux et les dessus-de-lit (pendant) deux années. _____
_____.

5. **Depuis quand** est-ce que tu m'attends _____?

6. Depuis quand suis-tu un régime? _____?

7. **Depuis quand** ta grand-mère regarde-t-elle **le** même **feuilleton télévisé (the soap opera)?** _____
_____?

8. **Depuis combien de temps** Madonna **tourne**-t-elle **un film (to film)** en Europe? _____
_____?

9. **Depuis combien de temps** Dee Duct et son mari paient-ils leurs dettes en ligne? _____
_____?

10. **Combien de temps y a-t-il que** tu traduis le français? _____
_____?

11. Mme Chariot fait des emplettes dans Walmart (pendant) plus de trois heures. _____
_____.

12. Est-ce que Minnie Rell boit assez d'eau pendant le temps chaud? _____
_____?

Sentences 5, 7, 8, 9 and 10 include phrases in bold type. Use a synonym for each of those terms and rewrite the questions. More than one response for each is possible.

5. _____?
_____?

7. _____?
_____?

8. _____?
_____?

9. _____?
_____?

10. _____?
_____?
_____

UNE REVUE - A Review

Les Pronoms Possessifs, Les Pronoms Démonstratifs, Les Pronoms Interrogatifs, Les Pronoms Relatifs and Special Uses of the Present Tense

Supporting the Sentence Structure- **Circle the letters of the answers to complete the sentences.**

1. French possessive pronouns ____.
a. are not preceded by definite articles
b. always follow contractions
c. begin with the same letters as possessive adjectives
d. each have three forms

2. ____ can substitute in French for possessive pronouns.
a. reflexive pronouns   b. 's   c. contractions and partitives   d. *à* + disjunctive pronouns

3. French demonstrative pronouns ____.
a. agree with the nouns they replace
b. have one singular and one plural form
c. are not followed by *-ci* or *-là*
d. include indirect object pronouns in their names

4. French demonstrative pronouns can precede phrases beginning with ____.
a. à   b. cela (ça)   c. de   d. en

5. French interrogative pronouns ____.
a. cannot be subjects   b. refer only to things   c. cannot be preceded by contractions
d. contain the names of interrogative adjectives

6. *Qui* and *ce qui* are ____.
a. interchangeable   b. subjects of relative clauses   c. objects of relative clauses
d. interrogative pronouns

7. The most precise translation for *ce qui* and *ce que* is ____.
a. that which   b. what   c. whom   d. that

8. *Dont* is used to replace ____.
a. interrogative words   b. verb phrases ending with *de*   c. all expressions with *avoir*
d. phrases ending with à

9. As relative pronouns, the four members of the *lequel* family ____.
a. are preceded by contractions
b. do not show agreement with antecedents
c. are objects of prepositions
d. cannot refer to people

10. Locations and expressions of time can be assigned to a member of the *lequel* family or to ____.
a. depuis   b. où   c. pendant   d. comment

'Fitting Comments' for a Puzzled Look- **Rearrange the pieces to form complete sentences.**

1. combien de temps/ se rase-t-il/ Nick/ Depuis

_____?

2. sur lequel/ ses pieds/ Le tabouret/ est fade/ il met

_____.

3. d'or/ ce qui/ n'est pas/ Tout/ **brille (shines)**

_____.

4. dont/ ces choses/ Où/ tu parles/ trouves-tu

_____?

5. des nouveaux-riches/ dans sa maison/ Chiffon préfère/ à ceux/ les meubles d'occasion

_____

6. de piscine/ nager/ tu n'as pas/ tu peux/ dans la mienne/ Comme

_____ .

_____

7. son petit/ ne voit pas/ dans ses mains/ ce que/ La mère/ tient/ **égarée (distracted)**

_____ .

_____

8. "à lui" et/ acheter/ avec les inscriptions/ blanches-là/ "à elle"/ Vont-elles/ ces serviettes?

_____

_____ ?

What's Going On? - Translate the underlined phrases.
1. <u>They have been thinking about you (*tu*)</u> depuis hier. _____
2. <u>I have been working</u> sur **le chemin de fer (the railroad)**. _____
3. <u>Since when has Kay Beck been staying</u> au Canada? _____

4. <u>How much time does James spend</u> au gymnase? _____

5. <u>How long have you (*tu*) been flying</u> cet hélicoptère? _____
_____ ou _____
6. <u>How long have they been living</u> dans le même voisinage? _____
_____ ou _____
7. <u>How long has Anne Surance been driving</u> la voiture de ses parents? _____
_____ ou _____
8. Je connais quelqu'un <u>who sits in a bathtub during a hurricane</u>. _____

_____

_____

LE PASSÉ COMPOSÉ - THE PAST TENSE
REGULAR VERBS CONJUGATED WITH AVOIR

The French have a composed approach when referring to a 'tense' situation. *Le passé composé,* the French past tense, always includes two components: a helping/an auxiliary verb and a past participle. Former experiences might give us "a heads up" about the present, but the reverse is true for this tense in French.

Le passé composé of *donner* is given here.

Donner - To Give

Singular	Plural
j'ai donné- I gave, did give, have given	nous avons donné- we gave, did give, have given
tu as donné- you gave, did give, have given	vous avez donné- you gave, did give, have given
il/elle/on a donné- he/she/it/one gave, did give, has given	ils/elles ont donné- they gave, did give, have given

----

Presents for Dealing with the Past

1. Notice the three translations for each form of *donner* in the model above! Though *j'ai donné* literally says, "I have given," it also means <u>I gave,</u> and <u>I did give</u>. This "3 for 1 rule" is very important when constructing negative and interrogative sentences *au passé composé.* (The French know how to economize.)

2. *Le passé composé* of a verb conjugated with *avoir* has a present tense form of that auxiliary + a past participle.

3. Infinitives and past participles of -<u>er</u> verbs sound the same. (The procedure is painless because the 'roots' aren't touched.)

Ex. Nous avons parlé de l'avenir. > We talked/did talk/ have talked about the future. (But that was in the past.)

4. The past participle (pp.) of a regular -<u>er</u> verb is formed by removing the <u>r</u> from the infinitive ending and changing the <u>e</u> to an <u>é</u>.

Exs. *fermer > fermé* (closed), *jouer > joué* (played), *parler > parlé* (spoken), *rester >resté* (stayed)

4a. Orthographic/stem changing verbs drop the final <u>r</u> and top the last <u>e</u> with an accent *aigu* to form their past participles.

Ex. Les pédiatres ont pesé les bébés et les jeunes enfants. > The pediatricians weighed the babies and the young children. (And measured them 'on a scale of 1 to 10.')

5. The past participle of a regular -<u>ir</u> verb is formed by dropping the final <u>r</u> from the infinitive. By doing so, you will have *fini* (finished) as well as *réussi* (succeeded).

Exs. *bâtir > bâti* (built), *choisir > choisi* (chosen), *rempli* (filled), *rougir > rougi* (blushed)

Ex. Ray Dar a ralenti aussitôt qu'il a remarqué la voiture de police. > Ray Dar slowed down as soon as he noticed the police car. (The officer may have already reserved a ticket for the performance.)

6. The past participle of a regular -<u>re</u> verb is formed by removing those two letters from the infinitive and adding a <u>u</u>. (The SS *Nothing* turns into a U-Boat.)

Exs. *attendre > attendu* (waited (for), *entendre > entendu* (heard), *perdre > perdu* (lost)

Ex. Son frère lui a demandé, "Tu m'as entendu quand j'ai chuchoté à Maman?" > Her brother asked her, "Did you hear me when I whispered to Mom?" (If the sister does not answer him, she's got her own secret.)

A very important note: All regular past participles end with a vowel (<u>e</u>, <u>i</u> or <u>u</u>).

7. <u>Has/have</u> + a past participle and <u>did</u> + a past participle are considered units. Direct, indirect and reflexive pronouns keep their present tense positions and precede the entire verb phrase.
Ex. Le marchand l'a vendu. > The merchant sold/did sell/has sold it. (Giving up the <u>e</u> on *le* was part of the deal.)

8. When an infinitive follows a past participle, the word order is identical to English.
Ex. Mes parents ont aimé bien regarder mes matchs de tennis. > My parents really liked to watch my tennis matches. (The term "love" was never used.)

8a. Object pronouns go between the verb *au passé composé* and the infinitive.
Ex. Ils ont décidé de le déplacer. > They decided to move it. (But then, they realized that <u>it</u> belonged between the two verbs.)

9. *Le passé composé* states or infers a completed past action. A time reference can be part of the sentence. Frequently used, chronological markers are *déjà, hier, hier soir- last night, avant-hier-* the day before yesterday, *le mois dernier, la semaine/l'année dernière, le mois passé, la semaine/ l'année passée.*

10. In past tense sentences, *il y a* means <u>ago</u>. The translations <u>there is/there are</u> are reserved for the present tense.
Ex. Il y a plus de **piétons** que des conducteurs à Paris. > There are more **pedestrians** than drivers in Paris. (It is a less stressful means of using one's 'motor skills.')
Ex. Il y a plusieurs années, sa famille a loué un chalet aux Alpes. > Several years ago, his/her family rented a chalet in the Alps. (Real estate was high, even then.)

'Let the Good Times Roll'- Write the following sentences *au passé composé*. Then translate the new versions with the three options.
Ex. M. Pasdesou dépense tout ce qu'il gagne. > M. Pasdesou a dépensé tout ce qu'il a gagné. >
Mr. Pasdesou spent/has spent/did spend all that he earned/did earn/has earned.

1. Chantal chante très bien ce soir. _____

_____.

2. Grâce remercie l'homme sympathique. _____

_____.

3. Quelques étudiants désirent poser des questions. _____

_____

_____.

4. Nous partageons un pied-à-terre près de la Sorbonne. _____

_____

_____.

5. Le fermier nourrit les animaux tôt le matin. _____

_____

_____.

6. Rose et Scarlett rougissent devant les garçons. _____

_____

_____.

7. Le docteur Rigoler guérit des patients. _____

8. Chanel et moi entendons les nouvelles. _____

_____

9. Je réponds au téléphone ce matin. _____

_____

10. Vous rendez ce que vous empruntez. _____

_____

Translating for a 'Past-time'- Use the correct forms of the infinitives in parentheses, and write the sentences in French.

1. (jouer) The little ones played marbles together. _____

_____

2. (acheter) Ken Tucqui bought a horse for Louis Ville. _____

_____

3. (porter) Demi Couvert wore a French bikini. _____

_____

4. (louer) Louie rented a cabin on **the hill (la colline)**. _____

_____

5. (bavarder) Ella Dutemps and I chatted yesterday. _____

_____

6. (nettoyer, briller) You (*vous*) cleaned so much that everything shined. _____

_____

7. (vieillir) Everyone got old suddenly. _____

8. (agir) You (*tu*) acted like a child. _____

9. (maigrir) Mrs. Peau and Mrs. Os lost too much weight. _____

_____

10. (interrompre) Someone interrupted him twice. _____

_____

11. (vendre) Henri Ford sold his car two hundred years ago. _____

_____

12. (perdre, trouver) I lost it, and you (*tu*) found it. _____

Le Passé Composé aux Formes Interrogatives

The four ways to ask a question in French *au temps présent* apply *au passé composé*. There is a little lilt in one's voice at the end of every type of question: intonation, *est-ce que*, *n'est-ce pas?* and inversion. Legally and grammatically, interrogation can precede or follow statements.

Since You Asked
With intonation
Ex. Une femme **déprimée** a trouvé quatre cents euros sur **le trottoir**? > A **depressed** woman found four hundred euros on **the sidewalk**? (She had previously 'been looking down.')

With est-ce que?
Ex. Est-ce qu'on a invité Daphne à la fête? > Did someone invite Daphne to the party? (To know her response, the first step is '*est-ce que*.')

With n'est-ce pas?
Ex. Fa So a demandé de l'argent à Rémy, n'est-ce pas? > Fa So asked Rémy for some money, didn't he? (Fa So could have said, "Do you have any dough, Rémy?")

With inversion
Ex. Ton professeur de musique a-t-il entendu ton solo hier soir ? > Did your music teacher hear your solo last night? (He might have wanted 'to take some notes.')

Le Passé Composé aux Formes Négatives

Many positive things can be said for knowing how to use negatives correctly *au passé composé*.

Forming Basic and Advanced 'K-nots'

1. Negative phrases surround the helping verb *au passé composé*. The past participle is usually the last word in the verb phrase.
Ex. Le novice n'a jamais attrapé de grandes pêches. > The novice never caught any big fish. (A true fisherman would not have used that 'line.')
Ex. Mme Casper n'a rien révélé du fantôme dans son grenier. > Mrs. Casper revealed nothing about the ghost in her attic. (The secret could come back to haunt her.)

2. Short adverbs often precede past participles. They include *bien*, *déjà*, *mal*, *peu* and *trop*.
Ex. Vous avez bien mangé hier soir au Café Rainforest. > You ate well last evening at the Rainforest Café. (Not 'a drop' was left on their plates.)

3. Terms with an Alternate Negative Approach

3a. *Personne* follows the past participle.
Ex. Nous n'avons rencontré personne **remarquable** pendant notre croisière. > We did not meet anybody **outstanding** during our cruise. (It's a matter of 'how one comes across.')

3b. *Que* follows the past participle and precedes the word(s) stressed.
Ex. Une bonne fée avec **une baguette magique** ne leur a donné que trois vœux. > A fairy godmother with **a magic wand** gave them only three wishes. (After her third strike, 'she was out.')

3c. *Nulle part*- nowhere follows the past participle. Its antonym is *partout*.
Ex. Mme Adage a cherché **le dicton** partout, mais elle ne l'a trouvé nulle part. > Mrs. Adage looked for **the saying** everywhere, but she found it nowhere. (Maybe it had 'a hidden meaning.')

3d. *Ne .. ni .. ni*- neither .. nor: *Ni* precedes each noun, pronoun or adjective stressed.
Ex. Le petit ami de Freida Looke a voyagé beaucoup l'été dernier. Il ne lui a envoyé ni les lettres ni les cartes postales. > Freida Looke's boyfriend traveled a lot last summer. He sent her neither letters nor postcards. (Nevertheless, 'she got the message.')

3e. *Aucun(e)*, a synonym for *pas un(e)*, means no/not one/not any. This negative has a singular from and precedes the nouns that it modifies. Its translations can be singular or plural.
Ex. Ces touristes inconsidérés-là n'ont laissé aucun pourboire. > Those inconsiderate tourists left no tip(s). (If only their servers could do without them.)

'It Can't Hurt to Ask.'- Change the interrogative and the negative present tense sentences into *le passé composé.*

Ex. Mme Gâtelesgosses grondé-t-elle ses petits? > Mrs. Gâtelesgosses a-t-elle grondé ses petits?
Ex. Di Ette ne goûte jamais de profiteroles. > Di Ette n'a jamais goûté de profiteroles.

1. Tu passes l'aspirateur partout? _____?

2. Est-ce que Polly et Esther aiment la même étoffe? _____
_____?

3. Prêtez-vous quelques euros à vos amis? _____
_____?

4. Le petit-fils joue-t-il aux dames avec son grand-père? _____
_____?

5. Où est-ce que Jett voyage? _____?

6. (2 verbes) Rougit-elle quand il lui donne un baiser? _____
_____?

7. (2 verbes) Larmette pleure quand elle mal place sa poupée, n'est-ce pas? ____
_____?

----

8. Raphael Rappelle n'oublie pas les mots à la chanson. _____
_____.

9. Leur mère ne laisse plus de gâteaux secs pour le Père Noël. _____
_____.

10. Les hôtes froids ne parlent guère aux invités. _____
_____.

11. (2 verbs) Ils m'accompagnent nulle part, et ils ne rencontrent personne. ____
_____.

The Times 'Across Words' Puzzle- Put the letters of the time expressions beside the numbers of the phrases that start the sentences.

_____ 1. Le vieux soldat américain a visité Paris

_____ 2. La nouvelle mariée a lancé son bouquet

_____ 3. Les jeunes femmes ont nettoyé à fond leurs penderies et leurs tiroirs

_____ 4. Michel a essayé d'obtenir son permis de conduire

_____ 5. L'enfant n'a pas assisté au cours aujourd'hui

_____ 6. Nous commençons à voir les modes

_____ 7. Tu as parlé français

_____ 8. Après minuit le premier janvier, M. Champagne a utilisé la phrase,

_____ 9. Le serveur m'a apporté un autre verre de vin

_____ 10. La mère a donné **un biberon (a baby bottle)** au petit enfant

A. parce qu'il a neigé trop hier.

B. aussitôt qu'il a pleuré.

C. "l'année passée."

D. que je connais déjà.

E. après la deuxième guerre mondiale.

F. dans son hôtel hier soir.

G. quand le client a payé.

H. le dimanche de Pâques.

I. encore une fois.

J. à l'âge de seize ans.

_____ 11. Le voyageur a regardé la télé
_____ 12. Que cette ville a grandi
_____ 13. M. et Mme Provence ont acheté une petite
        maison à Nice
_____ 14. M. Mauvaistemps a lavé sa voiture
_____ 15. Je n'ai pas désiré voir le même monument
_____ 16. Il n'a pas compté l'argent
_____ 17. À la soirée il m'a présenté aux gens
_____ 18. Je n'ai mangé ni le jambon ni le dinde

K. pendant sa réception de mariage.
L. quand ils ont déménagé en France.
M. la semaine passée à Montréal.

N. dès que j'ai fini le premier.
O. du siècle dernier.
P. depuis ma dernière visite ici.
Q. avant le vide-grenier.
R. juste avant la tempête.

Le Passé Composé aux Phrases Négatives-Interrogatives

A negative phrase generally surrounds the helping/auxiliary verb. A past participle is typically the last word of the negative-interrogative cluster.

Samples on a Negative-Interrogative Roll

Ex. Pourquoi n'a-t-il pas contesté le prix de son billet avant le vol? > Why didn't he dispute the price of his ticket before the flight? (Maybe he thought that 'it wouldn't get him anywhere.')

Ex. Est-ce que la belle-mère cruelle de Hansel et Gretel n'a jamais averti les enfants de **la** mauvaise **sorcière** dans les bois? > Didn't Hansel and Gretel's cruel stepmother ever warn the children of **the** evil **witch** in the woods? (She probably told them 'to just take a hike.')

'Twisting the Facts'- **Change the following statements into negative-interrogative forms. More than one question format is possible.**
Ex. Jules César a traversé cette rivière.
1. Est-ce que Jules César n'a pas traversé cette rivière?
2. Jules César n'a-t-il pas traversé cette rivière?

1. Tu as répondu à ton courrier électronique? _____
_____?

2. Dot Tedlyne a coupé **les bons de réduction (the coupons)** avant d'aller au supermarché. _____
_____?

3. Nous avons ramassé toutes les feuilles l'automne dernier. _____
_____?

4. Le prof a déjà expliqué la conjugaison des verbes. _____
_____?

5. Georges Curieux a posé la même question de nouveau. _____
_____?

6. Jade et son époux ont assisté à un cours de cuisine chinoise. _____
_____?

7. M. Swan a vendu son cottage près du lac. _____
_____?

Who Hasn't Mastered Negative-Interrogatives *au Passé Composé*? - Translate the following sentences.

1. Didn't it cost anything? _____?
2. Hasn't Slim Jim gotten thinner? _____?
3. We never erased it? _____?
4. Who has not eaten yet? _____?
5. Haven't you (*vous*) guessed the answer? _____
   _____?
6. Why haven't they built (*bâtir*) it? _____?
7. Haven't you (*tu*) thought more about it? _____
   _____?
8. Didn't Curt O'See ever interrupt anyone? _____
   _____?
   _____

LES PARTICIPES PASSÉS IRRÉGULIERS - Irregular Past Participles
La Première Partie

Many past participles take advantage of being the last word in verbal phrases. It's much easier to get to know them if the groups are approached separately.

Two And Three Letter Past Participles Ending with -U

1. avoir- eu (had)

2. boire- bu (drunk)
Ex. Un étranger à un bar a pleuré lorsqu'il a bu. > A stranger at a bar cried while he drank. (Some of the regulars referred to him as 'bu-who?')

3. croire- cru (believed) (*J'ai cru* sounds similar to a popular clothing chain.)

4. devoir- dû (had to) + an infinitive
Ex. Le malade a dû rester au lit pendant la tempête d'hiver. > The sick man had to stay in bed during the winter storm. (Why would he trade his comfort for 'sheets of ice' and 'blankets of snow'?)

5. lire- lu (read)
Ex. Tu m'as lu hier soir. > You read to me last night. (If you don't say the verb phrase, you 'skip *tu m'as lu*.')

6. plaire- plu (pleased)

7. pleuvoir- plu (rained)

An important note: *Plaire* and *pleuvoir* have identical past participles.
Ex. Il vous a plu quand il a plu. > It pleased you when it rained. (The bad weather gave them a sunny disposition.)

8. pouvoir- pu (could) + an infinitive
Ex. Les secrétaires n'ont pas pu sortir avec le patron. > The secretaries couldn't go out with the boss. (He was left 'in his own company.')

9. savoir- su (known): The past participle also means <u>found out</u>.

10. voir- vu (seen)
Ex. Est-ce que vous avez vu James Bond dans ce film-là? > Did you see James 'Bond' in that film?

(He does that with beautiful women in every movie.)
A helpful hint: Saying the past participles in this unit aloud is 'rhyme time' well spent.

Four, Five and Six Letter Past Participles Ending with -U

1. apparaître- apparu (appeared)
Ex. Le météore qui a apparu dans le ciel hier soir a atterri dans **un pâturage** de vache. > The meteor that appeared in the sky last night landed in a cow **pasture**. ("Let the chips fall where they may!")

2. connaître- connu (known): The Indian tribe, *les Su*, traveled by *connu*. (It is a 'known' fact.)

3. paraître- paru (seemed): Its synonym is *sembler*.

4. reconnaître- reconnu (recognized)
Ex. La jeune fille **a trébuché** juste au moment où elle a reconnu l'acteur célèbre. > The girl **tripped** the moment that she recognized the famous actor. (And then 'she fell for him.')

5. courir- couru (run)
Ex. Uri et Rush ont couru plus vite que leur père. > Uri and Rush ran faster than their father. (He just 'took it in his stride.')

6. tenir- tenu (held, grasped)

7. falloir- fallu (was necessary) + an infinitive
Ex. Il a fallu prendre le dernier rendez-vous avec son avocat spécialisé dans le divorce. > It was necessary to make the last appointment with her divorce lawyer. (Was there an 'x' by that date?)

8. vouloir- voulu (wanted)
Ex. Quelques touristes ont voulu se réveiller tôt pour voir **le lever de soleil**. > A few tourists wanted to wake up early to see **the sunrise**. (Most were not moved by the idea.)

It All Depends on 'U'- Write the correct forms of the following verbs *au passé composé*: apparaître, avoir, boire, connaître, courir, croire, lire, plaire, pouvoir, reconnaître, savoir, voir and vouloir. A couple of past participles can be used more than once.

1. Tous mes amis _____ _____ le film, <u>Manon de la Source</u>.
2. _____-tu _____ M. Short longtemps?
3. Je n'_____ pas _____ / _____ lui dire les mauvaises nouvelles.
4. _____-tu jamais _____ dans un marathon?
5. Personne n'_____ _____ l'histoire **du tyran (the bully).**
6. Qu'est-ce que vous _____ _____ savoir?
7. Quelques étudiants _____ _____ comme des trous lorsqu'ils _____ _____
l'occasion.
8. Nous _____ _____ le mec aussitôt que nous l' _____ _____.
9. Pierre Lapin n'_____ jamais _____. Il _____ _____ rester chez lui
pendant la fête de Pâques.
10. Comme Josephine ne comprend pas la philosophie, cela m'_____ _____ qu'elle _____
_____ un livre par Albert Camus.

Two Sets of False -RE Verbs au Passé Composé
La Deuxième Partie

Only two principle verbs, *mettre* and *prendre*, have past participles that end with -<u>is</u>. Yet, as the heads of large families, 'they put up with and take a lot.'

-<u>Is</u> in the Past
1. **admettre- admis (admitted)**
2. **commettre- commis (committed)**
3. **émettre- emis (emitted)**
4. **mettre- mis (put, placed, set). One of its synonyms is** *placer.*
Ex. Mme Seplaint a demandé à son mari, "Qui a mis la lessive dans le lave-linge?, qui a mis le couvert, et qui a mis les plats dans le lave-vaisselle?" > Mrs. Seplaint asked her husband, "Who put the laundry in the washing machine?, who set the table, and who put the dishes in the dishwasher?" (It was always '*mis, mis, mis.*')
5. **omettre- omis (omitted)**
6. **permettre- permis (allowed, permitted)**
Ex. Je ne sais pas qui a permis à l'imbécile de conduire. > I do not know who permitted the imbecile to drive. (Neither of them was a 'Rhodes' scholar.)
7. **promettre- promis (promised)**
Ex. Deb Itz a promis de rembourser tout l'argent qu'elle a emprunté. > Deb Itz promised to pay back all the money that she borrowed. (One might wonder which was kept.)
8. **remettre- remis (put back, put on again)**
9. **transmettre- transmis (transmitted)**

----

1. **apprendre- appris (learned)**
2. **comprendre- compris (understood)**
Ex. Le garçon n'a pas compris le sens du gros mot. > The boy did not understand the meaning of the curse word. (When confronted he said, "I don't know. I swear.")
3. **prendre- pris (taken)**
Ex. Pourquoi Mme Treize n'a-t-elle pas pris la médicine pour ses côtes douloureuses? > Why didn't Mrs. Treize take the medicine for her painful ribs? (Maybe she was afraid of its 'side effects.')
4. **reprendre- repris (taken again, taken back, resumed)**
5. **surprendre- surpris (surprised)**
Ex. La petite américaine a surpris le soldat français quand elle lui a parlé couramment en français. > The little American girl surprised the French soldier when she spoke to him fluently in French. (She 'caught him off guard.')

Some Recalls Are Necessary- Label the statements *vrai* or *faux.*
_____ 1. Past participles of regular -<u>er</u>, -<u>ir</u> and -<u>re</u> verbs end with vowels.
_____ 2. There is one translation for each verb form *au passé composé.*
_____ 3. Orthographic/stem changing verbs have past participles ending with an <u>é</u>.
_____ 4. Object pronouns precede helping verbs *au passé composé.*
_____ 5. *Il y a* has the same translation when used with present or past tense verbs.

_____ 6. Past participles are typically the last words of negative verb phrases.

_____ 7. Shorter adverbs always follow past participles.

_____ 8. *Personne* and *que* go after past participles.

_____ 9. *Pu* and *dû* are followed by infinitives.

_____ 10. Infinitives endings with -*aître* have past participles ending with a -u.

_____ 11. Past participles on "the *mettre* team" end with a -t.

_____ 12.The *mettre* and *prendre* families of verbs have the same past participle endings.

'An End in Sight'- **Circle the letters of the correct responses to complete the sentences.**

1. Pourquoi ton fils a-t-il _____ aussi vite que possible à l'école?

a. compris   b. remis   c. dû   d. couru

2. _____ le temps de préparer le dîner et mettre le couvert avant sept heures.

a. Personne n'a compris   b. On n'a pas eu   c. Il a dû   d. Ceux qui ont su

3. Anne Core achète le même vin que nous avons _____.

a. y omis   b. déjà transmis   c. bu hier soir   d. volé il y a longtemps

4. Il y a une heure il a _____, et les rues sont toujours trempées.

a. peu appris   b. plu beaucoup   c. trop pris   d. paru bien

5. Fabriquée ment si souvent que nous _____ sa dernière histoire.

a. n'avons pas cru   b. n'avons pu tenir   c. avons jeté   d. lui avons promis

6. Bonjour Alphonse, "Je _____ le moment où je _____."

a. lui ai appris .... lui ai lu   b. l'ai surpris .... l'ai permis   c. t'ai plu ... t'ai compris

d. t'ai reconnu .... t'ai vu

7. Mlle Cœurtendre _____ chez elle le chiot que personne _____.

a. a dû .... n'a lu   b. a remis .... n'a tenu   c. a pris .... n'a voulu   d. a nourri .... n'a connu

8. _____ faire les devoirs?

a. N'as-tu pas vu   b. N'as-tu pas pu   c. N'as-tu pas mis   d. N'as-tu pas apparu

----

Participes Passés Irréguliers - Irregular Past Participles
La Troisième Partie

Some verbs that are irregular in the present tense have regular past participles. Examples are *dormir > dormi, mentir > menti* **and** *sentir > senti.* **However, most irregular verbs have irregular past participles. Those endings can often be determined by common features in the infinitives.**

1. The infinitives of several irregular verbs end with -re. Their past participles are formed by dropping those two letters and replacing them with a t. In addition, those past participles are identical to their third person singular present tense forms.

a. dire- dit (said, told)

Ex. Leur mère frustrée a crié, "Je vous ai dit mille fois." > Their frustrated mother screamed, "I have told you a thousand times." (But, there is 'numb' in numbers and 'old' in told.)

b. décrire- décrit (described)

c. écrire- écrit (written)

Ex. Tout le monde sait que vous n'avez pas écrit le roman vous-même. > Everybody knows that you did not write the novel yourself. (It should be classified as fiction.)

d. faire- fait (made, done)

Ex. Qu'est-ce que ton chien a fait sur **la pelouse**? > What did your dog do on **the lawn**? (The answer can be found in the English translation.)

<u>A note</u>: **Le fait is <u>the fact</u>.** (It's "a done deal.")

2. The past participle of *être* is *été*, the French word for <u>summer</u>. With no other past participles in the group, *être* chose the season 'to take off on its own.'

Ex. Mme Glacée a été dans plusieurs villes dans l'Alaska. > Mrs. Glacée has been in several cities in Alaska. (She says, "There's no place like Nome.")

3. Verbs with -<u>rir</u> infinitive endings frequently form their past participles by exchanging those letters for <u>ert</u>.

a. couvrir- couvert (covered)

Ex. Entrenous a couvert la bouche de sa nièce aussitôt que la petite a mentionné le cadavre dans son placard. > Entrenous put his hand over his niece's mouth as soon as the little girl spoke of the skeleton in his closet. (Two things needed 'to be covered up.')

b. découvrir- découvert (uncovered)

c. ouvrir- ouvert (opened)

Ex. Pourquoi as-tu ouvert la fenêtre? Il fait froid dehors. > Why did you open the window? It's cold outside. (Closing it will not make it any warmer.)

d. souffrir- souffert (suffered)

<u>An exception</u>: **The past participle of *courir* is *couru*.** (You need to keep track of that one.)

4. Verbs with -<u>evoir</u> infinitive endings form their past participles by removing those five letters and adding a <u>u</u>. A cedilla is placed under the <u>c</u>. (It's a logical location for a fish hook.)

a. apercevoir- aperçu (caught sight of, noticed)

b. decevoir- déçu (disappointed)

Ex. Quand Pinocchio a menti, il a déçu ses maîtres. > When Pinocchio lied, he disappointed his teachers. (Did they 'suspend' him?)

c. recevoir- reçu (heard, received)

Ex. Nous t'avons reçu cinq sur cinq. > We heard you loud and clear. (The acoustics must have been good 'in those quarters.')

5. The past participles of *rire* and *sourire* are formed by dropping -<u>re</u> from the infinitives. The shorter word is *ri; souri* is broader.

Ex. En regardant un film des Marx Brothers, mes amis ont ri comme des **baleines**. > While watching a Marx Brothers' film, my friends laughed like **whales**. (That's a real belly laugh.)

6. The past participles of -<u>ivre</u> verbs such as *suivre* and *poursuivre* are formed by taking the -<u>re</u> off the infinitive ending and replacing it with an <u>i</u>. (You'll go along with that, right?)

Ex. Euclid a suivi bien en géometrie. > Euclid followed (did well in) geometry. (More than likely, he 'knew all the angles.')

6a. <u>Two exceptions</u>: The past participles of *vivre* is *vécu*; *survivre* is *survécu*. (They do not follow follow.)

Ex. M. Santé a survécu à l'âge de quatre-vingt-dix ans en mangeant beaucoup de légumes et fruits. > Mr. Santé lived to the age of ninety by eating a lot of vegetables and fruits. (Is that why it is called "a ripe old age"?)

7. Verbs with -<u>uire</u> infinitive endings form their past participles by deleting the -<u>re</u> and trading

it for a <u>t</u>.
a. conduire- conduit (conducted, driven, led)
b. constrire- construit (built, constructed)
c. détruire- détruit (destroyed, ruined)
Ex. Sandrine et une amie ont construit **un château de sable** énorme. Un tyran l'a détruit. > Sandrine and a friend built a huge **sand castle**. A bully destroyed it. (Doesn't that just 'go against the grain'?)
d. introduire- introduit (introduced, presented)
e. produire- produit (produced)
f. traduire- traduit (translated)
Ex. Elle a traduit "gratuit" pour l'américain. > She translated "free" for the American. (And 'he took her at her word.')
9. The past participles of -<u>indre</u> verbs are formed by taking -<u>dre</u> off the infinitive and replacing them with a <u>t</u>. The third person singular present tense forms of -<u>indre</u> verbs and their past participles are spelled the same.
a. atteindre- atteint (reached)
b. craindre- craint (feared)
Ex. Comme son fils a craint un monstre sous son lit, sa mère a installé **une veilleuse**. > Because her son feared a monster under his bed, his mother installed **a nightlight**. (Now, he can see for himself.)
c. éteindre- éteint (extinguisted, put out)
d. peindre- peint (painted)
Ex. Des joueurs ont peint les plafonds des hôtels à Las Vegas. > Some gamblers painted the ceilings of Las Vegas hotels. (The job called for 'high rollers.')

<u>Parsing the Participles</u>- Label the statements *vrai* or *faux*.

_____ 1. All verbs irregular in the present tense have irregular past participles.

_____ 2. The third person singular present tense forms of *dire, faire* and *écrire* and their past participles are identical.

_____ 3. The past participle of *être* can be grouped with other verbs.

_____ 4. Most -*rir* verbs have past participles ending with <u>i</u>.

_____ 5. The past participle of *courir* is *couru*.

_____ 6. The past participles of -<u>evoir</u> verbs end with a <u>t</u>.

_____ 7. To form the past participles of *rire* and *sourire,* delete -<u>re</u> from the infinitive endings.

_____ 8. The past participles of *suivre* and *poursuivre* end with an <u>i</u>.

_____ 9. The past participles of all -<u>ivre</u> verbs are formed the same way.

_____ 10. To form the past participles of -<u>uire</u> verbs, trade the <u>re</u> for an <u>s</u>.

_____ 11. -<u>Indre</u> verbs form their past participles by exchanging <u>dre</u> for a <u>t</u>.

_____ 12. Third person singular present tense -<u>indre</u> verbs and their past participles are the same.

'Putting It in Reverse'- Write these present tense sentences *au passé composé*.

1. M. et Mme Bellevue conduisent à la plage pour voir le lever du soleil. _____

_____.

2. Quel état, l'Idaho ou le Maine, produit plus de pommes de terre cette année? _____

_____?

3. Mon Dieu! Comment tu souffres! _____!

4. Faye Rien décrit sa vie comme banale. _____

_____ .

5. Ces pauvres familles-là survivent à un autre **tremblement de terre (an earthquake)**? _____

_____ ?

6. Les bonnes éteignent les veilleuses quand elles nettoient les chambres à coucher. _____

_____ .

7. Qu'est-ce que Mme Bacon découvre quand elle ouvre sa tirelire? _____

_____ ?

8. Nous ne voyons pas d'animal qui rit dans le pâturage. _____

_____ .

9. Quand on aperçoit une baleine, on prend une photo. _____

_____ .

10. Je ne le poursuis pas en justice parce que je ne connais pas d'avocat **peu coûteux (inexpensive)**.

_____

_____ .

'So the Story Goes'- Using the correct past tense forms of the verbs in parentheses and object pronouns, write original sentences (not more than seven words) to complete the scenarios.
Ex. (ouvrir) Thomàs a vu un paquet fermé de muffins sur le comptoir. > (Thomas saw a closed package of muffins on the counter.) > **Il l'a ouvert** or **Il ne l'a pas ouvert**.

1. (recevoir) Flaubert m'a envoyé un livre. _____ .
2. (prendre) Ils m'ont offert un billet. _____ .
3. (être) Passepartout a voyagé en Inde? _____ .
4. (couvrir) A-t-elle fait son lit ce matin? _____ .
5. (atteindre) Le petit a voulu le jouet sur la cinquième étagère. _____

_____ .

6. (pleuvoir) Tu as apporté ton parapluie à Londres. _____

_____ .

7. (boire) La mère a donné du lait au bébé? _____ .
8. (reconnaître) Elle nous a décrit le bistro. _____ .
9. (écrire) Ton oncle et ta tante t'ont envoyé des cartes postales. _____

_____ .

10. (croire) O. Courant a vu l'article dans le journal. _____

_____ .

11. (dire) Il leur a raconté des idées, n'est-ce pas? _____

_____ .

12. (traduire) Vous avez suivi **le discours (the speech)**. _____

_____ .

13. (construire) Est-ce que des ingénieurs ont bâti un pont? _____

_____ .

14. (offrir) On a donné un prix sur **le spectacle de réalité (reality show)**? _____

_____ .

_____

PAST PARTICIPLE AGREEMENT FOR VERBS CONJUGATED WITH *AVOIR*

Verbs conjugated with *avoir* often show 'a finishing touch' on *le passé composé*. What precedes the past participle determines its ending. The agreement is always seen but not always heard.

The Spin on Past Participles- Picking Vowels or Consonants

1. Because past participles agree in gender and in number with the preceding direct objects, it is frequently necessary to add an -e̲, an -s̲ or an -e̲s̲ to the verb ending.

2. With a masculine singular direct object pronoun, the past participle keeps its original form. The examples and exercises in this unit thus far have included only *le* or *l'*. (We had not reached an agreement.)

Ex. Elle a mis le couvert. > She set the table. Elle l̲'a mis̲. > She set it.

3. If the past participle ends with a vowel, its pronunciation is unchanged when an e̲ is added.

Ex. Nous ne l'avons pas vu̲e̲ hier. > We did not see her yesterday.

As the e̲ is silent, we never heard from her either.

4a. *Me* and *te* refer to both sexes. An e̲ at the end of a past participle refers to a feminine singular direct object.

Ex. Est-ce que **le berger** t'a remarqué̲e̲? > Did **the shepherd** notice you? (If he had looked at 'ewe,' he would have seen the feminine ending .)

4b. *Nous* refers to both genders; *les* replaces masculine and feminine nouns. When those plural pronouns are used, the past participle has an -s̲ or an -e̲s̲ ending.

Ex. Ils nous ont dirigé̲e̲s̲ à la Gare de Lyon. > They directed us to the Gare de Lyon.

The second e̲ on *dirigées* gives us 'a lead' that *nous* refers to just females. (Men would not have asked for directions.)

Ex. Ce conducteur **distrait**-là les a presque renversé̲s̲. > That **distracted** driver almost knocked them down. (That obviously made them 'cross' quickly.)

By paying attention to the s̲ ending, you notice just male or male and female pedestrians.

4c. *Vous* refers to one individual whom the speaker doesn't know well or to two or more people with whom he/she is or is not well acquainted. So, if *vous* is the direct object, the past participle is open to four possible endings: keep it as is, add an e̲, add an s̲ or add an e̲s̲.

Ex. Le détective vous a rencontré̲s̲ avant-hier. > The detective met you the day before yesterday.

The s̲ on *rencontrés*, with no additional e̲, indicates that *vous* includes men or men and women, but not just women. (Why hire a detective?)

5. Coincidentally, s̲ and t̲, the last two letters of past, are the only consonants at the end of past participles.

5a. A past participle ending with an s̲ is unchanged if it is preceded by a masculine singular or plural direct object.

Ex. Ma cousine, qui suit un régime, a pris des éclairs. Je les ai remis̲. > My cousin, who is on a diet, took some éclairs. I put them back.

No extra s̲ on *remis* and no additional calories were needed.

5b. If a past participle ending with a t̲ follows a masculine plural direct object, an s̲ is added to the verb. Neither consonant is pronounced.

Ex. Nous n'avons pas parlé lorsque l'agent de police nous a conduit̲s̲ **au commissariat**. > We didn't speak while the policeman drove us to **the police station**.

Like the t and the s, they 'reserved the right to remain silent.'

6. If the final unaccented e of a past participle is visible, its preceding consonant is audible.

Ex. L'artiste n'a pas essayé de cacher **la cicatrice** très **proéminente** de Mme Delapeau. Il l'a pein<u>te</u> comme ça. > The artist did not try to hide Mrs. Delapeau's very **prominent scar**. He painted it like that. **The scar and the t were 'pronounced' when it was** *peinte.*

6a. The s after the final e is silent.

Ex. Les voisins ont mangé des crêpes délicieuses chez nous. Mon père a annoncé fièrement, "Je les ai fait<u>es</u> moi-même." > The neighbors ate some delicious crêpes at our house. My father announced proudly, "I made them myself."

7. Past participle agreement rules apply to direct object nouns.

Ex. Combien de réponses avez-vous s<u>ues</u>, Sue? > How many answers did you know, Sue?

Sue knew that the past participle ends with <u>es</u> because *réponses* **is a feminine plural noun.**

Ex. Quels joueurs de football ont-elles **snob<u>és</u>**? > Which football players did they **snub**? (More than likely, those who were offensive and defensive.)

The <u>s</u> on *snobés* **shows that the past participle and** *joueurs* **are 'making a team effort.'**

8. The past participle in a relative clause beginning with *que* **generally agrees in gender and in number with the antecedent.**

Ex. Lona Toon chante constamment le rond qu'elle a appri<u>s</u> au camp. > Lona Toon constantly sings the round that she learned in camp.

Since *le rond* **is masculine singular, no e is added, and the <u>s</u> on** *appris* **is thankfully silent.**

Ex. Ce n'est pas la recette que Wolgang a cherch<u>ée</u>. > It is not the recipe that Wolfgang looked for.

***La recette* called for an extra e.**

Ex. Les parents de Mélodie n'ont pas payé pour les CDs qu'elle a choisi<u>s</u>. > Melody's parents didn't pay for the CDs that she chose.

***Choisis* picked up an <u>s</u> that no one can hear.**

When Past Participle Agreement Is Not in Effect

1. There is no past participle agreement if the sentence has an indirect object pronoun without an accompanying direct object pronoun.

Ex. Est-ce que leur mère leur a lu une fable? > Did their mother read a fable to them? (If the woman read them and not to them, she had 'medium' reading skills.)

2. The past participle of a verb is unchanged before an infinitive with its own direct object.

Ex. Ils sont au milieu de la circulation qu'ils ont voulu éviter. > They are in the middle of the traffic that they wanted to avoid. (If *la circulation* is bad, all of 'the arteries must be clogged.')

Because their goal is <u>to avoid traffic</u>, the past participle *voulu* **'is in park.'**

3. There is no past participle agreement with e*n***.**

Ex. Mon père est sûr que les soucoupes volantes n'existent pas, mais j'en ai vu deux. > My father is sure that flying saucers don't exist, but I have seen two of them. (That's another case in which there is no agreement.)

"All's Well That Ends Well"- With the provided infinitives and nouns as a reference, complete the sentences using the correct past participle forms.
Ex. (inviter/Minnie) Mickey l'a <u>invitée</u> au Cheesecake Factory.

1. (plier/les tables) M. Doublé les a _____.
2. (casser/les miroirs) Je ne les ai pas _____.
3. (expliquer/le code de Da Vinci) Leonardo l'a _____.
4. (**troquer- to trade**/les cartes de baseball) M. Diamond les a _____.
5. (finir/les devoirs) Vous les avez _____.
6. (cueillir/les fleurs) Est-ce que Mme Desjardins les a _____?
7. (vendre/la moto) M. Nerouleplus ne l'a jamais _____.
8. (lire/les œuvres de Shakespeare-m.) Mac et Beth les ont _____?
9. (prendre/les repas) Je ne les ai pas _____ au patio.
10. (écrire/**son autobiographie-f.**) Mlle L. Même l'a _____.
11. (apercevoir/l'étoile de Bethléem) Plusieurs gens l'ont _____.
12. (introduire/ Stephanie) L'entremetteuse l'a _____ à Étienne.
13. (connaître/les acteurs) Nous n'en avons pas _____.

Cutting and Pasting *le Passé Composé*- **Rewrite the sentences by changing the underlined noun phrases into pronouns and adding any necessary agreement.**
Ex. Pierre a frappé <u>les pierres</u> avec un baton. > Peter hit the stones with a stick.
    Perre <u>les</u> a frappées avec un baton.

1. Nous cherchons <u>un dictionnaire hollandais</u>. _____.
2. J'espère que les gendarmes ont attrapé <u>les vilains mecs</u>. _____
_____.
3. Guerlain a introduit <u>cette ligne de parfums</u>. _____.
4. Qui a mis **<u>les cartes de visite professionnelle</u> (business cards)** dans ce tiroir? _____
_____?
5. M. Raisin a bu <u>les meilleurs vins du pays</u>. _____.
6. Avez-vous protégé <u>vos plantes</u> de la tempête de neige? _____
_____?
7. Après six ans, son fils a reçu **<u>son diplôme universitaire</u>-m. (his college degree)**. _____
_____.
8. Mmes. Barton et Nightingale ont choisi <u>une carrière très **rémunératrice** (rewarding)</u>. _____
_____.
9. Les espagnoles ont combattu <u>les arabes</u> il y a longtemps. _____
_____.
10. Mme Byer a attendu **<u>ses ventes par correspondance</u>-f. (mail order)**. _____
_____.
11. Mathusalem a bien vécu <u>sa vie</u>. _____.
12. Je n'ai jamais voulu vendre <u>ma bague de diamants</u>. _____
_____.

Amended Agreements- Rewrite the sentences with any necessary additions *au passé composé*.
Ex. Voici les vitamines que le pharmacien recommande. > Voici les vitamines que le pharmacien a recommandées.

1. Mes copains nous rencontrent au spectacle. _____

_____.

2. La traduction? On la finit. _____.

3. Ce sont les passages que je ne comprends pas. _____

_____.

4. Combien de courriers électroniques reçoit-il? _____

_____?

5. Laisse-moi voir la lettre que tu n'envoies pas! _____

_____!

6. Pendant que je fais une mousse, tu la goûtes. _____

_____.

7. La clé? Pandora la tient dans sa main. _____

_____.

8. Laquelle de ces revues veulent-ils? _____

_____?

9. Il y a des choses que je ne dis pas. _____

_____.

10. Ma sœur lave les chemises, et je les repasse. _____

_____.

11. Flint allume des cigarettes, mais nous les éteignons. _____

_____.

12. Elle ne prête pas les livres de poche qu'elle lit. _____

_____.

13. Est-ce que Mai Zoreilles croit les rumeurs qu'elle entend? _____

_____?

14. Je lui apprends à le faire sans mon aide. _____.

_____

LE PASSÉ COMPOSÉ AVEC ÊTRE

You may think that you mastered *le passé composé* when you learned all the verbs conjugated with *avoir*, but alas, "it was not <u>to be</u>." Since *être* verbs do not take direct objects, the subjects and past participles must draft their own agreements.
Here's how the conjugation falls into place!

Tomber - To Fall

Singular	Plural
je suis tombé(e)- I fell, did fall, have fallen	nous sommes tombés(es)- we fell, did fall, have fallen
tu es tombé(e)- you fell, did fall, have fallen	vous êtes tombé(e),(s),(es)- you fell, did fall, have fallen
il est tombé- he/one fell, did fall, has fallen	ils sont tombés- they fell, did fall, have fallen
elle est tombée- she/one fell, did fall, has fallen	elles sont tombées- they fell, did fall, have fallen

----

'The Means to an End'
1. The past participles of verbs conjugated with *être* reflect the gender and the plurality of the subjects.
2. The four possible past participle endings are to leave it as is or to add an <u>e</u>, an <u>s</u> or an <u>es</u>.
2a. *Il, elle, on, ils* and *elles* form endings "are set in stone." (Some people never change.)
2b. *Je, tu* and *nous* form endings show the gender of the person(s) involved.
2c. *Vous* form endings are a tossup as both gender and plurality can be kicked around.
3. Verbs conjugated with *être au passé composé* have three translations.
Ex. Henri et Henriette sont tombés amoureux. > Henry and Henrietta fell in love/have fallen in love/ did fall in love.
4. "Vandertramps, MD," a fictitious physician, is an acronym identifying the verbs conjugated with *être au passé composé*. She offers a free 'initial' visit.

Initials	Infinitives	Past Participles
V	venir (to come)	venu
A	aller (to go)	allé
N	naître (to be born)	né
D	devenir (to become)	devenu
E	entrer dans (enter into)	entré
R	rentrer (to reenter), rester (to stay)	rentré, resté
T	tomber (to fall)	tombé
R	*retourner (to return), revenir (to come again)	*retourné, revenu
A	arriver (to arrive)	arrivé
M	mourir (to die)	mort
P	partir (to leave)	parti
S	sortir de (to go out)	sorti

M	*monter (to go up)	*monté
D	*descendre (to go down)	*descendre

'Doctoring' the Past Participles- Translate the following sentences.

1. You (sing.) went only once. _____

_____.

2. Dr. Frankenstein became a scientist. _____

_____.

3. Who came in, and who went out? _____

_____?

4. All of her children were born in June. _____

_____.

5. Vee Zeet stayed at my house (for) five days. _____.

_____.

6. I left, and they (fem.) arrived the same afternoon. _____

_____.

7. Leif and I fell off the roof last fall. _____

_____.

8. Dee Laid and her husband came home late this evening. _____

_____.

Abbreviating the Abbreviations

1. *Devenir* and *revenir* **have past participles similar to** *venir.*

Ex. Mlle Vandertramps, une étudiante, est devenue Vandertramps, MD. > Ms Vandertramps, a student, became Vandertramps, MD. (She also has verifiable experience as a file clerk.)

2. **Many of the verbs on the list can be paired as antonyms: venir-aller, naître-mourir, arriver-partir, monter-descendre and entrer dans-sortir de.**

Ex. Nina est entrée dans le salon, et Pinta est sortie. > Nina came into the living room, and Pinta left. (They were like 'two ships passing in the night.')

3. **Most past participles make the doctor's medicine easy to swallow. The irregular verbs** *aller,* *partir* **and** *sortir* **have regular past participle endings. In fact, aside from the** *venir* **trio, the only irregular past participles are** *né* **and** *mort.*

3a. **The feminine singular past participle of** *naître- née* **is sometimes seen on the society page of newspapers when the bride's maiden name is included in the wedding announcement.**

Ex. Rose N. Bloom, née Lipschitz (She may have married neither for love nor for money.)

3b. **Ending with a consonant,** *mort* **is the only Vandertramps, MD past participle that alters its pronunciation when an -e or an -es is added to make subject-verb agreement. Although** *mourir* **connotes the end of someone or something, its past participle begins** mortician, mortuary **and even unrelated** mortgage. (Some people consider it 'a killer.')

4. **As verbs conjugated with** *être au passé composé* **are intransitive, they do not deal with direct objects. (They just can't take** it.**)**

4a. **The verbs on the Vandertramps, MD list preceded by asterisks can be conjugated** *au passé composé* **with forms of** *avoir* **or** *être.*

Ex. Jacques et Gille ont monté la colline. > Jack and Jill went up the hill.

Because of the direct object *la colline*, the helping verb is *ont*. The past participle doesn't show agreement with the subject.
Ex. Jacques et Gille sont tombés. > Jack and Jill fell down.
With the helping verb *sont*, subject-past participle agreement is in effect. There is no object to their tumbling. (For centuries, some people have wondered what made them fall.)
4b. Vandertramps, MD also discharges *descendre*, *monter* and *retourner* if they happen to take nonprescribed direct objects.
4c. Those verbs that have no past participle agreement when direct objects/nouns follow them show agreement when direct objects/pronouns precede them.
Exs. Jacob et Esau ont monté l'échelle. > Jacob and Esau went up the ladder.
    Jacob et Esau l'a montée. > Jacob and Esau went up it.
With the direct object pronoun *l'* replacing ladder (f.), the agreement 'step' is necessary.
5. Adjectives ending in -ed in English and in *é* in French come from verbs. Preceded by a form of *être*, these predicate adjectives are dually past participles.
Ex. Les repas sont préparés. > The meals are prepared. (With an s 'on the side.')
Ex. Mlle Flask n'est pas attirée par le technicien de laboratoire. > Ms Flask is not attracted to the lab technician. (Perhaps, the right chemistry isn't there.)

Determining End Results- Circle the letters of the responses that best complete the sentences.
1. À quelle heure _____, François?
a. êtes-vous arrivé   b. êtes-vous arrivée   c. êtes-vous devenu   d. est-il tombé
2. Quand les touristes _____, ils ont parlé de leurs voyages récents.
a. ont éternué   b. sont sortis   c. sont revenus   d. sont descendus
3. Colton et moi _____ à chevaux à Besançon.
a. est monté   b. sommes montés   c. sommes descendus   d. sont allés
4. Toute la famille _____ pour fêter mon anniversaire de naissance.
a. est rentrée   b. sont rentrées   c. est entrée   d. est partie
5. Nanette et sa jumelle _____ le 12 avril.
a. est née   b. sommes nées   c. sont nés   d. sont nées
6. Mme Toussetrop _____ à son médecin parce qu'elle est encore malade.
a. a retourné   b. est retournée   c. a triché   d. l'a déçue
7. Nous ne _____ nulle part. Nous _____ chez nous.
a. sommes venus .... sommes descendus   b. avons survécu .... sommes morts
c. sommes allés ..... sommes restés   d. sommes partis. .... l'avons fait
8. La Blanche Neige se demande, "Les nains où _____?"
a. est-il allé   b. sont-ils ascendus   c. sont-ils retournés   d. sont-ils allés
9. Le petit-fils _____ le jour où son arrière-grand-mère _____.
a. sont sortis .... est montée   b. est revenu .... l'a laissé tomber   c. est né .... est morte
d. a été enrhumé .... est devenue handicapée
10. Le diable _____ quand l'ange _____.
a. est entré dans la salle à manger .... est revenu   b. est decendu en bas .... est monté en haut
c. est resté dans la salle de séjour .... y est retourné   d. est sorti du foyer .... l'a collé

378

'To Be' at Work- Rewrite the following sentences *au passé composé.*

1. Est-ce que le Jedi retourne? _____?

2. Les trains partent de Biarritz à l'heure. _____
_____.

3. Bunny et toi allez aux montagnes faire du ski. _____
_____.

4. Tes ventes par correspondance arrivent ce matin. _____
_____.

5. Les soldats meurent à cause de leurs blessures. _____
_____.

6. "Pourquoi rentres-tu à minuit, Cendrillon?" _____
_____?

7. Mes cousines fâchées sortent de ma maison sans dire "au revoir." _____
_____.

8. Grâce **aux bourses-f. (the scholarships)** et aux prêts, ils deviennent avocats. _____
_____.

9. Tu (f.) viens au club seule, et tu pars seule. _____
_____.

10. **Ce** petit **porcelet-ci (this piggy)** va au marché. Celui-ci reste chez lui. _____
_____.

LES VERBES RÉFLÉCHIS AU PASSÉ COMPOSÉ
La Première Partie

When reflexive verbs discuss the past, they generally relive their experiences with *être.* **Their past participles agree in gender and in number with the subjects of the sentences.**
Are you wondering how a reflexive verb looks conjugated *au passé composé?*

Se Demander - To Wonder (To Ask Oneself)

Singular	Plural
je me suis demandé(e)- I wondered, have wondered, did wonder	nous nous sommes demandé(e)s- we wondered, have wondered, did wonder
tu t'es demandé(e)- you wondered, have wondered, did wonder	vous vous êtes demandé(e)(s)(es)- you wondered, have wondered, did wonder
il s'est demandé- he wondered, has wondered, did wonder	ils se sont demandés- they wondered, have wondered, did wonder
elle s'est demandée- she wondered, has wondered, did wonder	elles se sont demandées- they wondered, have wondered, did wonder

-----

Reflexives- Past Agreements and Disagreements

1. Whether a sentence is in declarative, interrogative, negative or negative-interrogative form, the reflexive pronoun precedes the helping verb *au passé composé.*
Ex. Mes ancêtres ne se sont pas dépêchés en Californie au milieu du dix-neuvième siècle. > My an-

cestors did not hurry to California in the mid-nineteenth century. (They were not in any 'Rush.')

2. When the reflexive verb is not followed by a direct object, the past participle agrees with the subject in gender and in number.

Ex. Elle s'est douchée. > She showered.

Notice that an extra e 'glistens' at the end of the past participle!

3. When a reflexive pronoun acts as an indirect object, the past participle is unchanged.

Ex. Elle s'est rasé les jambes. > She shaved her legs.

The extra e has been 'nicked' because *les jambes* dangle after the verb.

4. Reciprocal reflexives have a plural form only. The three pronouns preceding those verbs are *nous, vous* or *se*.

Ex. M. et Mme Fiers se sont félicités. > Mr. and Mrs. Fiers congratulated themselves.

The husband and wife showed their pleasure with an s.

Ex. Les jumelles ne se sont pas entendues en partageant le studio. > The twin sisters didn't get along well while sharing the studio. (They made better 'womb mates' than roommates.)

Despite their quarreling, they showed agreement by adding an es to the past participle.

5. If a reciprocal/reflexive pronoun is used indirectly, the past participle remains as is.

Ex. Celine et Linette se sont téléphoné. > Celine and Linette called (to) each other.

No agreement was reached during their conversation because *téléphoner* is followed by *à*.

6. To reinforce the meaning of a reflexive pronoun, *l'un(e) l'autre* or *les un(e)s les autres*- each other/one another are sometimes added after reciprocal verbs.

Ex. Nous ne nous sommes pas disputés l'un l'autre **désormais**. > We didn't dispute each other **from then on**.

They specified their terms and ended it with an agreement.

Furnishing Empty Spaces- Fill in the blanks with the correct *passé composé* forms of the verbs in parentheses. Where there is a choice of gender, write the masculine form.

1. (se sécher) Mme S. Ouier _____.
2. (se mettre à) Axel Érateur _____ conduire très vite.
3. (se baigner) Est-ce que les petits _____ ensemble?
4. (se casser) Winnie l'Ourson _____ l'orteil.
5. (se promener) M. et Mme Walker _____ au quai.
6. (se rendre compte) Tu _____ du fait trop tard.
7. (se déshabiller, se coucher) Je _____ et, je _____
   tôt hier soir.
8. (s'endormir) Des enfants _____ avant l'arrivée de Wee Willie Winkie.
9. (se méfier de) Tu _____ clerc qui ne t'a pas donné un **reçu-m. (receipt)**?
10. (s'en aller) Mes beaux-parents _____ il y a deux jours.
11. (s'embrasser) Les Joyner _____ à l'aéroport.
12. (se rappeler) M. Oubliant et moi ne _____ pas _____ mettre les
    chèques dans **la boîte aux lettres (the mailbox)**.
13. (se raser) Est-ce que les bergers _____ les barbes l'été dernier?

LES VERBES RÉFLÉCHIS AU PASSÉ COMPOSÉ
La Deuxième Partie

Not all reflexive verbs share a meaning with their nonreflexive forms. (The presence or absence of a pronoun can make all the difference in the 'word.')

Unrelated Nonreflexive-Reflexive Sets
1. agir- to act vs. s'agir de- to be a question of
Ex. Pour plusieurs animaux **échoués**, il s'est agi de **survivance.** > For several **stranded** animals, it was a question of **survival.** (Their 'preyers' didn't help.)
2. garder- to keep vs. se garder de- to be aware of: People might keep themselves out of a difficult situation by being aware of it in advance.
3. mettre- to put vs. se mettre à- to begin to
Ex. Une étudiante s'est mise à se plaindre de l'accordance des verbes au passé composé. > A student started to complain about the past tense agreement of verbs. (Her teacher 'put an end to it.')
4. passer- to pass, to spend vs. se passer de- to do without: *Se débrouiller-* **to manage is related to the reflexive verb. Even after the prefix is 'lifted,' most of** *le brouillard-* **the fog remains.**
Ex. Elle s'est passée de la nourriture trois jours lorsqu'elle a eu la grippe. > She went without food three days while she had the flu. (Perhaps she kept it up because she could not 'keep it down.')

Additional Reflexive Verbs

Space for a Few Extra 'Selves'
1. s'arrêter- to stop oneself: Go ahead and picture an <u>s</u> after the <u>ê</u>!
2. se débarrasser de- to get rid of: The legal system gets rid of barristers by <u>disbarring</u> them.
Ex. Comment est-ce qu'il s'est débarrassé de toutes **les bosselures** sur sa voiture? > How did he get rid of all **the dents** on his car? (He did a 'knock out' job.)
3. se détendre- to relax: In its nonreflexive form, the verb means <u>to loosen.</u>
4. s'emparer de- to take hold of: Negative emotions can <u>impair</u> one from doing positive things.
Ex. La colère s'est emparée de Madeleine. > Anger took hold of Madeleine. (For her, it was just 'the latest rage.')
5. se faire à = s'habituer à- to get used to/to accustom oneself to: <u>Habitual</u> and the second verb phrase are cognates.
Ex. Les Lowenhigh ont grandi à Paris, mais ils se sont faits aux montagnes. > The Lowenhighs grew up in Paris, but they got used to the mountains. (They are 'like second nature' to them now.)
6. se fier à = avoir confiance en- to trust: *Se méfier de-* <u>to mistrust</u> **is its antonym.** (Miss Trust is not a good person 'to bank on.')
7. se figurer- to imagine: The connection between the two verbs is not "a figment of your imagination." What you figure and what you imagine are both possibilities.
8. se moucher- to blow one's nose: *Un mouchoir* **is used for its intended purpose or to swat** *une mouche-* **a fly.** (But only in that order.)
9. se pencher = s'incliner- to lean over, to bend: Those familiar with the word <u>penchant</u>, a particular liking for something, might be 'inclined' to see a similarity between the English and the

French verbs.

Ex. Pour leur donner l'impression de soulever sa propre valise, **la dorlotée** s'est penchée. > To give them the impression of lifting her own suitcase, **the pampered woman** leaned over. (Nobody would have expected her 'to bend over backwards.')

10. se noyer- to drown: This is appropriately a stem-changing verb. (If used in the present tense, something 'radical' needs to be done to help 'the subject.')

<u>**Self-Service**</u>- **Put the correct forms of the verb phrases from the following list in the blanks: s'arrêter de, se débarrasser de, se détendre, s'emparer de, se faire à, s'habituer à, se fier à, se figurer, s'incliner, se moucher, se pencher, se noyer (Two answers may are possible.)**

1. Sy Niss et Al Lergy _____ en classe ce matin.
2. Mon amie et moi _____ hier soir en lisant des catalogues de vente par correspondance.
3. Un diplôme universitaire dans sa main, Reims Bourser a trouvé un travail bien-payant. Il a dit "Je peux _____ mes dettes maintenant."
4. Personne ne les a **secourus (rescued, saved)**, et après quatre jours dans l'océan, tous les hommes

_____ .
5. Leur grand-mère française ne _____ jamais _____ vivre à Chicago.
6. Tu lui as dit ton **mot de passe (password)** parce que tu _____ lui.
7. M. Aboyer n'a pas pu _____ sa maison sans son chien.
8. Aussitôt que la sorcière _____ , Hansel l'a poussée dans le four.
9. La dépression _____ M. Bleu, et il ne s'est jamais **remis (recovered)**.
10. M. Maudire _____ jurer, et nous sommes **reconnaissants (grateful)**.

le Musée Rodin (Paris)

382

PERFECT PARTICIPLES WITH *AVOIR* AND *ÊTRE*

Participating Participles

1. The present participle is used when two actions occur at the same time. *Le participe présent* **is typically formed from the present tense** *nous* **form of the verb. The -<u>ons</u> is removed, and <u>ant</u> crawls into that spot.** *En* **(while) often precedes** *le participe présent.*

Ex. En se débarrassant des choses dans sa table de nuit, une femme a trouvé un vieux journal intime vide. > While getting rid of things in her night stand, a woman found an old empty diary. (She must have been 'at a loss for words.')

2. The perfect participle is used when one action precedes another. *Le participe parfait* **includes** *ayant* **(having) or** *étant* **(being) + a past participle.** (Thereby making *étant* 'the perfect being.')

2a. *Ayant* **precedes verbs conjugated with** *avoir au passé composé*; *étant* **goes before those conjugated with** *être.*

3. The past participle in a phrase with *ayant* **agrees with the preceding direct object.**

Ex. Ayant essuyé quelques tables après le happy-hour, la serveuse a remarqué un couple **au fond du** restaurant. > Having wiped a few tables after happy hour, the waitress noticed a couple **in the back of** the restaurant. (Would she be serving 'leftovers' for dinner?)

Replacing *quelques tables* **with** *les*, **the above sentence becomes:** *Les ayant essuy<u>ées</u>, la serveuse a remarqué un couple au fond du restaurant.* **An <u>és</u> is needed on** *essuyé* **because 'the original order' was changed.**

4. The past participle in a phrase with *étant* **agrees with the subject of the sentence.**

Ex. Étant rentré<u>e</u> chez elle après **l'heure d'affluence,** Malta s'est détendue avec une bière. > Having come home after **rush hour,** Malta relaxed with a beer. (Some 'bottlenecks' are easier to handle.)

5. The past participle in a phrase with *après avoir* **agrees with the preceding direct object.**

Ex. La jeune a demandé une explication de la reproduction de serpents. Après l'avoir entendu<u>e</u>, elle a fait un son **sinistre.** > The young girl asked for an explanation of the reproduction of snakes. After having heard it, she made an **ominous** sound. (It was not easy to differentiate 'the hiss' from hers.)

Ex. Deux cambrioleurs ont pris des articles d'un magasin de sports. Après les avoir volé<u>s</u>, les mecs ont vendu l'équipement à leurs amis. > Two burglars took some articles from a sporting goods store. After having stolen them, the guys sold the equipment to their friends. (The culprits may have been 'old pros.')

6. The past participle in a phrase with *après être* **agrees with the subject of the sentence.**

Ex. Après être devenu<u>s</u> pilotes, M. Hautenair et son fils ont volé seulement pendant le jour. > After becoming pilots, Mr. Hautenair and his son flew only during the day. (It allowed them time 'to take off on their own' at night.)

Ex. Après **s'être démis** l'épaule pendant **la bagarre** au bar, Herty n'y est jamais retournée. > After **dislocating** her shoulder during **the brawl** at the bar, Herty never returned there. (Did 'the joint' get back in shape?)

<u>**A reminder:**</u> **There is no <u>e</u> at the end of** *démis* **because the verb is followed by the direct object** *l'épaule.*

Accord or Discord?- Label the statements *vrai* or *faux*.

_____ 1. The pronunciation of verbs always changes if -<u>e</u>, -<u>s</u> or -<u>es</u> is added to the past participle.

_____ 2. The only consonants at the end of past participles are <u>s</u> and <u>t</u>.

_____ 3. There is one possible past tense ending when *nous* is the direct object.

_____ 4. If the preceding direct object is a noun, past participle agreement does not apply.

_____ 5. Past participles agree with the antecedents of relative clauses.

_____ 6. Past participles reflect agreement with preceding indirect objects.

_____ 7. Most Vandertramps, MD verbs do not take direct objects.

_____ 8. There are two possible pp. endings for the *vous* form of Vandertramps, MD verbs.

_____ 9. *Mort* is the only Vandertramps, MD pp. whose pronunciation changes with the addition of an <u>e</u> or an <u>es</u>.

_____ 10. There are several sets of antonyms on the Vandertramps, MD list.

_____ 11. Many past participles have identical adjectival forms.

_____ 12. Reflexive verbs are conjugated *au passé composé* with a form of *avoir*.

_____ 13. Past participle agreement is always in effect with reflexive verbs *au passé composé*.

_____ 14. Reciprocal reflexives are conjugated only in the plural.

_____ 15. Perfect participles consist of *ayant* or *étant* plus a past participle.

_____ 16. Past participles in phrases containing *ayant* do not agree with preceding direct objects.

_____ 17. Past participles in phrases beginning with *après* + *être* agree with the subject.

'Looking Over the Agreements'- Translate the following sentences.

1. The whales did not drown. _____.

2. We (f.) did not wake up early. _____.

3. They (f.) washed their hair yesterday. _____
_____.

4. Ambre and Delphine never spoke to each other again. _____
_____.

5. The burglars were not aware of the dangerous dog. _____
_____.

6. Because of **the cost (le coût)** of gas, you (f.s.) got rid of your car. _____
_____.

7. The grateful person relaxed when someone rescued him. _____
_____.

8. **Greed (l'avidité-f.)** took hold of the thief whom the police arrested today. _____
_____.

9. Jo Ly found the perfect evening gown. Having bought it, she wanted to go to the party. _____
_____

10. Not accustomed to using a broom or a mop, the pampered woman had to hire a maid. _____
_____

11. After having listened to his speech, we did not trust him. _____
_____.

12. After having gotten rid of the jewels, the two sisters realized their value. _____
_____
_____.

LA VOIX PASSIVE - The Passive Voice

In a passive voice construction, the subject does not perform the action. Nevertheless, it makes its presence known in a variety of ways.

How the Passive Voice Expresses Itself

1. The two components most often found in a passive construction are a form of *être* and a past participle that agrees in gender and in number with the subject.

Ex. Les portes sont ouvertes à dix heures. > The doors are opened at ten o'clock.

Understanding that the subject is inactive is the key to *la voix passive*.

1a. A past participle *à la voix passive* is also a predicate adjective. (les portes ouvertes = opened doors.)

2. When there are two consecutive past participles, the second one agrees with the subject.

Ex. Mme Présage a été avertie. > Mrs. Présage has been warned. (The unnamed informant also has a passive voice.)

Ex. Les manucures n'oublient plus leurs rendez-vous comme une secrétaire a été embauchée. > The manicurists do not forget their appointments any more as a secretary has been hired. (Now everyone has 'nail files.')

3. A phrase beginning with *par* (by) is used if the person(s) or thing(s) performing the action is/ are identified.

Ex. La voiture de la femme préoccupée est stationnée par son valet. > The preoccupied woman's car is parked by her valet. (The owner sometimes gives a tip 'when it comes to her.')

Ex. Quels oiseaux sont attirés par le toît de cette glacerie-là? > Which birds are attracted to the roof of that ice cream parlor? ("Baskin Robbins," of course.)

3a. An exception: The doer is introduced by *de* after certain verbs.

Ex. Les nouveaux-nés sont aimés de tous. > Newborns are loved by all. (But their parents and their nannies care for them the most.)

Ex. Au Festival du Cinéma à Cannes, M. Triche a été accompagné de sa maîtresse. > At the Cannes Film Festival, Mr. Triche was accompanied by his mistress. (He 'swept his wife under the rug' and gave her stand-in 'the red carpet treatment.')

4. The passive voice can be prompted by placing *se* in front of the third person form of a verb.

Ex. Plusieurs léopards se sont vus pendant notre safari africain. > Several leopards were seen during our African safari. (How many were 'spotted'?)

Ex. Tous, ça se voit. > All (of them). It's obvious.

5. *On* is used as a substitute for *la voix passive*.

Ex. On parle espagnol et français à Miami. > Spanish and French are spoken in Miami. (It is a coincidence that the translation, "My friend," houses both languages.)

Ex. On a cambriolé un théâtre à Broadway. > A Broadway theater was burglarized. (But the culprits 'didn't steal the show.')

Activating the Passive Voice - Rewrite the sentences by changing the subjects to *on*. Some will be *au temps présent*; others *au passé composé*.
Ex. Le son des cloches est entendu. > On entend le son des cloches.

1. La rue a été décorée. _____.
2. Les billets sont vendus au guichet. _____.
3. Les cousins n'ont pas été invités. _____.
4. Les pas sont balayés. _____.
5. Votre examen a été corrigé. _____.
6. La malade a été guérie. _____.
7. Les téléphones cellulaires sont activés. _____
_____.
8. Ma chambre à coucher est nettoyée. _____
_____.
9. Les batailles ont été gagnées. _____.
10. Les murs sont peints. _____.

'Secret and Identified Agents' - Translate the following sentences.
1. Dulcinea est aimée de Don Quichotte. _____
_____.
2. Les hôpitaux pêche sont construits par l'Entreprise Picchi. _____
_____.
3. Trop de boulots sont éliminés ces jours-ci. _____
_____.
4. Le patient du docteur Rigoler est conseillé de se reposer. _____
_____.
5. Pourquoi les étrangers n'y sont-ils pas accueillis? _____
_____ ?
6. Vous ne pouvez pas dire que vous n'avez pas été averti. _____
_____.
7. Selon Vénus, toutes les planètes n'ont pas été découvertes. _____
_____.
8. Georges a dit, "Notre drapeau a été cousu par Betsy." _____
_____.
9. Plus de trésors ont été trouvés sous la mer par M. Cousteau. _____
_____.
10. Les noms ont été changés pour protéger les innocents. _____
_____.

'It Can Be Taken Two Ways'- Change the sentences below from the passive to the active voice.
Ex. Cette chanson-là a été chantée par Edith Piaf. > Edith Piaf a chanté cette chanson-là.

1. Trois mille espions ont été embauchés par Interpol. _____
_____.

2. Le professeur Hawkins est respecté de tous ses collègues. _____
_____.

3. Le français se parle au Sénégal par ses citoyens. _____
_____.

4. Ces chocolats-ci ne sont pas faits par les belges. _____
_____.

5. Sa photo a été prise par un étranger. _____
_____.

6. Melissa et Jason ont été enseignés par les professeurs particuliers. _____
_____.

7. Les fleurs ont été placées sur **la tombe (the grave)** par le veuf. _____
_____.

8. Tous ses ex maris ont été poursuivis en justice par Mme Prendtout. _____
_____.

le Bois de Bologne, le Parc de Bagatelle (Paris)

UNE REVUE - Le Passé Composé et La Voix Passive

Rules Not Meant To Be Broken- Match the letters to the numbers of the phrases to form complete sentences.

_____ 1. The past participle agrees with the antecedent

_____ 2. Some verbs irregular in the present tense

_____ 3. The past participles of regular verbs

_____ 4. Direct, indirect and reflexive pronouns

_____ 5. _Le passé composé_ usually has

_____ 6. _Personne, ne que_ and _nulle part_

_____ 7. The pps. of -_uire_ and -_indre_ verbs

_____ 8. If a sentence contains only an indirect object or _en,_

_____ 9. The pps. of Vandertramps, MD verbs

_____ 10. S̲ and t̲ are the only consonants

_____ 11. When a sentence contains a form of _avoir_ + a pp. + an infinitive,

_____ 12. The past participle of the _vous_ form of an _être_ verb

_____ 13. When a Vandertramps, MD verb has a direct object,

_____ 14. The only Vandertramps, MD verb whose past participle

_____ 15. Predicate adjectives can be

_____ 16. Reflexive verbs are conjugated

_____ 17. If the reflexive pronoun acts as an indirect object,

_____ 18. Reciprocals are reflexives

_____ 19. Reciprocal verbs followed by _à_

_____ 20. When _ayant_ and _étant_ are placed in front of a past participle,

_____ 21. The verbs in perfect participle phrases agree with

_____ 22. _Après_ can be followed by

_____ 23. In a passive construction

_____ 24. The doer/agent in a passive construction is preceded

_____ 25. If a nonreflexive verb replaces the passive voice,

_____ 26. When _on_ replaces the passive voice in English,

A. has four possible endings.

B. three translations for each verb form.

C. in the past tense with _être._

D. found at the end of past participles.

E. ends with a consonant is _mourir._

F. _se_ is used.

G. have regular past participles.

H. the preceding direct object or the subject of the sentence.

I. the same words as past participles.

J. precede helping verbs _au passé composé._

K. that only have plural forms.

L. by _de_ or _par._

M. that precedes _que._

N. the perfect participle is formed.

O. end with a t̲.

P. the pp. is unchanged if the direct object belongs to the infinitive.

Q. _avoir_ or _être_ + a past participle.

R. end with é̲, i̲ or u̲.

S. the verb is in the third person singular.

T. the past participle is unchanged.

U. the pp. does not agree with the subject.

V. follow past participles.

W. take indirect objects.

X. the helping verb is a form of _avoir._

Y. a form of _être_ is typically used.

Z. agree in gender and in number with the subject of the sentence.

'If You So Choose'- Circle the letters of the answers that best complete the sentences.
1. Merci beaucoup pour les cadeaux. Je les _____ hier.
a. ai reçu   b. ai reçus   c. ai promis   d. ai envoyés
2. Pinocchio est **la marionnette (the puppet)** que Gepetto _____.
a. faisant   b. a fait   c. a faite   d. avoir faite
3. Mme Sanscanne a regardé soigneusement les pas lorsqu'elle _____ l'escalier roulant.
a. a monté   b. est montée   c. a prise   d. a atteint
4. Notre tante Lorraine? Nous _____ en Alsace le mois dernier.
a. l'avons visité   b. lui avons rendu visite   c. l'a connue   d. y sommes allés
5. Combien d'heures Hervé _____ hier soir dans la bibliothèque?
a. a-t-on été   b. a-t-il fallu   c. a-t-il dépensé   d. a-t-il passées
6. Sadie a le même nom que sa grand-mère qui _____.
a. est née   b. est mort   c. est morte   d. a descendu
7. Est-ce que Piaget et vous avez _____ toutes les pièces que Shakespeare _____?
a. assisté à .... a dessiné   b. compris .... a dit   c. vus .... a jouées   d. lu .... a écrites
8. En coupant le bœuf gelé, Mme Douloureuse _____ la main.
a. a donné   b. a plié   c. s'est blessé   d. s'est blessée
9. Comme il _____ avant hier, Colette _____ chez elle.
a. a plu .... est restée   b. l'a surprise .... est tombée   c. a neigé .... s'est trompée
d. l'a suivie .... s'est mise à boire
10. Ils _____ riches et fameux. Ceux-là sont les buts qu'ils ont _____ atteindre.
a. se sont faits .... espérés   b. sont devenus .... voulu   c. ont grandi .... choisis
d. se sont habitués .... commandés
11. M. Mauvaisyeux est **vexé (upset)**. Les lunettes qu'il _____ récemment sont déjà _____.
a. a vues .... noyées   b. a achetées .... perdues   c. a essuyées .... cassées
d. s'est débarrassées .... tuées
12. Jusqu'à la semaine dernière, Mlle Colère et Mme Fâchée _____ à merveille.
a. se sont penchés   b. se sont méfiées   c. se sont rencontrés   d. se sont entendues
13. Après _____, M. et Mme Lointain ne sont jamais _____.
a. être partis .... revenus   b. partant .... rentrés   c. ils sont partis .... retournés
d. l'avoir quitté .... apparus
14. Scarlett _____ de Rhett, n'est-ce pas?
a. s'aime   b. est aimée   c. se sont aimés   d. aime
15. La ville de Paris _____ la Seine.
a. divise dedans   b. a divisé de   c. est divisée par   d. s'est divisé par

---

Now and Then- Write the following sentences *au passé composé.*
1. Les prêtres sont debout devant l'église. _____
_____.
2. Quand je vois un bel arc-en-ciel, j'en prends une photo. _____
_____.
3. M. Touslesdeux embauche et renvoie des salariés le même jour. _____
_____.
4. Drew et moi admirons les tableaux magnifiques que vous dessinez. _____

389

5. Ima Dunne ne veut ni lui parler ni lui écrire encore. _____.

6. Qu'est-ce que les Homer font aussitôt qu'ils rentrent chez eux? _____
_____?

7. Quelques garçons s'asseyent au bord du lac pendant que des jeunes filles nagent. _____
_____
_____.

8. Évidemment, ceux qui ne meurent pas survivent. _____.

9. Mme Enbas n'entre pas dans le grenier parce que la porte est fermée à clé. _____.

10. Les marionnettes sont nommées Guignol et Gnafron. _____
_____.

la Cathédrale d'Amiens

LES PHOTOS VALENT MILLE MOTS - HUIT JOURS À PARIS
Pictures Are Worth A Thousand Words - Eight Days In Paris

| Doug | Dave | Jeff | Naomi |

Du Vocabulaire du Conte
1. bilingue- bilingual
2. entendre parler de- to hear about
3. La Ville des Lumières- The City of Lights (What Paris is often called)
4. Bon Voyage!- (Have a) good trip!

Maman et ses quatre enfants **bilingues** sont allés à Paris il y a vingt ans. Elle est retournée seule cet été-ci, et elle y a passé huit jours fabuleux. Aussitôt qu'elle est rentrée, Maman a invité ses enfants chez elle à **entendre parler de** son voyage. Pendant qu'elle a raconté ses excursions, les quatre ont posé des questions et ont fait des plaisanteries. Tout le monde s'est bien amusé.
Voici votre occasion de visiter Paris et connaître **"la Ville des Lumières."** Bon voyage!

A note: Well-known people and places are introduced in bold type.

Le Premier Jour

Du Vocabulaire du Conte
1. faire les gros titres- to make the headlines
2. fut- was
3. l'Exposition Universelle- The World's Fair
4. Charles de Gaulle- a major airport serving Paris
5. défaire- undo, unpack
6. transmettre des ondes- to transmit waves
13. la réclame- the advertisement
14. la vue d'ensemble- the overview
15. le séjour- the stay
16. dévorer- to devou
17. déroutant- confusing
18. bercer- to rock

7. **le Champ de Mars**- a promenade near the Eiffel Tower
8. **le Trocadéro**- the site of le Palais de Chaillot
9. **René Descartes**- a French writer and philosopher of the seventeenth century
10. **la Madeleine**- a neo-classical styled church
11. **la promo**- the promotion
12. **les Folies Bergère**- a famous Parisian cabaret where dancers are scantily clothed

----

Naomi: Où es-tu restée?

Maman: Le Paris Hilton.

Dave: Elle t'a invitée à rester chez elle?

Doug: Et cette histoire n'a pas **faite les gros titres** de l'Enquirer?

Maman: Soyez sérieux! De ma fenêtre je pouvais voir **la Tour Eiffel**. Savez-vous qu'elle **fut** bâtie pour **l'Exposition Universelle** de 1889? Voici des photos!

Jeff: Tu n'as pas fait de tours le premier jour?

Maman: Mais si! Mon vol a **atterri** à onze heures le matin. Le tour de taxi de **Charles de Gaulle** a pris seulement une heure. Après avoir **défait** mes valises, je suis allée à **la Tour Eiffel**. Au premier étage, il y a un piano bar.

Naomi: Quelle bienvenue à Paris!

Jeff: Je le trouve plutôt étrange qu'une tour utilisée pour **transmettre des ondes radio** est devenue une telle attraction avec les bars et les restaurants.

Doug: Gustave Eiffel les a utilisés pour attirer les clients.

Maman: De la Tour Eiffel j'ai traversé **le Champ de Mars**, et je me suis promenée au **Trocadéro**. J'ai visité brièvement les deux musées **au Palais de Chaillot**.

Dave: Je me rappelle vaguement leurs noms.

Maman: **Le Musée de la Marine** et **le Musée de l'Homme**. Le deuxième m'a intéressée plus.

Doug: As-tu rencontré de gentils mecs là?

Maman: Les collections anthropologiques et préhistoriques s'y trouvent.

Dave: Tu n'as pas encore répondu à sa question.

Maman: Alors, j'ai vu le cerveau de **René Descartes**.

Jeff: C'est lui qui a dit, "Je pense, donc je suis."

Dave: Quel dommage! Il ne peut plus éprouver son existence. C'est ton tour de parler, Maman.

Maman: On ne visite pas Paris sans aller aux grands magasins **les Galeries Lafayette** et **Au Printemps** au **Boulevard Haussmann**.

Doug: Et il faut y aller juste après être arrivé en ville.

Maman: Certainement! Les musées se ferment de bonne heure. Changer de sujet, une publicité sur un kiosque à journaux devant **la Madeleine** a attiré mon attention.

Jeff: Une promo pour **les Folies Bergère**?

Maman: Pas exactement! **La réclame** a décrit les tours en bateaux-mouches sur **la Seine**. Je pensais que cela me donnerait **une vue d'ensemble** pour **mon séjour** à Paris.

Naomi: Mon amie et son mari ont fait ce tour-là le soir, et ils ont pris le dîner sur le bateau.

Maman: Quant à moi, j'ai **dévoré** tout sans prendre un repas. J'ai passé sous **le Pont Neuf** qui joint **la rive gauche** à **la rive droite**.

Dave: Un nom **déroutant** pour le plus vieux pont de la ville.

Maman: C'est vrai. **Le Pont Charles de Gaulle** accueille maintenant la circulation de deux "grands projets," **la Très Grande Bibliothèque** et **Bercy**.

Doug: Les concerts de rock stars y ont lieu. C'est une coïncidence que le verbe est **bercer**?

Maman: Je pense que oui. Cette construction est une arène de sports.

Dave: On va voir si Maman suit **ce rythme** toute la semaine.

Maman: Je suis descendue au **Pont de l'Alma**, très prés de mon hôtel. Quinze minutes après entrer dans ma chambre, je me suis endormie.

Écrivez des réponses complètes en français aux questions suivantes.

1. L'avion de Maman a-t-il atterri à Orly ou à Charles de Gaulle? _____

_____.

2. Comment s'appelle la promenade où se trouve la Tour Eiffel? _____

_____.

3. Quels sont les deux musées au Palais de Chaillot? _____

_____.

4. Qu'est-ce qu'on voit dans le Musée de l'Homme? _____

_____.

5. Qu'est-ce qui sont les Galeries Lafayette et Au Printemps, et où se trouvent-ils? _____

_____.

6. Quelle église néo-classique Maman a-t-elle passée? _____

_____.

7. Pourquoi les bateaux-mouches sont-ils très populaires? _____

_____.

8. Comment s'appelle le plus vieux pont de Paris? _____

_____.

9. Quels sont les deux "grands projets?" _____

_____.

10. Où Maman est-elle descendue du bateau-mouche? _____

_____.

Le Deuxième Jour

le Penseur (the Thinker)

le Panthéon

Du Vocabulaire du Conte

1. monter en flèche- to sky rocket
2. les tapisseries- the tapestries
3. s'adresser à- to cater to
4. feuilleter- to leaf through

11. dénicher- to pick up
12. la correspondance- the transit connection
13. le Quartier latin- the area surrounding
    la Sorbonne, part of l'Université de Paris

5. la volonté- the willpower
6. le curé- the parish priest
7. le réseau de métro- the subway system
8. entretenu- kept, maintained
9. les chefs-d'œuvre- the masterpieces
10. Revenons aux moutons!- Let's return to the subject! ("Let's come back to the sheep!")

14. démolir- to demolish
15. raconter des souvenirs- to reminisce
16. le tombeau- the tomb
17. enterrer- to bury
18. apprécieraient- would appreciate

Maman: Le deuxième jour, j'ai fait un tour à pied de **la rive gauche**. Cette partie de Paris a changée énormément depuis notre visite il y a vingt ans. Les prix aux **boulevards St. Michel** et **St. Germain** sont **montés en flèche.**

Doug: Notre Maman a aidé l'économie française de toute façon.

Naomi: Mais il y a toujours tant de choses à voir et à faire qui ne coûtent pas cher.

Maman: Et j'en ai découvert beaucoup. Commençons avec ces photos-ci! D'abord, je suis allée **au Musée de Cluny**, célébré pour ses objets fabriqués au Moyen Âge surtout ses **tapisseries**. Ensuite, j'ai pris une place devant **le Café Deux Magots**. Ce n'est plus l'endroit de réunion des intellectuels bien connus, mais on aime penser qu'il **s'adresse** toujours **à l'élite**.

Dave: De cette photo, je crois que tu as été très impressionnée par le flan?

Maman: Tu as deviné juste.

Doug: Où est-ce que tu t'es arrêtée après cette pâtisserie-culturelle?

Maman: Au lieu d'entrer dans **le Saint-Germain-des-Prés,** je suis allée à **la Librairie Hachette**, et je me suis détendue **en feuilletant** des livres.

Naomi: Pas d'achats au 6e arrondissement?

Maman: Oui, bien sûr! J'ai perdu **ma volonté** dans des boutiques à **la Rue Grenelle** et à **la Rue de Rennes**. Quelques surprises pour toi sont en route.

Doug: La voilà! Une confession de Maman sans le besoin d'**un curé.**

Jeff: L'arrêt suivant?

Maman: J'ai pris un métro au **Musée Rodin**. **Le réseau de métro** à Paris est très commode et bien **entretenu**.

Doug: Les français ne considèrent pas les graffiti comme **les chefs-d'œuvre** d'art.

Maman: Revenons à nos moutons! Regardez ces cartes postales que j'ai **dénichées** dans **le Musée Rodin**. Voici **le Penseur, les Mains** et **le Baiser.**

Dave: Celle-ci est très amusante. Devant la photo du Baiser, il y a un signe qui dit, "Ne touchez pas, s'il vous plaît!"

Jeff: Trop tard! Les baisers l'ont déjà fait.

Maman: Je n'arrive pas à comprendre le réseau d'autobus. Trop de **correspondances** pour arriver à **l'Université de Paris!** J'ai pris un taxi là-bas.

Naomi: As-tu passé devant ton vieil appartement à **la Rue des Écoles**?

Doug: C'est un site historique maintenant?

Maman: Oui Naomi, et non Doug. Les bâtiments **du Quartier Latin** sont exactement comme je me les rappelle. Heureusement, les français ne **démolissent** pas les vieux édifices sans bonne raison.

Dave: Es-tu retournée à ton endroit préféré, **le Jardin du Luxembourg**?

Maman: Bien sûr, et Nicolas m'y a rencontrée.

Jeff: Je me le rappelle. Comment va-t-il?

Maman: Il va très bien. En **racontant nos souvenirs**, nous nous sommes assis près de la fontaine.

Doug: Je peux raconter des souvenirs aussi, surtout ce qui est arrivé après son cours d'anglais final. Il t'a donné **une carte de vœux** qui a dit, "With Sympathy."

Naomi: Et les ballons avec l'inscription, "Get Well Soon!"

Maman: Vous deux comprenez sa confusion? "Sympathy" l'a fait penser à "sympathique."

Jeff: Mais celle-ci est la meilleure histoire de Nicolas: Il a fait un voyage d'affaires à San Francisco, et Maman lui a envoyé un puzzle du Pont Golden Gate.

Dave: Après l'avoir reçu, il lui a écrit une carte de remerciements qui a dit, "Thank you for the gift. I play in my hotel room every night."

Maman: C'est amusant Dave, mais tu sais qu'en français, on joue à une casse-tête.

Jeff: Dites-nous ce que vous avez fait après votre promenade sur la ruelle des souvenirs.

Maman: Nous sommes allés au **Panthéon,** en face du Jardin du Luxembourg.

Doug: Je connais le Panthéon. On y trouve **les tombeaux** des français bien connus.

Maman: Tu as raison. Peux-tu me dire lesquels y sont **enterrés**?

Dave: Tous?

Maman: **Les Curie, Hugo, Voltaire** et **Braille apprécieraient** ton sens de l'humour. Sur un autre point, qui peut deviner avec qui Nicolas et moi avons diné ce soir-là?

Doug: Quelqu'un du **Panthéon**?

Maman: Non, avec Chrétien, l'oncle de Nicolas.

Doug: J'étais deux doigts de la réponse correcte.

Écrivez des réponses complètes en français aux questions suivantes.

1. Quels deux boulevards principaux sur la rive gauche est-ce que Maman a mentionnés? _____
_____.

2. Comment le quartier a-t-il changé depuis leur visite il y a vingt ans? _____
_____.

3. Qu'est-ce qu'il y a dans le Musée de Cluny? _____
_____.

4. Quel est le nom du café d'anciens intellectuels? _____
_____.

5. Qu'est-ce que Maman a fait au lieu d'aller au Saint-Germain-des-Prés? _____
_____.

6. Pourquoi Maman aime-t-elle le réseau de métro de Paris? _____
_____.

7. Quelles sont trois statues bien connues dans le Musée Rodin? _____
_____.

8. Comment s'appelle le quartier où l'Université de Paris se trouve? _____
_____.

9. Quel est l'endroit préféré de Maman? _____.

10. Qui est Nicolas? _____.

11. Donnez un exemple pour montrer qu'il n'a pas parlé anglais bien. _____
_____.

12. Nommez trois français enterrés dans le Panthéon. _____
_____.

Le Troisième Jour

la Sainte-Chapelle

la Conciergerie

Du Vocabulaire du Conte

1. autrefois- formerly
2. le rez-de-chaussée- the ground floor
3. Pas grave!- It's OK!, It's no big deal!
4. rigolo- funny
5. le réseau ferroviaire- the railway system
6. lier- to tie (in)
7. voudrait- would like, would want
8. le point de repère- the landmark
9. le VAT- the value added tax (known as TVA in French)
10. ingénieux- clever
11. les bouquinistes- the vendors along the banks of the Seine
12. les gargouilles- the gargoyles
13. gagner haute la main- to win hands down
14. la quintessence- the epitome
15. les vitraux- the stained glass windows
16. le manque- the lack
17. la rediffusion- the rerun
18. fit- made
19. arbriter- to house, to shelter
20. furent- were

Maman: J'ai commencé le troisième jour **aux Halles, autrefois** appelé "l'estomac de Paris."

Dave: Tu vas nous raconter ce qu'il y en a dedans?

Maman: Touché, Dave! **Le Forum des Halles** a remplacé l'ancien marché en plein air. Au-dessous **du rez-de-chaussée**, il y a maintenant des restaurants, une bibliothèque, et même un musée de cire, **le Musée Grévin.**

Doug: Nous l'avons visité ensemble.

Maman: Tu penses à Madame Tussard à Londres.

Jeff: Pas grave, Doug. Ce sont des musées de cire. D'habitude, on ne peut pas voir la différence.

Maman: Quel groupe **rigolo!** Qu'est-ce qui se trouve sur le niveau sous le musée?

Dave: Une usine de bougies?

Maman: C'est **Châtelet-les-Halles**, le centre **du réseau ferroviaire** parisien.

Dave: Cela explique comment tout est **lié.**

Maman: Qui **voudrait** voir plus de photos? **Des points de repère** de l'Île de la Cité?

Naomi: Laisse-moi les voir!

Dave: Je sais où tu les as prises. En haut du grand magasin **la Samaritaine**, n'est-ce pas?

Doug: De ce lieu, la vue panoramique de Paris est extraordinaire.

Maman: Je suis ravie qu'il y ait des faits que vous n'avez pas oubliés.

Jeff: Ce jour-là, nous avons bavardé avec de gentils vendeurs par la Seine. Maman, tu m'as ramené la poule que j'ai voulue?

Dave: Quelqu'un l'a servie pour un dîner il y a vingt ans.

Doug: À cause de cette poule, on a introduit **le VAT** européen.

Maman: Très **ingénieux**, Doug. Jeff, **les bouquinistes** sont toujours là. Les européens attachent une grande valeur aux choses d'anciennes époques.

Doug: Nous décorons nos jardins des **gargouilles**, mais les européens connaissent leurs origines.

Jeff: Celles sur **la Cathédrale de Notre Dame de Paris** sont formidables.

Maman: J'en tiens des photos. À mon avis, de toutes les églises célèbres du monde, **la Cathédrale de Notre Dame de Paris gagne haute la main.** C'est **la quintessence** d'architecture gothique.

Naomi: Je suis d'accord. Je me rappelle **ses** beaux **vitraux**.

Dave: Je me rappelle que Maman a acheté une petite statue de **Quasimodo** pour moi.

Maman: Voilà! Il n'y a pas **de manque** de culture parmi mes enfants.

Jeff: Nous auditionnons pour des rôles à **la Comédie Française.** C'est tout!

Maman: Je n'y ai pas vu de spectacle. Je n'ai pas assisté à **l'Opéra** non plus. Il est fermé en été.

Doug: Tu peux regarder **des rediffusions** des *Sopranos* à la télévision.

Jeff: Comment s'appelle l'église que nous avons visitée pas loin de la Notre Dame de Paris?

Maman: Tu parles de **la Sainte-Chapelle.** C'est aussi un exemple d'architecture gothique.

Doug: Raconte-moi un peu d'histoire de **la Conciergerie.** Je parle sérieusement pour un instant.

Naomi: La Conciergerie est un édifice **dans le Palais de Justice.** Ce nom est ironique parce qu'elle fut une prison pendant la Révolution française. Plusieurs personnes, compris **Marie Antoinette**, y **furent** guillotinées.

Maman: Très bien fait, Naomi. Doug, je suis curieuse. Pourquoi est-ce que l'histoire de ce point de repère t'intéresse.

Doug: Il me fascine qu'une prison est devenue un palais.

Dave: Tiens, tiens, mon jumeau philosophique!

Écrivez des réponses complètes en français aux questions suivantes.

1. Qu'est-ce qui a remplacé le marché en plein air? _____
_____ .

2. Quel est le nom du musée au-dessous du rez-de-chaussée? _____
_____ .

3. Où se trouve le centre du réseau ferroviaire? _____
_____ .

4. Dans quelle partie de Paris sont la Cathédrale de Notre Dame et la Sainte-Chapelle? _____
_____ .

5. Pourquoi monte-t-on au sommet de la Samaritaine? _____
_____ .

6. Qui sont les bouquinistes? _____
_____ .

7. Que Maman a-t-elle dit de la Cathédrale de Notre Dame de Paris? _____
_____ .

8. Que Naomi s'est-elle rappelée? _____

9. Qu'est-ce qu'elle sait de la Conciergerie? _____
_____ .

10. Quelle femme bien connue y est morte? _____ .

Le Quatrième Jour

le Louvre

la Joconde (Mona Lisa)

Du Vocabulaire du Conte

1. **le sous-sol**- the basement
2. **l'artiste (m./f.)**- the artist, the performer
3. **l'augmentation (f.) de salaire**- the raise in pay
4. **interdit**- forbidden
5. **le clou**- the highlight, the nail
6. **la Victoire de Samothrace**- <u>the Winged Victory</u>- a headless, female statue with wings
7. **l'aile (f.)**- the wing

8. **le marais**- the swamp
9. **s'arrêter en passant**- to stop by
10. **le tirage**-the print
11. **le pavé rond**- cobblestone
12. **pittoresque**- picturesque

13. **le bibelot**- the trinket

Maman: Ces photos représentent mon quatrième jour à Paris. Je l'ai passé sur **la rive droite**. Quelle journée extraordinaire! J'ai commencé mes aventures au **Centre Pompidou** que quelques parisiens appellent toujours **"Beaubourg."**

Jeff: C'est où il y a une structure ultramoderne qui ressemble **au sous-sol** d'une usine.

Maman: Des français partagent ton point de vue. Nous n'y sommes jamais entrés. Une bibliothèque et un musée se trouvent à l'intérieur.

Dave: Nous avons vu des clowns, des jongleurs et d'autres **artistes à la Place Pompidou**.

Maman: Et des mimes? Cette fois un m'a choisie du public. Il m'a fait l'imiter.

Dave: Ne me dis pas que tu n'as ni bougé ni parlé!

Doug: Maman ne va pas te répondre. Elle a une nouvelle carrière.

Maman: N'essaie pas de gâter mes deux minutes de gloire, Doug! Devinez ce que j'ai fait ensuite!

Jeff: Tu as demandé **une augmentation de salaire**?

Maman: Bien sûr, et plus tard, j'ai pris un métro au **Louvre**. Sa gare de métro est la plus belle de la ville. Elle donne un aperçu du musée. Il est **interdit** de prendre les photos à l'intérieur, mais j'ai des cartes postales qui vous montrent **les clous** de ma visite.

Doug: Je reconnais cette statue. C'est **la Victoire de Samothrace**. Elle a gagné la guerre, mais elle a perdu sa tête.

Dave: Et voici **la Vénus de Milo**! Puisqu'elle n'a pas de bras, la Victoire de Samothrace devrait lui donner **une aile**.

Naomi: Tu as vu **la Joconde**?

Maman: Oui, Naomi. Cette fois j'ai remarqué que le fond paraît préhistorique.

Jeff: Il ressemble à **un marais**.

Maman: Avant de sortir du musée, je me suis **arrêtée en passant** la librairie. J'y ai acheté une douzaine de **tirages**. Jeff, tu viens de mentionner **"marais."** Voici quelques photos que j'ai prises de ce quartier **pittoresque**. J'adore ses petites rues **aux pavés ronds**. Et rien ne compare à une charcuterie au 4ᵉ arrondissement. J'ai pris un déjeuner superbe à **la Rue des Rosiers**.

Naomi: Pas exactement la cuisine française, mais au moins tu as finalement mangé.

Maman: Au contraire! J'ai trop mangé à Paris. Après le repas, je me suis promenée par **la Place des**

Vosges, la plus vielle place de Paris. **La maison de Victor Hugo** est dans cette photo-ci.

Jeff: As-tu acheté des souvenirs au **Marais**?

Maman: Seulement un beau livre au **Musée Carnavalet**. On peut trouver tout de l'histoire de Paris là. J'admets que j'ai eu envie d'acheter beaucoup de **bibelots** uniques sur **la Rue St. Paul**. Mais, je n'ai que deux bras.

Dave: Tu as plus de chance que la Vénus de Milo.

Écrivez des réponses complètes en français aux questions suivantes.

1. Où Maman a-t-elle passé son quatrième jour à Paris? _____
_____.

2. Qu'est-ce qui se trouve à l'intérieur du Centre Pompidou? _____
_____.

3. Qu'est-ce que Maman a fait à la Place Pompidou? _____
_____.

4. Comment peut-on reconnaître la Victoire de Samothrace? _____
_____.

5. Qu'est-ce qui manque de la Vénus de Milo? _____.

6. Qu'est-ce que Maman a remarqué cette fois de la Joconde? _____
_____.

7. Comment savez-vous que le Marais est un quartier pittoresque? _____
_____.

8. Quelle est la plus vieille place de Paris? _____.

9. Quel auteur célèbre habita au Marais? _____.

10. Qu'est-ce qu'on trouve dans le Musée Carnavalet? _____
_____.

l'Hôtel de Ville

Le Cinquième Jour

le Musée d'Orsay

Du Vocabulaire du Conte

1. cliquer sur- to click on
2. le commentaire- the comment
3. Le Cardinal Richelieu- Louis XlII's chief minister
4. avoir du sens- to make sense
5. le jeu de mots- the play on words
6. au début- initially, originally
7. retourner- to return, to turn over

8. confondre- to confuse
9. le nu- the nude
10. le paysage- the landscape
11. autrement dit- in other words
12. faire une pause- to take a break
13. le plaisir spécial- the treat
14. le sac à provisions- the shopping bag

Doug: Maman vient de cliquer sur les photos du cinquième jour.

Maman: Ce jour-là, je suis retournée à la rive droite. Le matin j'ai rencontré un ami, Jean-Marc, et nous avons fait un tour en voiture des points de repère.

Dave: Voudrais-tu nous raconter de cet homme mystérieux?

Maman: Je suis restée chez ses parents il y a longtemps.

Naomi: Où êtes-vous allés ensemble?

Maman: Nous avons commencé un petit tour à **l'Hôtel de Ville**. Pas de **commentaires** suggestifs! L'Hôtel de Ville est la résidence du maire de Paris. De là, Jean-Marc a conduit à **la Place de la Bastille**. Il m'a expliqué que cette place touche trois arrondissements, le 4e, le 11e et le 12e.

Jeff: Vous deux avez visité quelques autres endroits ensemble?

Maman: Après m'avoir emmenée au **Palais Royal**, Jean-Marc est parti pour aller travailler.

Doug: Ton prince t'a abandonnée au palais!

Jeff: La fin du conte de fées! C'est quoi, le Palais Royal?

Maman: C'est où **le Conseil d'État** se rassemble. **Le Cardinal Richelieu** y habita au XVIIe siècle.

Dave: Cela **a du sens**. Richelieu dans un lieu riche.

Maman: Quel **jeu de mots**!

Naomi: Plus de photos?

Maman: J'en ai tant, mais personne ne va reconnaître les premières. Quand nous avons visité Paris, les peintures impressionnistes ont été au **Jeu de Paume**. Elles sont maintenant au **Musée d'Orsay**.

Naomi: Celui-ci ne ressemble pas à un musée.

Maman: **Au début**, c'était une gare.

Doug: C'est intéressant! Le musée a voyagé mais pas les voyageurs.

Maman: Regardez ces cartes postales sans les **retourner**! Qui reconnaît les artistes?

Jeff: Je **confonds Manet et Monet**.

Maman: Ils se sont connus. Manet a peint plus de **nus**. Les œuvres de Monet comprennent les gens, **les paysages** et les fleurs.

Dave: **Autrement dit**, c'est Monet qui a couvert tout.

Maman: Que tu aimes blaguer!

Naomi: Puis-je prendre ces cartes postales avec les ballerines de **Degas**?

Maman: Bien sûr! Prends-les!

Jeff: Tu es heureuse maintenant, Naomi? Tu as tous les tutus.

Dave: Faisons une pause! Nous avons passé cinq jours à Paris, et nous n'avons rien mangé.

Maman: J'ai apporté **des plaisirs spéciaux** avec moi.

Jeff: J'ai vu **le sac à provisions**.

Naomi: Mangeons-les en continuant notre tour de Paris pour le faire plus authentique!

Écrivez les réponses complètes en français aux questions suivantes.

1. Comment Maman connaît-elle Jean-Marc? _____

_____.

2. À quel point de repère ont-ils commencé le tour en voiture? _____

_____.

3. Qui habite dans cet édifice-là? _____.

4. Comment savez-vous que la Place de la Bastille est très grande? _____

_____.

5. Comment le Palais Royal est-il utilisé aujourd'hui? _____

_____.

6. Qu'est-ce que le Musée d'Orsay était autrefois? _____

_____.

7. Quels peintres impressionnistes Jeff confond-il? _____

_____.

8. Quelles cartes postales est-ce que Naomi a prises? _____

_____.

la Place de la Concorde

Le Sixième Jour

Napoléon Bonaparte

Du Vocabulaire du Conte

1. entrer tête baisée- to dive head first
2. l'agence (f.) de tourisme- the tourist agency
3. l'approche (f.)- the approach
4. subtil- subtle
5. le dessin- the design
6. alla- went
7. l'Obélisque de la Concorde- a monument that Egypt gave to France
8. le salon d'exposition- the showroom

9. selon ses moyens- within one's means
10. arriver à tomber sur- to come across, to stumble upon
11. le gros plan- the closeup
12. le flambeau- the flame
13. vivant- living, lively

Maman: Comme il y a tant de choses à voir sur la rive gauche, j'y suis allée une troisième fois. Qui se souvient de **la Place de la Concorde**?

Naomi: Je me rappelle même ce qui est arrivé l'après-midi que nous y sommes allés. Jeff est **entré tête baisée** dans la fontaine devant **la statue de Lille**.

Jeff: Je l'ai considérée être la plus belle des huit femmes. Je me rappelle que chacune représente une ville en France.

Dave: Je sais que ce n'est pas la fin de l'histoire.

Maman: Après avoir grondé Jeff, je suis entrée dans **une agence de tourisme** tout près pour acheter cinq billets pour "**Paris par Nuit**" en autobus. Quand le propriétaire a regardé par la fenêtre, il a vu ton frère se séchant sur la statue de **Jeanne d'Arc**.

Doug: Jeff, utilises-tu toujours une **approche** si **subtile** pour attirer l'attention de jolies filles?

Naomi: J'ai encore mes photos du tour "**Paris par Nuit**."

Maman: J'ai gardé un peu plus de souvenirs. Très embarrassée, je suis sortie du bureau aussitôt que possible. Ensuite, nous avons fait une promenade à **la Rue de Rivoli**. On ne s'habitue pas à voir une mère accompagnée d'un gosse trempé avec trois autres enfants dans ce quartier très chic. Heureusement, personne ne nous a annoncé à **l'Ambassade Américaine** qui est très proche.

Dave: La Place de la Concorde est au fond de **l'Avenue des Champs-Élysées**, n'est-ce pas?

Maman: Tu a raison. La place sépare le Louvre et le Jardin des Tuileries de l'Avenue des Champs-Élysées. Ces photos montrent la ressemblance entre **le dessin** de Paris et celui de Washington, DC.

Doug: **L'Obélisque de la Concorde** me fait penser au Washington Monument.

Jeff: Notre Capitole ne fut-il pas dessiné par un français?

Maman: Oui, **l'Enfant Plaza** tient son nom. Au fait, vous savez qu'il y a une petite reproduction de **la Statue de la Liberté** sur la Seine?

Doug: L'histoire française n'est pas mon point fort, mais je vous assure que ces Napoléons sont très délicieux. Je n'ai aucune idée pourquoi il **alla à l'École Militaire** après sa morte.

Jeff: Il ne fut pas enterré à l'École Militaire. Son tombeau est **aux Invalides**.

Doug: De toute façon, il alla au lieu incorrect à l'heure incorrecte.

Naomi: Encore un peu de vin, Doug?

Dave: Raconte-nous de ta promenade à l'Avenue des Champs-Élysées! Les parfumeries, les chocolatiers et **les salons d'exposition** ont-ils changé?

Maman: Ceux-là ne m'intéressent pas beaucoup, et les boutiques ultra-chères ne sont pas **selon mes moyens**. Mais je suis **arrivée à tomber sur** des arcades aux prix raisonnables.

Jeff: Je regarde **un gros plan** de l'Arc de Triomphe, et je ne vois pas le **flambeau** sur le **Tombeau du Soldat Inconnu**.

Naomi: Peut-être le drapeau tricolore le couvre.

Doug: N'est-il pas interdit de brûler le drapeau français?

Jeff: Il est ironique que le Soldat Inconnu français soit le meilleur connu.

Maman: Il y a une certaine vérité dans cela.

Doug: Je me rappelle qu'un musée militaire commémorant les batailles de Napoléon est au sommet de l'Arc de Triomphe.

Dave: Nous l'avons monté pour avoir une bonne vue de **l'Étoile.**

Jeff: C'est bon à savoir. Enfin, nous avons vu une personne **vivante**.

Naomi: L'Étoile n'est pas une vedette. Elle est formée par les huit boulevards qui émettent de l'Arc de Triomphe. Il est plus facile d'imaginer une étoile là que les vingt arrondissements concentriques autour de Paris.

Doug: Qui a pris ta photographie devant l'Arc de Triomphe?

Maman: Je ne sais pas.

Dave: C'était **le photographe** inconnu.

Écrivez des réponses complètes en français aux questions suivantes.

1. Qu'est-ce que Jeff a fait à la Place de la Concorde il y a vingt ans? _____

_____.

2. Pourquoi Maman est-elle entrée dans une agence de tourisme? _____

_____.

3. Quelle statue est devant l'agence? _____.

4. Comment est la Rue de Rivoli? _____.

5. Qu'est-ce que la Place de la Concorde sépare? _____

_____.

6. Pourquoi le dessin de Paris ressemble-t-il à celui de Washington, DC.? _____

_____.

7. Qu'est-ce qu'on voit à la Seine et à New York City? _____

_____.

8. Quelle erreur Doug a-t-il faite de Napoléon? _____

_____.

9. Où Napoléon fut-il enterré? _____.

10. Quels types de magasins sont à l'Avenue des Champs-Élysées? _____

_____.

11. Qu'est-ce que Jeff a remarqué en regardant un gros plan de l'Arc de Triomphe? _____

_____.

12. Qu'est-ce que Doug se souvient de ce point de repère-là? _____

_____.

13. Qu'est-ce qui est l'Étoile? _____

_____.

Le Septième Jour

la Basilique de Sacré Cœur

Du Vocabulaire du Conte
1. **demander des nouvelles de**- to ask about
2. **la basse-cour**- the barnyard
3. **reconnaîtriez**- would recognize
4. **le croquis**- the sketch
5. **lever une femme**- to pick up a woman
6. **la butte**- the mound
7. **le quartier des prostituées**- the red light district
8. **le fil des pensées**- the train of thought
9. **réunir des fonds**- to raise money
10. **la religieuse = la sœur**- the nun, the sister
11. **firent**- made
12. **devint**- became
13. **s'ouvrirent**- were opened
14. **le funiculaire**- the funicular- (a corded railway system for high altitudes)
15. **l'atelier (m.)**- the studio
16. **allumer**- to light
17. **le cierge**- the church candle
18. **le porte-clés**- the key chain
19. **la cigale**- the grasshopper, the cricket
20. **captivé**- fascinated
21. **tomber**- to drop off something, to fall
22. **donner sur**- to face, to overlook
23. **offrir à quelqu'un à**- to treat someone to
24. **le Vendôme**- a column in honor of Napoleon's victories

----

Maman: J'ai passé un très beau jour avec Isabelle. Elle a **demandé des nouvelles de** vous.

Naomi: Ah oui! L'étudiante du petit village dans le Jura. Elle est chouette.

Doug: Elle a toujours six chevaux, **une basse-cour** et deux saint-bernards?

Maman: J'espère bien que non. Isabelle habite à Paris maintenant. Elle a tant maigri que vous ne la reconnaîtriez pas.

Doug: Évidemment elle s'est débarrassée de plus que ses animaux.

Jeff: Qu'est-ce que vous deux avez fait pour vous amuser?

Maman: Sur notre chemin à **la Basilique de Sacré Cœur à Montmartre**, nous avons pris un café à **la Place du Tertre**. Quand nous étions prêtes à partir, un artiste âgé m'a donné **un croquis** de mon visage. Il a dit, "Je n'ai pas encore fini avec vous."

Dave: Quelle façon formidable de **lever une femme**!

Maman: Nous avons ri tout le long à la **butte** de Montmartre. Isabelle m'a dit des faits très intéressants du quartier.

Jeff: Le quartier des prostituées est à **la Place Pigalle**. C'est très proche à Montmartre.

Maman: Mes photos ont une valeur plus historique, mais elles sont liées à **ton fil des pensées**. Pour **réunir des fonds** pour l'église, les **religieuses firent** du vin, et ce quartier-ci **devint** connu pour son alcool. Après cela, des boîtes de nuit comme **le Moulin Rouge** et **le Chat Noir s'ouvrirent**.

Jeff: Buvons aux sœurs!

Naomi: Tu n'as pas pris **le funiculaire**?

Maman: Non. Isabelle voulait indiquer **les ateliers** de **Renoir** et **Utrillo** sur le chemin. Enfin, nous sommes arrivées à l'église. J'ai admiré la belle architecture, et Isabelle a **allumé des cierges**.

Doug: D'autres excursions avec elle?

Maman: Beaucoup plus. Nous sommes allées à **Barbès** qui n'est pas loin du Montmartre.

Dave: Qu'est-ce qui est là?

Maman: Qu'est-ce qui n'est pas là? C'est un mini-monde où tout se vend à bon prix. Je ne sais pas si Barbès est mentionné dans le Guide Michelin, mais je recommande ce quartier pour son ambiance exotique. Après un déjeuner délicieux, nous avons pris le métro à **la Porte de Clignancourt**.

Naomi: Un marché aux puces énorme est à Clignancourt. On y étale tout de **porte-clés** aux meubles de **Versailles**.

Jeff: Pensez-y! Les bateaux-mouches sont sur la Seine. On va à **la Cigale** voir un concert. On peut acheter tout au marché aux puces. Les français sont vraiment **captivés** par les insectes.

Maman: Alors, Isabelle a mis ses achats dans un taxi, et le chauffeur les a **tombés** chez elle. Nous l'avons suivi à son appartement.

Doug: Pour ça, elle a payé cher. Où habite-t-elle?

Maman: Boulevard Faubourg-St. Honoré.

Naomi: Incroyable! Ce voisinage est vachement chic.

Maman: Une de ses fenêtres **donne sur la Place Vendôme**; une autre sur **l'Hôtel Ritz**.

Dave: Et son palais est meublé des trucs de Barbès et Clignancourt?

Doug: C'est sa seule façon de payer son loyer.

Jeff: Je crois que non. Maman vient de me dire qu'Isabelle **lui a offert à dîner au Café de la Paix**.

Doug: Donne-moi le numéro de téléphone de cette femme!

Écrivez des réponses complètes en français aux questions suivantes.

1. Qu'est-ce que Naomi pense d'Isabelle? _____.

2. Où la Maman et Isabelle se sont-elles arrêtées en route à la Basilique de Sacré Cœur? _____
_____.

3. Qu'est-ce que l'artiste a dit après avoir donné le croquis à Maman? _____
_____.

4. Pourquoi le Montmartre devint-il célèbre pour son alcool? _____
_____.

5. Quels sont les noms des deux boîtes de nuits connues dans ce quartier? _____
_____.

6. Pourquoi les deux n'ont-elles pas pris le funiculaire? _____
_____.

7. Qu'est-ce qu'Isabelle a fait dans l'église? _____.

8. Comment Maman a-t-elle décrit Barbès? _____
_____.

9. Où est-ce qu'Isabelle et Maman sont allées après leur déjeuner? _____
_____.

10. Pourquoi Jeff pense-t-il que les français sont captivés par les insectes? _____
_____
_____.

11. Comment les achats d'Isabelle sont-ils arrivés chez elle? _____
_____

12. Comment s'appelle l'hôtel à la Place Vendôme? _____
_____.

13. Qu'est-ce que Dave demande des meubles d'Isabelle? _____
_____.

14. Où les deux femmes ont-elles dîné? _____
_____.

Le Huitième Jour

la Galerie des Glaces (the Hall of Mirrors)   **les Jardins de Versailles**

Du Vocabulaire du Conte

1. être tout ouïe- to be all ears
2. le défilé- the military parade
3. la chaleur- the heat
4. climatisé- air conditioned
5. se rassembler- to gather together
6. la visite guidée- the guided tour
7. la vie nocturne- the nightlife
8. le carrefour- the crossroads
9. l'industriel (m.)- the industrialist
10. abstrait- abstract

16. s'endormaient- used to fall asleep
17. fit mettre- had ____ put
18. l'insigne (m.)- the insignia
19. RER- Reseau Express Regional- the rapid transit system linking Paris to its suburbs
20. servit- served
21. le pouvoir- the power
22. à l'origine- originally
23. eut- had
24. se dévouer- to devote oneself

11. C'était un bon!- That was a good one!
12. payaient- used to pay
13. le sou- the cent
14. restaient- used to stay
15. dérangeait- used to bother

25. rejeter le blâme sur- to lay the blame on
26. couper le souffle de quelqu'un- to take one's breath away
27. les feux d'artifice- the fireworks

Maman: J'ai rempli mon jour final des activités extraordinaires.

Doug: Nous **sommes tout ouïe**.

Maman: C'était le 14 juillet. Pour cela, je suis allée aux Champs-Élysées regarder **le défilé**. Quelle foule énorme! Quelle **chaleur** incroyable!

Naomi: Tu es restée là?

Maman: Je suis entrée dans un Monoprix-Prisunic **climatisé** d'où la vue était plutôt bonne. Ensuite, j'ai pris un métro à **Montparnasse**, un quartier sur la rive gauche. Au début du dix-neuvième siècle, le monde artistique et intellectuel **s'y est rassemblé**.

Jeff: J'ai lu quelque part que les cafés les meilleurs connus à Montparnasse ont des noms comme **le Dôme, le Coupole** et **le Rotonde**. Pourquoi ont-ils ces termes architecturaux?

Maman: J'aurais dû poser cette question pendant **ma visite guidée**. Voici des photos du quartier.

Dave: Celle-ci est **le Cimetière Montparnasse**. Tes hôtes se sont levés pour t'accueillir?

Maman: Tu parles des écrivains **Baudelaire, Maupassant** et **Sartre** et de **l'industriel Citroën**. Un fait intéressant de Montparnasse: Entre 1910 et 1920, le centre de **la vie nocturne** était **le Carrefour Vavin**. Ces jours-ci on l'appelle **la Place Picasso**.

Doug: La raison du changement du nom est **abstraite**.

Naomi: C'était un bon, Doug.

Maman: Des artistes et des écrivains **payaient** quelques **sous** pour louer les tables aux cafés où ils **restaient** toute la nuit. Personne ne les **dérangeait** quand ils s'y **endormaient**.

Jeff: De mauvaises impressions mais de bons impressionnistes!

Doug: Es-tu allée à **Père Lachaise**? **Jim Morrison** y est enterré.

Maman: Ce cimetière-là est dans un autre quartier. **Jim Morrison** est en très bonne compagnie de **Fréderic Chopin** et **Édith Piaf**.

Jeff: Revenons aux vivants! **L'Observatoire de Paris** est à Montparnasse, n'est-ce pas?

Maman: Certainement! Jeff, tu sais qu'elle fut fondée par Louis XIV?

Dave: C'est pourquoi on l'appelle **le Roi Soleil?**

Naomi: Non, mais c'est une pensée amusante. Il **fit** mettre **l'insigne** du soleil partout.

Maman: J'ai vu **la Tour Montparnasse**, le plus haut immeuble de bureaux d'Europe. J'ai déjeuné dans une bonne crêperie bretonne, et j'ai pris **le RER** de **la Gare du Montparnasse**.

Jeff: Devinons où Maman est allée!

Maman: Je viens de nommer le roi qui y habita.

Naomi: Maman est allée au **Château de Versailles**.

Maman: Tu as raison.

Dave: Nous y sommes allés ensemble pendant notre voyage.

Jeff: Le palais absolument énorme **servit** du symbole du pouvoir absolu.

Naomi: Comment est-ce qu'on utilisa toutes les pièces?

Maman: À l'origine, le grand appartement du roi eut sept pièces consacrées aux planètes et aux dieux. Le grand appartement de la reine eut sept pièces aussi, mais pas consacrées de même.

Dave: Bien sûr que non. La reine **se dévoua** au Louis XIV qui se considéra le Dieu.

Jeff: Voilà Dave! Tu viens d'expliquer une cause de la Révolution française.

Naomi: Parlons un peu de **la Galerie des Glaces!**

Maman: D'accord! L'histoire de cette pièce si connue est ironique. Avec Wilhelm comme l'empereur, l'empire allemand y fut né. Pendant **la Conférence de Paix à Paris** on y a **rejeté le blâme sur l'Allemagne pour la Première Guerre Mondiale.** Les Chefs d'État se rencontrent toujours dans la Galerie des Glaces.

Jeff: On y a fait surtout des réflexions.

Naomi: Et **les Jardins de Versailles coupent le souffle** de tout le monde.

Doug: Certainement celui des jardiniers.

Dave: Où as-tu vu **les feux d'artifices?**

Maman: Á cause de la circulation, il a pris trois heures pour arriver à mon hôtel.

Jeff: Tu ne les as pas ratés?

Maman: Heureusement non. Je suis montée à l'étage le plus haut de la Tour Eiffel. J'ai bu un verre de champagne, tout en regardant le spectacle.

Naomi: Quelle fin parfaite de tes vacances! Tu as commencé et terminé ton voyage au même lieu.

Maman: Ah oui! Mon voyage dernier à Paris n'y sera pas mon dernier voyage.

Écrivez des réponses complètes en français aux questions suivantes.

1. Quelle est la signification du quatorze juillet en France? _____
_____.

2. Pourquoi Maman est-elle allée à l'Avenue des Champs-Élysées ce jour-là? _____
_____.

3. Où est-elle allée par métro? _____.

4. Qui s'y est rassemblé au début du vingtième siècle? _____
_____.

5. Quels écrivains sont enterrés dans le Cimetière Montparnasse? _____
_____.

6. Comment le Carrefour Vavin s'appelle-t-il aujourd'hui? _____
_____.

7. Quelles célébrités sont enterrées à Père Lachaise? _____
_____.

8. Pourquoi Louis XIV mérite-t-il le nom "le Roi Soleil"? _____
_____.

9. Quel est un fait intéressant de la Tour Montparnasse? _____
_____.

10. Quelle pièce est la meilleure connue du Château de Versailles? _____
_____.

11. Quelle ironie est associée à cette pièce-là? _____
_____
_____.

12. Qu'est-ce que Maman a fait en regardant les feux d'artifice? _____
_____.
_____

UNE REVUE - Let's Go Back To Paris!

Photos of Paris- Separating Positives from Negatives- Label the statements *vrai* or *faux*.

_____ 1. La Tour Eiffel fut construite pour l'Exposition Universelle de 1889.

_____ 2. Il y a deux musées au Palais de Chaillot.

_____ 3. Au Printemps et les Galeries Lafayette sont au Champ de Mars.

_____ 4. La Madeleine est un exemple d'architecture gothique.

_____ 5. La Seine sépare la rive gauche de la rive droite.

_____ 6. Le Musée de Cluny est connu pour ses objets du Moyen Âge.

_____ 7. La Victoire de Samothrace et la Vénus de Milo se trouvent dans le Musée Rodin.

_____ 8. La Sorbonne est dans le Quartier Latin.

_____ 9. Le Jardin des Tuileries n'est pas près du Panthéon.

_____ 10. Les Cathédrales de Notre Dame de Paris et Sainte-Chapelle sont sur l'Île de la Cité.

_____ 11. La Conciergerie est une partie du Palais de Justice.

_____ 12. Marie Antoinette fut guillotinée à la Place Pompidou.

_____ 13. On appelle "Mona Lisa" la Joconde en France.

_____ 14. La Vénus de Milo n'a pas de tête.

_____ 15. Le maire de Paris habite au Palais Royal.

_____ 16. La maison de Victor Hugo et le Musée Carnavalet sont dans le Marais.

_____ 17. Le Musée d'Orsay était autrefois une gare.

_____ 18. Degas est très célèbre d'avoir peint les danseuses.

_____ 19. Les statues à la Place de la Concorde représentent les batailles de Napoléon.

_____ 20. La Place de la Concorde est entre le Louvre et l'Avenue des Champs-Élysées.

_____ 21. Une reproduction de la Statue de la Liberté se trouve sur la Seine.

_____ 22. Napoléon fut enterré dans l'École Militaire.

_____ 23. L'Étoile est une grande rue à Montmartre.

_____ 24. Jim Morrison et Édith Piaf sont enterrés dans le Cimetière Montparnasse.

_____ 25. La Conférence de Paix à Paris eut lieu dans la Galerie des Glaces à Versailles.

_____ 26. Les Chefs d'États ne se rencontrent plus dans le Château de Versailles.

'Connecting the Right Bank to the Left Bank'- Match the letters to the numbers of the phrases to form complete sentences.

_____ 1. On appelle Paris

_____ 2. L'Ambassade Américaine

_____ 3. Le Châtelet-les-Halles

_____ 4. Le Tombeau de Napoléon

_____ 5. Les Folies Bergères

_____ 6. Le Penseur, les Mains et le Baiser

_____ 7. Au-dessous du Forum des Halles

A. est un cabaret bien connu.

B. qui fut prise pendant la Révolution française.

C. on trouve des boutiques très chères.

D. furent les peintres impressionnistes.

E. rencontre au Palais Royal.

F. sont dans le Marais.

G. se trouve dans les Invalides.

_____ 8. Charles de Gaulle et Orly   H. au Louvre et au Château de Versailles.

_____ 9. À la Rue de Rivoli   I. sont des boîtes de nuit à Montmartre.

_____ 10. La Joconde et la Vénus de Milo   J. de l'Université de Paris.

_____ 11. St. Michel et St. Germain   K. est le centre du réseau ferroviaire parisien.

_____ 12. La Rue des Rosiers et la Rue St. Paul   L. il y a une bibliothèque et le Musée Grévin.

_____ 13. Les bouquinistes vendent des livres   M. de la Cathédrale de Notre Dame de Paris.
           et des œuvres d'art

_____ 14. Le Musée de l'Homme   N. du Palais de Justice.

_____ 15. Le Conseil d'État   O. est près de la Place de la Concorde.

_____ 16. La Sorbonne est la plus grande   P. sont enterrés dans le Panthéon.
           succursale (branch)

_____ 17. Il y a des gargouilles à la façade   Q. sont deux aéroports près de Paris.

_____ 18. La Bastille est la prison   R. sont grands boulevards sur la rive gauche.

_____ 19. Les Curie, Victor Hugo et   S. la Ville des Lumières.
           Louis Braille

_____ 20. Louis XIV habita   T. sont les sculptures dans le Musée Rodin.

_____ 21. Edouard Manet et Claude Monet   U. est sous l'Arc de Triomphe.

_____ 22. La Conciergerie est une partie   V. aux quais de la Seine.

_____ 23. Le tombeau du Soldat Inconnu   W. commémore les victoires de Napoléon.

_____ 24. Le Moulin Rouge et le Chat Noir   X. contient des collections anthropologiques et
                                         préhistoriques.

_____ 25. Le Vendôme est une colonne qui   Y. les rues près de l'Arc de Triomphe.

_____ 26. L'Étoile est formée par   Z. sont dans le Louvre

'Circling Paris'- Select the letters of the answers that best complete the sentences.

A note: Some responses contain verbs _au passé simple,_ **but their stems will be familiar.**

1. Mme Arris voudrait une vue d'ensemble de Paris. Elle doit _____.
a. accueillir des étrangers   b. faire un tour sur un bateau-mouche   c. faire les gros titres
d. perdre sa volonté

2. On qui se promène au Champ de Mars voit la Tour Eiffel et _____.
a. Charles de Gaulle   b. le Boulevard Haussmann   c. l'île de la Cité   d. le Palais de Chaillot

3. Le plus vieux pont de Paris est le Pont _____.
a. d'Alma   b. Charles de Gaulle   c. Neuf   d. d'Avignon

4. Le Musée de Cluny est sur la rive gauche près de/du _____.
a. Saint Germain-des-Prés   b. la Cathédrale de Notre Dame   c. la Sainte-Chapelle
d. la Madeleine

5. Le Panthéon se trouve dans le même arrondissement que _____.
a. la Comédie Française   b. l'Opéra   c. le Jardin du Luxembourg   d. l'Étoile

6. Tous les suivants sont les grands magasins à Paris sauf _____.
a. la Samaritaine   b. au Printemps   c. les Galeries Lafayette   d. les Halles

7. Pour mieux comprendre l'histoire de Paris, Guillaume et moi sommes allés au _____.
a. Centre Pompidou   b. Musée de l'Homme   c. Musée Carnavalet   d. Jeu de Paume

8. M. et Mme Sourires regardent les jongleurs et les mimes _____.

a. à la Place Pompidou   b. aux quais de la Seine   c. au Marais   d. à Père Lachaise

9. La Place _____ touche trois arrondissements.

a. des Vosges   b. Vendôme   c. de la Bastille   d. Picasso

10. L'Obélisque et les statues qui représentent huit villes de France sont _____.

a. au Louvre   b. à la Place de la Concorde   c. à Barbès   d. à Montparnasse

11. Il y a une ressemblance entre Paris et Washington, DC. parce que (qu') _____.

a. la Seine est comme le Potomac   b. l'Enfant Plaza se trouve dans chaque ville

c. les deux villes ont une Statue de la Liberté   d. un français dessina les deux villes

12. Les Richelieu entrent dans des boutiques de grands couturiers et des parfumeries très chères. Ils sont _____.

a. sur l'Avenue Champs-Élysées   b. sur l'Île de la Cité   c. à la Porte de Clignancourt
d. près de la Sorbonne

13. Des religieuses firent du vin pour réunir des fonds pour _____.

a. la Place Pigalle   b. la Basilique de Sacré Cœur   c. le Château de Versailles
d. la Porte de Clignancourt

14. La Place de Tertre, un endroit pittoresque à Montmartre, est près _____.

a. de la Très Grande Bibliothèque   b. du Châtelet-les-Halles

c. d'anciens ateliers de Renoir et d'Utrillo   d. du Boulevard Faubourg-St. Honoré

15. Le Coupole, le Dôme et le Rotonde sont des _____.

a. cafés connus à Montparnasse   b. noms des cimetières célèbres

c. les grands appartements à Versailles   d. architectes français

16. Beaucoup de gens vont à l'Avenue des Champs-Élysées le 14 juillet _____.

a. faire des achats dans le Monoprix-Prisunic   b. regarder de l'art abstrait

c. allumer le flambeau au Tombeau du Soldat Inconnu   d. voir le défilé de la Fête Nationale

17. Louis XIV fut appelé "le Roi Soleil" parce qu'il _____.

a. fonda l'Observatoire de Paris   b. fit mettre l'insigne partout

c. décora tous les salons d'un thème céleste   d. ne dormit jamais à Versailles

18. Pour voyager à la banlieue de Paris on peut _____.

a. donner sur le paysage   b. prendre le RER   c. être tout ouïe   d. lever une femme

---

L'IMPARFAIT - THE IMPERFECT TENSE

Although the name suggests that it is flawed, the imperfect tense could be one of the easiest to master. Its pattern is 99% percent foolproof. (It never claimed to be perfect.) *L'imparfait* serves so many purposes that you may wonder how you <u>communicated</u>, <u>were communicating</u> or <u>used to communicate</u> in French without it.

Give its conjugation some thought!

Penser - To Think

<u>Singular</u>	<u>Plural</u>
je pens<u>ais</u>- I thought, was thinking, used to think	nous pens<u>ions</u>- we thought, were thinking, used to think
tu pens<u>ais</u>- you thought, were thinking, used to think	vous pens<u>iez</u>- you thought, were thinking, used to think
il/elle/on pens<u>ait</u>- he/she/it/one thought was thinking, used to think	ils/elles pens<u>aient</u>- they thought, were thinking, used to think

----

Creating the Perfect Imperfect

1. *L'imparfait* is derived from the present tense *nous* form of the verb. Remove the -<u>ons</u> to find the imperfect stem! And yes, the *nous* form of *avoir* 'flies as' *avions*.

2. The singular endings -<u>ais</u>, -<u>ais</u>, -<u>ait</u> and the third person plural ending, -<u>aient</u>, share an identical pronunciation. Consequently, the use of the correct subject pronoun takes center stage.

3. The *nous* and *vous* form endings, -<u>ions</u> and -<u>iez</u>, look like present tense regular -er/-re verbs preceded by an <u>i</u>.

4. Verbs *à l'imparfait* in statement form can have three translations: the verb in the past tense without an auxiliary/helping verb, was/were + a verb ending in -<u>ing</u> and used to + a verb.

Ex. Le vieux M. Bouquin vendait des tirages par la Seine. > Old Mr. Bouquin sold/was selling/used to sell prints by the Seine. (He may not be *au quai* now.)

Ex. Des artistes peignaient des nus dans leurs ateliers. > Some artists painted/were painting/used to paint nudes in their studios. (But then realized that it would be better to apply color to a canvas.)

5. The irregular imperfect stem of *être* is <u>ét</u>. Its present tense *nous* form doesn't end with -<u>ons</u>. Regular imperfect endings are added to its 'alien' base.

Ex. J'étais contente de regarder des rediffusions. > I was content to watch reruns. That translation is shown again as "I used to be content to watch reruns."

6. The imperfect stems of the impersonal verbs *falloir* and *pleuvoir* are *fall* and *pleuv*.

Ex. **Puisqu**'il pleuvait, elles ne sont pas allées à la campagne le week-end dernier. > **Since** it rained/was raining, they didn't go to the country last weekend. (The weather 'put a damper on' their plans.)

7. An <u>e</u> precedes all singular and third person plural imperfect endings of -<u>ger</u> verbs. They are 'boots' with additional <u>es</u> as inserts. (It is not 'the last' that you'll hear from the boot.)

Ex. Il s'endormait quand il voyageait par train. > He fell asleep/used to fall asleep when he traveled/used to travel by train. (Maybe he thought that the conductor said, "All are bored.")

Ex. Toutes les choses bougeaient partout pendant le tremblement de terre. > Everything moved/was moving everywhere during the earthquake. (No one could say that it was "his fault.")

8. A cedilla is placed under the <u>c</u> throughout the singular and in the third person plural imperfect forms of -<u>cer</u> verbs. You're 'off the hook' for the *nous* and the *vous*. (You were warned that

'the other boot' would drop.)

Ex. Le tyran menaçait les autres enfants. > The bully threatened/was threatening/used to threaten the other children. (He may also have been disturbed.)

9. Verbs including *étudier, oublier, rire* and *sourire* with an i in front of their present tense -<u>ons</u> endings have an <u>ii</u> in the imperfect *nous* and *vous* forms.

Ex. Nous souriions en voyant nos reflets dans les fenêtres. > We smiled/were smiling/used to smile while seeing our reflections in the windows. (They would have really liked '*rire*' view mirrors.)

<u>Backing Up the Statements</u>- Write the underlined verbs *à l'imparfait* on the spaces provided.

_____ 1. Les gosses <u>aiment</u> bien regarder le défilé.

_____ 2. La Sœur Bernadette <u>allume</u> les cierges dans la cathédrale.

_____ 3. Tout le monde <u>écrit</u> des cartes de remerciements.

_____ 4. La jeune fille au pair <u>berce</u> le bébé.

_____ 5. Ce chef-d'œuvre n'<u>est</u> pas dans le musée.

_____ 6. M. Peck et moi <u>avons</u> de la volaille dans notre basse-cour.

_____ 7. Vous <u>venez</u> chez moi pendant vos vacances scolaires.

_____ 8. Elles les <u>voient</u> pendant leurs séjours à Montpelier.

_____ 9. Qui sait ce qu'Anne Stitute y <u>apprend</u>?

_____ 10. Les mecs <u>veulent</u> lever des filles dans les endroits chics.

_____ 11. Je ne <u>comprends</u> pas les correspondances du métro parisien.

_____ 12. Ronald McDonald et moi <u>sourions</u> souvent.

_____ 13. Les balais et les serpillières ne <u>sont</u> pas dans le sous-sol.

_____ 14. Vous <u>faites</u> des achats à Barbès avec Barbara.

_____ 15. M. Colère et M. Fâché ne <u>s'entendent</u> pas.

<u>Using the *Nous* to Uncover the Past</u>- Change the sentences *du temps présent à l'imparfait*.

1. Hervé le lave. _____.

2. Julia et Robert habitent à Hollywood. _____

_____.

3. Rosa et Rose rougissent rarement. _____.

4. Le vendeur et vous vendez les vêtements le vendredi. _____

_____.

5. Étienne et moi y sommes en été. _____

_____.

6. Eva y va de temps en temps. _____.

7. Honoré et son frère ne mentent pas. _____

_____.

8. Je le dis toujours. _____.

9. Mai Fiée ne les croit pas. _____.

10. Ma grand-mère efface les tableaux noirs. _____

_____.

11. Il faut les savoir. _____.

12. Où étudiez-vous? _____?

13. Ils ne peuvent pas le faire. _____.

14. Thurston boit beaucoup d'Orangina. _____
_____.

15. Tu écris à Sean Penn? _____?

16. Nous ne nous asseyons pas ici. _____
_____.

17. Je m'amuse chez les Bontemps. _____
_____.

18. Dawn se réveille-t-elle tôt le matin? _____
_____?

UTILISER L'IMPARFAIT - Using the Imperfect Tense

Both *le passé composé* and *l'imparfait* express past actions. The following explanations feature the events behind their parting of the ways.

A Matter of Timing
1. Aside from their different translations, the primary difference between the two tenses is the frequency and duration of the actions involved. *Le passé composé* expresses 'a one time event' and states or implies its completion; *L'imparfait* relates a repeated past action or one that took place over a period of time.
1a. *Le passé composé* and *l'imparfait* can both be translated using a single verb. The imperfect tense is used when <u>was/were</u> or <u>used to</u> can be inserted.
Ex. Mort a visité le Panthéon. > Mort visited/ has visited/did visit the Pantheon
Ex. Mort visitait le Panthéon. > Mort visited/was visiting/used to visit the Pantheon.
In the first example, one visit to the tombs of famous French people was enough. In the second, Mort returned to the mausoleum. (Maybe to assure himself that everyone was 'still' there.)
Ex. Plusieurs religieuses ont porté les robes longues au Vatican. > Several nuns wore/have worn/did wear long dresses at the Vatican.
Ex. Plusieurs religieuses portaient les robes longues au Vatican. > Several nuns wore/were wearing/ used to wear long dresses at the Vatican.
The first example infers that the nuns were not in the habit of wearing a habit; the second one implies that their long attire was in effect for a lengthy period of time.
2. <u>Used to</u> is the most dependable term for labeling continuous and habitual past actions.
Ex. Nous nous levions toujours tôt pour exercer et nous baigner. > We always used to get up early to exercise and to bathe. (Now, they just 'jump in the shower.')
2a. <u>Was</u> and <u>were</u> translations occasionally call for *le passé composé*.
Ex. Es-tu né le onze février? > Were you born (on) February 11?
3. If <u>would</u> means <u>used to</u>, *l'imparfait* is used.
Ex. Jewel Tone envoyait les SMS à son ancien flirt. > Jewel Tone would send/used to send text messages to her former boyfriend. (Did her new guy 'get word of it?')
4. *L'imparfait* typically describes past events involving people, things or conditions.
Ex. Ce candidat-là portait un complet bleu, une chemise jaune, une cravate rouge et des chaussettes vertes. > That candidate wore/was wearing a blue suit, a yellow shirt, a red tie and green socks. (He

413

went all out for 'the primaries.')

Ex. Pendant que Blanche et sa maman faisaient des emplettes, il neigeait. > While Blanche and her Mom shopped/were shopping, it snowed/was snowing. (It was perfect weather for a White Sale.)

5. *L'imparfait* is used to express time in the past. *Était* precedes days of the week, months of the year and time on a clock.

Ex. C'était lundi, le 18 juin quand Eva est sortie avec le loser. > It was Monday, June 18, when Eva went out with the loser. (She remembers the date vividly because there wasn't a second one.)

6. *L'imparfait* is used more than *le passé composé* to relate prior emotions, thoughts and conditions because the feelings had been ongoing for an unspecified time. Verbs that apply to those categories include *aimer, croire, désirer, espérer, être, penser, pouvoir, préférer, regretter, savoir, souhaiter* and *vouloir*.

Ex. Aristotle et lui voulaient devenir philosophes. > Aristotle and he wanted/used to want to become philosophers. (They gave the idea a lot of thought.)

Ex. Barclay ne préférait-il pas sa banque à celle de ses parents? > Didn't Barclay prefer/used to prefer his bank to that of his parents? (His 'interest' must have changed.)

7. If a sentence contains two verbs stating simultaneous past action, both are in the imperfect.

Ex. Au moment où la femme finissait le roman, son mari commençait à le lire. > Just when the wife was finishing the novel, her husband was starting to read it. (There are two sides to every story.)

Ex. Lorsqu'ils attendaient un autobus, ils parlaient de leur ancienne liaison. > While they waited for a bus, they talked about/were talking about their former affair. (It was the perfect setting for 'an off again on again' romance.)

8. *L'imparfait* and *le passé composé* can be together in the same sentence. The imperfect relates the action that lasted longer; the past tense is a point on that time line.

Ex. Je me douchais quand le téléphone a sonné. > I was taking a shower when the telephone rang. (Showering takes more time than the ringing of a phone even with 'call waiting.')

Ex. Blinky a vu **le signal lumineux** au sommet de la Tour Eiffel quand il était à Paris. > Blinky saw/did see **the beacon** on top of the Eiffel Tower when he was in Paris. (But he did not consider it to be 'a high-light' of his trip.)

'As It So Happened'- Match the letters to the numbers of the phrases to form sentences.

_____ 1. Quand Matinée habitait à Manhattan,	A. C'était mercredi, le 21 juin.
_____ 2. John Lennon est né a Liverpool,	B. qu'il allait à la foire.
_____ 3. Hy Teck a pris son salaire de la semaine passée pour	C. Je pouvais **encaisser mes chèques (to cash my checks)** sans identification.
_____ 4. Je me rappelle l'événement clairement.	D. Enfin, il l'a fait aujourd'hui.
_____ 5. Il pleuvait deux jours,	E. à son récital de ballet.
_____ 6. Tu t'es perdu lorsque	F. mais il est mort à New York City.
_____ 7. Tout le monde à la banque me connaissait.	G. ce qu'elle a reçu.
_____ 8. Tu arrangeais le bouquet de fleurs,	H. et personne n'avait un parapluie.
_____ 9. Frank O'Phone voulait toujours être interprète.	I. seulement le dimanche.
_____ 10. Arabesque portait un tutu bleu	J. elle allait souvent au théâtre.
_____ 11. Le Petit Chaperon Rouge souriait	K. une nouvelle lune chaque nuit.
_____ 12. Monty demandait un poney chaque fois	L. et Violette cherchait un vase.

414

_____ 13. Mes parents cachaient nos cadeaux,

_____ 14. La famille s'asseyait dans le salon

_____ 15. Avant l'introduction des supermarchés,

_____ 16. Le bébé ne pouvait pas dire une phrase complète.

_____ 17. Quand j'étais une petite fille, je pensais qu'il y avait

_____ 18. Espoir ne voulait pas

M. acheter beaucoup de **dispositifs- m. (devices)** électroniques.

N. mais nous les trouvions toujours.

O. Cependant, il est devenu un professeur de français.

P. tu conduisais autour de Paris.

Q. on faisait les courses presque tous les jours.

R. avant d'entrer dans la chambre de sa grand-mère.

The Imperfect Tense with Time Phrases

(Note: The numbering is continued for an upcoming exercise.)

9. _L'imparfait_ is used to tell how long one <u>had been doing</u> something. _Depuis_ (since) and a time reference are usually included in the sentence.

Ex. M. Jetson et ses collègues volaient depuis jeudi. > Mr. Jetson and his colleagues had been flying since Thursday. (They finally 'got down to business.')

The imperfect tense is needed in the previous example because the action began and continued in the past.

9a. _Depuis combien de temps + l'imparfait_ and _depuis quand + l'imparfait_ are both formulas for making questions regarding ongoing past actions.

Ex. Depuis combien de temps/Depuis quand votre équipe de base-ball jouait-elle dans la chaleur? > How long had your baseball team been playing in the heat? (Maybe only a few minutes after 'warm-'ing up.')

10. _Cela (ça) faisait_ + a time reference + _que_ + the imperfect tense is synonymous with phrases beginning with _depuis_ + the imperfect.

Ex. Le pauvre Noé! Cela faisait quarante jours qu'il pleuvait. > Poor Noah! It had been raining (for) forty days. (His entire production was 'overcast.')

11. _Il y avait_ + a time reference + _que_ is a fourth way to relate actions or events that began and continued in the past.

Ex. Il y avait deux ans qu'elles prenaient soin d'un chien à un appétit énorme. > For two years, they had been taking care of a dog with an enormous appetite. (Did they have any luck 'curbing it?')

11a. The corresponding interrogative form is _Combien de temps y avait-il que ...?_

Ex. Combien de temps y avait-il que le voleur cachait dans l'agence de voyage? > How long had the thief been hiding in the travel agency? (It was an ideal spot to plan 'a getaway.')

12. A form of _venir de_ in the imperfect tense + an infinitive means <u>had just done something</u>.

Ex. Le meurtrier qui venait de s'échapper de la prison cherchait un boulot. > The murderer who had just escaped from prison was looking for a job. (He didn't 'have time to kill.')

Ex. **La garantie** sur leur **camionette** venait d'expirer quand **les freins** ont arrêté de marcher. > **The warranty** on their **van** had just expired when **the brakes** stopped working. (Since then, they've had 'nonstop problems.')

13. *L'imparfait* is used with adverbs and adverbial expressions indicating repeated or continuous past actions. Examples include:

a. autrefois- formerly

b. chaque jour, (semaine, mois, année)- each day, (week, month, year)

c. de temps en temps- from time to time

d. d'habitude- usually, habituellement- habitually

e. d'ordinaire- usually, ordinarily

f. en général- in general, généralement- generally

g. parfois/quelquefois- sometimes

h. souvent- often

i. toujours- always

j. tous les jours, (mois)- every day, month

k. toutes les semaines, (années)- every week, (year)

l. tout le temps- all the temps

Ex. Les petites croyaient autrefois **aux licornes.** > The little girls formerly believed/used to believe **in unicorns.** (At some point, they realized that there was no point.)

Ex. Tous les mois leur plan de lancer une montgolfière échouait. > Every month their plan to launch a hot air balloon failed. (It wasn't easy 'to get it off the ground.')

'Explaining It a Number of Ways'- Choose a reason from 2a. through 13. from the preceding lists that explains why the sentences are *à l'imparfait* or *au passé composé*, and translate them. **Ex. (6) Mlle J. Raison pensait qu'elle savait tout. > Ms J. Raison thought/used to think that she knew everything.**

1. _____ Catherine s'habillait élégamment même avant son mariage au prince. _____

_____ .

2. _____ Il était une heure quand la souris a monté l'horloge. _____

_____ .

3. _____ Cela faisait longtemps qu'Alice était au Pays des Merveilles. _____

_____ .

4. _____ La Blanche Neige aimait les sept nains. _____

_____ .

5. _____ Mickey et Minnie se disputaient de temps en temps. _____

_____ .

6. _____ Combien de temps y avait-il que Hansel et Gretel se promenaient dans la forêt? _____

_____ ?

7. _____ Depuis combien de temps La Belle au Bois Dormant y était-elle? _____

_____ ?

8. _____ Marie avait un petit agneau dont **la toison (the fleece)** était aussi blanche que la neige. ____

_____ .

9. _____ Calvin Coolidge, le trentième président des États-Unis est né le 4 juillet. _____

_____ .

10. _____ Des animaux se moquaient de Dumbo à cause de ses grandes oreilles. _____

_____ .

11. ____ Lorsque **la Boucle d'Or (Goldilocks)** dormait dans le petit lit, les trois ours sont rentrés.

_____.

12. ____ La cigale dansait et jouait du violon pendant que les fourmis travaillaient. _____

_____.

13. ____, ____ Le lapin ne croyait pas que la tortue gagnait la course. _____

_____.

14. ____, ____ Les trois petits chatons venaient de perdre leurs mitaines quand leur mère a annoncé que la tarte était prête. _____

_____.

15. ____, ____, ____ Après avoir fait la connaissance d'Aladdin, Jasmine pensait à se marier avec **un bourgeois (a commoner)** tout le temps. _____

_____.

Going, Went, Gone- Fill in the blanks with the correct present, past or imperfect forms of the verbs in parentheses.
Ex. (être, faire) Vous vous rappelez que quand vous <u>étiez</u> jeune, vous <u>faisiez</u> les bonhommes de neige en hiver.

1. (prendre, sortir) Penny _____ la monnaie quand elle _____ ce matin.
2. (encaisser, recevoir) Tu _____ les chèques que tu _____ hier?
3. (voyager, rester) Il y a quelques années ils _____ souvent à l'étranger. Ces jours-ci, ils _____ chez eux.
4. (pouvoir, savoir) Mireille ne _____ pas chanter la Marseillaise par cœur maintenant, mais elle _____ tous les mots autrefois.
5. (sourire, rêver) Nous _____ souvent parce que Faye Croire _____ des licornes toutes les nuits.
6. (être, courir, avoir) Quand tu _____ jeune, tu _____ seul dans les collines le soir. Tu n'_____ jamais peur.
7. (s'occuper de, peindre) Il y a longtemps Mme Ange _____ enfants pendant que Michel _____ les plafonds.
8. (se plaindre, aller) Sue Frire _____ / _____ de sa santé pendant un mois. Avant-hier, elle _____ à l'hôpital.
9. (suivre, admettre, être) Magellan _____ la fausse route jusqu'à sept heures du soir. Enfin, il _____, "Je n'ai aucune idée où je _____."
10. (venir de, apprendre) Vous _____ faire cet exercice avec trois temps parce que vous _____ les règles.

_____

LA VIE DANS UNE PETITE VILLE AU MAINE Il YA SOIXANTE ANS
Life in a Little City in Maine Sixty Years Ago
La Première Partie

Du Vocabulaire du Conte

1. se sentir en sécurité- to feel safe
2. abondant- plentiful
3. les œufs brouillés- the scrambled eggs
4. le laitier- the milkman
5. la porte arrière- the back door
6. les difficultés scolaires- the learning problems
7. saisir- to seize, to catch on
8. l'orthographie (f.)- the spelling
9. le correcteur orthographique- the spell check
10. le rapport- the report, the connection
11. le casse-croûte- the snack
12. la machine à écrire- the typewriter
13. les travaux scolaires- the schoolwork
14. la chaîne- the channel, the chain
15. tous les trente-six du mois- once in a blue moon
16. le ciné-parc- the drive-in movie
17. danser à quatre- to square dance
18. le carreau- the tile inside a building
19. orné- ornate
20. la poignée de porte- the doorknob
21. le sèche-linge = le sechoir- the dryer
22. étendre le linge- to hang clothes out to dry

Quand j'étais une jeune fille de neuf ans au Maine, le monde semblait immense, mais je **me sentais en sécurité** dans mon petit coin du globe.

Les jours quand j'allais à l'école ma mère me réveillait. Après que nous nous soyons habillés, mon frère, Myles, et moi mangions des petits déjeuners **abondants**. Ils comprenaient **des œufs brouilles**, du toast au beurre ou à la confiture et des céréales chaudes.

Le laitier laissait le lait frais par **la porte arrière**. S'il faisait mauvais temps, il mettait les bouteilles dans la cuisine. La porte n'était jamais fermée à clé.

À l'école, je faisais attention toujours à ce que mes maîtres enseignaient. Mes parents, surtout mon père, me disaient que les mauvaises notes n'étaient pas la faute des maîtres. De plus, il n'y avait pas de noms pour **des difficultés scolaires**. Les élèves qui apprenaient vite recevaient plus de travail. On s'attendait moins de ceux qui **saisissaient** lentement. Ces jours-là, nous étions encouragés à apprendre par cœur. La bonne écriture et **l'orthographie** parfaite étaient très importantes aussi. (Comme il n'y avait pas d'ordinateurs, nous ne pouvions pas compter sur le **correcteur orthographique**.) Pour écrire leurs **rapports**, les étudiants plus âgés les **tapaient** sur **une machine à écrire**.

À trois heures et demie de l'après-midi, Myles et moi rentrions. Nous prenions **un casse-croûte,** et nous faisions nos devoirs tout de suite. Notre mère était à la maison. Généralement, les épouses restaient chez elles pendant la journée. On n'avait plus d'argent qu'on a aujourd'hui, mais le coût de la vie n'était pas si haut.

Après avoir fini nos **travaux scolaires**, nous étions permis de regarder la télévision. Elle avait juste été inventée. Imaginez que les émissions n'étaient pas en couleur et que nous ne pouvions voir que trois **chaînes** clairement! En essayant d'obtenir la réception d'autres, nous bougions "les oreilles du lapin" dans toutes les directions. (C'était notre version d'un jeu de vidéo.)

Parfois le soir, nous nous asseyions devant la radio pour entendre nos programmes favoris. **Tous les trente-six du mois**, nous allions à **un ciné-parc**. Je m'y endormais avec une boîte de popcorn dans mes mains.

Ma famille demeurait dans une très grande maison que mon grand-père avait construite au début du vingtième siècle. Des locataires habitaient en haut. Ils **dansaient à quatre** le samedi soir.

Quant à ma maison, les sols étaient couverts de linoléum. Sur les plafonds il y avaient de beaux **carreaux ornés**. **Les poignées de porte** étaient de verre. N'oublions pas l'extérieur de la maison! Pour prendre soin de la pelouse, mon père poussait une tondeuse à gazon manuelle.

Des appareils qu'on utilise aujourd'hui n'existaient pas il y a soixante ans. Ma mère lavait les plats à la main. C'était juste avant le lave-vaisselle automatique était disponible. Nous avions un lave-linge, mais comme **le sèche-linge** n'avait pas encore été inventé, on **étendait le linge**. Plusieurs articles de vêtements étaient fabriqués de fibres synthétiques. Néanmoins, quelques gens passaient beaucoup de temps faisant le repassage.

Savoir rien d'inventions futures, notre mode de vie ne semblait pas difficile.

<u>Écrivez des réponses complètes en français aux questions suivantes.</u>

1. Quel âge la petite fille avait-elle quand cette histoire a eu lieu? _____
_____.

2. Qu'est-ce que les enfants mangeaient pour le petit déjeuner? _____
_____.

3. Qu'est-ce que ses parents pensaient de mauvaises notes? _____

4. Quelles matières scolaires étaient plus importantes il y a soixante ans qu'aujourd'hui? _____

_____.

5. Comment étaient les émissions de télévision il y a soixante ans? _____

_____.

6. Nommez deux choses qu'on faisait les soirs qu'on fait rarement ces jours-ci? _____

_____.

7. Qu'est-ce que les locataires faisaient le samedi soir pour s'amuser? _____

_____.

8. Comment son père prenait-il soin de la pelouse? _____

_____.

9. Quels appareils électroménagers que nous utilisons n'existaient pas il y a soixante ans? _____

_____.

10. Pourquoi la mode de vie ne semblait-elle pas difficile? _____

_____.

LA VIE DANS UNE PETITE VILLE AU MAINE IL Y A SOIXANTE ANS
Life in a Little City in Maine Sixty Years Ago
La Deuxième Partie

Du Vocabulaire du Conte
1. le propriétaire d'une entreprise- the business owner
2. s'absenter- to be away
3. les aliments congelés- the frozen food
4. la veille au soir- the previous evening
5. le chasse-neige- the snowplow
6. passer- to get through
7. le lendemain matin- the next morning
8. le coup de sifflet- the whistle
9. les congères (f.)- the snow banks
10. la poupée en papier- the paper doll
11. gagnerait- would win
12. l'éventail (m.)- the fan
13. le bonnet et les pantoufles de bain- the bathing cap and bathing slippers
14. le cornet de glace- the ice cream cone
15. Ça se dit- It is said
16. être en train de- to be in the act of
17. acquérir- to acquire
18. le dérivé- the by-product
19. le comportement- the behavior
20. la courtoisie- the courtesy
21. obligatoire- mandatory
22. plutôt que- rather than
23. importer- to matter

Les soirs, toute ma famille mangeait le dîner ensemble. Comme mon père était **propriétaire d'une entreprise**, il **s'absentait** très peu. Ma mère, portante souvent un tablier, servait les repas délicieux. Les fours à micro-ondes n'ont pas existés encore. En plus, elle considérait **les aliments congelés** en dernier ressort.

Vivre dans un climat très froid est difficile pour des adultes, mais il y a quelques avantages pour les enfants. Quelquefois, il neigeait tant **la veille au soir** que **les chasse-neige** ne pouvaient pas **passer le lendemain matin**. Le moment où nous entendions **un coup de sifflet** fort à sept heures du matin de la caserne de pompiers, nous savions que les écoles seraient fermées ce jour-là. Mon frère et moi nous habillions comme les esquimaux pour jouer dans **les congères**. Pendant ces tempêtes de neige, je passais aussi des heures dans ma chambre à coucher où je dessinais des vêtements pour mes **poupées en papier**. Les soirs je jouais des jeux de société avec Myles. (Il fallait lui promettre d'avance qu'il **gagnerait**.)

Nous nous rendions compte que l'été s'approchait quand il y avait **un éventail** ou une climatisation en boîte dans les fenêtres ouvertes. Pendant les vacances scolaires d'été, mon père me conduisait au moins une fois par semaine à un étang. Il fallait porter **un bonnet et des pantoufles de bain** quand on y nageait. Nous nous inquiétions de l'eau dans nos oreilles et du verre dans nos pieds mais jamais de la pollution. En rentrant, mon père et moi nous arrêtions à une glacerie. Il achetait **un cornet de glace** pour moi et une bouteille de coca pour lui-même. Nous aimions y écouter la musique rock du juke-box. (C'était juste avant Elvis Presley est devenu populaire.)

Certainement, le monde d'aujourd'hui est très différent de celui que je viens de décrire. Ces jours-ci, les ordinateurs nous permettent de faire les affaires, payer les factures, acheter tout et communiquer avec tout le monde sans sortir de nos maisons. En outre, on peut conduire ou voler d'un endroit à un autre aussi bien que préparer un repas en très peu de temps.

Ça se dit que la technologie moderne **est en train de** remplacer des emplois. Peut-être il faut perdre quelques choses pour **acquérir** d'autres.

Un dérivé du nouvel âge se manifeste dans **le comportement** des gens. Il y a ceux qui disent que la moralité du passé n'adapte pas à nos vies aujourd'hui. On rencontre même des personnes qui considèrent que **la courtoisie** commune n'est plus **obligatoire**. Pour ces individus, c'est le temps présent **plutôt que** le temps imparfait qui **importe**.

Écrivez des réponses complètes en français aux questions suivantes.

1. Qu'est-ce que le père de la petite fille faisait pour gagner une vie? _____
_____.

2. Comment savez-vous que sa mère cuisinait les repas **nutritifs (nutritious)**? _____
_____.

3. Pourquoi les écoles étaient-elles fermées parfois en hiver? _____
_____
_____.

4. Quelles trois activités la petite faisait-elle pendant ses jours de congé? _____

5. Comment savaient-ils que l'été venait? _____

6. Où est-ce que la petite fille allait avec son père en été? _____

7. Qu'est-ce que le père et sa fille faisaient en rentrant chez eux? _____

8. Quelles sont deux choses que les ordinateurs nous permettent de faire? _____

9. Qu'est-ce que la technologie moderne peut remplacer? _____

10. Selon l'auteur, comment le comportement de quelques gens a-t-il changé? _____
_____
_____

'Take My Words for It!'- Translate the following sentences.
1. The milkman used to leave the bottles of milk beside the fan. _____

2. My parents used a typewriter to do their school reports. _____

3. Handwriting and spelling were important school subjects. _____

4. We would open our windows to touch the snow banks. _____

5. The tenants who square danced would also go to drive-in movies. _____

6. The mornings after a big snowstorm we waited for the sound of a loud whistle. _____

7. Before going to school, we used to eat a healthy breakfast. _____

8. There were three television channels, and the programs were in black and white. _____

9. The mother hung out the wash while her daughter designed paper dolls. _____

10. The backdoor was never locked, but we used to feel safe. _____

11. It was obligatory to show courtesy to everyone. _____

12. Some people say that the children's behavior was better because their parents were rarely away.
_____
_____
_____

UNE REVUE DES PRONOMS OBJECTIFS
A Review of Object Pronouns

Like constructing a building, learning a foreign language involves reinforcing structures. The foundation of single object pronouns should be solid before moving up to a higher level.

The Ground Floor

1. When a subject and verb ask <u>whom</u>? or <u>what</u>?, a direct object answers. The translations for *me, te, le, la, l', nous, vous* **and** *les* **are <u>me, you, him, her, it, us, you</u> and <u>them</u> respectively.**
Ex. **Cet agent de change** informé lit the Wall Street Journal plusieurs heures chaque jour. > That in-informed **stockbroker** reads the Wall Street Journal several hours each day. (That's how 'he invests his time.')
If *le* **replaces <u>the Wall Street Journal</u>, the first example says:** *Cet agent de change informé <u>le</u> lit plusieurs heures chaque jour.* **> That informed stockbroker reads <u>it</u> several hours each day.**
<u>An important reminder</u>: **Direct object pronouns can replace noun phrases beginning with possessive or demonstrative adjectives.**
Exs. Quelqu'un a trouvé son I-Cosse. > Someone found his I-Pod.
  Quelqu'un l'a trouvée. > Someone found it. (That was 'music to his ears.')
2. Indirect object pronouns are *me, te, lui, nous, vous* **and** *leur***. Their translations are the same as direct object pronouns preceded by <u>to</u>.**
<u>An important reminder</u>: **The lists of English direct and indirect object pronouns are identical. The latter can speak <u>to</u> you because they are living; the former cannot.**
Ex. Le bijoutier a vendu une montre d'or à ma mère. > The jeweler sold a gold watch to my mother. (The jeweler sold my mother is a bad translation and a bad transaction.)
With *lui* **replacing** *à ma mère***, the sentence becomes** *Le bijoutier <u>lui</u> a vendu une montre d'or.* **> The jeweler sold a gold watch to her.** (That's how 'it finally winds up.')
3. Reflexive pronouns, with translations including -<u>self</u> and -<u>selves</u>, team up with subject pronouns to form the combos *je me, tu te, il/elle/on se, nous nous, vous vous* **and** *ils/elles se***.**
Ex. Le mec qui fait des tyroliennes s'appelle Encore. > The guy who yodels is called/calls himself Encore. (What an appropriate name! You can say that again!)
4. *Y***, typically translated as <u>there</u>, replaces prepositional phrases indicating location.**
Ex. Un des Beatles a offert une place à la jolie fille au concert. > One of the Beatles offered a seat to the pretty girl at the concert.
When *y* **substitutes for** *au concert***, the sentence says** *Un des Beatles <u>y</u> a offert une place à la jolie fille.* ("He Saw Her Standing There.")
5. *En* **replaces phrases beginning with** *de, du, de la, de l'* **and** *des***. Its translations are <u>some, any, of it, of them</u> and <u>from there</u>.**
Ex. Le café avait le goût **de boue**. > The coffee had the taste **of mud**. (Was it 'ground' recently?)
Using *en* **to fill in for** *de boue***, the sentence reads** *Le café <u>en</u> avait le goût.* **> The coffee had the taste of it.**
6. Object and reflexive pronouns can precede or follow conjugated verbs and imperatives.
Ex. Paula Cee a dit, "N'oubliez pas de **déposer une réclamation**!" > Paula Cee said, "Don't forget **to file a claim**!" (One could sense her 'unsettled' feeling.)
If *la réclamation* **is 'processed' as a pronoun, the sentence becomes** *Paula Cee a dit, "N'oubliez*

pas de __la__ déposer!" > Paula Cee said, "Don't forget to file <u>it</u>!

<u>An important exception</u>: **When a verb is affirmative imperative, the pronoun follows it.** (It is to be expected since the verb is in the 'command' form.)

Ex. "Jean, prends ma carte de crédit, et achète la batterie pour ma voiture!" > "Jean, take my credit card, and buy the battery for my car!" (Two' charges' will be involved.)

After taking away *ma carte de crédit* **and replacing** *la batterie*, **the sentence says,** *"Jean, prends-__la__, et achète-__la__ pour ma voiture!"*

DOUBLE OBJECT PRONOUNS

When a meeting of double object pronouns is called to order, practicality presides. Categories of pronouns are summoned together and cross-examined.

The Order of Double Object Pronouns before the Verb

<u>Box #1</u>	<u>Box #2</u>	<u>Box #3</u>	<u>Box #4</u>	<u>Box #5</u>	<u>Verb</u>
me (m')	le (l')	lui	y	en	
te (t')	la (l')	leur			
se (s')	les				
nous					
vous					
se (s')					

<u>'The Buddy System'</u>

1. To master the sequence of double object pronouns that precede verbs, you'll have 'to think outside the boxes.' Though Box #1 includes three types of pronouns, the reflexives are the only ones fully represented. Labeling Box #1 as "reflexives plus" enables the leftovers to go <u>directly</u> into Box #2 and <u>indirectly</u> into Box #3.

2. Marking the first three boxes "reflexive, direct and indirect" respectively provides an alternate route to 1. That packaging requires verification that the reflexives/direct/indirect object pronouns under Box #1 "go priority" as reflexives.

Ex. C'est incroyable! Mon voisin **radin** a un GPS, et il me l'a offert. > It's unbelievable! My **stingy** neighbor has a GPS, and he offered it to me. (They might both be headed in the right direction.)

3. *Y* before *en* is a secure combination. The reverse order, <u>some there</u>, is locked in English.

4. Double object pronouns usually precede conjugated verbs and infinitives. The order applies whether the sentence is in declarative, negative, interrogative or negative-interrogative form.

Exs. Elle ne se rappelle pas son premier baiser. > She doesn't remember her first kiss.

    Elle ne se le rappelle pas. > She doesn't remember it. (Maybe it wasn't a 'touching' moment.)

Exs. Qui a laissé le bébé sur **la cime d'arbre**? > Who left the baby on **the treetop**?

    Qui l'y a laissé/Qui l'a laissé là? > Who left him there? (Who 'put him up to it?')

A Double Header for Double Object Pronouns- Change the underlined phrases into pronouns, and rewrite the sentences with those pronouns placed correctly.
Ex. La vieille femme a caché <u>ses diamants</u> <u>sous son matelas</u>. > La vielle dame <u>les</u> <u>y</u> a cachés.

1. Le Louvre se trouve <u>près des Tuileries</u>. _____.
2. Le rock-star a donné <u>son autographe</u> **<u>à son admiratrice</u> (his admirer).** _____
_____.
3. Luc Attem indique <u>les sites historiques</u> <u>aux touristes</u>. _____
_____.
4. Brinks et moi nous sentions en sécurité <u>chez nous</u>. _____
_____.
5. L'agent de change a-t-il décrit <u>des bourses</u> <u>à ses clients</u>? _____
_____?
6. N'envoyez pas <u>la réclamation</u> <u>à ce bureau</u>! _____!
7. Le cochon aime avoir <u>de la boue</u> <u>à ses pieds</u>. _____
_____.
8. Mlle Trust dit <u>la vérité</u> <u>à ses parents</u> rarement. _____
_____.
9. Les pilotes voient <u>le signal lumineux</u> <u>au sommet de la Tour Eiffel</u>. _____
_____.
10. Ma mère ne me permettait pas de faire <u>mes devoirs</u> <u>devant la télévision</u>. _____
_____.
11. Qui peut **déchiffrer (decipher)** <u>l'écriture de médecin</u> <u>sur l'ordonnance</u>? _____
_____?
12. Ne donne plus <u>de jouets</u> <u>à ses enfants</u>! _____!

Objects without Objections- Change the underlined phrases into pronouns, and write affirmative answers for the questions. Add past participle agreement if necessary.
Ex. Est-ce qu'elles ont vu <u>la soucoupe volante</u> <u>a Roswell, Nouveau Mexique</u>? > Did they see the flying saucer in Roswell, New Mexico? Oui, ells l'y ont vu<u>e</u>. > Yes, they saw it there.

1. Ella Gante prenait-elle <u>ses repas</u> <u>dans la salle à manger</u>? _____
_____.
2. Faut-il donner <u>la réponse</u> <u>à Uri</u> tout de suite? _____
_____.
3. Polly Tesse a-t-elle envoyé <u>une carte de remerciements</u> <u>à son hôtesse</u>? _____
_____.
4. As-tu prêté <u>ton Blackberry</u> <u>à ton copain</u>? _____.
5. Est-ce que M. et Mme Fiddle se sont amusés <u>à la danse à quatre</u>? _____
_____.
6. La Boucle d'Or a mangé <u>du porridge</u> <u>chez les trois ours</u>? _____
_____.
7. Le coureur a-t-il porté <u>la torche</u> <u>aux Jeux Olympiques</u>? _____
_____.

8. M. Tweety a gardé <u>ses oiseaux</u> <u>dans son appartement</u>? _____
_____.

9. Sharette a montré <u>tes lettres</u> <u>à sa petite-fille</u>, n'est-ce pas? _____
_____.

10. Est-ce qu'on enseigne <u>les pilates</u> <u>aux personnes du troisième âge</u>? _____
_____.

<u>Taking "No" for an Answer</u>- **Exchange the underlined phrases for pronouns, and put them in negative-imperative responses. Unless otherwise indicated, use the *tu* form!**
Ex. Si j'achète <u>les bibelots</u> <u>au marché aux puces</u>? > How about my buying the trinkets at the flea market? > Ne les y achète pas! > Don't buy them there!

1. Je mets <u>du beurre</u> <u>sur le poisson</u>. _____!
2. Tu te préoccupes <u>de ses problèmes</u>. _____!
3. Si je donne <u>ton numéro de téléphone</u> <u>à l'entremetteuse</u>? _____
_____!
4. Je place <u>ces chandeliers</u> <u>dans la salle de séjour</u>. _____!
5. Si j'offre <u>des cuisses de grenouilles</u> <u>aux enfants</u>? _____!
6. Vous montez <u>les montagnes russes</u> <u>à la foire</u>? _____
_____!
7. Tu te plains <u>du service</u>. _____!
8. Nous faisons <u>notre réservation</u> <u>à l'Hôtel Lointain</u>. _____
_____!
9. Si je dis <u>le secret</u> <u>à ma meilleure amie</u>? _____!
10. Nous vendons <u>les blue-jeans</u> <u>à la famille Levi</u>. _____
_____!

DOUBLE OBJECT PRONOUNS WITH THE AFFIRMATIVE IMPERATIVE

In affirmative commands, double object pronouns are placed together <u>after the verbs</u>. It is not difficult to adapt to the sequence since most of the items in the boxes are stacked *à l'anglaise*.

The Order of Double Object Pronouns after the Verb

Verb	Box #1	Box #2	Box #3	Box #4
	le	moi (m')	y	en
	la	toi (t')		
	les	lui		
		nous		
		vous		
		leur		

Let's Be Positive about This!

1. There are four (not five) columns listing the order of double object pronouns for affirmative commands. Third person direct object pronouns take the lead. *Me* **and** *te* **change to** *moi* **and** *toi* **and are demoted from first to second place.**

Ex. Le conducteur de train a dit à son copain, "Apporte-moi un sandwich à midi, s'il te plaît!" > The train conductor said to his friend, "Bring me a sandwich at noon, please!"

Put on a double object pronoun track, the previous sentence arrives faster as *Le conducteur de train lui a dit,"Apporte-le-moi à midi, s'il te plaît!"* **> The train conductor said to him, "Bring it to me at noon, please!"** (Hopefully, he will 'get off for lunch.')

Ex. Jules César a dit, "Prêtez-moi vos oreilles!" > Julius Caesar said, "Lend me your ears!"

Replacing *vos oreilles* **with** *les,* **Caesar's order and that of the double object pronouns turns into** *"Prêtez-les-moi!"* **> "Lend them to me!"** (He expected 'no flap.')

An important note: A hyphen precedes each noncontracted pronoun in positive commands.

2. A mixed list with reflexive, indirect and direct object pronouns (excluding *le, la* **and** *les***) is in second place.**

Ex. Lis les comptines à Olivier! > Read the nursery rhymes to Oliver!

With the substituted pronouns, the request is *Lis-les-lui!* **> Read them to him!** (The triple l̲s in the abridged French version add 'a Twist.')

3. *Moi + en* **and** *toi + en* **contract to** *m'en* **and** *t'en.*

Ex. Ann Firmière a dit, "Donnez-moi **des pansements**, s'il vous plait!" > Ann Firmière said, "Give me **some bandages** please!"

She could have 'wrapped it up' with *"Donnez-m'en, s'il vous plaît!"* **> "Give me some, please!"**

Ex. Va-t'en! > Go away! (Only the t̲ has remained.)

A note: *S'en aller* is the infinitive for the preceding command. (In case you are wondering what is going *en*.)

4. French and English pronoun order for positive commands is usually identical.

Exs. Dis-le-moi! > Say/Tell it to me!, Montrez-les-nous! > Show them to us!

5. *Y* **and** *en* **are the exceptions to #4.** **Some there** **is transposed into French as** **there some.**

Ex. Rajoutez de l'eau à la soupe! > Add some water to the soup!

When *de l'eau* **and** *à la soupe* **'evaporate' and 'condense' into pronouns, the sentence becomes** *Rajoutez-y-en!* **> Add some to it!**

5a. Affirmative imperatives that have two object pronouns rarely end with *y.* **That pronoun is replaced with the adverb** *là-bas.*

Ex. Suivez-les là-bas! > Follow them there! (The words changed, but the meaning is still t̲here.)

Action after the Action Word- **Translate the pronouns in parentheses, and put them after the verbs!**

1. (them, to us) Explique- _____, s'il te plaît!

2. (some, to her) Prêtons- _____!

3. (them, to them) Servez- _____, s'il vous plaît!

4. (it, to her) Prends- _____!

5. (us, some) Envoie- _____, s'il te plaît!

6. (it, to them) Lisez- _____, s'il vous plaît!

7. (it, to us) Raconte- _____, s'il te plaît!

8. (them, there) Mettons- _____!
9. (them, to me) Enseigne- _____, s'il te plaît!
10. (yourselves, there) Amusez- _____!

'The Status of Your Order'- Make the negative commands affirmative!
1. Ne leur en donnons pas! _____!
2. Ne lui en prends pas! _____!
3. Ne la leur vend pas! _____!
4. Ne nous en achète pas! _____!
5. Ne les y laisse pas! _____!
6. Ne me le rends pas! _____!
7. Ne me les offrez pas! _____!
8. Ne le lui suggérons pas! _____!
9. Ne me les promettez pas! _____!
10. Ne vous en débarrassez pas! _____!

le Saint-Germain-des-Prés (Paris)

LES MÉTIERS et LES PROFESSIONS - Trades and Professions

The myriad of manual laborers, shop owners, public servants and titled professionals deserve formal introductions and tricks to help you remember their trades.

Shopkeepers with 'the Same End in Sight'

With their names ending in -<u>ier</u>, the merchants listed below are related. Two exceptions are *le boucher*- the butcher and *le boulanger*- the bread maker. (They need to 'keep an <u>i</u> out.')

1. le bijoutier- the jeweler, le bottier- the bootmaker, le charcutier- the (pork) butcher/the deli-man, le charpentier- the carpenter, le cordonnier- the shoemaker, l'épicier- the (green) grocer, le jardinier- the gardener, le joaillier- the jeweler, le maroquinier- the leather dealer, le menuisier- the carpenter, le papétier- the stationer, le pâtissier- the pastry maker, le poissonier- the fish merchant, le quincaillier- the hardware store owner, le teinturier- the dry cleaner

1a. *Le bijoutier* and *le joaillier* are both jewelers. (Which one do you think has 'a better ring'?)

1b. *Le charpentier* and *le menuisier* are both carpenters. (It might be easier to build your vocabulary with the first one.)

2. The female counterparts take the mens' names, insert an accent *grave* over the <u>e</u> before the <u>r</u>, and add an <u>e</u> at the end. *La menuisière* is among the women who make 'cabinet' decisions.

3. To find the majority of above named merchants in their places of business, delete the final <u>i</u> from the masculine singular job title, and attach an -<u>ie</u> ending.

Ex. Le charcutier travaille dans une charcuterie. > The deli man works in a deli. (He is 'sandwiched' between his livelihood and his shop.)

Not So Odd Jobs

1. *Le fabricant*- the manufacturer 'gets it together' *sans une devanture*- without a storefront.

2. *L'aubergiste*- the innkeeper and *l'hôtelier/l'hôtelière*- the hotel owner 'mind their business.' If a restaurant is included with the lodging, *le propriétaire* is known as *l'hôtelier-restauranteur* or *l'hôtelière-restauranteuse.*

3. *Le/La libraire*- the bookseller works in *la librairie*. That information should not be 'misfiled' under *les bibliothécaires*- the librarians who <u>take care</u> of books *dans une bibliothèque.* (Though they may 'text-message' each other to assist clients.)

4. *Le jardinier/La jardinière*- the gardener, rarely seen in *la jardinerie*- the garden shop, is more likely to do work outside. However, *le/la fleuriste*- the florist 'makes arrangements' and meets customers at *le magasin de fleurs*- the flower shop. For him/her, the job title and its workplace are 'planted.'

Workers with the Tools of the Trade

1. *L'électricien/L'électricienne*- the electrician has 'the power' to fix 'current' problems and to avoid future ones.
2. *Le mécanicien/La méchanicienne*- the mechanic figures out "what goes" if your car does not.
3. *Le plombier/La plombière*- the plumber has a 'draining' job to make things runs smoothly.
4. *Le réparateur/La réparateuse*- the repairman/the repair woman makes adjustments both on-site and in their schedules until their customers say, "That works for me."

Hands-On Helpers

1. *Le concierge/Le gardien/La gardienne d'immeuble*- the doorman/the porter/the caretaker has multiple names in both languages and wears several hats. (If they leave their jobs, there are a lot of vacancies in the building.)
A note: *Le concierge* is referred to as *un portier* or *un chasseur* in a hotel.
2. *La bonne* is the maid. (With all her cleaning supplies, she has her hands full.)
3. *Le maître*- the butler greets and seats household members and guests. Occasionally, he must delete visitors.
4. *La jeune fille au pair* and *le garçon au pair* are known simply as *au pair* in English. (It is a fitting term since one rarely sees either one unaccompanied by a child or children.)

Professions with a Protective Covering

1. *L'agent de police* is the local policeman; *la gendarme* is the national police officer. *La femme policier*- the policewoman flashes a different badge. Members of *les forces de l'ordre*- the police force are on patrol or in *le poste/le commissariat de police*- the police station. They receive their orders from *le préfet de police*- the chief of police.
2. *Le marin* and *le matelot* are sailors. <u>Marine</u> is a cognate of the first word, and <u>mate</u> is related to the second. Their 'terms of service' place them *dans la marine*- in the Marines (without an <u>s</u> but with a 'sea') or *dans la gendamerie maritime*- in the Coast Guard.
3. *Le soldat*- the soldier, having no 'uniform' location, can be stationed anywhere. The private life of *un simple soldat*- a private is unlike that of *le caporal-chef*- the corporal.
3a. *Le commandant en chef*- the commander in chief is in charge of *l'armée*- the Army, *l'armée de l'air*- the Air Force and *la marine*- the Navy. (He is at 'the head of the brass.')
4. *Le pompier*- the fireman can be seen inside or outside *la caserne de pompiers*- the fire station. *Le capitaine des pompiers,* the fire chief of *la brigade de sapeurs-pompiers*- the fire department, issues regulations. (He is 'higher up on the ladder.')

5. *Le garde forestier*- **the forest ranger gives directions and advice to campers.** (Assuming there are no fires, he lives a 'sheltered' existence.)

Employees with the Means to Make a Living

1. *Le chauffeur* **is the privately employed driver.** *Un chauffeur de taxi* **is a taxi driver.** (Both are available 'from the get-go.')

2. *Le conducteur d'autobus*- **the bus driver keeps a set schedule throughout town, but** *l'ambulancier*- **the ambulance driver is 'on call' to and from the hospital.** (Minnie Driver usually stays around Hollywood.)

3. *Le routier* **is the truck driver. Because he eats at so many** *restaurants routiers*- **truck stops, he knows where he'll get gas.**

4. *Le livreur/La livreuse*- **the delivery person carries anything from a pizza to a piano.** (He/She might enjoy the job even though 'their business is dropping off.')

5. *Le facteur*- **the postal carrier delivers** *le courrier* **in** *une voiture postale. Le postier*- **the postal clerk, seen in** *la poste/le bureau de poste,* **has a permanent work address.**

6. *L'éboueur*- **the trash collector has** *boue* **in his title, but one should not assume that his name is mud.** (His business 'is always picking up.')

7. *Le déménageur*- **the mover is hopefully not also a shaker.** (Broken items can't be 'replaced.')

8. *Le locataire de voitures*- **the rental car agent has 'a lot' to choose from. He's 'on a first name basis' with** *le locataire de vélos*- **the bike renter.**

9. *Le capitaine d'un navire de croisière*- **the captain of a cruise ship is the first to be notified of a good 'sail.'**

10. *Le pêcheur*- **the fisherman understands that the 'net' wage is what he takes home.**

11. *Le chef de train*- **the train conductor is not known for his** *haute cuisine.* **Yet, regional fares are offered on** *le chemin de fer*- **the railroad.**

12. *Le/La pilote*- **the pilot,** *l'hôte/l'hôtesse de la compagnie aérienne*- **the cabin/flight attendant and** *autres membres de l'équipage* **are usually 'suited' for their work. They aren't always reprimanded if they get up or come in late.**

13. *L'astronaute*- **the astronaut expects 'to get blasted' on the job** *dans un vaisseau spatial*- **in a space shuttle.**

'A Labor Union'- Match the phrases to the nouns with which they are closely associated.

_____ 1. le charcutier	A. les légumes et les fruits
_____ 2. le marin/le matelot	B. les outils et les provisions de ménage
_____ 3. le pompier	C. les chambres et les repas
_____ 4. le maroquinier	D. les meubles et les boîtes
_____ 5. l'astronaute	E. les baignoires et les toilettes
_____ 6. le cordonnier	F. les gâteaux et les tartes
_____ 7. l'aubergiste	G. le bois et la construction
_____ 8. le bijoutier/le joaillier	H. les sandwichs et les viandes froides
_____ 9. le chef de train	I. le vaisseau spatial et l'univers
_____ 10. l'épicier	J. le nettoyage à sec et le repassage

____ 11. le charpentier/le menuisier	K. le chemin de fer et les gares
____ 12. le déménageur	L. les fils métalliques et les courants
____ 13. le boucher	M. les bagues et les colliers
____ 14. le pâtissier	N. les incendies/les feux et les échelles
____ 15. le mécanicien	O. les valises et les sacs à main
____ 16. le teinturier	P. les lettres et les revues
____ 17. le quincaillier	Q. les chaussures et les sandales
____ 18. l'électricien	R. les voitures et les camions
____ 19. le facteur	S. les bateaux et les navires
____ 20. le plombier	T. la viande et la volaille

Careers That Take Old Records and All CDs into Consideration

1. *L'agent d'assurance-* **the insurance agent has plans that cover unexpected events.** (Their policies include deductibles, but with life insurance, only the deceased 'is taken off.')

2. *L'agent de change-* **the stockbroker invests his/her time investing other people's money.**

3. *L'agent immobilier/immobilière,* **the real estate agent, whose French title suggests that he/she is at a standstill, organizes an open house in hopes of 'closing the deal.'**

4. *L'agent de publicité-* **the advertising agent 'gets the word out' to pull clients in.**

5. *L'agent de voyage* **is the travel agent. He/she is consulted if one tries to book his own trip but doesn't get very far.)**

6. *L'agent secret* **is the secret agent.** (For security reasons, a job description is unavailable.)

Occupations with Give and Take

1. *Le prêteur/La prêteuse-* **the lender loans people funds that they don't have to purchase something that they don't have if they agree to pay for it 'on borrowed time.'**

2. *Le prêteur sur gages-* **the pawnbroker pays 'cold cash' for 'hot items' such as guns and gold.**

3. *Le caissier/La caissière-* **the bank teller/the cashier weighs incoming and outgoing resources to arrive at a balance.**

4. *Le percepteur/La perceptrice-* **the tax collector informs** *les contribuables-* **the taxpayers about their property's value.** ('For what it's worth,' *c'est seulement la perception du percepteur.*)

5. *Le/La comptable* **means** <u>the bookkeeper</u> **and** <u>the accountant</u>**. Since he/she profits in spite of a client's loss, people get credit for doing the books themselves.**

Jobs with a Selling Point

1. *L'homme d'affaires* **is the businessman, and** *la femme d'affaires* **is the businesswoman.** (Both have *affaires*, but that's their business.)

1a. *Le commis-voyageur* **is the traveling salesman. As** *commis* **means <u>committed</u>, it's ironic that the career is frequently associated with infidelity.**

2. *Le travailleur/La travailleuse à son compte,* **the self-employed individual, needs neither** *un(e) patron(ne)-* **a boss nor** *un(e) gérant(e)-* **a manager.**

3. *Le/La réceptionniste-* **the receptionist and** *le/la secrétaire-* **the secretary may answer to or for** *le patron.* (Others might 'pick up on it.')

4. *Le/La VRP-* **the sales representative is employed by most industries. After the 'initial' face-to-face call,** *le/la vente représentative (vrp)* **is easily recognizable.**

5. *Les commerçants/Les commerçantes* **and** *les marchands-* **the merchants include the -<u>ier</u>/-<u>ière</u> shopkeepers and merchants. The spelling connections between their French and English titles verify the importance of 'word of mouth.'**

6. *Les vendeurs/Les vendeuses* **are the salesmen/the saleswomen who may be dually referred to as** *les commis-* **the clerks. With either label, they are included as** *le personnel-* **the personnel.**

What Kind of Job Are They Doing?- Circle the letter of the answer that does not belong in the group.

1. a. le boucher	b. l'épicier	c. le quincaillier	d. le charcutier
2. a. le marin	b. l'ouvrier	c. le matelot	d. le soldat
3. a. l'éboueur	b. le routier	c. le déménageur	d. le percepteur
4. a. l'homme d'affaires	b. le commerçant	c. le VRP	d. le chauffeur
5. a. l'agent de voyage	b. le pilote	c. le garde forestier	d. l'astronaute
6. a. le comptable	b. le plombier	c. l'électricien	d. le mécanicien
7. a. le jardinier	b. le maroquinier	c. le cordonnier	d. le bijoutier
8. a. le menuisier	b. le fabricant	c. le tenturier	d. le constructeur
9. a. l'ambulancier	b. le joaillier	c. le conducteur	d. le livreur
10. a. la papêterie	b. l'argenterie	c. la pâtisserie	d. la parfumerie
11. a. le vendeur	b. le clerc	c. le commis	d. le métier
12. a. l'aubergiste	b. le libraire	c. la bibliothèque	d. l'hôtelier

---

'The Perfect Job Fit'- Match the letters to the numbers to form complete sentences.

_____ 1. M. Whistler, un chef de train,

_____ 2. Le préfet de police est le patron

_____ 3. Le locataire de vélos et le locataire de voitures

_____ 4. Les documents d'un agent d'assurance

_____ 5. Bill, un percepteur, nous informe

_____ 6. Le fabricant fait les articles

_____ 7. Après avoir fini l'affaire avec l'agent immobilier,

_____ 8. Le commandant en chef se charge

A. dont le menuisier et le réparateur ont besoin.

B. travaille pour les compagnies aériennes.

C. mais un portier se trouve à un hôtel.

D. passent leurs jours à la Bourse.

E. n'a ni un patron ni un gérant.

F. et il leur vend les produits de sa compagnie.

G. voyagent sur le chemin de fer.

H. donnent un sens de sécurité.

_____ 9. L'équipage de vol
_____ 10. Ona, une travailleuse de son compte,
_____ 11. Le routier voyage d'habitude loin de sa ville,
_____ 12. Le cordonnier et le bottier
_____ 13. Le concierge se voit à l'entrée d'un immeuble d'habitation,
_____ 14. Le VRP rend visite aux clients,
_____ 15. On appelle un agent de publicité
_____ 16. Le quincaillier vend des choses
_____ 17. M. Bond, un agent secret, ne peut pas
_____ 18. On va chez le papétier
_____ 19. Pas tous les agents de change
_____ 20. Le mécanicien répare les problèmes
_____ 21. Hans Zover, le caissier, vous donne

I. vendent ce qu'on porte aux pieds.
J. de l'agent de police et de la femme policier.
K. révéler les détails de son travail.
L. des impôts qu'il faut payer.
M. des forces militaires et marines.
N. acheter des articles de correspondance.
O. on téléphone au déménageur.
P. mais le livreur conduit localement.
Q. louent la transportation avec deux ou quatre **pneus (tires)**.
R. des billets et de la monnaie.
S. qui sont à vendre chez les commerçants.
T. si on ne fait pas de réclames lui-même.
U. avec la transmission et les freins.

Artisans Who 'Make' a Living

1. *L'ouvrier du bâtiment*- **the construction worker often labors with** *le menuisier/le charpentier* **and** *le maçon*- **the bricklayer. The last French term is 'cemented' to mason.**

1a. *Les sous-traitants*- **the subcontractors toil under the watchful eye of** *l'entrepreneur*- **the contractor. (If the work is poorly done, it is the contractor's job 'to make something out of it.')**

2. *Le grand couturier* **is the high fashion designer.** *Le couturier* **and** *la couturière* **are the dressmakers. (Even though a male seamstress might not follow our 'pattern' of thinking.)**

2a. *Le styliste*- **the stylist creates "knock-offs" and enables buyers 'to knock off' a large chunk from the original price.** *Les stylistes* **don't pay exorbitant rent for** *les maisons de haute couture*- **the high fashion houses.**

3. *Le mannequin*- **the female model has a masculine form in French. The male model poses as** *le mannequin masculin*.

4. *Le dessinateur/La dessinatrice* **are generic terms for designers who put their labels on everything except clothing.** *Dessiner* **and** *le dessin* **can be 'traced' to the job title.**

5. *Le/La peintre* **is the artistic painter.** *Les portraits, les paysages, la nature morte*- **the still lives and** *la vie urbaine*- **the city life are among his/her inspirations. (They 'canvas' a large area.)**

5a. *Le peintre en bâtiments* **is the house painter. (Never dressed in an artist's smock,** *le peintre en bâtiments* **usually puts on 'two coats.')**

6. *Le sculpteur/La sculpteuse*- **the sculptor can mold an entire human form or a smaller portion**

of the anatomy. (Those who want a replica of the top half of the body must specify 'the bust size.')

7. *L'architecte*- the architect could be 'drawn to' anything from blueprints to green roofs. (His/her plans are kept open.)

8. *L'ingénieur/L'ingénieuse* is the professional engineer who is involved in the field of *le génie*- engineering. He/she heads 'a support team' to construct *les ponts, les routes et les tours d'habitation*- high-rise buildings. (They might prefer skyscrapers since they 'build things to scale.')

9. *L'écrivain/La femme écrivain* is the writer by profession. Reading between the lines, you see that the title is close to *l'auteur/la femme auteur*- the author. The former who writes *un roman, un scénario*- a screenplay, or perhaps even *un livre de français*, becomes *un auteur/une femme auteur* once the work is published. (The warm-up exercise is done without 'a book jacket.')

An important note: Painters, sculptors and writers are often *des travailleurs/travailleureuses à leurs compte.* (Their income is 'in their own hands.')

10. *L'éditeur/L'éditrice*- the publisher has 'last writes.' Note that *l'éditeur* is not the translation for the editor!

11. *Le rédacteur/la rédactrice*- the editor usually makes changes to newspaper and/or magazine articles, while *le/la journaliste* fine tunes political and/or sports pieces. *Le directeur/la directrice* edits novels and texts. (Anyone confusing the terms may 'stand corrected.')

A note: *Le directeur/La directrice* can also be the director of a company or an institution.

Data Based Professions and Trades

1. *Le technicien* is an engineer by trade rather than by profession. *Un technicien d'ordinateur*- a computer technician is 'linked' to this category.

2. *Le concepteur de sites internet*- the website designer spins *les sites web/les sites internet*.

3. *Le programmeur/La programmeuse*- the programmer, like *le technicien d'ordinateur*, works in the computer generated domain of *l'informatique*- computer science.

4. *Le/La scientifique* and *le savant*- the scientists *font des recherches*. They hypothesize, analyze and test before publicizing their findings. (Scientists are not without principles.)

Careers Providing 'the Finishing Touches'

1. *Le décorateur/La décoratrice*- the decorator determines *l'ambiance*- the setting for the works of *les dessinateurs*- the designers. (However, anyone from an aspiring Martha Stewart to a licensed professional can be involved 'in the scheme of things.')

2. *Le coiffeur*- the barber/the hairstylist and *la coiffeuse* can wash and cut their clients' hair or create new looks for them. (Often privy to their personal lives, *la coiffeuse* knows their 'roots.')

3. *Le/La manucure*- the manicurist and *le/la pédicure*- the pedicurist use 'polished skills' when pampering their customers.

4. *Le masseur/La masseuse* is the masseuse. The feminine form offers 'a hands on' translation. *Le massager* is the soothing instrument.

5. *L'entraîneur/L'entraîneuse* is the trainer. Yet, one using their services is not a trainee.

Real Professions That Are Staged

1. *Le chanteur/La chanteuse-* **the singer has a strong voice in this category. These artists 'put a lot of themselves' into the infinitive** *chanter.*
2. *Le danseur/La danseuse* **is the dancer. The job title is 'an extension' of** *danser.*
3. *L'acteur/L'actrice-* **the actor/the actress can be cast in a 'play' mode, but bringing life to the characters they portray is serious business for them.**
3a. *La vedette-* **the star refers to a well-known actress or actor.** (If one is chosen over another for a leading role, does it produce <u>Star Wars</u> or 'a Universal clash'?)
4. *Le/La comique* **is the comedian/comedienne whose unique career is all 'funny business.'**
5. *Le musician/La musicienne-* **the musician is 'instrumental' in turning thoughts into music.**
6. *Le producteur/La productrice* **applies to the film producer only.**
6a. *Le metteur en scène* **is in charge of 'play production.'** (The description features an oxymoron.)
6b. *Le réalisateur/La réalisatrice-* **the producer fills the time slots for** *les émissions de télévision.* <u>A note</u>**: In the French entertainment media, the term "director" is 'spliced in' with the producer.** (They believe in sharing the credits.)
7. *L'athlète professionnel/L'athlète professessionelle-* **the professional athlete goes on this team because he/she makes a living by entertaining an audience.** (And is 'a good sport' about it.)

<u>Occupations That Speak to Us and for Us</u>

1. *Le prêtre* **and** *le curé* **are priests.** (They have two names but only one 'calling.')
2. *Le pasteur* **is the pastor/the Protestant minister.** *Le révérend* **identifies the leader of subcategories of Christian denominations.** (Contributions of all denominations are most welcome.)
3. *Les moines-* **the monks typically live in secluded locations.** (Excluding *Des Moines* in Iowa.)
4. *La sœur* **and** *la religieuse,* **like the sister and the nun, share two names.** (Which are not in 'any specific order.')
5. *Le rabbin-* **the rabbi encourages members of his/her synagogue to renew their subscriptions to the Old Testament.**
6. *L'avocat* **means** <u>the lawyer</u> **and** <u>the avocado</u>**.** (One must peel off a lot of 'green' for both.)
7. Le juge- **the judge exercises his/her authority by overruling and sustaining motions.** (But out of court exercises might include 'bar bells' and 'bench presses.')
8. *L'oratoire* **is the public speaker who voices an opinion to persuade an audience.** (If he/she has a good platform, questions will be 'raised.')
9. *Le présentateur/La présentatrice de journal télévisé-* **the television newscaster reports current events.** (There is a remote chance that they won't be 'turn-offs.')
10. *Les politicien(ne)s* **are politicians. Officials in the French 'tower of power' include** *le maire-* **the mayor,** *le membre de l'Assemblée Nationale-* **the member of the French National Assembly,**

436

le sénateur- the senator, *le Premier Ministre*- the Prime Minister, *le Président*- the President.
(Political correctness aside, "politics" is Latin for "many bloodsuckers.")

Work That Features Creatures

1. *L'éleveur/L'éleveuse* is the breeder. (Animal lovers find 'a perfect match' with this job.)
2. *L'exterminateur/L'exterminateuse*- the exterminator has 'a solution' for "what's bugging the customers."
3. *L'agriculteur/L'agricultrice* and *le fermier/la fermière* are farmers who are seen in *un champ, une basse-cour, une grange*- a barn, *une écurie*- a horse stable or *une étable*- a cow stable.
4. *Le/La vétérinaire*- the veterinarian views animals as his or her 'pet' projects. (Although their patients can't verbalize, they understand 'pat responses.')
5. *Le gardien/La gardienne de zoo*- the zookeeper works *dans un jardin zoologique*- in a zoo and offers cage services to wild animals in their 'roam away from home.'
6. *L'empailleur/L'empailleuse* and *le/la taxidermiste* are taxidermists who might raise the dead for display and 'stuff' like that.

'Filling a Vacancy'- Choosing from the following list, replace the blanks with correct answers. (Use articles if needed.) les décorateurs, les empailleurs, les entraîneurs, les grands couturiers, les ingénieurs, les maires, les mannequins, les metteurs en scène, les oratoires, les ouvriers du bâtiment, les programmeurs, les réalisateurs, les rédacteurs, les révérends, les sculpteurs

1. Cardin, Dior, Hermès et Givenchy sont _____ bien connus.
2. _____ travaillent avec les menuisiers et les maçons.
3. _____ s'habillent des dernières façons.
4. _____ trouvent de bonnes mises pour les travaux des dessinateurs.
5. Ceux qui s'occupent des productions de pièces sont _____.
6. Les personnes qui travaillent dans l'informatique sont _____.
7. Fiorella LaGuardia et Ed Koch sont deux _____ bien connus.
8. Ray Plica et son fils sont _____ qui font les statues des gens et des choses.
9. Mai Ermode et ses collaborateurs sont _____. Ils apprennent aux gens et aux animaux ce qu'il faut faire et ne pas faire.
10. _____ supervisent ceux qui construisent les routes et les bâtiments.
11. Marc Rouge édite le texte des journaux et des revues. Il est _____.
12. Les dirigeants des églises baptistes et méthodistes sont _____.
13. _____, comme Mona Vis et ses collègues, expriment leurs opinions pour convaincre le public.
14. Mme.Tyma Slotz et ses collaborateurs font les horaires pour les émissions de télévision. Ils sont

_____.
15. Mort Maisgardé et ses associés sont _____. Ils préservent les animaux qui ne vivent plus.

Professions That Come with Instructions

1. *Le maître* **and** *la maîtresse-* **the master and the mistress educate young children. Subbing for these teachers are:** *l'instituteur/l'institutrice* **and** *le professeur/la professeure des écoles. La maîtresse-* **the schoolteacher should not be confused with** *la maîtresse-* **the mistress.** (However, both provide services that may not be available at home.)

Important notes: While *le maître* **is also the male head of a household,** *le maître d'hôtel/de maison* **is the butler. Furthermore,** *le maître d',* **the lead waiter, oversees** *le serveur* **and** *la serveuse* **who carry out the orders that** *le chef* **prepares. In finer restaurants, one can expect a table call from** *le sommelier-* **the wine steward.** (The list gives new meaning to the term "restaurant chain.")

2. *Le professeur/La professeure-* **the teacher/the professor usually specializes in one area.** (Quite possibly the teachers' lounge.) *Les professeurs* **and** *les instructeurs* **offer their knowledge to those high school and college students who are not affiliated with the 'bored' of education.**

An important note: The term *l'éducation* **includes the upbringing cultivated at home as well as the subjects taught in school.**

Professionals Who Make a Living from Check-Ups, Check-Ins and 'Check-Outs'

1. *Le médecin* **and** *la femme médecin-* **the male/female doctor/physician tell patients what to cut out, but** *le chirurgien/la chirurgienne-* **the surgeon explains what he/she will cut out.** (Hospitals also 'get a cut.')

2. *Le/La spécialiste-* **the specialist such as** *le/la psychologue-* **the psychologist,** *le/la cardiologue-* **the cardiologist and** *l'ophtalmologiste-* **the ophthalmologist treat particular parts of the human body.** *Le/La radiologue-* **the radiologist interprets one kind of blur;** *le médecin anesthésiste-* **the anesthetist induces another. The specialists' labels ending in -**<u>logue</u> **make it easier to cata**<u>logue</u> **the illness.**

3. *L'infirmier/L'infirmière-* **the nurse watches over the patients and works with physicians who 'call the shots' and prescribe 'the rest.'**

4. *L'auxiliaire médical(e)* **is the paramedic. The French term confirms that help is on the way.**

5. *Le/La dentiste-* **the dentist drills and fills the patients' teeth. He/she often 'gets to the root' of the problem.** (Aware that clients could retaliate, the dentist is careful when he 'checks their bites.')

6. *Le pharmacien/La pharmacienne-* **the pharmacist dispenses medication and advice which are 'to be taken as prescribed.'**

7. *L'entrepreneur des pompes funèbres-* **the undertaker makes a living because others are not.** (He fittingly 'brings closure' to this chapter.)

Which One 'Works'?- Circle the letters of the responses to complete the job descriptions.

1. Les patrons des sous-traitants sont _____.

a. ouvriers du bâtiment   b. entrepreneurs   c. maçons   d. entraîneurs

2. Ceux qui **créent (create)** les modes pour les mannequins sont _____.

a. menuisiers   b. oratoires   c. stylistes   d. grands couturiers

3. Un architecte et _____ travaillent ensemble pour construire les gratte-ciel, les tours d'habitation et les ponts.

a. un peintre en bâtiments   b. un technicien d'ordinateur   c. un ingénieur   d. un chirurgien

4. Mlle A. Criture a un poste chez le Monde, un journal français. Elle est _____.

a. mannequin   b. rédactrice   c. moine   d. vedette

5. _____ s'occupe des productions de pièces dans un théâtre.

a. Le mettre en scène   b. L'aubergiste   c. Le réalisateur   d. Le maître d'

6. Celui qui lave et coupe les cheveux est _____.

a. masseur   b. agriculteur   c. savant   d. coiffeur

7. Un _____ prend soin des animaux, et il les vend aussi.

a. avocat   b. éleveur   c. exterminateur   d. rabbin

8. Tous les suivants enseignent les petits sauf _____.

a. les professeurs   b. les maîtresses   c. les institutrices   d. les professeurs des écoles

9. Ni le révérend ni _____ se trouve dans une église catholique.

a. le prêtre   b. le curé   c. le pasteur   d. la religieuse

10. M. Baum ne s'occupe pas de la santé de ses clients parce qu'il est _____.

a. pharmacien   b. infirmier   c. auxiliaire médical   d. entrepreneur des pompes funèbres

11. Les spécialistes de l'informatique sont _____.

a. écrivains et auteurs   b. avocats et juges   c. concepteurs de sites internet et programmeurs

d. présentateurs de journal télévisé

12. Mme I. Hertz, qui a mal aux yeux, consulte _____.

a. un artisan   b. un psychologue   c. un ophtalmologiste   d. une sculpteuse

---

'An Honest Day's Work'- Label the true statements *vrai* or *faux*.

_____ 1. Le scientifique et le savant sont des synonymes.

_____ 2. Les acteurs et actrices célèbres sont vedettes.

_____ 3. Les vêtements d'un styliste coûtent plus que ceux d'un grand couturier.

_____ 4. Les peintres sont spécialistes de génie.

_____ 5. Un avocat est un fruit aussi bien que quelqu'un qui représente ses clients.

_____ 6. Les mannequins ne sont pas faits de bois.

_____ 7. Un maître et une maîtresse enseignent dans une université.

_____ 8. Le manucure et le pédicure prennent soin des ongles.

_____ 9. Le dessinateur et le décorateur font la même chose.

_____ 10 Le libraire et le bibliothécaire ne font pas le même travail.

_____ 11. Le prêtre et le curé sont des synonymes.

_____ 12. L'éleveur et l'exterminateur travaillent ensemble.

_____ 13. Le Premier Ministre habite dans une écurie.

_____ 14. Ceux qui font de la politique sont souvent oratoires.

_____ 15. L'auxiliaire médical n'est pas chirurgien.

UNE REVUE - A Review

L'Imparfait, Double Object Pronouns, Les Métiers et Les Professions

Making Alternate Arrangements- Put the sections in the correct sequence to form sentences.

1. des secrets/ les/ ne voulait pas/ M. Houdini avait/ dire/ mais il/ nous

_____.

2. en ville/ allaient/ Quand il jouait/ voir/ mes grands-parents/ le

_____.

3. dans l'eau/ mais il / On l'a mis/ est échappé/ dans une boîte serrée/ s'en/ et l'a baissée

_____
_____.

4. que mon ami Rob/ mais elle ne/ des gâteaux secs/ Ma mère savait/ disait rien/ lui/ prenait

_____
_____.

5. des jours entiers/ mais ils/ Gill et Finn/ en attrapaient / passaient/ n'y/ à ce lac-là/ rien

_____
_____.

6. rencontrions/ y/ nous amusions/ nous/ les/ quand nous/ Néanmoins/ toujours

_____.

7. savions jamais/ mais nous ne/ dans le champ en automne/ les épouvantails/ qui les/ Nous voyions/ y mettait _____

_____.

Grammar 'Rules'! - Circle the letters of the responses that best complete the sentences.

1. The singular and the third person plural imperfect endings ____.
a. have the same spelling   b. have the same pronunciation   c. change according to the verb
d. show agreement with preceding direct object pronouns

2. The imperfect stems of all verbs except *être* are found ____.
a. by removing the infinitive ending   b. *au passé composé*   c. in their present participles
d. by deleting -<u>ons</u> from present tense *nous* form

3. *L'imparfait* is used more frequently than *le passé composé* to ____.
a. express thoughts and emotions   b. describe completed past actions
c. translate has/have or did   d. translate intransitive verbs

4. -<u>Cer</u> and -<u>ger</u> verbs ____ *à l'imparfait.*
a. do not have "boot" form conjugations   b. have irregular *nous* and *vous* form endings
c. have several spelling changes   d. have no changes in the *nous* and *vous* forms

5. When *le passé composé* and *l'imparfait* are in the same sentence, the latter tense ____.
a. is always preceded by *depuis*   b. does not describe an ongoing past action
c. tells the action that lasted longer   d. is never translated by "had been"

6. *Cela faisait* and *Il y avait* are followed by ____.
a. a verb *au passé composé*   b. an expression of time + *que*   c. an interrogative phrase
d. *l'imparfait* and an adverb

7. When double object pronouns precede the verb, _____.

a. reflexives follow directs　　　　　　　b. indirects are put before reflexives

c. reflexives come first　　　　　　　　　d. those beginning with an l are last

8. With double object pronouns in affirmative commands, third person direct object pronouns ____.

a. are placed between *y* and *en*　　　　b. are in the same box as indirect object pronouns

c. affect past participle agreement　　　　d. immediately follow the verb

9. When an infinitive follows a conjugated verb, double object pronouns ____.

a. go together before the conjugated verb　　b. have hyphens between them

c. are separated with one before and one after the conjugated verb

d. are placed after the second verb

10. French affirmative commands with double object pronouns ____.

a. place reflexives at the end　　　　　　b. have an order very similar to English

c. do not use contractions for *me* and *te*　d. have the same sequence as negative commands

---

'Available Openings'- **Choosing from the following nouns, replace the blanks with the correct answers: Use indefinite articles if necessary. (un) commandant en chef, (un) commis-voyageur, (un) concierge, (un) fabricant, (un) fermier, (une) hôtesse de compagnie aérienne, (une) infirmière, (une) maîtresse, (un) marchand, (un) pâtissier, (un) peintre, (un) pilote, (un) plombier, (un) prêteur, (un) prêteur sur gages, (un) réparateur, (un) sculpteur, (un) vétérinaire**

1. Fauché parle avec _____ à sa banque pour emprunter de l'argent.

2. M. Lointain reste fréquemment dans les hôtels. Il est _____.

3. Mon _____ fait les meilleures Charlottes russes.

4. _____ paie comptant si on lui donne quelque chose de valeur.

5. Un commerçant et _____ sont des synonymes.

6. _____ s'occupe des petits dans une école primaire.

7. _____ travaille souvent avec des spécialistes dans un hôpital.

8. Le Président des États-Unis est aussi _____.

9. Mlle Trempée a une inondation dans sa salle de bain. Elle fait venir _____.

10. _____ nous accueille au rez-de-chaussée d'un immeuble d'habitation.

11. _____ et _____ sont deux membres de l'équipage de vol.

12. Mlle Exigeante ne trouve pas ce qu'elle veut dans les grands magasins. Pour ça, elle va à l'usine d' _____.

13. Pat Lapeau aimait beaucoup les animaux. Est-il devenu _____ ou _____ ?

14. Art Istique veut être _____ ou _____ pour créer des chefs-d'œuvre dans un atelier.

Employment Opportunities - **Judging by their qualifications, circle the letters of the trades or occupations that best suit the individuals.**

1. M. Kasbah vendait des produits en cuir aux marchés. Il cherche un boulot chez _____.

a. un joaillier　　　b. un maroquinier　　　c. un grand couturier　　　d. un teinturier

2. Mlle Chiffres est douée en mathématiques. Gagner une vie comme un(e) _____ lui intéresse.

a. comptable   b. serveuse   c. masseuse   d. contribuable

3. Rhodes, qui s'habitue à être loin de sa maison, sait conduire les grands camions. Il doit **soliciter un poste (to apply for a job)** comme un _____.

a. éboueur   b. locataire de voitures   c. prêteur   d. routier

4. O. Céans aime faire le bateau à voile. Il cherche une carrière qui lui permet de voyager. Il pense à devenir _____.

a. soldat   b. salarié   c. matelot   d. caissier

5. Lise, qui adore lire tout, veut avoir sa propre boutique. Pourquoi ne devient-elle pas (un) _____?

a. bibliothècaire   b. livreuse   c. percepteuse   d. propriétaire d'une librairie

6. M. Litetpain travaillait comme un chef dans un hôtel où sa femme était serveuse. Ils pensent à être travailleurs à leurs comptes. S'ils deviennent _____?

a. agents immobiliers   b. déménageurs   c. aubergistes   d. sous-traitants

7. Sue Rire est très á l'aise lorsqu'elle raconte ses plaisanteries. On l'encourage à avoir une carrière comme un(e) _____.

a. agent de change   b. VRP   c. comique   d. savant

8. Pi Lule ne veut ni assister à l'école de médecine ni travailler dans un laboratoire. Cependant, elle fait très bien dans la chimie. Pourquoi ne devient-elle pas _____?

a. radiologue   b. institutrice   c. pasteur   d. pharmacienne

le Louvre (Paris)

LE TEMPS FUTUR - THE FUTURE TENSE

With *le passé composé,* we can talk about what did happen, and with *l'imparfait* we can discuss what was happening. *Le temps futur* enables us to express what <u>will happen</u>.
Since the future is now literally "in your hands," here is some choice advice:

Choisir -To Choose

<u>Singular</u>	<u>Plural</u>
je choisir<u>ai</u> - I will choose	nous choisir<u>ons</u> - we will choose
tu choisir<u>as</u> - you will choose	vous choisir<u>ez</u> - you will choose
il/elle/on choisir<u>a</u> - he/she/it/one will choose	ils/elles choisir<u>ont</u> - they will choose

----

Looking into *Le Futur*

1. *Le futur proche*, the near future, is derived from a present tense form of *aller* + an infinitive. It tells what one is going to do. There is a limited time in which to do it.
Ex. Madame Deuxalafois va nourrir ses petits jumeaux tout de suite. > Mrs. Deuxalafois is going to feed her little twins right away. (She plans to do it 'on the double.')
2. The key word associated with *le temps futur* is <u>will</u>. (However, a will contains important information from the 'passed.')
3. The future of regular -<u>er</u> and -<u>ir</u> verbs is formed by attaching -<u>ai</u>, -<u>as</u>, -<u>a</u>, -<u>ons</u>, -<u>ez</u> and -<u>ont</u> to the infinitive. The same endings are found in the present tense conjugation of *avoir*.
Ex. Ils fêteront leur soixante-deuxième anniversaire. > They will celebrate their 'sixty-second' anniversary. (Of course, they have been married for more than a minute.)
4. The future of regular -<u>re</u> verbs is formed by taking the last <u>e</u> off the infinitive before adding the future endings.
Ex. Toulouse ne perdra jamais ce que je lui ai donné. > Toulouse will never lose what I gave to him. (Even though he was born 'Tou-louse.')
4a. Many irregular -<u>re</u> verbs and their families have regular future stems. The last <u>e</u> is deleted from the infinitive before regular future endings are added. Examples include *boire, conduire, connaître, croire, devoir, dire, écrire, lire, mettre, plaindre, prendre, rire* and *suivre*.
Ex. Le routier conduira entre Lille et Nancy. > The truck driver will drive between Lille and Nancy. (They are distant relatives.)
Ex. Je me mettrai à étudier la semaine prochaine. > I will start to study next week. (There's no time like the present, unless it's the future.)
5. Orthographic/stem changing verbs that alter their appearances in a "boot" form *au présent* make the adjustments in a "box" form in future conjugations.

5a. Verbs with unaccentuated <u>es</u> preceding the infinitive ending have an accent *grave* in every form *au futur*. This category includes *acheter, achever, amener, emmener, mener, se promener, élever, enlever, lever, geler* and *peser*.

Ex. Les éleveurs anglais élèveront des chiots très chers. > The English breeders will raise some very expensive puppies. (And thereby increase the value of their 'pound.')

5b. Verbs that change <u>é</u> to <u>è</u> in a "boot" form in the present tense keep the final <u>é</u> *au futur* for the entire conjugation. *Célébrer, espérer, posséder, préférer, protéger* and *répéter* are some that save their infinitive resources for future needs.

Ex. Nous espérons que toutes ces précautions nous protégéront contre l'ouragan. > We hope that all these precautions will protect us against the hurricane. (And that only the storm 'will blow over.')

5c. Verbs that double the <u>l</u> or the <u>t</u> in the shape of a boot in the present tense wear those paired consonants throughout *le futur*.

Ex. Vous ne jetterez pas ces règles de grammaire dans la poubelle. > You won't toss these grammar rules into the wastebasket. (We shouldn't throw away the future.)

5d. Verbs with -<u>oyer</u> and -<u>uyer</u> infinitive endings change the <u>y</u> to an <u>i</u> in all future forms. This category includes *employer, nettoyer, se noyer, s'ennuyer* and *essuyer*.

Ex. Essuiera-t-elle toutes les bouteilles **poussiéreuses** de liqueur? > Will she wipe all the **dusty** bottles of liquor? (Why not let the guests 'polish them off'?)

5e. Verbs with -<u>ayer</u> infinitive endings keep the <u>y</u> throughout the future. Examples are *balayer, essayer* and *payer*.

6. The future is secure with these adverbial terms: *à l'avenir*- in the future, *demain*- tomorrow, *le lendemain*- the next day, *le mois prochain/suivant*- the next/following month, *la semaine prochaine/suivante*- the next/following week, *l'année prochaine/suivante*- the next/following year, *le siècle prochain/suivant*- the next/following century, *la prochaine fois*- the next time

-----

<u>**'Where There's a Will'**</u>- **Write the underlined verbs *au temps futur* on the spaces provided.**

_____ 1. Le bottier et le cordonnier <u>travaillent</u> ensemble.

_____ 2. Ce tirage <u>coûte</u> moins au bouquiniste que dans une librairie.

_____ 3. Qui <u>dessine</u> un mouton pour <u>le Petit Prince</u>?

_____ 4. Tu **bronzes (tan)** cet été.

_____ 5. Les Bienvenu <u>accueillent</u> les invités.

_____ 6. Je n'<u>accomplis</u> jamais toutes mes **tâches (tasks)**.

_____ 7. Nous vous <u>attendons</u> devant ce Monoprix-là.

_____ 8. Le prêteur sur gages <u>vend</u> ta montre d'or?

_____ 9. Est-ce que tu te <u>promènes</u> seule par nuit au Boulevard St. Denis?

_____ 10. Juan Segaine et toi <u>répétez</u> les phrases.

_____ 11. Mme Fontaine <u>lit</u> des fables aux petits.

_____ 12. M. O. Revoir <u>met</u> à la porte des salariés.

_____ 13. Qu'est-ce que vous me <u>dites</u>?

_____ 14. Je <u>prends</u> mon déjeuner dans le Marais.

_____ 15. M. Fer et M. Acier <u>construisent</u> des ponts.

_____ 16. Lin Guiste et moi <u>traduisons</u> plusieurs langues.

Verbs with Irregular Future Stems

1. aller- ir
2. avoir- aur
3. courir- courr
4. devoir- devr
5. être- ser
6. envoyer- enverr
7. faire- fer
8. falloir- faudr
9. mourir- mourr
10. pleuvoir- pleuvra
11. pouvoir- pourr
12. recevoir- recevr
13. savoir- saur
14. tenir- tiendr
15. valoir- (to be worth)- vaudr
16. venir- viendr
17. voir- verr
18. vouloir- voudr

Stems with a System

1. The future stems of *avoir* **and** *savoir* **are** <u>aur</u> **and** <u>saur</u> **resprctively. With just one letter different in their infinitives, it makes sense that their futures are intertwined.** (Watering them down makes it easier 'to pull up their roots.')

Ex. La femme enceinte a quatre filles. Elle ne saura pas jusqu'au mois prochain si elle aura un fils. > The pregnant woman has four daughters. She will not know until next month whether she will have a son. (The woman hopes that 'it will turn out' as she wants.)

2. The future stem of *être* **is** <u>ser</u>**; that of** *faire* **is** <u>fer</u>**. Like many irregular future stems, these two rhyme.**

Ex. Mlle Mince a dit, "Je pense que j'y serai la seule avec un cadeau bon marché." > Ms Mince said, "I think that I will be the only one there with an inexpensive gift." (It is the thought that counts, and she knows what people will be thinking.)

Ex. Le vieux roi Cole fera venir ses trois joueurs de violon. > Old King Cole will call for his fiddlers three. (His special pipe and bowl would make anyone 'a merry old soul.')

3. The future stems of *pouvoir-* <u>pourr</u> **and** *voir-* <u>verr</u> **contain double** <u>rs</u>**.** *Voir* **is inside** *pouvoir.*

Ex. Nous avons convaincu notre père que nous ne pourrons pas faire du camping sans une nouvelle tente. > We convinced our father that we won't be able to go camping without a new tent. (They are already 'breaking ground.')

3a. The future stem of *envoyer,* <u>enverr</u>, **is** <u>verr</u> **prefixed by** <u>en</u>**.**

Ex. Faye Beau leur enverra une carte postale de la plus grande ville sur la Côte d'Azur. > Faye Beau will send them a post card from the largest city on the French Riviera. (That would be Nice.)

4. The future stems of *courir* **and** *mourir,* <u>courr</u> **and** <u>mourr</u>**, have double** <u>rs</u>**.**

Ex. M. Éclat, qui s'est cassé la jambe, ne courra pas dans le marathon cette année. > Mr. Éclat, who broke his leg, will not run in the marathon this year. (He can't sprint with a splint.)

5. *Devoir, pleuvoir* **and** *recevoir* **have future stems ending with a single** <u>r</u>**. They are** <u>devr</u>**,** <u>pleuvr</u> **and** <u>recevr</u> **respectively.**

Ex. Comme Veetesse ne payera pas **sa contravention**, elle devra aller devant le juge. > As Veetesse will not pay **her fine**, she will have 'to go before' the judge. (Who would think that not paying a ticket would result in the death penalty?)

6. The future stems of several irregular verbs are 'doctored' with a <u>dr</u>**.**

6a. *Falloir* **will join in any conversation if the subject is the third person singular.** *Valoir-* **to be worth has a full conjugation, but it prefers to be seen with third person subjects. Their future**

stems are _faudr_ and _vaudr_.

Ex. Croyant que **ses épingles** ne vaudront plus à l'avenir, l'antiquaire les vend. > Believing that **his pins** won't be worth more in the future, the antique dealer sells them. (He doesn't want 'to be stuck with' them.)

6b. The future roots of _venir_ and _tenir_, _viendr_ and _tiendr_, sprout _is_.

Ex. La diseuse de bonne aventure nous dit que la bonne chance nous viendra bientôt. > The fortune teller tells us that good luck will come to us soon. (She may access more from the credit cards than from her Tarot cards.)

6c. The future stem of _vouloir_- _voudr_ has no corresponding verb as a partner. You will want to keep that in mind.

Ex. Personne ne voudra acheter ces plantes en soie. Je les donnerai à un hôpital. > Nobody will want to buy these silk plants. I will give them to a hospital. (Someone might find a use for the 'IV.')

7. The future stem of _aller_, -_ir_, not fitting into any of the above categories, must _go_ alone.

Ex. Ces jeunes mariés n'iront pas à Florence pour **leur voyage de noces/leur lune de miel**. > Those newly weds will not go to Florence for **their honeymoon**. (Why get a third person involved?)

A helpful hint: The word _futur_ and the future stems themselves end with an _r_. The final letter of the noun indicates the verb tense.

An interesting aside: The chemical symbols for gold, -_au_, and iron, -_fe_, are inside _aur_ and _fer_.

'Planting the Roots'- Put the verbs in parentheses into the correct future forms.

1. (faire) Mo Tivé _____ de son mieux **désormais (from now on)**.
2. (valoir) Anne Ticiper croit qu'il _____ **la peine (the trouble)**.
3. (mourir) L'herbe et les fleurs _____ sans eau.
4. (voir) Est-ce que nous te _____ en même temps l'année prochaine?
5. (falloir) Il _____ cliquer sur Mapquest plusieurs fois pendant notre voyage.
6. (vouloir) J'en ai besoin maintenant, mais je ne le _____ pas à l'avenir.
7. (être) Winnie Pegg et Van Couver _____ toujours au Canada.
8. (pouvoir) Earl Lee et toi ne _____ jamais le faire plus tard.
9. (envoyer, recevoir) Comment _____-vous et comment _____-vous vos SMS sans vos I-Cosses?
10. (aller, avoir) Tu _____ mieux bientôt, et tu _____ envie de le faire.

Special Uses of the Present and Future Tenses

1. When _quand_ precedes an action or an event that generally happens and can be translated by whenever, the verb following it is in the present tense.

Ex. Les petits canards aiment jouer dans **les flaques d'eau** quand il pleut. > The little ducks love to play in **the puddles** when(ever) it rains.

2. If the action refers to an event that has not yet occured, _quand, lorsque, aussitôt que_ and _dès que_- as soon as often require _le temps futur_. However, the present tense is normally used in the same cases in English.

Ex. Donne-lui un baiser dès que tu le verras! > Give him a kiss as soon as you (will) see him!

Alternate Future Plans- Circle the letters of the answers that correspond to the first sentences.

1. Nous célébrerons dans un endroit lointain.
a. On ne connaîtra pas ceux qui seront là.   b. On trouvera l'hôtel facilement.
c. Les invités ne sauront pas la date.   d. La fête n'aura pas lieu à un site proche.

2. Charles Maine jouera le rôle d'un roi du Moyen Âge.
a. Il ne devra pas s'habiller.   b. Il ne devra pas se raser.   c. L'acteur ne voudra pas le faire.
d. Il sera nécessaire pour lui de se dépêcher.

3. Mlle Colis enverra un paquet bientôt à M. et Mme Laboîte.
a. Ils le recevront dans quelques jours.   b. On pourra le prendre du tabac.
c. Ils le retourneront à la poste.   d. On ne devra pas l'ouvrir.

4. Les étudiants indépendants demanderont ton assistance s'ils en auront besoin.
a. Ils pensent qu'ils réussiront par hasard.   b. On ne saura pas quoi faire.
c. Ils essayeront de le faire eux-mêmes d'abord. d. Tu ne viendras pas les aider.

5. La malade mourra chez elle **entourée de (surrounded by)** sa famille.
a. Un spécialiste viendra la voir.   b. La femme sera guérie dans sa propre maison.
c. Son médecin lui rendra trop de visites.   d. Elle n'ira pas à une clinique.

6. M. et Mme Pressés n'auront pas le temps de prendre un repas avant leur vol.
a. Ils mangeront un casse-croûte dès qu'ils monteront à bord.
b. Ils diront au douanier qu'ils n'ont rien à déclarer.
c. Le couple demandera des bières après l'arrivée.
d. Ces gens-là offriront leurs cartes d'embarquement à l'équipage.

7. Nettie la bonne a tant de tâches ménagères à faire pour la grande soirée chez les Onttout.
a. On remplacera les vitraux et les lustres.   b. Elle polira l'argenterie et les chandeliers.
b. Elle essuiera les meubles dans l'écurie.   d. Les Onttout peindra les murs et les plafonds.

8. Qu'est-ce que M. Jaguar fera de sa contravention pour excès de vitesse?
a. Cet homme s'en plaindra aux pompiers.   b. Il sera en panne en route à **la cour (the court)**.
c. Il enverra un chèque dans le courrier.   d. Le juge conduira plus lentement à l'avenir.

9. Quand son enfant aura trois ans, sa mère lui enseignera à parler japonais.
a. La femme apprendra une deuxième langue aussi.   b. L'enfant frappera sa mère.
c. Le petit commencera à l'apprendre très jeune.   d. Sa mère ne comprendra pas ses mots.

10. Dans le parc ce matin, j'ai rencontré le prêtre que tu connais. Devine ce qu'il m'a demandé!
a. "Vaudra-t-il la peine d'aller à la messe?"   b. "M'expliqueras-tu les dix commandements?"
c. "Deviendras-tu bouquiniste?"   d. "Je te verrai à l'église dimanche?"

'Space Exploration in the Future'- Write the verbs in parentheses *au temps futur*.

1. (bâtir, détruire) Les trois petits cochons _____ trois maisons. Le méchant loup
ne _____ pas la troisième.

2. (apprendre, voyager) Fogg et Passepartout _____ des mœurs très fascinants
quand ils _____ autour du monde l'année prochaine.

3. (vouloir) Personne ne _____ y habiter après tous les cambriolages.

4. (pouvoir) "Chip, _____-nous remplacer les carreaux dans le foyer?"

5. (recevoir) Ce que tu vois est ce que tu _____.

6. (s'endormir) Les enfants ne _____ pas à cause du bruit en bas.

7. (faire, se geler) S'il _____ chaud cet hiver, cet étang ne _____ pas.

447

8. (prendre, être, avoir) Je _____ un grand déjeuner lorsque je _____ chez les Bouffe. Ainsi, je n' _____ pas faim ce soir.

9. (mettre, s'arrêter) "Mme Bonplan _____-vous les serviettes dans le sèche-linge dès que le lave-linge _____?"

10. (se marier) Roméo demande à Juliette, "_____-tu avec moi?"

A Step Ahead- Change the following sentences *au temps futur.*

1. Les Schwinn louent des bicyclettes à Amsterdam. _____

_____.

2. Qui m'attend devant le club? _____?

3. Il faut le faire aussitôt que possible. _____

_____.

4. Pat Terne et moi les cousons nous-mêmes. _____

_____.

5. Fergie suit le régime de Jenny Craig. _____

_____.

6. M. Ford doit réparer ses propres freins. _____

_____.

7. Font-ils leurs études à l'Université de Grenoble? _____

_____?

8. Je ne peux pas lire son écriture. _____

_____.

9. Raye Présente et les autres avocats deviennent sénateurs. _____

_____.

10. Notre fille au pair ne va pas en France avec nous. _____

_____.

11. Tu ris quand tu vois **ce dessin animé-ci (this cartoon).** _____

_____.

12. Les Partir ne se joignent pas à nous parce qu'ils partent pour l'Europe en juin. _____

_____

_____.

'Exercising Your Will Power'- Translate the following sentences.

1. What will Babette buy for the baby? _____

_____?

2. Don't worry (*vous*)! I will finish it next week. _____

_____.

3. Everyone will be happy to see them. _____

_____.

4. Cameron will want these beautiful photos. _____

_____.

5. M. Bogart will drive us to the dock where we will take a boat to Casablanca. _____

_____.

6. As soon as you (*tu*) come, we will leave together. _____

7. When their children are in school, Ty and Dee will straighten out the house. _____

_____ .

8. There will be so many people in their chalet. How will the Woods be able to rest? _____

_____ ?

la Villette, Cité des Sciences et de l'Industrie

LE TEMPS CONDITIONNEL - THE CONDITIONAL TENSE

Everything is on hand to create the conditional recipe. You just need to know how to blend the ingredients. Two timers are used. One is set to the future; the other to the imperfect.
For step by step directions, keep your eyes on the endings and instructions below!

Regarder - To Look At

Singular	Plural
je regarderais- I would look at	nous regarderions- we would look at
tu regarderais- you would look at	vous regarderiez- you would look at
il/elle/on regarderait- he/she/it would look at	ils/elles regarderaient- they would look at

----

Under All Conditions

1. The conditional expresses what <u>would</u> occur given certain circumstances.
2. Because the conditional of will is would, future and conditional tenses share the same stems. 'To apply conditioning' to those 'roots':
a. Use the entire infinitive for regular -<u>er</u> and -<u>ir</u> verbs.
b. Use the infinitive minus the final <u>e</u> for regular and most irregular -<u>re</u> verbs.
c. Allow the following list of common irregular future/conditional stems to set in:

1. aller- ir	10. pleuvoir- pleuvra
2. avoir- aur	11. pouvoir- pourr
3. courir- courr	12. recevoir- recevr
4. devoir- devr	13. savoir- saur
5. être- ser	14. tenir- tiendr
6. envoyer- enverr	15. valoir- vaudr
7. faire- fer	16. venir- viendr
8. falloir- faudr	17. voir- verr
9. mourir- mourr	18. vouloir- voudr

3. The imperfect endings -<u>ais</u>, -<u>ais</u>, -<u>ait</u>, -<u>ions</u>, -<u>iez</u> and -<u>aient</u> are 'the branches' attached to the future stems.
Ex. Qu'est-ce qu'ils feraient sans leurs courriers électroniques? > What would they do without their e-mails? (They might 'go postal.')
4. Orthographic/stem-changing verbs alter their spelling *au conditionnel* exactly as they do *au futur*.
4a. Those with an unaccented <u>e</u> in the syllable before the infinitive ending add an accent *grave* to that vowel throughout the conjugation.
Exs. je mènerais, tu mènerais, il/elle/on mènerait, etc. (You see where this 'is leading.')
4b. Those with é to è changes in "boot" form *au présent* keep the é throughout *le conditionnel*.
Exs. je préférerais, tu préférerais, il/elle/on préférerait, etc. (By retaining the accent *aigu*, they show a 'sharp' preference.)
4c. Verbs with -<u>ler</u> and -<u>ter</u> infinitive endings conjugated in "boot" form *au présent* double the <u>l</u> and the <u>t</u> in all conditional forms.

Exs. je (me) rappellerais, tu (te) rappellerais, il/elle/on (se) rappellerait, etc.

Recall with its double l is a reminder that "boot verbs" lose their shape *au futur* and *au conditionnel*. For those tenses, they remain in "a box."

4d. Y changes to i throughout the conditional conjugations of -oyer and -uyer verbs.

Exs. je nettoierais, tu nettoierais, il/elle/on nettoierait, etc. (The y has been 'cleaned out.')

4e. Verbs with -ayer infinitive endings keep the y throughout *le conditionnel*.

Exs. je payerais, tu payerais, il/elle/on payerait, etc. (One is not offered a choice of payments.)

5. A conditional form of *devoir* + an infinitive expresses should/ought to do something.

Ex. On devrait être poli. (Il faudrait être poli.) > One should be polite. (The 'respective' French sentence has more than one translation.)

Ex. Mlle Scarlett pense qu'Autant en Emporte le Vent devrait avoir une fin heureuse. > Ms Scarlett thinks that Gone with the Wind should have a happy ending. (Is she 'blown away' that it doesn't?)

6. A conditional form of *pouvoir* + an infinitive is used when could means should be able to.

Ex. L'agent de haute couture pourrait reconnaître l'avion de Mlle Vogue. > The high fashion agent should be able to recognize Ms Vogue's plane. (Even with several 'models on the runway.')

7. Conditional forms of *aimer, pouvoir* and *vouloir* make requests and replies more polite.

Ex. Pourriez-vous me donner des renseignements? > Could you give me some information?

Ex. Elle ne voudrait pas vous dire. > She would not want to tell you.

7a. *Vouloir* often translates as "to like" when used *au conditionnel*.

Ex. Voudriez-vous voir ce film-là avec moi? > Would you like to see that film with me? (The courteous use of the conditional gives one more 'lobbying power.')

Making Use of the 'Would' Pile- Fill in the blanks with the correct conditional forms of *aimer, boire, dépenser, employer, être, partager, payer, penser, pouvoir, ranger, rentrer, suivre* and *vouloir*. More than one verb is possible for some answers.

1. Les gosses _____ / _____ jouer dans ces flaques-ci.

2. Le clerc a dit, "Ça suffit." Il ne (n') _____ plus les marchandises.

3. Je ne _____ pas que les Jeter _____ leur fortune comme ça.

4. Personne ne (n') _____ / _____ / _____ les conseils du vieillard.

5. Est-ce que M. Fiat et toi _____ heureux avec un Citroën?

6. Il ne sera pas facile, mais un savant _____ découvrir un remède.

7. Je ne _____ pas de secrets avec cette dame à la langue pendue.

8. Qu'est ce que tu _____ / _____ prendre pour un rafraîssement?

9. M. Malpointe a dit qu'il ne _____ jamais la contravention.

10. Nous pensions que M. et Mme Noce _____ en France après leur lune de miel.

11. _____ / _____ / _____ -tu le Coca ou le Pepsi?

12. Cela n'est pas utile. Pourquoi nous ne l' _____ pas?

Conditions That Do Not Warrant the Conditional

1. When <u>would</u> carries the sense of <u>used to</u>, *l'imparfait* is needed.
Ex. **Des bûcherons** coupaient les arbres pour vendre le bois. > **Some woodcutters** used to cut trees to sell the wood. (They no longer 'saw' the profits.)
There is a wood cut but not a 'would' cut.
2. When <u>could</u> means <u>was able to</u>, *l'imparfait* or *pu* + an infinitive is used.
Ex. Sans rien déclarer, Heidi a pu passer par le douanier. > Without declaring anything, Heidi could/ was able to get by the customs official. (No one heard 'the baggage claims' from her luggage.)
3. When <u>would</u> implies <u>to be willing to</u>, *l'imparfait* or *voulu* + an infinitive are the options.
Ex. Aucune vendeuse ne voulait renoncer à cette **place de choix.** > No vendor would/was willing to give up that **prime spot.** (They may be at the same 'stand still.')
Ex. Les criminels n'ont pas voulu parler de leurs vies en prison. > The criminals would not speak of/ were not willing to speak of their lives in prison. (They just 'didn't want to go there.')

Changes in the Future- Put the underlined verbs *au conditionnel* on the spaces provided.

1. _____ M. Goodyear <u>vendra</u> de nouveaux pneus.
2. _____ Ben Sûr et moi <u>dirons</u> que tout est possible.
3. _____ Je te les <u>offrirai</u>.
4. _____ Les petits <u>auront</u>-ils peur de Casper?
5. _____ <u>Ira</u>-t-elle à la plage à Cannes ou à Nice?
6. _____ Le scout <u>fera</u> tout pour recevoir cet insigne-ci.
7. _____ Aida <u>saura</u> que faire en cas d'**urgence-f. (urgency, emergency).**
8. _____ Hy Cees et son équipage <u>devront</u> regarder une carte.
9. _____ Nous <u>pourrons</u> l'utiliser encore.
10. _____ Est-ce que tu t'en <u>fâcheras</u>?
11. _____ Il s'<u>agira</u> de la motivation pour Anne Duce.
12. _____ Des cadeaux comme ceux-là <u>seront</u> apprecíes de tous.

'Filling In on a Conditional Basis'- Replace the blanks with the correct conditional forms of the verbs in parentheses.

1. (aimer) Mon père sait que ma mère _____ mieux un bouquet de lilas.
2. (compter) "M. Doigts, je ne _____ pas sur eux."
3. (souhaiter) Jeannie nous a demandé, "Pour quoi _____-vous?"
4. (avoir) Il n'y _____ pas assez de dessert pour tout le monde.
5. (dire) Qu'est-ce que tu leur _____?
6. (aller) Lona Lee n' _____ jamais à l'étranger toute seule de nouveau.
7. (devoir) M. Faitrien et vous _____ trouver un boulot.
8. (vouloir) La Bête a demandé à La Belle, " _____-tu danser avec moi?"
9. (donner, essayer) _____-tu tes vêtements d'occasion à une organization carita-tive ou _____-tu de les vendre?
10. (devoir, se plaindre) Nous ne _____ pas _____ autant.

Conditions Subject to Change- Translate the following sentences.
A note: *Le conditionnel* **should not be used for the sentences preceded by asterisks.**

1. Bea Stro said that she would eat at the café this evening. _____
_____.

2. I knew that he would explain it to us again. _____
_____.

3. Honoré tells his children that they should not lie. _____
_____.

4. Caviar? Everybody should taste it once. _____
_____.

5. Would Manuel read the instructions before assembling the bookcase? _____
_____?

6. Linc and I should be able to find it on line. _____
_____.

7. Why would you (*tu*) make fun of him? _____?
8. Compton did not realize that the encyclopedias would be worth a lot of money. _____
_____
_____.

9. *The Sales would never wash their car. _____
_____.

10.*Many years ago we could run quickly as you (informal). _____
_____.

11.*Rose would blush when she was little. _____
_____.

12.*We would believe everything that they told us. _____
_____.

13.*I remember that Dinah would set the table for each meal. _____
_____.

14.*They could not understand her when Svetlana spoke to them in Russian. _____
_____.
_____

SI CLAUSES

Those who use *si* clauses correctly understand that two tenses are involved. Basic variations of these split sentences are featured below. Additional types will be 'unwrapped' in an upcoming chapter. All *si* clauses contain an <u>if</u> inside the 'gift.'

Si Clause/Dependent Clause	Independent/Main/Resulting Clause
Present >>>>>>>>>>>>>>>>>>>>>	Imperative, Present, Future
Imperfect >>>>>>>>>>>>>>>>>>>	Conditional

Beyond the *Si*

1. *Si* (if) introduces a dependent clause, a group of words that do not form a complete thought. The second part of the sentence, the independent/main/resulting clause, does relate a finished thought. It is not contingent upon the *si* clause. Either clause can precede the other.
1a. A *si* clause *au temps présent* can introduce or follow a main clause *à l'impératif*.
Ex. Si ton bébé pleure, donne-lui un biberon ou change sa couche! > If your baby cries, give him a bottle or change his diaper. (That advice was taken from 'the ins and outs of infant care.')
1b. A *si* clause *au temps présent* can introduce or follow a main clause *au présent*.
Ex. Si je renverse du vin rouge sur la moquette, j'enlève **la tache** avec le vin blanc. > If I spill some wine on the carpet, I remove **the spot** with white wine. (The rug might have a better 'nap.')
1c. A *si* clause *au temps présent* can introduce or follow a main clause *au futur*.
Ex. Si elles vont au supermarché, elles achèteront du yaourt et de la mayonnaise. > If they go to the supermarket, they will buy some yogurt and some mayonnaise.
Ex. Elles achèteront du yaourt et de la mayonnaise si elles vont au supermarché. > They'll buy some yogurt and some mayonnaise if they go to the supermarket. (Being so into 'culture,' they could also check out a local library.)
The clauses were reversed in the previous examples. (However, the dairy products didn't 'turn.')
2. When a *si* clause is *à l'imparfait*, the main clause is *au conditionnel*. As it is unlikely that the result will occur, such constructions are called "contrary to fact conditions."
Ex. Si **Bob l'Éponge** avait un choix, il prendrait ses vacances sur la Côte d'Azur. > If **Sponge Bob** had/were to have a choice, he would take his vacation on the French Riviera. (Where he could 'soak up some sun.')
2a. To reinforce the use of *l'imparfait* after *si*, you can insert <u>were to</u> before the verb instead of translating it as a single word.
Ex. Si Greeta venait aujourd'hui, tu l'accueillerais. > If Greeta came/were to come today, you would welcome her. (If she shows up tomorrow, she or her host 'might be put out.')
2b. *Le conditionnel* in the main clause parallels its use in English.
Ex. Si la bonne fortune vous souriait, vous gagneriez **la loterie**. > If good luck smiled/were to smile at you, you would win the lottery. (And if Lady Luck turned up, she wouldn't be turned down.)
3. The <u>i</u> in *si* is dropped only in front of *il* and *ils*. There is no contraction before *elle* or *elles*.
Ex. Clair Bleu ne verrait pas de nuages si elle regardait le ciel. > Clair Bleu wouldn't see any clouds if she looked at/were to look at the sky. (However, *s'il* and *si elle* have distinct 'formations.')

4. When *si* means <u>whether</u>, the clause may be *au présent, au passé composé, au futur ou au conditionnel.*

Ex. Je ne sais pas si tu as emprunté ou tu as volé le corrigé. > I do not know whether you borrowed or you stole the answer key. (It could be 'taken' both ways.)

<u>*'Si* Excursions'</u>- **Use the correct tenses of the verbs in parentheses to complete the sentences.**

1. (attirer) Si Mme Prada portait des vêtements bon marché, _____-elle autant d'attention?

2. (abondonner) M. Quitte _____ ce projet-là s'il ne réussit pas la première fois qu'il essaie de le faire.

3. (aller) Si je suivais les recommandations de mon médecin, j'_____ mieux.

4. (devenir) Si vos deux neveux assistent aux cours du droit, _____-ils avocats?

5. (dire) Si une fée t'**exauçait (to grant)** un vœu, qu'est-ce que tu lui _____?

6. (choisir) Si Brunhilde pouvait changer son nom, lequel _____-elle?

7. (faire) Tu monteras à cheval s'il _____ beau à Fontainebleau.

8. (accomplir) Si les amies passent tout l'après-midi au bistro, elles n'_____ pas leurs tâches ménagères.

9. (essayer) Si tu ne réussis pas d'abord, _____, _____ de nouveau!

10. (vouloir) Simone demanderait à Jean-Paul, si elle _____ comprendre l'existentialisme.

11. (avoir) Ryder et moi _____ un tour gratuit si **le contrôleur (the ticket taker)** ne prend pas nos billets.

12. (pouvoir) Si elles faisaient leurs valises maintenant, elles _____ visiter une attraction de plus avant leur vol.

<u>'Time Between the Connections'</u>- **Put the letters beside the numbers of the clauses that begin the sentences.**

_____ 1. Si je fais une erreur,

_____ 2. Si le VRP en vendait plus,

_____ 3. Les plantes ne fleurissent pas

_____ 4. Qu'est-ce que les piétons feraient dans les grandes villes

_____ 5. Si on ne l'arrête pas

_____ 6. Si Gully Bull la croit,

_____ 7. Achète un carnet de billets

_____ 8. Les Greenfield n'auraient pas beaucoup d'espace

_____ 9. S'il neige aujourd'hui,

_____ 10. Les enfants regardent des dessins animés

_____ 11. Si le téléphone sonnait au milieu de la nuit,

_____ 12. On pense que tu es gâté,

_____ 13. Si personne ne peut t'aider,

A. s'ils déménageaient à une grande ville.

B. la sourde ne l'entendrait pas.

C. si on ne parle pas arabe?

D. si vous n'avez ni le temps ni la patience!

E. où est-ce qu'Annette et Frankie resteront?

F. il ne pourrait pas soutenir le monde.

G. fais-le toi-même!

H. je la corrige aussitôt que possible.

I. si on ne les **arrose (to water)** pas.

J. si tu comptes sur d'autres pour faire tout.

K. s'ils n'ont rien d'autre à faire le samedi matin.

L. s'il n'y avait pas de vacances scolaires.

M. Phil Osophie parlera toute la nuit.

455

_____ 14. Peut-on être journaliste au Moyen-Orient

N. si j'oublie son anniversaire de naissance.

_____ 15. Des étudiants se plaindraient,

O. si vous visitez un pays étranger!

_____ 16. Elle sera désolée

P. il recevrait **une prime (a bonus).**

_____ 17. Si le cottage n'est pas disponible cet été,

Q. il est naïf.

_____ 18. N'essayez pas de le mettre ensemble

R. Les White et moi ferons du ski demain.

_____ 19. Si Atlas n'était pas si fort,

S. s'il n'y avait pas de feux de signalisations?

_____ 20. Respectez leurs mœurs

T. si tu prends le métro souvent!

If Conditions Permit- Translate the phrases in parentheses.

1. (If Grégorien sings) _____, tout le monde dans l'église peut l'entendre.

2. (if she comes) Je serai etonné _____.

3. (If you have a cold) _____, restes-tu au lit?

4. (If Coquille prepared snails) _____, les mangeriez-vous?

5. (if I went to the resort) Je m'amuserais _____.

6. (If you are not in a hurry) _____, prends un café avec moi!

7. (If Les Vin visit the Loire Valley), _____ _____, ils feront un tour des châteaux.

8. (if you saw her) La reconnaîtriez-vous _____?

9. (If we were hungry) _____, nous nous servirions.

10. (If Faye Dodo falls asleep) _____, ne la réveille pas!

11. (if their son becomes famous) Les parents d'Elvis seront contents _____ _____.

12. (If you receive their invitation) _____, réponds-y, s'il te plait!

13. (if I needed some money) Me le prêterais-tu _____ _____?

14. (If you're happy, and you know it) _____ _____, battez vos mains!

_____

UNE REVUE - A Review

Le Présent, Le Passé Composé, L'Imparfait, Le Futur, Le Conditionnel and *Si* Clauses

Checking Your 'Temps-erature'- Label the statements *vrai* or *faux*.

_____ 1. Future endings are very similar to the present tense conjugation of *avoir*.

_____ 2. Orthographic/stem-changing verbs keep their "boot" forms *au futur* and *au conditionnel*.

_____ 3. The future stem for all -er, -ir and -re verbs is the entire infinitive.

_____ 4. *Le futur* and *le conditionnel* have the same stems.

_____ 5. *L'imparfait* and *le conditionnel* have different endings.

_____ 6. Not all future and conditional stems end with a single r.

_____ 7. If *quand* translates as "whenever," the verb following it must be *au futur*.

_____ 8. If would means used to, *l'imparfait* is used.

_____ 9. When would translates as "to be willing to," *le conditionnel* is used.

_____ 10. A *si* clause may introduce or end a sentence.

_____ 11. *Si* clauses *au présent* are followed by main clauses *à l'impératif, au présent* or *au futur*.

_____ 12. *Si* clauses can be *au conditionnel*.

_____ 13. "Were to" is the best translation for verbs *à l'imparfait* in *si* clauses.

_____ 14. When *si* means whether, the main clause must be *au présent*.

Flexing 'Tense' Muscles- Write the forms of the verbs in parentheses for each tense shown.

Part 1

Le Présent	Le Passé Composé	L'Imparfait	Le Futur	Le Conditionnel
Ex. (faire-tu)				
tu fais	tu as fait	tu faisais	tu feras	tu ferais

1. (montrer-je) _____

2. (maigrir-on) _____

3. (rendre-ils) _____

4. (aller-je) _____

5. (avoir-elle) _____

6. (boire-je) _____

7. (conduire-il) _____

8. (connaître-tu) _____

9. (croire-je) _____

10. (devoir-vous) _____

11. (dire-tu) _____

12. (dormir-il) _____

13. (écrire-tu) _____

14. (envoyer-elle) _____

15. (être-il) _____

16. (falloir-il) _____

17. (lire-tu) _____

18. (mettre-je) _____

19. (mourir-elle) _____

20. (ouvrir-je) _____

21. (partir-ils) _____

22. (pouvoir-tu) _____

23. (prendre-il) _____

24. (recevoir-je) _____

25. (rire-nous) _____

26. (savoir-tu) _____

27. (sortir-vous) _____

28. (venir-elle) _____

29. (voir-tu) _____

30. (vouloir-je) _____

Change the singular verbs in bold in <u>Part 1</u> into the plural. First person sing. > first person plural, second person sing. > second person plural, third person sing. > third person plural.

<u>Part 2</u>

<u>Le Présent</u> (Ex. aller-je) nous allons	<u>Le Passé Composé</u> nous sommes allé(e)s	<u>L'Imparfait</u> nous allions	<u>Le Futur</u> nous irons	<u>Le Conditionnel</u> nous irions

1. _____

2. _____

3. _____

4. _____

5. _____

6. _____

7. _____

8. _____

9. _____

10. _____

11. _____

12. _____

13. _____

14. _____

15. _____

16. _____

17. _____

18. _____

COMPOUND PAST TENSES

If mastering the French language is viewed as putting a puzzle together, arranging compound past tense phrases might be thought of as interlocking verb sections. Since each piece has been inspected, grouping them as units should be 'a snap.'

Forms of Compound Past Tenses

Le Passé Composé
j'ai remplacé- I replaced, have replaced, did replace

Le Plus-Que-Parfait (The Pluperfect)
j'avais remplacé- I had replaced

Le Futur Antérieur (The Future Perfect)
j'aurai remplacé- I will have replaced

Le Conditionnel Passé (The Past Conditional)
j'aurais remplacé- I would have replaced

Le Passé Composé
je suis allé(e)- I went, have gone, did go

Le Plus-que-Parfait (The Pluperfect)
j'étais allé(e)- I had gone

Le Futur Antérieur (The Future Perfect)
je serai allé(e)- I will have gone

Le Conditionnel Passé (The Past Conditional)
je serais allé(e)- I would have gone

Le Passé Composé
je me suis souvenu(e)- I remembered, did remember, have remembered

Le Plus-Que-Parfait (The Pluperfect)
je m'étais souvenu(e)- I had remembered

Le Futur Antérieur (The Future Perfect)
je me serai souvenu(e)- I will have remembered

Le Conditionnel Passé (The Past Conditional)
je me serais souvenu(e)- I would have remembered

Getting it Together

1. Four time frames are included in compound past tenses. Each one has a form of *avoir* or *être* + a past participle. All agreement rules are in effect.

2. *Le passé composé*, conjugated with a present tense form or *avoir* or *être*, is translated by the past participle alone, has/have + a past participle or did + a past participle.

Ex. Se rappelant leur anniversaire de mariage, l'époux a envoyé des fleurs à son épouse. > Remembering their wedding anniversary, the husband sent/has sent/did send some flowers to his wife. (Forget-me-nots would have been appropriate.)

An exception: *Le passé composé* forms of *naître* produce only was/were born.

Ex. Des gens disent que Sir Winston Churchill est né dans une salle de bain pendant un bal. > Some people say that Sir Winston Churchill was born in a bathroom during a ball. (Could that explain his popularity with 'the House of Commons'?)

3. *Le plus-que-parfait*, the pluperfect, is composed of an imperfect form of *avoir* or *être* + a past participle. The only translation for the helping/auxiliary verb is <u>had</u>.

3a. If a sentence states or implies two past actions, <u>had</u> refers to the less recent one. (Making it

'the past past')

Ex. Leroi n'avait jamais eu les moyens d'acheter **un jeu d'échecs auparavant**, mais il en a acheté un ce matin. > Leroy had never had the means to buy **a chess set previously**, but he bought one (of them) this morning. (Maybe, he found an affordable one in 'a pawn shop.')

Ex. Sarah Mownie, qui était sortie avec tant de célibataires, s'est mariée enfin à/avec Justin Tyme. > Sarah Mownie, who had gone out with so many bachelors, finally married Justin Tyme. (Being her last hope, Sarah referred to him as "the expiration date.")

4. *Le futur antérieur*, **the future perfect, relates actions or events that will have been completed in the future. This tense could be thought of as "the future past." With forms of** *avoir* **or** *être* **as the helping/auxiliary, its translations are** <u>will/shall have</u> **+ a past participle.**

Ex. Par sa retraite, elle aura enseigné des centaines d'étudiants pas motivés. > By her retirement, she will have taught hundreds of unmotivated students. (That teacher might ask herself, "What's a little gray matter?")

Ex. **Dès lors**, les cousins de Faye Bull se seront rendus compte qu'elle leur a menti. > **By now**, Faye Bull's cousins will have realized that she lied to them. (While lies might leave permanent marks, the the truth usually comes out.)

4a. *Le futur antérieur* **relates probability or supposition in the past. Its translation is** <u>must have</u> **+ a past participle.**

Ex. Il est minuit, et Dracula n'est pas revenu encore au château. Il se sera arrêté pour un morceau. > It is midnight, and Dracula has not yet come back to the castle. He must have stopped off for a bite.

4b. *Lorsque, quand, après que, dès que* **and** *aussitôt que* **often signal** *le futur antérieur.*

Ex. Aussitôt que Tirée Lachasse aura bu sa troisième tasse de thé, ses invités partiront. > As soon as Tirée Lachasse will have drunk her third cup of tea, her guests will leave. (Tirée will probably 'have to go' too.)

5. *Le conditionnel passé,* **the past conditional, expresses actions or events that would/would not have taken place if something else had/had not occurred. Including a conditional form of** *avoir* **or** *être* **+ a past participle, its translations are** <u>would/would not have</u> **+ a past participle.**

Ex. Sans **l'héritage** de ton oncle très riche, tu n'aurais pas survécu. > Without your very rich uncle's **inheritance**, you would not have survived. (But the income changed the outcome.)

5a. A conditional form of *avoir* **+** *dû* **means** <u>should have</u>.

Ex. Dorothée a dit à son chien, "Toto, nous n'aurions jamais dû quitter le Kansas." > Dorothy said to her dog, "Toto, we never should have left Kansas." (Wait until they 'get wind of' Oz!)

6. All compound past tenses except *le plus-que-parfait* **contain** <u>has</u> **or** <u>have</u> **in their translations.**

Exs. Il a inclus- It included, It has included, It did include (*le passé composé*)

   Il aura inclus- It will have included (*le futur antérieur*)

   Il aurait inclus- It would have included (*le conditionnel passé*)

   Il avait inclus- It had included (*le plus-que-parfait*) (You should expect 'an imperfect helper' to be contrary.)

Breaking Down the Compounds- **Circle the letters of the answers that translate the underlined verb phrases.**

1. Tara <u>aura brûlé</u>.　　a. will burn　　b. has burned　　c. will have burned　　d. would have burned
2. Paul Revere <u>a crié</u>.　　a. is yelling　　b. did yell　　c. had yelled　　d. would yell
3. Tout le monde <u>avait veilli</u>.　　a. aged　　b. will age　　c. would have aged　　d. had aged
4. La Joconde <u>aurait souri</u>.　　a. would smile　　b. would have smiled　　c. did smile d. will have smiled
5. Georges Washington <u>avait dormi</u> là.　　a. would sleep　　b. had been sleeping　　c. had slept d. will have slept
6. Les soldats <u>auront combattu</u>　　a. had just fought　　b. were fighting　　c. could have fought d. will have fought
7. Nous l'<u>aurions peint</u>.　　a. would have painted　　b. could have painted　　c. must have painted d. would paint
8. L'<u>avez</u>-vous <u>voulu</u>?　　a. did want　　b. will have wanted　　c. would want　　d. had wanted
9. Tim et Lassie <u>sont rentrés</u>.　　a. are coming home　　b. have come home　　c. had come home d. will have come home
10. La neige <u>n'était pas tombée</u>.　　a. was not falling　　b. has not fallen　　c. had not fallen d. would not fall
11. La Grandma Moïse s'y <u>serait assise</u>.　　a. would sit　　b. must have sat　　c. should have sat d. would have sat
12. Qui s'en <u>sera souvenu</u>?　　a. will remember　　b. will have remembered　　c. had remembered d. would have remembered
13. Nous <u>aurions dû</u> le <u>savoir</u>.　　a. ought to know　　b. could have known　　c. should have known d. would have to know
14. Lady Godiva <u>aurait dû s'habiller</u>.　　a. should have dressed　　b. would dress　　c. had to dress d. must have been dressed

----

'Auxiliary Services'- **Fill in the blanks by translating the underlined helping verbs.**

1. She <u>did</u> not leave again. Elle ne (n') _____ pas repartie.
2. You <u>had</u> forgotten it. Vous l'_____ oublié.
3. Le fantôme <u>will have</u> disappeared. Le fantôme _____ disparu.
4. Who <u>would have</u> taken them? Qui les _____ pris?
5. Lee Berté <u>had</u> had the time to do it. Lee Berté _____ eu le temps de le faire.
6. Why <u>had</u> you left them? Pourquoi les _____ -vous laissés?
7. I <u>would have</u> done it myself. Je l'_____ fait moi-même.
8. Anne Avance <u>had</u> already driven there. Anne Avance y _____ déjà conduit.
9. Lerner and I <u>would have</u> understood her. Lerner et moi l'_____ comprise.
10. You <u>have</u> always protected her. Tu l'_____ protégée toujours.
11. Thierry <u>must have</u> pulled it by mistake. Thierry l'_____ tiré par erreur.
12. You <u>should have</u> warned them. Vous _____ dû les avertir.
13. Why <u>hasn't</u> Ben Venu arrived yet? Pourquoi Ben Venu n'_____ -il pas arrivé encore?
14. Ann Ouiée <u>would</u> not <u>have</u> stayed long. Anne Ouiée ne _____ pas restée longtemps.
15. Oréal and I <u>should have</u> put on make up. Oréal et moi _____ dû nous maquiller.

461

<u>**Another Helping of Helping Verbs and Past Participles**</u>- **Translate the following sentences.**

1. You (*tu*) have not studied enough. _____.

2. Sue Vent has been to France several times. _____
_____.

3. Tucker Dout had gone upstairs. _____.

4. Had the plane landed by midnight? _____
_____?

5. Mr. Despoils and I had not shaved. _____
_____.

6. I will have learned it well. _____.

7. You (*vous*) will have accomplished everything. _____
_____.

8. By now, Mr. Routier will have found the best exit. _____
_____.

9. How would I have ever known that? _____
_____?

10. Mrs. Serrer would not have opened the door. _____
_____.

11. Wouldn't she have been bored in a little village? _____
_____?

12. Mr. and Mrs. Claus would have had a good time in Florida. _____
_____.

AGREEMENT IN COMPOUND PAST TENSES

For those not sure where to 'plug in' past participle agreement, this refresher course will shed some additional light.

<u>**Honoring Verbal Agreements**</u>
1. Past participles agree in gender and in number with direct objects that precede the helping/ auxiliary verbs.
Ex. M. Porter a porté les paquets à la poste. Il les y a porté<u>s</u>. > Mr. Porter carried the packages to the post office. He carried them there.
Portés **is 'postmarked' with an s because** *les* **fills in for** *les paquets,* **a masculine plural noun.**
Ex. Mme Wheeler avait caché une nouvelle bicyclette dans le sous-sol, mais son fils l'y a trouvé<u>e</u>. > Mrs. Wheeler had hidden a new bicycle in the basement, but her son found it there. (There may have been an unidentified 'spokes-person.')
An additional <u>e</u> is spotted on *trouvée* **because** *l'* **replaces** *la bicyclette,* **a feminine singular noun.**
2. If direct object pronouns replace nouns of both genders, an s is added to the past participle.
Ex. N'aurait-il pas jeté dehors la vieille serpillière et le sceau cassé? Pourquoi les aurait-il gardé<u>s</u>? > Wouldn't he have thrown out the old mop and broken pail? Why would he have kept them? (Maybe he did not want to 'wring in the new.')
3. Past participles agree neither with preceding indirect objects nor with *en.*

Ex. Bert et Ernie nous ont montré les lettres de l'alphabet. > Bert and Ernie showed the letters of the alpabet to us. (Everyone knew 'Y.')

3a. If a sentence includes both indirect and direct object pronouns, past participle agreement is in effect.

Ex. Bert et Ernie nous les a montr<u>ées</u>. > Bert and Ernie showed them to us.

Montrées **is displayed with an** <u>es</u> **because** *les* **takes the place of** *les lettres*.

4. Past participles show agreement in relative clauses introduced by *que* **or any member of the** *quel* **family.**

Ex. Dora l'Exploratrice prête-t-elle les valises qu'elle a achet<u>ées</u>? > Does Dora the Explorer lend the suitcases that she bought?

Since the antecedent *les valises* **is a fem. plural noun, the past participle is 'tagged with' an** <u>es</u>.

Ex. Il y a plusieurs universités à Paris. À laquelle Grady a-t-il assist<u>ée</u> l'année dernière? > There are several universities in Paris. Which one did Grady attend last year?

Because the preceding interrogative pronoun *à laquelle* **is fem. singular, the past participle receives an** <u>e</u> **for 'additional credit.'**

5. Past participles of verbs conjugated with *être* **(Vandertramps, MD verbs) generally agree in gender and in number with the subjects.**

Ex. Superman et Super Souris sont rest<u>és</u> dans un hôtel près de l'aéroport hier soir. > Superman and Mighty Mouse stayed in a hotel near the airport last night. (They had an early morning flight.)

5a. Past participles of reflexive verbs usually agree in gender and in number with the subjects and their adjoining reflexive pronouns.

Ex. Les Sœurs Ensemble s'étaient habill<u>ées</u>. > The Ensemble Sisters had dressed themselves.

The subject, *s'* **and the past participle with an** <u>es</u> **added are well coordinated.**

<u>**An exception**</u>**: If the sentence includes a reflexive pronoun and a direct object, the past participle does not show agreement.**

Ex. Diane s'est teint les cheveux. > Diane dyed her hair.

With *les cheveux* **'hanging' at the end of the sentence, no** <u>e</u> **is added to** *teint*.

<u>**'Compounds Fractured'**</u>**- On the spaces provided, add an** <u>e</u>**, an** <u>s</u>**, an** <u>es</u> **or no letters to the past participles.**

1. Aurais-tu séché les cours? Oui, je les aurais séché ____.
2. M. Saumon a-t-il commandé la bouillabaisse? Oui, il l'a commandé ____.
3. Maman, as-tu mis les assiettes sales dans le lave-vaisselle? Oui chérie, je les y ai mis ____.
4. Jacques Sprat avait mangé la graisse, n'est-ce pas? Non, il ne l'avait pas mangé ____.
5. La bonne a-t-elle trouvé les boucles d'oreille que Mme Bijoux avait perdu ____? Non, elle ne les a pas trouvé ____.
6. Est-ce que le conducteur d'autobus aurait permis aux passagers de monter sans payer? Non, il ne l'aurait pas permis ____.
7. <u>Silas Marner</u> aurait offert la prime à ses commis? Non, il ne la leur aurait pas offert ____.
8. Une vedette a jamais répondu aux lettres de ta sœur? Oui, deux vedettes lui ont écrit ____.
9. Cézanne ou Seurat? Lequel a peint cette nature morte-là? Cezanne l'a peint ____.
10. Ce bûcheron-là a-t-il envoyé les photos des soucoupes volantes au gouvernement? Je pense qu'il les lui a envoyé ____.

Change and Exchange- **Add any necessary agreement to the past participles. Then, translate the sentences.**

1. Voici les Barbies que ma grand-mère a envoyé ____. _____

_____.

2. Les clés sont où tu les as laissé ____. _____

_____.

3. C'est une pensée que Plato et Aristotle auraient discuté ____. _____

_____.

4. Il y a des votes que la machine n'a pas compté ____. _____

_____.

5. Forrest Gump! Nous aurions aimé l'avoir rencontré ____. _____

_____.

6. Les petits ont commencé à pleurer le moment que leur mère a quitté ____ la maison. _____

_____.

7. Nous n'avons aucune idée quelle langue elle aurait appris ____ en Macédoine. _____

_____.

8. Marie n'a jamais grondé l'agneau qui l'a suivi ____ à l'école. _____

_____.

9. Cela ne concerne pas Monique. Je ne lui aurais rien dit ____. _____

_____.

10. La femme policier m'a demandé ____ si je les avais vu ____ récemment. _____

_____.

11. Ceux-ci ne sont pas les contes que j'aurais lu ____ à un enfant de son âge. _____

_____.

12. Les couches et les biberons? Faye Veur les a acheté ____ pour Jeanne Aibesoin parce qu'elle les
a voulu ____. _____

_____.

_____

SI CLAUSES WITH COMPOUND PAST TENSES

The 'sea claws' used with compound past tenses digs deeper than those that accompany single verbs. The support equipment includes imperfect and conditional forms of *avoir* or *être* plus a past participle. Having recently explored the compound past tenses, you are ready 'to take the plunge.'

Si Clause/The Dependent Clause >>>>>>>>>>>>> Main/Independent/Resulting Clause

Le Plus-que-Parfait/The Pluperfect > >>>> Le Conditionnel Passé/The Past Conditional

---

<u>Facts to Fathom</u>
1. *Si* clauses *au plus-que-parfait* express actions that would/would not have take taken place if other events had/had not occurred.
2. The translation of *le plus-que-parfait* (the pluperfect) includes the auxiliary <u>had</u>, while the *le conditionnel passé* (the past conditional) is helped by <u>would have.</u>
Ex. Si le caissier de banque avait fait attention, il n'aurait pas donné trop d'argent à Mme Deplus. > If the bank teller had paid attention, he would not have given too much money to Mrs. Deplus. (She said that there was no need to correct it 'on her account.')
3. A *si*/dependent clause can precede or follow a main/independent clause.
Ex. Le chef aurait fini de faire la crème brûlée s'il avait eu le temps. > The chef would have finished making *la crème brûlée* if he had had the time. (But it was 'left on the back burner.')
4. Past participle agreement is in effect with *si* clauses in compound past tenses.
Ex. Si l'épouse de Peter était restée, il l'aurait mise dans une coquille de citrouille. > If Peter's wife had stayed, he would have put her in a pumpkin shell. (Would he ever 'hold a candle to her'?)
Ex. Galahad et Lancelot seraient-ils devenus rois si l'histoire avait été différente? > Would Galahad and Lancelot have become kings if history had been different? (Maybe if they had agreed that once a 'knight' was enough.)
5. A pluperfect form of *pouvoir* expresses <u>could have/had been able.</u>
Ex. Si Désespérée avait pu le faire elle-même, elle ne vous aurait pas téléphoné à l'heure du dîner. > If Désespérée could have done it herself, she would not have called you at dinner time. (And gotten 'a busy signal.')
Ex. Si les beaux types avaient pu garder leurs yeux ouverts, ils auraient remarqué cette jeune femme flirtante avec eux. > If the handsome guys could have kept their eyes open, they would have noticed that young woman flirting with them. (Did they 'catch a few winks'?)

<u>'Initialing the Clauses'</u>- Write the letters of the phrases beside their corresponding numbers to form complete sentences.

_____ 1. Si le Comte Conte avait écrit son autobiographie,

_____ 2. Le commerçant aurait offert **une sucette (a lollipop)** à Suzette

_____ 3. Je n'aurais pas eu peur de te dire

_____ 4. Si j'avais reçu une telle lettre,

A. s'il avait neigé la vieille au soir?

B. si leur mère avait su cuisiner mieux.

C. si le prince n'était pas venu.

D. si nous n'avions pas porté de manteaux.

_____ 5. Si vous m'aviez rendu ce que vous me devez,

_____ 6. Nous ne serions pas nés

_____ 7. Si Blaise et Pascal s'étaient inquiétés de leur santé,

_____ 8. Est-ce que Faye Duski serait allée à Chamonix

_____ 9. Si Mme Lèche-Lèvres ne s'était pas arrêtée devant le chocolatier,

_____ 10. Nous aurions repris froid,

_____ 11. Auriez-vous fait la même chose

_____ 12. Tes copains t'auraient-ils rencontré pour une boisson

_____ 13. S'ils avaient cambriolé le château pendant la journée,

_____ 14. Si nous l'avions vue dans une foule,

_____ 15. Si Polly avait bouilli de l'eau,

_____ 16. Les enfants n'auraient pas été minces

_____ 17. S'il avait senti mauvais,

_____ 18. La Belle au Bois Dormant aurait dormi cent ans

_____ 19. Si tu avais pu payer comptant

_____ 20. Anne Guish n'aurait pas pleuré

_____ 21. Si vous aviez élevé douze enfants,

_____ 22. Ils n'auraient pas consulté un avocat

_____ 23. S'ils t'avaient menti une fois,

_____ 24. Si les billets avaient coûte moins

_____ 25. Est-ce que le mariage aurait duré

E. si tu les avais appelés au dernier moment?

F. vous n'auriez pas pu en gâter tous.

G. si la femme n'était pas partie pour les affaires fréquemment?

H. si tu m'avais déplu.

I. lui aurais-tu donné ta carte de crédit?

J. te serais-tu fié à eux encore?

K. si nos parents ne s'étaient pas rencontrés.

L. je ne l'aurais pas goûté.

M. si la petite s'était comportée bien.

N. un garde les auraient vus

O. s'ils avaient pu se mettre d'accord.

P. elle n'aurait pas été **tentée (tempted).**

Q. si vous l'aviez su à l'avance?

R. nous aurions bu du thé.

S. je vous aurais prêté plus.

T. auraient-ils assisté au concert?

U. ils auraient dû prendre un rendez-vous chez le médecin.

V. je l'aurais **déchirée (ripped/torn up).**

W. je l'aurais lue.

X. nous ne l'aurions pas reconnue.

Y. si son petit ami n'avait pas déçu ses espoirs.

Time to Fill- **Replace the blanks with the correct compound tense forms of the verbs provided. Ex. (habiter, être) Si M. Rogers <u>avait habité</u> dans ton voisinage, tu <u>aurais été</u> de bons amis. > If Mr. Rogers had lived in your neighborhood, you would have been good friends.**

1. (attendre, aider) Si Mme Hâte _____ _____, quelqu'un l'_____

_____.

2. (gronder, montrer) Est-ce que tes parents t'_____ _____ si tu n'_____
pas _____ la courtoisie aux vieillards?

3. (oser, téléphoner) Si Ann Timidée et moi _____ _____ le faire, nous _____
_____ à nos anciens flirts.

4. (avoir, pouvoir) Si la fête _____ _____ lieu samedi, Guillaume et Harry _____
_____ y assister?

5. (dire, savoir) Si Madame Vison ne nous _____ pas _____ que celles-là étaient les

fourrures fausses, nous ne l' _____ jamais _____.

6. (prendre, craindre) La Petite Mlle Muffet _____ _____ son déjeuner si elle n' _____ pas _____ l'araignée.

7. (croire, voir) Je ne l'_____ pas _____ si je ne l'_____ pas _____ de mes propres yeux.

8. (pleuvoir, aller) S'il n' _____ pas _____, _____-nous _____ à Rennes?

9. (recevoir, naître) Noëlle _____ _____ plus de cadeaux pour son anniversaire de naissance si elle n'_____ pas _____ en décembre.

10. (s'asseoir, trouver) Ils ____ _____ _____ s'ils _____ _____ une place disponible.

11. (venir, partir) S'ils n'_____ pas _____ par mercredi, Merced _____ _____.

12. (devenir, persuader) _____-elles _____ femmes médecins si leurs parents les _____ _____?

Some 'Iffy' Situations- Translate the following sentences.

1. If we had read everything, we would not have signed the papers. _____ _____.

2. If the Talons had ordered three lobsters, they would have shared them with us. _____ _____.

3. The soldiers would have died if they had stayed there. _____ _____.

4. If Robin Hood (*Le Robin des Bois*) had not given the money to the poor, would he have kept it for himself? _____ ?

5. If you (*tu*) had known the answer, you would not have asked the question. _____ _____.

6. Would Fifi have wanted a poodle if she could have owned a dog? _____ ?

7. Humpty Dumpty would not have fallen if he had not sat on a wall. _____ _____.

8. Would ET have returned home if he had not been sick? _____ ?

9. If Santa had come to my house, he would have eaten French pastry. _____ _____.

10. If the department stores had opened early (passive voice), the tourists would have gone shopping before their flight. _____ _____.

VERBS THAT REQUIRE NO PREPOSITIONS BEFORE INFINITIVES

With no preposition to split up the team, verb-on-verb phrases offer 'nonstop action.' You will recognize 'the lightweights' from previous 'rounds,' but after a warm up, the four newcomers will also 'fit like a glove.'

Verbs Followed Directly By Infinitives

1. adorer- to adore
2. aimer- to like/love
3. aimer mieux- to prefer
4. aller- to go
5. *compter- to intend
6. désirer- to wish/want
7. détester- to hate
8. devoir- to have to/be supposed to
9. entendre- to hear
10. envoyer- to send
11. espérer- to hope
12. faire- to make
13. *faillir- to almost do/just miss doing/to fail

14. falloir- to be necessary
15. laisser- to let/allow
16. oser- to dare
17. pouvoir- to be able
18. préférer- to prefer
19. *prétendre- to claim
20. savoir- to know (how)
21. souhaiter- to wish
22. *valoir mieux- to be better
23. venir- to come
24. voir- to see
25. vouloir- to want/wish

Concentrating on the Starred Contenders

1. *Compter-* to intend and *avoir l'intention de* are synonyms. *Compter sur* means to count on/to rely on.
Ex. Mlle Piggy compte demander à Kermit de l'épouser. > Miss Piggy intends to ask Kermit to marry her? (She might be waiting until 'Leap Year.')

2. *Faillir-* to almost do/just miss doing is the equivalent of *presque* (almost) + a verb.
Ex. Archie a failli **mettre dans le mille**. > Archie almost **hit the bull's eye**.

3. *Prétendre-* to claim/maintain/pretend: Its synonym is *revendiquer*.
Ex. Visa a prétendu être innocente de toutes ces charges. > Visa claimed to be innocent of all those charges. (Was there 'any credit to her account'?)

4. *Valoir mieux,* to be better, is literally "to be worth better."
Ex. Ne vaudrait-il mieux demeurer à la campagne qu'en ville? > Wouldn't it be better to live in the country than in the city? ("The grass is always greener ...")

Where's the Action?- Put the letters beside the numbers of the phrases to complete the ideas.

_____ 1. Le bébé dans le berceau au sommet de l'arbre

_____ 2. On n'éteint pas la veilleuse dans la chambre à coucher de Luz

_____ 3. Je n'aime pas son idée du tout,

_____ 4. La solution n'est ni noire ni blanche.

A. il ne faut pas réserver une table.

B. dès que nous entendions **la sonnerie (the ringing)** de la cloche.

C. qui commencent par, "Je voudrais vous informer que ...."

D. veut dire qu'il a failli le faire.

_____ 5. Mme Toile dépenserait moins en vêtements

_____ 6. M. Jean A. Peur n'est pas devenu **pilote de chasse (fighter pilot)**

_____ 7. Des courriers électroniques sont **les arnaques/les escroqueries (scams)**

_____ 8. Vous n'allez pas les convaincre

_____ 9. Il ne peut pas le faire aujourd'hui,

_____ 10. Puisqu'elle déteste faire la queue,

_____ 11. Comme la glace ne s'est pas gelée sur l'étang,

_____ 12. Au lieu d'être déprimé,

_____ 13. Pour dîner chez Didier

_____ 14. Je me demande où est Waldo.

_____ 15. Nous nous levions de nos places

_____ 16. Cette histoire était si triste

_____ 17. À cause de tant de **fourmis-f. (ants)** dans sa cuisine,

_____ 18. On qui dit qu'il a presque fini quelque chose

E. on ne peut pas y patiner.

F. qu'elle nous a fait pleurer.

G. Pourquoi n'est-il pas ici?

H. si elle savait coudre à machine.

I. parce qu'elle prétend voir des monstres dans le noir.

J. Comment sait-on quel choix vaudra mieux?

K. Laissez-les apprendre par l'expérience!

L. Colline a fait venir un exterminateur.

M. a failli tomber.

N. Mme Colis a fait son fils rendre l'achat.

O. parce qu'il n'ose pas sauter en chute libre.

P. et j'ai l'intention de lui dire.

Q. mais il espère l'accomplir ce week-end.

R. il aime mieux avoir des pensées agréables.

PREPOSITIONS THAT PRECEDE INFINITIVES

À and *de* join several conjugated verbs to infinitives. The following sections tighten those links and serve as a vocabulary renewal/expansion project.

Verbs That Require *À* Before Infinitives

1. **aider à-** to help to
2. **s'amuser à-** to have a good time
3. **apprendre à-** to learn to
4. **s'attendre à-** to expect
5. **avoir à-** to have to
6. **chercher à-** to try to
7. **commencer à-** to begin to
8. **continuer à-** to continue to
9. **consentir à-** to consent to
10. **décider à-** to decide to
11. **encourager à-** to encourage to
12. **forcer à-** to force to
13. **s'habituer à-** to get used to
14. **hésiter à-** to hesitate to
17. **se mettre à-** to begin to
18. **obliger à-** to obligate to
19. **passer (du temps) à-** to spend time
20. **penser à-** to think about
21. **persister à-** to persist in
22. **se plaire à-** to enjoy, to take pleasure in
23. **se préparer à-** to prepare to/get ready to
24. **renoncer à-** to give up
25. **se résigner à-** to resign oneself to
26. **rester à-** to remain to
27. **réussir à-** to succeed in
28. **servir à-** to be useful for
29. **songer à-** to think about
30. **suffire à-** to be enough to/for

15. inciter à- to incite to   31. tenir à- to insist on

16. inviter à- to invite to   32. travailler à- to work to/for

----

Using an 'À Frame' to Bridge the Gap

1. The foundation for this structure should be solid with *apprendre à, commencer à, s'habituer à, se mettre à, penser à, réussir à, servir à* **and** *songer à.*

A reminder: *Penser à*- to think about (to have on one's mind) and *songer à* are synonyms. *Penser de* **means** to have an opinion of.

2. Material needed to build the second level

2a. aider à- to help to

Ex. Le Dieu aida Moïse à mener le peuple de l'Égypte. > God helped Moses to lead the people from Egypt. (It was, after all, 'a dry run.')

2b. s'amuser à- to have a good time + a verb ending with -ing

Ex. La famille Haagen Daz s'est amusée à regarder la parade. > The Haagen Daz family had a good time watching the parade. (They might have been waiting for 'the ice cream float.')

2c. s'attendre à- to expect to

Ex. À cause de l'orage, des commerçants ne s'attendent pas à faire beaucoup d'affaires. > Due to the storm, some shopkeepers do not expect to do a lot of business. (On the contrary, bad weather might 'bring customers in.')

2d. avoir à- to have to: *Il faut* **is its synonym.**

Ex. L'entraîneur dit à M. Sitz qu'il a à passer plus de temps au gymnase. > The trainer tells Mr. Sitz that he has to spend more time at the gym. (He may have wanted 'to exercise other options.')

2e. chercher à- to try to: *Essayer de* **and** *tâcher de* **are its synonyms. When it is not followed by a preposition,** *chercher* **is on its own looking for someone or something.**

Ex. Nous avons cherché sans succès à **traire** la vache. > We tried without success **to milk** the cow. (They may have even 'had others pulling for them.')

3. Many verbs followed by *à* **are almost identical in spelling to their English cognates. The list includes** *consentir à, continuer à, encourager à, forcer à, hésiter à, inciter à, inviter à* **and** *obliger à.* **In addition, conjugated forms of** *encourager à, forcer à, inciter à, inviter à* **and** *obliger à* **can take direct objects in front of** *à* **and an infinitive.**

Ex. Sabrina et Venus ont invité des amis à voir leur match à Wimbledon. > Sabrina and Venus invited some friends to see their match at Wimbledon. (It was an 'open' invitation.)

Ex. Le propriétaire d'un hôtel exclusif a obligé ses ouvriers à attraper les souris. > The owner of an exclusive hotel obliged his workers to catch the mice. (And 'to keep their traps shut.')

4. *Suffire à/pour*- **to be enough to and** *travailler à/pour*- **to work to add either** *à* **or** *pour* **to their original translations without altering the meanings.**

Ex. Le capitaine du navire de croisière demande à son équipage, "Nos activités suffiront à/pour **divertir** les invités?" > The captain of the cruise ship asks his crew, "Will our activities be enough to **entertain** the guests?" (They can always 'be swayed.')

5. Besides the familiar reflexives *s'amuser à, s'attendre à, décider à, s'habituer à* **and** *se mettre à,* **two reflexive verbs requiring a 'to' step are** *se préparer à* **and** *se résigner à.*

Ex. Elle s'et résignée à accepter le marriage de sa fille à Faitrien. > She resigned herself to accept her daughter's marriage to Faitrien. (But 'a split decision' still crosses her mind.)

Constructions with the 'To Story'

1. The accompanying *à* **translates as "in" for** *réussir à, persister à* **and** *se plaire à*- **to enjoy, to take pleasure in.**

Ex. "Odette, ne te plaisait-il pas à écrire la poésie?" > "Odette, didn't you used to enjoy/take pleasure in writing poetry? (Perhaps, she can no longer do it 'justice.')

2. *Renoncer à*- **to give <u>up</u> and** *tenir à*- **to insist <u>on</u> are adamant about not being associated with other categories.**

Ex. Hogan dit qu'il renocera à lutter. > Hogan says that he will give up wrestling. (Some think that he will just 'put it on hold.')

Ex. Mme Têtue a tenu à contester l'évidence. > Mrs. Têtue insisted on disputing the evidence. (She was the only one left who thought she was right.)

'Deserving À Plus'- Put the following verbs beside their synonyms below: avoir à, s'attendre à, chercher à, consentir à, hésiter à, inciter à, se mettre à, se plaire à, renoncer à, réussir à, tenir à, suffire à/pour

1. motiver _____
2. accomplir _____
3. être obligé de _____
4. aimer _____
5. essayer de _____
6. accepter _____

7. s'arrêter _____
8. anticiper _____
9. quitter _____
10. commencer _____
11. être assez _____
12. insister sur _____

_____

'A' Go Between-Translate the following sentences.

1. Cent euros ne suffiront pas à payer l'addition. _____
_____.

2. Mme Veuttant n'est pas obligée à les acheter. _____
_____.

3. Ne t'attends pas à voir le Louvre entier dans un après-midi! _____
_____!

4. Les Messieurs Brown et McDonald tenaient à traire leurs vaches à main. _____
_____.

5. Les membres de la Croix Rouge aident à guérir les malades autour du monde. ____
_____.

6. À quoi pensez-vous quand vous ne songez pas à être en vacances? _____
_____.

7. Je pourrais renoncer à manger toutes les suceries à part les chocolats. _____
_____.

8. Mlle Poppins savait divertir les enfants. Ils s'amusaient à rester chez elle. _____
_____.

9. Si Dewitt Twyce avait pu s'habituer à vivre seul, le veuf ne se serait pas remarié. ____
_____.

10. Cherchons à apprendre tous les verbes suivis par à devant un infinitif! _____

Verbs That Require *De* Before Infinitives

1. accepter de- to accept to
2. accuser de- to accuse of
3. achever de- to finish
4. s'arrêter de- to stop from
5. cesser de- to stop
6. choisir de- to choose to
7. se contenter de- to be satisfied to/with
8. continuer de- to continue to
9. décider de- to decide to
10. se dépêcher de- to hurry to
11. s'efforcer de- to strive to
12. empêcher de- to prevent from
13. essayer de- to try to
14. s'étonner de- to be surprised at
15. éviter de- to avoid
16. féliciter de- to congratulate on/for
17. finir de- to finish
18. se garder de- to take care not to, to refrain from

19. mériter de- to deserve to
20. s'occuper de- to take care of
21. oublier de- to forget to
22. parler de- to speak about
23. se passer de- to do without
24. se plaindre de- to complain about
25. prier de- to ask to, to beg
26. refuser de- to refuse to
27. regretter de- to regret
28. remercier de/pour- to thank for
29. rêver de- to dream about
30. rire de- to laugh at
31. risquer de- to risk
32. se souvenir de- to remember
33. tâcher de- to try to
34. se vanter de- to boast of
35. venir de- to have just

De in the Supporting Role

1. You have already set a firm base with *essayer de, féliciter de, oublier de, parler de, se plaindre de, remercier de/pour, rêver de, rire de, s'occuper de, se souvenir de, tâcher de* **and** *venir de.*
Ex. Tu le remercies de/pour te donner **un bon d'épargne.** > You thank him for giving you **a savings certificate.** (It will eventually 'show it own appreciation.')
2. Those who don't act properly could be *accusé de* **not doing so.** *Se vanter de* **is being vain as it boasts of itself and/or its accomplishments.**
Ex. La famille de Mme Verser l'accuse de boire trop. > Mrs. Verser's family accuses her of drinking too much. ('Stoppers' should be available.)
Ex. Patti Série s'est vantée de faire les meilleurs desserts du monde. > Patti Série boasted of making the world's best desserts. (She was obviously not familiar with "humble pie.")
3. Nothing stops nor prevents *s'arrêter de* **and** *empêcher de* **from including** from **in their translations.**
Ex. Qu'est-ce qui a empêché Jacques de suivre une classe en ligne? > What prevented Jacques from taking an on-line course? (He may have found it 'virtually' impossible.)
4. *Venir de* **is used only** *au présent* **or** *à l'imparfait.* **Anyone who** has just **or** had just **done some- is** coming from **doing it.**
Ex. Juan et Juanita viennent de recevoir des billets gratuits pour voir **une corrida**. > Juan et Juanita have just received free tickets to see **a bull fight**. (It would be even better if no one were 'charged.')
5. Though *de* **usually means** of **or** from, **only a few listed verbs have those prepositions in their translations. However, 'de-tours' are available for some of the meanings.**
5a. Of **can substitute for** about **after** *parler de, se plaindre de* **and** *rêver de.*
Ex. M. Bruitfort a rêvé d'entendre des cloches, des sifflets et des **klaxons**. > Mr. Bruitfort dreamed

about/of hearing bells, whistles and **horns**. (He must be 'a sound sleeper.')

5b. Cognates translated by "to" but linked by *de* **are** *accepter de, choisir de, décider de, mériter de, refuser de, s'efforcer de-* **to strive to,** *prier de-* **to beg/to ask to and** *refuser de.*

Ex. Le méchant garçon qui a sonné l'alarme d'incendie a mérité d'être puni. > The naughty boy who rang the fire alarm deserved to be punished. (He won't 'pull that again.')

6. *Se garder de,* **to take care not to/to refrain from, demands attention because it is negative by nature.**

Ex. Mlle Sanssoin se garde d'acheter d'**arbustes** qui **requérissent** trop d'**entretien**. > Ms Sanssoin refrains from buying any **shrubs** that **require** too much **upkeep**. (She cringes at the idea of 'soiling her plants.')

7. The meaning of *s'efforcer de,* **to strive to, can be recalled with little** effort.

8. *Prier de* **is called upon in the expression,** *"Je vous en prie."* **> "I ask/beg/request it of you."**

Ex. Vous êtes priés d'éteindre vos téléphones cellulaires quand vous êtes à l'église. > You are asked to turn off your cell phones when you are in church. (It might enable other messages to be received.)

9. Some verbs that require *de* **+ an infinitive in French take no preposition in English. Instead, the second verb ends with -**ing**. Examples of such phrases are** *achever de, s'arrêter de, éviter de, finir de, regretter de* **and** *risquer de.*

Ex. Nous n'avons jamais regretté d'**ériger une clôture** entre notre maison et celle de nos voisins. > We've never regretted **putting up a fence** between our house and our neighbor's. (And 'they have never gotten over it.')

10. The model list has four possible ends **in sight. Even though** *achever de* **and** *finir de* **mean** to finish**, the former is actually** to finish off**.** *S'arrêter de* **and** *cesser de* **are synonyms.**

Ex. Après avoir goûté la cuisine de leur père, ils se sont arrêtés de taquiner leur mère de la sienne. > After having tasted their father's cooking, they stopped teasing their mother about hers. (They had to 'eat their words.')

11. A few verbs on the list that take *de* **are followed by various prepositions in English.**

11a. Those stray terms are *se contenter de-* **to be satisfied with,** *s'étonner de-* **to be surprised at,** *féliciter de-* **to congratulate on and** *se passer de-* **to do without. The relationship between** *s'étonner de* **and** astonish **is surprising.** *Se passer de-* **to do without is similar in meaning to** to pass on something**.**

Ex. B. Strong ne se passe pas de faire des exercices tous les matins. > B. Strong does not do without exercising every morning. (He just can't 'let it go.')

----

'Going Their Separate Ways'- **Put the following infinitives beside their antonyms: encourager à, accepter de, s'arrêter de, se contenter de, pleurer sur, s'efforcer de, oublier de, n'oser pas, détester, n'en dire rien**

1. empêcher de _____   6. continuer à _____
2. aimer _____   7. se vanter de _____
3. risquer de _____   8. se souvenir de _____
4. rire de _____   9. renoncer à _____
5. refuser de _____   10. se plaindre de _____

----

1. Je te prie d'écouter ses conseils. _____ .

2. Gardez-vous de klaxonner, ou vous serez obligé à payer une contravention! _____
_____ .

3. Mme Beau Tocs essaie d'empêcher le vieillissement. _____
_____ .

4. Le champion vient d'accomplir ce qu'il rêvait de faire longtemps. _____
_____ .

5. Bonnie Chance finit de réussir toujours quand elle décide de faire quelque chose. _____
_____ .

6. Rien n'empêchera Destin de tâcher d'atteindre son but. _____
_____ .

7. Tom Sawyer a su éviter de peindre la clôture lui-même. _____
_____ .

8. Si elle avait mérité de gagner le prix, nous lui en aurions félicité. _____
_____ .

9. Paon se vantait de recevoir de bonnes notes. Il n'a pas cessé d'en parler. _____
_____ .

Verbs That Require *À* + A Person + *De* + An Infinitive

The pluses for verbs followed by *à* and *de* are not just in the title. The rather short list includes familiar vocabulary. Furthermore, with one exception, both *à* after the conjugated verb and *de* before the infinitive are translated as "to." As a bonus, these double-preposition phrases share 'a personal touch.'

1. **commander à quelqu'un de-** to order someone to
2. **conseiller à quelqu'un de-** to advise someone to
3. **défendre à quelqu'un de-** to forbid someone to
4. **demander à quelqu'un de-** to ask someone to
5. **dire à quelqu'un de-** to tell someone to
6. **écrire à quelqu'un de-** to write to someone to
7. **interdire à quelqu'un de-** to forbid someone to
8. **offrir à quelqu'un de-** to offer to someone to
9. **ordonner à quelqu'un de-** to order someone to
10. **permettre à quelqu'un de-** to allow someone to
11. **promettre à quelqu'un de-** to promise someone to
12. **proposer à quelqu'un de-** to propose to someone to
13. **recommander à quelqu'un de-** to recommend to someone to
14. **reprocher à quelqu'un de-** to reproach someone for
15. **suggérer à quelqu'un de-** to suggest to someone to
16. **téléphoner à quelqu'un de-** to telephone someone to

Behind the Line Action

1. *Quelqu'un* **can be switched to a noun or an indirect object pronoun. The noun substitute follows the verb; the pronoun replacement precedes the verb.**

Ex. Une voix conseilla à Adam de ne pas être tenté par le serpent. > A voice advised Adam not to be tempted by the snake. (Everyone knows 'how it wound up.')

Ex. Liée contactait ses parents quand elle voyageait. Elle leur téléphonait à leur dire des nouvelles. > Liée used to contact her parents whenever she traveled. She phoned them to give them some news. (They referred to it as "remote control.")

2. Several verbs on the preceding list can be associated with English cognates. However, many of them include nuances in their translations.

2a. *Commander à quelqu'un de faire quelque chose* **and** *ordonner à quelqu'un de faire quelque chose* **both mean** <u>to order</u> **someone to do something. Yet,** *ordonner* **without an accompanying preposition =** *organiser*- **to organize. (Try to keep that straight!)**

2b. *Demander à quelqu'un de faire quelque chose* **is** <u>to ask</u> **someone to do something. The title, "**<u>commander</u> **in chief of the armed** <u>forces,</u>**" serves to separate** *commander* **from** *demander.*

Ex. M. Encolère a demandé au serveur de lui apporter un grand bifteck. Le serveur lui a apporté un petit. Le client fâché lui a commandé de faire chercher le propriétaire. > Mr. Encolère asked the server to bring him a large steak. The server brought him a small one. The angry customer ordered him to get the owner. ('Full satisfaction' cannot always be guaranteed.)

<u>A note</u>: *Demander quelqu'un en mariage*- **to propose marriage does not require a second verb.** (But an acceptance is followed by several parties.)

2c. *Conseiller à quelqu'un de faire quelque chose*- **to advise someone to do something offers its** *conseil*- **advice and is related to** <u>consul</u>**.**

Ex. Davidson a conseillé à Harley de porter son casque lorsqu'il monte à moto. > Davidson advised Harley to wear his helmet while he rides a motorcycle. (He didn't need 'a crash course.')

2d. *Défendre à quelqu'un de faire quelque chose*- **to forbid someone to do something is synonymous with** *interdire à quelqu'un de faire quelque chose.*

Ex. Votre père très strict vous défend d'être dehors après **votre couvre-feu** de minuit. > Your very strict father forbids you to be out after **your** midnight **curfew**. (His warning includes more than just what the hands of the clock might strike.)

<u>An important note</u>: **Everyone sees these notices in France:** *défense d'entrée* > **stay out,** *défense de fumer* > **no smoking and** *défense de stationner* > **no parking. Ironically, the people who put up the signs,** *défense d'afficher* > **no posting, don't take "no" for an answer.**

3. For several phrases listed with dual prepositions, translating *à* **and** *de* **as "to" facilitates the connection.**

3a. *Dire à quelqu'un de faire quelque chose*- **to tell someone to do something**

Ex. Ma sœur m'a dit de ne pas l'**avouer** à personne. > My sister told me not to **confess** it to anyone. (So there's no telling what happened.)

3b. *Écrire à quelqu'un de faire quelque chose*- **to write to someone to do something**

Ex. "Nous vous écrivons de vous informer que nous n'avons pas encore reçu votre réponse à notre **recensement**." > "We are writing to inform you that we have not yet received your response to our **census**." (Maybe 'the checks' are in the mail.)

3c. *Offrir à quelqu'un de faire quelque chose*- **to offer someone to do something**

Ex. J'ai dû offrir trente dollars à mon voisin de tailler mes arbustes. > I had to offer thirty dollars to my neighbor to trim my bushes. (He would not agree 'to cut the price.')

A note: An appropriate response to *une offre* is "*oui,*" "*merci (beaucoup)*" or both. Those who outwardly decline it do not show *la politesse*.

3d. *Permettre à quelqu'un de faire quelque chose-* **to allow someone to do something**

Ex. M. Parliament a dit à Mlle Lord, "Permettez-moi de vous offrir un verre!" > Mr. Parliament said to Ms Lord, "Allow me to buy you a drink!" (The bartender replied, "This one is on The House.")

3e. *Promettre à quelqu'un de faire quelque chose-* **to promise someone to do something**

Ex. Le roi Midas promit au peuple d'utiliser son pouvoir sagement. > King Midas promised the people to use his power wisely. (And his word was 'as good as gold.')

3f. *Proposer à quelqu'un de faire quelque chose-* **to propose/suggest to someone to do something**

Ex. Les trois femmes **potelées** lui ont proposé une formule de revenir en forme. > The three **chubby** women suggested a formula to her to get back in shape.

A note: *Porter un toast à la santé de quelqu'un-* **to propose a toast**

3g. *Recommander à quelqu'un de faire quelque chose-* **to recommend/suggest to someone to do something**

Ex. Mme Gibier a recommandé au gérant d'un restaurant d'offrir le faisan sous verre. > Mrs. Gibier recommended to the manager of a restaurant to offer pheasant under glass. (Will he 'look into it'?)

An important note: *Recommander* **is less forceful than** *commander.* **In fact,** *proposer, suggérer* **and** *recommender* **could be put inside 'the same suggestion box.'**

3h. *Téléphoner à quelqu'un de faire quelque chose-* **to telephone someone to do something**

Ex. Quand les télémarketeurs téléphonent à Elsa de vendre quelque chose, elle raccroche aux nez. > When telemarketers call Elsa to sell something, she hangs up on them. (But not before telling them that 'there is trouble with their line.')

4. *Reprocher à quelqu'un de faire quelque chose-* **to reproach/criticize someone <u>for</u> doing something: Not only does** *de* **translate as "for" but the verbs after it also end with -<u>ing</u>.**

Ex. Le premier avocat a reproché au deuxième de ne pas **révéler** toute la preuve. > The first lawyer reproached/criticized the second for not **revealing** all the evidence. (The prosecutor wouldn't 'allow the defense to rest.')

5. *Enseigner à quelqu'un à faire quelque chose = apprendre à quelqu'un à faire quelque chose-* **to teach someone to do something; They share the pattern: verb +** *à quelqu'un* **+** *à* **+ infinitive. However,** *enseigner* **+ should be reserved for school subjects.**

Ex. Quand j'étais une petite, ma tante Gertrude m'apprenait à tricoter les soirs. > When I was a little girl, my Aunt Gertrude used to teach me to knit in the evenings. (That was before 'cable.')

A Likely Response- Put the letters of the verb/verb phrases beside the numbers of those closest in meaning.

_____ 1. essayer de

_____ 2. penser à

_____ 3. désirer

_____ 4. achever de

_____ 5. se mettre à

_____ 6. préférer

_____ 7. enseigner à quelqu'un à

_____ 8. laisser quelqu'un faire quelque chose

A. quitter

B. inciter à

C. avoir à

D. permettre à quelqu'un de

E. être surpris de

F. prier de

G. interdire à quelqu'un de

H. accuser de

_____ 9. abandonner   I. apprendre à quelqu'un à

_____ 10. promettre à quelqu'un de   J. tâcher de

_____ 11. recommander à quelqu'un de   K. faire croire

_____ 12. demander à   L. commencer à

_____ 13. oser   M. cesser de

_____ 14. reprocher à quelqu'un de   N. se rappeler

_____ 15. causer   O. aimer mieux

_____ 16. commander à quelqu'un de   P. songer à

_____ 17. défendre à quelqu'un de   Q. suggérer à quelqu'un de

_____ 18. s'arrêter de   R. avoir l'intention de

_____ 19. falloir   S. finir de

_____ 20. feindre   T. donner sa parole

_____ 21. s'étonner de   U. être assez

_____ 22. se souvenir de   V. ordonner à quelqu'un de

_____ 23. compter   W. vouloir

_____ 24. suffire à/pour   X. avoir le courage de

Important Messages in the Letters- Circle the letters of the responses that best complete the sentences.

1. Pour avertir les pietons, des automobilistes _____ leurs klaxons.

a. veulent mettre   b. ont à utiliser   c. pensent à montrer   d. éviter de siffler

2. Tim Ide n'a pas _____ prendre une sucette de la petite corbeille dans la banque.

a. suffi à   b. empêché de   c. remercié de   d. osé

3. Tootsie Rolls _____ se passer des desserts sucrés.

a. a failli   b. a remercié de   c. s'est résignée à   d. a prié de

4. M. et Mme Jacques Pot ne se sont jamais _____ gagner la loterie à leurs amis.

a. vantés de   b. gardés de   c. tâchés de   d. achevés de

5. À cause des animaux sauvages dans notre voisinage, nous sommes _____ ériger une clôture.

a. incités à   b. accusés d'   c. interdits d'   d. obligés à

6. Mme Hier aime mieux les modes du bon vieux temps. Elle _____ mettre des couches de toile à son bébé.

a. sert à   b. consent à   c. tient à   d. prétend

7. Ray Ussir ne peut pas _____ recevoir de mauvaises notes.

a. valoir mieux   b. s'habituer à   c. compter   d. s'efforcer de

8. Vous vous _____ quitter ton boulot après avoir reçu une prime?

a. plaisez de   b. étonnez de   c. félicitez de   d. attendez à

9. L'avocat se méfie de Madame Cachée. Il lui _____ révéler tout.

a. ordonne de   b. défend de   c. permet de   d. offre de

10. On a _____ à 007 de (d') _____ la cassette immédiatement.

a. reproché .... écouter   b. proposé .... déchirer   c. conseillé .... détruire   d. promis .... copier

---

Provide the Missing Link- Insert *à*, *de*, *d'* or no preposition on the spaces provided.

1. Le clown se plaît _____ divertir la foule.
2. Harry Krishna a choisi _____ devenir moine.
3. Lee Zieux et moi avons décidés _____ passer notre jour de congé chez nous.
4. Adam et Eve s' habituèrent _____ habiter dans un jardin avec un serpent.
5. La loi nous défend _____ stationner devant la Maison Blanche.
6. Il vaut mieux _____ s'occuper des petits problèmes lorsqu'ils sont toujours petits.
7. Les maîtresses leur reprochent _____ mâcher le chewing-gum en classe.
8. Le guichet ne s'ouvre pas jusqu'à dix heures. Ne te dépêche pas là-bas _____ acheter de billets!
9. Quand l'économie est mauvaise, des gens se résignent _____ vivre sans luxe.
10. Il a fallu longtemps _____ trouver une place de stationnement. J'ai failli _____ rater mon vol.
11. Ne cherche pas _____ trouver un cadeau qui lui plaira! Elle se contentera juste _____ te voir.
12. Si vous étiez célèbre, qui aimeriez-vous _____ être?
13. Prudence se gardait _____ répéter ce que Mme Versetout tenait _____ raconter.
14. Le prêtre m'encourage _____ donner à la charité, mais il ne me force pas _____ le faire.
15. Madame Lesdeux se plaint _____ travailler trop, mais elle se vante aussi _____ passer les week-ends au bureau.

NOUNS AND ADJECTIVES FOLLOWED BY *À* AND *DE*

À and *de* could be considered fickle prepositions. After 'hooking up' with verbs, they 'go after' nouns and adjectives. Depending upon the specific function, *à* or *de* may be present.

How *À* and *De* Join the Conversation
Many nouns and adjectives welcome *de* before an infinitive. That preposition is included in an entourage of expressions such as:

1. **le besoin de**- the need to
2. **content de**- glad to, pleased to
3. **enchanté de**- delighted to
4. **heureux de**- happy to

5. **l'intention de**- the intention to (of)
6. **la peur de**- the fear of
7. **sûr de**- sure to (of)
8. **le temps de**- the time to

---

1. **To is an atypical translation for *de*.** Yet, between nouns or adjectives and infinitives, <u>*de*</u> often links those parts of speech <u>to</u> each other.

Ex. On serait heureux d'adopter ces chiots-là. > They would be happy to adopt those puppies. (But it involves so much 'paperwork.')

Some exceptions: Several common adjectives including *dernier, lent, prêt, premier* and *seul* are followed by *à* + an infinitive.

Ex. Monice Worth était la première à arriver et la dernière à partir. > Monice Worth was the first to arrive and the last to leave.

Ex. Je ne suis pas prêt à manger le petit déjeuner. > I am not ready to eat breakfast. (But the table is 'all set.')

2. **Impersonal expressions composed of *il* + *est* + an adjective take *de* in front of an infinitive.**

Ex. Il est fatiguant de préparer le dîner pour un mari ingrat tous les soirs. > It is tiring to prepare dinner for an ungrateful husband every evening. (Maybe she should 'have it out with him.')

3. Infinitives with a passive meaning are preceded by *à*.

Ex. Quelques gens réfléchissent à acheter sa voiture d'occasion qui est à vendre. > A few people are thinking about buying his used car which is for sale/to be sold. (He hopes that someone 'will break down' and purchase it.)

Ex. Cette eau-là n'est pas bonne à boire. > That water is not good to drink/to be drunk. (The advice and the water must come from 'a reputable source.')

4. Similar sentences can vary in meaning according to the preposition used.

Ex. Il est possible de faire cette traduction-ci. > It is possible to do this translation.
Doing it (the process) is a possibility.

Ex. Cette traduction-ci est possible à faire. > This translation (itself) is possible to do.
The tone is passive. (The project was tossed around, but it did not land on anyone's desk.)

5. Two distinct constructions follow *il est* and *c'est*. It has one translation in English.

Ex. Il est facile de conduire. > It is easy to drive. **Driving in general is easy.**

    C'est facile à conduire. > It is easy to drive. **A specific vehicle is easily handled.**

5a. This shortcut is even faster:

Il est + bon + de ....

C'est + bon + à .....

'Click on a Link'- Choose *à*, *d*, or *d'* to complete the following sentences.

1. La fondue est facile _____ préparer.
2. Mme Crise a toujours un problème _____ résoudre.
3. Ma mère sera ravie _____ te voir.
4. "Chers Messieurs, Je regrette _____ vous informer que ...."
5. Phil et Sophie ne sont pas les seuls _____ suivre cette philosophie.
6. Franklin D. Roosevelt a dit, " Il n'y a rien _____ craindre sauf la peur elle-même."
7. Il est fascinant _____ étudier **la génétique (genetics).**
8. M. Leconte a toujours le temps _____ nous lire.
9. Ma valise est pleine de vêtements prêts _____ porter.
10. Jim Nastiques a l'intention _____ faire des exercices au gymnase.
11. Il n'est pas prudent _____ dire tout à Mme Potin. Au contraire, il est sage _____ garder la bouche cousue devant elle.
12. C'est une bonne leçon _____ apprendre.

The Right Connections- Translate the following sentences.

1. Les Misérables is a wonderful novel to read. _____

_____.

2. Sue Rire was happy to go out with him. _____

_____.

3. It is forbidden to post signs here. _____

_____.

4. It is amusing to watch the cute babies. _____

_____.

5. There are many chateaux to see in France. _____

6. Tara Firma has no desire to mountain climb._____

_____.

7. I would be surprised to receive a gift from Mrs. Radine. _____

_____.

8. It is good to go home and to celebrate the holidays together. _____

_____.

9. According to Clara Fye, it is impossible to understand this explanation. _____

_____.

10. Is the newest technology easy to use? _____

_____ ?

11. Ms Gagner and I would be proud to show you our prizes. _____

_____.

12. It is rare to speak more than three languages fluently. _____

_____.

_____.

la Place des Vosges (Paris)

UNE REVUE - A Review

Compound Past Tenses, *Si* Clauses, Verbs with and without Prepositions + Infinitives, Nouns and Adjectives Followed by *À* and *De*

Truer Words May Have Been Spoken- Label the sentences *vrai* or *faux*.

_____ 1. Compound past tenses are composed of a form of *avoir* or *être* + a past participle.

_____ 2. Reflexive verbs are not conjugated with a form of *être* in compound past tenses.

_____ 3. If a reflexive pronoun acts as an indirect object, the past participle is unchanged.

_____ 4. *Le passé composé* can be substituted for *le plus-que-parfait*.

_____ 5. *Le plus-que-parfait* is the only compound past tense translated with one helping verb.

_____ 6. Will have is included in the translation of *le futur antérieur*.

_____ 7. *Le conditionnel passé* is used to translate must have.

_____ 8. A common translation of *le conditionnel passé* includes would have.

_____ 9. A present tense form of *devoir* + an infinitive expresses should have.

_____ 10. An independent (main clause) can be *au plus-que-parfait*.

_____ 11. Forms of *aimer mieux* and *préférer* are followed directly by infinitives.

_____ 12. No reflexive verbs are followed by *à* plus an infinitive.

_____ 13. The meanings of *rester*, *suffire* and *travailler* are changed if those verbs are followed by *à* + an infinitive.

_____ 14. Some verbs that take *de* + an infinitive require no preposition in English.

_____ 15. *Empêcher* is the only infinitive on the list with *de* translated as "from."

_____ 16. Constructions that include both *à* and *de* + an infinitive cannot contain nouns.

_____ 17. *Défendre à quelqu'un de faire quelque chose* and *interdire à quelqu'un de faire quelque chose* are synonyms.

_____ 18. *Pour* is the most common prep. to follow nouns and adjectives and precede infinitives.

_____ 19. *Il est* + an adjective is followed by *de* + an infinitive.

_____ 20. Infinitives with a passive meaning are preceded by *à*.

'What Are the Odds?'- Circle the letter of the response that is not related to the others in the group.

1. a. independent clause	b. main clause	c. *si* clause	d. resulting clause
2. a. parce que	b. aussitôt que	c. quand	d. dès que
3. a. valoir mieux	b. désirer	c. souhaiter	d. vouloir
4. a. ravi de	b. désolé de	c. heureux de	d. enchanté de
5. a. penser à	b. réfléchir à	c. songer à	d. servir à
6. a. se vanter de	b. devoir	c. avoir à	d. être obligé à
7. a. courir la chance	b. conseiller	c. oser	d. risquer
8. a. commencer à	b. débuter	c. achever	d. se mettre à
9. a. s'efforcer de	b. se tâcher de	c. essayer de	d. se garder de
10. a. demander	b. prier de	c. éviter	d. solliciter
11. a. proposer	b. interdire	c. suggérer	d. recommander
12. a. s'amuser à	b. se plaire à	c. s'attendre à	d. passer du bon temps

----

<u>**Widening the Passages**</u>- **Translate the phrases in parentheses to form complete sentences.**

1. Avant de partir de Barcelone, (Mrs. Taureau planned to attend a bullfight). _____
_____.

2. **Les ivrognes (the drunks)** qui ont incité la bagarre (just missed killing two customers). _____
_____.

3. Le voyeur a avoué (that he had hidden himself in the bushes). _____
_____.

4. Si tu avais regardé *Dancing with the Stars*, (you would have seen her). _____
_____.

5. Par la fin du procès, (the lawyers will have revealed everything). _____
_____.

6. On aurait imposé un couvre-feu, (if a war had taken place there)._____
_____.

7. M. Toute aurait klaxonné toute la journée, (if the law had permitted it). _____
_____.

8. (It is good to see) _____ tant de visages heureux.

9. (Chekov thinks that it is important to answer) _____
_____ _____ au recensement du gouvernement.

10. Vous n'êtes pas (the only ones to prefer ready-to-wear clothing). _____
_____.

la Jeune Fille au Chapeau Fleuri by Auguste Rodin (le Musée Rodin, Paris)

482

LE PASSÉ SIMPLE - The Simple Past (The Past Definite)

Since this tense specializes in historical past events and its conjugations consist of single verbs, the term *passé simple* is most fitting. Moreover, if those to whom this tense refers could speak, they might say that the simple past was indeed less complex than today's world. While *le passé composé* together with *l'imparfait* are used almost exclusively in French conversation, *le passé simple* partners with *l'imparfait* for historical and literary works.

Here's to a tense that has carried itself and worn well over the years!

Porter - To Carry, To Wear

Singular	Plural
je port<u>ai</u>- I carried/wore, did carry/wear	nous port<u>âmes</u>- we carried/wore, did carry/wear
tu port<u>as</u>- you carried/wore, did carry/wear	vous port<u>âtes</u>- you carried/wore, did carry/wear
il/elle port<u>a</u>- he/she/it carried/wore, did carry/wear	ils/elles port<u>èrent</u>- they carried/wore, did carry/wear

----

Presenting *le Passé Simple*

1. If you have a feeling of *déjà vu* when you look at the above conjugation, the credit should go to the people and facts mentioned in <u>Les Photos Valent Mille Mots - Huit Jours à Paris</u>.

2. The singular of most -<u>er</u> verbs *au passé simple*, **including** *aller*, **is formed by dropping the infinitive ending and attaching the singular present tense forms of** *avoir*, -<u>ai</u>, -<u>as</u>, -<u>a</u>. (It's true that history repeats itself.)

Ex. Napoléon Bonaparte alla du général à l'empereur rapidement. > Napoleon Bonaparte went from general to emperor quickly. (He did it 'in short order.')

3a. The unique plural forms show that French is indeed a foreign language. The *nous* **and** *vous* **endings, -<u>âmes</u> and -<u>âtes</u>, have a circumflex above the <u>a</u>.**

<u>A helpful hint</u>: *Les âmes* are <u>the souls</u>. **Picturing that noun with the** *vous* **form ending will help connect you** *au passé simple*.

3b. The *ils/elles* **form offers an alternate 'means to an end'; Attach -<u>èrent</u> to the stem or -<u>ent</u> to the entire infinitive. Either way, an accent** *grave* **goes over the next to last <u>e</u>.**

Ex. Georges et Marthe dansèrent **le menuet**. > George and Martha danced **the minuet**. (The women showed their membership to 'a fan club.')

4a. All endings of -<u>ger</u> verbs *au passé simple* **are preceded by an <u>e</u>. That vowel has a previously reserved spot in the third person plural.**

Ex. Louis XIV obligea tous ses sujets à s'incliner devant lui. > Louis XIV obligated all his subjects to bow in front of him. (The women responded with the 'curtsy' of a reply.)

4b. Excluding the third person plural, -<u>cer</u> verbs *au passé simple* **have a cedilla under the <u>c</u>.**

Ex. Des chevaliers menacèrent leurs ennemis en **brandissant** leurs épées faites en Bretagne. > Some knights threatened their enemies by **brandishing** their swords made in Brittany. (Even today, people are familiar with the name "Britney Spears.")

All regular and many irregular -ir and -re verbs share the same endings *au passé simple.* **Here's 'the skinny' on one such verb.**

Maigrir - To Lose Weight

Singular	Plural
je maigris- I lost weight, did lose weight	**nous maigrîmes**- we lost weight, did lose weight
tu maigris- you lost weight, did lose weight	**vous maigrîtes**- you lost weight, did lose weight
il/elle maigrit- he/she/it lost weight, did lose weight	**ils/elles maigrirent**- they lost weight, did lose weight

---

1. The singular *passé simple* **-ir endings are identical to those of present tense -ir verbs.** (Their conjugations 'see i to i.')

2. The -is, -is, -it, -îmes, -îtes -irent endings are added to -ir/-re infinitive stems.

3. Aside from the third person plural, the only difference between -er and -ir/-re *passé simple* **endings is the exchange of an a for an i.**

Ex. Plusieurs artistes **affamés** vendirent leurs autoportraits. > Several **starving** artists sold their self-portraits. (They were 'beside themselves' for money.)

4. *Le passé simple* **is rarely used in the first and second persons.**

Backing Up the Facts- **Change the underlined verbs** *au passé simple.*

A note: The irregular verbs in this exercise have regular forms in the simple past.

1. Gaugin <u>a passé</u> des années à Tahiti. _____
2. Les œuvres de Rabelais <u>captivaient</u> François Premier. _____
3. Est-ce qu'une baleine <u>a avalé</u> Jonah? _____
4. Les Curie <u>travaillaient</u> ensemble dans un laboratoire. _____
5. On <u>considérait</u> les femmes potelées être magnifiques. _____
6. Mary Shelley, pas le docteur Frankenstein, <u>a crée</u> un monstre. _____
7. **Les hommes des cavernes (the cavemen)** <u>mangeaient</u> avec leurs mains. _____
8. Louis XIV <u>a déménagé</u> de Paris à Versailles. _____
9. **Les Rois mages (The three wise men)** <u>sont allés</u> à Bethléem. _____
10. Les papes **bénissaient (blessed)** des chevaliers. _____
11. Christophe Colomb <u>a découvert</u> l'Amérique en 1492. _____
12. En quelle année les colons <u>sont</u>-ils <u>partis</u> pour la Virginie? _____
13. Robin Hood ne <u>rendait</u> jamais ce qu'il <u>volait</u>. _____, _____
14. La famille de Roméo <u>combattait</u> celle de Juliette. _____

Les Verbes Irréguliers au Passé Simple
La Première Partie

The past participles of many irregular verbs ending with a -<u>u</u> provide the stems for their *passé simple* conjugations.

Infinitives	Passé Simple Stems	Infinitives	Passé Simple Stems
1. avoir	eu	9. pleuvoir	plu
2. boire	bu	10. pouvoir	pu
3. connaître	connu	11. recevoir	reçu
4. courir	couru	12. savoir	su
5. croire	cru	13. valoir	valu
6. devoir	dû	14. vivre	vécu
7. falloir	fallu	15. vouloir	voulu
8. lire	lu		

Le passé simple conjugation of <u>lire</u> has the following' booking':

Singular	**Plural**
je lu<u>s</u>- I read, did read	nous lû<u>mes</u>- we read, did read
tu lu<u>s</u>- you read, did read	vous lû<u>tes</u>- you read, did read
il/elle lu<u>t</u>- he/she/it read, did read	ils/elles lu<u>rent</u>- they read, did read

----

Keeping *le Passé Simple* Uncomplicated

1. The endings -<u>s</u>, -<u>s</u>, -<u>t</u>, -<u>mes</u>, -<u>tes</u> and -<u>rent</u> are attached to the past participles of the irregular verbs listed above. The *nous* and *vous* forms top the <u>u</u> with a circumflex.

Ex. Josephine, la femme de Napoléon, connut ses maîtresses parce qu'elles restèrent fréquemment à Fontainebleau. > Josephine, Napoleon's wife, knew his mistresses because they frequently stayed at Fontainebleau. (They met 'on common ground.')

Ex. Beethoven ne put pas entendre. Cependant, il composa la très belle musique. > Beethoven could not hear. However, he composed very beautiful music. (His writing skills were 'sharp,' but his auditory ability was 'flat.')

Ex. Les dinosaures ne vécurent pas dans le Parc de Jurassic. > The dinosaurs did not live in Jurassic Park. (They were only 'produced' there.)

2. The only simple past forms of *falloir* and *pleuvoir* are *fallut* and *plut* respectively.

Ex. Pendant que Noé navigua son arche, il plut pendant quarante jours et nuits. > While Noah sailed his ark, it rained for forty days and nights. (Did his 2 x 4s 'weather the storm' as well as his 2 x 2s?)

Passed On Past Facts- Write the correct *passé simple* forms of the infinitives in parentheses to complete the sentences.

1. (vouloir) Christophe Colomb _____ trouver une route d'Europe en Asie.
2. (savoir) Les anciens romains _____ parler latin.
3. (vivre) Georges Washington et Thomàs Jefferson _____ en Virginie.
4. (recevoir) Grâce à Paul Revere, les citoyens de Boston _____ des nouvelles.
5. (boire) Plusieurs artistes _____ beaucoup d'alcool tous les jours.
6. (avoir) Benjamin Franklin _____ plus de quatre-vingts ans quand il signa la Déclaration de l'Indépendance.
7. (pouvoir) La plupart des personnes ne _____ pas lire pendant le Moyen Âge.

Les Verbes Irréguliers au Passé Simple
La Deuxième Partie

This category of irregular verbs has two features in common. They sport regular -**ir/-re** simple past conjugations, and all but *s'asseoir* and *voir* have infinitives ending with -**re**.

Irregular Verbs with Irregular Passé Simple Stems

Infinitives	Passé Simple Stems	Infinitives	Passé Simple Stems
1. s'asseoir	s'ass	8. mettre	m
2. conduire	conduis	9. naitre	naqui
3. construire	construis	10. peindre	peign
4. dire	d	11. prendre	pr
5. écrire	écriv	12. rire	r
6. faire	f	13. traduire	traduis
7. joindre	joign	14. voir	v

The conjugation of *faire* shows how they did things *au passé simple.*

Singular
je f<u>is</u>- I did, did do, made, did make
tu f<u>is</u>- you did, did do, made, did make
il/elle f<u>it</u>- he/she/it did, did do, made, did make

Plural
nous f<u>î</u>mes- we did, did do, made, did make
vous f<u>î</u>tes- you did, did do, made, did make
ils/elles f<u>irent</u>- they did, did do, made, did make

Classified Information
1. Regular -**ir/re** *passé simple* endings -<u>is</u>, -<u>is</u>, -<u>it</u>, -<u>î</u>mes, -<u>î</u>tes and -<u>irent</u> are added to the irregular roots listed above. The *nous* and *vous* forms have circumflexes for 'i-brows.'
2. With one letter stems, *dire, faire, mettre, rire* and *voir* put 'the simple' in *le passé simple.*

Ex. Albert Einstein ne dit rien jusqu'à l'âge de trois ans. > Albert Einstein did not say anything until the age of three. (It took him a few years 'to digest his formula.')

3. *Dire, rire, sourire, conduire, construire* and *traduire* retain their singular present tense forms in the simple past.

Ex. Da Vinci sut pourquoi la Joconde sourit. > Da Vinci knew why Mona Lisa smiled. (He'd given her some 'great lines.')

Ex. Si Gustave Eiffel pouvait parler, il dirait, "Je construis cette tour pour l'Exposition de 1889." > If Gustave Eiffel could speak, he would say, "I built that tower for the Exposition of 1889." (Today, he is praised for being 'level-headed.')

4. *Le passé simple* stems of *écrire- écriv, joindre- joign* and *peindre- peign* are the same as their present tense plural roots.

Ex. Diderot et d'Alembert écrivirent l'Encyclopédie. > Diderot and d'Alembert wrote <u>The Encyclopedia.</u> (Nowadays, most people do research on the computer and 'turn down the volume.')

5. *Le passé simple* conjugations of *apprendre, comprendre, entreprendre, reprendre* and *surprendre* take after *prendre* by adding prefixes to its <u>pr</u> stem.

Ex. Quand une pomme tomba sur sa tête d'Isaac Newton, il comprit la loi de gravité. > When an apple fell on Isaac Newton's head, he understood the law of gravity. (That's when 'it hit him.')

6. *Le passé simple* conjugations of *admettre, commettre, omettre, permettre, promettre, remettre, sousmettre* and *transmettre* are identical to *mettre* but with prefixes added to the <u>m</u> stem.

Ex. On promit aux voyageurs du Titanic de belles **cabines de luxe,** des repas délicieux et la musique extraordinaire. > They promised the passengers of *the Titanic* beautiful state rooms, delicious meals and extraordinary music. (And that was just 'the tip of the iceberg.')

<u>'Digging Up the Roots'</u>- Répondez en français aux questions suivantes.

1. Quel auteur français écrivit Les Misérables? _____
_____.

2. Où Jésus Christ naquit-il? _____.

3. Qui construisirent les Pyramides? _____
_____.

4. Quel romain bien connu dit "veni, vidi, vici"? _____
_____

5. Qu'est-ce que The Wright Brothers firent à Kitty Hawk, North Carolina en 1903? _____
_____

6. Qu'est-ce que le peuple de Paris prit le 14 juillet 1789? _____
_____

7. Quel américain bien connu conduisit les premières expériences avec l'électricité? _____
_____

8. Quelles deux personnes commirent **le péché (the sin)** originel? _____
_____

9. Nommez un pays qui se joignit à la France pendant les deux guerres mondiales. _____
_____

10. Quel président des États-Unis permit la libération **des esclaves-m./f. (slaves)**? _____
_____
_____

Les Verbes Irréguliers au Passé Simple
La Troisième Partie

Être, Mourir et Venir

Having novel stems and/or endings, *être*, *mourir* and *venir* 'are at odds' with the other verbs *au passé simple.* (They just won't 'let bygones be bygones.')
Their unique forms are:

Être

Singular	Plural
je fus- I was	nous fûmes- we were
tu fus- you were	vous fûtes- you were
il/elle fut- he/she/it was	ils/elles furent- they were

Mourir

Singular	Plural
je mourus- I died, did die	nous mourûmes- we died, did die
tu mourus- you died, did die	vous mourûtes- you died, did die
il/elle mourut- he/she/it died, did die	ils/elles moururent- they died, did die

----

Venir

Singular	Plural
je vins- I came, did come	nous vînmes- we came, did come
tu vins- you came, did come	vous vîntes- you came, did come
il/elle vint- he/she/it came, did come	ils/elles vinrent- they came, did come

----

Distinguishing Looks *du Passé Simple*

1. *Faire* and *être* both have an <u>f</u> as the first letter of their conjugations *au passé simple.* **The <u>i</u> to <u>u</u> vowel switch is the only difference between the simple past forms of the two verbs.**
Ex. Louis Pasteur fut le savant qui fonda la bactériologie moderne. > Louis Pasteur was the scientist who founded modern bacteriology. (His theory was "What you don't see is what you might get.")
2. The last letters of the conjugations of *être* and *mourir* are identical to each other as well as to other simple past verbs whose stems ends with a <u>u</u>.
Ex. Louis XVI et Marie Antoinette furent guillotinés pendant la Révolution française. Ils moururent ensemble. > Louis XVI and Marie Antoinette were guillotined during the French Revolution. They died together. (They had been warned that the citizens would be 'clamping down' on royalty.)
<u>A note</u>: In the above example, *fut* + a past participle constitutes the passive voice.
2a. The stem of *mourir* is easily accessed with the phrase: "One died and was no '*mour.*'"
2b.The first and second persons singular and plural of *mourir* are just for show in past tenses.
(Assuming that the deceased have ceased to communicate.)
Ex. John Adams et Thomàs Jefferson moururent le quatre juillet de la même année. > John Adams and Thomas Jefferson died July 4th of the same year. (After they 'declared their independence.')

3. With their irregular stems and endings, *venir* and *tenir* and their families resemble no other verbs *au passé simple*. Nevertheless, the hospitable first and second person singular of *venir* do offer French wines while they 'have a roof over their heads' in the *nous* and *vous* forms.

Ex. L'idée du premier bureau de poste vint de Benjamin Franklin. > The idea for the first post office came from Benjamin Franklin. (The Pony Express had 'run out of steam.')

3a. *Devenir, prévenir, revenir, se souvenir de* and *survenir*- to happen unexpectedly are modeled after *venir* in the simple past. *Contenir, détenir, maintenir, obtenir, retenir* and *soutenir* are 'beholding' to *tenir*.

Translating Past Times for a Pastime- Write the following sentences in English.

1. Des artistes affamés du dix-huitième siècle s'habituèrent à vivre de jour en jour. _____
_____.

2. Les chevaliers parlèrent de leurs ennemis qui moururent en bataille. _____
_____.

3. Louis XVI écouta sa femme Marie Antoinette qui lui donna de mauvais conseils. _____
_____.

4. Des citoyens furent tentés de ne pas s'incliner devant le roi. _____
_____.

5. Avec toutes leurs tâches, Georges et Marthe n'eurent pas le temps de jouer aux sports. _____
_____.

6. Les femmes potelées furent à la mode il y a deux cents ans. Ainsi, elles ne tinrent jamais à suivre les régimes. _____
_____.

7. François Premier, le roi français pendant la Renaissance, fit construire de beaux châteaux le long de la Loire. _____
_____.

8. Selon la comptine anglaise, Wee Willie Winkie courut au travers de la ville pour être sûr que tous les enfants furent aux lits par huit heures du soir. _____
_____.
_____.

Finishing Fascinating French Facts- Put the infinitives in the correct forms *du passé simple* to complete the sentences.

1. (devenir, avoir) Louis XIV _____ roi quand il _____ neuf ans.
2. (être, prédire) Nostradamus _____ clairvoyant qui _____ sa propre mort.
3. (s'appeler, être) Avant la naissance de Jésus Christ, la France _____ la Gaule et Paris _____ Lutèce.
4. (donner, dire, avoir) Sainte Geneviève, la patronne de Paris, _____ le courage au peuple. Elle _____ que les Huns n'attaqueraient pas, et elle _____ raison.
5. (être, écrire, raconter) Charlemagne _____ le souverain le plus fort du Moyen Âge. On ne sait pas encore qui _____ la Chanson de Roland, **le** premier **chef-d'œuvre (the masterpiece)** de la littérature française. Dans cette histoire- là, l'auteur _____ les guerres de Charlemagne et Roland contre les Sarrasins de l'Espagne.
6. (mourir, brûler) Jeanne d'Arc, l'héroïne nationale de la France, _____ à l'âge

de dix-neuf ans quand les anglais la _____ vive.

7. (vendre, être) Napoléon Bonaparte _____ la Louisiane aux États-Unis. Le Code Napoléon, qui forme la base des lois françaises, _____ créé par lui.

8. (diriger, devenir) Le Général Charles De Gaulle _____ le mouvement de résistance contre l'Allemagne pour libérer la France. Il _____ aussi Président de la Cinquième République.

9. (considérer, peindre) On _____ Molière être le plus grand écrivain des comédies classiques. Il _____ les vices humains d'une façon humoristique.

10. (montrer, se faire) Voltaire, un écrivain très populaire au dix-huitième siècle, _____ un esprit satirique pendant qu'il _____ le défenseur de l'humanité et la liberté.

11. (lire, vivre, gagner, être) Nous lisons aujourd'hui, comme on _____ au dix-neuvième siècle, des romans de Jules Verne. Ils comprennent Vingt Mille Lieues sous les Mers (<u>Twenty Thousand Leagues under the Sea</u>) et Le Tour du Monde en Quatre-Vingt Jours (<u>Around the World in 80 Days</u>). Guy de Maupassant, qui _____ en même temps, _____ la réputation du "grand maître de contes." Deux travaux, La Parure (<u>The Necklace</u>) et La Ficelle (<u>The String</u>) _____ (et sont toujours) ses publications les plus connues.

12. (se développer, faire) À la deuxième moitié du dix-neuvième siècle, le style d'impressionnisme _____ à partir du réalisme. Ses maîtres, Manet, Degas, Monet et Renoir, _____ la lumière l'objet essentiel de leurs peintures.

13. (éviter, déformer) Des artistes comme Cézanne, Gaugin et Van Gogh _____ la réprésentation photographique. À sa place, ils _____ la nature et le corps humain pendant l'époque de post-impressionnisme.

14. (choisir, devenir) Louis XIV _____ Jean-Baptiste Lully être directeur de l'Opéra de Paris. Deux siècles plus tard, Hector Berlioz _____ le compositeur le plus connu de l'époque romantique.

LES ANIMAUX - ANIMALS

LES MAMMIFÈRES - Mammals

From the bottom of an ocean to the top of a mountain, there are creatures that provide us with work, food, clothing, transportation, entertainment and companionship. Because animals have varying degrees of intelligence, they do not belong 'in the same class.' It is more appropriate to visit them at home with their families.

Les Animaux Domestiques et Les Animaux de Ferme - Domestic and Farm Animals

A Standing Ovation for Four-Legged Friends

1. *Le chat*- the cat has its own chair (<u>h</u>) to curl up in. *La chatte* gives birth to *le chaton*- the kitten. (The mother is not 'fined for littering.')

Expressions for This 'Cat-egory'

a. **avoir un chat dans la gorge- to have a frog in one's throat** (But he/she isn't ready 'to croak.')

b. **avoir d'autres chats à fouetter- to have other fish to fry: Its word-for-word translation is "to have other cats to whip."**

c. *Quand le chat n'est pas là, les souris dansent.* > **When the cat isn't there, the mice dance. In a similar American idiom, the rodents play.** (If French cats danced, they might do 'le cha-chat.')

----

2. *Le chien* is the male dog; *la chienne* is the female (and *un gros mot*). A puppy- *un <u>chiot</u>* starts out looking like its parents. *Le caniche* is <u>the French poodle</u>.

See 'a Dog Show' in These Idioms!

a. **entre chien et loup- at dusk** (When canines decide whether to prowl or howl.)

b. **s'entendre comme chien et chat- to get along like cats and dogs: The animals show their differences by reversing their order and plurality.** (Then, they go at it 'paws and claws.')

c. *Chien méchant!* > **Beware of the dog!** (This sign is an eye-catcher if no dogcatcher is around.)

d. *C'est une vie de chien.* > **It's a dog's life.** (The relaxed lifestyle and the translation are easy.)

e. *Elle a du chien!* > **She's striking!** (Obviously, she is 'well-groomed.')

f. *Quel chien du temps!* > **What foul weather!** (It's said when what's overhead is not fit for what's under foot.)

----

3. *Le cheval* is the male horse. *La jument* is the mare. (Though he may gallop off everywhere, she prefers 'a stable environment.')

A 'Mane' Expression Associated with the Horse

a. **être très à cheval sur le règlement- to be a stickler for the rules** (The phrase applies to anyone who prefers horse sense over nonsense.)

----

4. *La vache*- **the cow;** *Le taureau*- **the bull is her masculine companion.** (Taurus is the 'constellation prize' derived from the French word.)

<u>**Sayings 'Herd' through the Bovine**</u>

a. faire un coup en vache à quelqu'un- to play a dirty trick on someone (That gives the victim 'a legitimate beef.')

b. une période de vaches maigres pour l'économie- lean times for the economy (When very few people are 'living high off the cow.')

c. *Ah la vache!*- **Wow!** (Said if someone is 'utterly' surprised)

----

5. *Le(s) bœuf(s)* **is/are the ox(en).** (The plural is needed for those 'in it for the long haul.')

6. *Le mulet* **and** *la mule* **are mules.** (There's an extra letter in the 'male.')

7. *L'âne* **is the ass/the donkey.** (And "smart ass" is an oxymoron.)

----

8. *La chèvre*- **the nanny goat is 'the big cheese' around** *le bouc*- **the billy goat.** (That could make him gruff.)

<u>**Idioms Milked from** *la Chèvre*</u>

a. prendre la chèvre- to take offense (A possible result when someone doesn't 'butt out.')

b. devenir chèvre- to go crazy (Maybe 'the kids' are to blame.)

----

9. *Le mouton* **might be found curling up with** *la brebis*- **the ewe/the female sheep. They produce** *l'agneau*- **the lamb** (Could animal activists who are opposed to slaughtering this animal be referred to as 'bleating' hearts?) *La brebis galeuse* **is the black sheep** (Which disapproving family members might call 'ewe.')

<u>**Phrases Clipped from** *le Mouton*</u>

a. suivre quelqu'un comme des moutons- to follow someone like sheep (The translations for both expressions also conform perfectly.)

b. *C'est un mouton.* **> He's easily led.** (It's no problem 'to pull the wool over his eyes.')

c. *Revenons à nos moutons!* **> Let's get back to the subject!** (Said if someone has 'strayed.')

----

10. *Le cochon*- **the pig is not formally 'be-trough-ed' to** *la cochonne* **who gives birth to** *le porcelet*- **the piglet.** *Le porc*- **the hog and** *la truie*- **the sow can be spotted in 'pig tales.'**

<u>**A Saying from 'the Pig's Pen'**</u>

a. comme un cochon- like a pig (Such behavior leaves others dis-'grunt'-led.)

----

11. *Le lapin* **is the rabbit/the bunny.** (The double English translation is fitting for an animal known for its multiplication skills.) *Le lièvre* **is the hare. Don't confuse that word with** *la lèvre*- **the lip!**

----

12. *Les rongeurs*- **rodents include** *la souris*- **the mouse and** *le rat*- **the rat.**

<u>**Expressions That Vermin Gnaw into**</u>

a. un rat de bibliothèque- a bookworm (He might wish to be in 'a higher class.')

b. *Ce type est un vrai rat.* **> That guy is really stingy.** (He may just 'rat-ion' everything.)

13. *La chauve-souris*- **the bat is literally "the bald mouse."** (A vampire, not an umpire, is familiar with this type of bat.)

<u>Les Animaux Qui Habitent dans les Bois - Animals That Live in the Woods</u>

<u>Mammals with a Wild Side and on Their Own</u>
1. *Le castor* **is the beaver.** (Busy with its 'dam'project, it has no time for bridgework on its teeth.)

2. *L'écureuil* **is the squirrel.** (The 'cache' is available when it digs into its savings.)

3. *Le tamia*- **the chipmunk is also called** *l'écureuil à rayures*- **the striped squirrel.** *Le tamia* **ends with an atypical <u>a</u>.** (And a very bushy tail.)

4. *La mouffette* **is the skunk.** (It never keeps its anger 'bottled up' inside.)

5. *Le porc-épic* **is the porcupine.** (This animal is offended if anybody says that its name sounds like Porky Pig. (It is 'sharper' than one might think.)

6. *Le raton-laveur* **is the raccoon. The masked scavenger got its French name for washing what it eats.** (The raccoon might say, "That's garbage!")

7. *La marmotte d'Amérique*- **the groundhog comes out of its burrow February 2nd and forecasts when winter will end.** (Whatever its prediction, there is always 'a shadow of a doubt.')

----

8. *Le loup* **is the wolf.** (One hears 'night howls' when a full meal or a full moon is in view.)
<u>'A Lone Wolf' Phrase</u>
a. un loup déguisé en agneau- a wolf in sheep's clothing (It's not made of 100 percent wool.)

----

9. *Le renard* **is the fox.** (This animal is sly enough to feed off livestock while running its own news broadcasting company.)

10. *La biche* **is the doe/the female deer.** (Pronouncing a <u>t</u> in the middle of her name could signal a cross deer but not a deer crossing.) *Le cerf/le daim* **is the male deer.** (Hunters enjoy the sport even though it might not involve 'big bucks.')

11. *L'élan* **is the elk/the moose. The same French word means <u>momentum</u>.** (The noun applies to both simultaneously if 'the moose is loose.')

----

12. *L'ours* **is the male bear. The <u>s</u> at the end is pronounced.** *L'ourse*- **the female** bears *l'ourson*- **the bear cub.** (Thus making her 'a den mother.')
<u>Idioms with a Trapped Bear</u>
a. l'ours en peluche- the teddy bear (For sleepy small children, it hibernates 'on call.')

b. *Il ne faut pas vendre la peau de l'ours avant de l'avoir tué!* > **"You must not sell a bear's skin before having killed it." We recognize this idiom as "Don't count your chickens before they've hatched!** (It is good advice whether a creature is coming into or leaving the world.)

'Vetting' the Animals- Put the letters of the phrases beside the numbers of the animals to form complete sentences.

_____ 1. La jument   A. a une barbe et deux cornes.

_____ 2. L'âne   B. est noire et vole.

_____ 3. La brebis   C. est **le compagnon (companion)** de la vache.

_____ 4. L'écureuil   D. est de la même famille que le lapin.

_____ 5. La chauve-souris   E. est très grand et utilisé pour tirer de lourdes **charges (loads, burdens)**.

_____ 6. La marmotte d'Amérique   F. est chassé et mangé en automne.

_____ 7. Le renard   G. ressemble au mulet.

_____ 8. Le bouc   H. construit les barrages

_____ 9. L'élan   I. est un rongeur au manteau aigu.

_____ 10. Le rongeur   J. donne le lait et est plus petite que la vache.

_____ 11. Le porc-épic   K. se voit souvent avec un noix dans ses joues.

_____ 12. Le taureau   L. est un membre sauvage de la famille de chien.

_____ 13. La mouffette   M. est **la compagne (companion)** du cheval.

_____ 14. Le cerf   N. est le nom de famille qui inclut la souris et le rat.

_____ 15. Le lièvre   O. est **rusé (sly)** et **rougeâtre (reddish)**.

_____ 16. Le bœuf   P. est connue pour son parfum spécial.

_____ 17. La chèvre   Q. est la compagne du mouton.

_____ 18. Le raton-laveur   R. est plus grand que le daim mais de la même famille.

_____ 19. Le loup   S. a des cercles autour ses yeux et une queue rayée.

_____ 20. Le castor   T. prévoit le temps par son ombre.

Interpreting Animals' Expressions- Circle the letters of the idioms to complete or rephrase the scenarios.

1. Monsieur Tousyeux regarde une très belle femme. Il dit à son ami, "_____!"
a. Un ours en peluche!   b. Elle a du chien!   c. Elle prend la chèvre!   d. Quel chien du temps!

2. On qui ne peut pas dire les mots _____.
a. est un loup déguisé en agneau   b. devient chèvre   c. a l'élan   d. a un chat dans sa gorge

3. Puisque leurs parents ne sont pas chez eux, Vinnie et Ginnie font un boum impromptu.
a. Ils suivent leurs parents comme des moutons.   b. Ils ont d'autres chats à fouetter.
c. Quand le chat n'est pas là, les souris dansent.   d. C'est une vie de chien.

4. M. Avare donne comme des cadeaux ce qu'il achète dans les vide-greniers.
a. Ce type est un vrai rat.   b. Ah la vache!   c. Il est entre chien et loup.   d. C'est un mouton.

5. Mon frère a déguisé sa voix quand il m'a téléphoné, et il a feint d'être mon professeur.
a. Il revient à ses moutons.   b. Il m'a fait un coup en vache.   c. Chien méchant!
d. Nous nous entendons comme chien et chat.

Les Mammifères au Jardin Zoologique, au Cirque et sur les Plaines Africaines
Mammals in a Zoo, at the Circus and on the African Plains

Whether these mammals are seen in man-made enclosures or in their natural habitats, human visitors either pay per view to watch the show or are billed for 'roaming fees.' (And if agitated, these animals have been known 'to charge.')

Performing Mammals with Permanent Work Visas
1. *Le lion* is *le mâle,* and *la lionne* is *la femelle.* (Her roar does not have a nasal sound.)
A Tame Saying Featuring *le Lion*
a. se tailler la part du lion- to get the lion's share (Thus making it 'the king's ransom.')
----

2. *Le tigre* is the tiger. He is attracted to *la tigresse* with her very feminine ending.
3. *Le léopard* is the leopard. (An accent mark reveals the difference in one spot.)
4. *Le jaguar* is the jaguar. (Both the cat and the car have a sleek body and a powerful motion.)
5. *La hyène*- the hyena can be heard laughing hysterically. (Not even its <u>h</u> is silent.)
6. *Le cougouar/le couguar*- the cougar, *la panthère*- the panther and *le puma*- the puma are listed in <u>the Guinness Book of Records</u> as the animal with the most names. (If you have seen one, you've seen 'em maul.')
7. *La girafe* is the giraffe. (Except for the extra <u>f</u> in English, the two words 'are neck and neck.')
8. *La gazelle* is the gazelle; *l'antilope* is the antelope. (They're at home where 'the buffalo roam.')
9. *Le lama* is the llama. This beast of burden is often seen carrying a backpack. (Although there are no dallying llamas in South America, there is a Dalai Lama in Tibet.)
10. *Le chameau*- the camel's identity includes an <u>h</u> for hump. This animal enjoys drinking *eau* found at the end of its name.
11. *Le rhinocéros*- the rhinoceros has 'a sharp horn' over the <u>e</u>. (Its diminutive name is "rhino," but a diminutive form of the animal does not exist.)
12. *L'éléphant*- the elephant is used as a means of transportation and entertainment. (Yet, it is always ready 'to work for peanuts.')
13. *Le zèbre* is the zebra. (This member of the horse family shuns the gray mare and prefers things in 'black and white.')
----

14. *Le singe* is the monkey. (His 'swinging business' has many branches.) ***Le grand singe*, the ape, is a synonym for *le gorille*. Through the evolution of language, this beast has changed only one letter.** (It 'hung on to' everything else.) ***L'orangutan* is the orangutan.** (The family members have reddish-brown (orange) hair.)
An Idiom That Shows off *le Singe*
a. faire le singe- to monkey around (Given enough rope, someone might 'go bananas.')
----

15. *Le kangourou* **is the kangaroo. The French refer to a Snuggly (a baby carrier) as** *une poche kangourou.* (Should they be credited with having an 'aboriginal' idea?)

16. *Le koala-* **the koala is a marsupial and is not a member of the bear family.** (The female from Down Under is 'up front' about showing off her pouch.)

A note: Except for *le chameau* **and** *le singe,* **the French and English animal names listed in this category share a very strong resemblance.**

Les Mammifères Aquatiques - Aquatic Mammals

Warm Blooded Creatures That Thrive in Cold Water
1. *La baleine* **is the whale.**
An Expression with 'a Whale Sighting'
a. rire comme une baleine- to laugh hysterically (Or to have tons of fun.)

----

2. *Le dauphin* **is the dolphin. The French word also applies to the king's oldest son.** (One entertains an audience by jumping into the air; the other by reigning as an heir.)
3. *L'hippopotame-* **the hippopotamus, a massive river-land animal, has a cute sounding French label.** (Tame in its name is another mismatch.)
4. *Le lamantin* **is the manatee/the sea cow.** (Shallow water is 'the Habitat for Hugh Manatee.')
5. *La loutre de mer-* **the sea otter has the densest coat of fur of any animal.** (Is there any creature hotter than the otter?)
6. *Le marsouin-* **the porpoise is more difficult to train than** *le dauphin.* (Entertaining is rarely the purpose of the porpoise.)
7. *Le morse* **is the walrus.** (To verify that its name comes from 'whale-horse,' you could change the first letter or use Morse code.)
8. *L'ours polaire* **is the polar bear.** (At home in the Arctic Region, they are 'just chillin.')
9. *Le phoque* **is the seal.** (Beware of letting the incorrect pronunciation slip!)

Pick of the 'Letter'- Circle the letters of the answers that match the animals described.
1. Cet animal fort se voit aux fermes aussi bien qu'aux spectacles en Espagne. C'est ___.
a. un écureuil   b. un élan   c. un tamia   d. un taureau
2. On trouve cet animal divertissant dans un jardin zoologique ou à un cirque. Il n'est pas amusant de le rencontrer dans la forêt. C'est ___.
a. un ours   b. une truie   c. une brebis   d. un lièvre
3. Le zèbre est de la même famille que ___.
a. la hyène   b. le cheval   c. le mouton   d. le kangourou
4. Nous considérons cet animal aquatique être le plus intelligent des mammifères. C'est ___.
a. le dauphin   b. l'ours polaire   c. l'âne   d. le daim
5. Cet animal noir aime nager, mais si on lui donne du poisson à manger, il est content de rester par terre. C'est ___.
a. une panthère   b. un phoque   c. une mouffette   d. une chauve-souris
6. Le cougouar et la panthère sont de la même famille que ___.
a. la baleine   b. la girafe   c. le puma   d. la gazelle

7. Aux climats chauds, on monte à cet animal et l'utilise pour porter des choses. C'est ___.

a. une chèvre   b. une biche   c. une loutre de mer   d. un chameau

8. Cet animal énorme se trouve dans un fleuve boueux et sur la terre sèche. C'est ___.

a. un gorille   b. un rhinocéros   c. un hippopotame   d. un lamantin

9. En voyageant en Australie, les gens voient ce marsupial dans la campagne. C'est ___.

a. un raton-laveur   b. un koala   c. un marsouin   d. un lama

10. Cet animal agile est très intelligent et facile à apprendre. C'est ___.

a. un morse   b. un rongeur   c. un éléphant   d. un singe

LES OISEAUX – Birds

Because they can be found on a swing, on a farm, on exhibit or on their own, the best locale to get 'a bird's eye view' of them is in their typical domains. (That is better than having them drop in unexpectedly or, worse yet, 'leave a calling card.')

La Volaille et Les Oiseaux Non Comestibles - Poultry and Nonedible Birds

Fowl and nonaquatic birds are obviously not 'of the same feather.' However, those that share a country home may flock together.

'The Pecking Order'

1. *Le poulet, la poule, le coq, le canard, le dindon, le faisan* and *l'oie* have waddled and perched throughout the book. Before meeting their demise, they are entitled to 'last writes.'

a. ma poule- my pet (Being hand-picked trumps being hen-pecked.)

b. donner la chair de poule à quelqu'un- to give someone goose bumps: The French version is "to give someone hen's flesh." (It could 'come up in conversation.')

c. passer du coq à l'âne- to jump from one subject to another (This idiom applies when neither the tales nor the tails have anything in common.)

Birds Not Invited to Dinner

1. *L'aigle* (m.) is the eagle. This national symbol 'keeps its eye on' American currency.

2. *L'alouette* (f.) is the lark as well as the subject of a popular French children's song that tells how this bird is deplumed. (Nevertheless, judging by its popularity in cheese departments, *l'alouette* has managed 'to feather its nest.')

3. *L'autruche* (f.)- the ostrich is the largest species of bird. (It lays its egg at the beginning of the English noun.)

497

L'Autruche Sticks Its Neck out for This Saying
a. faire l'autruche- to bury one's head in the sand (A suitable gesture if one 'has made waves.')

---

4. *Le coucou* **is the cuckoo. As 'crazy' as it may seem, the females identify themselves by using the** *coucou* **sound to attract males.** (Their biological 'clocks' can be heard ticking.)

5. *La colombe* **is the dove.** (Are the words "lovey dovey" together because of the rhyming sound or the flutter?)

6. *Le corbeau/la corneille* **is the crow.** (The gender can be established 'as the crow flies.')

7. *Le hibou/la chouette* **is the owl. The male has ear tufts to help him decipher the aspirated h. The female is "the little cabbage."** (They are listed separately in 'Who's Hoo.')

8. *La hirondelle-* **the swallow is adept at locating and eating insects while it is in the air.** (With no 'down time,' the swallow swallows quickly and 'eats on the fly.')

9. *Le kiwi-* **the kiwi, a flightless bird found in New Zealand, is an endangered species.** (It could be leaving after all.)

10. *Le merle* **is the blackbird.** (Four and twenty were baked in a pie for the king who did not want 'to eat crow.'

11. *L'oiseau-mouche-* **the hummingbird is the only one in its class that can fly backwards.** (We don't know the reason because 'it's not singing.')

12. *Le paon* **is the peacock** (This bird is so proud that it can make anyone 'a fan' instantly.)

13. *Le perroquet* **is the parrot. Colorful in appearance and sometimes in its language,** *le perroquet* **is similar to** *la perruche-* **the parakeet.**

14. *Le pic-* **the woodpecker drills on trees to extract food.** (It just needs little 'bits.')

15. *Le pigeon* **is the pigeon. Nothing is added to either spelling.** (However, something could possibly be 'dropped.')

16. *Le rossignol* **is the nightingale.** (It is seen both on tree branches and on ski slopes.)

17. *Le rouge-gorge* **is the robin red breast.** (The French variety has only a painted throat while the English one is more revealing.)

18. *Le toucan-* **the toucan is a brightly colored, tropical bird with a very large 'bill.'** (It needs to find a mate so that the 'tou-can' share expenses.)

Species That Do Not Eat like Birds
1. *Le faucon-* **the falcon/the hawk is known for its visual acuity.** (If looks could kill, ...)

2. *Le vautour-* **the vulture devours the carcasses of wounded and dead animals.** (And therefore, it cannot be classified as 'a picky eater.')

Les Oiseaux Aquatiques - Aquatic Birds

Those Made to Wade
1. *L'aigrette* **(f.)- the egret is a member of the heron family. When it was popular to adorn hats with their white feathers, these wading birds were hunted relentlessly.** (The herons still 'harbor their egrets.')

2. *La cigogne-* **the stork is fabled to carry newborns into the world.** (Since this bird is mute, the only proof is its very large 'bill.')

3. *Le cygne*- the swan belongs to the same family as ducks and geese but has a different *nom de plume.*

4. *Le flamant rose* is the flamingo. Those viewing these pink, spindly-legged birds are asked not to feed them. (Somehow they manage 'to support themselves.')

5. *La grue*- the crane is known 'to whoop it up' with its courting dances. (Not many maneuvers are beyond the reach of cranes.)

6. *Le manchot* is the penguin. (Strutting in its permanent tuxedo, this bird puts on a one 'man-chot' 'to break the ice.')

7. *La mouette*- the seagull spreads its wings over water. (While a 'ba-gle' 'wings its spreads' over coffee.)

8. *Le sterne/la hirondelle de mer* is the tern. (The translation for this migratory bird 'can go either way.' A double 'tern' is allowed.)

'Calling All Birds'- Pluck the names from the following list 'to feather the empty nests.'
l'aigle, l'aigrette, l'autruche, la colombe, le coucou, le cygne, le faisan, le faucon, la grue, le hibou, la hirondelle, l'oiseau-mouche, le manchot, le merle, la mouette, le paon, le perroquet, le pic, le toucan, le vautour

1. L'oiseau sage qu'on voit la nuit est _____.
2. Le seul oiseau qui peut voler en arrière est _____.
3. Un oiseau qu'on voit à la plage ou au-dessus de la mer est _____.
4. L'oiseau qui mange les animaux morts ou blessés est _____.
5. L'oiseau blanc et élégant qui nage dans les lacs est _____.
6. L'oiseau chauve qu'on trouve sur les billets américains est _____.
7. Un oiseau noir qu'on voit partout est _____.
8. L'oiseau qui fait le même son que son nom est _____.
9. L'oiseau blanc associé avec l'amour est _____.
10. L'oiseau qui peut voir **sa proie (its prey)** de très lointain est _____.
11. L'oiseau aux belles plumes dans sa queue est _____.
12. Le plus grand de tous les oiseaux est _____.
13. L'oiseau qui trouve sa nourriture tout en volant est _____.
14. L'oiseau dont les plumes décoraient les chapeaux est _____.
15. L'oiseau noir et blanc qui habite dans les climats très froids est _____.
16. L'oiseau qui fait les trous dans les arbres pour chercher la nourriture est _____.
17. Un oiseau chassé et servi dans des restaurants chers est _____.
18. L'oiseau parlant qu'on associe avec les pirates est _____.
19. L'oiseau qui **tend (stretches)** son cou et danse exotiquement est _____.
20. Un oiseau aux couleurs brillantes et un long bec est _____.

LES REPTILES et LES AMPHIBIES - Reptiles and Amphibians

While *les serpents* have slithered around and 'wound up' on several pages, *les grenouilles* have leaped throughout the chapters and onto French menus. Some of the dangerous but hospitable reptiles would be delighted 'to take you in.' The more sociable amphibians would welcome you as well, providing that you 'catch them at home.'

A Clarification
Amphibians are water breathing newborns with gills which metamorphose into air breathing adults with lungs. (It is so convenient that these babies can 'change' themselves.) **Reptiles, on the other 'tail,' come into the world with a formed set of lungs.**

Amphibians with a *Pied-à-Terre* and 'a Pad' on the Water
1. *Le crapaud*- the toad has shorter legs than *la grenouille*. (That possibly explains why the game 'leap toad' is not popular.)
2. *Le triton*- the newt, a member of *la famille salamandre*, can regenerate its body parts. (Its life insurance policy is always stamped 're-newt.')
3. *Le têtard*- the tadpole becomes *une grenouille* or *un crapaud*. (Toad is haphazardly formed in-inside the word tadpole.)

Warming Up To Cold-Blooded Reptiles

1. *L'alligator* is the alligator. The only difference between the two nouns is the definite article. (The prices of alligator shoes and purses definitely make those articles significant.)
2. *Le crocodile*- the crocodile gives up nothing as it transforms from French into English. (But French ones offer 'a dile' (a deal) at the end.)
3. *Le lézard*- the French lizard molts its i for an é. The family, which includes dragons, geckos, iguanas- *les iguanes* and chameleons- *les caméléons*, is seen all over the globe. (Chameleons are known for 'changing their spots.')
4. *La tortue*- the tortoise is a land-dwelling, slow moving reptile. (However, the race was not won by a 'hare.') ***La tortue de mer*- the turtle lives by the water.** (But it goes inside frequently.)

LES POISSONS et LES CRÉATURES DE MER - Fish and Sea Creatures

A healthy portion of fish including *le thon*, *le saumon*, *la truite* and *le flétan* has been offered on lines throughout the book. Crustaceans have also been served on many occasions. This section looks below the surface at fish and sea creatures which are, for the most part, inedible.

Tackling the Fish and Their Associates

1. *L'anguille* (f.) is the eel. The English word resembles this fish's snakelike movement.

An Idiom that *l'Anguille* Slips into

a. *Il y a une anguille sous la roche.* > There's something going on. (The culprit might try 'to wiggle his way out of it.')

A note: *L'anguille* has not been "black listed" as inedible for Oriental cuisine.

2. *La bernache*- the barnacle forms 'strong attachments' to anything near it while pumping its poisonous tentacles to bring in clients.

3. *L'espadon* (m.)- the swordfish, a member of the marlin family, is hooked and cooked. (Most fishermen who 'cast for' marlin and sailfish put their trophy above a mantle.)

4. *L'étoile de mer*- the starfish has two stomachs, enabling it to ingest food much larger than itself. (Fish and mollusks try to avoid "the star of the sea" on 'opening nights.')

5. *L'hippocampe* (m.) is the sea-horse. When it is threatened by prey and during courtship, this creature camouflages itself by changing hues. (That's 'a horse of a different color.')

6. *La méduse*- the jellyfish is named for the marine goddess whose tendrils were snakes. (If she were having 'a bad hair day,' her locks looked 'ratty.')

7. *L'oursin* (m.) is the sea urchin. Only one letter differentiates *l'oursin* from *l'ourson*- the bear cub. (With outer spines to protect itself, *l'oursin* does better on its own than the 'pandered' bear.)

8. *La raie*- the ray flaunts 'extended' privileges. *La pastenague*- the sting ray houses venomous barbs in its tail. (Faites attention au poison dans ce poisson!)

9. *Le requin*- the shark is the largest and most ominous fish. It lives way below sea level. (But it instictively knows 'to rise' if guests come by.)

10. *Le vairon*- the minnow is the largest family of fish found in North America. One member is *le poisson rouge*- the goldfish. (Not everyone learns how to distinguish colors in 'schools.' A group of these fish is "a troubling," and therein lays the problem.)

A note: Most minnows are the perfect size for bait, but *la carpe*- the carp and the catfish (with no French translation) are edible. (Do you need a 'purr-mit' to catch catfish?)

Weighing In Creatures with 'Scales'- Circle the letters of the correct responses to complete the descriptions.

1. L'amphibie qui ressemble à une grenouille aux jambes plus courtes est _____.
a. la tortue de mer   b. la méduse   c. le crapaud   d. le vairon

2. Une créature de mer qui change sa couleur quand il/elle est près d'une proie est _____.
a. l'espadon   b. l'hippocampe   c. l'étoile de mer   d. l'oursin

3. La créature de mer au poison dans sa queue est _____.
a. le requin   b. le poisson rouge   c. l'anguille   d. la pastenague

4. Les reptiles aux mâchoires très fortes sont ____.

a. les iguanes et les caméléons   b. les alligators et les crocodiles   c. les raies et les têtards

d. les serpents et les lézards

5. ____ peut régénérer les parties de son corps.

a. Le triton   b. Le dragon   c. L'oursin   d. L'hippocampe

6. Le plus grand poisson du monde est ____.

a. le vairon   b. le flétan   c. le requin   d. l'espadon

7. Une créature de mer aux deux estomacs est ____.

a. la méduse   b. l'anguille   c. la bernache   d. l'étoile de mer

8. ____ devient une grenouille ou un crapaud.

a. une pastenague   b. une carpe   c. un têtard   d. un lézard

---

LES INSECTES - Insects

Except for *le papillon* (the butterfly), insects do not have 'widespread' popularity. In fact, they are viewed as the lowest species. Yet, insects should not be considered paupers. They have the means to travel anywhere they want, eat whatever they want and stay wherever they want.

An important note: *L'insecte* is the generic term for **the bug.** (Exterminating the last <u>e</u> will leave 'insect-inside.')

'Frequent Flyers'

1. *L'abeille* (f.) is the bee. The first two letters of the French noun are also its translation. (That makes it 'a free bee' and 'a buzzword.')

2. *La demoiselle* is the dragonfly/the damselfly. (Though swatted, she still remains 'a near miss.')

3. *Le frelon*- the hornet and *la guêpe*- the wasp belong to the same family. They usually keep to themselves unless someone knocks on their nests and invites them out. (They enjoy the movies. Their favorite 'pic-ture' show is *The Sting*.)

4. *Le lampyre/la luciole* are interchangeable terms for the firefly/the lightning bug. (The nouns introduce themselves in a 'flashy' manner.)

5. *La mante (religieuse)* is the (praying) mantis. Being predatory, these insects are also preying mantises. (They eventually 'get what is coming to them.')

6. *La mouche*- the fly 'earned its wings' as part of both *le bateau-mouche* and *l'oiseau-mouche*. (So, it is not in danger of a confrontation with the SWAT team.) *La mouche du vinaigre* is the fruit fly. (The French 'soured' on this insect long ago.)

A 'Catchy' Fly Expression

a. *Quelle mouche t'a piqué?* > **What has gotten into you?** (It is obviously something that the person couldn't just 'brush off.')

---

7. *Le moustique* is the mosquito. (This is likely the first insect people want to 'scratch off the list.')
8. *Le papillon*- the butterfly reigns as the handsomest specimen of the insect kingdom. (Perhaps that explains why one is referred to as "a monarch.") ***Le papillon de nuit* is the moth. *La mite* is the clothes moth.** (These 'fly-by-nights' are seen near light fixtures but not near light fabrics.)
<u>A note</u>: *Un papillon* **is slang for** *une contravention*- **a parking ticket.** (Collecting them is not a fun hobby.)

'Down to Earth' Insects
1. *L'araignée* (f.) is the spider. The web mistress weaves *une toile d'araignée*- **a spider web and deposits her eggs there.** (After the death of daddy long legs, the mother becomes 'a black widow.')
La tarentule- **the tarantula is the hairy member of the spider family.**
2. *La chenille*- the caterpillar is the larva of a moth or butterfly. *Une autochenille* is a Caterpillar Tractor. (The insect's development is arrested at a crawl, but the farm vehicle 'plows on ahead.')
3. *La cigale*- the cicada, *le criquet*- the locust, *le grillon*- the cricket and *la sauterelle*- the grass- hopper could all show up as unwanted guests at a lawn party. (*La <u>sauterelle</u>* would 'jump at the opportunity.')
<u>A helpful hint</u>: **To distinguish** *le criquet* **from** *le grillon*, **visualize the double <u>ll</u> in** *grillon* **as that insect's legs rubbing together to produce the chirping noise.**

---

4. *Le cafard* is the cockroach. (Awards should be given for capturing this most unwanted insect.)

Le Cafard Can Be Seen in This 'Crack'
a. avoir le cafard- to be feeling down/to have the blues. (The problem might be solved if the indi- vidual were granted one 'squish.')

---

5. *La fourmi* is the ant. (Maybe the carpenter ant, at least, has a 'constructive' purpose.)
6. *Le pou*- the louse is one of *les poux*- the lice. (The <u>x</u> is an attempt to eradicate them.) -
7. *La puce* is the flea. (It thrives on its host's blood and 'sticks to business.')

La Puce 'Markets Itself' with the Following Phrases
a. ma puce- my dear (This is a term of affection, not infection.)
b. mettre la puce à l'oreille- to get someone thinking: The French idiom parallels "to put a bee in one's bonnet." (If one is not 'bugged,' the idea might be well received.)

---

8. *Les scarabées*- the beetles are the insects with the largest number of known species. (Few of the hard shelled varieties fly; most remain on 'crawl-by.') *La coccinelle*- **the ladybug is a member of the Beetles Band.** (She shows her feminine side with *elle*.)
<u>Interesting notes</u>: **Although** *le scarabée* **ends with a double <u>e</u>, it is masculine. The unrelated bee 'bee-gins' the English translation, but it is 'bée-hind' in the French word.**

---

9. *Le termite*- the termite feeds on wood. (One of them was brazen enough to crawl into a pub and ask, "Is the 'bar tender' here?")

10. *La tique*- the tick is a parasite that dines at the host's expense. (Who then becomes known as "a lunch tick-et.")

---

11. *Le ver* is the worm. While *le ver de terre* is the earthworm, *le ver luisant* is the glow worm. (*Le vers* by itself is only 'a segment.')

Where the Verbally Versed *Ver* Is Viewed
a. tirer les vers du nez à quelqu'un- to worm information out of someone. The actual meaning is "to pull worms from someone's nose." (The informed person is just not ready 'to blow it.')
A note: *Le ver à soie*- the silkworm is really a moth and not a worm. Its cocoon is used to make silk thread. (Does that 'put a new spin on things'?)

Which Ones Should Be Zapped?- Circle the letter that does not belong in the group.

1. a. le cafard   b. le scarabée   c. le termite   d. le papillon
2. a. la puce   b. la cigale   c. le criquet   d. la sauterelle
3. a. la guêpe   b. l'abeille   c. le vers luisant   d. le frelon
4. a. la demoiselle   b. le lampyre   c. la coccinelle   d. la luciole
5. a. l'araignée   b. la tarentule   c. le cafard   d. la mouche du vinaigre
6. a. la mite   b. la chenille   c. le vers à soie   d. la mante religieuse
7. a. la tique   b. la mouche   c. la puce   d. le pou
8. a. le termite   b. le moustique   c. l'abeille   d. la guêpe

Un bateau-mouche sur la Seine (Paris)

UNE REVUE - A Review

Le Passé Simple, Les Mammifères, Les Oiseaux, Les Reptiles et Les Amphibies, Les Poissons et Les Créatures de Mer, Les Insectes

'His-story' and Her Story- Circle the letters of the best responses to complete the sentences.
1. Les hommes et les femmes de caverne ____.
a. allèrent au marché troquer leurs animaux   b. vécurent à une vieillesse
c. chassèrent et dessinèrent sur les murs   d. élevèrent leurs fils pour devenir médecins
2. Pendant l'époque de Jules César, les romains ____.
a. lurent des nouvelles d'Antoine et Cléopâtre   b. se rassemblèrent pour discuter la philosophie
c. montèrent **en char-m. (chariot)** pour tuer les piétons   d. furent en vacances après le 15 mars
3. Comme on n'eut pas de technologie médicale, des gens ____.
a. moururent des maladies qui n'existent plus   b. fondèrent des hôpitaux près des fermes
c. furent guéris le siècle suivant   d. prirent leurs ordonnances aux laboratoires lointain
4. Quand Colombe arriva en Amérique du Nord, les indiens ____.
a. l'accueillirent en parlant anglais   b. lui apprirent à faire un feu   c. furent déjà là
d. célébrèrent le jour de grâces avec lui et son équipage
5. On qui assista aux bals à la fin du dix-septième siècle ____.
a. connut tout le monde qui habita dans le palais   b. voulut cambrioler les meubles
d. mangea avant d'aller à la soirée   d. sut danser le menuet
6. Après l'invention de l'électricité, les gens ____.
a. ne lavèrent jamais leurs vêtements   b. n'ont pas dû de brûler des bougies la nuit
c. purent lire mieux sans lunettes   d. envoyèrent des cadeaux à Thomàs Edison

---

Remembering Your 'Past-Words'- Write the underlined verbs *au passé simple*.
1. Les esclaves worked. _____ .
2. Jeanne d'Arc led. _____ .
3. La guerre began. _____ .
4. Les Grecs believed. _____ .
5. Baudelaire drank. _____ .
6. Les gens learned. _____ .
7. Descartes said. _____ .
8. Les rois were born. _____ .
9. Les étrangers came. _____ .
10. Les coureurs hurried. _____ .
11. Le Louvre was built. _____ .
12. Les lois were written. _____ .

Famous 'Name Us' Characters - Match the letters of the nouns to the well-known creatures.

____ 1. Kermit	A. un élan
____ 2. Bambi	B. une mouffette
____ 3. Porky	C. un dauphin
____ 4. Dumbo	D. un singe
____ 5. Penny	E. un écureuil
____ 6. Smokey	F. un alligator
____ 7. Pepé Le Pew	G. une girafe
____ 8. Black Beauty	H. une biche
____ 9. Tony	I. un bœuf
____ 10. Donald	J. un cheval
____ 11. Flipper	K. un lapin
____ 12. Polly	L. un tamia
____ 13. Geoffrey	M. un éléphant
____ 14. Moby Dick	N. une marmotte d'Amérique
____ 15. Rocky	O. un tigre
____ 16. Wanda	P. un ver de terre
____ 17. Babe	Q. une grenouille
____ 18. Mickey	R. un chat
____ 19. Punxatawney Phil	S. un grillon
____ 20. Bullwinkle	T. un ours
____ 21. Peter Cottontail	U. un chien
____ 22. Curious George	V. un canard
____ 23. Felix	W. une brébis
____ 24. Alvin	X. une souris
____ 25. Lacoste	Y. un cochon
____ 26. Jiminy	Z. une baleine
____ 27. King Kong	AA. un poisson
____ 28. Lassie	BB. un perroquet
____ 29. Dolly	CC. un gorille
____ 30. Lowly	DD. une poule

How Do These Sound to You? - Label the statements *vrai* or *faux*.

_____ 1. Le caniche est un type de chat.

_____ 2. Le cheval est le mâle, et la jument est la femelle de la même famille.

_____ 3. L'âne et le bouc sont les synonymes.

_____ 4. La brebis et le mouton sont les parents de l'agneau.

_____ 5. La cochonne est la mère du porcelet.

_____ 6. L'écureuil et le tamia ne se ressemblent pas.

_____ 7. Le castor a un parfum spécial.

_____ 8. La chauve-souris et le raton laveur sortent le soir.

_____ 9. Le tigre et le zèbre sont rayés.

_____ 10. Le gorille et le grand singe sont des synonymes.

_____ 11. Il n'y a pas de différence entre le dauphin et le marsouin.

_____ 12. Le requin est le plus grand mammifère.
_____ 13. L'ours polaire et le manchot habitent où il fait très froid.
_____ 14. La cigogne le plus grand oiseau.
_____ 15. Le corbeau/la corneille et le merle sont des oiseaux noirs.
_____ 16. La colombe **frime (shows off)** ses plumes.
_____ 17. Le faucon et le vautour mangent d'autres oiseaux.
_____ 18. La mouette et le sterne se trouvent près de la mer.
_____ 19. L'aigrette, le cygne et le flamant rose préfèrent rester dans les eaux profondes.
_____ 20. L'alouette et le rossignol ne chantent pas.
_____ 21. Le têtard devient un crapaud ou une grenouille.
_____ 22. L'hippocampe et la méduse nagent verticalement.
_____ 23. Le poisson rouge est un membre de la famille de vairon.
_____ 24. Le frelon et la guêpe font le miel.
_____ 25. Les fourmis et les vers ne peuvent pas voler.

When Animals Have Their Say- Circle the letters of the idioms that complete or correspond to the scenarios.

1. À notre avis, ceux qui font mal aux animaux domestiques devraient ____.
a. faire le singe   b. faire l'autruche   c. passer du coq à l'âne   d. être notre puce

2. L'entraîneur strict ne changera rien dans son horaire.
a. C'est une période de vaches maigres pour nous.   b. Ce type est un vrai rat.
c. Il est très á cheval sur le règlement.   d. C'est un loup déguisé en agneau.

3. Quand le renard entre dans sa basse-cour, le fermier est si fâché qu'il ____.
a. a un chat dans la gorge   b. se taille la part du lion   c. rit comme une baleine   d. devient chèvre

4. Les animaux timides dans les bois doivent faire attention aux animaux sauvages qui ____.
a. ont d'autres chats à fouetter   b. les ont à l'œil
c. mettent la puce à leurs oreilles   d. reviennent à leurs moutons

5. Ses amis remarquent que Tweety a le cafard, et ils lui demandent "___?"
a. Quelle mouche t'a piquée?   b. Est-il entre chien et loup?
c. Pouvons-nous te faire un coup de vache?   d. Pourquoi n'es-tu plus notre poule?

6. Le flamant rose et le cygne ne sont pas jaloux du paon, mais ils se demandent, "Pourquoi est-ce qu'on ne dit jamais _____?"
a. que nous sommes des moutons   b. qu'il y a une anguille sous la roche
c. que nous avons du chien   d. que nous prenons la chèvre

7. La biche et le cerf rusés rient des chasseurs qui pensent à les attraper cet automne. Ils leur donnent ces conseils:
a. "Quand le chat n'est pas là, les souris dansent."
b. "Vous ne pouvez pas tirer les vers de nos nez."
c. "Vous nous donnez la chair de poule."
d. "Ne vendez pas la peau de l'ours avant de l'avoir tué."

_____

LE PRÉSENT DU SUBJONCTIF - THE PRESENT SUBJUNCTIVE

Le subjonctif typically expresses uncertainty and emotion. It is used far more often in French than in English. (Even though you may wish that it <u>were</u> not so.)
The following conjugation will give you a sense of the present subjunctive's mood.

Sentir - To Feel, To Perceive, To Smell

<u>Singulier</u>	<u>Pluriel</u>
je sent<u>e</u>- I feel, perceive, smell	nous sent<u>ions</u>- we feel, perceive, smell
I do feel, perceive, smell	we do feel, perceive, smell
I am feeling, perceiving, smelling	we are feeling, perceiving, smelling
tu sent<u>es</u>- you feel, perceive, smell	vous sent<u>iez</u>- you feel, perceive, smell
you do feel, perceive, smell	you do feel, perceive, smell
you are feeling, perceiving, smelling	you are feeling, perceiving, smelling
il/elle sent<u>e</u>- he/she/it feels, perceives, smells	ils/elles sent<u>ent</u>- they feel, perceive, smell
he/she/it does feel, perceive, smell	they do feel, perceive, smell
he/she/it is feeling, perceiving, smelling	they are feeling, perceiving, smelling

----

Getting into the Mood

1. One subjunctive stem is the third person plural present tense form of the verb. After -<u>ent</u> is deleted, the endings -<u>e</u>, -<u>es</u>, -<u>e</u>, -<u>ions</u>, -<u>iez</u> and -<u>ent</u> are added. Those attachments fit perfectly on all regular -<u>er</u>, -<u>ir</u> and -<u>re</u> verbs.
1a. Singular and third person plural subjunctive endings mirror those of regular present tense -<u>er</u> verbs. The *nous* and *vous* forms have imperfect endings. (The 'boots' are back in style.)
Ex. Il est bon que le psychiatre arrive à ses rendez-vous de bonne heure. > It is good that the psychiatrist arrives at his appointments early. (He can check to see if his patients 'are all there.')
Ex. Il est très important que nous practiquions le français autant que possible. > It is very important that we practice French as much as possible. (The advantages speak for themselves.)
1b. An alternate route to the subjunctive root is via the present participle. The -<u>ant</u> is removed and regular subjunctive endings are added. But #1 offers better access to -<u>cer</u> and -<u>ger</u> verbs.
2. The third person plural and the present participle are home bases for many irregular verbs and their families including *conduire, connaître, courir, couvrir, dire, dormir, écrire, lire, mettre, offrir, ouvrir, partir, rire, sentir, servir, sortir, traduire* and *vivre*.
Ex. Il est dommage que les cambrioleurs courent plus vite que cet agent de police. > It is a pity that the robbers run faster than that policeman. (The thieves must be as happy 'as all get-out.')
Ex. Il faut que je couvre les fenêtres avant que l'ouragan arrive. > It is necessary/I have to cover the windows before the hurricane comes. (The thought makes most people 'shutter.')
3. Four factors are generally responsible for putting the subjunctive 'in its mood.'
3a. an independent/main clause and a dependent/subordinate clause in the same sentence
3b. *que* (and occasionally other relative pronouns) joining the clauses
3c. a different subject in each clause
3d. a lead-in phrase that is expressed in the main/independent clause. These variables 'set off' *le subjonctif* **and thereby enable 'a mood swing.'**
Ex. Il est étonnant qu'elle maigrisse sans suivre un régime. > It is amazing that she is losing weight

without being on a diet. (Maybe it just 'comes off' like that.)

The catalyst in the preceding sentence is the impersonal expression *Il est étonnant.*

4. *Le présent du subjonctif* expresses both present and future actions.

Ex. Il est douteux que notre avion décolle demain. > It is doubtful that our plane will take off tomorrow. (Though it is certain that the plans are 'up in the air.')

5. The subjunctive is often used in French where the English translation includes an infinitive.

Ex. **Ce machiste-là** pense qu'il est bon que son épouse travaille mi-temps. > **That male chauvinist** thinks that it is good for his wife to work/that his wife work part-time. (As long as she is at home for 'the better half.')

Impersonal Expressions of Opinion

Verbs are *au subjonctif* following impersonal expressions of opinion. They consist of *Il est* + an adjective or *Il* + a verb in the third person singular.

1. Il est amusant- It is amusing	**14. Il est intéressant- It is interesting**
2. Il est bon- It is good	**15. Il est ironique- It is ironic**
3. Il est convenable- It is fitting	**16. Il est juste- It is juste**
4. Il est dommage- It is a pity/It is too bad	**17. Il est mauvais- It is bad**
5. Il est douteux- It is doubtful	**18. Il est nécessaire- It is necessary**
6. Il est essentiel- It is essential	**19. Il est normal- It is normal**
7. Il est étonnant- It is amazing	**20. Il est possible- It is possible**
8. Il est gentil/agréable- It is nice/It is kind	**21. Il est préférable- It is preferable**
9. Il est impératif- It is imperative	**22. Il est surprenant- It is surprising**
10. Il est important- It is important	**23. Il est temps- It is time**
11. Il est impossible- It is impossible	**24. Il est triste- It is sad**
12. Il est indispensable- It is indispensable	**25. Il est urgent- It is urgent**
13. Il est injuste- It is unfair	**26. Il est utile- It is useful**

----

1. Il convient- It is fitting (proper)	**4. Il semble- It seems**
2. Il faut- It is necessary	**5. Il suffit- It is enough**
3. Il se peut- It is possible	**6. Il vaut mieux- It is better**

A note: When *il semble* includes an indirect object, the verb following it is in the indicative.

Ex. Il nous semble que notre voisine hostile grossit. > It seems to us that our unfriendly neighbor is gaining weight. (Maybe they would just like 'to see less of her.')

Getting to Know Impersonal Expressions- **Fill in the blanks with correct responses.**

1. The antonym of *Il est bon* is _____.

2. The synonymn for *Il est essentiel* is _____.

3. A phrase very close in meaning to *Il est étonnant* is _____.

4. The synonym for *Il est impératif* is _____.

5. The antonym of *Il est impossible* is _____.

6. The antonym of *Il est injuste* is _____.

7. The synonym for *Il est préférable* is _____.

8. The synonym for *Il est possible* is _____.

9. The synonym for *C'est assez* is _____.

10. The synonym for *Il paraît* is _____.

A bonus: A synonym for *Il n'est pas sûr* is _____.

Meeting the Subjunctive on Impersonal Terms- Fill in the blanks with the correct forms of the verbs in parentheses.

A note: The irregular verbs below are conjugated regularly in the subjunctive.

1. (louer) Il est bon que la famille Décidons _____ la maison avant de l'acheter.

2. (choisir) Il vaut mieux que ma petite ne _____ pas les vêtements qu'elle porte à l'école.

3. (perdre) Il semble que Piaget et moi _____ notre temps.

4. (offrir) Il convient que Mme LeVerre _____ à boire à ses invités.

5. (mentir) Il est triste que ses gosses _____ fréquemment.

6. (partir) Il est dommage que vous deux _____ bientôt.

7. (dormir) Il est normal qu'un nouveau-né _____ presque toute la journée.

8. (mettre) Il est nécessaire qu'on le _____ dans le four.

9. (conduire) Il est impératif qu'Otto et moi _____ soigneusement.

10. (traduire) Il est intéressant que des gens bilingues ne _____ pas.

11. (connaître) Il est ironique que je _____ Marc aussi.

12. (dire) Il se peut que Mlle Cachepeu me _____ plus tard.

13. (se rencontrer) Il est agréable que vous _____ cet après-midi.

14. (s'entendre) Il est surprenant que mon chien et mon chat _____ bien.

More Contributions to the Subjunctive Cause

1. Verbs and expressions of volition including *aimer mieux, désirer, préférer, souhaiter, vouloir* and *vouloir bien* are followed by the subjunctive mood.

Ex. Le patron de Faye Tout voudrait qu'elle porte les colis à la poste. Il désire aussi qu'elle y passe prendre son courrier. Enfin, il préfère qu'elle achète des timbres là-bas et pas au bureau de tabac. > Faye Tout's boss wants/would like her to carry parcels to the post office. He also desires/wants her to pick up his mail there. Finally, he prefers that she buy some stamps there and not at the tobacco shop. (Faye will find another "most wanted list" at the post office.)

1a. The above example and its translation reveal a less than perfect fit. In the English version, the boss wants/would like, desires and prefers Faye. Linking the boss and the employee grammatically rather than romantically, the French adjust the sentences to read that he would like, desire and prefer <u>that</u> Faye/she .... (Nothing beats French tailoring!)

Verbs with a Persuasive Tone

1. **commander**- to order
2. **consentir**- to consent
3. **défendre**- to forbid
4. **empêcher**- to prevent
5. **exiger**- to demand

6. **insister**- to insist
7. **interdire**- to forbid
8. **ordonner**- to order
9. **permettre**- to permit

----

1. 'Forceful verbs' push dependent clauses into a subjunctive mood; verbs with a conciliatory tone nudge them into it.

Ex. Les maisons de haute couture exigent que leurs **postulants** remplissent plusieurs formulaires. > The high fashion houses demand that their **applicants** fill out several forms. (Their designers seem most interested in background 'checks' and finger 'prints.')

Ex. Le Général Moteurs insiste que la climatisation dans ses véhicules marche très bien. > General Motors insists that the air-conditioning in his vehicles works very well. (He won't permit 'a dishonorable discharge.')

2. Two verbs listed <u>order</u>, and two <u>forbid</u>. (The subjunctive manages 'to follow' both messages.)

Ex. Ray Compense ordonne que sa fille paresseuse finisse ses devoirs avant de regarder *Glee*. > Ray Compense orders that his lazy daughter finish her homework before watching *Glee*. (Her father has the 'whether' channel turned on.)

A note: The nine verbs on the above list appeared under *À* + a Person + *De* + an Infinitive.

'Reasoning with the Subjunctive'- Translate the following sentences.

1. We want you (*tu*) to succeed. _____.

2. Ms. Allée Vouzen wants the customer to leave right away. _____
_____.

3. Does she want Ron Fler to sleep in the guest room? _____
_____?

4. I would like you (*tu*) to tell me as soon as possible. _____
_____.

5. Bea Shore suggests that you (*vous*) read the letter again before sending it. _____
_____.

6. It is doubtful that we will sell our house this year. _____
_____.

7. It is ironic that Belle Voix's daughter does not sing well. _____
_____.

8. It is surprising that Earl E. Rizer is waking up late. _____
_____.

9. It is not fitting that **the bride (la jeune mariée)** dress in black. _____
_____.

10. Her father forbids her to talk to them. _____
_____.

Avoir et Être au Subjonctif

As you might expect, the subjunctive conjugations of *avoir* and *être* are irregular. Nonetheless, their uses are so commonplace that the forms will soon fit as comfortably as 'those old boots.'

Avoir -To Have

Singular	Plural
j'aie- I have, do have, am having	nous ayons- we have, do have, are having
tu aies- you have, do have, are having	vous ayez- you have, do have, are having
il/elle/on ait- he/she/it/one has, does have, is having	ils/elles aient- they have, do have, are having

----

Être -To Be

Singular	Plural
je sois- I am	nous soyons- we are
tu sois- you are	vous soyez- you are
il/elle/on soit- he/she/it/one is	ils/elles soient- they are

Trying *Avoir* and *Être* On for Size

1. The entire singular and the third person plural subjunctive forms of *avoir* start with <u>ai</u> and share an identical pronunciation. (It's a custom-made boot.)

1a. The third person endings, -<u>ait</u> and -<u>aient,</u> look familiar because they are found in the same locations in both the imperfect and the conditional tenses.

1b. In the *nous* and *vous* forms, a <u>y</u> replaces the <u>i</u>. ('Keep your <u>i</u>s out' for them!)

2. The subjunctive conjugation of *être* also fits into a boot. The *je* and *tu* forms have one sound and one spelling. The entire singular and the third person plural forms are pronounced like *la soie*- the silk. (It provides a very comfortable lining for the footwear.)

2a. Taking after *avoir,* the *nous* and *vous* subjunctive forms of *être* have a <u>y</u>.

3. *Avoir* and *être* are the only verbs with irregular endings *au subjonctif.*

A reminder: The *tu, nous* and *vous* forms of *être* and the *nous* and *vous* forms of *avoir* are also their imperatives. The *tu* form command *aie* becomes a subjunctive *aies.*

Ex. Soyez prêts à utiliser ces formes-ci de nouveau! > Be ready to use these forms again!

'Matching Pairs of 'Boot Verbs''- Put the letters of the dependent clauses beside the numbers of the independent clauses to complete the sentences.

____ 1. Il est très ironique

____ 2. Le général dit qu'il est impératif

____ 3. Rencontrez-nous au restaurant! Nous voudrions bien

____ 4. La courtoisie ne change pas. Il est toujours essentiel

____ 5. Écris-nous! Il est important

A. qu'elles se rencontrent à Paris en juillet.

B. que nous ayons de mauvaises notes.

C. qu'elle ait quinze paires de chaussures.

D. qu'un scolaire à l'étranger **ait la nostalgie (be homesick).**

E. que G.I. Joe suive les ordres.

_____ 6. Nos parents ne permettent pas

_____ 7. Les médecins le considère très
        surprenant

_____ 8. L'adolescente dépendante insiste

_____ 9. Mon couvre-feu est à minuit
        Ma mère commande

_____ 10. Les correspondantes souhaitent

_____ 11. Il est plus pratique et préférable

_____ 12. Quand on passe la douane, il faut

_____ 13. Selon des étudiants qui voyagent
        souvent, il est normal

_____ 14. Puisque que tu es en train de faire
        tes valises, il semble

_____ 15. Le temps passe si vite. Il ne semble
        pas possible

_____ 16. Les agriculteurs pensent qu'il est
        douteux

_____ 17. Mme Souliers en voudrait plus.
        Il ne suffit pas

_____ 18. Le Président de France et son
        épouse voudraient

F. que leur fils soit heureux dans une ville.

G. que nous ayons des nouvelles de toi lorsque
   tu es lointain.

H. que tu ne sois pas prêt à partir.

I. que Germain Vais ait un travail avant de
   déménager à une autre ville.

J. que Jennie Ration et moi ayons cinquante ans.

K. qu'on soit poli.

L. qu'Ann Croyable, dans un état critique, **ait
   bonne mine (looks well).**

M. que les Clinton soient leurs invités d'honneur.

N. que vous **soyez des nôtres (join us).**

O. que je sois chez moi cinq minutes en avance.

P. que ma mère et ma tante aient des jumeaux.

Q. qu'on ait tous les documents dans ses mains.

R. que son petit ami soit avec elle tous les jours.

Knowing the Subjunctive Personally

**Whether feelings are expressed by "emotional" adjectives or via "emotional" verbs, they vent
themselves in subordinate clauses *au subjonctif*. The terms are addressed first one by one and
then by categories.** (Their mood benefits from individual and group therapy.)

Adjectives with Emotional Attachments to the Subjunctive

1. **agacé- annoyed**
2. **content- glad, happy**
3. **désolé- distressed, sorry**
4. **embarrassé- embarrassed**
5. **enchanté- delighted**
6. **énervé- irritated**
7. **ennuyé- annoyed**
8. **étonné- astonished**
9. **fâché- angry**
10. **fier- proud**

11. **flatté- flattered**
12. **furieux- furious**
13. **gêné- bothered**
14. **heureux- happy**
15. **irrité- irritated**
16. **malheureux- unhappy**
17. **mécontent- displeased**
18. **ravi- delighted**
19. **surpris- surprised**
20. **triste- sad**

----

1. Unlike impersonal expressions that exist only in the third person singular, personal expressions can include any conjugated form of *être*.

Ex. Auntie Gravity est extrêmement fière que ses neveux soient astronautes. > Auntie Gravity is extremely proud that her nephews are astronauts. (They may be 'beaming,' too.)

Ex. Les clercs pas motivés sont ravis que leur gérant soit en vacances. > The unmotivated clerks are delighted that their manager is on vacation. (If he knows that little work is being done, he is not that 'far off.')

1a. The impersonal adjectives *étonnant* and *surprenant* placed 'a personal listing' in this directory under *étonné* and *surpris*.

1b. *Agacé, ennuyé, ennuyé, fâché, gêné, irrité* and *mécontent* are classified solely as "emotional" adjectives. (They provide their own 'cross' references.)

<u>**A Display of Emotional Adjectives**</u>- **Complete the following sentences.**
1. Enchanté et _____ sont des synonymes.
2. Deux antonymes d'heureux sont _____ et _____.
3. Ennuyé et _____ sont des synonymes.
4. Deux antonymes de content sont _____ et _____.
5. Deux synonymes d'irrité sont _____ et _____.
6. On qui est très fâché est _____.
7. On qui est très surpris est _____.
8. On qui a honte est _____.
9. On qui regrette quelque chose est _____.
10. Si on fait un compliment sur quelqu'un, celui-ci est _____, _____,
ou _____.

----

2. Where English includes a form of <u>to be</u> + an adjective to express fear or shame, French uses a form of *avoir*. The conjugated forms of *avoir peur, avoir honte* and *avoir crainte*- to be afraid/ to have fear precede dependent/subordinate clauses.

Ex. La mère de Rose n'a pas honte que sa fille rougisse facilement. > Rose's mother is not ashamed that her daughter blushes easily. (But the girl should be used to hearing 'colorful' language.)

2a. Affirmative expressions of fear take *ne* before the verb in a subjunctive/dependent clause. The 'half-negative' does not affect the translation.

Ex. Solly Citude a peur qu'un extraterrestre n'atterrisse dans son jardin de derrière. > Solly Citude is afraid that an extraterrestrial will land in her backyard. (Who knows where that 'comes from'?)

2b. When an expression of fear is negative or interrogative, *ne* is not found in the subjunctive/ dependent clause.

Ex. David ne craint pas que Goliath le tue. > David is not afraid that Goliath will kill him. (Still, the boy does feel tension in his hand.)

3. Verbs showing emotion in front of subjunctive clauses include *se fâcher, regretter, s'étonner, craindre*- to fear and *se réjouir*- to rejoice, to be happy.

Ex. Je regrette que mes parents n'aient pas les moyens de prendre leur retraite. > I am sorry that my parents do not have the means to retire. (It's known as 'the empty nest-egg syndrome.')

Verbal Expressions with Mood Swings

Indicators of the Indicative

1. être sûr(e)(s)- to be sure
2. être certain(e)(s)- to be certain
3. Il est certain- It is certain
4. Il est clair- It is clear
5. Il est évident- It is evident, It is obvious

6. Il est exact- It is exact
7. Il paraît- It appears, It seems
8. Il est probable- It is probable
9. Il est sûr- It is sure
10. Il est vrai- It is true

----

1. The present tense is used after affirmative phrases of certainty and probability.
Ex. Il est vrai qu'un poney reste un poney. > It is true that a pony stays a pony. (Neither the cute animal nor the type of conjugation changes its form.)
1a. If the expressions above are negative or interrogative, doubt or uncertainty is implied, and the verb is *au subjonctif* in the dependent/subordinate clause.
Ex. Est-il évident que Dick et Jane ne soient pas si heureux ensemble? > Is it obvious that Dick and Jane are not so happy together? (Maybe, they are just not 'on the same page.')
1b. However, if the phrases above are negative-interrogative, they precede the indicative tense. No uncertainty and little or no doubt is implied. (Some people might question that.)
Ex. Ne paraît-il que les chariots dans ce supermarché sont difficiles à séparer? > Doesn't it seem that the grocery carts in that supermarket are difficult to separate? (Even though they're attached to each other, they never make it 'down the aisle' together.)
2. Forms of *croire*, *espérer* and *penser* take the indicative tense in affirmative sentences.
Ex. Notre fille espère que nous lui donnons un petit téléphone **de haute technologie** ce Noël. > Our daughter hopes that we (will) give her a small **high-tech** telephone this Christmas. (She would like a visit from 'the Blue Tooth fairy.')
2a. Forms of *croire*, *espérer* and *penser* are followed by the subjunctive mood if those verbs are negative or interrogative.
Ex. Crois-tu tout ce qu'il te dise? > Do you believe everything that he tells you? (Does the truth 'lie' within?)
Ex. Tinker ne pense pas que les nouvelles voitures aient jamais besoin de réparations. > Tinker does not think that new cars ever need repairs. (He must be betting on 'the dealer.')
2b. When little or no doubt is implied, forms of *croire* and *penser* go before the indicative tense in negative and interrogative constructions. However, if doubt is inferred with forms of either of these verbs, the verb in the dependent clause is *au subjonctif*.
Ex. Personne ne pense qu'elles sont assez vieilles pour vivre seul. > Nobody thinks that they are old enough to live on their own.
In that example, the speaker is positive about his/her negative assessment.
Ex. Quelqu'un pense qu'elles soient assez vieilles pour vivre seul? > Does anyone think that they're old enough to live on their own?
In that example, the subjunctive mood is used because the speaker is not sure whether his/her question will elicit a positive or a negative response.

'Let's Be Reasonable!' - Put the infinitives in parentheses into indicative or subjunctive forms, and write brief explanations to account for the answers.
Ex. (aimer mieux) Le colonel Sanders <u>aime mieux</u> que nous mangions son poulet frit.
The subjunctive is used after verbs and expressions of volition.

1. (exister) Casper est sûr que les fantômes _____.

_____.

2. (porter) Tu ne crois pas que les chats noirs _____ malheur?

_____.

3. (perdre) Franc et Sou ont peur que nous ne _____ nos boulots.

_____.

4. (mettre) Il est convenable que Mme Négoces _____ un ensemble professionnel.

_____.

5. (courir) On interdit que vous _____ dans les couloirs.

_____.

6. (dormir) M. Auberge espère que ses invités _____ bien.

_____.

7. (traduire) Nous ne voulons pas que vous _____ mot pour mot.

_____.

8. (exiger) Il est clair que Ray Glèment _____ toujours la perfection.

_____.

9. (avoir) Il est ironique que les deux meilleures amies _____ le même prénom.

_____.

10. (être) Je suis agacé que ta fiancée ne (n') _____ pas plus polie.

_____.

11. (se méfier) Est-il possible que tu _____ de M. Rusé?

_____.

12. (être) Nous nous réjouissons que vous _____ ici.

_____.

Verbs with One Irregular Subjunctive Stem

The irregular stems for *faire*, *pouvoir* and *savoir* are *fass*, *puiss* and *sach* respectively.
1a. *Fass* and *puiss* have a double s.
1b. The three verbs have regular subjunctive endings.
Ex. Les Woods veulent que je fasse du camping avec eux ce week-end. > The Woods want me to go camping with them this weekend. (There is 'an outside chance.')
Ex. Il est surprenant qu'on puisse trouver les cow-boys à Beverly Hills. > It's surprising that one can find cowboys in Beverly Hills. (Perhaps, they are shopping on Rodeo Drive.)
Ex. Comment est-il possible que vous sachiez le score du match avant qu'il ne commence? > How is it possible for you to know the score of the match before it begins? (Before it starts, it is 0 to 0.)
2. The only subjunctive form of *falloir*, an impersonal verb, is *faille*.
Ex. Eve ne suggère pas qu'il faille punir Adam. > Eve does not suggest that it is necessary to punish

Adam. (She just hopes that he will 'turn over a new leaf.')

A Form Fitting Foundation- Fill in the blanks with the correct subjunctive spellings of *falloir*, *faire*, *pouvoir* and *savoir*.

1. Mes parents sont fiers que je le _____ moi-même.
2. Penses-tu que Jay Ographie _____ les noms de tous les départements français?
3. Faye Deaudeau voudrait que ses petits enfants _____ la grasse matinée.
4. Crois-tu que Judi Ciare et moi _____ réussir à l'examen de droit?
5. Il convient que vous _____ un tour de Tours avec vos invités.
6. Il est étonnant que la diseuse de bonne aventure _____ décrire tant de détails.
7. Je ne pense pas qu'il _____ la dorloter tout le temps.
8. Vos copains sont très surpris que vous _____ / _____ le faire.
9. Nous sommes désolés que les Hyer ne _____ pas prendre tous les postulants.
10. Il se peut que tu _____ que celle-ci est la dernière phrase de l'exercice.

The Subjunctive Has Its Doubts

1. *Le subjonctif* follows an independent/main clause that expresses doubt. Terms leading to the mood are *douter*- to doubt and its synonyms *n'être pas sûr* and *n'être pas certain*.
Ex. Ivan Idea doute que **le réchauffement de la planète** soit une réalité. > Ivan Idea doubts that **global warming** is a reality. (He may prefer not 'to get into a heated argument.')

2. *Nier* means <u>to deny</u>. The verb after it is *au subjonctif* since the speaker's message might cast doubts. (One should always consider 'the source of De-Nile.')
Ex. Je nie que nous trichions sur les examens. > I deny that we cheat on the exams. (Everyone seems 'to say the same thing.')

3. *Le subjonctif* is used in a dependent clause if an indefinite person or thing is sought. Because the individual(s) or object(s) might not be found, doubt is implied. (However, once 'the party' is located, there is no need for a subjunctive mood.)
Ex. Les deux femmes cherchent une boutique **dans les quartiers chics** où elles puissent acheter des vêtements classiques. > The two women are looking for a boutique **uptown** where they can buy vintage clothing. (They might have better luck browsing in 'the '20s and '30s.')
Ex. Connais-tu quelqu'un qui puisse parler Latin couramment? Do you know anyone who is able to speak Latin fluently? (I might be able 'to dig up somebody.')
<u>An important note</u>: In the two preceding examples, the dependent/subordinate clauses do not begin with *que*. The first starts with *où* and the second with *qui*.
4. *Le subjonctif* is used after superlative terms including *le seul*, *le premier* and *le dernier* when expressing an opinion.
Ex. Elle pense que la mouffette soit le seul animal qui émette de telle mauvaise odeur. > She thinks that the skunk is the only animal that emits such a bad odor. (The others 'don't even come close.')
4a. However, when the superlative is followed by *de*, *du*, *de la*, *de l*, or *des*, or if the statement is factual, the indicative is used.
Ex. Le Maine est le seul état des États-Unis qui a seulement une syllabe. > Maine is the only state in the United States that has only one syllable. (The subjunctive is 'on vacation' there.)

5. The subjunctive is used in clauses beginning with <u>certain indefinite</u> pronouns. A few phrases that fit into this "oxymoron" category are:
a. où que- wherever
b. quel que- whatever (an adjective)
c. quelque ... que and si ... que- however- (followed by a form of *être*)
Ex. Quelque riche qu'il soit, on ne saura jamais. > However rich he is, one will never know. (That is just something else that he is saving.)
d. qui que- who(m)ever
e. quoi que- whatever (a pronoun)
Ex. Quoi que cette publicité prétende, une taille ne va pas à tout. > Whatever that ad claims, one size does not fit all. (Some consumers are not 'comfortable' with it.)
<u>An important note</u>: **The French terms above end with *que;* their translations end with <u>ever</u>.**
6. The third person singular subjunctive form expresses a wish or a command.
Exs. Vive la France! > Long Live France!
    Ainsi soit-il! > Amen. So be it!

<u>'In Case There's Any Doubt'</u>- **Fill in the blanks with correct forms of the verbs in parentheses.**
1. (être) Fidélité nie que ses amis _____ coupables.
2. (avoir) Je ne suis pas certain que vous _____ tout ce dont vous avez besoin.
3. (savoir) Thomas doute que tu _____ la réponse correcte.
4. (pouvoir) Cherche-t-il quelqu'un qui _____ lui prêter un MP3?
5. (sortir) Qui que _____ avec Anne Huieuse ne s'amuse pas.
6. (marcher) Où que nous _____, nos ombres nous suivent.
7. (être) Le livre le plus populaire du monde _____ la Bible.
8. (servir) Connaissez-vous un restaurant qui _____ le dîner à dix heures le soir?
9. (pouvoir, être) Les cadeaux chics? Il est possible que tu _____ les trouver dans le 6ᵉ arrondissement. Mais, je ne suis pas sûre que les prix _____ raisonnables là-bas.
10. (vivre) Les hommes et les femmes ne sont pas toujours d'accord. _____ la différence!

<u>Branching Out -Verbs in the Subjunctive with Two Stems</u>

Irregular verbs in "boot" form kick off the final section of the present subjunctive. The entire singular and the third person plural turn in one direction; the *nous* and *vous* forms in another. These distinctions are clearly seen with the conjugation of *voir*.

<u>Singular</u>	<u>Plural</u>
je voie- I see, do see, am seeing	**nous voyions- we see, do see, are seeing**
tu voies- you see, do see, are seeing	**vous voyiez- you see, do see, are seeing**
il/elle/on voie- he/she/ it/one sees,	**ils/elles voient- they see, do see, are seeing**
** does see, is seeing**	

<u>Pursuing Alterate 'Roots'</u>
1. Verbs *au subjonctif* **with two stems have regular -e, -es, -e, -ions, -iez, -ent endings.**
2. *Voir, envoyer, renvoyer* **and** *croire* **have a y in the** *nous* **and** *vous* **forms.**
Ex. Une élève française dit à l'autre, "Il n'est pas possible que nous voyions les mêmes émissions de télévision que les anglais." > One French pupil says to the other, "It is not possible for us to see the same television programs as the English." (However, they do have 'a Channel' in common.)
3a. Orthographic/stem changing verbs with an è in their 'boots' in the present indicative leave them on in the subjunctive. In fact, aside from the i before the *nous* **and** *vous* **form subjunctive endings, the two conjugations are identical.**
Ex. Faut-il qu'un chauve enlève son chapeau quand il rencontre une femme? > Is it necessary for a bald man to remove his hat when he meets a lady? (Only if he wants to show that he is 'polished.')
3b. Verbs that double l's and t's in "boot form" in the present tense do so in the subjunctive.
Ex. Le gynécologue doute que la patiente enceinte se rappelle son rendez-vous. > The gynecologist doubts that the pregnant patient will remember her appointment. (She might not 'show.')
3c. -Cer verbs have no cedillas, and -ger verbs need no inserted es because no endings *au subjonctif* **begin with -a, -o or -u.**
Ex. Il est bon que nous partagions un chalet **au versant de** la montagne. > It's good that we're sharing a chalet **on the side of** the mountain. (Private rentals are 'over the top.')
3d. Paralleling *l'imparfait,* **-oyer and -uyer verbs keep the y in the** *nous* **and** *vous* **forms before adding -ions and -iez. The remainder of the conjugation is identical to the present indicative.**
Ex. Des parents disent à leurs adolescents, "Il est très important que vous nettoyiez vos chambres à coucher. > Some parents say to their teenagers, "It's very important that you clean your bedrooms." (Nobody seems to be able 'to get through.')
<u>An exception:</u> **-Ayer verbs keep the y in their stems throughout the subjunctive conjugation.**
Ex. Les locataires futures demandent au propriétaire, "Faut-il que nous payions autant que les gens dont les appartements ont un balcon?" > The future tenants ask the landlord, "Do we have to pay as much as the people whose apartments have a balcony? (They don't want 'to overlook' anything.)

The *prendre* **and the** *tenir/venir* **families include double n's throughout the singular and in the third person plural but not in the** *nous* **and** *vous* **forms.**

<u>Singular</u>	<u>Plural</u>
je prenne- I take, do take, am taking	**nous prenions- we take, do take, are taking**
tu prennes- you take, do take, are taking	**vous preniez- you take, do take, are taking**
il/elle/on prenne- he/she/it/one takes,	**ils/elles prennent- they take, do take,**
does take, is taking	**are taking**

<u>Singular</u>	<u>Plural</u>
je vienne- I come, do come, am coming	**nous venions- we come, do come, are coming**
tu viennes- you come, do come, are coming	**vous veniez- you come, do come, are coming**
il/elle/on vienne- he/she/it/one comes,	**ils/elles viennent- they come, do come,**
does come, is coming	**are coming**

<u>Taking It as It Comes</u>
1. Prefixed associates of the preceding families of verbs that sport a double <u>n</u> in "boot" format include *apprendre, comprendre, entreprendre, reprendre, surprendre, appartenir, contenir, déte-nir, maintenir, obtenir, retenir, soutenir, devenir, prévenir* and *revenir*.
<u>An important note</u>: **Like the *voir* and *croire* groups, *prendre, venir/tenir* and their related verbs are identical in the third person plural indicative and subjunctive forms.**
Ex. Les gosses veulent que le Père Noël vienne à leurs maisons avec beaucoup de jouets. > The kids want Santa to come to their homes with many toys. (But they have 'to drop off' first.)
Ex. Il vaut mieux qu'ils prennent un dîner léger avant de se coucher. > It is better for them to have a light dinner before going to bed. (Yet, some people are always 'up for' a heavy meal.)

The *nous* and *vous* subjunctive forms of *aller, boire, devoir, mourir, recevoir* and *vouloir* are the same as those in the imperfect tense.
The conjugation of *<u>aller</u>* just 'goes to show you.'

<div align="center">**Singular**</div>	<div align="center">**Plural**</div>
j'aille- I go, do go, am going	nous allions- we go, do go, are going
tu ailles- you go, do go, are going	vous alliez- you go, do go, are going
il/elle/on aille- he/she/it/one goes, does go, is going	ils/elles aillent- they go, do go, are going

----

Here's what you get with *<u>recevoir</u>*.

<div align="center">**Singular**</div>	<div align="center">**Plural**</div>
je reçoive- I receive, do receive, am receiving	nous recevions- we receive, do receive, are receiving
tu reçoives- you receive, do receive, are receiving	vous receviez- you receive, do receive, are receiving
il/elle/on reçoive- he/she/it/one receives, does receive, is receiving	ils/elles reçoivent- they receive, do receive, are receiving

----

<u>"Boots" with an Imperfect Fit</u>
1. *Aller* and *vouloir* are 'ill'-fitted boots. Those three letters 'squeeze in' after <u>a</u> in the first verb and after <u>eu</u> in the second one. (Exs. j'aille, je veuille)
Ex. Le père, qui n'est pas du tout riche, est mécontent que ses enfants aillent commander le canard à l'orange. > The father, who is not at all rich, is not pleased that his children are going to order duck with orange sauce. (Maybe he should 'stick them with the bill.')
Ex. Cette maîtresse-là est frustrée qu'un élève veuille rester dans une boîte. > That schoolteacher is frustrated that a pupil wants to stay in a box. (Did someone suggest that 'he contain himself'?)
<u>An important note</u>: **The subjunctive forms of *avoir* have a clipped, long <u>a</u> sound, while the sub-junctive 'boot' of *aller* produces a clipped, long <u>i</u> sound.**
2. -<u>Oiv</u> is 'the subjunctive insole' for *boire, devoir* and *recevoir*.
Ex. Ces parents sont inquiétés que des étudiants dans l'université boivent comme des trous. > Those parents are concerned that some students in the university drink like fish. (What are they learning in

'schools' these days?)

3. *Mourir* is an unmatched 'boot.' The <u>e</u> blacks out when the <u>o</u> 'comes back to life' in the *nous* and *vous* forms. (Exs. il meure, vous mouriez)

Ex. Il est ironique que des époux séparés meurent d'ennui. > It is ironic that some separated spouses are bored to death. (It is the result of 'having nothing to do with each other.')

Mapping 'the Roots' - Write the subjunctive forms (with pronouns) for the verbs below.
1. aller- third person singular _____
2. aller- first person plural _____
3. boire- first person singular _____
4. boire- second person plural _____
5. croire- third person singular _____
6. croire- first person plural _____
7. devoir- second person singular _____
8. devoir- second person plural _____
9. mourir- first person plural _____
10. mourir- third person plural _____
11. prendre- second person singular _____
12. prendre- second person plural _____
13. recevoir- first person singular _____
14. recevoir- second person plural _____
15. venir- first person plural _____
16. venir- third person plural _____
17. voir- first person singular _____
18. voir- first person plural _____
19. vouloir- second person singular _____
20. vouloir- second person plural _____

'You Don't Say!' - **Put the affirmative indicative sentences below into the negative subjunctive. Ex. Il est sûr que cette voiture-là appartient à un visiteur. > Il n'est pas sûr que cette voiture-là appartienne à un visiteur.**

1. Il pense que nous le comprenons bien. _____
_____.

2. Je suis certaine que Polly Tout va nettoyer l'argenterie ce matin. _____
_____.

3. Votre famille croit que vous voyagez trop. _____
_____.

4. Il est vrai que le prince vient de réveiller La Belle au Bois Dormant. _____
_____.

5. Kent Waite est sûr que je reçois les nouvelles aujourd'hui. _____
_____.

6. Il est évident que mon ancien flirt veut me parler. _____
_____.

7. Je connais quelqu'un qui peut m'apprendre à danser le zumba. _____

_____.

8. Ils sont certains que Mme Bulles boit seulement lors d'occasions spéciales. _____

_____.

Que Is the Cue

Several adverbial conjunctions precede the subjunctive mood. They can introduce the first or last clauses of sentences. Ending with *que*, they are easy to recognize. However, because some conjunctive phrases are followed by the present indicative, knowing when 'to hit the switch' is essential. (There are two tracks at 'conjunction junction.')

Conjunctions in Conjunction with the Subjunctive

The following conjunctions, which means <u>meeting</u>, have specific functions.
1. <u>To Express Time</u>
en attendant que- until
jusqu'à ce que- until
avant que- before
Ex. Nous ne pouvons pas **emménager** jusqu'à ce que vous signiez le contrat. > We cannot **move in** until you sign the contract. (That's 'the bottom line.')
Ex. La secrétaire de la parfumerie finit **les tâches administratifs** avant que son patron *ne s'attende les voir. > The secretary in the perfume shop finishes **the paperwork** before her boss expects to see it. ('Time is of the essence.')
<u>Important reminders</u>: *Jusque/Jusqu'*- as far as/until is a preposition followed by an adverb or a noun. (Ex. jusqu'à demain)
Avant de/d'- before is a preposition followed by an infinitive.** (Ex. avant de le faire)
2. <u>To Express Purpose</u>
afin que- in order that, so that
pour que- in order that, so that
The two expressions above are interchangeable. (They serve one purpose.)
Ex. Votre mère **télécharge** Skype pour que la famille puisse se voir sur l'ordinateur. > Your mother is **downloading** Skype so that the family can see one another on the computer. (They all must 'look forward to it.')
3. <u>To Express Conditions</u>
à condition que- on the condition that, provided that
pourvu que- provided that
à moins que- unless
Ex. Auntie Social reste toujours chez elle à moins que quelqu'un *ne la persuade de sortir. > Auntie Social always stays home unless someone persuades her to go it. (And that becomes 'a drag.')
4. <u>To Express Concession</u>
bien que- although
encore que- although

quoique- although

The three preceding conjunctions can substitute for each other. (Thus allowing for concession)

An interesting fact: *Quoique* **is the only conjoined conjunction followed by the subjunctive.**

Ex. Bien que le maçon surfe sur Internet constamment, il ne peut trouver un travail. > Although the mason surfs the Internet constantly, he cannot find a job. (Maybe, he should 'pound the pavement.')

5. To Express Negation

sans que- without

A helpful hint: Sanka coffee is made <u>without</u> caffeine.

Ex. Mlle Poêle veut **sauter** le dîner sans que tu l'aides. > Ms Poêle wants **to stir fry** dinner without your helping her. (She prefers to 'wok' alone.)

6. To Express Fear

de crainte que- for fear that (derived from *craindre*)

de peur que- for fear that

The two conjunctions above are interchangeable.

Ex. Aisle Cee n'achète pas les billets en avance de peur que quelques amies *n'**annulent** au dernier moment. > Aisle Cee isn't buying tickets in advance for fear that some friends will **cancel** at the last minute. (She may be judging by 'past performances.')

<u>Very important notes</u>

1. When adverbial conjunctions are used, the subject of the independent and dependent clause may be the same.

2. Unlike other subjunctive "lead-ins," adverbial conjunctions can begin or end sentences.

3. *Ne*, which is not translated, follows *avant que*, *à moins que*, *de crainte que* and *de peur que*. The 'half-negative' does not affect affirmative translations.

<u>There Is More to It Than "That"</u>

Some adverbial conjunctions precede the indicative tense. Many of those refer to time; none of them expresses fear.

<u>When the Indicative Is Indicated</u>

1. après que- after: To differentiate this conjunction from its antonym, *avant que*, which is followed by the subjunctive, remember not to get into a mood <u>after</u> it.

2. aussitôt que and dès que- as soon as: These synonyms can be used before verbs *au futur*.

3. parce que- because: Just because *que* is part of the term is not just cause for the subjunctive.

4. pendant que and tandis que- while: The latter one also means <u>whereas</u>, whereas *pendant que* does not.

5. puisque- since: This adverb stands out <u>since</u> it is the only one in the category that consists of one word.

<u>Joining Good 'Clauses'</u>- **Circle the letters of the best answers to complete the sentences.**

1. _____ Shrek soit très grand, il n'a pas beaucoup de muscles.

a. Á condition que   b. Bien que   c. De crainte que   d. À moins que

2. La mère regarde son petit fils de la fenêtre _____ il joue sur le gazon.

a. sans qu'   b. de peur qu'   c. puisqu'   d. pendant qu'

3. Mon père rentre du bureau _____ nous nous asseyons à table.

a. aussitôt que   b. pour que   c. pourvu que   d. encore que

4. Getta Clue m'envoie les SMS sans cesse _____ je n'y réponde jamais.

a. à moins que   b. quoique   c. en attendant que   d. tandis que

5. Prends le courrier maintenant _____ nous n'oubliions pas de le faire plus tard!

a. jusqu'à ce que   b. parce que   c. afin que   d. dès que

6. Les rues sont glissantes même _____ il pleut.

a. lorsqu'   b. aussitôt qu'   c. avant qu'   d. après qu'

7. Les élèves ne vont pas au jardin zoologique _____ vous les accompagniez.

a. sans que   b. de crainte que   c. parce que   d. pour que

8. Le machiste veut annuler leur mariage _____ sa mariée ne soit pas d'accord.

a. de façon que   b. bien que   c. puisque   d. dès que

9. _____ je ne me perde, je ne demande jamais la route.

a. Sans que   b. En attendant que   c. À moins que   d. Quoique

10. _____ son vol atterrit, Thierry téléphone à ses parents.

a. Encore que   b. Pendant que   c. Tandis que   d. Après que

---

Napoleon's Tomb (les Invalides, Paris)

LE PASSÉ DU SUBJONCTIF - THE PAST SUBJUNCTIVE

It is apropos that the final concept of this book discusses finished events. Helpers are on hand to make the past subjunctive "a done deal."
I am delighted that students <u>have learned</u> French and <u>had a good time</u> in the process!

Apprendre au Passé du Subjonctif

<u>Singulier</u>	<u>Pluriel</u>
j'aie appris- I learned, have learned, did learn	nous ayons appris- we learned, did learn, have learned
tu aies appris- you learned, did learn, have learned	vous ayez appris- you learned, did learn, have learned
il/elle/on ait appris- he/she/it/one learned, has learned, did learn	ils/elles aient appris- they learned, did learn, have learned

----

S'Amuser au Passé du Subjonctif

<u>Singulier</u>
je me sois amusé(e)- I enjoyed, have enjoyed, did enjoy myself
tu te sois amusé(e)- you enjoyed, have enjoyed, did enjoy yourself
il se soit amusé- he enjoyed, has enjoyed, did enjoy himself
elle se soit amusée- she enjoyed, has enjoyed, did enjoy herself

<u>Pluriel</u>
nous nous soyons amusé(e)s- we enjoyed, have enjoyed, did enjoy ourselves
vous vous soyez amuse(é)(s)(es)- you enjoyed, have enjoyed, did enjoy yourself/selves
ils se soient amusés- they enjoyed, did enjoy, have enjoyed themselves
elles se soient amusées- they enjoyed, have enjoyed, did enjoy themselves

----

<u>Back Tracking into the Past</u>
1. The past subjunctive contains a present subjunctive form of *avoir* or *être* + a past participle. Except for its subjunctive auxiliary/helping verbs, *le passé du subjonctif* is identical to *le passé composé*.
2. The independent/main clause is in the present tense. The dependent/subordinate clause is in the past subjunctive.
Ex. Nous ne pensons pas que le père ait voulu **conduire** sa fille **à l'autel**. > We do not think that the father wanted **to give** his daughter **away**. (Maybe he expected something in exchange.)
<u>A note</u>: *Conduire à l'autel* literally means "to lead to the altar."
Ex. Il est possible que nos grands-parents aient économisé longtemps pour acheter un congélateur. > It is possible that our grandparents saved for a long time to buy a freezer. (After that, all 'their assets were frozen.')
3. Like other compound tenses with a form of *être* as the helping verb, past participles *au passé du subjonctif* agree with the subjects in gender and in number.

525

Ex. Ken nie que Barbie soit née quelques années avant lui. > Ken denies that Barbie was born a few years before him. (He always liked 'to date' her.)

Ex. Al Cool est surpris que des invités **soient devenus pompettes** de bonne heure. > Al Cool is surprised that some guests **got tipsy** early. (They 'beat him to the punch.')

4. The grammatical features for present and past subjunctives are the same. If the two clauses have different subjects, they are usually linked by *que*. Expressions of opinion, emotion, doubt, denial, volition, request, along with commands, indefinite pronouns ending with *que* and some adverbial conjunctions ensure that verbs *au passé du subjonctif* will follow them.

'That' Makes More Sense- Use *que* to make the two sentences into one *au passé du subjonctif*.
Ex. Il est peu probable. Les banlieusards se sont détendus comme ça. > Il est peu probable que les banlieusards se soient détendus comme ça. > It is unlikely that the commuters relaxed like that.

1. Il est étrange. La recluse a voulu aller à l'étranger avec toi. _____
_____.

2. Je suis étonnée. Personne n'a conduit Blanche à l'autel. _____
_____.

3. Les bonnes d'hôtel ne sont pas heureuses. Nous avons fait la grasse matinée. _____
_____.

4. Il est très normal. Les petits dans la colonie de vacances ont eu la nostalgie. _____
_____.

5. Il vaut mieux. Claire a acheté les rideaux fleuris au lieu des **stores-m. (blinds)** noirs. _____
_____.

6. Il est triste. Le riche est mort tout seul. _____
_____.

7. Es-tu fâché? Je suis partie sans t'embrasser. _____
_____?

8. Il est ironique. Mlle Champagne est devenue pompette. _____
_____.

'Closing Remarks'- Complete the sentences by translating the clauses in parentheses.
1. La jeune fille au pair doute (that the baby slept well last night). _____
_____.

2. J'ai honte (that my children forgot to invite her). _____
_____.

3. Il est remarquable (that we wrote it perfectly). _____
_____.

4. Les trois ours sont agacés (that La Boucle d'Or stayed in their house). _____
_____.

5. (Although he died several years ago) _____
_____, Elvis Presley est toujours populaire.

6. Penses-tu (that Di Vertir et Anne Tertaine had a good time last week)? _____
_____?

7. Mme Peacock est fière (that you (*vous*) have learned so much). _____

_____ .

8. Il a fallu chuchoter (so that the little ones could not hear us). _____

_____ .

9. (Unless you (*tu*) made more of them) _____

_____ , il n'y a pas de croissants.

10. (Before they went to the supermarket) _____

_____ , Améal leur a demandé, "Qu'est-ce qui est pour le dîner?"

_____

Church of the Dome, les Invalides (Paris)

UNE REVUE - A Review

Le Subjonctif du Présent et le Subjonctif du Passé

Balancing the Subjunctive Account- Label the sentences *vrai* or *faux*.

_____ 1. Regular -<u>er</u>, -<u>ir</u> and -<u>re</u> present tense verbs have the same subjunctive endings.

_____ 2. All irregular verbs have irregular subjunctive stems.

_____ 3. The present subjunctive also expresses future action.

_____ 4. All impersonal expressions begin with *Il est*.

_____ 5. *Faire*, *pouvoir* and *savoir* each have one subjunctive stem.

_____ 6. *Avoir* and *être* are the only subjunctive verbs with irregular endings.

_____ 7. The subjunctive mood is used after verbs in a negative-interrogative form.

_____ 8. Verbs expressing belief, hope and thought must be in a negative or an interrogative form to take the subjunctive.

_____ 9. The subjunctive mood is used after expressions of certainty.

_____ 10. If there is little or no doubt in the speaker's mind, forms of *croire* and *penser* go before the indicative tense.

_____ 11. A dependent clause containing a verb *au subjonctif* must begin with *que*.

_____ 12. The subjunctive is used if the antecedent in the main clause has been located.

_____ 13. Indefinite expressions followed by the subjunctive have the English suffix -<u>ever</u>.

_____ 14. Commands may include a verb in the third person singular subjunctive.

_____ 15. Superlatives followed by a partitive do not take the indicative tense.

_____ 16. Imperfect tense and present subjunctive *nous* and *vous* forms of -<u>yer</u> verbs are the same.

_____ 17. Subjunctive verbs with two stems are always in "boot" form.

_____ 18. The subjunctive mood is used after all adverbial conjunctions.

_____ 19. *À moins que*, *avant que*, *de peur que* and *de crainte que* take *ne* before the verb.

_____ 20. *Le passé du subjonctif* includes the present indicative of *avoir* or *être*.

Resembling and Assembling- Match the letters to the numbers of the phrases that are closest in meaning.

____ 1. Il est préférable que	A. de peur que
____ 2. être heureux que	B. Il se peut que
____ 3. commander que	C. ne pas être sûr que
____ 4. à condition que	D. exiger que
____ 5. être malheureux que	E. être irrité que
____ 6. être enchanté que	F. Il est étonnant que
____ 7. douter que	G. se réjouir que
____ 8. bien que	H. pour que
____ 9. être énervé que	I. interdire que
____ 10. être très désolé que	J. souhaiter que
____ 11. de crainte que	K. être agacé que
____ 12. être embarrassé que	L. être triste que
____ 13. Il est très surprenant que	M. Il vaut mieux que
____ 14. être très fâché que	N. nier que
____ 15. vouloir que	O. jusqu'à ce que

_____ 16. demander que   P. avoir honte qu

_____ 17. en attendant que   Q. être ravi que

_____ 18. être ennuyé que   R. ordonner que

_____ 19. Il faut que   S. encore que

_____ 20. défendre que   T. être furieux que

_____ 21. Il est possible que   U. regretter beaucoup que

_____ 22. ne pas admettre que   V. Il est nécessaire que

_____ 23. afin que   W. pourvu que

'Tense or in a Mood?'- Circle the letters of the correct answers, and briefly state the reasons for your choices.

Ex. Il vaut mieux que Corinne ne (b) pas seule le soir.

a. sort   **b. sorte**

The subjunctive is used after impersonal expressions of opinion.

1. Nous sommes ravis que vous ___ des nôtres.

a. êtes   b. soyez

_____.

2. Voulez-vous que M. Ombre vous ___ partout?

a. suit   b. suive

_____.

3. Il est probable que nous ___ tous les postulants.

a. employons   b. employions

_____.

4. Je suis surpris qu'Hugh Midité ne _____ pas la signification du réchauffement de la planète.

a. comprend   b. comprenne

_____.

5. M. et Mme Règles exigent que leurs enfants ___ un couvre-feu.

a. ont   b. aient

_____.

6. Il leur semble que les vêtements dans les boutiques classiques ___ très chers.

a. sont   b. soient

_____.

7. Penses-tu pas que M. Attrapé ___ faire un aveu?

a. veut   b. veuille

_____.

8. Nous espérons que tu ___ à tes examens.

a. réussis   b. réussisses

_____.

9. Que le pape ___ tout!

a. bénit   b. bénisse

_____.

10. Des **familles d'accueil (host families)** ont peur que leurs étudiants d'échange ne/n' ___ rentrer chez eux trop tôt.

a. vont   b. aillent

---

11. Ma mère est la femme la plus intelligente du monde qu'il ___.
a. connaît   b. connaisse

---

12. Qui que ___ un enfant affamé a la pitié de lui.
a. voit   b. voie

---

13. Avez-vous jamais rencontré quelqu'un qui ___ toujours la vérité?
a. dit   b. dise

---

14. Bien que Demie Joie ___ bonne mine, nous savons qu'elle est malheureuse.
a. a   b. ait

---

15. Puisqu'il ___ toujours, votre avion ne va pas décoller.
a. pleut   b. pleuve

---

16. L'infirmière ferme les stores pour que les malades ___ s'endormir.
a. peuvent   b. puissent

'Write' This Way!- Translate the sentences. A choice of wording is possible for some of them.
1. It is ironic that such handsome beasts are dangerous. _____

2. It is not enough that Raye Connaissant simply says, "Thank you." _____

3. The new laws prevent people from smoking in front of some buildings. _____

4. Goofy is flattered that someone takes him for Pluto. _____

5. We are sorry that no one can wait for him. _____

6. Do you (vous) believe that we live more than once? _____
_____?

7. Nanette denies that Noé does not know how to swim. _____

8. I doubt that everyone is coming, but I hope so. _____

9. Évite Lesfoules is looking for someone who has a private plane. _____

10. Don't leave (tu) Paris without my seeing you! _____
_____!

11. It is not good that so many commuters did not have seats. _____

12. Mr. and Mrs. Partir are the only ones who did not stay. _____
_____.

13. Do you *(vous)* think that Ms Espoir is going to marry the man whom the fairy godmother chose?
_____
_____?

14. The writer is delighted that we have read her book. _____
_____.

les Champs-Élysées et l'Arc de Triomphe (Paris)

CPSIA information can be obtained
at www.ICGtesting.com
Printed in the USA
BVOW07s1352211116

468472BV00027B/57/P